THE DYNASTY OF CHERNIGOV, 1146–1246

Historians in pre-revolutionary Russia, in the Soviet Union, in con-temporary Russia, and the West have consistently relegated the dynasty of Chernigov to a place of minor importance in Kievan Rus'. This view was buttressed by the evidence that, after the Mongols invaded Rus' in 1237, the two branches from the House of Monomakh living in the Rostov-Suzdal' and Galicia-Volyn' regions emerged as the most powerful.

However, careful examination of the chronicle accounts report-ing the dynasty's history during the second half of the twelfth and the first half of the thirteenth century shows that the Ol'govichi of Chernigov successfully challenged the Monomashichi for supremacy in Rus'. Through a critical analysis of the available primary sources (such as chronicles, archaeology, coins, seals, "graffiti" in churches, and architecture) this book attempts to correct the pervading erro-neous view by allocating to the Ol'govichi their rightful place in the dynastic hierarchy of Kievan Rus'.

MARTIN DIMNIK is Professor of Medieval History, Senior Fellow and President Emeritus, Pontifical Institute of Medieval Studies, Toronto, and Professor of Medieval History, University of Toronto. His previous publications include *Mikhail, Prince of Chernigov and Grand Prince of Kiev, 1224–1246* (1981), and *The Dynasty of Chernigov, 1054–1146* (1994).

THE DYNASTY OF CHERNIGOV, 1146–1246

MARTIN DIMNIK

CAMBRIDGE
UNIVERSITY PRESS

PUBLISHED BY THE PRESS SYNDICATE OF THE UNIVERSITY OF CAMBRIDGE
The Pitt Building, Trumpington Street, Cambridge, United Kingdom

CAMBRIDGE UNIVERSITY PRESS
The Edinburgh Building, Cambridge, CB2 2RU, UK
40 West 20th Street, New York, NY 10011–4211, USA
477 Williamstown Road, Port Melbourne, VIC 3207, Australia
Ruiz de Alarcón 13, 28014 Madrid, Spain
Dock House, The Waterfront, Cape Town 8001, South Africa

http://www.cambridge.org

© Martin Dimnik 2003

First published 2003

Printed in the United Kingdom at the University Press, Cambridge

Typeface Adobe Garamond 11/12.5 pt.   *System* LᴬTEX 2ε   [TB]

A catalogue record for this book is available from the British Library

Library of Congress Cataloguing in Publication data applied for

ISBN 0 521 82442 7 hardback

Frontispiece   The miraculous icon of the Mother of God from the Eletskiy Monastery, Chernigov (seventeenth century)

Contents

Figures

Maps

Genealogical tables

Preface

Like its predecessor, *The Dynasty of Chernigov 1054–1146*, this book is based on an examination of primary sources. From among these, the chronicles of Rus' have once again served as the main reservoir of information. Nevertheless, they cannot be taken at face value. We must keep in mind that not one chronicle copy from the twelfth or the thirteenth century has survived. Chronicles written at the courts of the princes under investigation were incorporated into later compilations and have come down to us, for the most part, in those from the fifteenth and the sixteenth centuries. Consequently, in evaluating chronicle accounts, we must keep in mind the biases of the original chronicler and of later compilers. Moreover, errors crept into the texts during the course of recopying when scribes inadvertently made mistakes through ignorance, carelessness, or fatigue. In some instances compilers changed the text when they sought to improve the original in the light of their own world-view.

The dating also produces special difficulties. The chroniclers use two systems of dating: the March (*martovskiy*) Year and the Ultra-March (*ul'tramartovskiy*) Year. Both years begin with March. When the chronicle uses the March Year, the correct January year of the Christian or Common Era is obtained by taking the chronicle date, for example 6732, the date from the creation of the world according to the Byzantine calendar, and subtracting 5508, the year before Christ in which, according to Byzantine reckoning, the world was created. This gives us the January year 1224 CE. If the chronicler is using the Ultra-March Year of 6732, it is necessary to subtract 5509 to obtain the correct January year, 1223 CE.[1] It is not always clear which system was being used. In later compilations, entries included under one year frequently represent a mixture of the two styles; the compiler incorporated into his text entries from some chronicles which used the one system and some which used the other. In determining the correct

---

[1] See also *Mikhail*, pp. x–xii, and *Dynasty*, pp. xvi–xvii.

dates for the Hypatian Chronicle (Ipat.), the Laurentian Chronicle (Lav.), and the Novgorod First Chronicle (NPL), N. G. Berezhkov's study has been used as a guide.[2]

The chroniclers frequently refer to events as happening during the spring, the summer, the autumn, or the winter. Each season lasted three months. Spring began on March 8, summer on June 9, autumn on September 10, and winter on December 9. Thus, in the March Year, winter came during the last three months of the year: December, January, and February. According to the January calendar, however, the three months belong to two different years: December falls at the end of one year while January and February come at the beginning of the next. Thus, the winter that occurred in the March Year of 6732 corresponded to December of 1224 and January and February of 1225 in the January calendar, while the winter that occurred in the Ultra-March Year of 6732 corresponded to December of 1223 and January and February of 1224. It is also useful to note that the ice on the rivers usually melted in April.

The main source of southern Rus' information has been the Hypatian Chronicle, which is named after its oldest manuscript from the beginning of the fifteenth century.[3] The chronicle can be divided into three parts: the so-called Primary Chronicle up to the year 1117, the South-Russian *svod* completed in 1200 at the Vydubichi Monastery, and the chronicle of Galicia and Volyn' covering the years 1200 to 1292.[4] G. A. Perfecky translated the Galician–Volynian text into English.[5] The complete chronicle has also been translated into Ukrainian. The latter edition is particularly useful for its explanatory notes, maps, and geographical identifications.[6]

In 1377, the monk Lavrenty copied the so-called Laurentian Chronicle from a defective manuscript.[7] It records events up to the year 1305 and is the oldest source of information for Suzdalia, especially for the thirteenth century. Up to the year 1240 it also reports events from the Chernigov and Kievan lands. The chronicle incorporates the "*svod* of 1239" kept at the court of Yaroslav Vsevolodovich and the "*svod* of 1263" kept at the courts of Konstantin Vsevolodovich and his sons in Rostov.[8] Written by Suzdalian scribes, this compilation of the Monomashichi on occasion expresses hostility towards the Chernigov dynasty.

[2] Berezhkov.   [3] Ipat.
[4] L. V. Cherepnin, "Letopisets Daniila Galitskogo," *Istoricheskie zapiski* 12 (1941), 228–53; D. S. Likhachev, *Russkie letopisi i ikh kul'turno-istoricheskoe znachenie* (M.-L., 1947), pp. 431–3; O. P. Likhacheva, "Letopis' Ipatevskaya," SKKDR, 235–41.
[5] Perfecky.   [6] Makhnovets'.   [7] Lav.
[8] Yu. A. Limonov, *Letopisanie Vladimiro-Suzdal'skoy Rusi* (L., 1967); Likhachev, *Russkie letopisi*, pp. 427–31; Ya. S. Lur'e, "Letopis' Lavrent'evskaya," SKKDR, 241–5.

The Novgorod First Chronicle gives information mostly about Novgorodian affairs. Two of its copies have been published. The *Sinodal'nyy spisok*, or older redaction, was compiled during the fourteenth century and records events up to the middle of that century. The *Komissionnyy spisok*, or younger redaction, was compiled in the fifteenth century and records events up to the middle of that century.[9] Although the two copies have almost identical texts for the period under investigation, the younger redaction can at times be used to fill lacunae in the older. When quoting from the Novgorod First Chronicle two references will usually be given, the first to the older redaction and the second to the younger. The chronicle is of special importance to our study because it describes the involvement of the Ol'govichi in Novgorod during the first third of the thirteenth century.

In addition to these, all the chronicles in the series *Polnoe sobranie russkikh letopisey* (PSRL) were examined. Many of them are late compilations from the fifteenth to the seventeenth century which, in the main, repeat the information of the three oldest chronicles listed above. Nevertheless, they occasionally contain unique items of news. Of special value are a number of compilations that derive their information from the hypothetical source known as the *svod* of Feodosy and Filipp (1472–9).[10] Among these are the "Moskovskiy letopisniy svod kontsa XV veka," also known as "the Moscow *svod* of 1479" (Mosk.) which frequently expands or clarifies the Laurentian Chronicle, the "Ermolinskaya letopis'" (Erm.), the "L'vovskaya letopis'" (L'vov), and the "Patriarshaya ili Nikonovskaya letopis'" (Nikon.). The latter has been used sparingly because of its late provenance and the questionable reliability of its amplifications.[11] Another hypothetical source, the so-called *svod* of 1448, contains entries with different information.[12] It was evidently used by the Novgorodian chronicles known as the "Sofiyskaya pervaya letopis'" (Sof. 1) and the "Novgorodskaya chetvertaya letopis'" (N4).[13] These supplement the information given by the Novgorod First Chronicle.

The seventeenth-century "Gustinskaya letopis'" (Gust.) belonged to the Gustinskiy Monastery in the district of Poltava southeast of Kiev. In 1843, it

---

[9] NPL; see Likhachev, *Russkie letopisi*, pp. 440–4, and B. M. Kloss, "Letopis' Novgorodskaya pervaya," *SKKDR*, 245–7.

[10] A. N Nasonov, "Moskovskiy svod 1479 i ego yuzhnorusskiy istochnik," *Problemy istochnikovedeniya* 9 (M., 1961), 350–85. For a more detailed bibliography, see *Mikhail*, pp. ix–x.

[11] Mosk., Erm., L'vov, Nikon. 9, and Nikon. 10.

[12] Ya. S. Lur'e, "Obshcherusskiy svod-protograf Sofiyskoy I i Novgorodskoy IV letopisey," TODRL 28 (1974), 114–39.

[13] Sof. 1 and N4.

was published as a supplement to the Hypatian Chronicle in PSRL.[14] Unfortunately, it was not included in the 1908 republication. The "Gustinskaya letopis'" is important because it incorporates in its first part a manuscript similar to the Hypatian Chronicle. Consequently, a comparison of the two helps us to determine the correct dates of events. The "Radzivilovskaya letopis'" is of interest for its more than six hundred miniatures. Although these were drawn towards the end of the fifteenth century when the chronicle was written, a number of them are evidently direct copies of older, probably contemporary, miniatures.[15]

V. N. Tatishchev's *Istoriya Rossiyskaya* has been used sparingly. He produced two redactions of the work. The first, the more trustworthy, is contained in volume four of his *Istoriya Rossiyskaya*. He used sources that have since been lost and was thus able to incorporate new information. The second redaction, in volumes two and three, was a revision of the first. Although Tatishchev added more unique news from new chronicles and foreign sources, the second redaction is suspect. He wrote the text in contemporary Russian and therewith frequently changed the meaning of the original. He also inserted his own explanations without identifying them as such. For the purposes of our investigation the first redaction will be treated as the more reliable. Even so, his work will be referred to, in the main, only when both redactions have identical information.[16] It should also be noted that the Polish historian J. Długosz wrote a twelve-volume history in which he incorporated excerpts from Kievan and Galician–Volynian chronicles. Certain items of news concerning southern and southwestern Rus' are found only in his work.[17]

Non-chronicle texts are also valuable sources. One of these is the *Paterik* of the Kievan Caves Monastery, compiled during the first third of the thirteenth century.[18] It is made up mainly of letters written by Bishop Simeon of Vladimir in Suzdalia and the monk Policarp from the monastery. The accounts contain useful references to princes and religious personages

[14] Gust.; see D. I. Myshko, "Hustynsk'kyi litopys iak istorychne dzherelo," UIZh 4 (1971), 69–73.
[15] *Radzivilovskaya ili Kenigsbergskaya letopis'*, Komitet Imperatorskago Obshchestva Lyubiteley Drevney Pis'mennosti, 118 (Spb., 1902) (photoreproduction). Concerning the miniatures, see O. I. Podobedova, *Miniatyury russkikh istoricheskikh rukopisey* (M., 1965).
[16] Tat.; see A. A. Shakhmatov, "K voprosu o kriticheskom izdanii Istorii Rossiyskoy V. N. Tatishcheva," *Dela i Dni*, Kniga pervaya (Peterburg, 1920), 80–95; *Mikhail*, pp. xiii–xiv, and "Pitfalls," 137–53.
[17] J. Długosz, *Longini canonici Cracoviensis, Historiae Polonicae* (Leipzig, 1711), bk. 6. See also Yu. A. Limonov, "Pol'skiy khronist Yan Dlugosh o Rossii," *Feodal'naya Rossiya vo vsemirno-istoricheskom protsesse* (M., 1972), 262–8.
[18] D. Abramovich, *Kievo-pecherskiy Paterik* (K., 1930); M. Heppell (trans.), *The "Paterik" of the Kievan Caves Monastery* (Cambridge, Mass., 1989); L. A. Ol'shevskaya, "Paterik Kievo-Pecherskiy," SKKDR, 308–13.

Preface xix

of this period. The *Lyubetskiy sinodik* is an important source for helping us to determine the identities of the princes of Chernigov. The work contains a list of deceased princes of the dynasty to be commemorated by the monks at the Monastery of St. Anthony in Lyubech. R. V. Zotov compared the list of names in this source to the princes known from the chronicles and established the identities, the baptismal names, and monastic names of many individuals.[19]

A short account known as the "Slovo pokhval'noe na prenesenie moshchey Svv. Borisa i Gleba" exhorts the princes of Chernigov to live in brotherly love.[20] The anonymous work was presented on the feast of the translation of the relics of SS. Boris and Gleb. It appeals to the younger princes to be submissive to the elder ones and to cease their rivalries. The unknown author points to David Svyatoslavich (d. 1123) as an ideal prince and extols his princely behaviour and Christian virtues. The context of the *Slovo* reveals that it is a Chernigov work written after David's death.[21]

Hagiographic literature and religious accounts also provide useful information. The most important of these are the Life (*Zhitie*) of St. Evfrosinia of Suzdal'[22] and the account of the miraculous cure of Mikhail Vsevolodovich as a youth.[23] A unique source of written information is the fund of graffiti surviving on the walls of churches, notably in St. Sofia in Kiev. These inscriptions were meticulously studied by S. A. Vysotsky.[24] The epic poem "The Lay of Igor's Campaign" (*Slovo o polku Igoreve*) has not been used as a source.[25] Although it is useful insofar as it reflects the spirit of the age, it is unreliable as political evidence and provides no information that the chronicles do not give.

In addition to written works, other primary sources have been used. These include archaeological, architectural, artistic, sphragistic, and numismatic evidence. During the 1990s, Ukrainian archaeologists published valuable material concerning the Chernigov lands. Unfortunately for the political historian, much of the information is of greater value to the

[19] Zotov.
[20] Kh. Loparev (ed.), "Slovo pokhval'noe na prenesenie moshchey Svv. Borisa i Gleba," *Pamyatniki drevney pis'mennosti 98* (Spb., 1894).
[21] M. A. Salmina, "Slovo o knyaz'yakh," *SKKDR*, 429–31.
[22] V. T. Georgievsky, "Zhitie pr. Evfrosinii Suzdal'skoy, s miniatyurami, po spisku XVII v.," *Trudy Vladimirskoy uchenoy arkhivnoy komissii* (Vladimir, 1899), bk. 1.
[23] "Kniga stepennaya tsarskogo rodosloviya," PSRL 21, chast' pervaya (Spb., 1908), 248–9.
[24] *Drevne-russkie nadpisi Sofii Kievskoy XI–XIV vv.*, vyp. 1 (K., 1966) and his *Kievskie graffiti XI–XVII vv.* (K., 1985).
[25] V. P. Adrianova-Peretts (ed.), *Slovo o polku Igoreve* (M., 1950); J. Fennell and D. Obolensky (eds.), "The Lay of Igor's Campaign," *A Historical Russian Reader: A Selection of Texts from the XIth to the XVth Centuries* (Oxford, 1969), pp. 63–72; O. V. Tvorogov, "Slovo o polku Igoreve," *SKKDR*, 435–7.

study of the ethnic and material culture of the region. In like manner, the
evidence of medieval architecture and art is of greater use to students of
architecture and art than to political historians. Relying on seals and coins
as sources is also problematic. Specialists frequently disagree in attributing
these objects to specific princes. Moreover, there is insufficient evidence and
a lack of consensus among investigators concerning the princes' personal
signs such as those found on building materials. Consequently, a political
historian must use all this potentially valuable evidence with caution.

The book is, in effect, a compilation of virtually all the information that
the chronicles give on the dynasty of Chernigov for the period under investigation. Accordingly, events are examined chronologically in imitation
of the method used by the chroniclers. Since most readers are unfamiliar
with the dynasty's history, it is hoped that this method of presentation will
give them a clearer understanding of it. Moreover, it will give them an appreciation of what events the chroniclers and their contemporaries considered
to be noteworthy. This approach will also give the reader a cross-section
view of the political, ecclesiastical, and personal lives of members of the
dynasty. For easier reading each chapter is divided into subsections with
headings.

Problems arise in writing Slavic place names, proper names, and titles
in English. The term Rus' has been used to designate the so-called kernel
of the original state. For our purposes this includes the lands of Kiev,
Chernigov, and Pereyaslavl', along the central Dnepr region. The terms
patrimony (*otchina*) and domain (*volost'*) are used interchangeably. Place
names and proper names (such as Igor', Mikhail, Pereyaslavl', Zadesen'e)
have been transliterated from the forms found in the indexes of the relevant
chronicles. When chroniclers give different forms of a name, significant
variants are noted the first time the name appears (for example, Trubetsk,
Trubchesk, Trubech). For foreign names that have commonly accepted
forms in English, the latter have been used (for instance, Chingis Khan,
John de Plano Carpini, but Baty instead of Batu).

In speaking of dynasties, we have adopted the terminology of the chroniclers, who referred to members of a particular princely family by the collec-
tive form of the progenitor's name. For example, the descendants of Svyatoslav Yaroslavich of Chernigov (d. 1076) were called the Svyatoslavichi, and
those of Vladimir Monomakh (d. 1125) the Monomashichi. With growth in
numbers, one dynasty sometimes split up into several dynasties. In this way,
for example, the Svyatoslavichi became the Ol'govichi of Chernigov, the
Davidovichi of Chernigov, and the Yaroslavichi of Murom and Ryazan'.
The Ol'govichi in turn bifurcated into the senior branch and the cadet

branch. The Monomashichi split up into the Mstislavichi of Volyn', the Rostislavichi of Smolensk, and the Vsevolodovichi of Suzdalia.

Russian words have been transliterated according to the British system of Latinisation given in *The Slavonic and East European Review*.[26] Some minor modifications, however, have been made to this system. For example, e and ë are always transliterated as e (thus "ego" and not "yego"); the endings –yy and –iy are rendered –y in first names (as in Antony, Yury) and in modern surnames (Golubovsky, Vysotsky); however, in adjectival endings –yy and –iy are used (Pecherskyy, Vizantiyskiy); and feminine names ending in –iya are spelled –ia (Sofia, Agafia). For the transliteration of Ukrainian words and names we have followed the system adopted by *The Journal of Ukrainian Studies* published by The Canadian Institute of Ukrainian Studies in Toronto. Greek, Polish, German, and other foreign names are transliterated according to the forms found in *The Cambridge Medieval History*. Russian diacritical marks have not been used.

Abbreviations are explained in the list of abbreviations, where bibliographical information is found for the frequently used abbreviated titles. For unabbreviated titles, the first reference to a work is given in its complete form while subsequent references consist of the author's name, a key word or words from the title, and the page reference.

[26] W. K. Matthews, "The Latinisation of Cyrillic Characters," *The Slavonic and East European Review* 30, nr. 75 (1952), 531–48.

Acknowledgments

The plan to investigate the history of the dynasty of Chernigov was conceived some twenty years ago. The intention was to write the history in one book, but it soon became clear that a single volume would not do justice to all the available material. During the course of writing this, the second book on the dynasty of Chernigov, I received much valuable assistance from colleagues and friends whom I wish to thank.

First, I wish to acknowledge my indebtedness, albeit posthumously, to my former supervisor John Fennell, who encouraged me to take up the project and guided me with his insightful observations until his death. The late Sir Dimitri Obolensky advised me on Orthodox practices and Jonathan Shepard apprised me of Byzantine political traditions.

Ukrainian colleagues also helped in my research. Volodymyr Mezentsev was a mine of information on Chernigov's architectural heritage. Until his death, S. A. Vysotsky kept me abreast of his findings on the graffiti in the Cathedral of St. Sofia in Kiev. Over a number of years Mikhaylo Sagaydak and Volodymyr Kovalenko organized expeditions to medieval sites in Ukraine. We walked in the footsteps of the princes in Chernigov, Novgorod Severskiy, and Lyubech. We visited the Zadesen'e and the Posem'e district where V. V. Pryimak also offered his specialist's knowledge on that region. Expeditions to the south of Kiev took us to the river Ros' region. En route to Vladimir in Volyn' we visited Vruchiy, famous for its purple slate deposits. And from Galicia we retraced the route that merchants took to Kiev and Chernigov. In Kiev Gleb Ivakin and Volodymyr Zotsenko introduced me to its historical sites. I am also grateful to these colleagues for providing me with the most recent Ukrainian publications on Rus'. Other scholars and local officials whom I have not singled out also helped us on the expeditions. I wish to thank them all for their generous assistance and for their ubiquitous spirit of camaraderie.

A number of librarians merit a special note of thanks. At Oxford, Mrs. Carole Menzies of the Slavonic Reading Room in the Bodleian Library unflaggingly looked after my numerous requests. The staff at the Slavonic Section of the Taylorian Institute Library was always most accommodating. At the Pontifical Institute of Mediaeval Studies, Toronto, Caroline Suma cheerfully gave expert assistance.

I am indebted in a special way to Patricia Ellsworth for her enthusiastic assistance and for her optimistic efforts at trying to improve my grammatical and stylistic infelicities. I am grateful to Gerald Dimnik for his valuable technical assistance. My heartfelt thanks go to Karen Dinsdale who, as my administrative assistant, gave me most welcomed support and encouragement.

The Social Sciences and Humanities Research Council of Canada helped to finance the research for this book. It awarded me a three-year Standard Research Grant (1990–3) and summer grants in the years 1994, 1995, 1998, and 2000 administered through the University of St. Michael's College, Toronto. Moreover, I am grateful to the SSHRCC and to Ted Zakharchuk for partially funding my participation in the joint Canada–Ukraine Archaeological Expedition to Crimea in August 1996, which was organized by the Archaeological Institute of the Ukrainian Academy of Sciences.

Many other colleagues, librarians, and friends helped and advised me in my investigations. Although I have not singled them out by name, I wish to assure them that I greatly value their assistance and express my sincere thanks to them.

Toronto
July 2002

Chronological table of events

1151 – Vladimir Davidovich falls in battle
  – Izyaslav Davidovich occupies Chernigov
1152 – Izyaslav Mstislavich and his allies demolish Yury's Gorodets
  – Yury and Svyatoslav Ol'govich retaliate against them
1153 – Izyaslav Mstislavich and his allies attack Svyatoslav
1154 – November 14: Izyaslav Mstislavich dies in Kiev
  – Vyacheslav Vladimirovich dies in Kiev
  – Izyaslav Davidovich occupies Kiev
1155 – March 20: Yury occupies Kiev
1156 – Svyatoslav Vladimirovich seizes Vshchizh from his uncle Izyaslav
  – Svyatoslav Vsevolodovich rebels against his uncle Svyatoslav
1157 – May 15: Yury dies in Kiev
  – May 19: Izyaslav Davidovich occupies Kiev
  – Svyatoslav Ol'govich occupies Chernigov
  – Svyatoslav Vsevolodovich occupies Novgorod Severskiy
1158 – Izyaslav Davidovich and Svyatoslav Ol'govich conclude a pact
    at Lutava
  – Izyaslav flees from Kiev to the Vyatichi
  – Rostislav Mstislavich occupies Kiev
1159 – Izyaslav Davidovich fails to drive out Svyatoslav's son Oleg from
    Putivl'
  – Izyaslav fails to capture Chernigov
  – Izyaslav joins Svyatoslav Vladimirovich in Vshchizh
1160 – Izyaslav pillages the Smolensk lands
  – Svyatoslav Ol'govich and his allies storm Vshchizh
  – Svyatoslav Ol'govich sends his son Oleg to visit Rostislav in Kiev
  – Izyaslav Davidovich deceitfully wins over Oleg and other
    Ol'govichi
1161 – February 12: Izyaslav captures Kiev
  – March 6: Izyaslav dies in battle
1163 – Bishop Leon of Suzdal' visits Svyatoslav Ol'govich
1164 – February 15: Svyatoslav Ol'govich dies
  – Svyatoslav Vsevolodovich occupies Chernigov
  – Oleg Svyatoslavich occupies Novgorod Severskiy

THE FOURTH GENERATION: 1164–1201

1166 – Svyatoslav Vladimirovich dies in Vshchizh
  – Svyatoslav Vsevolodovich and Oleg Svyatoslavich fight over his
    domains

1181 – Svyatoslav fails to free Gleb from Suzdalia
– Svyatoslav becomes prince in Novgorod
– Svyatoslav and the Ol'govichi attack Drutsk
– Svyatoslav occupies Kiev
– Ryurik's troops rout Igor' and the Polovtsy at Dolobsk
– Ryurik cedes Kiev to Svyatoslav but keeps the Kievan land
1182 – The Novgorodians expel Svyatoslav's son Vladimir
– Vsevolod of Suzdalia sets Svyatoslav's son Gleb free
1184 – February 23: Konchak raids the lands of Pereyaslavl'
– Igor' pursues the pillagers and takes captives
– July 30: Svyatoslav and Ryurik defeat the Polovtsy at the river Erel'
– Igor' defeats nomads at the river Merla
1185 – January 1: Svyatoslav consecrates the Church of St. Vasily
– Svyatoslav and Ryurik defeat Konchak
– Svyatoslav goes to Karachev
– April 23: Igor' marches against the Donets Polovtsy
– May 12: Igor' is defeated at the river Kayala and taken captive
– Igor' escapes from Konchak's camp
1186 – March 25: Svyatoslav consecrates the Church of the Annunciation
– Porfiry fails to pacify Vsevolod of Suzdalia with the princes of Ryazan'
1187 – Konchak plunders the river Ros' region
– Polovtsian bands raid Chernigov lands
– October 1: Yaroslav Osmomysl dies in Galich
1188 – Svyatoslav and Ryurik campaign against the Polovtsy along the Dnepr
– Vladimir Igorevich returns from captivity with Konchak's daughter
– Roman Mstislavich of Volyn' seizes Galich
– Bela III drives out Roman from Galich
– Svyatoslav sends his son Gleb to the king in Galich
– Ryurik refuses to give Svyatoslav his Kievan domains in exchange for Galich
1190 – Kuntuvdey incites the Polovtsy to pillage the Ros' region
– Svyatoslav calls a *snem* of the Ol'govichi in Chernigov
1192 – Igor' defeats the Polovtsy
– Igor' and the Ol'govichi campaign against the Polovtsy a second time

1205 – June 19: Roman of Galich is killed
  – Ryurik seizes Kiev
  – Ryurik and the Ol'govichi fail to capture Galich
1206 – The Ol'govichi hold a *snem* in Chernigov
  – The Ol'govichi and Ryurik march against Galich
  – Vladimir Igorevich occupies Galich
  – Vsevolod Chermnyy evicts Ryurik and occupies Kiev
  – Vsevolod appoints his son Mikhail to Pereyaslavl'
  – Ryurik evicts Vsevolod from Kiev and Mikhail from
  Pereyaslavl'
1207 – Vsevolod drives out Ryurik from Kiev
  – August 19: Vsevolod Bol'shoe Gnezdo sets out against
  Chernigov
  – He diverts his attack against Ryazan'
  – Ryurik evicts Vsevolod Chermnyy from Kiev and occupies it
1208 – Roman Igorevich drives out his brother Vladimir from Galich
  – September 4: the Galicians give Galich to Ryurik's son Rostislav
  – Ryurik Rostislavich dies in Kiev
  – Vsevolod Chermnyy occupies Kiev
  – The Galicians evict Rostislav and reinstate Roman Igorevich
1209 – The Hungarians expel Roman and place Benedict in charge
  of Galich
1210 – Vsevolod Chermnyy sends Metropolitan Matfey to Vsevolod
  Bol'shoe Gnezdo
  – The Galicians ask Vladimir Igorevich to return to Galich
1211 – The Galicians hang three Igorevichi
1212 – Vsevolod Chermnyy drives out the Rostislavichi from their
  Kievan domains
  – April 13: Vsevolod Bol'shoe Gnezdo dies
  – The Rostislavichi attack Kiev
  – Vsevolod Chermnyy flees to Chernigov where he dies
  – Vsevolod's brother Gleb replaces him as senior prince
  – Mstislav Romanovich of Smolensk occupies Kiev
1218 – February 2: Konstantin Vsevolodovich dies and Yury succeeds
  him in Suzdalia
  – Mstislav Mstislavich Udaloy occupies Galich
1220 – The Lithuanians pillage Chernigov lands
  – Mstislav Svyatoslavich of Chernigov pursues the raiders
1223 – May 31: the Tatars defeat the princes of Rus' at the river Kalka
  – Mstislav Svyatoslavich of Chernigov is killed
  – Mstislav Romanovich of Kiev is killed

THE SIXTH GENERATION: 1223–1246

1223 – June 16: Vladimir Ryurikovich occupies Kiev
 – Mikhail Vsevolodovich occupies Chernigov
1224 – Yury of Suzdalia asks the Novgorodians to accept Mikhail as prince
1225 – Mikhail reconciles the Novgorodians with Yury
 – Yaroslav Vsevolodovich replaces Mikhail in Novgorod
1226 – Yury helps Mikhail against Oleg of Kursk
1228 – Vladimir Ryurikovich and Mikhail attack Daniil Romanovich
 in Kamenets
1229 – Mikhail rules Novgorod as an autonomous prince
 – Mikhail leaves his son Rostislav in Novgorod as prince
1230 – Bishop Spiridon cuts Rostislav's hair in Novgorod
 – Vladimir Ryurikovich and Mikhail send a peace delegation
 to Suzdalia
 – A famine hits the entire land
 – *Posadnik* Vnezd Vodovik and Rostislav flee to Chernigov
1231 – March 25: princes attend a *snem* in Kiev
 – Mikhail attacks Vladimir Ryurikovich in Kiev
 – Yaroslav Vsevolodovich attacks Serensk and Mosal'sk
 – *Posadnik* Vnezd Vodovik dies in Chernigov
1232 – Vodovik's supporters leave Chernigov
1233 – Izyaslav Vladimirovich pillages Daniil's town of Tikhoml'
 – Mikhail and Izyaslav threaten to march against Daniil
 – The Galicians invite Daniil to be their prince
1234 – Mikhail attacks Kiev
1235 – Vladimir and Daniil attack Mikhail in Chernigov but he drives
 them off
 – Izyaslav Vladimirovich brings the Polovtsy to Mikhail's aid
 – Mikhail defeats Vladimir and Daniil at Torchesk
 – The Polovtsy take Vladimir captive
 – Mikhail occupies Kiev
 – Daniil flees from Galich
 – Mikhail appoints Izyaslav Mstislavich to Kiev and occupies Galich
 – Vladimir returns to Kiev from the Polovtsy
1236 – Daniil and Yury of Suzdalia join forces against Mikhail
 – Yaroslav Vsevolodovich replaces Vladimir Ryurikovich in Kiev
 – Mikhail campaigns against Daniil in Volyn'
 – Daniil attacks Mikhail and Rostislav in Galich
 – Mikhail gives Daniil Peremyshl' and they conclude peace

- The Tatars defeat the Volga Bulgars
- Yaroslav departs from Kiev and returns to Suzdalia
- Mikhail appoints Rostislav to Galich and he occupies Kiev
1237 – Rostislav leads a campaign against the Lithuanians
- The Galicians invite Daniil to Galich and Rostislav flees
  to Hungary
- December 21: Baty invades Ryazan'
1238 – Baty razes Kozel'sk in the Vyatichi lands
1239 – March 3: the Tatars sack Pereyaslavl'
- Yaroslav Vsevolodovich takes Mikhail's wife captive at Kamenets
- October 18: Chernigov falls to the Tatars
1240 – Mikhail executes Tatar messengers and flees to Hungary
- Bela IV expels Mikhail and Rostislav from Hungary
- Mikhail and Rostislav go to the Poles
- Mikhail is pacified with Daniil and the latter returns Kiev to him
- December 6: Baty takes Kiev
1241 – Mikhail and his family flee to Mazovia and Silesia
- Mikhail returns to Kiev and appoints Rostislav to Chernigov
1242 – Rostislav seizes Galich
- Rostislav flees to Hungary and marries the king's daughter
- Baty sets up the Kipchak Khanate at Saray
1243 – Baty appoints Yaroslav Vsevolodovich prince of Kiev
- Mikhail visits Bela IV who rebuffs him
- Mikhail disowns Rostislav
1245 – October 26: Baty gives Daniil the *yarlyk* to rule Galicia and Volyn'
1246 – September 20: Baty kills Mikhail and his *boyar* Fedor at Saray
- September 30: Yaroslav Vsevolodovich is poisoned at Karakorum

Glossary

artel'   a team of craftsmen commissioned to build masonry structures
detinets   citadel
druzhina   a prince's private detachment of troops, bodyguard
druzhinnik   member of the *druzhina*
dvor   a prince or nobleman's household, court, courtyard
gramota   a letter, an official document of a treaty, law, or deed
grivna   monetary ingot, coin
igumen   abbot, father superior of a monastery
izgoi   a debarred prince, one ineligible to rule a town
konets   a suburb of a town, a town quarter
kuna   pelt of marten, monetary unit
letopis'   chronicle, annals
ostrog   a suburb of a town surrounded by a palisade
podol'   the lower town with a port and market
posadnik   mayor, chief executive official in a town, a prince's lieutenant
postrig   hair-cutting ceremony initiating a youth to majority
shurin   brother-in-law (wife's brother)
sinodik   book containing the names of those deceased whom the faithful
wished to have commemorated in church services
skhima   the schema or the great habit, the strictest monastic observance
in the Orthodox Church.
skhimnik   a monk having taken the vows of the *skhima*
snem   council of princes, congress, meeting, assembly
spisok   manuscript copy
strastoterpets   martyr, literally "passion-sufferer"
svat   son-in-law's father; daughter-in-law's father
svod   chronicle compilation, codex
test'   father-in-law (wife's father)
tiun (tivun)   town official, administrator
tysyatskiy   commander of a town militia, police chief

ustav   statute
veche   popular assembly, town assembly
voevoda   military commander
volost'   district, domain, administrative unit
yarlyk   charter, Tatar patent for a throne, document of privilege
Zhitie   'Life', narrative account of a saint's life or death
zyat'   son-in-law, brother-in-law

Abbreviations

Ak. sp.	"Suzdal'skaya letopis': Prodolzhenie po Akademicheskomu spisku," PSRL 1, second edition (L., 1928)
AN SSSR	Akademiya nauk Soyuz Sovetskikh Sotsialisticheskikh Respublik
Av.	"Letopis' Avraamki," PSRL 16 (Spb., 1889)
Barsov	N. Barsov, *Materialy dlya istoriko-geograficheskago slovarya Rossii: Geograficheskiy slovar' Russkoy zemli (IX-XIV st.)*, Vil'na, 1865
Barsukov	N. P. Barsukov, *Istochniki russkoy agiografii*, Spb., 1882
Baum.	N. de Baumgarten, *Généalogies et mariages occidentaux des Rurikides Russes du Xe au XIIIe siècle (Orientalia Christiana)*, vol. 9, no. 35 (Rome, 1927)
Baum. 2	N. de Baumgarten, *Généalogies des branches régnantes des Rurikides du XIIIe au XVIe siècle (Orientalia Christiana)*, vol. 35, no. 94 (Rome, 1934)
Berezhkov	N. G. Berezhkov, *Khronologiya russkogo letopisaniya*, M., 1963
bk.	book
chast'	part
Chteniya	*Chteniya v Imperatorskom Obshchestve istorii i drevnostey rossiyskikh pri Moskovskom universitete*
col.	column
Crisis	John Fennell, *The Crisis of Medieval Russia 1200–1304*, London and New York, 1983
d.	died
Dynasty	M. Dimnik, *The Dynasty of Chernigov, 1054–1146*, Toronto, 1994

Emergence of Rus	S. Franklin and J. Shepard, *The Emergence of Rus 750–1200*, London and New York, 1996
Erm.	"Ermolinskaya letopis'," PSRL 23 (Spb., 1910)
FOG	*Forschungen zur osteuropäischen Geschichte*
Golubovsky	P. V. Golubovsky, *Istoricheskaya karta Chernigovskoy gubernii do 1300 goda*, M., 1908
Gust.	"Gustinskaya letopis'," PSRL 2 (Spb., 1843)
H.	Heft
HUS	*Harvard Ukrainian Studies* (Cambridge, Mass.)
IKDR	*Istoriya kul'tury drevney Rusi*, Domongol'skiy period: I "Material'naya kul'tura," N. N. Voronin (ed.), (M.-L., 1948)
Ipat.	"Ipat'evskaya letopis'," PSRL 2, second edition (Spb., 1908)
Istoriia	M. Hrushevs'kyi, *Istoriia Ukrainy-Rusy*, 10 vols. (New York, 1954–1958, a reprint of the second enlarged edition of L'vov, 1905)
JBfGOE	*Jahrbucher für Geschichte Osteuropas*, Neue Folge (Wiesbaden)
K.	Kiev, Kyiv
kn.	kniga
KSIA	*Kratkie soobshcheniya o dokladakh i polevykh issledovaniyakh Instituta arkheologii* (AN SSSR, M.)
KSIIMK	*Kratkie soobshcheniya o dokladakh i polevykh issledovaniyakh Instituta istorii material'noy kul'tury* (AN SSSR, M.)
L.	Leningrad
Lav.	"Lavrent'evskaya letopis'," PSRL 1, second edition (L., 1926)
L'vov	"L'vovskaya letopis'," PSRL 20 (Spb., 1910)
M.	Moscow
Makhnovets'	L. Ie. Makhnovets' (trans.), *Litopys rus'kyi (za Ipats'kym spyskom)*, S. A. Zakharova (ed.), K., 1989
Maz.	"Mazurinskiy letopisets," PSRL 31 (M., 1968)
Mikhail	M. Dimnik, *Mikhail, Prince of Chernigov and Grand Prince of Kiev, 1224–1246*, Toronto, 1981
Mosk.	"Moskovskiy letopisniy svod kontsa XV veka," PSRL 25 (M.-L., 1949)
n.	note

N4	"Novgorodskaya chetvertaya letopis'," PSRL 4 (P., 1915)
N5	"Novgorodskaya pyataya letopis'," PSRL 4, (ii), (P., 1917)
Nasonov	A. N. Nasonov, *"Russkaya zemlya" i obrazovanie territorii drevnerusskogo gosudarstva*, M., 1951
Nikon. 9	"Patriarshaya ili Nikonovskaya letopis'," PSRL 9 (Spb., 1862)
Nikon. 10	"Patriarshaya ili Nikonovskaya letopis'," PSRL 10 (Spb., 1885)
NPL	*Novgorodskaya pervaya letopis' starshego i mladshego izvodov*, A. N. Nasonov (ed.), M.-L., 1950
nr.	number
P.	Petrograd
Perfecky	*The Hypatian Codex, Part Two: The Galician–Volynian Chronicle*, G. E. Perfecky (trans.), Munich, 1973
Pisk.	"Piskarevskiy letopisets," PSRL 34 (M., 1978)
"Pitfalls"	M. Dimnik, "A Bride's Journey from Kiev to Vladimir (1211): Pitfalls in Using V. N. Tatishchev as a Source," *Roma, magistra mundi. Itineraria culturae medievalis*. Mélanges offerts au Père L. E. Boyle à l'occasion de son 75e anniversaire édités par J. Hamesse (Fédération Internationale des Instituts d'Etudes Médiévales. "Textes et études du moyen âge," X), vol. 1 (Louvain-la-Neuve, 1998), 137–53
Pskov	*Pskovskie letopisi*, A. N. Nasonov (ed.), 2 vols., A.N. SSSR, 1941, 1955
PSRL	*Polnoe sobranie russkikh letopisey*, vols. 1–41 (Spb., L., M., 1841–1995)
pt.	part
Rapov	O. M. Rapov, *Knyazheskie vladeniya na Rusi v X-pervoy polovine XIII v.*, M., 1977
Rappoport	P. A. Rappoport, *Russkaya arkhitektura X-XIII vv. Katalog pamyatnikov*, in the series *Arkheologiya SSSR Svod arkheologicheskikh istochnikov* (E1–47), L., 1982
Rog.	"Rogozhskiy letopisets," PSRL 15 (P., 1922)
s.a.	*sub anno*
SA	*Sovetskaya arkheologiya*
Sim.	"Simeonovskaya letopis'," PSRL 18 (Spb., 1913)

SKKDR	*Slovar' knizhnikov i knizhnosti Drevney Rusi*, vyp. 1 (XI-pervaya polovina XIV v.), D. S. Likhachev (ed.), L., 1987
Sof. 1	"Sofiyskaya pervaya letopis' (vyp. pervyy)," PSRL 5, second edition (L., 1925)
Spb.	St. Petersburg
Sviatyi kniaz'	*Sviatyi kniaz' Mykhailo chernihivs'kyi ta ioho doba*, V. P. Kovalenko *et al.* (eds.), Chernihiv, 1996
svod 1493	"Sokrashchennyy letopisnyy svod 1493 g.," PSRL 27 (M.-L., 1962)
svod 1495	"Sokrashchennyy letopisnyy svod 1495 g.," PSRL 27 (M.-L., 1962)
Tat.	V. N. Tatishchev, *Istoriya Rossiyskaya*, 7 vols., M.-L., 1962–1968
Tip.	"Tipografskaya letopis'," PSRL 24 (P., 1921)
TL	*Troitskaya letopis', rekonstruktsiya teksta*, M. D. Priselkov (ed.), M.-L., 1950
TODRL	*Trudy Otdela drevnerusskoy literatury*, A.N. SSSR, Institut russkoy literatury (Pushkinskiy Dom, M.-L.) volume
Tver.	"Tverskaya letopis'," PSRL 15 (Spb., 1863)
UIZh	*Ukrains'kyi istorychnyi zhurnal* (K.)
var.	variant
Vlad.	"Vladimirskiy letopisets," PSRL 30 (M., 1965)
VOIDR	*Vremennik Obshchestva istorii i drevnostey rossiyskikh pri Moskovskom universitete*
vol.	volume
Vosk.	"Voskresenskaya letopis'," PSRL 7 (Spb., 1856)
vyp.	vypusk
Yanin 1	V. L. Yanin, *Aktovye pechati Drevney Rusi X-XV vv.*, vol. 1, Pechati X-nachala XIII v., M., 1970
Yanin 3	V. L. Yanin and P. G. Gaydukov, *Aktovye pechati Drevney Rusi X-XV vv.*, vol. 3, Pechati, zaregistrirovannye v 1970–1996 gg., M., 1998
Zaytsev	A. K. Zaytsev, "Chernigovskoe knyazhestvo," *Drevnerusskie knyazhestva X-XIII vv.*, L. G. Beskrovny (ed.) (M., 1975), 57–117
Zemlya Vyatichey	T. N. Nikol'skaya, *Zemlya Vyatichey. K istorii naseleniya basseyna verkhney i sredney Oki v IX-XIII vv.*, M., 1981

Zh. M. N. P.   *Zhurnal ministerstva narodnago prosveshcheniya* (Spb.)

Zotov   R. V. Zotov, *O Chernigovskikh knyazyakh po Lyubetskomu sinodiku i o Chernigovskom knyazhestve v Tatarskoe vremya*, Spb., 1892

Introduction

The history of the dynasty's first hundred years appeared in 1994 as *The Dynasty of Chernigov 1054–1146*. It began with the year in which Svyatoslav Yaroslavich became the autonomous prince of Chernigov and ended with the year in which his grandson Vsevolod Ol'govich died as prince of Kiev. The present volume continues with the succession of Vsevolod's brother Igor' to Kiev and ends with the year 1246, when Vsevolod's great-grandson Mikhail Vsevolodovich died as the last autonomous senior prince of the dynasty. Although his career was investigated in the monograph *Mikhail, Prince of Chernigov and Grand prince of Kiev, 1224–1246* (Toronto, 1981), it merits a re-examination because of the new studies that have appeared over the past twenty years. In this work Mikhail's career will also be looked at chronologically rather than thematically and his achievements will be evaluated in the light of those of his ancestors.

The reasons for writing a new history of the dynasty were discussed in the earlier study, but it will be useful to review them. As it was pointed out, the first written source of Rus' to mention Chernigov is "The Tale of Bygone Years," also known as the "Primary Chronicle."[1] It reports the origin of the dynasty under Svyatoslav Yaroslavich and tells of his activities and those of his sons up to 1117, the year in which it ends. After that a number of Svyatoslav's descendants kept chronicles at their courts, but none of them has survived. The main reason for this is that in the middle of the thirteenth century the Tatars eliminated the princes of Chernigov as a political force. At the same time, the Monomashichi of Suzdalia found favor with the new overlords and, on becoming the supreme rulers in Muscovy during the fifteenth and sixteenth centuries, had their scribes produce compilations assimilating information from older extant chronicles.

---

[1] *Dynasty*, pp. 7–8.

I

We do not know if any of the Chernigov chronicles survived to the fifteenth century. If they did, hostile copyists probably discarded them. Moreover, in assembling information to record the history of their masters, the Muscovite scribes frequently ignored, rejected, or altered the information of the Chernigov sources. Their compilations therefore contain only passing and often deprecatory references to the princes of Chernigov because the latter had been the rivals of the Monomashichi in Rus'. In addition to the Muscovite compilations, a number of regional ones (such as those from Galicia-Volyn', Novgorod, and Pskov) have also survived.

Muscovite chronicle compilations, with their emphasis on the achievements of the Monomashichi, have influenced and even dictated the views of historians. Consequently, although the dynasty of Chernigov did not become ineffectual until the middle of the thirteenth century, many historians relegated it to a place of little importance even before that date. General histories of Rus' written up to the end of the nineteenth century illustrate the relatively insignificant role that their authors attributed to Svyatoslav's descendants. These works are primarily paraphrases of chronicle accounts. Their authors devote little space to examining the aspirations and achievements of the dynasty or to investigating the degree to which its princes observed or transgressed the practices of succession and inheritance.[2]

During the last quarter of the nineteenth century a number of historians examined the histories of individual principalities. Two of them, P. V. Golubovsky and D. Bagaley, investigated the history of Chernigov.[3] These were important studies because, for the first time, the authors assembled all the available chronicle information on the activities of the House of Chernigov. The two historians made little headway towards evaluating the successes of the princes, however, and towards placing them on the proper rung of political importance in Rus'. At a later date Golubovsky also published the first critical identification of the towns that the chronicles reported in the Chernigov lands.[4]

One important nineteenth-century study is different in nature. R. V. Zotov set out to identify all the princes of Chernigov from the time of the Tatar invasion to the year 1362, when Ol'gerd of Lithuania occupied Kiev. In order to do so, however, he also had to identify all the princes before

---

[2] See, for example, I. Belyaev, *Razskazy iz russkoy istorii*, second edition (M., 1865), bk. 1; M. Pogodin, *Drevnyaya russkaya istoriya do mongol'skago iga* (M., 1872), vol. 1; N. M. Karamzin, *Istoriya gosudarstva Rossiiskago*, third edition (Spb., 1830–1), vol. 3; S. M. Solov'ev, *Istoriya Rossii s drevneyshikh vremen* (M., 1962, 1963), kn. 1 and 2, and others.
[3] P. V. Golubovsky, *Istoriya Severskoy zemli do poloviny XIV stoletiya* (K., 1881); D. Bagaley, *Istoriya Severskoy zemli do poloviny XIV stoletiya* (K., 1882).
[4] Golubovsky.

the Tatar invasion, beginning with the dynasty's progenitor, Svyatoslav Yaroslavich. By comparing the names of princes and princesses that he found recorded in the previously little-studied *Lyubetskiy sinodik* with the names that the chronicles reported, he was able to verify and expand the list of known princes.[5] Since, however, his objective was to establish the correct genealogy of the dynasty, he did not investigate its political history.

In 1891, the Ukrainian historian M. Hrushevsky wrote the most penetrating study so far on the political activities of the princes of Chernigov.[6] Since his main task was to write the history of Kiev, however, he studied the activities of the princes of Chernigov only insofar as they affected Kiev. Later, he published another analysis of the dynasty's activities in his work on Ukraine-Rus'.[7] Since this was a general history, he again failed to adequately examine the importance of the House of Chernigov.

Soviet academics generally belittled the history of Chernigov. Following the examples of their nineteenth-century predecessors, they focused their attention on the dynasties of Suzdalia, Galicia-Volyn', Smolensk, Ryazan', and the town of Novgorod. Their failure to produce a monograph on Chernigov during the course of some seventy years shows how little importance they attached to the dynasty. There were, nevertheless, dissenting voices. A. N. Nasonov challenged the accepted Soviet view. He argued that in the twelfth century two of the strongest principalities, Chernigov and Rostov-Suzdal', initiated a struggle for supremacy in Rus'.[8] Moreover, B. A. Rybakov was one of the most prolific Soviet archaeologists writing on the Chernigov lands. The number of his published works in the bibliography, notably his oft-cited study on Chernigov's antiquities,[9] testifies to the importance that he attached to the town.

Some twenty-five years ago, the Soviet scholar A. K. Zaytsev wrote a study on the principality of Chernigov.[10] His focus, however, was the identification of the principality's towns, boundaries, and districts. Two Ukrainian scholars also wrote important theses on Chernigov and its lands, but their works never appeared in published form. V. I. Mezentsev examined the historical topography of the town. He argued persuasively that in the twelfth

---

[5] Zotov.
[6] *Ocherk istorii Kievskoy zemli ot smerti Yaroslava do kontsa XIV stoletiya* (K., 1891).
[7] *Istoriia.*
[8] "Vladimiro-Suzdal'skoe knyazhestvo," *Ocherki istorii SSSR: period feodalizma IX–XV vv.*, B. D. Grekov (ed.) (M., 1953), pt. 1, pp. 320–34.
[9] "Drevnosti Chernigova," *Materialy i issledovaniya po arkheologii drevnerusskikh gorodov*, N. N. Voronin (ed.), vol. 1, in *Materialy i issledovaniya po arkheologii SSSR* (M.-L., 1949), nr. 11, pp. 7–93.
[10] Zaytsev M., 1975, pp. 57–117.

and thirteenth centuries Chernigov outstripped Kiev in size and successfully competed with it for supremacy.[11] V. P. Kovalenko investigated the
provenance of chronicle towns in the Chernigov lands from the ninth to
the thirteenth centuries.[12] His many publications are based on the extensive excavations that he has conducted on the citadels of many of these
towns.

Since 1990, Ukrainian and Russian archaeologists have excavated new
medieval sites in the Chernigov lands and published their findings. T. N.
Nikol'skaya is doing extensive work on the Vyatichi lands; G. P. Polyakov
is studying Karachev and the surrounding district; A. P. Motsya and the
now deceased A. V. Kuza studied medieval Novgorod Severskiy and other
towns; E. A. Shinakov and V. V. Minenko specialize in the towns of the
Podesen'e; O. A. Makushnikov is researching Gomiy and its environs; A. V.
Shekun and E. M. Veremeychik are investigating the towns and trade routes
in the region around Lyubech; Yu. N. Sytyy specializes in the towns of the
Zadesen'e; O. V. Sukhobokov, V. V. Pryimak, and Yu. Yu. Morgunov are
specialists on the Seym river basin; L. N. Bol'shakov studies the architecture
of Chernigov; and V. Ya. Rudenok is investigating its monastic history.

The present volume continues our study of the long-neglected and con-
troversial political history of the dynasty. It should be pointed out once
again, however, that the available sources provide little information on the
social and agrarian conditions of the period under investigation. We also
know little about the nature of landownership, legal administration, and
the tribute system. Archaeological, sphragistic, architectural, artistic, and
numismatic findings have thrown light on such matters as crafts, masonry
architecture, and trade between the towns of Rus' and with other lands.
It is the chronicles, however, that remain the chief source of information
on the personal and political lives of the princes. They record their births,
marriages, deaths, building projects, relations with the Church, oath taking, oath breaking, alliances, squabbles, internecine wars, and campaigns
against the Polovtsy. Consequently the chronicles will, to a large extent,
determine the course of our investigation.

The main purpose of this book is to examine the achievements and fail-
ures of the princes of Chernigov in order to put them into their proper place
in the political history of Rus'. We will attempt to establish how powerful
different senior princes were in relation to each other and in relation to

[11] *Drevniy Chernigov: Genezis i istoricheskaya topografiya goroda,* Doctoral dissertation, The Institute of
History of the Ukrainian Academy of Sciences, K., 1981.
[12] *Proiskhozhdenie letopisnykh gorodov Chernigovo-Severskoy zemli (IX–XIII vv.),* Avtoreferat dissertatsii
na soiskanie uchenoy stepeni kandidata istoricheskikh nauk, K., 1983.

senior princes of other dynasties. We will attempt to ascertain whether, in their contests with other dynasties, the princes of Chernigov violated the tradition governing succession to Kiev. We will examine the role that marriage alliances played in inter-dynastic relations. We will also evaluate whether, in their rivalries among themselves, the princes of Chernigov breached the practice of inheritance and the system of lateral succession. In order to determine the latter, it will be necessary to establish, insofar as available evidence allows, the identities of all the princes and their places in the dynasty's order of genealogical seniority.

THE FIRST HUNDRED YEARS

The princes of Chernigov owned one of the largest domains in Rus'. Even after they lost the Murom and Ryazan' lands in the 1120s, their territorial base was second only to Novgorod's seemingly limitless hinterland. During the second half of the twelfth and the first half of the thirteenth centuries, they controlled the vast territories stretching from below Moscow in the north to the reaches of the upper Donets river in the south, from the Dnepr in the west to Kursk in the east. Chroniclers identify by name some seventy towns in this domain, but the total number was closer to several hundred. Numerous smaller settlements also dotted the countryside. In the central region of Chernigov alone, archaeologists have identified more than 500 settlements. Indeed, they assert that the princes of Chernigov ruled a larger population than any other dynasty (map 1).[13]

Chernigov, the dynastic capital, testifies to the political importance, wealth, cultural enterprises, and foreign contacts of its princes. It is located on the river Desna some 150 km northeast of Kiev. Specialists have estimated that, at its zenith in the late twelfth and early thirteenth centuries, it covered an area of some 400–450 hectares and was arguably the largest town in Rus'. Kiev encompassed some 360 to 380 hectares.[14] Chernigov, unlike Kiev, had a hereditary dynasty. Its bishop was second in importance to the metropolitan in Kiev. It was a major hub of crafts and commerce; its merchants, as we shall see, traded with the Rhine region, the Volga Bulgars, Novgorod, and Byzantium.

---

[13] V. P. Kovalenko, "Chernigovo-Severskaya zemlya v sisteme Drevnerusskikh knyazhestv XII–XIII vv.: istoriograficheskie traditsii i real'nost'," *Otechestvennaya i vseobshchaya istoriya: metodologiya, istochnikovedenie, istoriografiya* (Bryansk, 1993), 83–5.

[14] Mezentsev, *Drevniy Chernigov*, p. 150, and his "The Territorial and Demographic Development of Medieval Kiev and Other Major Cities of Rus': A Comparative Analysis Based on Recent Archaeological Research," *The Russian Review* 48 (1989), 161–9.

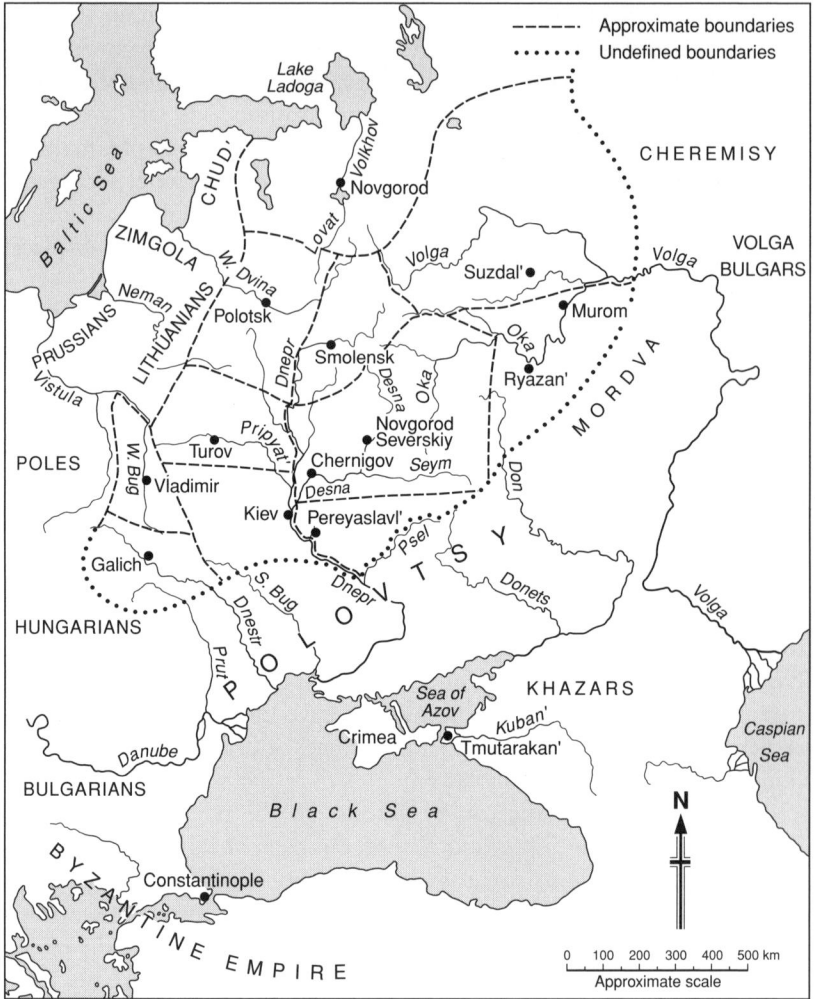

Map 1   The lands of Rus' in the middle of the twelfth century

As a cultural center it competed with Kiev and had its own school of architecture. Three of its eleventh- and twelfth-century masonry churches have survived: the bishop's Cathedral of the Transfiguration on the citadel (figure 1), the Church of the Assumption at the Eletskiy Monastery, and the Church of St. Elias at the entrance to the Caves Monastery. Two of its medieval churches have been restored: the Paraskeva Pyatnitsa in the market square and the Church of SS. Gleb and Boris on the citadel. Written sources

Figure 1   Holy Saviour Cathedral and medieval Chernigov: a fragment from the icon of
the Eletskiy Monastery

and archaeological probes conducted during the Soviet period testify to the existence of episcopal courts, princely courts, and other masonry buildings on the citadel (map 2).

No chronicle has survived from Chernigov, but others that have come down to us have copious information concerning its princes. This is so because the latter were closely associated with the history of Kiev. Indeed, their involvement in the inter-dynastic rivalries for supremacy in Rus′ helps us to understand better the fluctuating balance of power between the dynasties, the process of succession, and the practice of inheritance. As has been noted, the history of their first hundred years was examined in *The Dynasty of Chernigov 1054–1146*. Since these events influenced the policies of later princes, let us review the more important developments.

From the vantage point of hindsight it would appear that, from the earliest times, the princes of Rus′ apparently acknowledged a practice of succession governed by genealogical seniority. According to this tradition, after the prince of Kiev died his eldest surviving brother succeeded him. After all the brothers had ruled in rotation, succession passed to the genealogically eldest surviving relative in the next generation. Svyatoslav Igorevich (d. 972), who had no brothers, seemingly followed this practice by appointing his genealogically eldest relative, his son Yaropolk, to Kiev. Yaropolk and his younger brothers Oleg and Vladimir were evidently the first princely family which had the opportunity of putting the principle of the so-called "lateral system of succession" into practice. Nevertheless, their conduct neither confirms nor refutes the observation that they were expected to occupy Kiev in rotation. Yaropolk killed Oleg and, in revenge, Vladimir killed Yaropolk and became the sole ruler. In the test case, so to speak, fratricide pre-empted any advocated peaceful process of succession.

Even though Vladimir himself used violence to seize supreme power, the chronicler claims that before his death he designated his successor to Kiev according to a recognized procedure. Contrary to his own wishes, he conceded that his alleged eldest son Svyatopolk was the rightful claimant.[15] According to another tradition, Svyatopolk was the son of Vladimir's eldest brother Yaropolk. The latter, we are told, had abducted a Byzantine nun. When she was already pregnant with Svyatopolk, Vladimir, in turn, abducted her from Yaropolk after killing him.[16] According to this view, therefore, Svyatopolk was Vladimir's eldest surviving nephew. In either case, whether Svyatopolk was Vladimir's eldest nephew or his eldest son,

---

[15] M. Dimnik, "Succession and Inheritance in Rus′ before 1054," *Mediaeval Studies* 58 (Toronto, 1996), 87–117.
[16] *Emergence of Rus*, pp. 190–1.

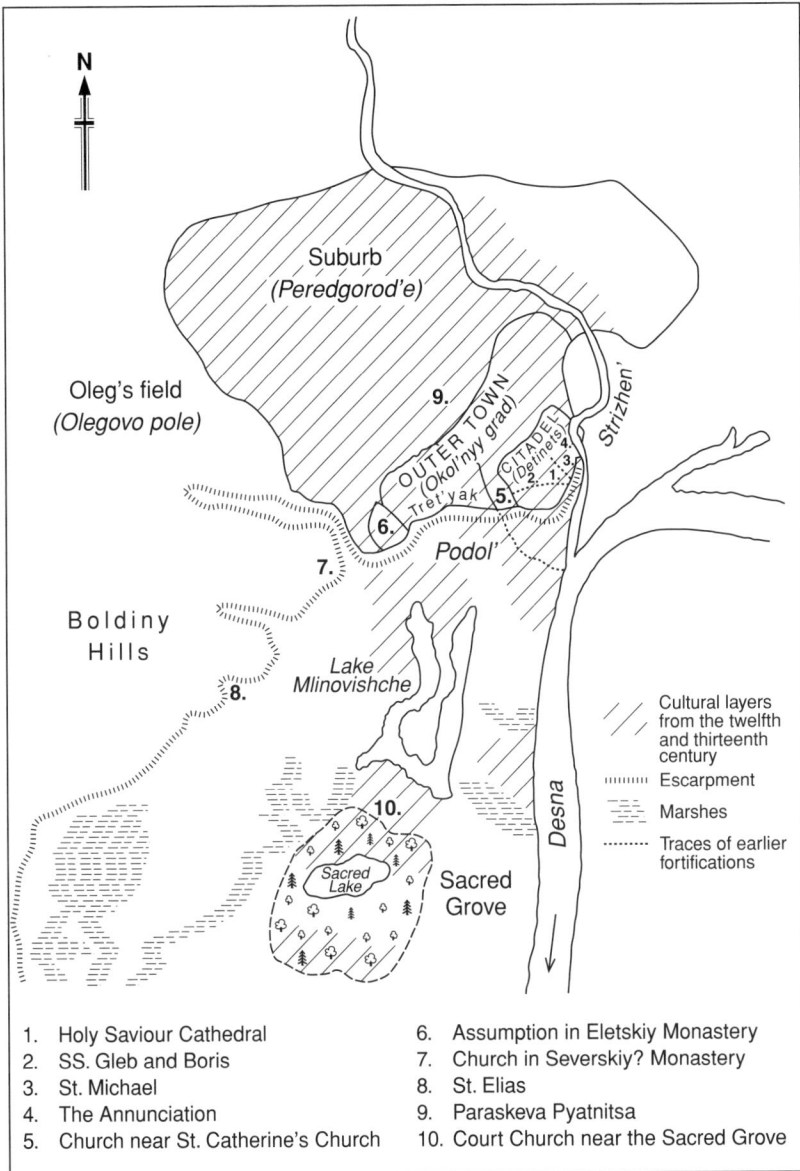

N

Suburb
(Peredgorod'e)

Oleg's field
(Olegovo pole)

9.

OUTER TOWN
(Okol'nyy grad)

Strizhen'

CITADEL
(Detinets)
4.
2. 1. 3.

Tret'yak 5.

6.

Podol'

7.

Boldiny
Hills

8.

Lake
Mlinovishche

10.

Sacred
Lake

Sacred
Grove

Desna

	Cultural layers from the twelfth and thirteenth century
	Escarpment
	Marshes
	Traces of earlier fortifications

1. Holy Saviour Cathedral	6. Assumption in Eletskiy Monastery
2. SS. Gleb and Boris	7. Church in Severskiy? Monastery
3. St. Michael	8. St. Elias
4. The Annunciation	9. Paraskeva Pyatnitsa
5. Church near St. Catherine's Church	10. Court Church near the Sacred Grove

Map 2   Chernigov in the twelfth and thirteenth century (adapted from B. A. Rybakov)

the news that he recognized Svyatopolk as his rightful successor shows that
Vladimir acted, or reveals that a later chronicler writing the report believed
that Vladimir acted, in keeping with a principle of succession governed by
genealogical seniority.

The inheritance of patrimonies was distinct from succession. Vladimir,
like his father Svyatoslav, allocated to each of his sons a domain that was
evidently to become his permanent possession. Despite Vladimir's seeming
desire to abide by pre-existing practices of succession to Kiev and of granting
patrimonies, his sons violated the process of the peaceful transition of power
once again. Many Kievans opposed Svyatopolk's occupation of Kiev and
supported his younger brother Boris. Svyatopolk's fear of usurpation, and
his determination to consolidate his rule by depriving his brothers of their
patrimonies, prompted him to initiate fratricidal wars. In the end, his
younger brother Yaroslav, who became known as "the Wise" (*Mudryy*),
emerged the victor.[17]

Yaroslav adopted his father's practice of allocating hereditary domains
by giving each of his sons a patrimony. He also honored the system of
lateral succession as it was generally practiced. He changed the procedure
of succession to Kiev, however, in order to obviate future internecine wars.
He designated his three eldest surviving sons and their descendants as
successors to Kiev. For convenience let us speak of these three families as
the "inner circle." Yaroslav therewith debarred his two youngest sons from
occupying Kiev. He named his eldest son, Izyaslav, as his successor. After
Izyaslav died he was to be replaced, in a peaceful manner, by Svyatoslav, the
next in precedence. After he died the youngest, Vsevolod, would occupy
Kiev. After Vsevolod's death, succession would pass to the next generation,
presumably, to Izyaslav's eldest surviving son. The process would then be
repeated according to genealogical seniority among the members of the
inner circle.

To ensure that the prince of Kiev was the most powerful of the three
and able to maintain order among the other princes, Yaroslav gave his three
eldest sons patrimonies adjacent to Kiev. Izyaslav got Turov, Svyatoslav got
Chernigov, and Vsevolod got Pereyaslavl'. As each, in turn, occupied Kiev
he would rule the Kievan land in addition to his patrimony. This, Yaroslav
believed, would give the prince of Kiev military superiority over each of his
brothers. The system was based on the premise that the three princes would
live in brotherly love and abide by Yaroslav's directive to succeed each other
peacefully. This, to judge from the evidence, was Yaroslav's innovation to

[17] Concerning the power struggle, see *Emergence of Rus*, pp. 184–93.

the system of succession to Kiev.[18] His sons put the viability of the scheme to the test.

Svyatoslav of Chernigov suffered from an incurable ailment. In 1072, at the translation ceremony of the relics of SS. Boris and Gleb in Vyshgorod, he sought a miraculous cure by placing on the sore on his shoulder the hand of St. Gleb, whom he had adopted as the patron saint of the family. He was not healed. Consequently he anticipated, rightly as it turned out, that he would predecease his elder brother, Izyaslav. He would thus fail to rule Kiev according to the peaceful order of succession that his father had advocated. Consequently, none of his sons would have the right to rule Kiev. They could not have recourse to the age-old maxim that they had the right "to sit on the throne of their father." Svyatoslav therefore used force, a proven means of laying claim to Kiev. He persuaded his brother Vsevolod to join him in overthrowing Izyaslav. The brothers therewith violated Yaroslav's directive to live in brotherly love. By breaking it, however, Svyatoslav secured for his sons the right "to sit on the throne of their father."

Each dynasty of the "inner circle" was to adopt for its dynastic capital the practice of succession that Yaroslav had instituted for Kiev. In Chernigov, for example, Svyatoslav's eldest son would succeed him, and then the latter's eldest surviving brother and so on. No prince could claim Chernigov as his hereditary domain. Moreover, as Svyatoslav's sons came of age, he gave each of them a patrimony in the Chernigov lands. Consequently, Svyatoslav's successor would occupy Chernigov while retaining control of his patrimonial domain. The prince of Chernigov, as the dynasty's senior prince, also had the right to succeed to Kiev when the dynasty's turn came to rule it according to genealogical seniority within the "inner circle."

Despite Svyatoslav's violation, Yaroslav's system of succession to Kiev worked more or less successfully during the first generation of the "inner circle." Izyaslav succeeded Yaroslav the Wise. Svyatoslav and Vsevolod deposed him, but after four years Svyatoslav died and Izyaslav returned to Kiev. Following Izyaslav's death, Vsevolod occupied the throne. After him, Kiev passed peacefully to Izyaslav's eldest surviving son, Svyatopolk. Svyatopolk and Vsevolod's son Vladimir Monomakh, however, changed Yaroslav's scheme.

Oleg, Svyatoslav's eldest surviving son, was the rightful ruler of Chernigov. By 1096, however, Svyatopolk and Monomakh had deprived him of his patrimonial lands. In the following year, they imposed their

[18] M. Dimnik, "The 'Testament' of Iaroslav 'The Wise': A Re-Examination," *Canadian Slavonic Papers* 29, nr. 4 (1987), 369–86.

terms on the helpless prince at the Congress of Lyubech. First they humiliated Oleg by demoting him as senior prince. They also deposed him as sole ruler of Chernigov and made him co-ruler with his brother David. They made the less-energetic David the politically senior of the two. At that time, it appears, they confirmed Novgorod Severskiy as Oleg's patrimony and allotted an unidentified domain, perhaps Lyubech, to David. Their youngest brother, Yaroslav, got the lands of Murom and Ryazan'. The dynastic capital of Chernigov became their common patrimony. At Lyubech the princes also placed David's sons before Oleg's sons in political precedence, designating David's to rule Chernigov ahead of Oleg's.

Svyatopolk and Monomakh also penalized the dynasty as a whole. They advanced Monomakh up a rung on the ladder of succession to Kiev ahead of the princes of Chernigov. Accordingly, after Svyatopolk's death, Monomakh and not Oleg would occupy Kiev. By changing the order of seniority, Monomakh successfully debarred the princes of Chernigov from ever ruling Kiev because both Oleg and David predeceased him. Their sons therefore became *izgoi*. At the same time, Monomakh secured succession to Kiev for his own descendants. His self-orchestrated promotion was another violation of Yaroslav's system of succession to Kiev. Thus, after vanquishing Oleg and depriving him of his military resources, Monomakh and Svyatopolk reaped their reward by relegating his dynasty to the bottom rung of the inner circle. Oleg, for his part, never rebelled against the penalties his cousins imposed on him because he also had scored a victory. He had won the permanency of family patrimonies.

Monomakh's ambitions did not stop at demoting the Svyatoslavichi. After Svyatopolk's death he formed an alliance with Oleg and David to debar Svyatopolk's heirs from Kiev. They therewith abolished the "inner circle" in that the three-family system of succession created by Yaroslav the Wise ceased to exist. But Monomakh had still greater ambitions for his family. Whereas his grandfather Yaroslav the Wise had designated his three eldest sons and their descendants as claimants to Kiev, before his death, in 1125, Monomakh made a deal with the Kievans to accept the family of his eldest son Mstislav as their resident dynasty. In this way, he debarred his four youngest surviving sons.

When Monomakh died, Oleg and David's youngest brother, Yaroslav, was prince of Chernigov. According to the Lyubech agreement, he was to succeed Monomakh to Kiev. He, however, lacked the leadership qualities needed to challenge Monomakh's son Mstislav. Consequently, Yaroslav and his sons also became debarred. His genealogically eldest surviving nephew, Oleg's son Vsevolod, was made of different metal. In 1127, he evicted Yaroslav from Chernigov and assumed the role of senior prince. Mstislav of Kiev, his father-in-law, confirmed the usurpation. They relegated Yaroslav to Murom and Ryazan', made the towns his permanent domain, and deprived him and his heirs of the right to rule Chernigov. Vsevolod also reinstated the Ol'govichi ahead of the Davidovichi in the order of succession to Chernigov.

In 1132, after Mstislav died, Monomakh's descendants squabbled over succession. Mstislav's sons argued that, according to Monomakh's agreement with the Kievans, they were the rightful claimants. Mstislav's younger brothers, in particular Yury, later called "Long-arm" (*Dolgorukiy*), insisted that they had prior claims according to the system ordained by Yaroslav the Wise. During the rivalry, Vsevolod Ol'govich usurped Kiev. He refused to submit to the injustice that Monomakh had done in pre-empting the claim of his father Oleg. Since the latter had never ruled the town, Vsevolod could not claim the right to sit on the throne of his father. He had a right, however, insofar as he was the senior prince of the dynasty and usurpation was a recognized form of seizing power. Through usurpation, therefore, Vsevolod secured the right for his sons to rule Kiev. Moreover, he imitated Monomakh in attempting to make the town the hereditary domain of the Ol'govichi. Before his death, he designated his younger brother Igor' to succeed him. Given Vsevolod's success in asserting his authority over the princes in Rus', he either persuaded them or intimidated them, including the Kievans, into pledging their support for Igor'.

At the time of Vsevolod's death, therefore, the system of succession to Kiev initiated by Yaroslav the Wise had become defunct. The three families of the "inner circle" (Izyaslav, Svyatoslav, and Vsevolod's) that he had designated to rule Kiev had been reduced to two: Svyatoslav's descendants had lost their claim, but Vsevolod Ol'govich had regained it for his family by usurping Kiev; Vsevolod Yaroslavich's descendants had never lost their claim thanks to the machinations of his son Vladimir Monomakh. Moreover, by ignoring the traditional system of lateral succession, he sought to give Kiev to the family of his eldest son. Vsevolod Ol'govich, abiding by the practice of genealogical seniority, designated his younger brother to replace him. It remained to be seen whom the Kievans would elect. Would they keep their promise to Monomakh and welcome the heirs of his son Mstislav, or would they keep their pledges to Vsevolod and enthrone his younger brother Igor'?

I

The third generation continued: 1146–1164

Vsevolod, the eldest Ol'govich in the third generation of the princes of Chernigov, had risen to the pinnacle of political power in the dynasty and in Rus' by becoming senior prince of the dynasty and by ruling Kiev. It fell to his brother Igor', the next in seniority, to maintain the supremacy of the Ol'govichi in Rus'. To do this he had to secure his authority as senior prince of the dynasty, consolidate the superiority of the Ol'govichi over his cousins the Davidovichi, and replace his brother as prince of Kiev. He could look forward to facing these challenges with the loyal support of his brother Svyatoslav.

The chroniclers describe Igor''s ephemeral reign in Kiev in vivid detail. Their preoccupation with his career can be explained, as we shall see, by the significance of his failure and by the unprecedented nature of his death. In evaluating their accounts, we should keep in mind that the chroniclers had different views of Igor' at different stages of his life. Before his death they speak of him as having a violent nature and accuse him and his brother Svyatoslav of being cunning, greedy, and dishonest. They also accuse the brothers of breaking promises, instigating plots, and forcing reconciliation.[1] After Igor''s death, as we shall see, the chroniclers looked upon him as a good man, a defender of his patrimony, and a saint. Consequently, when examining the accounts, we must keep in mind the biases of hostile anti-Ol'govichi detractors, of loyal Chernigov subjects, and of pious proponents of Igor''s martyrdom.

IGOR' FAILS IN KIEV

After Yaroslav the Wise, Igor' was the third prince from the dynasty of Chernigov to occupy Kiev. His grandfather Svyatoslav and his elder brother, Vsevolod, had usurped power. Igor', however, was the first who succeeded

---

[1] *Dynasty*, pp. 369–83.

14

to the capital of Rus′ through peaceful means. His reign began under auspicious conditions. Before his death in 1146, Vsevolod seemingly took the necessary measures to secure Igor′'s peaceful succession. He persuaded the princes of Chernigov, a number of the Monomashichi, and the Kievans to pledge their loyalty to Igor′ as his designated successor.[2] Consequently, after Vsevolod's death, it should have been merely a formality for the same princes and the townsmen to renew their pledges. Unfortunately for Igor′, this was not to be the case.

After Vsevolod's death, the Kievans had to acknowledge Igor′ as their prince with a new oath of allegiance and negotiate the terms of his rule. Accordingly, he summoned them to Yaroslav's court on the hill, his home ground so to speak, where the Kievans kissed the Holy Cross to all his terms. They refused, however, to install him as prince. This is implied by the chronicler's failure to record the enthronement ceremony in St. Sofia Cathedral at which a new prince pledged his oath to the Kievans by kissing the icon of the Mother of God. Instead, the townsmen went to the *podol′*, where they traditionally met in *veche*. They summoned Igor′ to come and kiss the Holy Cross to all their terms. Their actions indicate that they distrusted him.[3]

Seeing that at least some Kievans were reluctant to accept him, Igor′ demonstrated his desire to begin his reign on the right footing by delegating his younger brother, Svyatoslav, to negotiate on his behalf. Given his allegedly volatile nature, this was a prudent tactic. To judge from the reports of chroniclers, his contemporaries looked upon Igor′ with hostility. According to one albeit late source, Vsevolod had coerced the Kievans into kissing the Holy Cross to Igor′ and they neither liked him nor wanted him to be their prince. The other princes also disliked him and the Ol′govichi. It was said that no prince of Rus′ was of the same mind as Igor′ except for his brother Svyatoslav.[4] Consequently, Igor′ may well have sent his brother to parley with the Kievans because he was aware of his own unpopularity.

Nevertheless, Igor′'s willingness to have an intermediary negotiate on his behalf showed that he was capable of discretion. He also demonstrated patience by attempting to appease the *veche* through negotiation rather than by forcing his authority on the people. Such behavior contradicts

---

[2] *Dynasty*, pp. 404–11.
[3] Ipat., cols. 321–2; Mosk., p. 37. See also I. Ya. Froyanov, "Vechevye sobraniya 1146–1147 gg. v Kieve," *Vestnik* Leningradskogo Universiteta, 8, Seriya Istoriya, Yazyk, Literatura, vyp. 2 (1977), 31.
[4] Gust., p. 298. Elsewhere, under 1146, the two Davidovichi accuse Igor′ of malice towards Izyaslav Mstislavich and to them (Ipat., col. 329). Other anti-Ol′govichi sources observe that Igor′ was replaced in Kiev by Izyaslav Mstislavich, "the offshoot of a good root" (svod 1493, p. 233; svod 1495, p. 319).

the chroniclers' claim that he was a bellicose prince. Igor′ also took wise precautions. He rode to the lower town with his *druzhina*, but remained at a safe distance from the Kievans while his brother negotiated with them. In this way he not only stayed out of harm's way should the townsmen resort to violence, but also kept his retinue menacingly near to the assembly in a show of force to intimidate it into concluding a speedy settlement. But Svyatoslav was not merely Igor′'s figurehead. The brothers proposed to act as co-rulers. When Svyatoslav negotiated with the Kievans they instructed him to kiss the Holy Cross in his own name and in the name of his brother. They also made him promise that either he or Igor′ would judge their grievances. Finally, after Svyatoslav agreed to their terms they proclaimed, "Igor′ your brother is our prince and so are you," and they promised to betray neither the one nor the other.[5]

Igor′'s decision to rule Kiev with Svyatoslav had precedent. As has been shown elsewhere, their father, Oleg, and their uncle David had ruled Chernigov together after the Congress of Lyubech (1097).[6] That dual rule was accepted practice in Rus′ during the middle of the twelfth century was later demonstrated by Igor′'s successor Izyaslav Mstislavich who, as we shall see, would rule Kiev with his uncle Vyacheslav Vladimirovich. Igor′, as the elder brother, would presumably assume the role of the senior partner while Svyatoslav, the junior brother, would act as the commander of military operations. Such an arrangement would be a coup for the dynasty of Chernigov. Having its two genealogically senior princes in Kiev would ensure that the capital of Rus′ remained in the hands of the Ol′govichi even after Igor′'s death.

The *veche* seemingly had no grievances against Igor′ himself. Rather, it objected to the practices of Vsevolod's former administrators (*tiuni*), Ratsha and Tudor. It demanded that Igor′ neither condone such activity during his reign nor reappoint Vsevolod's officials. He agreed and granted the Kievans a *tiun* of their own choosing.[7] It is impossible to determine how much credence we can give to the citizens' accusations. Disgruntled subjects who had not profited from his administration levied criticisms against any former ruler. Moreover, partisan Kievans were especially hostile to a prince of a rival dynasty, particularly to one who showed signs of insecurity. Since Igor′'s foothold in Kiev was still unsure, the *veche* adopted the tactic of discrediting the rule of his brother Vsevolod, who had designated him as the successor. In doing so, it pressured Igor′ into granting it greater concessions.

[5] Ipat., cols. 321–2; Mosk., p. 37.   [6] *Dynasty*, pp. 213–15.   [7] Ipat., cols. 321–2; Mosk., p. 37.

Igor′'s readiness to yield to the *veche* once again suggests that he was not as bellicose as some chroniclers claimed. Indeed, his actions reveal his sensitivity to the precarious nature of his candidacy. He realized that to antagonize the townsmen before securing his rule in Kiev would be foolhardy. In the recent past they had effectively assumed the role of kingmakers and had favoured candidates from the House of Monomakh.[8] Igor′ could not afford to give the *veche* a pretext for selecting a prince from the rival dynasty.

After Igor′ kissed the Holy Cross and departed for dinner, the chronicler reports, townsmen pillaged the court of the erstwhile *tiun* Ratsha and those of other officials. Igor′ dispatched Svyatoslav to quell the riot. He also sent envoys to Izyaslav Mstislavich in Pereyaslavl′, demanding his support. But Izyaslav refused to give it. The Kievans therefore invited Izyaslav to be their prince because they did not want the Ol′govichi.[9]

The sources do not agree why the Kievans rioted. The Hypatian chronicler implies that Igor′'s personal conduct was not the cause. At first he writes that the townsmen rioted against Vsevolod's former officials. Later, however, when the Kievans invited Izyaslav to Kiev, their main grievance was directed against the Ol′govichi as a family. They objected to Igor′ and Svyatoslav's rule because they wished to prevent Kiev from becoming the inheritance of the Ol′govichi.[10] Nevertheless, other sources unequivocally state that the Kievans were displeased with Igor′. One claims that they were coerced into kissing the Holy Cross to him although they neither liked him nor wanted him to be their prince.[11] Yet another asserts that they sent for Izyaslav because Igor′, after occupying the throne, acted contrary to the promises he had made to the *veche*.[12]

It is difficult to assess the veracity of these reports. More than likely, Svyatoslav and the *veche* conducted their negotiations in good faith, but a bellicose anti-Ol′govichi faction rioted because it wanted to take revenge on Vsevolod's former officials and to undermine Igor′'s authority. This pro-Izyaslav group undoubtedly claimed that the townsmen were coerced into kissing the Holy Cross to Igor′. Indeed, it must have been in reference to this faction that, at an earlier date, a pro-Chernigov chronicler (to judge from his bias) wrote that the Kievans had deceived Igor′ when Vsevolod had insisted that they pledge their allegiance to his brother.[13] Thus, an

---

[8] Vsevolod, Igor′'s elder brother who, in 1139, usurped Kiev, was preceded on that throne by Vladimir Monomakh and three of his sons, Mstislav, Yaropolk, and Vyacheslav (*Dynasty*, pp. 312–50).

[9] Ipat., col. 322.   [10] Ipat., col. 323.   [11] Gust., p. 298.   [12] Mosk., p. 37.

[13] Ipat., cols. 320–1; *Dynasty*, p. 410. See Hrushevsky, *Ocherk istorii Kievskoy zemli*, pp. 169–70. Concerning the tendentious reporting of the Chernigov chronicler, one probably employed by Svyatoslav Ol′govich, see S. M. Solov'ev, *Istoriya Rossii* (M., 1963), kn. 2, vol. 3, pp. 112–13.

undercurrent of opposition to the Ol'govichi had already existed when Vsevolod attempted to secure his brother's succession.

The chroniclers fail to record whether Igor' broke his agreement with the *veche* before or after the mob plundered Ratsha's court. Consequently, we must determine the sequence of the two events if we are to establish who broke their oath first. According to the Hypatian account, the rioters attacked the courts of the officials immediately after Igor' took his oath and rode to dinner. Such a rapid sequence of events would not have given Igor' sufficient time to make administrative appointments. We may conclude therefore that the anti-Ol'govichi mob violated the *veche's* oath and therewith freed Igor' of his promises to the Kievans.

The misconduct of Vsevolod's *tiuni*, his alleged coercion of the Kievans to support Igor', the latter's unpopularity, and his reappointment of Vsevolod's officials were all reasons that helped to persuade the malcontents to rebel against the Ol'govichi. But the most cogent consideration for them was that they did not wish to become an inheritance for the Ol'govichi. Their accusation implies that the princes of Chernigov were attempting to secure their permanent rule over Kiev by handing over control of it from one senior prince to the next. This news supports our contention that Igor' and Svyatoslav were initiating dual rule. According to such an arrangement, Igor' would be succeeded by the eldest surviving Ol'govich, who, presumably, would be Svyatoslav.

Significantly, the Kievans did not object to becoming the patrimony of one princely family; they objected to becoming the inheritance of the Ol'govichi. They, or those supporting the Mstislavichi, had already adopted Vladimir Monomakh and his descendants as their dynasty.[14] Following Monomakh's death in 1125, the Kievans had selected, according to the order of lateral succession, Monomakh's eldest surviving sons: Mstislav, Yaropolk, and Vyacheslav.[15] In 1139, Vsevolod Ol'govich foiled their plans by evicting Vyacheslav from Kiev. Before his death, he had designated Igor' as his successor presumably with the intention of displacing the Monomashichi permanently and making the Ol'govichi Kiev's hereditary dynasty. In 1146, by inviting Izyaslav, the citizens not only demonstrated their intention to reinstate the Monomashichi, but also to confine their choice to the family of Monomakh's eldest son, Mstislav.

As a result of this rivalry, the system of lateral succession, which Yaroslav the Wise had allegedly inaugurated, once again underwent modification.[16]

[14] *Dynasty*, pp. 267–72, 276–7, 298–300, 305–8.   [15] *Dynasty*, pp. 305–50.
[16] Concerning Yaroslav's alleged system of succession, see Dimnik, "Testament,", pp. 369–86 and *Dynasty, passim.*

Izyaslav violated the genealogical order of succession within his dynasty because according to it, he was not in line to rule Kiev. His uncles Vyacheslav of Turov and Yury Dolgorukiy of Suzdalia were on higher rungs. By accepting the summons to Kiev, therefore, Izyaslav challenged the Ol'govichi and pre-empted the claims of his uncles. As a result, the prospects for peace looked bleak. Fortunately for Izyaslav, his uncles were unable to challenge him immediately because of the distance that separated them from Kiev.

Izyaslav's main concern was to evict the Ol'govichi. In addition to the Kievans, he had at his disposal the pagan Black Caps (*Chernye klobuki*) and the inhabitants of the entire Ros' river basin (Poros'e).[17] Just the same, Izyaslav's address to his supporters reveals that he considered it important to establish his claim according to moral legitimacy in addition to military might. He therewith implicitly acknowledged that he was violating the traditional practice of succession and the oath that he had made to Igor'. Izyaslav justified his usurpation by explaining that he had acknowledged Vsevolod's political seniority out of respect for his age and owing to their personal bond.[18] As has been shown elsewhere, Vsevolod had indeed used his various associations with Izyaslav to make him pledge support for Igor'.[19] Following Vsevolod's death, however, Izyaslav considered himself released from any promises he had made to Vsevolod under duress.

Moreover, Izyaslav did not hesitate to point out that even though Igor' was the designated successor and his own uncles were ahead of him in genealogical seniority, he also had a legitimate claim. He had recourse to the age-old maxim that Kiev had been the throne of his grandfather and father. Igor' was unable to back his claim with similar authority. He had failed to obtain it because Monomakh had pre-empted his father, Oleg, and denied him his rightful turn in Kiev. Therefore, according to the age-old maxim and Yaroslav's system of lateral succession, Igor' had no claim to Kiev.

Igor' ignored the objection that his father Oleg had not ruled Kiev. He had arguments in support of his succession that, in his view, outweighed that criterion. First, there was the genealogical argument: he was the rightful successor to Vsevolod because as the next in seniority he replaced Vsevolod as the senior prince of the dynasty. Second, he was Vsevolod's designated successor to Kiev. Since Vsevolod's rule was recognized as legitimate, he had the authority to name his successor. Third, Igor' had right on his side

---

[17] The princes of Rus' allowed nomads expelled from the steppe by the Polovtsy to settle the Poros'e. These nomads (Torki, Pechenegs, and Berendei) became collectively known as the Black Caps. They occupied towns such as Yur'ev, Torchesk, Korsun', and Dveren (see B. A. Rybakov, *Kievskaya Rus' i russkie knyazhestva XII–XIII vv.* [M., 1982], pp. 488–90).

[18] Ipat., cols. 323–4.   [19] Ipat., cols. 317–18; *Dynasty*, pp. 404–5.

because twice, once before and once after Vsevolod's death, the Kievans had acknowledged him as their prince.

But the pro-Izyaslav chronicler had additional arguments supporting Izyaslav's legitimacy. Before setting out from Pereyaslavl', Izyaslav turned to the highest moral authority to sanction his usurpation. He went to the Church of St. Michael, where he asked God to assist him. He also obtained the blessing of Bishop Evfimy. Later, before setting out with his troops, Izyaslav once again invoked divine approbation for his usurpation by declaring that God and the power of the Life-giving Cross would give the victory either to him or to the Ol'govichi.[20] In other words, if he defeated the Ol'govichi his claim would be justified because God Himself would have granted him the victory. In this way he would be vindicated for his usurpation and exonerated for breaking the pledges that he had sworn to the Ol'govichi.

Igor' commanded the allegiance of the Ol'govichi and he controlled Kiev, but he was unaware of the treachery of his alleged Kievan supporters. The backing of the other princes, who had pledged allegiance to him earlier, was also questionable now that Vsevolod was dead. Consequently, Igor' sent messengers to Vladimir Davidovich and his brother Izyaslav in Chernigov asking if they intended to honour their oaths to him. The Davidovichi took advantage of their cousin's vulnerability by demanding that he grant them additional domains. After Igor' succumbed to their extortion, they kissed the Holy Cross "to Igor' and to his brother Svyatoslav."[21] With this remark, the chronicler once again alludes to the dual rule of the Ol'govichi. The Hypatian chronicler also adds news that was evidently written by a pro-Ol'govichi chronicler. He reports that after the Davidovichi took their oaths in the Holy Saviour Cathedral (the Cathedral of the Transfiguration of Our Lord), they set out for Kiev. Bishop Onufry, before whom the princes had taken their oaths, proclaimed to the local priests that if anyone violated the promise that he had made to the Ol'govichi, he would be damned.[22]

In asking for more towns the Davidovichi demonstrated the opportunism of princes pledging allegiance to one whose power was insecure. In

---

[20] Ipat., col. 323.   [21] Ipat., col. 324.

[22] Ipat., cols. 324–5; compare Tat. 4, p. 202 and Tat. 2, p. 163. The pro-Ol'govichi and pro-Izyaslav biases in the Hypatian account reveal that the compiler used chronicles written at the courts of princes who were involved in these rivalries. Depending on his political affiliation, one chronicler might praise the action of a prince as a divinely inspired act while another might condemn it as the machinations of the Devil (Rybakov, *Kievskaya Rus'*, p. 491). According to some, extracts from Chernigov chronicles were incorporated into the so-called Kievan Chronicle of the Hypatian account (Bagaley, *Istoriya Severskoy zemli*, pp. 299–300; *Istoriia*, vol. 2, p. 332).

this instance, it was also a continuation of the rivalry that the Ol'govichi and the Davidovichi had initiated after Vsevolod occupied Kiev. At that time Igor' and Svyatoslav had challenged their elder brother over the towns that he had allocated to the Davidovichi.[23] When Igor' attempted to secure his position as prince of Kiev, therefore, Vladimir and Izyaslav seized the opportunity to weaken his territorial base. Although the location of the domains in question is not revealed, some of them must have been in the Chernigov lands. Since Igor' had not yet secured his rule over the right bank, it is unlikely that the Davidovichi would have been content with grants of land solely from that side of the Dnepr.

After the Kievans broke their oath to Igor' by inviting Izyaslav to be their prince, he reneged on his promise to them and reappointed two of Vsevolod's former officials: the *tysyatskiy* Uleb (Ouleb) and the *voevoda* Ivan Voitishich.[24] Igor' no doubt expected them to be more reliable than the officials Svyatoslav had selected at the Kievans' behest. His main objective in conscripting the two, undoubtedly, was to win the backing of the townsmen who had supported the two officials in the past. Igor''s plan had promise insofar as he appointed men from Kiev rather than *boyars* (noblemen) from Chernigov to the Kievan posts. Its weakness lay in the consideration that many Kievans allegedly hated Uleb and Ivan because they had been Vsevolod's henchmen. Surprisingly, the two did win the confidence of the citizens, but for reasons unexplained they deserted Igor' and became ringleaders of the pro-Izyaslav group.[25] Consequently, the very men Igor' had conscripted to help him win Kievan support fomented the rebellion. Ironically, one of the pretexts the townsmen used for rejecting Igor' was his reappointment of Uleb and Ivan.

The conspirators also won over the two Davidovichi.[26] The treachery of the brothers was unexpected for two reasons: Igor' had just made territorial concessions to them and they had never before severed their political affiliation with the Ol'govichi. After 1127, when Vsevolod usurped Chernigov, the Davidovichi had always collaborated with their cousins against the Monomashichi. Nevertheless, as has been noted, they had established closer ties with Vsevolod than with his brothers. Uleb and Ivan would have used this rivalry to their advantage. For the first time, therefore, the descendants of Oleg and David found themselves in opposing camps.

---

[23] *Dynasty*, pp. 376–7.
[24] In 1117 Ivan Voitishich was one of Vladimir Monomakh's commanders (Ipat., col. 284); in 1128 he served Monomakh's eldest son Mstislav in the same capacity (Ipat., col. 292); in 1141, however, he served Vsevolod Ol'govich (Ipat., col. 307).
[25] Ipat., col. 324.   [26] Ipat., cols. 324–5.

The two Kievan traitors persuaded Izyaslav to attack the town by promising him that the town militia would desert the Ol'govichi. Meanwhile, they
deceitfully advised Igor' and his brother to march against their foe. Before
going into the field, Igor' and Svyatoslav proclaimed their innocence and
accused Izyaslav of treachery because he had promised them not to seek
Kiev. After that, the two sides engaged in a fierce battle and the Ol'govichi
were soundly defeated.[27]

In defeating Igor', we are told, Izyaslav violated the oath that he had
made promising not to take Kiev and pledging his allegiance to Igor' and
Svyatoslav. This evidence gives us a new insight into the history of the
Ol'govichi. As we have seen, Izyaslav had pledged his loyalty to Igor' only
once, in Vsevolod's presence. Consequently, it must have been on that
occasion that Izyaslav made his pledge to both Igor' and Svyatoslav. This
reveals that it was Vsevolod who ordained that his brothers should act as
co-rulers.

The military support that Izyaslav received from the towns of the Poros'e
region bespeaks widespread disaffection with the Ol'govichi in the Kievan
land. Although Igor' must have realized that there was also Kievan opposition to him, he evidently did not anticipate Uleb and Ivan's treachery. Nevertheless, he retained the backing of the Vyshgorodians, who traditionally worked hand in glove with the Kievans.[28] Surprisingly, Igor'
did not summon the Polovtsy even though they had served as auxiliaries
for the princes of Chernigov during the reigns of his grandfather and
father.

Izyaslav's enthronement in Kiev was undoubtedly the same as the ceremony used in Chernigov. As he approached the town the townspeople,
abbots, monks, and priests dressed in their vestments went out to greet him.
The procession entered Kiev through the Golden Gates and wended its way
to the metropolitan's St. Sofia Cathedral. There, on Tuesday August 13,
Izyaslav venerated the icon of the Mother of God.[29] He also ratified his
promise to defend the town and to abide by the agreements that he had
made with the *veche*. Finally, he "sat on the throne of his grandfather and
father" located in the center balcony facing the main altar. The metropolitan
ordinarily presided over the installation.

[27] The most detailed report of the battle is found in Ipat., cols. 325–8. Brief accounts are found in
Mosk., pp. 37–8; Lav., cols. 313–14 and elsewhere.
[28] Since some forces of the Ol'govichi fled to Vyshgorod, its inhabitants were probably Igor''s allies.
The town's close association with the dynasty of Chernigov was demonstrated in 1115, when Oleg
consecrated the Church of SS. Boris and Gleb (*Dynasty*, pp. 276–82) and in 1146, when Igor''s
brother Vsevolod chose to be buried in Vyshgorod (*Dynasty*, p. 411).
[29] Ipat., col. 327.

The Ol'govichi, in the meantime, were in disarray. Igor''s brother, Svyatoslav, escaped but found himself the odd man out in the Chernigov lands where the Davidovichi had sided with Izyaslav. Moreover, the latter neutralized Svyatoslav Vsevolodovich, his and Igor''s nephew, by coercing him into pledging his allegiance. Izyaslav also took captive Igor' and Vsevolod's retainers in the Kievan land,[30] pillaged their possessions, and confiscated their lands. His forces also desecrated monasteries belonging to the Ol'govichi,[31] while the Black Caps and the Berendei defiled ecclesiastical institutions.[32]

Izyaslav dealt with Igor' most ruthlessly of all. After his forces gained the upper hand in the fighting, Igor' fled to the marshes at Dorogozhichi northwest of Kiev. When his horse got stuck in the mire he was unable to move because he had an infirmity in his legs. Four days later, the enemy found him floundering in the swamps. Izyaslav had the hapless fugitive taken to Pereyaslavl' and thrown into a pit in the Monastery of St. Ioann.[33] Such conduct was unprecedented among the Monomashichi and the Ol'govichi.[34] The chronicles report only two earlier occasions on which princes had been incarcerated in like fashion.[35] Instead of keeping Igor' in Kiev, however, Izyaslav sent him to Pereyaslavl' where he could not solicit assistance from his Kievan supporters.[36] Izyaslav's treatment of Igor' demonstrated that he was prepared to use the most extreme measures short of killing him to remove him as a rival. By incapacitating Igor' he dashed any immediate hopes that the Ol'govichi may have had of ruling Kiev.

---

[30] Ipat., col. 328. The reference to both Igor' and Vsevolod's retainers is further evidence of the continuity of policy and personnel from Vsevolod to Igor'.

[31] In Kiev, the dynasty's monastery was that of St. Simeon in the Kopyrev suburb (*Dynasty*, pp. 114–15). Outside the town, Vsevolod had founded the Monastery of St. Cyril at Dorogozhichi (*Dynasty*, pp. 389–94).

[32] The compiler evidently copied this news from a pro-Monomashichi chronicler, who refused to censure Izyaslav for the impious behavior of his troops in the manner that an earlier chronicler had condemned Igor''s father Oleg for allowing his Polovtsian allies to commit similar atrocities (see s.a. 1094: Ipat., cols. 216–17; *Dynasty*, pp. 185, 189).

[33] Ipat., cols. 326–8.

[34] In the light of the anti-Ol'govichi sentiments expressed by chroniclers and historians, it is worth noting that the princes of Chernigov never mistreated a rival prince by throwing him in a pit. On the contrary, they had a tradition of providing sanctuary to refugee princes. For example, Vsevolod Ol'govich had given sanctuary to Ivan Berladnik (Ipat., cols. 316–17; *Dynasty*, pp. 403–4). As we shall see, Svyatoslav Vsevolodovich would provide a safe haven for the brothers Vsevolod and Mikhalko, as well as their nephews, whom their elder brother Andrey would expel from Suzdalia. Igor' Svyatoslavich of Putivl' would give sanctuary to Vladimir Yaroslavich of Galich.

[35] Yaroslav the Wise threw his brother Sudislav into a pit (Ipat., col. 139). Yaroslav's son Izyaslav threw Vseslav of Polotsk and his two sons into a pit in Kiev (Ipat., col. 156).

[36] His decision to imprison Igor' outside of Kiev was undoubtedly influenced by the example of Vseslav of Polotsk. In 1068, the disaffected Kievans had rebelled against Izyaslav Yaroslavich, released Vseslav from the pit, and proclaimed him prince (Ipat., cols. 160–1; *Dynasty*, p. 66).

Igor′'s reign in Kiev lasted less than two weeks. A number of factors contributed to his downfall. Most important was the Kievans' opposition. Although Vsevolod had named Igor′ his successor, the townsmen refused to accept him. Assuming the role of kingmakers once again, they helped Izyaslav to stop Oleg's descendants from making Kiev their hereditary domain, just as in 1139 Vsevolod had prevented Monomakh's heirs from achieving the same objective. As a result, neither dynasty secured an undisputed right of succession to the capital of Rus′. Instead, it would become the prize for the strongest contenders from among Vsevolod Ol′govich's sons and from the House of Monomakh. Igor′'s fate, therefore, was a milestone in the history of succession to Kiev.

Igor′'s pride and volatile personality were handicaps to his success. As we have seen, the chronicler claimed that, aside from his brother Svyatoslav, Igor′ had no friends either among the Kievans or the princes. It is not surprising, therefore, that he failed to win the support of all the princes who had backed his brother Vsevolod. A number of those who had promised the latter that they would be loyal to Igor′ did so from fear of Vsevolod; after he died, therefore, they deserted Igor′. Among these, as we have seen, were the Davidovichi and Izyaslav of Pereyaslavl′. Nevertheless, following Izyaslav's usurpation, the relationship of the Ol′govichi to a number of other princes improved. Volodimerko Volodarevich of Galich had challenged Vsevolod for control of Volyn′. After Vsevolod died, that controversy ceased and the opportunity for restoring amicable relations between the two families returned. Izyaslav also estranged his uncles Yury of Suzdalia and Vyacheslav of Turov, who had prior claims to Kiev. Their strained relations enabled the Ol′govichi to approach the two uncles as allies.

Another reason for Igor′'s failure was his relatively small territorial base. Before Vsevolod occupied Kiev he had all the resources of Chernigov at his command. At the time of Vsevolod's death, however, the Davidovichi and not Igor′ ruled the dynastic capital. In keeping with his seniority among the Ol′govichi, Igor′ probably governed the provincial capital of Novgorod Severskiy.[37] Moreover, unlike Vsevolod, whose personal domain lay in the extensive Vyatichi lands, Igor′ owned a smaller domain constituting the regional center of Gomiy, on the river Sozh, and three towns in its vicinity.[38]

[37] The evidence, as we shall see, that his brother Svyatoslav fled to Novgorod Severskiy after he escaped from Izyaslav's pursuers confirms that the stronghold of the Ol′govichi remained loyal to Igor′ throughout the crisis. Concerning the towns that traditionally belonged to the Novgorod Severskiy territories, see Zaytsev, pp. 80–1.
[38] Ipat., col. 311; *Dynasty*, pp. 373, 375; O. A. Makushnikov, "K voprosu o topografii letopisnogo Gomiya," *Tezisy* Chernigovskoy oblastnoy nauchno-metodicheskoy konferentsii, posvyashchenoy

As we shall see, he also controlled an unspecified number of smaller settlements scattered throughout the Chernigov and Kievan lands.[39] The chronicles tell us nothing about Gomiy, but archaeological excavations have revealed that it was a strong economic center with a *detinets*, suburbs, and trading quarters. The fortified part of the town was some three times larger than the ones at Lyubech, Trubchevsk, Vshchizh, and Putivl', but less than half the size of that in Novgorod Severskiy. The chronicles do not report the existence of any monasteries, but the discovery of cells in caves reveals that Gomiy had a cave monastery like Lyubech, Chernigov, and Kiev. Consequently, it probably also had regular monasteries.[40] As we shall see, later when Igor' requested Izyaslav Mstislavich to let him adopt the monk's habit, he explained that he had considered becoming a monk when he was still living in his domain.[41] Since Igor' was favourably disposed to monasticism, he may have founded a monastery in his administrative center.

We also learn that Igor''s health was unsound. The chronicler states enigmatically that his legs failed him in the marshes. Circumstantial evidence suggests that his ailment may have been sufficiently debilitating to hinder his military activity. It is noteworthy that before the 1140s the chroniclers mention Igor' less frequently than his younger brother, Svyatoslav.[42] The chronicler refers to him for the first time after Vsevolod usurped Kiev.[43] This is surprising since, given Igor''s seniority, he should have played a more prominent role than Svyatoslav. Furthermore, as we have seen, Igor' delegated Svyatoslav to negotiate with the Kievan *veche*. It is not unreasonable to assume that one reason why Igor' kept a low profile on that occasion was his infirmity. From the time of Vladimir Monomakh the Kievans

20-letiyu Chernigovskogo arkhitekturno-istoricheskogo zapovednika (sentyabr' 1987 g.) (Chernigov, 1987), pp. 46–8; Zaytsev, p. 104.

[39] Concerning Igor''s village located near Novgorod Severskiy, see below, p. 32. In 1142, Vsevolod had granted Igor' the towns of Gorodets Osterskiy (Gorodok) and Rogachev on the right bank of the Dnepr. Neither was located in the patrimony of the Ol'govichi (Ipat., col. 312; *Dynasty*, p. 376). Igor' presumably lost control of these after he was imprisoned.

[40] See O. A. Makushnikov, "O meste letopisnogo Gomiya v sisteme gorodskikh tsentrov Chernigovo-Severshchiny," *Arkheolohichni starozhytnosti Podesennia*: Materialy istoryko-arkheolohichnoho seminary, prysviachenoho 70-richchiu vid dnia narodzhennia H. O. Kuznetsova, O. P. Motsia (gen. ed.) (Chernihiv, 1995), pp. 96–7, also V. Ya. Rudenok and O. A. Makushnikov, "Pervye speleo-arkheologicheskie issledovaniya v Gomele," *Gomel'shchina: arkheologiya, istoriya, pamyatniki*: Tezisy Vtoroy Gomel'skoy oblastnoy nauchnoy konferentsii po istoricheskomu kraevedeniyu, 1991 g., O. A. Makushnikov and A. I. Drobushevsky (eds.) (Gomel', 1991), pp. 55–6.

[41] Ipat., col. 337; Mosk., p. 38.

[42] For example, in 1136, Vsevolod did not send Igor' but the younger Svyatoslav to rule Novgorod (NPL, pp. 24, 209; *Dynasty*, pp. 337–8). In 1139, when Vsevolod usurped Kiev, Igor' again is not mentioned as assisting Vsevolod, while Svyatoslav is named (Ipat., col. 302; *Dynasty*, pp. 349–50).

[43] Ipat., col. 302; *Dynasty*, pp. 349–50, 352–3.

consistently selected military champions as their princes; they looked upon older or physically debilitated candidates as undesirable. Because of Igor's handicap, therefore, the hard-nosed Kievans probably preferred to have the healthier Izyaslav as prince.

Igor's defeat had catastrophic results on his political career. He lost the position of senior prince in Rus' and, following his incarceration, he became an ineffectual senior prince of the Ol'govichi. Moreover, his deposition had serious repercussions on the fortunes of the Ol'govichi. In addition to losing Kiev, he also lost control of all the Kievan towns that fell under the jurisdiction of the prince of Kiev.[44] The Ol'govichi therewith not only forfeited the primacy that they had enjoyed in Rus' during Vsevolod's lifetime, but were also relegated to a position of the least importance in their dynasty. Within some two weeks they lost two senior princes, Vsevolod and Igor'. This limited the number of active princes in the family to the two Svyatoslavs. Igor's brother assumed the role of acting senior prince. He had to champion the cause of the Ol'govichi alone, however, because Izyaslav placed his nephew, Svyatoslav Vsevolodovich, under house arrest. Svyatoslav Ol'govich's task was made all the more difficult because the resources of the Davidovichi were greater. What is more, they enjoyed Izyaslav's favour.

SVYATOSLAV OL'GOVICH FIGHTS FOR SURVIVAL

During the course of two tumultuous weeks the balance of power in the dynasty had swung sharply in favour of the Davidovichi while the fortunes of the Ol'govichi had plummeted. Following the death of Svyatoslav Yaroslavich in 1076, when the political lot of his sons had reached its nadir, the task of championing the dynasty's cause had fallen on Oleg. After Igor's capture in 1146, the task of keeping the Ol'govichi politically alive fell to Oleg's youngest son, Svyatoslav.

Before investigating his fight for survival, let us acquaint ourselves with his relatives. His deceased brother Vsevolod was survived by his wife Maria, the sister of Izyaslav of Kiev,[45] and by his sons, Svyatoslav and Yaroslav.[46] Vsevolod also had two daughters; almost nothing is known of the one, while the other, Zvenislava, married Boleslav "the Tall" (*Wysoki*) of the

---

[44] The chronicles identify some eighty urban centers within the boundaries of the Kievan land (P. P. Tolochko, *Drevnyaya Rus'*, Ocherki sotsial'no-politicheskoy istorii [K., 1987], p. 117).

[45] *Dynasty*, pp. 254–5.

[46] Svyatoslav's date of birth is unknown, but he had become politically active by the early 1140s, suggesting that he was born in the 1120s (*Dynasty*, pp. 362–3). Yaroslav was born in 1139 in Kiev (Ipat., col. 306; *Dynasty*, pp. 361–2).

Piast dynasty.[47] Igor′'s unidentified wife, as we shall see, was living in Novgorod Severskiy; the couple evidently had no children.[48] Svyatoslav himself married a Polovtsian princess in 1108, with whom he had Oleg and a daughter.[49] His wife died before 1136 because in that year he married a Novgorodian woman.[50] The chronicles have not yet reported the existence of their children. Even less is known of the Davidovichi. From later information, however, we learn that Vladimir had a son named Svyatoslav and that Izyaslav had an unnamed daughter.[51] From genealogical considerations, therefore, the future of the Ol′govichi looked more secure than that of the Davidovichi who were dangerously close to extinction.

After Igor′ was defeated in August 1146, Svyatoslav fled to Chernigov. He sent messengers to Vladimir and Izyaslav asking them if they had remained faithful to the Ol′govichi. The brothers confirmed their loyalty.[52] It is surprising to discover that his cousins were in Chernigov because the last news we had of them was that they had set out to help Igor′ and then that they had deserted him. Nevertheless, their presence in Chernigov shows that they had not joined Izyaslav. This is confirmed by the information that they had returned to Chernigov ahead of Svyatoslav, who had fled directly from the battlefield. Furthermore, Svyatoslav's query if they were still loyal to the Ol′govichi is proof that the brothers had not helped Izyaslav, because if they had Svyatoslav would have witnessed their treachery. The Davidovichi were vacillating in their loyalty and if their reply to Svyatoslav was true, they had changed their minds yet again by deserting Izyaslav in favour of the Ol′govichi.

On becoming the most senior active Ol′govich, Svyatoslav considered it mandatory to occupy Novgorod Severskiy, which Igor′ had undoubtedly ruled before moving to Kiev.[53] We are not informed why, when faced with the urgency of consolidating his authority, he took the circuitous route via Kursk.[54] As has been shown elsewhere, he had ruled the town in 1141, and we may assume that he still controlled it five years later.[55] Most likely,

[47] Ipat., col. 308; *Dynasty*, p. 383. Zvenislava's sister, according to some investigators, was named Anna and married a prince of Galicia (Zotov, pp. 268–9; Baum., IV, 22–5).
[48] Zotov, pp. 263–4; Baum., IV, 13.
[49] Concerning their marriage, see Lav., cols. 282–3; *Dynasty*, p. 241.
[50] NPL, p. 209; *Dynasty*, pp. 337–8; Zotov, pp. 39, 265.
[51] Zotov, pp. 266–7.   [52] Ipat., col. 328.
[53] The chronicles do not state that Igor′ was prince of Novgorod Severskiy, but circumstantial evidence supports this contention. As we shall see, he left his wife in Novgorod Severskiy when he moved to Kiev, evidently intending to send for her after he had secured his position in Kiev.
[54] Ipat., col. 328.
[55] Ipat., cols. 308–9; *Dynasty*, p. 369. Concerning Kursk, see also A. K. Zaytsev, "Do pytannia pro formuvannia terytorii davn′orus′kykh kniazivstv u XII st.," UIZh, nr. 5 (1974), 43–53.

therefore, he visited the eastern outpost to collect his family and the families of his retinue. His occupation of Novgorod Severskiy was a declaration to the princes of Rus′ that he had assumed command of the Ol′govichi in Igor′'s absence.

The fickle Davidovichi finally decided that, with Izyaslav's backing, they could assert their dominance over the Ol′govichi. Accordingly, adopting a merciless policy towards Igor′, they requested Izyaslav to remove him from the political scene by keeping him in the pit permanently. They also sought to deprive Igor′ of all family support by insisting that Svyatoslav abandon him and never attempt to free him. After neutralizing Igor′ they intended to seize his domains. Their insistence that Svyatoslav vacate Novgorod Severskiy and return to his patrimony of Putivl′ suggests that they wanted to appropriate the family capital of the Ol′govichi on the pretext that its rightful ruler was still Igor′.[56] But Svyatoslav refused to budge. He also remained adamant in his demand that Izyaslav release Igor′.[57]

By ordering Svyatoslav to pledge allegiance to them, the Davidovichi demanded that he formally acknowledge the new status quo. Under Vsevolod, the Ol′govichi had been the dominant family in the dynasty, but following Igor′'s capture the balance of power had shifted to the Davidovichi. Since they controlled Chernigov and enjoyed Izyaslav's backing, the Davidovichi commanded the military clout to make unprecedented demands on Svyatoslav. They therefore threatened to confiscate his domains if he refused to pledge allegiance. He had to submit to them or go to war.

Significantly, the brothers consistently acted as one. They both pledged allegiance to Igor′ and they both deserted him. When Svyatoslav came to Chernigov he found both of them there and obtained pledges from both. Later, they both sent him the ultimatum. After that, as we shall see, they would always act as one, whether it was in their negotiations with Izyaslav or in their dealings with Svyatoslav. Consequently, their conduct bespeaks a sharing of power. Just as Igor′ and Svyatoslav had proposed to rule jointly in Kiev, the Davidovichi acted as co-rulers in Chernigov.[58]

---

[56] Novgorod Severskiy evidently became the patrimonial capital of the Ol′govichi in 1097 at the Congress of Lyubech (*Dynasty*, pp. 219–21, 255–61). As such, it could not become the hereditary domain of any one Ol′govich. After Igor′'s death, it would pass on to his eldest surviving brother, and if there were none, to his eldest surviving nephew. This system of succession could, of course, be disrupted by force. Since, as we shall see, Svyatoslav's personal patrimony was Putivl′, the Davidovichi evidently wanted him to relinquish control of Novgorod Severskiy and reside in Putivl′.

[57] Ipat., cols. 328–9.

[58] In a number of instances where princes were co-rulers, the younger prince appeared to be the dominant partner. Thus, Svyatoslav assumed a more active role than Igor′; as we shall see, Izyaslav Mstislavich would be stronger than his uncle Vyacheslav Vladimirovich. Later evidence suggests that Vladimir's brother Izyaslav was also the dominant partner of the two Davidovichi.

Svyatoslav prepared for war by turning for help to Yury Dolgorukiy in Suzdalia, who championed the succession rights of the Monomashichi. He maintained that he and his brother Vyacheslav had prior claims to Kiev over their nephews, the Mstislavichi.[59] Vladimir Svyatoslavich of Murom also brought reinforcements.[60] This rare reference to the Murom line, which was also descended from the House of Chernigov, is noteworthy. In 1127 Svyatoslav's brother Vsevolod had usurped Chernigov from Vladimir's grandfather Yaroslav.[61] Vladimir's friendship therefore signifies that he did not condemn the Ol'govichi as a family for Vsevolod's transgression. Svyatoslav also won the support of his brother's ally Ivan Rostislavich nicknamed Berladnik. Vsevolod had probably given him a Kievan domain from which Izyaslav evicted him.[62] Finally, the Polovtsy joined Svyatoslav. He summoned his Polovtsian father-in-law, Aepa the son of Girgen,[63] who immediately sent 300 horsemen.[64] In this way Svyatoslav kept alive his father's practice of summoning the nomads to help him in inter-dynastic wars.

Izyaslav in Kiev expressed no immediate interest in Svyatoslav's preparations for war. Instead, he consolidated his authority on the right bank of the Dnepr by evicting his nephew Svyatoslav Vsevolodovich from Vladimir in Volyn', which the latter's father had given him. Izyaslav compensated the Ol'govich with five lesser towns, including Bozh'skyy (Buzh'skyy) and Mezhibozh'e in the southwest corner of the Kievan land.[65] Since the two towns were located in the region that was later referred to as the Bolokhov lands,[66] all five towns were more than likely in that district. As we shall see, during the first half of the thirteenth century the princelings of that region

<hr/>

[59] During the reign of Yury's brother Yaropolk in Kiev, and later during the reign of Vsevolod Ol'govich, Yury opposed Yaropolk's efforts to place the Mstislavichi on the throne of Kiev and Vsevolod's efforts to place the Mstislavichi on the patrimonial throne of Pereyaslavl'. In both instances Yury and his brothers argued that, according to genealogical seniority, they had prior claims (*Dynasty*, pp. 324–32).

[60] Vladimir was the grandson of Svyatoslav's uncle Yaroslav (Baum. 2, XIV, 7).

[61] *Dynasty*, pp. 303–8, 314–20.

[62] During the winter of 1144 Volodimerko of Galich had expelled Ivan from Zvenigorod after the latter attempted to usurp Galich. Later, Vsevolod Ol'govich gave Ivan sanctuary in Kiev (Ipat., cols. 316–17; *Dynasty*, pp. 403–4).

[63] The chronicler claims that the Polovtsian khan was the brother of Svyatoslav's mother (*ui*). Svyatoslav's father Oleg had married a Greek noblewoman (*Dynasty*, p. 160) and it was Svyatoslav who, in 1108, married a Polovtsian princess (Lav., cols. 282–3; *Dynasty*, p. 241). Thus, in 1146, Svyatoslav probably asked his Polovtsian father-in-law to send troops. As we have seen, in 1136 Svyatoslav was married a second time to a Novgorodian woman (NPL, p. 209; *Dynasty*, pp. 337–8).

[64] Ipat., col. 329.

[65] *Bouzh'skyi i Mezhibozh'e pyat' gorodov* (Ipat., col. 330). Under 1147, we are told that Svyatoslav controlled Bozh'skyy, Mezhibozh'e, Kotel'nitsa, "all five towns" (*vsekh pyat' gorodov*, Ipat., col. 343) indicating that, in 1146, Svyatoslav had received five towns in all (*Mikhail*, p. 119).

[66] Concerning the Bolokhov towns, see *Mikhail*, pp. 117–19; also, see below, p. 327.

were allied to the Ol'govichi. It may well be that their loyalty stemmed from the days of Svyatoslav's rule in those towns.

After evicting Svyatoslav from Vladimir, Izyaslav discovered that his immediate enemy was not the Ol'govichi but his own kin. Vyacheslav spurned Izyaslav's authority, seized Vladimir, and repossessed the towns that he had lost to Vsevolod Ol'govich. He alluded to the crux of the problem when he declared that he placed his hope in his seniority. That is, he rejected Izyaslav's usurpation of Kiev because he adhered to the principles of succession prescribed by Yaroslav the Wise. According to genealogical seniority, Vyacheslav was the rightful claimant to Kiev. Moreover, he had been prince there in 1139, when Vsevolod Ol'govich had usurped power. Izyaslav retaliated by dispatching his brother Rostislav of Smolensk and Svyatoslav Vsevolodovich to subdue Vyacheslav. The Ol'govich obeyed and demonstrated his willingness to assist his uncle, at least against princes from the House of Monomakh.[67]

Meanwhile, the Davidovichi reasoned that since they had initiated an evil plot they should carry it out to its logical conclusion by killing Svyatoslav.[68] Their merciless plan was unprecedented in the dynasty. Ironically, the villains were the sons of the pious David and the brothers of the monk Svyatosha, one of the first princes of Chernigov to be canonized.[69] We are told that, after Izyaslav Davidovich was allegedly cured from a fatal illness through Svyatosha's intercession, he wore his brother's hair shirt into battle to ensure his safety.[70] In this way he sacrilegiously used the relic with the assumption that his sainted brother would pray for his safety while he was executing the evil deed.

In addition to appropriating Igor''s domain, the Davidovichi also resolved to steal Svyatoslav's lands and asked Izyaslav Mstislavich for help. The princes therefore held a meeting in Chernigov to concoct their heinous plan. Thus, unlike Izyaslav's grandfather Vladimir Monomakh and Svyatopolk Izyaslavich of Kiev, who had used the council at Lyubech in 1097 to secure peace among all the princes in a spirit of reconciliation, Izyaslav and the Davidovichi sought to annihilate the Ol'govichi in a spirit of treachery. Izyaslav commanded the Davidovichi, his son Mstislav, and the Berendei, to march against Svyatoslav. They besieged Novgorod Severskiy

---

[67] Ipat., cols. 329–30; Mosk., p. 38.   [68] Ipat., col. 330.

[69] According to popular tradition, David died under an aura of sanctity (Loparev, "Slovo pokhval'noe," pp. 16–7, 25–7, 29–30). He became venerated as a saint locally (Arkhimandrit Leonid [L. A. Kavelin], *Svyataya Rus'* ili svedeniya o vsekh svyatykh i podvizhnikakh blagochestiya na rusi [do XVIII veka]. Obshche i mestno chtimykh [Spb., 1891], p. 32). See also *Dynasty*, pp. 301–2.

[70] Filaret, Archbishop of Chernigov, *Russkie svyatiye*, third edition (Spb., 1882), vol. 3, pp. 225–7; Heppell, *The "Paterik,"* pp. 135–6; *Dynasty*, p. 398.

and slaughtered many inhabitants of the outer town. Later, they withdrew to a village called Meltekove and sent men to seize Igor' and Svyatoslav's herds: they captured 3,000 mares and 1,000 horses. Others plundered the surrounding villages and set grain and courts ablaze.[71]

In the meantime, Svyatoslav asked Yury for assistance. Pledging to help set Igor' free, he rode to Svyatoslav's aid. By campaigning in person he demonstrated his determination to challenge Izyaslav's rule, but at the same time he learned, to his chagrin, that this left Suzdalia exposed to attack. Izyaslav instructed Rostislav Yaroslavich in Ryazan' to invade Yury's lands.[72] Rostislav's willingness to pillage Suzdalia shows that the prince of Kiev commanded the loyalty of at least one prince from Ryazan' or, rather, that Rostislav backed the Davidovichi. As we have seen, Svyatoslav had solicited the support of Vladimir Svyatoslavich of Murom. Thus we see that the princes of Murom and Ryazan' were divided in their loyalties to their relatives in Chernigov.

When Yury reached Kozel'sk[73] in the Vyatichi lands, he learned that Rostislav was plundering his domain. He therefore sent his son Ivanko to Svyatoslav's assistance and returned home. Svyatoslav gave Ivanko the town of Kursk with its Posem'e district.[74] For an Ol'govich not only to relinquish control of a domain but also to give it to a prince of another dynasty was extraordinary. On the one hand, Svyatoslav's action bespeaks desperation. On the other hand, he probably wished to placate Yury for his loss of Gorodets Osterskiy in the southwest corner of the Chernigov lands. Four years earlier, Svyatoslav's brother Vsevolod had taken Gorodets Osterskiy from Yury and given it to Igor'.[75] Since Izyaslav undoubtedly seized the town after he captured Igor', Svyatoslav could not return it to Yury. He therefore compensated Yury with Kursk. Located on the southeastern periphery of the Novgorod Severkiy lands, it was the most vulnerable town of the Ol'govichi to nomadic incursions. What is more, the Monomashichi had controlled it in the past and its ownership was not yet determined.[76] Consequently, Svyatoslav gave Kursk away because it was his most expendable domain.

[71] Ipat., cols. 330–2; compare Tat. 4, p. 204 and Tat. 2, pp. 166–7.
[72] Ipat., col. 332. Rostislav of Ryazan' was Svyatoslav's cousin, the son of his youngest uncle, Yaroslav (Baum. 2, XIV, 4; compare Baum. IV, 17).
[73] The town was located on the steep left bank of the river Zhizdra, a tributary of the Oka. It is mentioned here for the first time (Nasonov, p. 225; *Zemlya Vyatichey*, pp. 128–30).
[74] Ipat., col. 332. The Kursk Posem'e included the districts of Kursk, Ol'gov, and Ryl'sk (Zaytsev, pp. 95–6).
[75] Ipat., col. 312; *Dynasty*, pp. 366, 376.
[76] In 1095 Monomakh's son Izyaslav had ruled it before capturing Murom (Ipat., col. 220; Lav., col. 229; *Dynasty*, p. 193). In 1127 Mstislav took it from Vsevolod Ol'govich and gave it to his son Izyaslav, who now ruled Kiev (*Dynasty*, p. 336).

32   *The Dynasty of Chernigov*

After welcoming Ivanko, Svyatoslav sent his priest to the Davidovichi suing for peace and condemning them for pillaging his lands and for attempting to kill him. The Davidovichi spurned his rebuke and repeated their demand that he desert Igor' and conclude peace. Once again he refused. They therefore plundered Igor''s village and set off for Putivl'.[77] The chronicler leaves no doubt that the town was Svyatoslav's domain. Since he had given Kursk to Ivanko, we may conclude that Putivl' was the more important of the two towns. Svyatoslav therefore looked upon Putivl' as his patrimonial capital. Izyaslav arrived at the town after the Davidovichi had captured it; the citizens capitulated to him, but just the same, the attackers sacked the town.[78]

The chronicler's description of the plundering deserves comment. First, his detailed list of the items pillaged – 900 stacks of corn, 500 *berkovets* of honey,[79] eighty jugs of wine, two silver vessels, altar cloths, fabrics sewn with gold thread, vestments, two censers, an incense bowl, the Gospels with covers made of forged metal, bells, and 700 servants – suggests that he worked for one of the Ol'govichi. Second, the plenitude of provisions in the princes' larders bespeaks their wealth. Third, since the allies set out from Igor''s village to Putivl' on Christmas Day, they would have attacked Novgoród Severskiy a few weeks earlier, probably in November. By that time the crops had been harvested and the warehouses were brimming over with produce. Clearly, one reason why they chose that time of year to attack was to rape the barns of the Ol'govichi of their winter stores. Fourth, the numerous metal objects testify to flourishing local crafts. Fifth, the plundering testifies to the egalitarian conduct of the princes. Each participant received a share of the spoils from the prince's court in Putivl'.[80] Accordingly, Izyaslav divided Svyatoslav's possessions into four portions, one for each prince: himself, his son Mstislav, and the two Davidovichi.

To judge from the information that the princes plundered no monasteries, it appears that two of the most important domains belonging to the

---

[77] The location of Igor''s village (*Igoreve sel'tso*) is not known. According to one view, it was located some 9 km south of Novgorod Severskiy near the river Desna on the road to Putivl' (Golubovsky, p. 19). This view has been challenged; see V. P. Kovalenko, "Knyazheskie sela v okrestnostyakh Novgorod-Severskogo v XII v.," *Drevnerusskiy gorod Putivl'*, Tezisy dokladov i soobshcheniy oblastnoy nauchnoy konferentsii, posvyashchennoy 1000-letiyu g. Putivlya, A. V. Lugovskoy *et al.* (eds.) (Putivl', 1988), pp. 16–17.

[78] Ipat., cols. 332–4. The Hypatian Chronicle has a lacuna in Svyatoslav's peace proposal to the Davidovichi. The complete text is in Mosk., p. 38 and Erm., p. 32.

[79] A *berkovets* was a weight equivalent to ten poods or 360 lb avoirdupois.

[80] The prince's court was located on the *detinets*; see V. A. Bohusevych, "Rozkopky v Putyvl's'komu kremli," *Arkheolohiia* 15 (K., 1963), pp. 171–4 and O. V. Sukhobokov, "K vozniknoveniyu i ranney istorii Putivlya," *Drevnerusskiy gorod*, Materialy Vsesoyuznoy arkheologicheskoy konferentsii, posvyashchennoy 1500-letiyu goroda Kieva (K., 1984), p. 120.

Ol'govichi, Novgorod Severskiy and Putivl', had no monastic institutions before the middle of the twelfth century.[81] The allies did, however, desecrate churches. Since the pillagers set fire to Igor''s church, we may conclude that it was made of wood. Moreover, he probably built it as it was dedicated to his patron St. George. The attackers also plundered the Church of the Ascension in Putivl'. To date, archaeologists have not unearthed any masonry foundations of the edifice, suggesting that it also was a wooden structure.[82] The chronicles do not disclose the identity of its founder, but he was not Svyatoslav's father, Oleg. There is no evidence that he ever resided in the town. Moreover, Svyatoslav's elder brother, Vsevolod, inherited the Vyatichi lands as his patrimony, and Igor' ruled Gomiy near the Dnepr. Their youngest brother, Gleb, who died in 1138, had been prince of Kursk.[83] Consequently, Svyatoslav probably erected the church in his patrimonial capital.

It is noteworthy that the citizens of Putivl' refused to capitulate to the Davidovichi and insisted on surrendering only to Izyaslav Mstislavich. Tatishchev has a unique passage in which the elders of Putivl' rebuked the Davidovichi as follows:

Princes, we have kissed the Holy Cross to our prince [Svyatoslav] and cannot violate our oath. But you are breaking your oaths to your brothers [the Ol'govichi] and placing your hope in your military might. You are forgetting how God punishes either the offenders themselves or their children. Do you not remember how Oleg Svyatoslavich [Svyatoslav's father] violated his oath by fighting his brothers, by devastating the lands of Rus' with the Polovtsy, and by carrying off the inhabitants into captivity? And even though he acquired much wealth, do you not see how God is avenging Himself on his children? Princes, consider your own conduct! We, however, will not violate the oaths we have made on the Holy Cross for as long as we live.[84]

If the information is true, it reveals the popular sentiments of the citizens in Putivl' and, perhaps, of many inhabitants in Rus'. According to this view,

---

[81] Bagaley claimed that the Davidovichi, Vladimir and Izyaslav, founded the Monastery of the Transfiguration (*Spasopreobrazhenskiy monastyr'*) located one quarter of a *verst* to the south of Novgorod Severskiy overlooking the Desna. He based his observation on the evidence (which he failed to describe) provided by a stone found, in 1787, in the old monastery wall when it was being quarried for stones (*Istoriya Severskoy zemli*, p. 291). It is highly unlikely that the Davidovichi founded a monastery in the patrimonial capital of the Ol'govichi. Moreover, if the monastery existed in 1146, the besiegers would have plundered it when they besieged Novgorod Severskiy, and the chronicler would have reported the event.

[82] Archaeologists have discovered the foundations of a masonry church in Putivl', but they believe it was built at the beginning of the thirteenth century (see below, p. 248).

[83] Concerning Gleb, see NPL, pp. 25, 210; *Dynasty*, pp. 174–5, 342.

[84] Tat. 4, p. 205; compare Tat. 2, pp. 167–8.

the Davidovichi were perfidious and the Ol'govichi were suffering divine retribution for their father's perjury.

Having laid waste to Svyatoslav's town of Putivl', Izyaslav and the Davidovichi once again advanced against Novgorod Severskiy intending to launch an all-out attack. On this occasion they were determined to fight until Svyatoslav capitulated.[85] This, at least, is how he interpreted their intent after his father's erstwhile retainer reported Izyaslav's approach. The attendant, who came from Vladimir's retinue, was privy to the plans of the Davidovichi and his information was trustworthy. The chronicler, at any rate, does not accuse him of treachery. We are not told why the unnamed *boyar* changed his allegiance when Svyatoslav's fortune was at such low ebb. It may be that, like the inhabitants of Putivl', he condemned the Davidovichi for their treachery.

SVYATOSLAV FLEES TO THE VYATICHI LANDS

Svyatoslav realized that his personal fortune and the fate of the Ol'govichi were at stake. He therefore took the precaution of weeding out the disloyal from the loyal supporters. Before abandoning Novgorod Severskiy, he gave his retainers the choice of joining him on his odyssey, as it turned out to be, or remaining to seek their fortunes with the Davidovichi. His faithful retainers Ivanko Yur'evich, Vladimir Svyatoslavich of Murom, Ivan Berladnik, and the Polovtsian khan Tyunrak Osulukovich with his brother Kamosa accompanied him to the "forest land" (*lesnaya zemlya*).[86] Significantly, the reference, the first, to Svyatoslav's wife, children, and Igor's wife shows that he organized a wholesale evacuation of his family. He sought safety in the lands of the Vyatichi, where Karachev, the regional center of the forest land, was his first stop.[87]

---

[85] Ipat., cols. 334–5; Mosk., pp. 38, 389; Vosk., pp. 36–7. A late source claims that the Davidovichi intended to blind Svyatoslav and then kill him (Nikon. 9, p. 170).

[86] The Hypatian chronicler wrongly refers to the two Polovtsian khans as Svyatoslav's uncles, that is, the brothers of his mother (*ui*) (Ipat., col. 334). If they were related to him they must have been his brothers-in-law because Svyatoslav's first wife, and not his mother, was a Polovtsian princess (*Dynasty*, p. 241).

[87] Karachev (Korachev), mentioned here for the first time, was located on the site of the present-day Karachev on the river Snezhet' in the forest land. The latter was located to the east of the Podesen'e between Novgorod Severskiy and the Vyatichi lands. According to A. K. Zaytsev, the Chernigov Vyatichi lands were a separate administrative region in the twelfth century encompassing a smaller area than the ethnic tribal lands of the Vyatichi. The Chernigov Vyatichi lands lay to the east and north of a line formed by Bleve, the Podesen'e, Karachev, and Mtsensk ("Domagoshch i granitsy 'Vyatichey' XII v.," *Istoricheskaya geografiya Rossii XI-nachalo XX v.* [M., 1975], pp. 23–30). Compare T. N. Nikol'skaya, who places the towns north of Kromy, including Karachev, Spas, and Mtsensk

The inhabitants of Novgorod Severskiy sent word to Izyaslav, the Davidovichi, and Svyatoslav Vsevolodovich that Svyatoslav had fled to Karachev. On hearing the news, Izyaslav Davidovich was furious and persuaded his allies to let him follow in pursuit. Accompanied by 3,000 men travelling on horseback without supply wagons, he took the fastest route via Sevsk[88] and Boldyzh.[89] His unexpected arrival placed Svyatoslav in a quandary: he could either flee, thereby placing his wife, children, and *druzhina* at Izyaslav's mercy, or he could stay and fight, thereby endangering his own life. He resolved to fight and, on January 16, 1147, he defeated the Davidovich. Izyaslav of Kiev learnt of Svyatoslav's victory while he was still some distance from Karachev. He arrived at the town only to discover that Svyatoslav had fled deeper into the forests.[90]

Izyaslav had made use of his stopover at Putivl' not only to appoint his *posadniki* over the Seym towns, but also to reorganize his troops. Significantly, after Putivl' fell we learn that Svyatoslav Vsevolodovich accompanied Izyaslav. Svyatoslav's name was not included among the four princes who pillaged Novgorod Severskiy, Igor''s village, and Putivl', indicating that he was not present for the initial part of the campaign. He therefore joined Izyaslav at Putivl', probably after completing his attack on Vyacheslav in Turov. At the same time, Izyaslav removed his son Mstislav from the campaign. The next time we meet him, he will be ruling Kursk, which Svyatoslav had given to Ivanko. Izyaslav probably dispatched Mstislav to take over that town after Putivl' fell.

Earlier, before Izyaslav came to Putivl', an important event took place in Pereyaslavl'. In the autumn of 1146, Igor', languishing in the pit in the Monastery of St. Ioann, became grievously ill.[91] He therefore asked Izyaslav to let him adopt the monk's habit before he died.[92] He explained that he had already considered entering a monastery while he was still ruling his

---

in the Vyatichi lands ("K istoricheskoy geografii zemli Vyatichey," *SA*, nr. 4 [M., 1972], pp. 158–70, and her *Gorodishche Slobodka XII–XIII vv.* [M., 1987], pp. 144–51).

[88] Sevsk (Sev'sk, Sev'sko) was located on the river Seva, a tributary of the Desna to the east of Novgorod Severskiy (Nasonov, p. 230; Makhnovets', p. 569).

[89] T. N. Nikol'skaya points out that Izyaslav followed the traditional route which went from Putivl' via Sevsk, Boldyzh, Karachev, Serensk, and Lobynsk to Moscow. She also believes that the remains of Boldyzh, which she calls Bol'shoe Slobodinskoe gorodishche, are located on the high right bank of the river Navla northwest of Kromy (*Gorodishche Slobodka*, pp. 5, 136 and *Zemlya Vyatichey*, pp. 160–4).

[90] Ipat., cols. 335–6; Mosk., pp. 389–90; Lav., col. 314. Tatishchev claims that in the fighting Svyatoslav was wounded in the hand by a spear (Tat. 2, pp. 168–9).

[91] A number of the sources say that Igor' fell ill in the autumn (NPL, pp. 27, 213; Tver., col. 207).

[92] Taking tonsure before death was a common practice for princes. Igor''s elder brother, Vsevolod, became a monk before his death and evidently took Gabriel (Gavriil) as his monastic name (*Dynasty*, p. 410; Zotov, pp. 262–3).

domain. Izyaslav ordered his men to dismantle the cage over the pit and to release Igor'. The latter, however, was so feeble that he had to be lifted out of the pit and carried to a cell. Unable to eat or drink, he lingered on the brink of death for eight days, but "God returned his soul to him." On January 5, 1147 Bishop Evfimy tonsured him.[93] Later, they transferred him to the monastery of St. Fedor in Kiev where he took the vows of the great habit (*skhima*), the strictest monastic observance in the Orthodox Church and, evidently, adopted the name Ignaty.[94]

On becoming a monk, Igor' renounced his political career and therewith forfeited the post of senior prince of the Ol'govichi.[95] The mantle of office passed to his brother, Svyatoslav. Izyaslav of Kiev would have informed the Davidovichi of this important development after Christmas when he joined them at Putivl'. We must therefore view Izyaslav Davidovich's battle with his cousin, on January 16, 1147, in that light. Svyatoslav himself was probably unaware of his brother's abdication, but Izyaslav knew and this probably antagonized him even more against Svyatoslav. He realized that he was challenging the new senior prince of the Ol'govichi and killing him now took on an added significance. At the same time, Svyatoslav's main demand that Igor' be released no longer contained the same political importance.

After Izyaslav Mstislavich and his allies captured Karachev and plundered it, he declared to the Davidovichi that he had fulfilled his promise by giving them all the domains of the Ol'govichi that they had sought, including Igor''s patrimony, Svyatoslav's domain, and Novgorod Severskiy.[96] Igor''s territories, or part of them, were located around the town of Gomiy. The center of Svyatoslav's patrimony was Putivl'. Novgorod Severskiy held a status similar to Chernigov: it never became a prince's private domain but remained the common property of all the Ol'govichi. Their senior prince was its ruler. Significantly, the Davidovichi agreed that Izyaslav had fulfilled his promise. Nevertheless, they had failed to kill Svyatoslav. They

[93] For the date, see Lav., col. 314.

[94] Ipat., cols. 337–8; Mosk., pp. 38–9. The chronicles do not report the names Igor' adopted on becoming a monk and a *skhimnik*. One view has it that the names were Georgy (baptismal), Gavriil (monastic), and Ignaty (*skhimnik*); see M. N. Berezhkov, *Blazhennyy Igor' Ol'govich, knyaz' Novgorodseverskiy i velikiy knyaz' Kievskiy* (Chernigov, 1893), p. 42. According to another view, the names were Georgy, David, and Ignaty (Zotov, pp. 263–4).

[95] See similar instances with Svyatosha (*Dynasty*, pp. 253–4) and Ryurik Rostislavich (see below, pp. 247–8).

[96] Ipat., cols. 336–7; Mosk., pp. 390, 38. According to Tver., Izyaslav also gave some of the seized possessions, domains, and towns to Svyatoslav Vsevolodovich (Tver., col. 207; compare Nikon. 9, pp. 170–1).

therefore renewed their pursuit and were joined by a new representative of the Mstislavichi, Rostislav of Smolensk.

The latter is mentioned as participating in the chase for the first time. He evidently attached himself to the Davidovichi at Dobryansk (Bryansk)[97] to replace his brother Izyaslav, who had returned to Kiev. His arrival may help to explain, in part, why the Davidovichi went west rather than north to Kozel'sk in pursuit of Svyatoslav. Meanwhile, heeding the warning his nephew sent from Karachev, Svyatoslav Ol'govich went east to Dedoslavl';[98] from there he proceeded north to the Osetr, a tributary of the Oka.[99] At that point Ivan Berladnik deserted him and joined Rostislav of Smolensk.[100]

Surprisingly, Svyatoslav Vsevolodovich, who was allied to Izyaslav of Kiev and the Davidovichi, warned Svyatoslav Ol'govich that the Davidovichi were still pursuing him. It would appear that Izyaslav, believing his nephew's loyalty to be genuine, allowed him to remain in Karachev. Izyaslav, however, miscalculated. On escaping the clutches of his uncle Izyaslav of the Mstislavichi, Svyatoslav demonstrated his ambivalent loyalties by warning his uncle Svyatoslav of the Ol'govichi of the danger he still faced. His conduct is not surprising. After all, he had joined the Monomashichi under duress, and his natural preference was for his father's family since his political future lay with it. Besides, Izyaslav and the Davidovichi had antagonized him by plundering Karachev, allegedly to punish its inhabitants for helping the fugitive. As his patrimonial capital, the town probably held Svyatoslav Vsevolodovich's main court whose storerooms he had to replenish after the pillaging.

While Svyatoslav was at Koltesk, north of the river Osetr, Yury sent 1,000 men from Beloozero to join him.[101] From there he went west to Lobynsk and rested.[102] Consequently, by the end of February, after evading his pursuers for some two months, he found respite in the northeast corner of the Vyatichi lands, the most distant terminus from Novgorod Severskiy in the

[97] The town, mentioned for the first time, was located on the river Desna. According to archaeological evidence, it arose around the middle of the twelfth century (T. V. Ravdina, "O vremeni vozniknoveniya Bryanska," KSIA 135 [1973], pp. 66–71).
[98] The town was located on the river Shivorona, a tributary of the Upa that flows into the Oka from the east. It is mentioned for the first time (Nasonov, p. 224; *Zemlya Vyatichey*, pp. 130–1).
[99] One source claims that from Dedoslavl', Svyatoslav travelled through a number of towns in the lands of Ryazan' (Nikon. 9, p. 171), but this is spurious information (Nasonov, pp. 209–11).
[100] Ipat., col. 338; Mosk., p. 39.
[101] Koltesk, mentioned for the first time, was located near the boundary of Suzdalia on the river Oka, east of the river Protva (Nasonov, pp. 225–6; *Zemlya Vyatichey*, pp. 131–3).
[102] Mentioned for the first time, the town was located at the mouth of the Protva that flows into the Oka from the northwest (Nasonov, p. 226).

territories of the Ol'govichi. Most of the towns at which he stopped are mentioned for the first time. The identification of the heretofore-unrecorded citadels implies that other settlements, which the chronicler failed to mention because Svyatoslav did not stop there, also existed.

His plight was desperate but not hopeless because he successfully mustered loyal support. Of vital importance was the passive backing that the Vyatichi gave him. To judge from the welcome that he received in the towns that he used as staging posts, no local populace denied him sanctuary. Moreover, no band of Vyatichi took advantage of his vulnerability by attacking his train as it wended its way through the forests. Indeed, the Vyatichi demonstrated their loyalty to Svyatoslav by resolutely refusing to be bribed by the Davidovichi to kill him.

The fugitive also obtained active military support. At first, Svyatoslav's nephew Svyatoslav Vsevolodovich campaigned against his uncle because Izyaslav of Kiev forced him to do so, but secretly he assisted Svyatoslav when given the opportunity to express his true sentiments. Svyatoslav Ol'govich also received uncharacteristically loyal backing from his Polovtsian in-laws, who remained at his side until the Davidovichi gave up the chase. His greatest coup, however, was winning over Yury Dolgorukiy. His help gave Svyatoslav a viable chance of success because Yury's resources were greater than those of any other prince in the House of Monomakh barring, perhaps, Izyaslav of Kiev. When the Davidovichi learnt that Svyatoslav had received reinforcements from Yury, they returned to Chernigov. Significantly, by throwing in his lot with Yury, Svyatoslav acted contrary to the policy that his deceased brother Vsevolod had followed. Whereas the latter had supported the nephews, Izyaslav and the Mstislavichi, in their quarrel with their uncles, Yury and the Monomashichi,[103] Svyatoslav joined forces with the uncles.

Unlike his brother Igor', who allegedly had a volatile personality, Svyatoslav had a more amenable disposition. He was also a prudent tactician and when circumstances demanded, he advisedly retreated. Thus, when enemy forces overwhelmed him at Novgorod Severskiy, he followed the advice of his counsellors and withdrew to the safety of the forested districts. When battle was unavoidable, however, he demonstrated outstanding leadership. During the course of his meanderings, he prudently eschewed antagonizing the Vyatichi by not pillaging their towns. He also placed compassion ahead of his political objectives. When the reinforcements from Beloozero gave him the advantage over the Davidovichi, he refused to pursue them in order to remain at the bedside of the dying Ivanko. After the latter died on

[103] *Dynasty*, pp. 328–31.

February 24, 1147, Svyatoslav sent his body to his father Yury in Suzdalia. The latter showed his appreciation by promising to send another son to replace Ivanko.[104]

Thus we see that the year 1146 was momentous for the dynasty of Chernigov. At the time of his death, Vsevolod had held supreme authority in Rus'. When his youngest brother, Svyatoslav, assumed the office of senior prince, he was a fugitive. Igor' had been the weak link in the chain of leadership among the Ol'govichi.

BISHOP ONUFRY CHAMPIONS KLIM SMOLYATICH

After Izyaslav returned to Kiev, the Davidovichi withdrew to Chernigov, and Svyatoslav regrouped in the Vyatichi lands, Rus' experienced an ecclesiastical crisis in which Bishop Onufry of Chernigov played a leading role. In 1143, Vsevolod Ol'govich and Metropolitan Mikhail had appointed him bishop of Chernigov[105] after Bishop Panteleymon "the Blessed" had died in the previous year.[106] In 1146, as we have seen, Onufry witnessed the oath that the Davidovichi pledged to Igor'. The following year, after the death of Metropolitan Mikhail,[107] Izyaslav selected the *skhimnik* Klim (Kliment) Smolyatich, a native of Rus', to replace Mikhail and instructed the bishops to invest him in office on their own authority.[108]

In the dispute over Klim's installation, Onufry articulated the majority's view that the assembled bishops had the authority to create a metropolitan in the absence of a patriarch. Some have argued that he supported Klim because he belonged to the faction advocating the appointment of a native of Rus' as metropolitan. To judge from the available information, it is unlikely that nationalism was at the hub of the dispute. Nifont of Novgorod and Manuel of Smolensk were not opposed to Klim's candidacy because he was from Rus'. Rather, they argued that the bishops lacked the authority to appoint anyone, from Rus' or from Greece; that prerogative belonged to the patriarch alone.

Onufry's main objective, it seems, was to convince the bishops that they should install Klim because, owing to the ecclesiastical controversies in Byzantium, no one knew how long the patriarchal throne would remain

---

[104] Ipat., cols. 338–9; Mosk., p. 39; compare Tat. 4, p. 206 and Tat. 2, p. 170.
[105] Ipat., col. 313.
[106] Ipat., col. 309. Panteleymon became venerated locally as a saint (Arkhimandrit Leonid, *Svyataya Rus'*, p. 35).
[107] Mikhail died in Byzantium after he went there in 1145 (Lav., col. 312).
[108] Gust., pp. 298–9.

vacant.[109] He defended the power of the synod to install Klim by calling on the mandate of the canons and the practice of the Orthodox Church. Moreover, he pointed out that it was valid for the bishops to install Klim because they had a relic of St. Clement which they could use,[110] just as the Greeks used the hand of St. John to bless a newly appointed metropolitan. On July 27, the bishops, presided over by Onufry, consecrated Klim as bishop, installed him as metropolitan, and blessed him with the head of St. Clement.[111]

The bishop of Chernigov gained no ecclesiastical benefits by supporting Klim's appointment. On the contrary, after the latter assumed office, his own authority would diminish because he would cease functioning as the acting metropolitan. Just the same, in supporting Izyaslav's appointee, Onufry seemingly acted with duplicity. Since Izyaslav's usurpation of Kiev and imprisonment of Igor´ had evidently not alienated Onufry from him, the bishop could be accused of supporting Izyaslav's allies, the Davidovichi. That is, he sided with the brothers after they betrayed the Ol´govichi even though, a year earlier, he had threatened with damnation all those who broke their oaths to Igor´.

As for Izyaslav, he wanted the highest-ranking church official in Rus´ to be his man. While the office of metropolitan was vacant, as already noted, Onufry acted in his stead. Onufry's first loyalty, undoubtedly, was to the prince of Chernigov. Because of the conflict raging between the Ol´govichi and the Davidovichi, and because of the latter's political fickleness, it was not inconceivable that Onufry could at some point become estranged from the prince of Kiev. Klim's appointment would obviate that problem for Izyaslav. As for the princes of Chernigov, the silence of the chronicles suggests that the two families did not challenge Onufry. On the one hand,

---

[109] For an examination of the controversy over Klim's appointment, see D. Obolensky, "Byzantium, Kiev and Moscow: A Study in Ecclesiastical Relations," *Byzantium and the Slavs* (New York, 1994), pp. 142–9; S. Franklin (trans. and intro.), *Sermons and Rhetoric of Kievan Rus´* (Harvard University Press, 1991), pp. xlv–lviii; S. Senyk, *A History of the Church in Ukraine*, vol. 1, To the End of the Thirteenth Century (Rome, 1993), pp. 108–18; and *Istoriia*, vol. 3, pp. 262–5.

[110] According to tradition, Clement, purportedly the third successor of St. Peter in Rome, was exiled to Crimea, where he was martyred. In the ninth century Constantine (St. Cyril), allegedly discovered his relics (A. P. Vlasto, *The Entry of the Slavs into Christendom* [Cambridge, 1970], pp. 35–6). Around 988, Vladimir, the Christianizer of Rus´, took some of the relics from Kherson to Kiev (Lav., col. 116; S. H. Cross and O. P. Sherbowitz-Wetzor [trans.], *The Russian Primary Chronicle: Laurentian Text* [Cambridge, Mass., 1953], pp. 116, 249). Vladimir evidently had the relics placed in one of the side altars of the Tithe Church (*Desyatinaya tserkev*) which he built (Ya. N. Shchapov, *Gosudarstvo i tserkov´ Drevney Rusi X–XIII vv.* [M., 1989], p. 29).

[111] Ipat., cols. 340–1; Mosk., pp. 39–40; Lav., col. 315 gives the date. This was evidently only the second occasion in the history of Rus´ on which a native was appointed metropolitan. The first was in 1051, when Hilarion (Ilarion) was made metropolitan (Lav. col., 155). Concerning Klim's career, see Shchapov, *Gosudarstvo i tserkov´*, pp. 196–7.

the Davidovichi, as Izyaslav's allies, would have supported Klim's appointment. On the other hand, Svyatoslav, as we shall see, would later refuse to cooperate with Klim.[112] At the beginning of 1147, however, he was a refugee in the Vyatichi lands and too preoccupied with regaining control of his patrimony to make any effective protest against Klim's appointment.

SVYATOSLAV RECOVERS THE VYATICHI LANDS

In the spring, Svyatoslav Ol'govich had a stroke of good fortune when Yury Dolgorukiy kept his promise by coming to his assistance. This enabled him to retaliate against his enemies. Surprisingly, the two did not direct their initial attacks against the Davidovichi and Izyaslav of Kiev, but against the latter's younger brothers Svyatopolk of Novgorod and Rostislav of Smolensk.[113] The latter, as we have seen, had joined the Davidovichi at Dobryansk to pursue Svyatoslav, but Svyatopolk had not participated in the campaign. By seizing Novyy Torg (Torzhok) and the river Msta region in the Novgorod lands, Yury drew Svyatopolk into the conflict. His objective, it would appear, was to vent his anger against the Mstislavichi as a family for pre-empting his claim to Kiev.

After returning from the campaign, Yury invited Svyatoslav to Moscow and the latter came on Friday April 4.[114] The visit gave Yury the opportunity to meet the Ol'govich in his capacity as the senior prince for the first time. It also enabled the princes to express their goodwill towards each other: they exchanged gifts, feasted, and rejoiced. The main purpose of the meeting, however, was political. After pledging oaths, they discussed what strategy they would adopt against their enemies. This is implied by Yury's promise to send another son with troops.

The political pact also had a personal dimension. The chronicler suggests this by drawing attention to Svyatoslav's son Oleg, who is mentioned by name for the first time. His advance arrival in Moscow and his errand to present the skin of a snow leopard to Yury seemingly had an unrevealed purpose, but one that was germane to the meeting. We can surmise that purpose from the news that, three years later, Oleg married one of Yury's daughters.[115] Consequently, Yury probably used the Moscow visit to meet his future son-in-law and to arrange the match with Svyatoslav. In this way the princes cemented their political pact with a personal bond. After

---

[112] See below, pp. 78–9.   [113] Ipat., col. 339; Mosk., p. 39.
[114] Ipat., cols. 339–40; compare Mosk., p. 39; Tat. 2, pp. 170–1. Concerning the date, see Berezhkov, p. 147.
[115] See below, p. 59.

being reassured of Yury's friendship, Svyatoslav returned to Lobynsk, went to Nerinsk, crossed the Oka, and set up camp.[116]

Svyatoslav launched a two-pronged counter-attack: the first against Rostislav of Smolensk and the second against the Davidovichi. By sending his troops into Smolensk districts, he repaid Rostislav for his part in pillaging the Vyatichi lands. He also accommodated Yury, whose fight was with the Mstislavichi. This favour may have prompted Yury to send his son Gleb with greater dispatch; the latter joined Svyatoslav at Devyagorsk.[117]

Svyatoslav's Polovtsian allies, the Toksobichi and the Brodniki, also came from the eastern bank of the river Donets (Severniy Donets).[118] The Toksobichi came, in part, because of their marital tie with Svyatoslav. The consideration that he was now the senior prince of the Ol'govichi was also a factor. Most inviting, however, were the opportunities to undermine princely unity and to indulge in looting. Consequently, the nomads, Gleb, and Vladimir of Murom provided Svyatoslav with a force that outnumbered every retinue that the *posadniki* of the Davidovichi commanded. Moreover, to judge from the earlier response of the Dedoslavl' inhabitants, the Davidovichi could not count on Vyatichi support. In face of the overwhelming odds, the *posadniki* abandoned their posts, and Svyatoslav reclaimed all the Vyatichi towns[119] stretching from Bleve,[120] Dobryansk, and Vorobeyna in the west, to Domagoshch[121] and Mtsensk in the east.[122]

Sometime after Svyatoslav initiated his counter-attack against the Davidovichi, his nephew Svyatoslav Vsevolodovich vacated Karachev and went

---

[116] The location of Nerinsk has not been determined. Since Svyatoslav began his return journey southward at this time, if such a town existed it was probably on the left bank of the river Oka (he crossed over to the right bank after coming to Nerinsk) evidently upstream from Lobynsk, that is, to the south in the direction of Dedoslavl'. A number of investigators claim, however, that the name Nerinsk is a corruption and that it should read Serensk (see *Zemlya Vyatichey*, pp. 136–7).

[117] Devyagorsk is mentioned for the first time. Its exact location has not been determined, but it was located between Dedoslavl' and Mtsensk (Makhnovets', p. 548).

[118] Concerning the Toksobichi, see S. A. Pletneva, "Polovetskaya zemlya," *Drevnerusskie knyazhestva X–XIII vv.*, L. G. Beskrovny (ed.) (M., 1975), p. 277 and her *Polovtsy* (M., 1990), pp. 97–8. The Brodniki, mentioned for the first time, evidently came from the extreme northeastern region of the Polovtsian steppe to the east of Kursk (Pletneva, "Polovetskaya zemlya," pp. 280–1, 298–9).

[119] Concerning the towns of the Vyatichi lands, see Nikol'skaya, "K istoricheskoy geografii zemli Vyatichey," pp. 158–70; Zaytsev, pp. 99–103.

[120] Also referred to as Oblov' and Oblove, the town was located at the source of the river Bolva, a northeastern tributary of the Desna, and lay on the boundary between the Chernigov and Smolensk lands (Nasonov, p. 221; *Zemlya Vyatichey*, pp. 77–8).

[121] Domagoshch, mentioned for the first time, was probably located northwest of Mtsensk, on the left bank of the Oka near the mouth of the river Zusha (Zaytsev, "Domagoshch i granitsy 'Vyatichey' XII v.," pp. 27–9; *Zemlya Vyatichey*, pp. 147–8).

[122] Zaytsev, pp. 99–100. Mtsensk, mentioned for the first time, was located on the site of present-day Mtsensk on the river Zusha, a right tributary of the river Oka (*Zemlya Vyatichey*, pp. 141–4).

to Vladimir Davidovich in Chernigov. Svyatoslav Ol'govich probably bypassed Karachev because its people had given him sanctuary and because
the town belonged to his nephew. Meanwhile, Izyaslav Davidovich had
occupied Novgorod Severskiy and evidently also imposed his rule over
Starodub and the surrounding towns of the Ol'govichi.[123] His stay there
was short-lived, however, because Svyatoslav's advance forced him to flee
to Chernigov.

From Mtsensk, Svyatoslav set out for Kromy, which lay on the southern
frontiers of the Vyatichi lands.[124] Since Mstislav Izyaslavich controlled the
town, it belonged to his Kursk domain.[125] Svyatoslav therewith began the
next phase of his attack: the drive to recover his towns of Putivl' and
Kursk in the Posem'e. Before he reached Kromy, however, messengers sent
by Vladimir Davidovich and Svyatoslav Vsevolodovich intercepted him
at Spas, proposing a settlement.[126] They relinquished their claims to the
Vyatichi lands, to Putivl', and to Novgorod Severskiy to which Svyatoslav
returned. Since only Vladimir and Svyatoslav sent the delegation, Izyaslav
Davidovich had either not yet reached them or was opposed to the proposal.
Indeed, the offer was full of duplicity. The news that Izyaslav of Kiev was
not party to it means that Vladimir and Svyatoslav acted independently
of their ally, therewith betraying him. The chronicler's curt comment that
"they kissed the Holy Cross, but they were not reconciled," also suggests
that they had a secret agenda.[127]

THE DAVIDOVICHI PLOT TREACHERY

The Davidovichi did make their offer of peace to Svyatoslav in bad faith.
They plotted against him anew. Vladimir sent his brother to Izyaslav in Kiev
complaining, deceitfully a number of sources claim, that Svyatoslav had
seized his Vyatichi domain. He asked Izyaslav to help the Davidovichi drive

[123] Concerning Starodub, see V. P. Kovalenko and E. O. Shinakov, "Litopysnyi Starodub (do pytannia
pro lokalizatsiiu)," *Liubets'kyi z'izd kniaziv 1097 roku v istorychnii doli Kyivs'koi Rusi*, Materialy
mizhnarodnoi konferentsii prysviachenoi 900-littiu z'izdu kniaziv Kyivs'koi Rusi u Liubechi, P. P.
Tolochko (gen. ed.) (Chernihiv, 1997), pp. 89–101.
[124] Kromy, mentioned for the first time, was located south of Mtsensk on the left bank of the river
Nedna, not far from where it flows into the river Kroma (*Zemlya Vyatichey*, pp. 144–6).
[125] The sources do not give the prince's first name, just his patronymic. But he can be no other than
the son of Izyaslav of Kiev who participated in the attack on Putivl' and then received Kursk from
his father.
[126] Spas (Spash') mentioned for the first time, was located between Mtsensk and Kromy. The alleged
site of the now extinct town was located on the river Nepolod, a left tributary of the Oka (*Zemlya
Vyatichey*, pp. 74–7).
[127] Ipat., cols. 341–3; compare Mosk., p. 40.

out Svyatoslav from the Vyatichi lands. He also proposed that they march against Yury either to conclude peace or to wage war. Izyaslav agreed.[128]

Meanwhile, Svyatoslav Vsevolodovich, to whom Izyaslav had given five towns in the southwest corner of the Kievan land, came to Kiev.[129] He asked Izyaslav to let him return to the Chernigov lands because his entire 'livelihood' (*zhizn'*) was there. Svyatoslav feared being relegated to the backwater towns in the Kievan frontier because his political future lay with his own dynasty. If he remained away from his patrimony for too long, another might seize it. He, however, had to retain possession of it if he hoped to climb to the top of the dynastic ladder. Izyaslav therefore let him return to his patrimony but ordered him to join the campaign against Svyatoslav and Yury.[130]

Izyaslav also invited the Kievans to join his campaign against Yury. They, however, refused to march against the House of Monomakh, but agreed to fight the princes of Chernigov. Moreover, they advised him to be reconciled with Yury and not to trust the Davidovichi. Acting on their advice, Izyaslav sent a man to Chernigov to appraise the intentions of the Davidovichi. The official discovered that they and Svyatoslav Vsevolodovich had formed a pact with Svyatoslav Ol'govich and had informed Yury of their alliance. They also conspired to take Izyaslav captive or to kill him. Izyaslav therefore demanded that the Davidovichi confirm their oath. But they refused, declaring that they were greatly aggrieved because he was holding Igor' captive, and would be reconciled only if he released Igor'. Izyaslav's messenger accused the brothers of violating their oath and declared war.[131]

Thus we see that, after the Davidovichi failed to kill Svyatoslav Ol'govich and to appropriate all the lands of the Ol'govichi, they plotted against Izyaslav. They hoped to realize their policy of aggrandizement by winning Kiev for Vladimir. Since their father David had not ruled the town, they could not claim the right to sit on the throne of their father. Their only recourse was usurpation. Significantly, this was the optimum time for them to initiate their challenge because they enjoyed supremacy in the dynasty.

[128] Ipat., col. 343; Mosk., p. 40; compare a number of sources, which state that the Davidovichi deceived Izyaslav with their request (for example, Erm., p. 34 and L'vov, p. 109). Before the account describing the delegation to Izyaslav, Nikon. claims that Andrey Rostislavich, prince of Elets in Ryazan' (*iz Rezani s Eltsa*), came to Chernigov and formed a pact with the Davidovichi (Nikon. 9, p. 173). Andrey was the son of Rostislav Yaroslavich of Ryazan' (Baum. 2, XIV, 8) who had invaded Yury's Suzdalian lands (see above, p. 31).

[129] The five towns included Bozh'skyy, Mezhibozh'e, and Kotel'nitsa (see above, p. 29).

[130] Ipat., col. 343; Mosk., p. 40.

[131] Ipat. cols. 343–7; Mosk., pp. 40–1; Erm., p. 34. Compare Nikon., which claims that the princes of Ryazan' formed an alliance with the Davidovichi (Nikon. 9, pp. 173–4).

Moreover, the brothers won over Svyatoslav to their camp by promising to fight for Igor''s release. They seemingly forgot, however, that in addition to Izyaslav they also had to contend with the Kievans.

IGOR''S DEATH

Izyaslav of Kiev inadvertently provided the Kievans with the pretext for committing an unprecedented act of treachery. He marshaled his troops and set out against the Davidovichi. From his camp near the river Supoy north of Pereyaslavl', he sent messengers to his brother Vladimir, whom he had left in charge of Kiev, to Metropolitan Klim, and to the *tysyatskiy* Lazar' (Lazor') ordering them to assemble a *veche* at the Cathedral of St. Sofia. Izyaslav's men reminded the citizens how they had offered to march against the princes of Chernigov. Izyaslav summoned the townsmen to arms now not only because the Davidovichi and Svyatoslav Vsevolodovich had betrayed him, but also because the Davidovichi intended to uproot the citizens. The Kievans agreed to come.

One man declared that before leaving Kiev they should remember what happened during the reign of Izyaslav Yaroslavich (d. 1078). At that time malicious men freed Vseslav of Polotsk from the pit and enthroned him.[132] As a result Kiev suffered great woe. In 1147 Igor' was imprisoned in the Monastery of St. Fedor and posed a similar threat. The speaker proposed, therefore, that they kill the prince before joining Izyaslav. The people agreed. Vladimir attempted to stop them declaring that his brother had not ordered them to kill Igor'. He mounted his horse in the hope of arriving at the monastery ahead of them, but they blocked his way.

Igor', as was his wont, visited the Church of St. Fedor at midday. He sought solace in prayer and resigned himself to becoming a martyr if that was God's will.[133] The rabble found him in the church and seized him. He accused them of being lawbreakers who, having kissed the Holy Cross to him as their prince, now sought to kill him. But they ripped the cassock from his back and led him away naked. Vladimir confronted them at the gate of the monastery. He jumped off his horse and covered the hapless victim with his cloak. Once more he pleaded with the mob not to commit

---

[132] See Ipat., cols. 160–1; Lav., cols. 170–1; *Dynasty*, p. 66.
[133] In the 1880s, the miraculous icon of the Mother of God, before which Igor' had prayed when the mob dragged him away, was preserved in the Church of the Assumption in the Caves Monastery. The icon was popularly called Igor''s icon (Barsukov, col. 215). The church was destroyed during the Second World War.

this evil deed and, taking Igor′, sought sanctuary in his mother's court. But the pursuers broke down its gate. On spotting Igor′ on the balcony they tore it down and, grabbing Igor′, killed him.[134]

Tying his feet together with a rope, they dragged his body to a nearby market, placed it on a cart, and took it to the market square in the *podol′*. There, they dumped it on the ground for ridicule. Igor′, "a good man and a defender of his patrimony," won the "crown of martyrdom" on Friday September 19.[135] On discovering the body, "righteous men" covered it with their cloaks. They told Vladimir where it lay and he sent Lazar′ to retrieve it. On arriving at the market, the *tysyatskiy* accused the culprits standing there of killing the prince. They replied, however, that it was not they, but the Davidovichi and Svyatoslav Vsevolodovich who were responsible for his death because they had plotted to kill Izyaslav. Lazar′ then took the body to the nearby Novgorodian church of St. Mikhail.

That night "God bestowed a great favour." All the candles around Igor′'s body came alight. The Novgorodians reported this wonder to the metropolitan, but he forbade them to repeat it to anyone. He also sent *Igumen* Ananiya (Onaniya) from the Monastery of St. Fedor to bury the prince. The monk clothed the naked corpse in princely garb, sang the customary hymns over it, and had it interred in the Monastery of St. Simeon founded by Igor′'s grandfather, Svyatoslav, and patronized by Igor′'s father, Oleg.[136]

The callous intervention of the townsman confirms two things. First, the pro-Izyaslav faction's manipulation of the *veche* demonstrates its continued dominance in the town. Significantly, Metropolitan Klim evidently belonged to this group. He revealed his anti-Ol′govichi bias by prohibiting the Novgorodians from announcing God's favor to the murdered prince. The manifestation would have been interpreted as divine condemnation of the faction's crime. Second, the speaker's proposal reveals that the Ol′govichi still had supporters in Kiev whom Izyaslav's partisans could not trust. The passers-by in the market who covered Igor′'s body undoubtedly belonged to that loyal group. The Novgorodians were also friendly to Igor′, to judge from the news that Lazar′ placed his body in their church. Later, they demonstrated their favourable disposition by proclaiming God's favour to the murdered prince. Finally, judging from the tenor of the Hypatian account, its author was also friendly to Igor′. We do not know, however, whether he praised the prince because he favoured the House of Chernigov

---

[134] Lav., col. 318.   [135] Concerning the date, see Berezhkov, p. 147.
[136] Ipat., cols. 347–55; Lav., cols. 316–18; Mosk., pp. 41–2; N4, pp. 151–2. Concerning Svyatoslav's association with the monastery, see *Dynasty*, pp. 113–19.

or because, as a pious Christian, he deemed it inappropriate to speak ill of a martyr.

The deed was unprecedented in Rus': never before had a prince been the victim of mob hatred. Its savagery was also unwarranted: the Kievans attacked the defenseless Igor' by exposing him to ridicule, by beating him to death, and by desecrating his body. The horrendousness of their crime was magnified in that they defiled one who had dedicated himself to God. Even so, the Kievans argued that they were free of guilt because they had merely turned the tables on the Davidovichi. What the latter failed to do to Izyaslav, the Kievans succeeded in doing to Igor'.

Significantly, the Mstislavichi were not implicated in the atrocity. Izyaslav was in the field at the time of the crime. Moreover, in the past he had demonstrated a modicum of compassion towards Igor' by allowing him to become a monk when he was at death's door. More importantly, Izyaslav's brother Vladimir valiantly defended the Ol'govich.[137] His efforts were genuine since the pro-Ol'govichi chroniclers report them.

We know little about Igor' as a man. As we have seen, some chroniclers tell us that princes and people alike disliked him because he was proud and had a violent temper. Tatishchev alone offers a more detailed description of Igor', seemingly given by a personal acquaintance of the prince:

This Igor' Svyatoslavich [that is, Ol'govich] was a courageous man and an avid hunter with dogs and birds. He read many books and was educated in liturgical hymnody. He frequently sang in the church when he was in Vladimir [*sic*].[138] He had little respect for priests and refused to keep the fasts. Because of this the ordinary people had little affection for him. He was of medium height, skinny, and of dark complexion. He wore his hair long as a priest's, as was the custom, and his beard was narrow and short. When he lived in the monastery he observed all the rules like a monk, but whether he pretended or was truly repentant I do not know. God knows.[139]

Igor' may have been lukewarm in his piety, but his passive acceptance of a violent death at the hands of fellow Christians won him the status of passion-sufferer (*strastoterpets*).[140] He therewith joined the illustrious

---

[137] Vladimir's support of Igor' is not surprising in the light of later evidence. As we shall see, his son Mstislav would marry a daughter of Svyatoslav Vsevolodovich (see below, pp. 135–6).
[138] This is evidently an error. According to chronicle information, Igor' never lived in a town called Vladimir.
[139] Tat. 4, pp. 210–11 and Tat. 2, p. 176. According to Rybakov, Tatishchev quoted the *boyar* author Petr Borislavich, who wrote the family chronicle of the Mstislavichi (*Kievskaya Rus'*, pp. 484–5).
[140] The term refers to Christians who suffered a violent death at the hands of fellow Christians as victims of treachery. SS. Boris and Gleb, who were killed by their elder brother Svyatopolk in 1015, were the first *strastoterptsy* of Rus' (E. Golubinsky, *Istoriya kanonizatsii svyatykh v russkoy tserkvi*, second edition [M., 1903], pp. 43–9, 58).

company of SS. Boris and Gleb. Thus, even though many of their contemporaries and later chroniclers condemned the Ol'govichi for their alleged treachery, a member of that very family was exalted by the Orthodox
Church. The Ol'govichi might well argue, therefore, that Igor' helped to
wash away the stains of their dynasty's disgrace with his martyr's blood.

On January 5, 1147, when Igor' became a monk, he exempted his brother,
Svyatoslav, from the political obligation of rescuing him from the pit. Eight
months later, on September 19, when the Kievans killed Igor', they released Svyatoslav from the moral duty of freeing him from captivity in
the monastery. At that time, however, they imposed a new responsibility on Svyatoslav. He became in honor bound to seek retribution for the
ignominious crime that the Kievans had committed against Igor'.

SVYATOSLAV RECLAIMS THE POSEM'E

Towards the end of September 1147, Svyatoslav Ol'govich learnt of his
brother's murder. At the same time Gleb Yur'evich came from Suzdalia and
together they set off against Mstislav Izyaslavich in Kursk.[141] Surprisingly,
after receiving the news of Igor's death, Svyatoslav did not take immediate
retaliatory action against the Kievans or Izyaslav. Instead, he set out to
retrieve the confiscated Posem'e towns. Even though the chronicler makes
it appear as if Igor's murder was the stimulus for the campaign, this was
not the case. Gleb's arrival merely coincided with Igor's death. Svyatoslav
and Gleb had planned the expedition earlier in the year after Svyatoslav had
regained control of his Vyatichi towns. Moreover, after he was reconciled
with the Davidovichi and Svyatoslav Vsevolodovich, they demonstrated
their support by helping him to evict the Mstislavichi from the Posem'e
lands.

Svyatoslav's objective in repossessing Kursk and its outposts was to give
them to Gleb. In this way, he hoped to retain the support of Gleb's father
in Suzdalia. The town capitulated without a battle because its inhabitants
refused to fight a descendant of Monomakh. The people of Kursk therefore
demonstrated the same readiness to oppose the Ol'govichi and refusal to
fight the Monomashichi as the citizens of Kiev had done.

Earlier in the year, as we have seen, when Izyaslav Mstislavich withdrew
from the campaign against Svyatoslav, he stated that he had given the Davidovichi all the lands of the Ol'govichi, including Svyatoslav's entire domain.

---

[141] Ipat., cols. 355–9. In the spring of 1147, as we have seen, Gleb had helped Svyatoslav regain control
of his Vyatichi lands. He must have returned home to Suzdalia after Svyatoslav was reconciled with
the Davidovichi but came south again in the autumn to help Svyatoslav campaign in the Posem'e.

Since Izyaslav did not give them Kursk, this meant that he and the Davidovichi did not consider it to belong to the patrimony of the Ol'govichi. Indeed, the evidence that Putivl', and not Kursk, was Svyatoslav's personal capital, and the information that he was willing to part with Kursk by giving it to Gleb, confirms that the Ol'govichi did not consider Kursk to be part of their inheritance. It was still a contested domain which had changed hands between the prince of Chernigov and the prince of Pereyaslavl' on a number of occasions.[142] Thus, in 1147 the local inhabitants did not universally acknowledge the Ol'govichi to be the rulers of the Posem'e region. At Vyr',[143] V'yakhan',[144] and Popash,[145] Svyatoslav encountered obstinate resistance even though he sought to capture the towns for Gleb. Significantly, the people preferred Izyaslav of Kiev. In other words, all the anti-Ol'govichi towns did not prefer the same Monomashichi. Nevertheless, the news that Svyatoslav attempted to retake the three towns shows that they belonged to Kursk. They evidently formed the western boundary of the Kursk district south of the Seym.

Significantly, Svyatoslav and his allies did not attack Glebl' but Izyaslav Mstislavich did.[146] He also besieged Vsevolozh,[147] Unenezh,[148] Belavezha

---

[142] When Vladimir Monomakh ruled Chernigov (1078–94), he gave Kursk to his son Izyaslav, who remained there until 1095 (Ipat., col. 220; *Dynasty*, pp. 193–4). In 1127 Monomakh's son Mstislav gave Kursk to his son Izyaslav and, at the same time, Mstislav's brother Yaropolk of Pereyaslavl' controlled the Seym region through his *posadniki* (Lav., cols. 296–7; *Dynasty*, p. 314). It was not until 1136, it appears, that the Ol'govichi regained control of Kursk from Yaropolk (*Dynasty*, p. 336). At the beginning of 1147, therefore, control of the town went to the House of Monomakh once again.

[143] The town Vyr' was located near the river Vyr', a tributary of the Seym between the latter and the Sula (Nasonov, p. 223). Concerning Vyr' and the Polovtsian route to the Posem'e, see V. G. Lyaskoronsky, "K voprosu o Pereyaslavl'skikh Torkakh," Zh. M. N. P., chast' 358 (Spb., 1905), 278–302; Yu. Yu. Morgunov, "Letopisnyy gorod Popash," SA, nr. 1 (M., 1985), 241–9; V. V. Pryimak, "Deiaki pidsumky vyvchennia davn'orus'koho mista Vyr i Vyrivs'koi volosti," *Problemy rann'oslovians'koi i davn'orus'koi arkheolohii Poseim'ia*, O. P. Motsia *et al.* (eds.) (Bilopillia, 1994), pp. 38–42. See also Zaytsev, pp. 96–7.

[144] V'yakhan', mentioned for the first time, was located southwest of Vyr' on the river Terna, a tributary of the Sula (Nasonov, p. 223; Makhnovets', p. 546). See also Yu. Yu. Morgunov, "Letopisnyy gorod V'yakhan'," SA, nr. 2 (M., 1982), 237–45.

[145] Mentioned for the first time, Popash was probably located on the river Popad'ya, a tributary of the Sula (Nasonov, p. 229; Makhnovets', p. 565). See also Morgunov, "Letopisnyy gorod Popash," SA, nr. 1 (M., 1985), 241–9.

[146] Mentioned for the first time, Glebl' was located west of Popash, probably on the river Romen, a tributary of the Sula; see Golubovsky, pp. 9–10; Nasonov, pp. 223–4; Makhnovets', p. 547; P. V. Golubovsky, "Gde nakhodilis' sushchestvovavshie v domongol'skiy period goroda: Vorgol, Glebl', Zartyy, Orgoshch', Snovsk, Unenezh, Khorobor'?" Zh. M. N. P., chast' 347 (Spb, 1903), 111–35.

[147] Mentioned for the first time, Vsevolozh was located southeast of Chernigov in the Zadesen'e (Golubovsky, pp. 8–9; Nasonov, p. 223; Makhnovets', p. 546). The outposts of Unenezh, Belavezha, Glebl', and Bakhmach were located one day's march (some 30 km) from it (Zaytsev, p. 79).

[148] Mentioned only in this instance, Unenezh was located on the river Oster, on the site of the present-day Nezhin (Nasonov, pp. 232–3).

(Belaya Vezha),[149] and Bakhmach,[150] thus revealing that the Chernigov dynasty controled these towns. They were not, however, among the towns that Svyatoslav attempted to reclaim for himself. Therefore, they did not belong to the Ol'govichi but to the Davidovichi. The inhabitants confirmed this. When they fled in the face of Izyaslav's attack they sought sanctuary in the Davidovichi capital of Chernigov rather than in Svyatoslav's patrimony of Putivl', even though Belavezha and Bakhmach were closer to Putivl' than to Chernigov. In the light of this information, we may conclude that Izyaslav attacked only the domains of the Davidovichi.[151] This is not surprising since, after he discovered their plot to kill him, Izyaslav would have directed his wrath against the two brothers.

In razing the Zadesen'e, Izyaslav struck a severe blow to the livelihood of the Davidovichi. It has been estimated that the district contained some fourteen towns and eighty villages.[152] What is more, Vsevolozh served as the center of defense against nomadic attacks and controlled the caravan route from the steppe to Chernigov. The most important overland route was the one traders used to travel from the Volga Bulgars, via Kiev and Galich, to Central Europe. Merchants using the route crossed the upper reaches of the river Oster to the south of Glebl'. At that point the main route took them south of the Oster to Kiev, but they could also take the northern fork to Glebl', Vsevolozh, and Chernigov. In setting fire to the towns of the Davidovichi, Izyaslav disrupted the lucrative trade passing through the Zadesen'e.[153]

---

[149] Mentioned for the first time, Belavezha was located in the upper reaches of the river Oster (Nasonov, p. 221; Makhnovets', p. 540; V. P. Kovalenko and Yu. N. Sytyy, "Letopisnaya Belavezha [K voprosu o lokalizatsii]," *Arkheologiya slavyanskogo Yugo-Vostoka*, A. G. D'yachenko (gen. ed.) [Voronezh, 1991], pp. 59–66).

[150] Mentioned for the first time, Bakhmach is the present-day village of Bakhmach on the river Borzna, a tributary of the Desna (Nasonov, p. 222; Makhnovets', p. 542).

[151] At a later date, the Davidovichi accused Izyaslav of devastating their towns in the Zadesen'e (see below, p. 57).

[152] V. P. Kovalenko, "K voprosu o vzaimootnosheniyakh feodal'nykh gorodov i okrugi v Chernigovo-Severskoy zemle," *Iz istorii Bryanskogo kraya* (Bryansk, 1995), p. 65; Zaytsev, pp. 78–80. The western boundary of the Zadesen'e ran along the river Desna from Chernigov to the mouth of the river Oster; the southern boundary ran along the river Oster to its source and continued east to the region of Glebl'; the eastern boundary ran from Glebl' longitudinally to the river Seym; the northern boundary ran along the Seym to its confluence with the Desna and then along the latter to Chernigov (Yu. N. Sytyy, "K istorii izucheniya Chernigovskogo Zadesen'ya," *Problemy arkheologii Yuzhnoy Rusi*, P. P. Tolochko (gen. ed.) [K., 1990], pp. 62, 65).

[153] Concerning the trade route and the importance of Vsevolozh, see V. P. Kovalenko and Yu. N. Sytyy, "Torgovo-ekonomicheskie vzaimosvyazi Chernigovo-severskoy zemli s volzhskoy Bulgariey v IX–XIII vv.," *Put' iz Bulgara v Kiev*, A. Kh. Khalikov (gen. ed.) (Kazan', 1992), pp. 57–9 and Yu. N. Sytyy, "Chernigovsko Zadesen'e v sostave votchiny chernigovskikh knyazey," *Istoriko-arkheologicheskiy seminar "Chernigov i ego okruga v IX–XIII vv.,"* (26–28 sentyabrya 1988 g.), Tezisy dokladov (Chernigov, 1988), pp. 35–6.

According to the account, Izyaslav's brother Rostislav caused much damage to the Chernigov districts on his way south from Smolensk. Since he travelled down the left bank of the Dnepr, he probably pillaged Chichersk[154] and Gomiy. The latter, as we have seen, had belonged to Igor' and thus would have been among the towns that Izyaslav had given to the Davidovichi. We have no way of knowing whether they returned it to Svyatoslav Ol'govich after their *rapprochement*. As for Lyubech, Rostislav undoubtedly identified only it by name because it was the most important citadel that he sacked, and it was probably the patrimonial domain of the Davidovichi. Thus, in addition to helping Izyaslav raze the Zadesen'e towns, Rostislav made his brother's revenge all the sweeter by destroying the capital of the Davidovichi family.[155]

After his tour of pillaging, Izyaslav withdrew to Kiev, where he instructed his troops to re-assemble for a campaign against Chernigov as soon as the rivers froze. After the ice formed, however, it was the Ol'govichi and the Davidovichi who sent their troops and the Polovtsy to pillage Bryagin, a Kievan town across the Dnepr from Lyubech.[156] This is the only occasion on which the chronicler mentions the town. It is also the first time the princes of Chernigov pillaged that district of the Kievan land. Indeed, it appears surprising on first sight why they attacked a town that seemingly had no special significance. The most plausible explanation is that they retaliated against Rostislav's sack of Lyubech by destroying the nearest Kievan stronghold across the Dnepr.

The Hypatian chronicler concludes his account for the year 1147 by reporting that Gleb Yur'evich captured his father's town of Gorodets Osterskiy[157] from Izyaslav of Kiev. The latter attacked Gleb who, on failing to obtain reinforcements from Vladimir Davidovich and Svyatoslav Ol'govich, capitulated. After Izyaslav returned to Kiev, however, Gleb informed Vladimir that he had pledged his allegiance to Izyaslav against his will. Therefore, after the danger passed, he renewed his alliance with the prince of Chernigov.[158] As has been noted, when Vsevolod Ol'govich had been prince of Kiev he had taken Gorodets Osterskiy from Yury and had given it to his brother Igor'.[159] Izyaslav Mstislavich assumed control of the

---

[154] Nasonov, p. 233.
[155] Concerning Lyubech, see Golubovsky, pp. 20–1. For a reconstruction of the town, see Rybakov, *Kievskaya Rus'*, pp. 423–8.
[156] Ipat., col. 359. Bryagin was located on the river Braginka, a tributary of the Pripyat' (Makhnovets', p. 542).
[157] The town was located near the mouth of the river Oster, an eastern tributary of the Desna. The Oster formed the boundary between the lands of Chernigov and Pereyaslavl'.
[158] Ipat., cols. 359–60; compare s.a. 1148: Mosk., pp. 43–4.   [159] *Dynasty*, pp. 366, 376.

town after Igor''s death when he sent his brother Vladimir to govern it.[160] Therefore, Gleb had to evict Vladimir to reclaim the town in his father's name. He therewith stoked the conflict that had already engulfed southern Rus'.

THE PRINCES OF CHERNIGOV AND IZYASLAV
OF KIEV RECONCILED

In 1148 the princes of Rus' re-established the political alignments that had existed two years earlier. When the ice began to thaw, we are told, Izyaslav once again marched against Chernigov. He took up position west of the town at the place known as "Oleg's field" (*Olegovo pole*), where he remained for three days.[161] Because Chernigov was impregnable he avoided storming it, and the princes of Chernigov refused to confront him before they received reinforcements from the Polovtsy and the princes of Ryazan'. Indeed, this is a rare occasion on which the princes of Ryazan' came to Chernigov from their distant domain. Presumably, the Davidovichi had summoned them since, as we have seen, in the previous year they had assisted the Davidovichi by pillaging Yury's lands in Suzdalia. As it turned out, after they joined the Davidovich, they achieved nothing because a river near Lyubech prevented them from attacking Izyaslav.

The latter, for his part, also failed to confront his enemies in open battle, but he satisfied his appetite for revenge. His troops ravaged the Chernigov district by setting fire to the villages and to the entire livelihood in the region up to the river Belous (Bolovos).[162] From there he led his forces to the district of Lyubech, "where they [that is, the Davidovichi] had all their livelihood."[163] Thus, the Davidovichi incurred all the losses because it was they who controlled the districts of Chernigov and Lyubech.

---

[160] Ipat., col. 355.   [161] Ipat., cols. 360–3.

[162] The chronicler calls it Bolovosa (Golubovsky, pp. 5–6; Nasonov, p. 222). The Belous was one of the two rivers (the other being the Muravlya) constituting the water route from Chernigov to Lyubech. The overland route also traveled along the Belous through the many settlements along the river's course (A. V. Shekun, "Drevniy sukhoputnyy put' mezhdu Chernigovom i Lyubechem," *Arkhitekturni ta Arkheolohichni Starozhytnosti Chernihivshchyny*, M. M. Holodna *et al.* (eds.) [Chernihiv, 1992], pp. 70–4).

[163] It has been estimated that some twenty-six towns and 190 villages existed in the region between Lyubech and Chernigov (Kovalenko, "K voprosu o vzaimootnosheniyakh feodal'nykh gorodov i okrugi v Chernigovo-Severskoy zemle," pp. 65–6; Zaytsev, pp. 78–80). For a list of all the known settlements in the region, see A. V. Shekun and E. M. Veremeychik, "Selishcha IX–XIV vv. v mezhdurech'e nizoviy Desny i Dnepra," *Chernigov i ego okruga v IX–XIII vv.*, A. A. Zolotareva (ed.) (K., 1988), pp. 93–110. Since the district of Lyubech constituted the heart of the lands belonging to the Davidovichi, this evidence supports the argument that Lyubech was their patrimonial domain.

They therefore agreed to be reconciled and, with the Ol'govichi, kissed the Holy Cross to Izyaslav in the Holy Saviour Cathedral. They agreed not to hold him accountable for Igor''s fate, to protect the land of Rus', and to live at peace with everyone.[164] The reason for their change of heart was Yury's failure to bring military aid. True, he had sent token forces with Ivanko and Gleb, but this had also been a self-serving gesture that enabled him to obtain towns in the Kursk region for his sons. Disgruntled with Yury's tepid support, the princes of Chernigov demanded that he come in person. His unwillingness to do so dashed their hopes of achieving a decisive victory over Izyaslav. They treated his refusal as a violation of his pledge and as the license to renege on their own oaths. Because of the damage Izyaslav had wrought on their lands and the destruction he might still inflict, their best means for protecting their domains was to be reconciled with him.

Despite the past perfidy of the Davidovichi, Izyaslav gave them the benefit of the doubt. Nevertheless, he imposed important demands on them. He insisted that the Ol'govichi swallow their pride by promising not to seek restitution for Igor''s murder. He undoubtedly reminded them of his innocence in the crime by pointing out that he had been in the field at the time and that his brother Vladimir had valiantly attempted to save Igor' life. The Davidovichi, for their part, had to cease plotting Izyaslav's death and to abandon their quest for Kiev. Both families accepted Izyaslav's terms.

This was the first occasion after the death of Vsevolod Ol'govich on which the princes of Rus' negotiated peace. The alliance between the dynasty of Chernigov and the Mstislavichi thus became, notionally at any rate, the most powerful in the land. It left Yury Dolgorukiy the odd man out. The number of prominent Church officials present at the oath taking highlighted the importance of the agreement. Izyaslav sent Bishop Fedor of Belgorod and *Igumen* Feodosy of the Caves Monastery to witness the pledges that the four princes took in the Holy Saviour Cathedral, where Bishop Onufry of Chernigov would have presided.

At an unspecified time before the reconciliation, an event took place which probably helped to strain relations between the Ol'govichi and Yury. He sent his son Rostislav with reinforcements for the Ol'govichi. On the way south, however, Rostislav decided not to assist them because they had been the enemies of his grandfather and his uncles. He therefore went to Kiev and asked Izyaslav for a domain. The latter gave him Bozh'skyy,

---

[164] Ipat., cols. 363–6.

Mezhibozh'e, Kotel'nitsa, and two other towns.[165] On learning that the military assistance Yury sent with his son Rostislav never reached them, the Ol'govichi probably reconsidered the effectiveness of their alliance with Yury and insisted, unsuccessfully, that he come in person.

Meanwhile, Rostislav's brother Gleb remained loyal to his father. For this Izyaslav evicted him from Gorodets Osterskiy and advised him to obtain a domain from the Ol'govichi since he had come to them in the first place.[166] Gleb's political isolation in Rus' is confirmed by the information that he did not remain in Chernigov with the now hostile Davidovichi, but returned to his father in Suzdalia. Significantly, on leaving Rus' he also forfeited control of Kursk. We learn later that Izyaslav repossessed it.

In the autumn, Izyaslav tested his alliance with the princes of Chernigov by summoning them to a *snem* at Gorodets Osterskiy.[167] His uncle Yury, he declared, was harassing the Novgorodians where his son was prince.[168] He therefore asked his allies to march against Yury to settle the dispute. The Ol'govichi did not come to the meeting and Izyaslav looked upon their non-attendance as insubordination. He reminded Vladimir Davidovich that all the princes of Chernigov had promised to campaign with him. The Davidovichi assured him of their constancy and promised to persuade Svyatoslav Ol'govich to join the campaign. They agreed to set off for Suzdalia after the rivers froze and to rendezvous at the Volga.[169] The Davidovichi thus expressed their willingness to honour their pledges to Izyaslav even if it meant antagonizing Yury.

As was frequently the case when princes formed alliances, the Mstislavichi and the Ol'govichi followed up their political union with a personal one. Rostislav of Smolensk arranged for his son Roman to marry a daughter of Svyatoslav Ol'govich. On January 9, 1149, the unnamed girl arrived in Smolensk from Novgorod Severskiy.[170] She was the first child that Svyatoslav gave away in marriage. Consequently, she was probably older than her brother Oleg, who, as we shall see, would marry in the following year. Her sister Maria would be born on August 7, seven months after her marriage.[171] Her remaining siblings were also not yet born.

[165] These were evidently the same five towns that he had given to Svyatoslav Vsevolodovich in 1146 (see above, p. 29). According to the Hypatian Chronicle, Rostislav came to Kiev after departing from Suzdalia in a huff because his father refused to give him a domain (Ipat., cols. 366–7).
[166] Lav., cols. 319–20; Mosk., p. 44.
[167] According to Tatishchev the date was September 14 (Tat. 4, p. 215 and Tat. 2, p. 185).
[168] Izyaslav sent his son Yaroslav to rule Novgorod in the autumn (NPL, pp. 28, 214).
[169] Ipat., cols. 366–8.
[170] Ipat., col. 368. Concerning the date, see Berezhkov, pp. 147–8.
[171] The chronicler reports that at sunrise on Sunday a daughter was born to Svyatoslav, presumably in Novgorod Severskiy, and she was christened Maria (Ipat., col. 376).

Rostislav and Izyaslav probably negotiated the marriage with Svyatoslav after the latter failed to attend the *snem*. Given his lukewarm commitment to the alliance, the Mstislavichi hoped to firm up their political pact with a personal tie. Their strategy, in the short term, was to assuage Svyatoslav's outrage over his brother's murder. The marriage bond, the first between the Ol'govichi and the Mstislavichi since Svyatoslav's elder brother Vsevolod had married the sister of the Mstislavichi, was also important in the long term.[172] On the one hand, Svyatoslav was the senior prince of the Ol'govichi. As such, he was the main challenger to the Davidovichi for supremacy in the dynasty. On the other hand, Rostislav was next in seniority after Izyaslav. Consequently, he had a good chance of becoming senior prince of the Mstislavichi. The marriage tie between the two families therefore held great promise for their future collaboration.

THE OL'GOVICHI HELP YURY CAPTURE KIEV

Soon after the marriage, the Mstislavichi discovered the true sentiments of the Ol'govichi. According to their agreement at Gorodets Osterskiy, the Davidovichi and the Ol'govichi were to join the Mstislavichi at the Volga. Instead of keeping their word, the princes of Chernigov stopped in the Vyatichi lands to monitor Izyaslav's campaign. By refusing to attack Suzdalia, they made their inclinations clear. They confirmed Izyaslav's suspicions that they wavered in their loyalty to him, and they let Yury know that they were reticent about antagonizing him. It appears that the Ol'govichi, aided and abetted by the Davidovichi, refused to attack Suzdalia in the hope that, should opportunity allow, they could revive their pact with Yury.

Around Palm Sunday, when the spring thaw had already set in, the Mstislavichi stopped pillaging Yury's domains.[173] After Izyaslav returned to Kiev in the early summer of 1149, evildoers accused Yury's son Rostislav of plotting to seize Kiev in Izyaslav's absence. Rostislav denied the accusations, but Izyaslav forced him to return to his father in Suzdalia. Offended by the shame that Izyaslav had heaped on his son, Yury assembled his forces and, on July 24 set off across the Vyatichi lands. Thus after all the entreaties of the Ol'govichi had failed to entice Yury to lead a campaign against his nephew in Kiev, Izyaslav's mistreatment of his son catapulted him into action.

Meanwhile, Vladimir Davidovich promised Izyaslav that the Davidovichi would help him against Yury. Izyaslav asked Vladimir to persuade Svyatoslav Ol'govich to join them. When the Davidovichi messengers came

[172] *Dynasty*, pp. 254–5.
[173] Ipat., cols. 368–72; Mosk., pp. 45–6. In 1149, Palm Sunday fell on March 27 (Berezhkov, p. 147).

to Novgorod Severskiy, however, Svyatoslav placed them under guard and sent his own men to Yury asking if his intention was to attack Izyaslav or to devastate Svyatoslav's Vyatichi lands. Yury assured Svyatoslav that his purpose was to avenge himself for the dishonour his nephew had heaped on him by devastating his Suzdalian lands, by refusing to give Rostislav domains, and by expelling the latter from Rus'.[174] After receiving Yury's reply, Svyatoslav sent messengers to Izyaslav offering to join him if he returned at least some of Igor''s possessions. Izyaslav was furious. He reminded Svyatoslav that he had sworn to renounce his antagonism over Igor' and had pledged to be loyal to Izyaslav. Moreover, Svyatoslav had agreed to join Izyaslav at the Volga but had broken that promise too. Izyaslav therefore declared war on Svyatoslav.[175]

At first glance, Svyatoslav showed little respect for the sacredness of oaths. It was such seemingly unprincipled conduct which prompted the chronicler to retort that the citizens of Rus' placed little trust in the promises made by the princes of Chernigov. Svyatoslav's conduct, however, suggests that he viewed the sanctity of oaths taken voluntarily, and of those taken under duress, differently. He believed that defending family rights was a greater moral obligation than fulfilling oaths taken under threat. That is why he had demonstrated such unwavering resolve to free his brother Igor'. And that is why he looked upon his task of regaining Igor''s possessions in the same light. After his brother's deposition, Svyatoslav inherited the task of reviving his family's fortunes. His long-term objective was to restore the Ol'govichi to that height of political power which would enable one of them to make a bid for Kiev. Consequently, he was disinclined to respect oaths forced upon him by a hostile challenger for Kiev. As opportunities arose, he considered it his obligation to join ranks with princes who would help to advance the fortunes of the Ol'govichi.

Thus, in the summer of 1149, he attempted to take advantage of the inter-family squabble in the House of Monomakh. Even though he had repeatedly begged Yury to march against Izyaslav, Svyatoslav did not jump at the chance of joining him after he finally embarked on his campaign. Yury could return Igor''s possessions to him only after defeating Izyaslav. The more direct course of action was to ask Izyaslav himself to return the confiscated property. Unfortunately for Svyatoslav, his threat of joining Yury failed to intimidate Izyaslav. The latter's refusal therefore drove Svyatoslav into

---

[174] Since, as we have seen, Izyaslav had given Rostislav five towns in the southwest corner of the Kievan land, Yury undoubtedly meant that Izyaslav refused to give to Yury's family the patrimonial domains of Gorodets or Pereyaslavl'. This is corroborated by later evidence.

[175] Ipat., cols. 372–6; Mosk., pp. 45–6; Lav., cols. 320–1.

Yury's camp once again. Svyatoslav's negotiations with Yury and Izyaslav demonstrate that he had a private agenda for the Ol'govichi. Accordingly, his political objectives and not his blood ties dictated his relationship with the Davidovichi.

On August 7,[176] Svyatoslav joined Yury and declared that Izyaslav was their mutual enemy because he had killed Igor'. They sent messengers to Chernigov inviting the Davidovichi to join them, but the brothers refused, declaring that their earlier pact with Yury had been useless. Because of his inactivity, Izyaslav had pillaged their towns in the Zadesen'e. Yury and Svyatoslav therefore rode to the river Supa near Pereyaslavl', where Svyatoslav Vsevolodovich and a multitude of Polovtsy joined them. Meanwhile, Izyaslav rendezvoused with Izyaslav Davidovich and Rostislav of Smolensk. They crossed the Dnepr and proceeded to the river L'to (Al'ta), where they confronted Yury.

He proposed a peaceful settlement. Because Izyaslav had devastated his lands and deprived him of his seniority (*stareshinstvo*), he asked Izyaslav to hand over Pereyaslavl' so that he could give it to his son. Izyaslav, Yury conceded, could keep Kiev. But Izyaslav refused and attacked. In the evening, when Svyatoslav Ol'govich and Svyatoslav Vsevolodovich withdrew to their camps, Izyaslav pursued them. Yury and the Ol'govichi counter-attacked. When Izyaslav's contingents from the river Ros' region fled, the Kievans and Izyaslav Davidovich followed suit. Finally, the citizens of Pereyaslavl' also abandoned the field proclaiming Yury to be their prince. On seeing the mass desertions, Izyaslav himself fled. Four days later, on August 27, when Yury arrived before Kiev, Izyaslav asked the citizens to help him defend the town. They, however, advised him and his brother to flee. Nevertheless, they assured the Mstislavichi that they would support them in their future battles with Yury. Izyaslav therefore went to Volyn' and Rostislav returned to Smolensk.[177]

Let us make a number of brief observations. First, Svyatoslav's declaration to Yury that Izyaslav was their mutual enemy because he had killed Igor' is the first chronicle evidence that, contrary to his promise to Izyaslav, Svyatoslav held the former responsible for his brother's death. Second, Rostislav's willingness to fight against Svyatoslav Ol'govich demonstrates that their children's marriage earlier in the year was too weak a bond to keep the fathers from waging war. Third, by accusing Izyaslav of pre-empting his seniority in the House of Monomakh, Yury confirmed that he observed

---

[176] Ipat., col. 376. Concerning the date, see Berezhkov, p. 148.
[177] A small number of chronicles say that Izyaslav fled to Vladimir (for example, Ipat. cols. 376–83; NPL, pp. 28, 215), but most say he fled to Lutsk (for example, Lav., cols. 321–2; Mosk., p. 46).

the lateral system of succession advocated by Yaroslav the Wise. Finally, as
Izyaslav and Rostislav fled from Kiev, its citizens proclaimed their intention
to oppose Yury. They proposed to tolerate his presence for only as long as
they had to, and promised to fight for the return of the Mstislavichi.

After Yury entered Kiev he summoned the hostile Vladimir Davidovich,
who came from Chernigov and submitted to him. His ally Svyatoslav
Ol′govich, however, requested that Yury return the patrimonial domains
of the Ol′govichi. Yury complied and gave him Kursk, the Posem′e region, the Snovskaya *tysyacha*,[178] Sluchesk, Klechesk, and all the Dregovichi
lands.[179] Svyatoslav was therewith appeased and returned to his domain.[180]
As Izyaslav's successor, Yury assumed not only control of the lands that the
former had appropriated as prince of Kiev, but also the authority to return
them to the Ol′govichi. Izyaslav had probably assumed jurisdiction of the
Snovskaya *tysyacha* and the Dregovichi territories west of the Dnepr after
evicting Igor′ from Kiev. He had seized Kursk and the Posem′e region from
Gleb Yur′evich after driving him out of Gorodets Osterskiy. Significantly,
after that date the Ol′govichi never again lost Kursk. Even though it had
belonged to his son Gleb, Yury laid no claim to it because he won control
of the more important Pereyaslavl′ which he gave to his son Rostislav.

Yury's compliance with Svyatoslav's request shows that, in his view, all the
specified domains belonged to the Ol′govichi. We can also take the silence
of the Davidovichi as tacit confirmation of the validity of the territorial
transfer. Consequently, Svyatoslav finally repossessed all the patrimonial
domains that the Ol′govichi had held during the reign of his eldest brother,
Vsevolod.

The land settlement significantly strengthened the power of the
Ol′govichi in relation to the Davidovichi. The chronicles do not identify
all the towns that the Davidovichi held at that time, but as we have seen,
in addition to the Chernigov domain they owned the Zadesen′e district
and the Lyubech region.[181] Therefore, in the light of Svyatoslav's increased

---

[178] According to one view, the Snovskaya *tysyacha* was the old territorial core of the Chernigov
lands along the river Snov′, which included Snovsk, Starodub, and Novgorod Severskiy (Nasonov,
pp. 57–9). Another view has it, probably correctly, that Novgorod Severskiy was not part of the
original Snovskaya *tysyacha* (Zaytsev, pp. 81–9).

[179] The Dregovichi lands were probably given to Oleg Svyatoslavich at Lyubech in 1097, as part of
the territorial settlement (*Dynasty*, p. 220; see also Zaytsev, pp. 104–9, and his "Do pytannia pro
formuvannia terytorii davn′orus′kykh kniazivstv u XII st.," pp. 43–53).

[180] Ipat., cols. 384–94; Lav., cols. 322–6; Mosk., pp. 46–7; compare Gust., pp. 299–300.

[181] Bagaley cites the statement that Vladimir Davidovich made to Izyaslav Mstislavich, under 1147,
when he said, "Brother, Svyatoslav Ol′govich has seized my domain, the Vyatichi" (Ipat., col. 343)
as proof that the Davidovichi owned the Vyatichi lands (*Istoriya Severskoy zemli*, p. 132). Although

military resources and the consideration that he, and not the Davidovichi, now had the backing of the prince of Kiev, it was an opportune time for him to strengthen his position against his cousins even further.

He did so by forming a personal pact with Yury. The Hypatian chronicler begins his entries for the year 1150 by announcing that Yury gave a daughter in marriage to Svyatoslav's son Oleg.[182] As has been suggested, the princes probably arranged the match in Moscow three years earlier.[183] For the immediate future, Svyatoslav's family tie with Yury was of greater benefit than the one he had concluded in the previous year with Rostislav of Smolensk. Nevertheless, even though Yury was the most powerful prince in the land, his rule was contentious. His elder brother, Vyacheslav of Turov, had first claim to Kiev. Yury's rule was also precarious because the Kievans were hostile to him and his nephew Izyaslav still coveted the throne. In light of the unsettled nature of princely relations, therefore, Svyatoslav could find consolation in the knowledge that he also enjoyed a personal tie with the Mstislavichi.

SVYATOSLAV TRANSLATES IGOR'S BODY TO CHERNIGOV

In the same year, 1150, Svyatoslav Ol'govich also transferred Igor''s body from the Monastery of St. Simeon in Kiev to Chernigov, where it was interred 'in the tower' (*v tereme*) adjacent to the Holy Saviour Cathedral.[184] Even though Igor' had been buried in the patrimonial monastery in Kiev, Svyatoslav resolved to repatriate him. He was motivated to do so by the same family loyalty that had compelled him to fight for Igor''s release and to avenge his murder. Granted, Igor' had ruled Kiev and merited burial there. Indeed, he was the only prince of Chernigov whose remains were laid to rest in one of Kiev's main suburbs, the Kopyrev *konets*.[185] Under more pacific circumstances, the Ol'govichi might have looked upon his interment there as a singular honour. Because of the hostility of the Kievans, however, Svyatoslav wished to remove the body from that town to obviate any further desecration. He had failed to transfer it for almost three years while Izyaslav

the Davidovichi controlled Vyatichi lands in 1147, there is no evidence that their father David received these as his patrimony. In 1147, the Vyatichi lands that Vladimir owned were the ones the Davidovichi had appropriated from the Ol'govichi after Izyaslav captured Igor'.

[182] Ipat., col. 394; Gust., p. 300.   [183] See above, p. 41.

[184] Ipat., col. 408; compare Gust., p. 300.

[185] As has been shown elsewhere, in 1143 Svyatosha, the eldest brother of the Davidovichi, was buried outside of Kiev in the Caves Monastery, and three years later Vsevolod Ol'govich was interred in the Church of SS. Boris and Gleb in Vyshgorod (*Dynasty*, pp. 398, 409–10).

had control of Kiev. The favorably disposed Yury, however, granted him permission.[186]

The chronicles do not record the date of the translation ceremony, but historians generally agree that it was June 5, the day on which the Orthodox Church celebrates Igor's feast.[187] Frequently, the Church chose the day of martyrdom to commemorate a saint, but it did not with Igor', who died on September 19. This suggests that Metropolitan Klim did not establish the feast while Igor's body lay in Kiev because, during that period, the only eligible date for his commemoration was the day of his murder. Klim's reticence to canonize Igor' is not surprising to judge from his efforts to silence the Novgorodians from reporting the divine manifestation surrounding the prince's body in their church. Moreover, the Kievans who killed Igor' would have opposed his canonization. Izyaslav also would have objected had the metropolitan proposed establishing a feast for his erstwhile enemy. Understandably, therefore, Svyatoslav brought Igor's body to Chernigov, where he would be buried in friendlier surroundings and given due ecclesiastical recognition.

Popular belief in the divine favour bestowed on Igor' and the chronicler's insistence on calling his remains relics, confirm that many Kievans and, presumably, inhabitants in Chernigov, looked upon him as a *strastoterpets* immediately following his murder.[188] The obvious occasion for his canonization was the translation ceremony since, according to custom, that day was also celebrated as the saint's feast.[189] The duty of canonizing Igor' fell on the unidentified bishop of Chernigov.[190] Although the chronicler does not describe the event, Svyatoslav probably imitated the ceremonies of 1072 and 1115 when the relics of SS. Boris and Gleb were translated in Vyshgorod.[191]

In preparation for the canonization, Svyatoslav, the bishop, and Igor's widow would have ordered the necessary hymns to be composed, icons

---

[186] The chronicles do not identify Yury as the prince who gave Svyatoslav the permission. But the chronicler interjects the news of Igor's translation into a very long account of the rivalry between Yury and Izyaslav at the point when Yury was prince of Kiev.

[187] Zotov, p. 264; Barsukov, col. 211.   [188] See also Barsukov, col. 214.

[189] For example, on May 2 the Orthodox Church celebrates the Translation of the Relics of SS. Boris and Gleb to commemorate the event that occurred in 1072 (Lav., col. 182; compare Ipat., col. 172, which gives the date as May 20; see also *Dynasty*, pp. 76–81).

[190] In 1146, as we have seen, the bishop had been Onufry. His death is not reported, but after 1147 he is never mentioned again. Consequently, by 1150 he may have been replaced by another. According to Bagaley, Evfimy was the bishop when Igor's remains were translated (*Istoriya Severskoy zemli*, p. 284).

[191] Concerning the two ceremonies, see *Dynasty*, pp. 76–81, 276–91.

and other devotional objects to be made, and liturgical prayers and a *Zhitie* to be written.[192] On the designated day, Igor''s remains would have been taken out of Kiev on a sledge escorted by Svyatoslav, other princes, their retinues, pro-Ol'govichi abbots, priests, and townspeople. Before they entered the main gate of Chernigov, the cortège would have been greeted by the Davidovichi, Igor''s widow if she was alive, the bishop, the abbots, the clergy, and the faithful. They would have escorted the relics with candles, censers, and singing. In the cathedral the bishop would have canonized Igor' and proclaimed his feast day with the appropriate liturgy. After the body was interred, Svyatoslav and the Davidovichi would have held a feast for all present. This was a momentous day for the dynasty and, in particular, for the Ol'govichi. Igor' was not only their first *strastoterpets* but also their first saint whose relics were buried in Chernigov.[193] Moreover, by bringing Igor''s remains to Chernigov and by formalizing his sainthood, Svyatoslav promoted his cult and enhanced the prestige of the Chernigov eparchy.

Svyatoslav also had the task of finding a burial site for Igor'. Significantly, he rejected Novgorod Severskiy, the capital of the Ol'govichi, where he was prince and where Igor' himself had ruled before going to Kiev. No prince had yet been interred there and the town had no suitable church for such an important entombment.[194] He therefore chose Chernigov, the traditional burial ground for the dynasty. He had to obtain permission, however, from Vladimir Davidovich. The latter consented, seemingly without objection, realizing that the Davidovichi could poach some of the glory from the Ol'govichi by providing a shrine for the *strastoterpets*. As the official patrons of Igor''s canonization, the Davidovichi would enhance their own prestige.[195]

[192] The seventeenth-century Gustinskiy is the only chronicle that testifies to the existence of a *Zhitie* (Gust., p. 300). A *Zhitie* is recorded in the *Kniga Stepennaya tsarskogo rodosloviya*, PSRL 21, chast' pervaya (Spb., 1908), pp. 203–6. See also Berezhkov, *Blazhennyy Igor'*, pp. 41–2; Barsukov, cols. 214–5; and Golubinsky, *Istoriya kanonizatsii svyatykh*, pp. 58–9.
[193] We do not know whether Igor' was the first of the dynasty to be canonized. His cousin Svyatosha Davidovich who died in 1143 was canonized at an undisclosed date (*Dynasty*, p. 398). Both princes were venerated as saints soon after their deaths.
[194] The only recorded stone church existing in the town in 1150 was that of St. Michael mentioned by the chronicler under 1180 (Ipat. col. 613). It is generally believed that Svyatoslav's father Oleg built the church in honor of his patron St. Michael (*Dynasty*, p. 257; A. V. Kuza, V. P. Kovalenko, and A. P. Motsya, "Chernigov i Novgorod-Severskiy v epokhu 'Slova o polku Igoreve'," *Chernigov i ego okruga v IX–XIII vv.*, A. A. Zolotareva [ed.] [K., 1988], p. 61).
[195] The situation is reminiscent of the one in the Church of SS. Boris and Gleb in Vyshgorod in 1115, when Vladimir Monomakh attempted to steal some of the glory from Svyatoslav's father Oleg, who had built the church in honor of the two *strastoterptsy* (*Dynasty*, pp. 278–82).

Igor's body was placed in a *terem* beside the cathedral.[196] He could not be buried inside the church because he had never ruled Chernigov. Only princes who ruled the dynastic capital enjoyed the privilege of being buried inside Holy Saviour Cathedral.[197] Nevertheless, it is surprising that the princes did not make an exception in Igor's case given his exalted status in the Church. His relics could have been entombed in a side chapel.[198] Svyatoslav and the bishop could not have overlooked such an opportunity for honoring the saint. If either one suggested that Igor' be laid to rest in a prominent place inside the cathedral, the Davidovichi had the authority to forbid it. Although the accusing finger points at the two brothers, the chronicler reports no controversy over the placement of the relics.[199]

VLADIMIR DAVIDOVICH FALLS IN BATTLE

The translation ceremony was a peaceful interlude in an otherwise turbulent year. While the Davidovichi and the Ol'govichi dutifully supported Yury in Kiev, the major political rivalry became the conflict between him and his nephew Izyaslav Mstislavich. They adopted the rationale that they were both illegal claimants to Kiev and that Vyacheslav of Turov, Yury's elder brother, was the rightful candidate. Vyacheslav, however, was incapable of asserting his claim. Yury and Izyaslav therefore proposed a *modus operandi*: each sought to rule Kiev with Vyacheslav as his senior partner. Their recriminatory accusations turned into open conflict around the spring of 1150, when all of southern Rus' became involved in the dispute.

We are told that Yury brought his brother Vyacheslav to Vyshgorod in the hope of strengthening his position in Kiev. Just the same, Izyaslav, with the help of the Kievans, his son Mstislav, his brothers, princelings from Volyn', the Hungarians, the Poles, the Black Caps, and the Berendei, attacked Kiev forcing Yury to seek sanctuary in Gorodets Osterskiy. He, in turn,

---

[196] Although the exact meaning of *terem* is difficult to determine in this context, it refers to a structure like a tower, a porch, or a gallery with burial vaults abutting on or adjacent to the cathedral. The exact location of the *terem* has not been determined (Bagaley, *Istoriya Severskoy zemli*, pp. 288–9; Berezhkov, *Blazhennyy Igor'*, pp. 31, 40, and Golubinsky, *Istoriya kanonizatsii svyatykh*, p. 59).

[197] Igor's grandfather, Svyatoslav, and father, Oleg, both ruled Chernigov and were buried inside the cathedral (*Dynasty*, pp. 127–8, 292–3). Igor's eldest uncle, Gleb, never ruled Chernigov and was buried in a chapel adjacent to the cathedral (*Dynasty*, p. 146).

[198] This practice is testified to in Chernigov in the middle of the thirteenth century. In 1246, as we shall see, Mikhail Vsevolodovich and his *boyar* Fedor were martyred in Saray. Their bodies were later brought to Chernigov and entombed in a side-chapel dedicated to them in the Holy Saviour Cathedral (*Mikhail*, p. 143).

[199] Such a controversy arose in 1115 over the placement of the relics of SS. Boris and Gleb. At that time Vladimir Monomakh attempted to overrule the wishes of Oleg and his father Svyatoslav, who built the church (*Dynasty*, pp. 280–1).

summoned the Davidovichi, the two Ol'govichi, Volodimerko (Vladimir) from Galich, and the Polovsty, evicted Izyaslav, and reoccupied Kiev. That winter Izyaslav set out to capture Kiev once again. Along the way he encountered strong opposition from Volodimerko of Galich. When he arrived at Belgorod, however, he caught Yury unprepared. The latter fled to Gorodets Osterskiy once again and Izyaslav occupied Kiev the second time. Volodimerko was furious. He found it incomprehensible how Yury, who had one son in Peresopnitsa on the western frontier of the Kievan land and another in Belgorod the western outpost of Kiev itself, was not informed of the approaching enemy. He therefore abandoned Yury and returned to Galich. Meanwhile, Izyaslav went to Vyacheslav in Vyshgorod, where he acknowledged Vyacheslav as his father and Vyacheslav recognized Izyaslav as his son. The two occupied Kiev as co-rulers and Vyacheslav became the senior partner.[200]

On this occasion, Izyaslav became more securely ensconced because he and Vyacheslav worked out an unprecedented arrangement. Joint rule was common enough in Rus'. The two Davidovichi, as we have seen, were acting as co-rulers in Chernigov. The duumvirate of Vyacheslav and Izyaslav, however, was unusual in that it was the first time that an uncle and a nephew had created such a partnership. As for Yury, it is noteworthy that, whereas Volodimerko of Galich deserted him, the princes of Chernigov, uncharacteristically it might be said, remained loyal.

In the spring of 1151, Yury summoned Vladimir Davidovich and Svyatoslav Ol'govich to attack Kiev. Svyatoslav set off on Monday April 2.[201] The following day, his wife in Novgorod Severskiy gave birth to his second son whom he christened Yury and gave the princely name of Igor'.[202] By giving the child the baptismal name of Yury, Svyatoslav acknowledged his friendship with Yury. In choosing Igor' for the boy's princely name, he testified to the close bond that had existed between him and his deceased brother. Indeed, by selecting the name Igor' and by participating on the campaign against Izyaslav, Svyatoslav showed that his brother was on his mind. He was marching against Igor''s enemy in retribution for the injustices Izyaslav had inflicted on his brother. It is also interesting to note that the two Igor''s, the uncle and the nephew, would attain fame, ironically, for their misfortunes. The already dead Igor' achieved acclaim for his martyrdom. The newly born Igor' would become renowned, as we shall see, for his disastrous campaign against the Polovtsy.

---

[200] Ipat., cols. 394–418; Mosk., pp. 47–50, 390; Erm., p. 37.
[201] For the date, see Berezhkov, p. 152.   [202] Ipat., col. 422.

Svyatoslav spent Easter Sunday, April 8, in Blestovet (Blestovit) and then went to Chernigov, where he joined Vladimir Davidovich.[203] They travelled by boat to Gorodets Osterskiy, where they joined Yury to celebrate his feast day on April 23. Meanwhile, Vladimir's younger brother, Izyaslav, joined Yury's enemies Vyacheslav and Izyaslav. Thus, apparently for the first time, the two Davidovichi threw in their lots with rival princes. Tatishchev alone gives a plausible explanation why the brothers parted ways:

> At first, neither brother wished to oppose Izyaslav Mstislavich because they believed he and Vyacheslav had right on their side. Moreover, Vladimir's *tysyatskiy* Azary Chudin appealed to Vladimir not to go to war. Svyatoslav, however, accused Azary of being in Izyaslav Mstislavich's pay and of counselling against war because he was loath to leave his young wife. Svyatoslav also warned Vladimir that if Yury captured Kiev the latter would deprive him of Chernigov. Consequently, even though Vladimir did not wish to join Yury, Svyatoslav persuaded him to do so.[204]

As Yury set off for Kiev, many Polovtsy joined him, but at the Dnepr, Izyaslav's men patrolling the river in boats prevented his troops from crossing. We are told in detail how Yury's forces eventually crossed the Dnepr, how the Kievan alliance took up defensive positions around the town, how Vyacheslav admonished Yury before the latter attacked, how Yury failed to take Kiev, how Izyaslav counter-attacked, how Yury waited in vain for Volodimerko to bring Galician reinforcements, and how the Ol'govichi and the Polovtsy contrived to continue the battle by intercepting messengers carrying proposals of peace. In the end, Vyacheslav and Izyaslav were victorious.

Vladimir Davidovich fell in the battle and Izyaslav of Kiev instructed Vladimir's brother to take his body to Chernigov.[205] Izyaslav Davidovich travelled post-haste via Vyshgorod and the next day arrived in Chernigov, where he buried Vladimir in the Holy Saviour Cathedral.[206] His haste was prompted by his desire to secure control of Chernigov before the Ol'govichi seized it. We should also note that, unlike Igor', Vladimir was buried inside the Holy Saviour Cathedral alongside his predecessors who had ruled the dynastic capital. Significantly, he was the first Davidovich to merit this distinction because he was the first of David's sons to rule Chernigov.

We know little about Vladimir's personal life. In 1144, as has been noted elsewhere, he had married a daughter of Vsevolodko Davidovich of Gorodno, a town northwest of Turov.[207] After his death, his widow fled

---

[203] Blestovit was located on the right bank of the river Pulka, a tributary of the Desna to the east of Chernigov (Golubovsky, p. 5; Nasonov, pp. 221–2; Makhnovets', p. 540).
[204] Tat. 4, p. 232; Tat. 3, pp. 28–9.   [205] Lav., col. 334.   [206] Ipat., cols. 423–40.
[207] *Dynasty*, pp. 387–8; Zotov, pp. 261–2; Baum., IV, 9 and VII, 1.

to the steppe and married the Polovtsian khan named Bashkord.[208] His son Svyatoslav, who has not yet been mentioned by the sources, also survived Vladimir.[209]

One chronicler describes Vladimir as a "good and gentle prince." Despite this compliment, other chroniclers criticize the two Davidovichi for their infidelity to oaths. This dichotomy of views suggests that Vladimir may have been readily influenced by others. The observation is reinforced by Tatishchev's claim, if true, that Svyatoslav persuaded Vladimir to remain loyal to Yury even though his brother Izyaslav joined Izyaslav Mstislavich's camp. Indeed, circumstantial evidence suggests that Vladimir's brother dictated their policies during their joint rule in Chernigov. Thus, whereas Vladimir's meekness made him shun rivalries, his brother's bellicosity drove him to initiate them. In this Vladimir was the son of his father David, who advocated a pacific life.[210] Vladimir was also seemingly made from the same mould as his eldest brother, Svyatosha, who rejected worldly power for the monastic life.[211]

Vladimir's cultural activities are not recorded. Basing our observation on the evidence of one artifact that has been attributed to him, however, we have evidence that he patronized culture at least to a limited degree (figure 2). The object is a large silver cup with the inscription: "This cup belongs to Prince Vladimir Davidovich. May he who drinks from it have good health and thank God and his lord the grand prince."[212]

The cup would have been used at feasts, like those held at the conclusion of alliances, where it was passed from guest to guest.[213] Vladimir probably commissioned it from a Chernigov craftsman after 1146, that is, after the death of Vsevolod Ol'govich. It was only then that, as prince of Chernigov, he became the most powerful prince in the dynasty. In the light of his political authority he considered it his prerogative to call himself grand (*velikiy*)

---

[208] See s.a. 1159: Ipat., col. 501; Mosk., p. 65. [209] Zotov, p. 266; Baum., IV, 20.
[210] *Dynasty*, pp. 301–2. [211] *Dynasty*, pp. 252–4.
[212] "A se chara knya[zhya] volodimirova davydov[i]cha kto iz nee p'[e] tomu na zdorov'e a khvalya boga [i?] svoego ospodarya velikogo knya[zya]" (B. A. Rybakov, "Russkie datirovannye nadpisi XI–XIV vekov," *Arkheologiya SSSR,* Svod arkheologicheskikh istochnikov, E 1–44, B. A. Rybakov [ed.] [M., 1964], p. 28, and A. A. Medyntseva, "Chara Vladimira Davydovicha," *Problemy arkheologii Yuzhnoy Rusi,* T. N. Telizhenko [ed.] [K., 1990], pp. 128–35). The cup was discovered in 1843 at Saray Berke, the former capital of the Golden Horde. According to Rybakov it was probably part of the booty the Tatars seized in 1239, when they captured Chernigov ("Russkie datirovannye nadpisi," p. 28; concerning the sack of Chernigov, see below, pp. 349–50). Medyntseva suggests that the cup may have fallen into Tatar hands via the Polovtsy. As we have seen, after Vladimir's death, his wife married Khan Bashkord. In going to live with the Polovtsy, she may have taken her dead husband's ceremonial cup with her. ("Chara Vladimira Davydovicha," p. 134; concerning Vladimir's widow, see above, pp. 64–5).
[213] A. Andersson, *Mediaeval Drinking Bowls of Silver Found in Sweden* (Stockholm, 1983), p. 2.

Figure 2   Ceremonial bowl of Vladimir Davidovich

prince. The designation distinguished him from the status of the genealogically senior (*starshiy*) prince, which Igor' and then Svyatoslav Ol'govich held. This is one of the oldest references to a grand prince in Rus'.[214]

Vladimir's death deprived the Davidovichi of their military superiority in the dynasty. Moreover, the ratio of princes between the Davidovichi and the Ol'govichi now favored the latter. On the one hand, Svyatoslav recently had a second son born to him, and his nephews, Svyatoslav and Yaroslav, were also raising families. On the other hand, only two Davidovichi remained. Of these, Izyaslav had only a daughter,[215] and his nephew Svyatoslav Vladimirovich was not yet married. Nevertheless, Izyaslav had one important advantage. He was allied to Vyacheslav and Izyaslav Mstislavich of Kiev. Consequently, after he stepped into his brother's shoes, the realignment of princely power in the dynasty remained to be tested.

IZYASLAV DAVIDOVICH IN CHERNIGOV

As Izyaslav Davidovich was burying his brother, the vanquished princes were dispersing in all directions. Svyatoslav Ol'govich and his nephew Svyatoslav Vsevolodovich fled to Gorodets Osterskiy.[216] We are told that the uncle "was of heavy build and had difficulty in fleeing." He therefore

---

[214] Compare Rybakov, who suggests that the cup was made in 1239 after Vladimir occupied Chernigov ("Russkie datirovannye nadpisi," p. 28).

[215] In 1155, Izyaslav's daughter, whose name is not revealed, would marry Yury's son Gleb (Ipat., col. 482; Zotov, pp. 266–7).

[216] Tatishchev reports a related incident. When Vladimir's *tysyatskiy* Azary learnt of his prince's death and discovered that Svyatoslav was fleeing from the field of battle, he pursued Svyatoslav to the Dnepr wishing to avenge Vladimir's death. Svyatoslav escaped, but Azary, on capturing two of Svyatoslav's advisers, sent their heads to Svyatoslav in revenge (Tat. 4, p. 235; Tat. 3, p. 33).

sent his nephew ahead to Chernigov undoubtedly to seize the dynastic capital. The Ol′govichi believed that the Davidovichi controlled it unjustly.
According to lateral succession, after Igor′ lost Kiev he should have acquired
Chernigov and, after his death, it should have gone to his brother Svyatoslav.
The latter therefore looked upon Vladimir's death as an ideal opportunity
for capturing the town. When Svyatoslav Vsevolodovich reached the Desna,
however, he learned that Izyaslav was already there. He therefore withdrew
and Svyatoslav Ol′govich went to Novgorod Severskiy. Meanwhile, around
July 24, Vyacheslav and Izyaslav besieged Yury in Pereyaslavl′ and commanded him to return to Suzdalia. He agreed promising never again to
seize Kiev from them and to sever his alliance with Svyatoslav Ol′govich.
They gave him a month's grace to remain at Gorodets Osterskiy.[217]

As was the practice at the time of the transfer of power in the dynasty, all
the princes of Chernigov had to swear allegiance to Izyaslav Davidovich.
He, for his part, confirmed them in their domains. If he saw fit, he would
also grant additional towns to princes who supported him or confiscate
lands from those princes who opposed him. Given his recent battle with
the Ol′govichi, it was conceivable that he might punish them by denying
them towns. Thus, after Svyatoslav returned to Novgorod Severskiy, he
proposed peace and articulated his terms to Izyaslav as follows:

We have two patrimonies. One is from my father Oleg and the other is from your
father David. You, my brother, are a Davidovich, and I am an Ol′govich. You,
my brother, take the patrimony of your father David, and give us the one that
belonged to Oleg. Let us divide the patrimonies in this fashion.[218]

Izyaslav, we are told, acted in a Christian manner. He welcomed the
Ol′govichi, allowed them to keep Oleg's lands, and retained his father's
patrimony for himself.

Svyatoslav was confident in making his demand because he read the political situation correctly. The two families had been in a state of almost
constant warfare for five years during which time they had sustained increasing manpower losses. If Izyaslav refused Svyatoslav's demand he faced
the danger of going to war yet again and incurring even greater losses.
Moreover, he was not prepared to go to war because, as the new senior
prince, he had not yet consolidated his authority. Significantly, in granting
the Ol′govichi their father's patrimony, Izyaslav himself would not forfeit
control of any lands. The Ol′govichi already ruled their entire patrimony.

---

[217] Ipat., cols. 440–4; see s. a. 1150: Mosk., pp. 390–1, 50–4; see s.a. 1152: Lav., cols. 330–6; compare
s.a. 1151: Tat. 4, pp. 231–6 and Tat. 3, pp. 26–35.
[218] Ipat., col. 444.

By accepting the status quo, therefore, Izyaslav renounced his former objective of seizing the lands of the Ol'govichi and endorsed the patrimonies that the princes at Lyubech had created for the two families.[219]

Accordingly, Svyatoslav Ol'govich retained Novgorod Severskiy and his patrimonial domain of Putivl', which once again included Kursk. His nephew Svyatoslav Vsevolodovich controlled Karachev. Most likely, the uncle also gave him most of the neighboring Vyatichi districts but kept for himself Igor''s Gomiy district, the Dregovichi lands, and the Snovskaya *tysyacha*. The Davidovichi controlled the Chernigov domain, the Zadesen'e, and the Lyubech region.

The disparity in sizes of the patrimonies of the Davidovichi and Ol'govichi is glaringly obvious. The Davidovichi lands, however, were more desirable. They were closer to Kiev and belonged to what is known as the kernel of Rus'. They held important trade routes, were more densely populated, had richer craft and trade centers, and had more fertile soil. Moreover, they had Chernigov, the political, commercial, ecclesiastical, and cultural capital of the dynasty. In comparison, although the lands of the Ol'govichi encompassed a larger area, they included the sparsely populated and impassable forests of the Vyatichi, the distant Dregovichi lands, and the less colonized Posem'e frontier which was the object of Polovtsian raids.

Meanwhile Yury overstayed his welcome in Gorodets Osterskiy. Izyaslav of Kiev, Izyaslav Davidovich, Svyatoslav Vsevolodovich, and troops sent by Svyatoslav Ol'govich attacked him. He fled to Suzdalia leaving his son Gleb behind. En route he stopped at Novgorod Severskiy, where Svyatoslav welcomed him, provided him with wagons, and saw him on his way.[220] This report reveals that, in addition to being reconciled with Izyaslav Davidovich, the Ol'govichi also formed a pact with Izyaslav Mstislavich. The only condition under which they would have joined him against Yury was if they had pledged allegiance to him. Significantly, Svyatoslav Ol'govich complied by sending troops. We are not told whether his obesity prevented him from campaigning in person or if he did not wish to antagonize Yury. In any case, by sending troops he satisfied Izyaslav and by not going in person he avoided offending Yury. The latter confirmed this by visiting Svyatoslav. Their meeting was a warning to Izyaslav Mstislavich and to Izyaslav Davidovich that Svyatoslav continued being as faithful to Yury as circumstances allowed.

---

[219] Concerning the territorial allocations made at Lyubech, see *Dynasty*, pp. 219–21.
[220] Ipat., col. 445.

Meanwhile, the Ol'govichi continued to foster the friendly relations with the citizens of Polotsk (Polochane) that their grandfather Svyatoslav had initiated.[221] Only sporadic reports of such contacts have survived in later compilations. Indeed, we have learned nothing about the relations of the Ol'govichi with Polotsk since 1143, when Svyatoslav Vsevolodovich married a princess from that town.[222]

Under the year 1151 we are told that, after deposing Rogvolod Borisovich and replacing him with an unidentified Glebovich,[223] the Polochane considered it necessary to form an alliance with Svyatoslav Ol'govich. They asked him to be their guardian and to protect them from any injustices that their new prince might inflict upon them. More importantly, they asked him to condone their deposition of Rogvolod because, as we shall see, the latter was evidently Svyatoslav's preferred ruler of Polotsk. In return, they promised to be at Svyatoslav's call.[224] This undoubtedly appealed to him because it meant that they became a useful counter-balance to the princes of Smolensk. Granted, Svyatoslav had formed a marriage alliance with Rostislav Mstislavich. As we have seen, however, the latter and his son Roman, Svyatoslav's son-in-law, had assisted Izyaslav of Kiev in the latest campaign. The Ol'govichi could therefore use the Polochane, the western neighbours of Smolensk, as an effective lever against Rostislav's family.

The decision of the Polochane to become Svyatoslav's allies is noteworthy for additional reasons. It meant that they preferred to have an Ol'govich as their protector rather than a prince from the House of Monomakh. The *veche* evidently wished to retain its independence from the Monomashichi who controlled the neighbouring domains of Turov, Smolensk, and Novgorod. What is more, it meant that the Polochane selected Svyatoslav Ol'govich over his cousin Izyaslav Davidovich of Chernigov. The latter was the more powerful of the two because he was the political head of the dynasty. Nevertheless, the *veche* preferred Svyatoslav because, as already noted, the Ol'govichi had established marital ties with the dynasty of Polotsk and they ruled Dregovichi towns which bordered on Polotsk. This

---

[221] *Dynasty*, pp. 91, 96.
[222] The chroniclers tell us that Svyatoslav married Vasil'ko's daughter (Ipat., col. 313; Lav., col. 310). According to one view, the father of the bride Maria was Vasil'ko Svyatoslavich (Baum., VIII, 33), but another view has it that he was Vasil'ko Rogvolodich (Zotov, p. 267). See also *Dynasty*, p. 384.
[223] According to Baum., the patronymic Glebovich refers to Gleb Vseslavich (d. 1118) who had three sons: Rostislav, Volodar, and Vsevolod (VIII, 6, 12–14). To judge from later evidence, the Glebovich in question was Rostislav.
[224] Ipat., cols. 445–6; see s.a. 1150: Mosk., p, 54.

gave them personal, political, and commercial interests in common with the Polochane.

THE RAZING OF GORODETS AND YURY'S REVENGE

Meanwhile, after expelling Yury from Rus', Vyacheslav and Izyaslav realized that they could not prevent him from renewing his bid for Kiev. They could, however, thwart his military operations in Rus' by destroying his only military outpost in the south. According to Tatishchev, Izyaslav Davidovich persuaded the duumvirs to level Gorodets Osterskiy:

Izyaslav Davidovich declared to the other princes that as long as Yury controlled Gorodets it presented a great danger to Rus' and they should destroy it. Yury's son who administered it could summon the Polovtsy while Yury attacked from Suzdalia, making it impossible for the princes to defend their lands. But if they had only Yury to contend with, they could be forewarned of his attack. Moreover, he suggested that they buy the services of the Polovtsy before Yury and Svyatoslav Ol'govich did so. The princes therefore conscripted nine Polovtsian khans into their service, but not the in-laws of Svyatoslav Ol'govich.[225]

Consequently, in the winter of 1152, Izyaslav Mstislavich, Izyaslav Davidovich, and Svyatoslav Vsevolodovich rode against Gorodets Osterskiy, dug up its earthen wall, and set a torch to it.[226] Thus, the co-rulers of Kiev tested the loyalty of the princes of Chernigov once again, and once again Svyatoslav Ol'govich was truant. Although he did not even send troops on this occasion, the chronicler does not report any dissension among the princes, thereby implying that Svyatoslav had not rejected his Kievan allies. His excuses, as before, were probably his inability to ride a horse and his friendship with Yury. Perhaps, just as Svyatoslav Ol'govich's personal bond with Yury made him reluctant to campaign against his Suzdalian in-law, Svyatoslav Vsevolodovich's family tie with Izyaslav made him reticent to disobey his uncle in Kiev.

Although razing Gorodets may have had merit as a long-term measure for safeguarding Rus' from Polovtsian attacks, in the short term it was a gross miscalculation. It precipitated the very evil the princes had sought to prevent – another attack on Rus'. Yury decided to exact retribution for the destruction of his family possession. He summoned the Polovtsy and set off for Rus' with Rostislav Yaroslavich of Ryazan'[227] and the princes of Murom.

[225] Tat. 4, p. 237; Tat. 3, p. 36.
[226] Ipat., col. 446; Mosk., p. 54; Tver., col. 219. One source states that this occurred in the winter (L'vov, p. 115).
[227] In 1146, as we have seen, Rostislav Yaroslavich of Ryazan' pillaged Yury's domain after Izyaslav Mstislavich ordered him to do so (see above, p. 31).

On first sight the objects of his attack, the lands of the Chernigov princes, appear surprising. Since the duumvirs had ordered the destruction of his stronghold he should have vented his fury against them. Instead, he began by pillaging the Vyatichi lands through which he passed. Surprisingly, he repeated his attack on the same lands on his return journey to Suzdalia, even after being reconciled with Svyatoslav Ol'govich. In the light of their pact, it is unlikely that he devastated his ally's towns. Therefore, he must have directed his anger against Svyatoslav Vsevolodovich who had partic-ipated in the destruction of Gorodets Osterskiy. Since the latter had his patrimonial capital at Karachev, and Svyatoslav Ol'govich's patrimony was in the Posem'e, much of the Vyatichi territory probably belonged to the nephew.

Yury launched his primary attack against Izyaslav Davidovich. We have seen that, according to Tatishchev's account, Izyaslav had suggested to the duumvirs that they raze Gorodets. If the information is true, then it is understandable why Yury led his entire host against Chernigov. Although he achieved no decisive victory, he assuaged his thirst for revenge to a significant degree. He and Svyatoslav reduced the outer town (*ostrog*) and all the suburbs of Chernigov to smouldering embers.[228] Moreover, the Vyatichi lands lay devastated and the Polovtsy indulged in their customary rapine as they passed through the Zadesen'e of the Davidovichi and the Posem'e of the Ol'govichi on their way to the steppe. Consequently, after Yury withdrew in the spring of 1153, the duumvirs could sit back smugly realizing that, even though they had been the cause of Yury's attack, they had escaped the brunt of his reprisals.

Not surprisingly, Svyatoslav Ol'govich joined his in-law in the campaign, but the chronicler would have us believe that he did so reluctantly. There may be an element of truth in this contention. His defection from the Kievan alliance placed him in jeopardy. After Yury departed, he was vul-nerable to attack from the co-rulers because he was the odd man out in Rus'. When Svyatoslav pointed out his vulnerability to Yury before the latter returned to Suzdalia, Yury left behind his son Vasil'ko with a small *druzhina*. In February of 1153 Izyaslav Mstislavich, his nephew Roman from Smolensk, Izyaslav Davidovich, and Svyatoslav Vsevolodovich attempted to score a decisive victory against Svyatoslav by capturing Novgorod Severskiy.

---

[228] The *ostrog* surrounded by a palisade was usually the most poorly defended suburb of a town. For a description of the different parts of Chernigov, see: V. A. Bohusevych, "Pro topohrafiiu drevn'oho Chernihova," *Arkheolohiia* 5 (K., 1951), 116–26; V. P. Kovalenko, "Do vyvchennia chernihivs'kogo peredgoroddia," *Slov'iano-rus'ki starozhytnosti pivnichnoho livoberezhzhia*, Mate-rialy istoryko-arkheolohichnoho seminaru, prysviachenoho 60-richchiu vid dnia narodzhennia O. V. Shekuna (19–20 sichnia 1995 r. m. Chernihiv) O. P. Motsia (gen. ed.) (Chernihiv, 1995), pp. 40–5; and *Dynasty*, pp. 11–17.

They could do no more, however, than destroy the town's suburbs and negotiate an unwanted pact.[229]

Later, in the autumn, Svyatoslav met Izyaslav Davidovich at Khorobor,[230]
where they agreed to work as one and returned home.[231] Around that time,
Svyatoslav undoubtedly was also reconciled with his nephew in Karachev.
It is unlikely, however, that the *rapprochement* with his relatives forced him
to break off his friendly relations with Yury of Suzdalia.

Over the next few years Kiev became the object of rivalry for a number of princes. Under the year 1153, in describing Izyaslav Mstislavich's
campaign against Yaroslav Osmomysl,[232] the chronicler also reports that
Izyaslav Davidovich sent his forces to accompany the prince of Kiev.[233]
Given their pledge of loyalty, the princes of Chernigov were expected to
assist Izyaslav of Kiev when summoned to war. The Ol'govichi did not
send troops but this was probably not an act of insubordination. More
than likely, Svyatoslav Ol'govich either was allied with Yaroslav of Galich,
or his town had been so seriously devastated that he successfully begged
to be exempted from sending auxiliaries. Significantly, Izyaslav of Kiev insisted that Izyaslav of Chernigov send his troops. Perhaps the memory of
the Davidovichi plot to kill him compelled him to take the precaution of
having Izyaslav's forces at his side rather than in Chernigov, from where they
could be deployed against Kiev in his absence. Izyaslav Davidovich proved
his loyalty, but in doing so he exposed Chernigov to attack from Svyatoslav
Ol'govich. The latter also kept his oath to his cousin, and peace was
maintained.

The year 1154 was uneventful for the dynasty of Chernigov until the
autumn. Nevertheless, one event occurred earlier in the spring or the summer that presaged war. Yury set off for Rus' with the forces of Rostov and
Suzdal'. As his troops were travelling through the Vyatichi lands, a plague
struck their horses and he was forced to abort the campaign. When the

---

[229] Ipat., cols. 455–61; Mosk., pp. 56–8.
[230] The town, located on the right bank of the Desna almost equidistantly between Chernigov and
    Novgorod Severskiy, was probably near the boundary of the two domains (Golubovsky, pp. 42–50;
    Nasonov, p. 232; Makhnovets', p. 575).
[231] Ipat., col. 465; Mosk., p. 58. The information concerning the pact appears to be a continuation of
    the entry which reports events that occurred in the autumn.
[232] Yaroslav became prince of Galich at the beginning of 1153 after the death of his father Volodimerko
    (Ipat., col. 463; Mosk., p. 58; Lav., col. 340).
[233] Ipat., cols. 465–8.

Polovtsy joined him, he ordered his son Gleb to accompany them to the steppe and to recruit more horsemen. He, however, returned to Suzdalia.[234] Tatishchev suggests, probably correctly, that his objective was to force his brother and nephew in Kiev to give him a domain in Rus' in compensation for Gorodets Osterskiy.[235]

In the autumn, Rus' was thrown into turmoil. Izyaslav Mstislavich died on Sunday night, November 14.[236] Because Vyacheslav's old age prevented him from going into the field, Izyaslav's death left Kiev without a commander-in-chief. A potential threat presented itself immediately when Izyaslav Davidovich came to Kiev, allegedly to pray at the dead man's grave. Vyacheslav, however, refused him entry. After testing the waters he withdrew to Chernigov, but his motive was transparent. Seizing Kiev was on his mind.

Izyaslav's unchallenged arrival at the doorstep of Kiev alerted Vyacheslav to the threat that the absence of a military commander presented to his safety. While he awaited his nephew Rostislav from Smolensk, he demonstrated unexpected acumen in selecting his bodyguard. He could have called upon Izyaslav's youngest brother, Vladimir of Dorogobuzh, who had served as Izyaslav's lieutenant in Kiev at the time of Igor''s murder.[237] A closer choice was Izyaslav's son Mstislav of Pereyaslavl', who had come to Kiev to bury his father. Surprisingly, Vyacheslav selected the Ol'govich, Svyatoslav Vsevolodovich. We must remember, however, that the latter was also the maternal nephew of the Mstislavichi and, if we are to believe the chronicler, both Vyacheslav and Rostislav loved him as their favourite son. But even more important, by enlisting Svyatoslav's help Vyacheslav divided the House of Chernigov. Whereas Svyatoslav joined Vyacheslav who had summoned Rostislav from Smolensk to replace his brother Izyaslav, Izyaslav Davidovich and Svyatoslav Ol'govich summoned Yury Dolgorukiy to replace his deceased nephew.

Svyatoslav later admitted to Yury that he had acted like a fool. As the eldest of his generation, he was the heir apparent to Svyatoslav Ol'govich as senior prince of the Ol'govichi. By opposing his uncle he alienated himself from the family of which he could one day become head. His action, at best, bespoke a man torn in his loyalties to his father's brother and to his mother's brother. Ultimately, he chose to reap the immediate rewards the

[234] Ipat., col. 468; Mosk., p. 58; Lav., col. 341.   [235] Tat. 4, p. 244; Tat. 3, pp. 47–8.
[236] Ipat., cols. 468–9; NPL, pp. 29, 215. Other sources give the date November 13 (for example, Mosk., p. 58; Lav., cols. 341–2); see Berezhkov, p. 156.
[237] Concerning Vladimir, see Ipat., cols. 446, 465. Izyaslav's younger brother Svyatopolk died at the beginning of 1154 (Ipat., col. 468).

Mstislavichi offered in preference to the long-term benefits the Ol'govichi promised. His choice bespoke his political shortsightedness.

Rostislav rewarded him with the towns of Turov and Pinsk. These domains were evidently meant to replace the ones Svyatoslav forfeited in his Chernigov patrimony on joining the Mstislavichi. The new territorial grants, however, made him completely dependent on the princes of Kiev. He would be allowed to keep them only as long as Vyacheslav and Rostislav remained in power or as long as he enjoyed their good graces. Rostislav tested Svyatoslav's loyalty almost immediately by commanding him to help defend Pereyaslavl' against Gleb Yur'evich and the Polovtsy. The real test of his allegiance came, however, when Rostislav declared his intention to attack Chernigov. Svyatoslav had no choice but to join him if he wished to keep Turov and Pinsk.

As Rostislav was leading his troops against Chernigov, Vyacheslav died. This precipitated a succession crisis. Granted, the *veche* had assured Rostislav that he could remain prince of Kiev after his uncle's death. But Yury disagreed. Following his elder brother's death, he became the eldest prince in the House of Monomakh. In keeping with the traditional system of lateral succession, Yury considered himself to be the rightful claimant to Kiev from among Monomakh's descendants. Accordingly, Svyatoslav Vsevolodovich could no longer argue that he was supporting the rightful claimant. Having committed himself to Rostislav, however, he remained loyal to his pledge.

Rostislav believed that the most important step for securing his rule in Kiev was to solicit Izyaslav Davidovich's recognition of his succession. He therefore attempted to make Izyaslav renounce his own claim. But the latter refused to be cowed into submission because Rostislav's rule was disputed and his military strength untested. Rostislav had the advantage only while he remained in Kiev, where he had the support of the townsmen. In the open field, Izyaslav had reason to be confident in the superior strength of his forces, especially after Gleb Yur'evich had brought the Polovtsy. Izyaslav's gamble paid off. He defeated Rostislav, who fled to Smolensk.

Svyatoslav Vsevolodovich was less fortunate. In addition to losing Turov and Pinsk, the Polovtsy took him captive. Thanks to the mediation of Izyaslav and his unnamed wife, who was probably a Polovtsian princess,[238] the hapless prince was set free and shepherded back into his dynasty's fold with his tail between his legs. As we shall see, Svyatoslav Ol'govich penalized

---

[238] According to the account, Izyaslav's wife helped to secure the release of Svyatoslav Vsevolodovich from the Polovtsy. Since she is singled out as a mediator, the implication is that she played a deciding role. It is reasonable to assume that she was in a favored position to be influential because she was of Polovtsian blood.

him for his disloyalty by returning to him only a few of his towns. To judge from the report, the princes settled their dynastic discipline problem without a conflict. Indeed, by intervening on Svyatoslav's behalf, Izyaslav expressed his desire to re-establish harmony between the two families.

Meanwhile, Izyaslav made his bid for supreme power in Rus'. In a veiled threat, he announced to the citizens that he was coming to Kiev. This placed the *veche* in a quandary. The townsmen needed a prince to defend them against the Polovtsy whom Gleb had brought, but they did not want Izyaslav. If they refused to invite him, however, they would have to contend with his *druzhina* in addition to the nomads. Grudgingly, therefore, they accepted him as prince. For the first time, therefore, a Davidovich occupied Kiev. Moreover, he was only the fourth prince from the House of Chernigov to hold that office. His predecessors had been the ill-fated Igor', the ruthless Vsevolod Ol'govich, and the progenitor of the dynasty, Svyatoslav Yaroslavich.

Izyaslav had no claim to the capital of Rus'. His father, David, had never ruled Kiev so he could not invoke the maxim that he had the right to sit on the throne of his father. The justification for his usurpation lay in the consideration that he was the political head of the House of Chernigov. In that capacity he could claim Kiev in the name of his dynasty.

But was Izyaslav's occupation of the town viable? His directive to Svyatoslav to occupy Chernigov shows that he believed his rule was secured. The glory of Kiev unfortunately blinded Izyaslav to his inevitable fate. Svyatoslav was more realistic. He calculated that he and his cousin could not defeat Yury. After all, the Polovtsy who had helped Izyaslav overpower Rostislav had been brought by Gleb at Yury's behest. They would probably join Yury against Izyaslav. Moreover, while passing through the Smolensk lands, Yury was reconciled with Rostislav, the senior prince of the Mstislavichi. Finally, because of the Kievans' avowed hatred for the dynasty of Chernigov, and their proclivity for supporting Monomakh's descendants, the *veche* was bound to favour Yury. In the light of these considerations, Svyatoslav did not share Izyaslav's optimism.

Significantly, after the death of Izyaslav Mstislavich but before that of Vyacheslav, Svyatoslav Ol'govich decided to back Yury's claim for Kiev. He therefore joined Izyaslav Davidovich in summoning Yury from Suzdalia. Since the latter had upheld Vyacheslav's right to Kiev, Svyatoslav envisioned Yury assuming the role of co-ruler in place of the deceased Izyaslav. After Vyacheslav himself died, however, Yury became the rightful claimant. Svyatoslav therefore confirmed his support for Yury when the latter travelled via "Sinin most" in the Chernigov lands. At Starodub, his nephew, Svyatoslav

Vsevolodovich, still smarting from his confessed blunder, ingratiated himself to both princes by submitting to them.[239] The pact of the Ol'govichi with Yury Dolgorukiy therefore alienated them from Izyaslav in Kiev. The latter, nevertheless, had a valid reason for his intransigence. He argued that his rule was legitimate because the Kievans had invited him. From practical considerations, however, his position was untenable: Yury had the military advantage. Finally, after Yury promised not to punish him, Izyaslav left Kiev.[240] He negotiated safe passage out of the town seemingly without penalties. Yury undoubtedly treated him with clemency because the Ol'govichi were favourably disposed to him and because he had acted generously towards Yury's son Gleb in giving him Pereyaslavl'. Despite Yury's leniency, however, Izyaslav refused to pledge him allegiance. Consequently, the first and only Davidovich to rule the capital of Rus' sat on the throne for even a shorter period of time than the ill-fated Igor'. On March 20, 1155, Yury was installed as prince.[241]

But Izyaslav's sojourn in Kiev had whetted his appetite for the so-called "golden throne" and, in the autumn, he prepared to attack Yury. Svyatoslav stopped him from the foolhardy venture because Yury had strengthened his position by placating the Mstislavichi. Moreover, he enjoyed the support of his son-in-law, Yaroslav Volodimerovich Osmomysl of Galich. After Izyaslav reluctantly capitulated, Yury sought to secure his and Svyatoslav's support by allotting a town in the Kievan land to each one of them. To Izyaslav he gave Korchesk (Korechesk),[242] and to Svyatoslav he gave Mozyr'.[243] Later, at the *snem* that Yury held at Lutava, a Chernigov border town on the west bank of the Desna near Gorodets Osterskiy,[244] he also

---

[239] "Sinin most" was located east of Starodub (see Nasonov, pp. 229, 231; Golubovsky, pp. 31, 37–8). Since Svyatoslav Ol'govich met Yury at "Sinin most," the town was probably part of his Novgorod Severskiy domain. Because Svyatoslav and his nephew had not yet been reconciled, it is unlikely that Svyatoslav Vsevolodovich would have come to his uncle's domain to greet Yury. Therefore, the region around Starodub where the nephew met Yury was probably his domain. This suggests that the region around "Sinin most," Radoshch (Radogoshch), and Starodub formed the boundary between the domains of the uncle and nephew.
[240] Ipat., cols. 468–78; Mosk., pp. 58–61; Lav., cols. 341–5.
[241] NPL, pp. 29, 215–16. Concerning the date, see Berezhkov, p. 64.
[242] The town was located to the east of Dorogobuzh, on the boundary of the Kievan and Volyn' lands (Makhnovets', p. 555; compare Barsov, p. 104).
[243] The town was located on the right bank of the river Pripyat', north of Vruchiy. Although some place it in the Turov lands, it, like Korchesk, was probably in the Kievan lands (Makhnovets', p. 559; compare Barsov, p.126).
[244] See Golubovsky, p. 20; Nasonov, p. 227; V. P. Kovalenko and O. V. Shekun, "Do lokalizatsii litopysnoy Lutavy," *Slov'iany i Rus' u naukovii spadshchyni D. Ia. Samokvasova*. Materialy istoryko-arkheolohichnoho seminaru, prysviachenoho 150-richchiu vid dnia narodzhennia D. Ia. Samokvasova (14–16 veresnya 1993 r., m. Novgorod-Sivers'kyi), P. P. Tolochko (gen. ed.) (Chernihiv, 1993), pp. 101–2; A. L. Kozakov, "De vidbuvalysia kniazivs'ki 'snemy' 1155 ta 1159 rr.

attempted to obviate any future opposition from the troublesome Davidovich by cementing the political pact with a personal bond. He arranged for his son Gleb to marry Izyaslav's unnamed daughter, evidently his only child, who arrived in Kiev that winter.[245]

In the autumn, Svyatoslav Ol'govich also took steps to bind the Ol'govichi closer together. The Hypatian Chronicle gives unique information probably taken from Svyatoslav's chronicle. After being reconciled with his uncle at Starodub, Svyatoslav Vsevolodovich confirmed his loyalty some six months later by kissing the Holy Cross. The repentant deserter presumably came to beg for his remaining towns. His uncle granted him only three, but the chronicler fails to identify them. Nevertheless, he reveals that Svyatoslav Ol'govich had already returned a number of towns to him on a previous occasion, namely sometime after his nephew had been released from captivity but before he met Yury near Starodub. At that time, the elder Svyatoslav evidently allotted Starodub to his nephew. In the autumn, however, he still withheld Snovsk (Snov'sk),[246] Karachev, and Vorotinesk (Vorotynsk)[247] seemingly the wealthiest districts of his nephew's domain. Since Svyatoslav Vsevolodovich had formerly controlled Snovsk in addition to Starodub, it appears that after Yury returned Igor''s domains to the Ol'govichi, the heart of Svyatoslav's holdings had been the Snovskaya *tysyacha*.[248]

Svyatoslav Ol'govich imposed a severe penalty on his nephew for his delinquency, but we are not told whether this punishment was to be a temporary or a permanent measure. The younger prince seemingly resigned himself to paying a high price for his unfaithfulness. Svyatoslav Ol'govich's treatment of his nephew shows that granting or confiscating domains was the standard procedure for rewarding loyalty or punishing treachery. Appropriating and allocating such domains was the prerogative of a senior prince whether he was the politically senior prince of Rus' (such as Yury

(istoryko-arkheolohichnyi aspekt lokalizatsii litopysnoi Lutavy)," *Liubets'kyi z'izd kniaziv 1097 roku v istorychnii doli Kyivs'koi Rusi*, Materialy mizhnarodnoi konferentsii prysviachenoi 900-littiu z'izdu kniaziv Kyivs'koi Rusi u Liubechi, P. P. Tolochko (gen. ed.) (Chernihiv, 1997), pp. 101–8.

[245] Ipat. cols. 479–82; compare Lav., col. 346. Gleb's first wife died in the previous year (Ipat., col. 468).

[246] The town (present-day Sednev) was located northeast of Chernigov, probably on the river Snov', close to where it flows into the Desna (Nasonov, p. 231; Golubovsky, pp. 38–40; Zaytsev, p. 69).

[247] The town was located on the river Vyssa, a left tributary of the Oka in the Vyatichi lands (T. N. Nikol'skaya, "Vorotynsk," *Drevnyaya Rus' i slavyane*, T. V. Nikolaeva [gen. ed.] [M., 1978], pp. 118–28; *Zemlya Vyatichey*, p. 148).

[248] Ipat. col. 479. We have seen that after occupying Kiev, Yury returned to Svyatoslav Ol'govich his entire patrimony, including the Snovskaya *tysyacha*. Svyatoslav must have given it to his nephew soon after Yury returned it to the Ol'govichi. As we have seen, both Snovsk and Starodub probably belonged to the Snovskaya *tysyacha* (see above, p. 58).

in Kiev), the politically senior prince of a dynasty (such as Izyaslav in Chernigov), or the genealogically senior prince of a family within a dynasty (such as Svyatoslav Ol'govich of the Ol'govichi). Moreover, in the instance of Svyatoslav Vsevolodovich, the evidence that Izyaslav Davidovich played no part in depriving him of lands reveals that none of the towns that Svyatoslav had controlled before his desertion fell under Izyaslav's jurisdiction. They all belonged to the patrimony of the Ol'govichi.

THE PRINCES OF CHERNIGOV AND THE CHURCH

Under the year 1156 the chronicler interjects a colourful passage to inform us of the roles that the princes of Chernigov played in the life of the Church. He tells us that, in 1156, Bishop Nifont of Novgorod travelled to Kiev to greet the newly appointed Metropolitan Konstantin coming from Constantinople. Before the latter arrived, however, Nifont became ill and died in April; he was buried in Abbot Feodosy's cave. Three days before his illness, however, he dreamed that he was praying in Svyatosha's stall in the Church of the Assumption in the Caves Monastery. In answer to his prayers, one of the monks led him to Abbot Feodosy's tomb where the saint appeared to him and foretold his death. Next the chronicler discusses Nifont's opposition to Klim's appointment as metropolitan and concludes by stating that Nifont and Svyatoslav Ol'govich "had love for one another because Svyatoslav occupied Novgorod without him."[249]

From this chance reference to Svyatosha we see that the memory of Izyaslav Davidovich's eldest brother was flourishing thirteen years after his death. This is confirmed by the news that Nifont considered the prince's stall to be a hallowed place. Since only Svyatosha and Feodosy, two of the monastery's holiest monks, favoured the bishop with his vision, the reference to them implies that they interceded with God on his behalf. Nifont's testimony to Svyatosha's sanctity, therefore, bolstered his cult and also enhanced the prestige of the Davidovichi.

The report of Nifont's friendship with Svyatoslav Ol'govich is surprising. Moreover, it appears to be out of context because Svyatoslav had nothing to do with the bishop's visit to Kiev. There is no record of the two meeting after 1136, when Svyatoslav ruled Novgorod. Indeed, at that time Nifont objected to the prince's marriage.[250] The account is also imprecise. It states

[249] Ipat. cols. 483–4; N4, pp. 155–7. Another source says that Nifont was on friendly terms with Svyatoslav because the latter had formerly resided in Novgorod (Heppell, *The "Paterik,"* pp. 110–12).
[250] NPL, pp. 24, 209; *Dynasty*, pp. 337–8.

that Nifont and Svyatoslav "had love for one another because Svyatoslav occupied Novgorod without him."[251] If we attempt to interpret the passage as a reference to Svyatoslav's rule in the northern emporium it makes no sense given Nifont's hostility to Svyatoslav at that time. If, however, we place it in the context of the entire report of the marvellous vision, it takes on a different meaning. The reference to Svyatoslav is preceded by an explanation of Nifont's crusade against Metropolitan Klim. By treating the reference to Svyatoslav as a continuation of the report on Nifont's rivalry with the metropolitan, it may be interpreted as follows: Nifont and Svyatoslav became friends because Svyatoslav occupied Novgorod (Severskiy) without him (that is, without Klim's blessing).[252]

If the latter interpretation is correct, the statement is intriguing. One reason why the author of Nifont's vision singled out Svyatoslav may have been because he was the prince's personal scribe. A second reason may have been because, given their former hostility in Novgorod, the *rapprochement* between the two men was so extraordinary it was noteworthy. They were probably reconciled around 1147 because of their mutual objection to Klim's appointment. Finally, Svyatoslav's opposition to the metropolitan sheds light on another incident. As we have seen, Klim did not canonize Igor′ while the latter was interred in Kiev. Another reason why he refused to do so, therefore, may have been his hostility towards Svyatoslav, the main champion of Igor′'s canonization.

JUNIOR OL′GOVICHI AND DAVIDOVICHI REBEL

Even though Izyaslav Davidovich and Svyatoslav Ol′govich remained loyal to Yury, their nephews rebelled against them. We are told that in 1156 Svyatoslav Vladimirovich[253] abandoned his domain of Berezyy[254] and rode north where he captured Vshchizh,[255] on the Desna west of Bryansk, and all

[251] "Lyubov zhe imesta s Svyatoslavom. s Olgovichem. be bo Svyatoslav sel bez nego Novegorode" (Ipat., col. 484).

[252] Concerning this interpretation, see Makhnovets′, p. 268.

[253] The Hypatian Chronicle does not identify the Svyatoslav mentioned here for the first time. Under the year 1159, however, it refers to him as Izyaslav's nephew Svyatoslav Vladimirovich (Ipat., col. 502; Zotov, p. 266).

[254] Berezyy was located near the river Svin′, a tributary of the Desna (Nasonov, p. 221; compare Golubovsky, pp. 2–5).

[255] Nasonov, p. 223; Makhnovets′, p. 546. Concerning Vshchizh, see B. A. Rybakov, "Stol′nyy gorod Chernigov i udel′nyy gorod Vshchizh," *Po sledam drevnikh kul′tur* (Drevnyaya Rus′), G. B. Fedorov *et al.* (eds.) (M., 1953), pp. 98–120.

the towns of the Podesen'e region that belonged to his uncle Izyaslav.[256] The
Davidovichi had controlled the region since 1142, when Vsevolod Ol'govich
had given it to them.[257] We are not told when Vsevolod had appropriated
the territory from the Davidovichi, but it was probably after 1127, when
he became prince of Chernigov. That the Podesen'e was not a part of the
inheritance of the Ol'govichi is supported by the news that in 1149, when
Yury returned all their patrimonial lands to the Ol'govichi, he did not hand
over the Podesen'e.[258]

We are not told why Svyatoslav Vladimirovich rebelled. It is possible,
however, that his bid for additional domains was triggered by his uncle's
failure in Kiev. After occupying that town, as we have seen, Izyaslav had
ceded control of Chernigov to Svyatoslav Ol'govich. In the light of his
increased territorial holdings in the Kievan land, Izyaslav undoubtedly also
gave Svyatoslav Vladimirovich more domains, perhaps the very Podesen'e
towns that the latter seized. After losing Kiev and being forced to reclaim
Chernigov, Izyaslav would also have repossessed the towns that he had given
to his nephew. Having tasted new power, however, the latter refused to be
denied.

At the same time Svyatoslav Vsevolodovich, who was living at Starodub,
solicited the help of his maternal uncle Rostislav of Smolensk, and waged
war against his paternal uncle Svyatoslav Ol'govich. He saw Svyatoslav
Vladimirovich's occupation of the Podesen'e towns as an opportunity for
retrieving the domains that he had lost to his uncle Svyatoslav. He undoubtedly intended to capture the Podesen'e towns and barter them for
the return of his own domains. In part, he was motivated to take military
action by the consideration that Svyatoslav Vladimirovich's appropriation
of the Podesen'e was unlawful. What is more, Svyatoslav Vsevolodovich
could argue that he himself had a claim to that district because his father
had ruled it before him.

Meanwhile, as was the practice after a new prince assumed control of the
capital of Rus', Yury Dolgorukiy went to negotiate peace with the Polovtsy.
His allies from Chernigov joined him. After the negotiations were successfully completed, Izyaslav invited the tribesmen, presumably his in-laws, to
help him drive out the upstart Ol'govich from the town of Berezyy, which

[256] It has been suggested that the other towns in the Podesen'e region were Ormina, Vorobeyna,
and Rosus' (Zaytsev, p. 98). See also E. A. Shinakov and V. V. Minenko, "'Goroda' Chernigovo-
smolenskogo pogranich'ya: faktory i etapy razvitiya," *Rol' rannikh mis'kykh tsentriv v stanovlenni
Kyivs'koi Rusi*, Materialy pol'ovoho istoryko-arkheolohichnoho seminaru. Serpen' 1993 r., s. Zelenyi
Hai Sums'koho r-nu Sums'koi obl., O. P. Motsia (gen. ed.) (Sumy, 1993), pp. 20–7.
[257] *Dynasty*, p. 376.   [258] See above, p. 58.

belonged to the Davidovichi. Meanwhile, Svyatoslav Ol'govich accompanied his in-law Yury to Kiev, where they rejoiced over their pact with the
nomads and Yury's newly won supremacy. Their celebration bespeaks a
close camaraderie.

Izyaslav failed to subdue the rebellious Ol'govich so he joined forces
with Svyatoslav Ol'govich against both nephews. The chronicler gives few
details of their campaign. It seems, however, that the uncles marched against
Svyatoslav Vsevolodovich in Starodub and Svyatoslav Vladimirovich in
Vshchizh. They pursued their prey into the Smolensk lands, but we are
not told why they did so. Perhaps Svyatoslav Vsevolodovich went there to
seek help from his maternal uncle Rostislav. In any case, the chase ended
happily, especially for the malcontents. In order to restore family harmony,
the uncles made concessions. Izyaslav, as we shall see, allowed his nephew
to keep Vshchizh. In like manner, we may assume, Svyatoslav Ol'govich
returned to his nephew one or more towns from among Snovsk, Karachev,
and Vorotinesk.[259]

YURY'S DEATH

Meanwhile, there was growing opposition to Yury in Kiev. In the winter
of 1156 he ordered his men in Suzdalia to bring Ivan Rostislavich Berladnik
to Kiev because he proposed to hand over the captive to his son-in-law
Yaroslav Osmomysl in Galich. Metropolitan Konstantin and all the abbots
interceded on Ivan's behalf, accusing Yury of condemning the man to certain death.[260] Moved by their entreaties, he sent Ivan back to Suzdalia in
chains. Izyaslav, however, dispatched horsemen to intercept the detachment
escorting the captive and had him brought to Chernigov.[261]

Ivan Berladnik and the princes of Chernigov had expressed their friendship for one another on a number of occasions. As already noted, in 1145
Vsevolod Ol'govich had given him sanctuary in Kiev after he failed to capture Galich from Yaroslav Osmomysl's father, Volodimerko.[262] Following
Vsevolod's death, Ivan supported Svyatoslav Ol'govich against the Davidovichi. But in 1147, he deserted Svyatoslav to join Rostislav of Smolensk
and the Davidovichi. Ten years later, Izyaslav showed that the two were still
friends by rescuing Ivan and giving him sanctuary.

[259] Ipat., cols. 484–5; compare Mosk., p. 61; Vosk., pp. 64–5; Gust., p. 304.
[260] The Hypatian chronicler reports that Metropolitan Konstantin, who replaced Klim, arrived in Kiev
after Yury was reconciled with the Polovtsy at Zarub (Ipat., col. 485).
[261] See s.a. 1157: Ipat., col. 488; compare s.a. 1156: Mosk., p. 62. The dating in the Hypatian Chronicle
for the next twenty years is under the Ultra-March year (Berezhkov, pp. 157, 168).
[262] See above, p. 23.

The spring of 1157 witnessed a major reorientation in alliances. Although Yury retained the support of his two in-laws, Svyatoslav Ol'govich and Yaroslav Osmomysl, he lost the backing of the Mstislavichi of Smolensk and of Volyn'. The latter deserted Yury after he attacked them. Before his younger brother Andrey had died in 1142, Yury had promised to find a domain for Andrey's son Vladimir. Accordingly, during the winter of 1156, Yury and Yaroslav Osmomysl unsuccessfully endeavoured to drive out Mstislav Izyaslavich from Vladimir in Volyn'.²⁶³ Izyaslav Davidovich found the time to be propitious for making an offer to Rostislav of Smolensk. If the latter and his relatives helped him to occupy Kiev he promised, as we shall see, to provide a domain for Rostislav's younger brother Vladimir, who had lost Vladimir in Volyn' to his nephew Mstislav.²⁶⁴ Their support gave Izyaslav powerful backing from the House of Monomakh for the first time. Unfortunately for the dynasty of Chernigov, however, his ambition once again pitted him against the Ol'govichi.

The Kievans also opposed Yury. As we have seen, in 1149 the chronicler recorded their antagonism towards him before he occupied Kiev. As Izyaslav and Rostislav fled from the capital, the citizens proclaimed their intention to tolerate Yury's presence for only as long as they had to; they declared their determination to fight for the return of the Mstislavichi.²⁶⁵ Their avowed antagonism therefore predisposed them to a hostile act. Consequently, there is reason to believe that the Kievans were responsible for Yury's untimely death on May 15. The chronicler singles out a drinking spree at the home of a certain Petrilo as the cause of the prince's demise. More than likely, Petrilo had the prince poisoned.²⁶⁶ After all, the Kievans had demonstrated their readiness to use extreme measures against an unwanted prince when they had murdered Igor'.

IZYASLAV DAVIDOVICH IN KIEV

Following Yury's death, the Kievans invited Izyaslav to be their prince. Their action is surprising because of their traditional antagonism towards the Davidovichi. They could argue, of course, that he was in command of a powerful coalition preparing to attack Kiev and their invitation to him was

---

²⁶³ Ipat., cols. 485–8; Mosk., pp. 61–2; Lav., col. 347.
²⁶⁴ Ipat., cols. 484–5.   ²⁶⁵ Ipat., col. 383; see above, p. 57.
²⁶⁶ The circumstances of Yury's death are not unlike those of Rostislav Vladimirovich of Tmutarakan'. In 1066 after the latter drank the wine into which a Greek official had inserted poison, the conspirator predicted that Rostislav would die within seven days (Ipat., col. 155; Lav., col. 166; *Dynasty*, p. 59). It is therefore possible that Yury was killed with a similar slow-working poison.

an act of expediency. Another reason why they opted for Izyaslav was that he won the support of his most powerful rival, Rostislav of Smolensk. After Yury's death, the mantle of the senior prince of the House of Monomakh passed to Rostislav, the eldest-surviving son of Monomakh's eldest son, Mstislav. To judge from subsequent events, he pledged to support Izyaslav and to go into battle under his command. Since the head of Kiev's favourite princely family deferred to Izyaslav, the townsmen resigned themselves to accepting him as their prince.[267]

On Pentecost Sunday, May 19, 1157, Izyaslav sat on the throne of Kiev the second time. On this occasion, he faced no opposition from the Kievans or from rival princes. But an immediate threat to his rule existed in his own dynasty. After occupying Kiev, he was expected to hand over the dynastic capital to another prince. The report that Svyatoslav Ol'govich arrived at its gates intending to occupy it bespeaks a predetermined order of succession. Presumably, it was to be the same arrangement that the princes had followed after Izyaslav had seized Kiev the first time. On that occasion, he had given Chernigov to Svyatoslav Ol'govich. Significantly, a different relationship existed between the two princes when he occupied Kiev the second time. On the first occasion Svyatoslav had been his ally; on the second occasion Svyatoslav had supported Yury against him. To his chagrin, therefore, when Svyatoslav attempted to enter the dynastic capital, Izyaslav's nephew Svyatoslav Vladimirovich refused him entry.

Svyatoslav had skipped two important steps. He had neither been reconciled with Izyaslav nor pledged loyalty to him. Fortunately for the peace of the dynasty, he was able to follow the road of conciliation. As we have seen, Svyatoslav had refused to back Izyaslav's bid for Kiev out of fidelity to the incumbent, Yury Dolgorukiy. Following the latter's death, therefore, Svyatoslav pledged loyalty to his cousin and the latter handed over Chernigov. Because Svyatoslav Ol'govich replaced his cousin in the dynastic capital, Svyatoslav Vsevolodovich replaced his uncle in Novgorod Severskiy, the capital of the Ol'govichi. After the usual celebrations, Izyaslav departed from Chernigov and returned to Kiev with his wife, children,[268] and *druzhina*.[269] On this occasion, therefore, the system of rotation between

---

[267] See s.a. 1158: Ipat., cols. 488–9; Gust., p. 304; compare s.a. 1157: Mosk., pp. 62–3; Lav., col. 348. Compare also Tolochko who suggests that a powerful Chernigov faction in Kiev supported Izyaslav, preventing Rostislav Mstislavich from occupying Kiev (*Drevnyaya Rus'*, pp. 128–9.)

[268] The reference to Izyaslav's family reveals that he had a number of children in addition to the daughter who married Gleb Yur'evich of Pereyaslavl' in 1156 (Ipat., col. 482). The children are neither identified nor mentioned again.

[269] See s.a. 1158: Ipat., col. 490; compare s.a. 1157: Mosk., p. 63. Concerning the date, see Berezhkov, p. 168.

the Davidovichi and Ol'govichi, as well as within the family of Ol'govichi, worked smoothly.

According to later information, as we shall see, Izyaslav handed over the town of Chernigov and seven other towns to Svyatoslav, but he did not hand over the Chernigov domain. He kept the latter for himself and for his nephew Svyatoslav Vladimirovich. The chronicler neglects to tell us the latter's territorial holdings. To judge from the information that some ten years later he would die in Vshchizh,[270] however, it appears that in 1156 his uncle allowed him to keep that town and probably the other towns that he had seized in the Podesen'e.

After being pacified with the Ol'govichi, Izyaslav performed one of the most important duties he had towards the inhabitants of Rus': he concluded peace with the Polovtsy at Kanev.[271] He also reached a settlement with Yaroslav Osmomysl, Yury's son-in-law. This is confirmed, as we shall see, by their collaboration later in the year. In this way Izyaslav restored harmony in his dynasty, consolidated his supremacy in Rus', and secured the safety of the inhabitants from nomadic attacks.

Later that year, Izyaslav besieged Yury Yaroslavich in Turov.[272] The composition of his troops, in the main Mstislavichi, and the purpose of the campaign, to procure a domain for Vladimir Mstislavich, suggest that Izyaslav led the attack in payment to the Mstislavichi for helping him to occupy Kiev. Rostislav evidently promised his dynasty's backing if Izyaslav agreed to compensate his younger brother, Vladimir, for his loss of Vladimir in Volyn'. Since Turov and Pinsk had belonged to his uncle Vyacheslav who died heirless, Rostislav laid claim to them. Granted, after Vyacheslav's death Yury Yaroslavich, a descendant of Izyaslav Yaroslavich of Turov (d. 1078), had repossessed his patrimonial towns. The Mstislavichi, however, justified their claim by arguing that Yury's father, Yaroslav,[273] had never ruled Turov and this made Yury an *izgoi*. The latter, for his part, pointed to the valiant stand that the townsmen put up in his defense, thereby testifying that they preferred his rule. Moreover, Yury could argue that God Himself supported his claim because He had intervened on his behalf by sending a plague on Izyaslav's horses. Izyaslav therefore failed to take Turov and Pinsk and to fulfill his promise to the Mstislavichi.[274]

---

[270] See s.a. 1167: Ipat., col. 525; see below, p. 109.   [271] Ipat., col. 490; Mosk., p. 63.

[272] Yury, the son of Yaroslav Svyatopolchich (Baum., II, 18) was descended from Izyaslav, the son of Yaroslav the Wise, to whom the latter had bequeathed Turov (see Dimnik, "Testament," pp. 383–5).

[273] Yaroslav Svyatopolchich was assassinated in 1123, when he was prince of Vladimir in Volyn' (Ipat., col. 287; *Dynasty*, p. 303).

[274] See s.a. 1158: Ipat., cols. 491–2; compare s.a. 1157: Mosk., p. 63.

SVYATOSLAV OL'GOVICH INTERVENES IN POLOTSK

In 1158 the chronicler once again refers to the less-publicized relations between Chernigov and Polotsk by reporting how the Ol'govichi helped to
bring about a change of rule. Under the year 1151, as we have seen, he had
recounted how the Polochane revolted against Rogvolod Borisovich,[275] sent
him under guard to Minsk, enthroned Rostislav Glebovich as prince, and
asked Svyatoslav Ol'govich to be their father.[276] Later, we are told, Rogvolod
escaped from Minsk, sought refuge with Svyatoslav, and asked the latter to
help him repossess his patrimony. In 1158 Svyatoslav provided him with a
military force and allowed him to use the town of Sluchesk in the Dregovichi
lands, which belonged to the Ol'govichi, as a base from which to launch
his attack. The evidence that Svyatoslav assisted the fugitive in every way
short of accompanying him testifies to their friendship.

Thus, even though in 1151 Svyatoslav had promised the Polochane to be
their father, seven years later he backed the very prince that they had evicted.
In assisting Rogvolod, Svyatoslav would have argued that he did not break
his oath to the townspeople because Rogvolod was not seeking Polotsk. He
wished to reclaim his patrimony of Drutsk that Rostislav Glebovich and the
latter's brothers had stolen from him. Indeed, as it turned out, Svyatoslav
did not break his promise to the Polochane because they themselves had
a change of heart. After Rogvolod occupied Drutsk, they evicted Rostislav
Glebovich and invited Rogvolod to return as prince. He occupied Polotsk
in July.

In addition to Svyatoslav, Rostislav of Smolensk also helped Rogvolod.
This is noteworthy for it reveals that Svyatoslav and Rostislav shared a common policy for Polotsk. Svyatoslav's primary purpose, it would appear at first
glance, was to reinstate Rogvolod in Drutsk, while Rostislav's intention was
to return Rogvolod to Polotsk. Nevertheless, it is more than likely that helping Rogvolod to reoccupy Polotsk was also Svyatoslav's ultimate objective.
To this end, Rogvolod would have kept Svyatoslav's military force at his side
until he was reconciled with Rostislav Glebovich. Moreover, following his
uncle's example, Svyatoslav Vsevolodovich of Novgorod Severskiy probably
gave troops to Rogvolod. He had a personal interest in Rogvolod's rehabili-
tation because his brother-in-law, Bryacheslav Vasil'kovich, was Rogvolod's
ally.[277] With the assistance of the Ol'govichi, therefore, Rogvolod was also

---

[275] Concerning Rogvolod, see Baum., VIII, 15.
[276] Concerning Rostislav Glebovich, see Baum., VIII, 12.
[277] Concerning Bryacheslav Vasil'kovich, see Baum., VIII, 30. In 1143 Svyatoslav Vsevolodovich married
the daughter of Rogvolod's cousin Vasil'ko Svyatoslavich, that is, Bryacheslav's sister (Ipat., col. 313;
Dynasty, pp. 384–7; Baum., VIII, 33).

able to reinstate Bryacheslav in his patrimonial domain of Izyaslavl'. More importantly, however, the new prince of Polotsk was now indebted to Svyatoslav Ol'govich.[278]

IZYASLAV LOSES KIEV

After reporting the Polotsk power struggle, the chronicler gives a long description of the fighting which arose in southern Rus', mainly because of Izyaslav Davidovich's pertinacity. Unfortunately for him, his obstinate support of Ivan Berladnik proved to be his undoing. Because of his seniority, Ivan was a rival to Yaroslav Osmomysl in Galich.[279] A faction of Galicians supported Ivan's candidacy so Yaroslav took his threat seriously.[280] Failing to neutralize Ivan through peaceful means, Yaroslav rallied the princes of Volyn' against Izyaslav. We are not told why the Mstislavichi, who had earlier supported Izyaslav's bid for Kiev, now sought to depose him. Since they had no vested interest in defending Yaroslav against Ivan, we may assume that they used Yaroslav's dispute with Izyaslav as a pretext for achieving their own end. Izyaslav, as we have seen, had failed to fulfill his promise to them by not capturing Turov for Vladimir Mstislavich. Their aim, undoubtedly, was to seize Kiev for Rostislav Mstislavich, who, they hoped, would demonstrate more determination in accommodating his brother with a suitable domain.

The threat to his rule prompted Izyaslav to seek support from the Ol'govichi. Relations in the House of Chernigov, however, were strained. After occupying Kiev, Izyaslav had acted in a heavy-handed manner towards the Ol'govichi. Svyatoslav Ol'govich accused him of refusing to give him the entire Chernigov domain, which, in his opinion, Izyaslav should have done. Instead, Izyaslav had given him Chernigov with a number of allegedly desolate towns. Izyaslav was aware of his cousin's discontent because, in the face of the impending attack on Kiev, he attempted to appease Svyatoslav by giving him the towns of Mozyr' and Chichersk.[281] As we have seen, Yury had already given Mozyr' to Svyatoslav at an earlier date.[282] Since

---

[278] See s. a. 1159: Ipat., cols. 493–6.

[279] Ivan's father Rostislav had been the elder brother of Yaroslav's father Volodimerko (Baum., III, 12).

[280] Hrushevsky suggests that Izyaslav hoped to occupy the throne of Galich by supporting the pretender Ivan (*Istoriia*, vol. 2, pp. 323–4). There is no chronicle evidence that Izyaslav hoped to capture Galich for himself.

[281] The town was located in the Chernigov lands north of Gomiy where the river Chichera flows into the Sozh (Nasonov, p. 233; Makhnovets', p. 576).

[282] In 1155 Yury had given Mozyr' to Svyatoslav in appreciation for his support (see above, p. 76). Izyaslav appropriated the town after he replaced Yury in Kiev.

it belonged to the Kievan domain, however, Svyatoslav had lost it with Yury's death. Controlling Chichersk would have pleased Svyatoslav more. It probably belonged to the Chernigov domain that Svyatoslav demanded from Izyaslav.[283]

The cousins celebrated their territorial settlement with a political *rapprochement* at Lutava. The identities of the princes who attended the meeting are noteworthy. The last surviving Davidovichi, Izyaslav and his nephew Svyatoslav Vladimirovich, represented their family. The Ol'govichi had more than twice that number. Svyatoslav Ol'govich came with his sons, Oleg and Igor'. The reference to Igor', the first since 1151 when he was born, shows that Svyatoslav's second son had now entered the political arena even though he was only seven years of age. Svyatoslav was also accompanied by his nephew Svyatoslav Vsevolodovich and probably the latter's younger brother Yaroslav, who ruled Ropesk.[284] In addition to firming up family relations, Izyaslav's show of dynastic solidarity dissuaded his enemies in Galich and Volyn' from attacking him.

Izyaslav, however, refused to let sleeping dogs lie. He declared war on Yaroslav Osmomysl. From a moral standpoint his action was commendable. In his alleged testament to his sons, Yaroslav the Wise had decreed that it was the duty of the prince of Kiev to assist a prince whose domain was attacked. In the middle 1140s, Ivan had lost his patrimony of Zvenigorod to Yaroslav's father Volodimerko, albeit after Ivan himself had failed to usurp Volodimerko's patrimony of Galich.[285] By attacking Galicia on Ivan's behalf, Izyaslav could argue that he was helping a victimized prince regain his patrimony. Just the same, how realistic was Izyaslav's objective? Earlier in the year Yaroslav had solicited overwhelming support, from princes and foreign rulers, against Izyaslav's patronage of Ivan. In the light of the intimidating opposition, what reasons could possibly have compelled Izyaslav to continue championing Ivan's seemingly hopeless cause?

He had, or believed he had, strong military support. Understandably, he counted on the now mollified Ol'govichi to help him. He could also summon the ever-willing Polovtsy and the tribesmen from the Poros'e region. But above all, to judge from the account, he was spurred into

[283] Zaytsev, p. 104.
[284] The town, located southwest of Starodub, lay on the river Irpa, a tributary of the Snov' (Golubovsky, pp. 32–3; Nasonov, pp. 229–30; Makhnovets', p. 567; E. A. Shinakov and V. V. Minenko, "Lokalizatsiya Orminy i Ropeska – letopisnykh tsentrov Chernigovskoy zemli," *Slov'iany i rus' u naukovii spadshchyni D. Ia. Samokvasova. Materialy istoryko-arkheolohichnoho seminaru, prysviachenoho 150-richchiu vid dnia narodzhennia D. Ia. Samokvasova* [14–16 veresnya 1993 r., m. Novgorod-Sivers'kyi], P. P. Tolochko [gen. ed.] [Chernihiv, 1993], pp. 42–3).
[285] *Dynasty*, pp. 403–4.

action by citizens in Galich. Partisans loyal to Ivan promised to betray Yaroslav Osmomysl and open the town's gates. The Galicians' offer of support also prompted Izyaslav to raise his sights. Initially, when he had agreed to secure a domain for Ivan, he presumably had Ivan's patrimony of Zvenigorod in mind. After the Galicians invited Ivan to be their prince, however, Izyaslav decided to challenge Yaroslav himself for his patrimony. Izyaslav therewith broke the directive of Yaroslav the Wise instructing him to assist the wronged party. His support of Ivan was no longer justified on moral grounds because the latter became, yet again, a would-be usurper.

The Davidovich miscalculated on three counts. First, he misjudged the loyalty of the Ol'govichi. Svyatoslav objected to fighting an offensive war, especially one that was of no benefit to a prince of their dynasty. He was willing to defend Kiev, but he refused to fight for the profit of Ivan Berladnik. Svyatoslav undoubtedly remembered how Ivan had deserted him in the Vyatichi lands when he was fleeing from the Davidovichi. Second, Izyaslav's plan to besiege Galich misfired. Yaroslav Osmomysl, Mstislav Izyaslavich, and Vladimir Mstislavich pre-empted his attack by marching against Kiev. Moreover, they forced him to confront them in the open field.

Izyaslav's third setback came when the Berendei and Torki deserted him. Moreover, during the fighting Khan Bashkord, Svyatoslav Vladimirovich's foster father, had arrived with 20,000 Polovtsian reinforcements, but these fair-weather friends fled as soon as they sensed defeat. In the short term, the treachery of the Poros'e tribesmen led to Izyaslav's downfall. But their disloyalty also had long-term importance. Unlike the Polovtsy from the steppe whose fickleness was of transitory significance, the Berendei and Torki were residents of the river Ros' frontier. Their support was vital for Izyaslav's rule in Kiev. What is more, after they threw in their lot with Mstislav Izyaslavich, the Kievans inevitably followed suit. Izyaslav was defeated on December 22, 1158; he had no choice but to flee. His reign in Kiev had lasted less than two years.

In the meantime, the Ol'govichi sat at home disgruntled. Following Izyaslav's threat to evict Svyatoslav from Chernigov because he boycotted the campaign, we learn that Svyatoslav remained unappeased with Mozyr' and Chichersk. Indeed, his response gives us new information concerning the nature of Izyaslav's territorial allocations to him. Svyatoslav accused Izyaslav of keeping the Chernigov domain for himself. Although the chronicler does not identify the towns it contained, Svyatoslav states that in addition to Chernigov, Izyaslav gave him seven towns including Moroviysk (on the Desna south of Chernigov), Lyubech, Orgoshch',[286] and Vsevolozh. These had all been devastated by the Polovtsy and were inhabited by dog herders. Since he accused Izyaslav of keeping the towns of the Chernigov domain for the Davidovichi, the seven towns obviously were not from that domain but from the patrimony of the Davidovichi. Izyaslav most likely gave them to Svyatoslav because they lay in ruins.[287] His refusal to grant the Ol'govichi their territorial demands fortified their resolve to boycott his campaign. Izyaslav, for his part, resented their lack of support.

Even in defeat he refused to restrain his rage. First, he fled to his town of Gomiy, where he orchestrated his wife's escape from Kiev.[288] She circumvented Chernigov and used towns belonging to Izyaslav and his allies as staging posts. He undoubtedly warned her to avoid the domains of the Ol'govichi because he had declared war on them. Despite Izyaslav's hostility, however, the Ol'govichi displayed no animosity towards his wife. Yaroslav Vsevolodovich testified to this by showing her every courtesy when she came to Ropesk. Izyaslav, however, rejected the token of friendship and alienated Svyatoslav Ol'govich by devastating Bleve (Oblov), which the latter's wife had probably received as a wedding gift.[289] Later he satiated his thirst for vengeance by pillaging the Vyatichi towns, which included the patrimony of Svyatoslav Vsevolodovich. In this way Izyaslav's foolhardy policy cost him Kiev and his unbridled wrath antagonized the Ol'govichi. He became an outcast.

The Mstislavichi reaped the fruits of Izyaslav's folly. Significantly, not one of the three victors (Mstislav Izyaslavich, Vladimir Mstislavich, and Yaroslav Osmomysl) attempted to occupy Kiev. Rostislav Mstislavich was

---

[286] The town, located some 19 km northwest of Chernigov in the upper reaches of the river Belous, lay on the route from Chernigov to Lyubech (Golubovsky, pp. 29–30; Nasonov, p. 228).

[287] Many towns belonging to the Davidovichi had been devastated by the Mstislavichi. In 1147, as we have seen, Rostislav had set fire to Lyubech and ravaged the districts around it. On the same campaign, the Mstislavichi destroyed Vsevolozh and other towns in the Zadesen'e (see above, pp. 49–51). The following year, the Mstislavichi once again pillaged the district of Lyubech (see above, p. 52).

[288] In 1142, when Vsevolod ruled Kiev, his younger brother Igor' ruled Gomiy (Ipat., cols. 311–12; *Dynasty*, p. 375), but we are not told whether Vsevolod gave it to Igor' when he was prince of Chernigov or after he occupied Kiev. The Davidovichi evidently took it from Igor' in 1146, after he was taken captive by Izyaslav. In 1158 Gomiy belonged to Izyaslav Davidovich. It has been suggested, correctly it would seem, that the town had been part of the patrimony of the Davidovichi (Zaytsev, p. 104).

[289] On a number of occasions, the chroniclers report how the bride's father-in-law gave her a town as a wedding gift. In 1188 Ryurik Rostislavich gave his new daughter-in-law Verkhuslava, Bryagin (Ipat., col. 658), and in 1211 Vsevolod Yur'evich gave his new daughter-in-law Agafia, Yur'ev (Tat. 4, p. 340 and Tat. 3, p. 183; see also "Pitfalls," p. 150). Since Svyatoslav Ol'govich's father was dead in 1136, when he married the Novgorodian bride (NPL, pp. 24, 209), Vsevolod Ol'govich, as senior prince of the Ol'govichi, probably gave a town to his new sister-in-law.

the undisputed claimant in the House of Monomakh according to the traditional system of succession Yury had championed, and according to the practice of succession Vladimir Monomakh had advocated. The two systems had converged on one candidate. After the death of his brother Izyaslav, Rostislav became the eldest surviving Mstislavich, and after the death of his uncle Yury, Rostislav also became the genealogically eldest prince in Monomakh's dynasty. He therefore had the right to rule Kiev on both counts. Surprisingly, Rostislav made the appointment of the metropolitan a condition of his acceptance. His objection to re-instating Klim and Mstislav Izyaslavich's rejection of Konstantin drew Svyatoslav Ol'govich into the dispute because Konstantin sought safety with Svyatoslav in Chernigov.[290]

METROPOLITAN KONSTANTIN'S DEATH IN CHERNIGOV

The chronicler once again interjects a pious episode. With this entry he hoped to exonerate Metropolitan Konstantin of any wrongdoing and to reproach the princes who opposed him. He reports that in the spring of 1159 the metropolitan was living out his last days in Chernigov in the company of Svyatoslav Ol'govich and Bishop Antony. The arrival of the latter, a Greek bishop, was not reported,[291] but his immediate predecessor had been Onufry.[292] In 1147, as we have seen, the latter had spearheaded the appointment of Klim Smolyatich as metropolitan. Antony, however, rejected Onufry's policy and supported Konstantin. Since Svyatoslav Ol'govich was hostile to Klim, Antony would have been swayed to adopt his prince's position. Moreover, Antony, whom the patriarch had appointed bishop of Chernigov, would have favoured Konstantin because the latter had also received the patriarch's blessing. The canonicity of Konstantin's appointment, unlike that of Klim, was never questioned.

Konstantin died in the spring and extraordinary manifestations surrounded his death. The three pillars of fire rising up to heaven over his body signified God's blessing on his appointment as metropolitan and on his holiness. By association, they exonerated Svyatoslav Ol'govich and

---

[290] See s.a. 1159: Ipat., cols. 496–504; Mosk., pp. 64–6; compare Gust., pp. 305–6. These chronicles do not report Konstantin's flight to Chernigov, but see Erm., p. 42 and L'vov, p. 119. Tatishchev alone, and only in his second redaction, claims that Konstantin returned to Chernigov, where he had been bishop (Tat. 3, p. 67).

[291] Under the year 1164 the chronicler tells us that Antony was a Greek (Ipat., col. 523).

[292] Compare Bagaley, who claims a certain Evfimy served as bishop of Chernigov between Onufry and Antony (*Istoriya Severskoy zemli*, p. 284).

Bishop Antony, who supported him. Moreover, the tranquility that reigned over Chernigov during the three days that his body lay exposed outside the town was an expression of divine favor. Concomitantly, the storm that struck Kiev with such force that it shook the earth, the blinding flashes of lightning, and the deafening claps of thunder, signified divine displeasure. The chronicler himself attests that the signs were meant to castigate the Kievans for their sins against Konstantin. The terrifying disturbances were also a condemnation of those who supported Klim, namely Mstislav Izyaslavich, his father who appointed Klim, and even Rostislav Mstislavich, who failed to reappoint Konstantin as metropolitan. Indeed, Rostislav was encamped on the prairie near Vyshgorod during the storm and the wind ripped his tent to shreds. In an admission of guilt, he ordered the Kievans to do penance in all-night vigils for the injustice they had inflicted on the Greek cleric.

In the eyes of the Orthodox faithful, Konstantin's fate was comparable to that of Igor'. The Kievans had rejected both: they had murdered the prince, and they had forced the metropolitan to flee for his safety. Konstantin himself identified his contentious career with Igor''s. In imitation of the prince whose body was desecrated by the Kievans, the deposed metropolitan had made a most unusual demand on Bishop Antony: "After I die do not bury my body, but throw it on the ground, bind the feet together with rope, drag it out of the town, and leave it there for the dogs to savage."[293] Svyatoslav also acknowledged the similarity in the fates of the two men by interring Konstantin next to Igor'. Consequently, the town grew in religious prestige as a place of shrines. Moreover, Konstantin's fate enhanced the reputation of its princes as defenders of righteousness and patrons of victims of Kievan injustice.

IZYASLAV THE FUGITIVE

Meanwhile, the enemies of Izyaslav Davidovich consolidated their alliance against him. Rostislav Mstislavich had occupied Kiev on Easter Sunday, April 12. Later, on May 1, he invited Svyatoslav Ol'govich to a feast at Moroviysk. They celebrated with great merriment and Rostislav showered Svyatoslav with gifts: furs from sable, ermine, black marten, polar fox, white wolves, and fish teeth. The next morning Svyatoslav invited Rostislav to a feast and they made merry as on the previous day. Svyatoslav gave Rostislav

---

[293] Mosk., pp. 66–7; Lav., col. 349; Vlad., p. 68. Concerning Konstantin's career, see Shchapov, *Gosudarstvo i tserkov'*, pp. 197–8.

the coat of a snow leopard, two swift steeds, and saddles decorated with hammered gold. After that they returned home.[294]

Ironically, Svyatoslav and Rostislav, who had kept aloof at the battle at Belgorod where Izyaslav Davidovich was defeated, benefited most from it. Rostislav occupied Kiev and Svyatoslav remained in Chernigov. Significantly, the latter's refusal to return Chernigov to his cousin contravened the decision of the Congress of Lyubech in 1097, where the princes of Rus' pronounced the Davidovichi to be politically senior to the Ol'govichi.[295] By usurping the dynastic capital, Svyatoslav secured for the Ol'govichi their rightful political seniority in the House of Chernigov.

Izyaslav had little recourse after Svyatoslav fortified his position by forming a pact with Rostislav at Moroviysk. In addition to being in-laws, the two men were drawn together by their similar objectives: to keep out Izyaslav from Kiev and from Chernigov. They formed the most powerful alliance in Rus'. Rostislav enjoyed the loyalty of all the princes of his dynasty ruling the Smolensk and Volyn' lands. Moreover, he had the backing of the prince of Galich, the citizens of Kiev, and the tribesmen of the Poros'e region. To this array of allies Svyatoslav brought the Ol'govichi. Although Izyaslav was greatly outnumbered he was not isolated. He could count on receiving token assistance from his nephew Svyatoslav Vladimirovich and capricious support from the Polovtsy. His plight, nevertheless, was critical. At the beginning of 1159 he was a fugitive just as Svyatoslav had been in 1146, after his brother Igor' lost Kiev.

After announcing Svyatoslav's pact with Rostislav, most chronicles report Izyaslav's attempts to retake Chernigov. After venting his rage against the Ol'govichi by devastating their Vyatichi towns, he went south to the Seym region. His strategy, it appears, was to capture Svyatoslav's patrimony and use it to barter for Chernigov. In the summer, therefore, he besieged Putivl' to where Svyatoslav had appointed his son Oleg. Failing to take the town he captured Vyr', located southeast of Putivl'. He selected the outpost as his marshaling ground because it was adjacent to his own Zadesen'e patrimony from which he could summon loyal troops. Moreover, it was close to Putivl', which he was attempting to capture. Finally, it was in an excellent location for rendezvousing with the Polovtsy. That Izyaslav summoned a band of nomads to attack Putivl' is confirmed by the news that Oleg killed their khan Santuz.[296]

[294] Ipat., col. 504; compare Tat. 4, p. 256 and Tat. 3, pp. 68–9.
[295] Concerning the agreement reached at Lyubech, see *Dynasty*, pp. 207–23.
[296] Mosk. p. 67. Compare the Hypatian Chronicle, which has a corrupt text and states, wrongly, that Yury Yaroslavich of Turov attacked Putivl' (Ipat., cols. 504–5).

After failing to seize Svyatoslav's patrimonial capital, he attacked the even better fortified Chernigov. But his determination to reoccupy the dynastic capital was no match for the Ol'govichi resolve to keep it. Moreover, they had the backing of Rostislav and all the princes of Rus' who had helped to evict Izyaslav from Kiev. Although the latter assembled a huge Polovtsian force, its main objective, as always, was to plunder. His only princely ally was the outcast Ivan Berladnik, who had remained loyal to him after the Belgorod fiasco. In the end, he failed to take Chernigov, but given his stubbornness he refused to admit defeat.

Although the chronicler's main objective is to describe Izyaslav's attack on Chernigov, he also gives new information about Svyatoslav's family. He introduces us to the prince's third son, Vsevolod, whom Svyatoslav sent to Rostislav in Kiev as a guarantee of his loyalty.[297] We also learn that, in addition to his Novgorodian wife, a number of his unidentified children accompanied Svyatoslav on a Sunday outing. Of his sons, Oleg was in Putivl' and Vsevolod, as noted, was in Kiev. The only son who remains unaccounted for is Igor'. Since he was born in 1151 and was only eight years of age, he may have been at his father's side. As for Svyatoslav's daughters, we have seen that his unnamed eldest girl had married Roman Rostislavich and had moved to Smolensk. In 1149, a second daughter, Maria, had been born. She was ten years of age and, as we shall see, still unmarried. Svyatoslav also had a third daughter, whose existence is known only from a graffito written on a church wall.[298] The two girls, most likely, were also with their parents.[299]

After failing to capture Chernigov, Izyaslav adopted a new strategy for the third phase of his campaign. Assembling a fresh force of the ever-accommodating nomads, and probably Ivan Berladnik, he attacked towns in the upper reaches of the Desna. At first glance this appeared to be no more than wanton destruction. As a prelude, he razed the towns of Vorobeyna[300]

---

[297] Zotov, p. 271; Baum, IV, 29.
[298] In 1972, S. A. Vysotsky uncovered a twelfth-century graffito in the northern choir in the Cathedral of St. Sofia in Kiev. The inscription reads as follows: "Vladimir's wife. The grief-stricken Andrey's daughter-in-law was here [in St. Sofia]. [She is] the sister of Oleg and Igor and Vsevolod. The priest Vanko, *vladyka's* man, wrote this." Vysotsky identified, correctly in our view, the brothers Oleg, Igor', and Vsevolod as the sons of Svyatoslav Ol'govich. He also suggested, again correctly, that their sister, Vladimir's wife, married the son of Andrey Vladimirovich (Monomakh's youngest son), who ruled Dorogobuzh in Volyn' during the 1160s. See S. A. Vysotsky, "Nadpis' s imenami geroev 'Slova o polku Igoreve' v Kievskoy Sofii," TODRL 31 (L., 1976), pp. 327–33. Concerning Vladimir and Andrey, see Baum., V, 17, 31.
[299] Ipat., cols. 505–8; compare Makhnovets', pp. 276–7; Mosk., pp. 67–8.
[300] Vorobeyna was probably located on the upper reaches of the river Teremushka (Teremka), to the southwest of Dobryansk (Golubovsky, pp. 7–8; Nasonov, pp. 222–3; Makhnovets', p. 545).

and Rosus' (Roksous'),[301] possessions of the Ol'govichi on the northern periphery of the Starodub district. His main objective for going to the Podesen'e, however, was to join his nephew Svyatoslav Vladimirovich in Vshchizh. Using that town as his base, he launched an invasion of the Smolensk lands. If, as the chronicler claims, the Polovtsy took 10,000 captives to sell into slavery, the breadth of his operation suggests that Izyaslav's immediate purpose was to deprive Rostislav's patrimony of manpower. In the long term, however, he hoped that his attack would force Rostislav to pressure Svyatoslav into returning Chernigov to him. But in addition to instilling terror into his enemies' subjects, Izyaslav also schemed to win new allies.[302]

From the Smolensk lands he sent matchmakers to Andrey Yur'evich, later known as Bogolyubskiy,[303] and asked for his daughter's hand in marriage for Svyatoslav Vladimirovich. He also requested military aid. Andrey responded by sending his son Izyaslav with troops. Earlier that winter, we are told, Svyatoslav Ol'govich and the princes of Rus' had attacked Vshchizh, but the townsmen staunchly defended it for five weeks while waiting for Izyaslav Davidovich to bring help. When the Ol'govichi learned that Andrey's son was finally coming to help the citizens, they concluded peace. At that time Svyatoslav Vladimirovich pledged allegiance to Svyatoslav of Chernigov. On learning that the siege had ended, Izyaslav Davidovich went to Volok,[304] where he met Andrey with his daughter.[305] Izyaslav escorted her to Vshchizh.[306]

Let us determine the order of events by first establishing the date on which Andrey's daughter arrived in Vshchizh. To judge from the account, the bride probably reached Vshchizh a few weeks after the Ol'govichi lifted their five-week siege. Since they had initiated it in the winter, which the chronicler reckoned to begin in the first half of December, we may conclude that the marriage took place in February or March of 1160. Accordingly, since Izyaslav and the Ol'govichi had both launched their campaigns in the winter, the two groups waged war no earlier than mid-December of the previous year. Indeed, the Ol'govichi probably attacked Vshchizh in

---

[301] The town was located north of Starodub, not far from Vorobeyna (Nasonov, p. 230). Some investigators call it Rosukha (Golubovsky, p. 33; Makhnovets', p. 567).

[302] Ipat., col. 508.

[303] He received the sobriquet from the palace he built at the village of Bogolyubovo near Vladimir.

[304] Volok Lamskiy was a Novgorodian outpost located on the river Lama, southwest of Rostov (Barsov, pp. 38–9).

[305] Tatishchev calls her Rostislava, but only in his second redaction (Tat. 3, p. 70; Baum., VI, 21).

[306] The Hypatian chronicler reports the attack of Svyatoslav of Chernigov on Vshchizh in two entries. Since all the other sources record only one attack, it seems that the Hypatian chronicler is reporting the same attack in both entries (Ipat., cols. 508–9; Mosk., p. 68; Lav., col. 350).

retaliation for Izyaslav's devastation of Vorobeyna and Rosus'. They also attempted to stop his marauding of Smolensk lands by forcing him to come to his nephew's assistance. The tactic evidently worked: the chronicler's comment that the citizens of Vshchizh were waiting for Izyaslav to bring reinforcements indicates that they had sent him an appeal for help. Consequently, it would appear that Izyaslav contacted Andrey in Suzdalia after receiving word of the Ol'govichi attack from the beleaguered citizens.

On seeing that his tactic to terrorize the Ol'govichi and the Rostislavichi had backfired, Izyaslav sought to befriend Andrey, who had succeeded his father Yury Dolgorukiy in Suzdalia. He asked Andrey for a marriage alliance undoubtedly in the hope of achieving his main objective, a political pact. The latter would place the Davidovichi in a favoured position with Andrey to solicit his military aid. Their unexpected good fortune made the Davidovichi serious rivals to the Ol'govichi once again. This was dramatically illustrated when the mere news that Andrey's son was bringing troops prompted the Ol'govichi to negotiate a hasty peace with Svyatoslav Vladimirovich.

Surprisingly, Andrey accepted Izyaslav's proposal for an alliance despite the latter's seemingly hopeless predicament. His motive, it appears, was to curb the growing power of the Mstislavichi. After Rostislav occupied Kiev, we are told, he also asserted his control over Novgorod.[307] Rostislav's success frustrated Andrey's ambitions because he was also attempting to assert his authority in Novgorod. By supporting Izyaslav, presumably with the intention of reinstating him in Kiev, Andrey hoped to remove Rostislav's appointees from Novgorod. Andrey made his intention ominously clear to the Novgorodians when he warned them that he intended to rule their town even if he had to take it by force.[308]

In the meantime, Svyatoslav Ol'govich had failed to capture Vshchizh, but he believed that he had scored an important victory.[309] After receiving Rostislav's support for his rule in Chernigov, he undoubtedly also obtained pledges of loyalty from all the Ol'govichi. The two Davidovichi were the exceptions. Izyaslav's devastation of his towns in the Starodub district gave Svyatoslav the pretext for attacking Vshchizh and subduing them. In forcing Svyatoslav Vladimirovich to obey him, Svyatoslav Ol'govich probably hoped that he had driven a wedge between the two Davidovichi. But it is doubtful that he truly won over the young Svyatoslav since he had taken his oath under duress. Moreover, at the time that he was pledging his allegiance

[307] NPL, pp. 30–1, 218. [208] Ipat., cols. 509–10.
[309] The ability of the townsmen to fend off Svyatoslav's siege for five weeks suggests that the new earthen and wall defenses around the town and *detinets* had been completed (see below, pp. 109–10).

to Svyatoslav of Chernigov, his uncle Izyaslav was negotiating a pact with Andrey in the name of both Davidovichi. Indeed, Izyaslav was arranging for his nephew to become Andrey's son-in-law. Consequently, Svyatoslav of Vshchizh had to choose between conflicting allegiances.

IZYASLAV'S INTRIGUE

After Izyaslav's attempts to capture Chernigov failed he had recourse to intrigue, a tactic that the Davidovichi had used with limited success in the past. As we have seen, their nefarious conspiracies had included unsuccessful attempts to kill Svyatoslav Ol'govich and Rostislav's elder brother, Izyaslav. Given Izyaslav Davidovich's continued scheming, there is little doubt that he had been the main instigator of the treachery that he and his brother Vladimir had plotted. Izyaslav's newest conspiracy was to undermine Rostislav's alliance so that he could drive out Rostislav from Kiev. To achieve this end, he sought to alienate the Ol'govichi from Rostislav by convincing them that Rostislav was planning to give Chernigov to him.

The latter evidently began his machinations after he returned to Vshchizh with his nephew's bride. This is implied by the news that he won the two Vsevolodovichi, Svyatoslav and Yaroslav, to his side before approaching Oleg in the autumn. Since the brothers joined his camp, we may assume that fighting Rostislav was their commitment to him. In payment, Izyaslav probably promised to give them Kievan domains.

Following the settlement at Vshchizh sometime in the early part of 1160, Rus' enjoyed a period of peace until a gesture of friendship was malevolently turned into an occasion of mistrust. Rostislav wished to cultivate friendship with the Ol'govichi and asked Svyatoslav to send his son Oleg to Kiev so that he could meet prominent Kievans, Berendei, and Torki.[310] Svyatoslav complied, not suspecting any treachery. Unfortunately for the princes, the well-organized network of Izyaslav's agents in Kiev and Chernigov undermined their friendship. When Oleg visited Rostislav, the latter's disloyal retainer deceived him into believing that Rostislav wanted to take him captive in order to pressure his father into abdicating from Chernigov.

The chronicler's preoccupation with Oleg and his knowledge of family details suggest that he was Oleg's personal scribe. Nevertheless, he leaves one question unanswered, probably intentionally, because it places his prince in a bad light. He does not explain why Oleg, after fleeing from Rostislav's

---

[310] The date is suggested by the preceding entry, which states that an eclipse of the moon occurred on August 20 (Ipat., col. 512).

camp, became angry with his seemingly obliging father in Chernigov. Since Oleg's request for Kursk is probably associated with his ire, his discontent may have been prompted by his father's allocation of domains. We are not told where Oleg had been ruling before he visited Rostislav. A year earlier, however, he had defended Putivl' against Izyaslav. Since he asked his father for Kursk, this suggests that he was not happy living in Putivl', perhaps because he considered Kursk to be of greater importance.

Surprisingly, the conspirators duped even the veteran Svyatoslav Ol'govich by convincing him that Rostislav intended to hand over Chernigov to Izyaslav. If, however, Svyatoslav supported Izyaslav's claim to Kiev, the latter would confirm his rule in Chernigov. Nevertheless, after Svyatoslav purportedly threw in his lot with his cousin, he hedged his bets by refusing to leave Chernigov to join Izyaslav in the field. In doing so, he prevented his enemies from deposing him in his absence, and avoided antagonizing Rostislav. But there was another reason why Svyatoslav remained at home: he was too heavy to mount a horse.

Izyaslav's machinations paid off: he won the support of all the Ol'govichi. Even though Izyaslav mustered a powerful force, his talents as a military commander were not on a par with his skills at plotting subversion. He turned tail when he learnt that Rostislav was marching against him. In Izyaslav's defense it could be argued that, having failed to secure the support of Gleb Yur'evich in Pereyaslavl', he feared that his son-in-law would attack him from the rear if he rode to confront Rostislav at Trepol'.[311]

IZYASLAV DIES FIGHTING FOR KIEV

Despite his failure to confront Rostislav in battle, Izyaslav was determined to regain control of Kiev. In 1161, Svyatoslav once again attempted, unsuccessfully, to stop him from waging war. But even though he insisted that Izyaslav cancel his attack on Kiev, Svyatoslav refused to hand over Chernigov to him. In any case, Izyaslav's quest for a domain compelled him to seek the ultimate prize, the capital of Rus'. He almost succeeded. On February 8, his troops captured Kiev, forcing Rostislav to flee to Belgorod.[312]

At that time, the chronicler reports, a terrifying sign appeared in the sky. The moon traversed the firmament from east to west, changing its appearance as it journeyed. It waned slowly and then completely disappeared. At first its face was as black as pitch, but later it seemed to become steeped in

---

[311] See s.a. 1161: Ipat., cols. 512–14; compare s.a. 1160: Mosk., pp. 69–70.
[312] See s.a. 1161: Ipat., cols. 515–16; Makhnovets', pp. 280–1; see s.a. 1160: Mosk. p. 70.

blood. It had two faces, one green and the other yellow. In the middle of the moon people claimed they saw what looked like two warriors striking each other with swords, one had blood gushing from his head and the other milk. Old people were convinced that the portent presaged the death of a prince.[313]

Because controlling Kiev required a total victory over Rostislav, Izyaslav pursued him to Belgorod. During the siege, Svyatoslav sent messengers to him requesting him to conclude peace. If Rostislav refused to be reconciled, Svyatoslav advised him to return across the Dnepr because that was the righteous thing to do. Izyaslav spurned his cousin's advice. He replied that if the two Vsevolodovichi and Oleg returned to the left bank, they could retire to their domains, but he had no home there. He refused to live with the Polovtsy or to occupy the devastated outpost of Vyr', where he would starve to death. He preferred, he declared, to die fighting for Kiev.[314]

Unfortunately for Izyaslav, the battle dragged on for too long a time allowing Mstislav Izyaslavich to bring reinforcements to Rostislav. Moreover, the support of Izyaslav's allies was fickle and his talents as a military commander were wanting. At Belgorod, for the second time, Mstislav and his associates proved to be his undoing. The chronicler reports that after the prince fled from the field of battle, Rostislav and Mstislav rode in pursuit. They found him at the lakes hiding in a pine grove. A certain Voibor Genechevich attacked him and repeatedly struck him on the head with a sabre while another Tork stabbed him in the thigh with a spear until Izyaslav fell off his horse. Rostislav and Mstislav approached him as he lay dying. Rostislav lamented:

Brother Izyaslav, are you satisfied now? Ruling Chernigov was not enough for you so you evicted me from Kiev. But even then you were not content and tried to drive me out of Belgorod as well.

Izyaslav asked for water, but they gave him wine. He drank it and, on March 6, 1161, "gave up the spirit."[315]

According to pious tradition, the prince was killed because he failed to take the usual precaution. He did not wear the hair shirt that had once belonged to his eldest brother, Svyatosha, who had died a monk.[316] One source describes Izyaslav's death as follows:

---

[313] Ipat., col. 516; Mosk., p. 70.
[314] Ipat., cols. 516–17. The Hypatian chronicler ended his account for the year 1161 at this point and continued the narrative under the year 1162.
[315] Ipat., cols. 517–18; Makhnovets', pp. 281–3; Mosk., pp. 70–1; N4, p. 159. Concerning the dates, see Berezhkov, p. 173.
[316] *Dynasty*, p. 398; see above, p. 30.

Whenever he went on a campaign, he wore the hair shirt, and so remained unhurt. But once he had committed a sin and did not dare to put it on, and so he was killed in battle; he had previously given instructions that he was to be buried in it.[317]

The monastic author does not identify Izyaslav's transgression, but the sin he may have had in mind was Izyaslav's slanderous accusations of Rostislav.[318]

Izyaslav's body, like that of his cousin Igor' fifteen years earlier, was temporarily placed in the Monastery of St. Simeon in Kiev. Later it was moved to Chernigov where it was interred on March 13. Izyaslav had ruled Chernigov and thus merited being buried inside its Holy Saviour Cathedral. Surprisingly, however, he was laid to rest next to his father, David, in the Church of SS. Gleb and Boris. Was Izyaslav's burial in his father's church deemed a greater honor then being entombed in the dynasty's mausoleum (figure 3)?

Although Svyatoslav and Izyaslav had been nominal allies before Izyaslav's death, Svyatoslav had reason to be displeased with his cousin. He disapproved of Izyaslav's intrigues and wars. More important, perhaps, was the consideration that at the time of Izyaslav's death he was not the prince of Chernigov. Indeed, he was an *izgoi*, and it was perhaps because of this status most of all that Svyatoslav refused to inter him in the dynasty's cathedral. In burying him in the smaller edifice, therefore, Svyatoslav slighted the erstwhile prince of Chernigov. It was the final humiliation of a bellicose prince who had fought ruthlessly to attain supreme power in Rus'.

Izyaslav's death was of great importance for the dynasty. It left the ranks of the Davidovichi at a dangerously low ebb. He evidently had no sons. What is more, in 1161 his four deceased brothers were survived by only one male offspring, Svyatoslav Vladimirovich.[319] It became his lot to champion the family's political claims and to propagate its line. Svyatoslav, however, who had married only a few months earlier, had not yet produced an heir. By contrast, the Ol'govichi were burgeoning: Svyatoslav Ol'govich boasted of having three sons and two nephews. The future of the dynasty therefore appeared to rest in their hands. In effect, Izyaslav's demise signalled the death-knell for the Davidovichi as a political force.

His death was also of great importance for inter-dynastic relations. It meant that Rostislav Mstislavich had lost his most bellicose rival for Kiev. Since no other challenger declared his hand, peace had a chance of returning

---

[317] Heppell, *The "Paterik,"* pp. 135–6.
[318] Under the same year, the chronicler tersely reports that Ivan Berladnik died in Solun' (Thessalonica), where it was generally believed that he was poisoned (Ipat., col. 519; Mosk., p. 71).
[319] Zotov, pp. 261–2.

Figure 3   A princely sarcophagus made from Vruchiy slate in the Church of SS.
Gleb and Boris, Chernigov

to Rus′. The most critical question was what policy Rostislav would adopt towards the Ol′govichi. Would he overlook their collaboration with Izyaslav because conspirators had duped them, or would he demand retribution for their betrayal? Significantly, Rostislav's last words to Izyaslav suggested that he held the dead prince responsible for the turmoil that had engulfed Rus′. But whether Rostislav chose to punish the Ol′govichi or not, he and Svyatoslav must have been relieved to see the cause of their recent wars irrevocably buried.

SVYATOSLAV OL′GOVICH AS SENIOR PRINCE

After the death of Izyaslav Davidovich, Svyatoslav Ol′govich, now the undisputed prince of Chernigov, chose to work in concord with Rostislav who was reinstated in Kiev. On the one hand, the latter pardoned the Ol′govichi for their disloyalty and, on the other, Svyatoslav, his three sons, and his two nephews kissed the Holy Cross to him.[320] Svyatoslav Vladimirovich of the Davidovichi, as we shall see, also joined Rostislav's alliance.

In the following year, 1162, Rostislav faced insubordination in his own dynasty. His younger brother Vladimir Mstislavich seized Sluchesk sometime after Rogvolod had used it as a sanctuary in the previous year.[321] By capturing the domain of the Ol′govichi he transgressed against Svyatoslav, whose rights Rostislav had pledged to defend. Rostislav therefore sent a number of junior princes to expel his brother. These included Rostislav's son Ryurik, Svyatopolk Yur′evich (whose father's domain of Turov was adjacent to Sluchesk),[322] three Ol′govichi (Svyatoslav Vsevolodovich, his brother Yaroslav, and Oleg Svyatoslavich), Svyatoslav Vladimirovich of Vshchizh, and the 'Krivskie princes'.[323] The latter probably included Rogvolod and Bryacheslav Vasil′kovich, who was Svyatoslav Vsevolodovich's brother-in-law. On seeing their large force Vladimir sued for peace and went to his brother Rostislav in Kiev.[324] Consequently, the alliance between Rostislav and Svyatoslav passed its first test.

---

[320] Mosk., p. 71; Erm., p. 45; L′vov, p. 122; s.a. 1162: Ipat., col. 520.
[321] In 1161, Volodar of Gorodets drove out Rogvolod from Polotsk forcing him to flee to Sluchesk (Mosk., p. 71; Ipat., col. 519).
[322] Baum., II, 22.
[323] Under the year 1129, when the chronicler speaks of the Krivskie princes, he identifies them as princes of Polotsk (Mosk., p. 31).
[324] Ipat., col. 521. A number of sources erroneously call the town in question Lutsk instead of Sluchesk (for example, Mosk., p. 72; Erm., p. 45).

During the early 1160s, while the princes of Rus' were preoccupied with their political squabbling, they also became embroiled in a passionate religious dispute. Contrary to custom, Bishop Leon of Suzdal' advocated rigorous fasting practices. Our purpose is not to examine Leon's heresy, as his teachings became known, but to determine Svyatoslav's role in the dispute.

We are told that, in 1161, Andrey Bogolyubskiy expelled Leon from Suzdal' and, in the following year, allowed him to return to Rostov. After some four months the prince asked him for permission to eat meat on Wednesdays and Fridays from Easter to the Feast of All Saints. Leon granted him permission to eat meat only on the Wednesday and the Friday of Easter week, insisting that he scrupulously observe the fasts during the remaining weeks. The bishop also ordered him to abstain from meat on the feasts of Christmas and the Baptism of Our Lord if they fell on a Wednesday or a Friday. Andrey expelled Leon from his lands, we are told, because the bishop's false teaching threw the Christians into great consternation.

Sometime in 1163, it would seem, Leon arrived at Svyatoslav Ol'govich's court in Chernigov. The prince placated him and then sent him to Rostislav in Kiev. The news that Leon stopped in Chernigov on his way to Kiev is noteworthy. Since Chernigov was the second most important eparchy in Rus', he probably made a special effort to persuade its prince to support his position. Svyatoslav, after all, had demonstrated his pro-Constantinopolitan bias earlier, in 1158, when he had given sanctuary to the deposed Metropolitan Konstantin. As noted above, Svyatoslav had supported Konstantin, a Greek whom the patriarch had appointed as metropolitan, and not Klim, a native of Rus' whom the local bishops had appointed as metropolitan. The prince's pro-patriarchal leanings probably led Leon to believe that Svyatoslav was also favorably disposed to his stringent position on fasting because it was the patriarch's view.[325] The news that Svyatoslav consoled Leon and that the two parted as friends suggests that the prince welcomed the bishop either out of courtesy or out of sympathy for his teaching.

In Kiev, however, Metropolitan (*Vladyka*) Fedor condemned Leon's views.[326] Towards the end of the year, or perhaps at the beginning of 1164, he

[325] E. S. Hurwitz, *Prince Andrej Bogoljubskij: The Man and the Myth* (Firenze, 1980), p. 26.
[326] The text is unclear concerning Fedor. Since, however, the only known bishop of Suzdalia who may have been alive at this time was Leon's predecessor Nestor (Lav., cols. 351–2) the *vladyka* (that is, bishop, archbishop, or metropolitan) to whom the chronicler refers must be Metropolitan Fedor, whom Leon visited in Kiev. The metropolitan died in 1163 (Mosk., p. 72; Erm., p. 46; compare Ipat., col. 522; see Berezhkov, pp. 175–6).

therefore went to Constantinople to exonerate himself. On the bank of an unnamed river, Archbishop Andrian of Bulgaria condemned Leon's views before Manuel I Comnenus. When the bishop challenged the emperor, Manuel's aides struck him down and wanted to drown him. All the envoys who had come from Kiev, Chernigov, Suzdal', and Pereyaslavl' witnessed the incident.[327]

According to the report, a number of princes sent envoys to monitor Leon's fate in Byzantium. That these envoys were not resident officials in Constantinople but men especially selected to accompany Leon from Rus' is suggested by the information that they searched out Manuel I at some unidentified river between Kiev and Constantinople, where the emperor was evidently conducting military maneuvers.[328] Surprisingly, Leon sought endorsement for his teaching from the emperor, who supported the lenient view on fasting, rather than from the patriarch, who championed the strict observance. It is unlikely that Leon made this blunder intentionally. More than likely the princes' envoys, who sought to justify their customary ways, steered him towards the emperor. We are not told. In the light of the evidence that the chronicler considers Leon's defeat to be approbation of the traditional fasting practices in Rus', it seems likely that the prince, the bishop, and the people of Chernigov rejected Leon's heresy.

SVYATOSLAV'S DEATH

The prince to whom the envoys reported Leon's fate may not have been Svyatoslav Ol'govich, but his successor. At the beginning of 1164, Svyatoslav became grievously ill and summoned his son Oleg from Kursk. The latter's *druzhinniki* advised him to go quickly to Chernigov because his cousin, Svyatoslav Vsevolodovich of Novgorod Severskiy, was not on friendly terms with either him or his father and might conspire against him. Oleg therefore rode quickly to Chernigov but arrived only to discover that his father had died three days earlier, on February 15.[329]

---

[327] Ipat., col. 520; Mosk., p. 72; compare Tip., pp. 79–80; s.a. 1164: Lav., cols. 351–2. Concerning the chronology of events, see Berezhkov, pp. 174–5. For somewhat different interpretations of the events, see Senyk, *A History of the Church in Ukraine*, p. 151, and Hurwitz, *Prince Andrej Bogoljubskij*, pp. 26–9.

[328] It has been suggested that Leon met Manuel I at the Danube where, in 1164, the emperor was preparing to attack the Hungarians (Berezhkov, p. 333, n. 106).

[329] Ipat., cols. 522–4; Makhnovets', pp. 285–6. Tatishchev provides the introduction to the account that is missing in the Hypatian Chronicle (Tat. 4, p. 268; Tat. 3, p. 79). Compare Mosk., pp. 72–3. Concerning the date, see Berezhkov, p. 176.

Svyatoslav's demise did not come as a surprise. His health had been failing for a number of years to judge from the chronicler's reference to his obesity, which debilitated his movements. Before his death Svyatoslav, whose baptismal name was Nikolay, put on the monastic habit and adopted the name Gavriil.[330] He would have been interred inside the Holy Saviour Cathedral. Since he had married his first wife, a Polovtsian princess, in 1108, he must have been in his sixties when he died.[331] His second wife, the Novgorodian Catherine (Ekaterina), and six children survived him.[332] Of the latter, neither Oleg nor the daughter who married Roman Rostislavich of Smolensk attended his burial. Because they were significantly older than the other children, their mother had probably been Svyatoslav's first wife. Igor', Vsevolod, and Maria, however, were most likely in Chernigov with their mother, Catherine.[333] Her second daughter, whose existence is known only from a graffito found on a choir wall in St. Sofia in Kiev, was probably also living at home.[334]

Svyatoslav expressed an active interest in religion and culture. As we have seen, he opposed the appointment of Metropolitan Klim and became involved in Leon's controversy. Indeed, he demonstrated an active interest in religious issues as early as 1137, when he produced a statute (*ustav*) regulating the relationship between the bishop and prince in Novgorod.[335] He evidently built the wooden Church of the Ascension in his patrimony of Putivl'. Moreover, as senior prince, it was his duty to oversee the dynastic monasteries in Chernigov and St. Simeon's in Kiev. We have examined a number of unique accounts concerning the Ol'govichi that were written either in great detail or presented as short entries. Much of this information was recorded in the family chronicle that he commissioned and, as we shall see, his sons Oleg and Igor' continued.[336] Finally, it has been suggested that after he became prince of Chernigov, he ordered a silver ceremonial cup to be made in Constantinople in imitation of the one that his predecessor Vladimir Davidovich had owned (figure 4).[337]

---

[330] Zotov, pp. 264–5.   [331] *Dynasty*, p. 241.   [332] Zotov, p. 265; *Dynasty*, p. 338.

[333] Concerning Svyatoslav's five children known from the chronicles, see Zotov, pp. 269–71.

[334] See above, p. 93.

[335] Three copies of the statute have survived (Ya. N. Shchapov, *Knyazheskie ustavy i tserkov' v Drevney Rusi XI–XIV vv.* [M., 1972], p. 150; *Dynasty*, pp. 100–1).

[336] M. D. Priselkov, *Istoriya russkogo letopisaniya XI–XV vv.* (L., 1940), pp. 50–2; Likhachev, *Russkie letopisi i ikh kul'turno-istoricheskoe znachenie* (M.-L. 1947), pp. 183–9; A. N. Nasonov, *Istoriya russkogo letopisaniya XI-nachala XVIII veka* (M., 1951), p. 107; A. A. Shakhmatov, *Obozrenie russkikh letopisnykh svodov XIV–XVI vv.* (M.-L., 1938), p. 72.

[337] The cup, along with two others, was part of a hoard discovered in 1985 on the citadel of Chernigov; see V. P. Kovalenko, "Chasha kniazia Ihoria," *Istoriia Rusi-Ukrainy* (Istoriko-arkheolohichnyi zbirnyk), O. P. Motsia (gen. ed.) (K., 1998), pp. 142–51. Concerning Vladimir's ceremonial cup, see above, pp. 65–6.

Figure 4   Ceremonial bowl of Svyatoslav Ol'govich

Most important for the Ol'govichi, however, were Svyatoslav's political achievements. After his brother Igor' was taken captive, he saved the
patrimonial domains of the Ol'govichi, including the capital of Novgorod
Severskiy, the Vyatichi lands, and the Posem'e region, from the predatory
claws of the Davidovichi. His plight echoed that of his father, Oleg, who in
1096 fought successfully to prevent his patrimony from being appropriated
by his hostile cousins.[338] Moreover, after salvaging the political fortunes of
the Ol'govichi, Svyatoslav usurped Chernigov from Izyaslav Davidovich.
He therewith reasserted the hegemony of the Ol'govichi in the dynasty.
Consequently, even though Svyatoslav never attained supreme authority
as prince of Kiev, his achievements for the Ol'govichi were of paramount
importance.

RIVALRY FOR SUCCESSION TO CHERNIGOV

Svyatoslav was the last prince of the third generation. After his death seniority in the dynasty passed into the hands of the next generation of Ol'govichi.

---

[338] Concerning Oleg's fights with Svyatopolk Izyaslavich and Vladimir Monomakh, see *Dynasty*,
pp. 194–207.

We must remember that Svyatoslav had been the youngest of four brothers (Vsevolod, Igor', Gleb, and Svyatoslav) and that the eldest, Vsevolod, was the only other brother who had sons. Therefore, at the time of Svyatoslav's death, the Ol'govichi were divided into two branches: the senior branch made up of Vsevolod's sons Svyatoslav and Yaroslav, and the junior or cadet branch constituting Svyatoslav's sons Oleg, Igor', and Vsevolod. Consequently, according to genealogical seniority, Svyatoslav Vsevolodovich of Novgorod Severskiy was the rightful successor to Chernigov. Even so, the pro-Oleg chronicler accuses Bishop Antony of acting perfidiously in informing Svyatoslav of his uncle's death. Granted, breaking his oath not to tell Svyatoslav was a grievous moral transgression. But to give the bishop his due, by informing the rightful successor that the throne was vacant, he was honouring the system of lateral succession.

Svyatoslav Ol'govich's advisers recognized Svyatoslav Vsevolodovich's claim and plotted against him. They feared that, on occupying Chernigov, he would uproot them from their positions of favor and replace them with his own officials. They therefore handed over the town to Oleg who demonstrated no desire to usurp the town. His objectives evidently were to rescue his father's wealth, to protect his stepmother and half-siblings, and to acquire the best possible domains for the cadet branch.

On assuming control of Chernigov, Svyatoslav Vsevolodovich would become the chief dispenser of domains. In that capacity, he was expected to respect existing practices, above all, the right of each prince to rule his patrimony. Accordingly, members of the senior branch would keep the Vyatichi lands while members of the cadet branch would retain the Posem'e region. Moreover, he would assume jurisdiction over the distribution of domains that over the years had reverted to the senior prince from princes who had died without heirs or who had forfeited control of their domains. Examples of such territories were Igor''s patrimony and the lands of the Davidovichi. Oleg's intention was to obtain from Svyatoslav as generous an allocation of these lands as possible before relinquishing control of Chernigov to him. But whatever towns Svyatoslav pledged to hand over to Oleg and to his half-brothers Igor' and Vsevolod, he broke his promise.[339]

On becoming prince of Chernigov, Svyatoslav, who had held Novgorod Severskiy in his capacity as the eldest prince of the senior branch, relinquished it to Oleg as the eldest prince of the cadet branch. In doing so, he bypassed his younger brother, Yaroslav who, as Oleg's genealogical senior, had prior claim to the town. Svyatoslav therewith changed the order of

---

[339] Ipat., cols. 522–4; compare Mosk., pp. 72–3.

succession to the patrimonial capital of the Ol'govichi. After that, Novgorod Severskiy would, in effect, become the capital of the cadet branch. We are not told what town, if any, became the capital of the senior branch. Most likely, Svyatoslav anticipated that Chernigov would serve that function. He probably believed that from then on the senior branch would continuously produce the dynasty's senior princes according to the system of genealogical seniority and they would become the sole claimants for the dynastic capital.

Svyatoslav Vsevolodovich had excellent credentials for becoming senior prince. His father, Vsevolod, had been a powerful prince of Kiev who had organized a cadre of supporters there. Svyatoslav could also profitably use his family relationship to his mother's brothers, the Mstislavichi, whose eldest surviving member, Rostislav, was the prince of Kiev. Svyatoslav's ambition would also be a determining factor. In the rivalry between his uncles Izyaslav Mstislavich and Svyatoslav Ol'govich, he had demonstrated judicious compliance. Granted, his growing ambition drove him to foolishly side with Vyacheslav of Kiev against his own dynasty. But by doing so, he ingratiated himself with Rostislav. After Svyatoslav Ol'govich's death, his expeditious appointment of his son, probably Vladimir,[340] to Gomiy,[341] and his *posadniki* to other Chernigov towns, bespoke his resolve to secure his supremacy in the dynasty. He also demonstrated ruthlessness by breaking his promises to Oleg. Finally, Svyatoslav was fortunate to attain the office of senior prince in his prime. In 1164 he was not yet forty years of age.[342] As we shall see, his reign as senior prince would last for thirty years.

---

[340] This is the first time the chronicler mentions not only that Svyatoslav had children, but that he had a son already politically active. Zotov proposes, correctly it would seem, that the son in question was Vladimir (Zotov, p. 272; see also Makhnovets', p. 286).

[341] To judge from the information that Svyatoslav sent his only active son to rule Gomiy, it was still an important regional center. Earlier, the town had belonged to Svyatoslav's murdered uncle Igor' (see above, p. 24). After the latter's death, it was appropriated by Izyaslav Davidovich, who fled to it for safety in 1158 after being driven from Kiev (see above, p. 89).

[342] Since his parents were married before 1127, he was probably born before that date (*Dynasty*, p. 362).

2

The fourth generation: 1164–1201

Since owning towns was one of the main sources of princely power, control of domains had been one of the main bones of contention between the Ol′govichi and the Davidovichi in their rivalry for supremacy in the dynasty. Later, a similar rivalry arose among the Ol′govichi. We have seen that Svyatoslav Vsevolodovich of Chernigov, the first senior prince of the fourth generation, refused to hand over to Oleg Svyatoslavich of Novgorod Severskiy the domains that he had promised. This was the first occasion after the 1140s, when Igor′ and Svyatoslav had argued over domains with their brother Vsevolod of Kiev,[1] that the Ol′govichi quarreled among themselves over territorial allocations. In this rivalry, the senior prince of the senior branch was pitted against the senior prince of the cadet branch. Nevertheless, after Svyatoslav occupied Chernigov, Oleg refrained from immediately challenging him over his breach of promise.

BIRTHS, MARRIAGES, AND DEATHS

For the next few years an atmosphere of peace settled on the Chernigov lands. It was highlighted by dynastic births, marriages, and deaths. On June 29, 1164, Oleg Svyatoslavich married Agafia the daughter of Rostislav Mstislavich of Kiev.[2] His first wife, the daughter of Yury Dolgorukiy, had evidently died. After losing his personal tie with the dynasty of Suzdalia, it is not surprising that Oleg chose his second wife from the House of Smolensk since, as we have seen, four years earlier Rostislav had demonstrated a special fondness for him.[3] By becoming Rostislav's son-in-law, Oleg offset the advantage that Svyatoslav of Chernigov had over him as Rostislav's nephew. In 1165 the cadet branch formed yet another personal tie with the prince of Kiev. Oleg's sister Maria married Rostislav's nephew, Yaropolk

---

[1] See for example, *Dynasty*, pp. 369–76.
[2] See s.a. 1165: Ipat., cols. 524–5; Gust., p. 308; see Berezhkov, p. 176.
[3] See above, p. 96.

Izyaslavich of Buzhsk.[4] In the same year, however, Oleg's Novgorodian stepmother died.[5] Following her husband's death in Chernigov, she had probably accompanied Oleg to her former home of Novgorod Severskiy, where Igor', Vsevolod, and her two daughters had been born. Finally, two years after Oleg and Agafia were married they had a son. They christened him Boris but gave him the secular name of Svyatoslav.[6]

Under the year 1166, the chronicler also gives family news about the senior branch. First, he reports that Yaroslav Osmomysl of Galich brought Boleslava, a daughter of Svyatoslav Vsevolodovich, as wife for his eldest son and heir apparent, Vladimir.[7] The union created a promising family relationship for Svyatoslav's sons, who became Vladimir's brothers-in-law. More importantly, however, Svyatoslav himself benefited from the marriage alliance. It strengthened his bargaining power with the prince of Kiev who had to keep in mind that Svyatoslav and Yaroslav, his neighbours to the northeast and the southwest, were allies.

Second, the chronicler reports that the daughter of Andrey, who had married Oleg, the son of Svyatoslav, died.[8] Circumstantial evidence shows that the Oleg in question was the son of Svyatoslav Vsevolodovich of Chernigov.[9] Thus, while Oleg of Novgorod Severskiy was ingratiating himself with the Mstislavichi of Smolensk, Svyatoslav established marital ties with the Monomashichi in Suzdalia. Unfortunately for Svyatoslav, the untimely demise of the princess dealt a serious blow to his plans for establishing a family association with Andrey Bogolyubskiy.[10]

But the most important death in 1166 occurred sometime in the spring. Svyatoslav Vladimirovich, the grandson of David, died in Vshchizh.[11] At the time of his death, Vshchizh was a strongly fortified town. This is testified to by the news that, in 1160, it withstood a siege for five weeks.[12] Indeed,

---

[4] Maria was evidently Yaropolk's second wife; see s.a. 1166: Ipat., col. 525; Gust., p. 308; Berezhkov, p. 177; Zotov, p. 271. Concerning Yaropolk, see Baum., V, 40.

[5] Catherine died in 1165; see s.a. 1166: Ipat., col. 525; Gust., p. 308. Concerning the date, see Berezhkov, p. 177.

[6] See s.a. 1167: Ipat., col. 526; Gust., p. 308; s.a. 1166: Mosk., p. 74. Concerning the date, see Berezhkov, p. 177.

[7] See s.a. 1167: Ipat., col. 527; Gust., p. 308.

[8] See s.a. 1167: Ipat., col. 527; compare Gust., p. 308.

[9] See, for example, s.a. 1166: Mosk., p. 74 which mistakenly identifies Oleg the son of Svyatoslav Vsevolodovich (who married Andrey's daughter) as Oleg the son of Svyatoslav Ol'govich (who married Andrey's sister). Concerning Oleg's identity, see Zotov, p. 272.

[10] It has been suggested that Oleg's wife was the daughter of Andrey Vladimirovich prince of Vladimir in Volyn' (Baum., V, 17); see A. Ekzemplyarsky, "Chernigovskie knyaz'ya," *Russkiy biograficheskiy slovar'* (Spb., 1905; reprint, Kraus, 1962), vol. 22, pp. 252–3. Since Oleg was born after Andrey Vladimirovich died in 1142, it is unlikely that Oleg married the daughter of this Andrey.

[11] See s.a. 1167: Ipat., col. 525.   [12] See above, p. 94.

archaeological evidence shows that, during the middle of the twelfth century, the old defensive wall was torn down, the old ditch was filled in, and the town's boundaries were expanded. The citizens built two new earthen walls and a deep ditch around the outer town. At the same time, they erected a stronger fortification made of oak trees around the *detinets*.[13] Since Svyatoslav was evidently the first resident prince of Vshchizh, he probably initiated the rebuilding projects. His death was a milestone in the dynasty. Because he evidently had no sons, it signaled the demise of the already politically powerless Davidovichi. Consequently, the Ol'govichi became the only family in the dynasty.[14] They acquired sole rights to the office of senior prince, to the patrimonial capital of Chernigov, and to all the Chernigov lands, including the towns of the defunct Davidovichi.

SVYATOSLAV VSEVOLODOVICH FACES TWO PROBLEMS

Early in his reign as senior prince, Svyatoslav was introduced to the two problems that would eventually preoccupy him in Chernigov. The first was the rivalry over disputed domains. Since the earliest days of princely rule in Rus', custom held that if a prince died without an heir his surviving brothers divided his domain among them.[15] Because Svyatoslav Vladimirovich had no surviving brothers, his domain passed to the closest living relatives, the Ol'govichi. Svyatoslav, as the senior prince of the Ol'govichi, held the authority to allocate the dead prince's domains. Unfortunately for Oleg, Svyatoslav sought to increase the landholdings of his own family at the expense of the cadet branch. When Oleg challenged his preferential treatment of the senior branch by demanding an equitable share of the domains, it became clear that the territorial disputes, which had alienated the Ol'govichi from the Davidovichi for the past twenty years, had not disappeared with the demise of the latter. Rather, they were merely transferred to the senior and cadet branches of the Ol'govichi.

---

[13] B. A. Rybakov, "Raskopki vo Vshchizhe v 1948–1949," KSIIMK 38 (1951), pp. 34–41, and his "Vshchizh – udel′nyy gorod XII veka," KSIIMK 41 (1951), pp. 56–8. Archaeologists also discovered the remains of a three-nave masonry church, which was built at the end of the twelfth or the beginning of the thirteenth century (Rappoport, pp. 48–9).

[14] We should keep in mind that after 1127 the Yaroslavichi, the descendants of Yaroslav the youngest brother of Oleg and David, became the ruling dynasty in the lands of Murom–Ryazan' and lost all claims to the Chernigov lands (*Dynasty*, pp. 319–20).

[15] The chronicles report a number of earlier instances when brothers asked that they be given a share of the lands that belonged to their deceased brother or brothers. For example, around 980 Vladimir made this demand to his elder brother Yaropolk and, around 1026, Mstislav made the same demand to his elder brother Yaroslav the Wise (Dimnik, "Succession and Inheritance," pp. 102–3, 112–3). For additional examples, see *Dynasty*, pp. 89–90, 139–40.

The chronicler gives only a vague description of the disputed domain. We know, for example, that Svyatoslav kept the best districts for his family. Accordingly, he gave Vshchizh to one of his sons.[16] Surprisingly, even though Vshchizh was the regional capital of the domain, the chronicler claims that Svyatoslav gave his brother Yaroslav the choice district. Although he does not identify it, indirect evidence points to Starodub. Since Oleg challenged Svyatoslav's allocations by attempting to capture Starodub, it evidently formed part of the dead prince's domain. Moreover, the news that its citizens invited Oleg to rule them shows that they preferred him to Svyatoslav's appointee, Yaroslav of Ropesk. The latter's appointment would also explain why he sent troops to Starodub and why they arrived ahead of Oleg. They were the contingent commanded by the *posadnik* whom Yaroslav sent to administer the town.

We are not told what towns Svyatoslav allotted to Oleg. The latter's dissatisfaction, however, shows that he believed them to be less important than Vshchizh and Starodub. Despite his discontent, Oleg had to sue for peace because he fell ill. Svyatoslav therefore gave him four unidentified towns, which implies that these did not include Vshchizh and Starodub.[17] Thus, Svyatoslav's allocations remained inequitable because he kept the choice towns for the senior branch.

The second problem that Svyatoslav would have to address was the attacks of the Polovtsy. Oleg, the chronicler tells us, did not renew the rivalry over domains after recovering from his illness. Instead, he campaigned against Khan Kobyak (Karlyevich) and defeated the Polovtsy.[18] We are not told whether he engaged in a defensive battle or if he launched an offensive raid. If it was the former, Oleg was probably defending his patrimonial possessions in the Kursk region, which were extremely vulnerable to nomadic attack. If his campaign was an offensive expedition, we can find at least one motive for his retaliation. During his conflict with Svyatoslav the latter had used the nomads for attacking Novgorod Severskiy. Granted, they terminated the attack before reaching the town, but on their way home to their tents the tribesmen undoubtedly pillaged Oleg's Posem'e districts.

Additional entries under 1166 show that the nomads were intensifying their raids on Rus'. On seeing how the Ol'govichi were living in strife, the nomads attacked merchants coming from the Greeks. Rostislav of Kiev

[16] One view has it, probably correctly, that the son was Oleg (Makhnovets', p. 287). As we have seen, the son who occupied Gomiy at an earlier date was probably the elder Vladimir.

[17] See s.a. 1167: Ipat., cols. 525–6; s.a. 1166: Mosk., pp. 73–4.

[18] According to Pletneva, Kobyak was a khan of the Lukomorskie Polovtsy from the region of the Black Sea and the Sea of Azov (*Polovtsy*, p. 147).

therefore sent troops to defend the caravans as they travelled along the Dnepr rapids.[19] Moreover, at about the time of Oleg's campaign, a Polovtsian band captured a certain Shvarn beyond Pereyaslavl' and massacred his *druzhina*.[20] That winter, the chronicler continues, the Ol'govichi led more campaigns against the nomads. Oleg captured the tents of Khan Koza,[21] carried away his wife and children, and seized his silver and gold. Yaroslav Vsevolodovich, for his part, destroyed the camp of Khan Beglyuk (Beluk).[22] Even though the chronicles do not report all the Polovtsian raids, the Ol'govichi campaigns suggest that the nomads were directing most of their attacks against the Chernigov lands. The Kievan side of the Dnepr was spared for the time being. The Polovtsy had not raided Rus' for over a generation. From now on their attacks would escalate until they reached their climax in the mid-1180s. Significantly, Svyatoslav Vsevolodovich chose not to risk going into battle in person.

THE MSTISLAVICHI FIGHT FOR KIEV

Soon after succeeding to Chernigov, Svyatoslav also monitored the first power struggle for Kiev. Towards the end of 1166, Rostislav Mstislavich set off for Novgorod. When he reached Chichersk on the river Sozh', Oleg and Agafia met him.[23] It appears that, after being alerted to the trip Agafia's father was making through Oleg's lands, the couple went from Novgorod Severskiy to greet him. As the host, Oleg entertained his father-in-law with a feast. Rostislav reciprocated with a similar gesture of friendship. Exchanging gifts formed part of the ritual greetings. Undoubtedly, an important objective of Rostislav's visit, but one the chronicler does not mention, was to see his new grandson Svyatoslav. From Chichersk he continued his trip to Novgorod. On March 14, 1167 he died on his way home from Smolensk.[24]

His death set in motion the process of succession to Kiev. Such a period of political instability normally found the princes of Chernigov renegotiating alliances, going to war if a succession rivalry broke out, or making their

---

[19] Ipat., col. 526; Mosk., p. 74.   [20] See s.a. 1167: Ipat., col. 527; s.a. 1166: Mosk., p. 74.
[21] He was evidently Koza Sotanovich (Pletneva, *Polovtsy*, pp. 151–2).
[22] See s.a. 1168: Ipat., col. 532; compare Makhnovets', p. 289; s.a. 1167: Mosk., p. 75. The Ol'govichi campaigned during the same winter in which Rostislav travelled to Novgorod, namely in 1166 (Berezhkov, p. 178). Since the princes attacked during the heart of winter, this must have been either in January or February of 1167.
[23] As we have seen, in 1158 Izyaslav Davidovich as prince of Kiev had given Chichersk to Oleg's father Svyatoslav (see above, p. 86). The latter treated it as his personal possession rather than as a domain that he acquired in his capacity as prince of Chernigov. This is suggested by the news that, after his death, it passed to his son Oleg rather than to his nephew Svyatoslav Vsevolodovich, his successor on the throne of Chernigov.
[24] See s.a. 1168: Ipat., cols. 528–32; compare s.a. 1167: Mosk., pp. 74–5; Lav., col. 353; s.a. 1166: NPL, pp. 32, 219. Concerning the date, see Berezhkov, pp. 67, 177–9.

own bid for Kiev. On this occasion, Svyatoslav Vsevolodovich expressed no desire to occupy the capital of Rus'. In accordance with the system of lateral succession, he expected Vladimir Mstislavich of Dorogobuzh to replace his deceased brother.[25]

On May 19, 1167 Mstislav Izyaslavich of Vladimir in Volyn' was installed on his father's throne in Kiev. In seizing the capital of Rus', however, he violated the lateral system of succession in denying his uncle, Vladimir Mstislavich, his rightful place in Kiev. At first, Vladimir himself supported Mstislav's selection. He was undoubtedly influenced to do so by the groundswell of opposition to his own claim. On the one hand, the Mstislavichi backed Mstislav because they thought, wrongly, that they could manipulate him. On the other hand, the Kievans preferred Mstislav because his leadership qualities outshone those of Vladimir. What is more, Mstislav was the son of the popular Izyaslav Mstislavich, whom the Kievans had avidly supported against Igor' Ol'govich. Vladimir, however, had defended Igor' from the Kievan mob and therewith demonstrated pro-Ol'govichi sentiments.

Vladimir proved their suspicions to be correct by fleeing to the Radimichi lands of the Ol'govichi.[26] This is not surprising since, as we shall see, his son Mstislav had married one of Svyatoslav Vsevolodovich's daughters.[27] Moreover, while fleeing through the Chernigov lands, he sought out his half-sister Maria in Glukhov, north of Putivl',[28] entrusted his wife and children to her,[29] and then sought safety in Ryazan'. By helping the fugitive, Maria indirectly drew her son Svyatoslav of Chernigov into Vladimir's camp. Svyatoslav's Novgorodian step-grandmother drew him into Vladimir's camp even further.[30] After Mstislav expelled her from Kiev because her son

---

[25] Baum., V, 32.
[26] The Radimichi lands were located east of the Dnepr along the basins of the rivers Sozh and Iput', and included the towns of Chichersk and Gomiy which belonged to the Ol'govichi.
[27] See below, pp. 135–6.
[28] Maria's presence in Glukhov suggests that the town was her personal possession, which she may have received as a wedding gift from her father-in-law Oleg (d. 1115) (see above, p. 89). Maria probably moved to Glukhov around 1146 or as soon as was conveniently possible after her husband's death. Consequently, in 1167 Glukhov was not part of Oleg's patrimonial domain in the Posem'e district.
[29] Ipat., col. 537. Maria's father Mstislav Vladimirovich (d. 1132) had married twice. His second wife, the daughter of a Novgorodian *posadnik* whom he married in 1122 (NPL, pp. 21, 205; Mosk., p. 28), was the mother of the Vladimir who left his wife in Glukhov. Maria's mother was Mstislav's first wife, the Swedish princess Christina, who died in 1122 (NPL, pp. 21, 205; Mosk., p. 28). This is supported by the news that Maria married Vsevolod Ol'govich before 1127 (*Dynasty*, pp. 313–14). Maria was therefore Vladimir's half-sister (Baum. V, 7, 22, 30). She was, of course, the mother of Svyatoslav Vsevolodovich of Chernigov.
[30] She was also Mstislav's step-grandmother. His father Izyaslav was born of Mstislav Vladimirovich's Swedish wife who died before Mstislav's second marriage in 1122 (Baum. V, 7, 23, 36). Since Izyaslav is reported as being politically active in 1127 (Lav., cols. 296–7; Mosk., p. 30), he would have been no more than four years of age had his mother been the Novgorodian second wife.

Vladimir was seeking to depose him, she fled to Svyatoslav. In welcoming her, Svyatoslav demonstrated that he remained on friendly terms with his step-uncle Vladimir even though he had pledged allegiance to Mstislav.[31]

AN ALL-RUS' CAMPAIGN AGAINST THE POLOVTSY

Svyatoslav's loyalty to Mstislav Izyaslavich was put to the test at the beginning of 1168, when the latter summoned the princes of Rus' to join him against the Polovtsy. The Ol'govichi sent the two Vsevolodovichi, Svyatoslav and Yaroslav, as well as Oleg Svyatoslavich and his youngest brother, Vsevolod. The Monomashichi were represented by Ryurik Rostislavich from Vruchiy (Ovruch), Yaroslav Izyaslavich from Lutsk, Gleb Yur'evich from Pereyaslavl', and many others. They set out on March 2.

Mstislav's decision to lead an all-Rus' campaign against the nomads shows that their raids had intensified. He accused them of two offenses. First, despite their pacts with the princes, they carried off Christians into captivity. Mstislav's main objective, therefore, was to stop the loss of vital human resources. Second, the tribesmen cut off trade on the southern routes to Kiev: the route from the Greeks along the Dnepr, the route along which salt was brought overland from Crimea along the Dnepr, and the overland route from the Caspian region, the so-called Zaloznyy put'. Mstislav's secondary objective, therefore, was to restore the uninterrupted flow of trade to Rus'.[32]

The Ol'govichi willingly joined the expedition because their domains suffered on both counts. We have already seen how the princes of the senior and cadet branches joined forces to conduct retaliatory raids against tribes that took booty and captives from the Posem'e and the Zadesen'e regions. As for trade, merchants conducting business in Kiev normally also visited Chernigov. Consequently, any disruption to Kievan trade affected the flow of goods through Chernigov.

On March 11 the princes reached the Polovtsian camps on the rivers Ugla (Orel') and Snoporod (Samara),[33] but the tribesmen had fled abandoning their wives, children, and possessions. Mstislav led the main force in pursuit,

---

[31] See s.a. 1169: Ipat., cols. 532–7; Makhnovets', pp. 289–92; compare s.a. 1168: Mosk., pp. 75–7. Concerning the date, see Berezhkov, pp. 179–80.

[32] It has been suggested that the periodic disruptions to trade along these routes did little permanent damage to the economy of Rus' (see P. B. Golden, "Aspects of the Nomadic Factor in the Economic Development of Kievan Rus'," *Ukrainian Economic History: Interpretive Essays*, I. S. Koropeckyj [ed.] [Cambridge, Mass., 1991], pp. 97–9).

[33] The rivers, both eastern tributaries of the Dnepr, are located south of the Vorskla, southeast of the Pereyaslavl' lands (Makhnovets', p. 293).

routed the enemy at the Black Forest (*Chernyy les*),[34] and sent troops after the nomads who had fled east beyond the river Oskol.[35] After their victory, the men of Rus' set free the captive Christians and seized much booty. Mstislav, however, alienated all the princes because, without informing them, he allowed his men to plunder the camps secretly at night. The princes returned home on Easter Day, March 31.[36]

Mstislav's all-Rus' campaign against the Polovtsy was the first since 1129, when his grandfather Mstislav Vladimirovich (d. 1132) drove the tribesmen beyond the Volga.[37] Although princes from both sides of the Dnepr participated in the campaign, they attacked tribes on the east bank. According to the few entries which have reported nomadic raids to date, these occurred in the Pereyaslavl' and Chernigov lands. On this occasion, the princes scored an overwhelming victory, but their very success led to dissension. Mstislav's surreptitious conduct antagonized his relatives and the Ol'govichi.

THE PRINCES OF RUS' SACK KIEV

During the remainder of the year animosity towards Mstislav grew and disaffected *boyars* levied false accusations against him. They told David Rostislavich that Mstislav was planning to take him and his brother Ryurik captive. Even though Mstislav kissed the Holy Cross to them, they distrusted him. Soon after, Mstislav offended Vladimir Andreyevich of Dorogobuzh by refusing to give him additional domains. Meanwhile, the Novgorodians expelled Svyatoslav thereby angering not only his brothers, the Rostislavichi, but also Andrey Bogolyubskiy, who supported his rule. When, on April 14, Mstislav sent his son Roman to Novgorod, most of the princes condemned his action. They spent the rest of the year conspiring and forming alliances against him.[38]

While the princes were plotting how to rid themselves of Mstislav, they were also growing increasingly disgruntled with his friend Metropolitan Konstantin for his "falsehood" (*nepravda*).[39] Towards the end of 1168, he

---

[34] This was located east of the river Ugla along the river Donets (Severniy Donets) at the mouth of the Oskol (Makhnovets', p. 576). According to another view, the forest was in the Pereyaslavl' lands (L. L. Murav'eva and L. F. Kuz'mina [compilers], *Imennoy i geograficheskiy ukazateli k Ipat'evskoy letopisi* [M., 1975], p. 111).

[35] The chronicle calls the river Vskol' (Vorskol) (Ipat., col. 540; compare Makhnovets', p. 293).

[36] See s.a. 1170: Ipat. cols. 538–40; compare s.a. 1168: Mosk., pp. 77–8; and s.a. 1167: NPL, pp. 32–3, 220. Concerning the date, see Berezhkov, p. 180.

[37] Mosk., p. 31; *Dynasty*, p. 322.

[38] See s.a. 1170: Ipat., cols. 540–3; s.a. 1168: Mosk., p. 78; s.a. 1167 and 1168: NPL, pp. 32–3, 219–20.

[39] Under the year 1167, a number of the chronicles report that Metropolitan Konstantin, evidently a Greek, came to Rus' (for example, NPL, pp. 32, 219).

placed *Igumen* Policarp of the Caves Monastery under a ban forbidding him to eat butter and drink milk on Christmas and Epiphany, when these fell on a Wednesday or a Friday. Bishop Antony of Chernigov supported the metropolitan and repeatedly condemned Svyatoslav Vsevolodovich for eating meat on those feast days. Svyatoslav cautioned Antony to stop reproaching him on pain of being evicted from the eparchy. But the bishop persisted in his pestering so Svyatoslav expelled him from Chernigov.[40] His action would have increased his popularity with the townspeople but strained his relations with Mstislav.

In rejecting the strict observance of fasting, Policarp and Svyatoslav upheld the practices of the Caves Monastery and the populace. Konstantin and Antony, however, adhered to Leon's so-called heresy.[41] The chronicles do not say if popular antagonism was directed only against the metropolitan or also against the prince of Kiev. In the light of Mstislav's refusal to censure Konstantin either for his intransigence or for his injustice towards Policarp, however, we may assume that it was.

That winter, Andrey Bogolyubskiy sent his son Mstislav with troops from Suzdalia to attack Mstislav Izyaslavich in Kiev. Andrey's alliance was made up of eleven princes including five of his relatives (a son, two of his brothers, one of his nephews, and a cousin from Dorogobuzh), four Rostislavichi, and two Ol'govichi. Additional reinforcements evidently came from Polotsk, Murom, Ryazan', and Beloozero.[42] At the eleventh hour, the alliance received assistance from the Torki and the Berendei, who deserted Mstislav Izyaslavich. Despite the large number of princes who wished to evict Mstislav from Kiev, not all deserted him. Andrey's brother Mikhalko remained loyal,[43] as did Mstislav's brother Yaroslav and the Kievans. Also numbered among his friends was Yaroslav Osmomysl, his uncle Vladimir Mstislavich, Svyatopolk Yur'evich of Turov, and, significantly for our investigation, Svyatoslav of Chernigov with his brother Yaroslav. Unfortunately for Mstislav, aside from his brother Yaroslav and the traitorous tribesmen, no allies came to his aid when Andrey's alliance attacked.

[40] See s.a. 1168: Lav., cols. 354–5; Mosk., p. 79. According to a number of sources, the metropolitan imprisoned Policarp (for example, s.a. 1169: L'vov, p. 124). The compiler of Nikon. alone adds that Antony went to Kiev and stayed with the metropolitan (see s.a. 1168: Nikon. 9, p. 236). These events happened shortly before the sack of Kiev in March of 1169 because, as we shall see, the chronicler refers to the metropolitan's falsehood as one of the reasons why Kiev suffered the catastrophe.
[41] Concerning the fasting controversy, see above, pp. 102–3.
[42] See s.a. 1171: Ipat., cols. 544–6; compare Makhnovets', pp. 294–6; s.a. 1168: Lav., cols. 354–5; Mosk., pp. 78–9. Concerning the troops from Polotsk, Murom, and Ryazan', see NPL, s.a. 1168: pp. 33, 220–1. Concerning the troops from Beloozero, see s.a. 1169: L'vov, p. 124; Erm., p. 47.
[43] On his march south, Mstislav took captive Andrey's younger brother Mikhalko, whom Mstislav Izyaslavich had sent to assist his son in Novgorod (s.a. 1170: Ipat., cols. 543–4).

To judge from later information and from the news that the princes spent most of the summer negotiating the terms of their collaboration against Mstislav Izyaslavich, we may assume that they agreed on the following issues: their willingness to conduct the campaign under Andrey's command, and their acceptance of his younger brother Gleb as Mstislav's replacement in Kiev. Why did they concede to Andrey on both counts? His military might was a compelling consideration which they could not ignore. Nevertheless, there were probably more important reasons for their concurrence. He was the genealogically eldest prince of the coalition and a rightful claimant to Kiev.

After Rostislav's death, as we have seen, the genealogically senior prince among the Mstislavichi was his youngest brother, Vladimir Mstislavich of Dorogobuzh. After he failed to occupy Kiev, however, he was debarred. The next in seniority were his cousins, the sons of Yury Dolgorukiy; the eldest of these was Andrey Bogolyubskiy.[44] His seniority gave him the right to act as commander-in-chief of the coalition. Refusing to participate in the campaign in person, however, he delegated command to his eldest son. More importantly, hoping to turn Vladimir on the Klyaz'ma into a Kiev of the north, he refused to occupy the capital of Rus' and appointed his younger brother Gleb to rule it in his stead. As the next in precedence, Gleb also had the right to sit on the throne of his father. Indeed, all of Yury's sons had a prior claim to Mstislav Izyaslavich. In this way, the capital of Rus' once again became the bone of contention between two families in the House of Monomakh, the Yur'evichi and the Mstislavichi.

The Ol'govichi were also divided. We must remember that Svyatoslav Vsevolodovich was of the same generation as Andrey so he enjoyed comparable seniority in his dynasty. Moreover, Svyatoslav's father had occupied Kiev giving him the right to sit on the throne of his father. Despite this right, however, he expressed no overt interest in ruling the capital of Rus' but remained loyal to Mstislav Izyaslavich. He was probably motivated to do so by his oath of allegiance and by the family tie to his cousin. Oleg, however, collaborated with Yury's family just as his father Svyatoslav had done. Indeed, Oleg had married Andrey's sister. More importantly, the princes of the cadet branch had grievances against Mstislav going back some twenty years. They recalled how he had helped his father Izyaslav expel their father Svyatoslav from Novgorod Severskiy and Putivl', and how he had occupied Kursk.

---

44 Baum., V, 16; VI, 4.

Although the main objective of the coalition was to evict Mstislav from Kiev, the two-day rampage shows that the troops from Smolensk, Suzdal', Chernigov, and Oleg's *druzhina*, had a deep-seated resentment of the Kievans. Their ill will was undoubtedly motivated by their jealousy of Kiev's commercial prosperity, cultural riches, and ecclesiastical splendor. Moreover, Yury's sons probably exacted compensation from the Kievans for their complicity in his death. As for Oleg and Igor' of the cadet branch, they avenged the murder of their uncle, Igor'. This may explain why the chroniclers single out Oleg's *druzhina* as being especially zealous in pillaging Kiev.

The victors plundered the *podol'* and the citadel including St. Sofia, the Tithe Church, and the monasteries. The pagans set fire to the Caves Monastery and desecrated churches before putting them to the torch. Sparing no one, they led into captivity those Christians who survived the slaughter. The chronicler concludes by reporting that the catastrophe befell Kiev "because of our sins" and "for the metropolitan's falsehood." On March 8, 1169,[45] Andrey's son Mstislav appointed his uncle Gleb of Pereyaslavl' to Kiev and returned to his father in Suzdalia with great glory and honor.[46]

There is no evidence that the allies sought to destroy Kiev. The Mstislavichi and the Ol'govichi, in particular, had vested interests in maintaining its pre-eminence because they were claimants to its throne.[47] As was to be expected, the damage to the town was temporary because the Kievans demonstrated uncanny resiliency. Archaeological excavations reveal that the town preserved its role as a center of commerce and that its trade flourished during the twelfth and the first half of the thirteenth century. The period witnessed spectacular growth in its industrial output and in the export of its manufactured articles. Its craftsmen produced items such as glassware, glazed ware, and jewelry. It was the leading producer of religious goods, amber items, and objects made from Vruchiy slate.[48]

---

[45] According to Berezhkov, the date was March 12, 1169 (p. 181).

[46] Concerning the campaign, see s.a. 1171: Ipat., cols. 544–6; compare Makhnovets', pp. 294–6; s.a. 1168: Lav., cols. 354–5; Mosk., pp. 78–9. See also, J. Pelenski, "The Sack of Kiev in 1169: Its Significance for the Succession to Kievan Rus'," in *The Contest for the Legacy of Kievan Rus'*, East European Monographs 377 (Boulder, 1998), pp. 46–8.

[47] There has been much debate among historians whether or not Kiev lost its pre-eminence in Rus' after it was sacked by Andrey's alliance. Concerning the discussions, see Tolochko, *Drevnyaya Rus'*, pp. 138–42; *Emergence of Rus*, pp. 323–4; *Crisis*, p. 6.

[48] T. S. Noonan, "The Flourishing of Kiev's International and Domestic Trade, ca. 1100–ca. 1240," *Ukrainian Economic History: Interpretive Essays*, I. S. Koropeckyj (ed.) (Cambridge, Mass., 1991), pp. 115, 131, 137, 145–6, and D. B. Miller, "The Kievan Principality in the Century before the Mongol Invasion: An Inquiry into Recent Research and Interpretation," HUS 10, nr. 3/4 (1986), 215–23.

Chronicle information confirms that it retained its status as the political, ecclesiastical, and cultural capital of Rus' up to the Tatar invasion.

THE AFTERMATH

Following the sack of Kiev, Gleb Yur'evich consolidated his rule. His tasks included subduing the Polovtsy on both sides of the Dnepr,[49] but his greatest challenge came from Mstislav Izyaslavich. In February of 1170, while Gleb was visiting his son in Pereyaslavl', Mstislav attacked Kiev. His brother Yaroslav, his uncle Vladimir Mstislavich, Yaroslav Osmomysl's troops from Galich, and Svyatopolk Yur'evich from Turov accompanied him. Svyatoslav of Chernigov and his brother Yaroslav also sent troops.[50] The Kievans opened the gates to Mstislav, but when he besieged Vyshgorod, David Rostislavich resisted. On April 13, Gleb came across the Dnepr with reinforcements forcing Mstislav to withdraw. David sent the Polovtsy in pursuit. As they passed the town of Mikhailov[51] they routed the princeling Vasil'ko Yaropolchich when he confronted them.[52] Later, Gleb destroyed Mikhailov but allowed Vasil'ko to seek asylum with Svyatoslav in Chernigov.[53] From this we see that Svyatoslav demonstrated his solidarity with Mstislav by helping him against Gleb and by offering sanctuary to Mstislav's nephew Vasil'ko.[54]

In addition to Mstislav's failure to regain Kiev, the chroniclers report a number of noteworthy events. On January 28, 1170, before Mstislav attacked Kiev, his enemy Vladimir Andreyevich of Dorogobuzh died. Vladimir Mstislavich, who in the meantime had returned from Ryazan', seized his town.[55] On August 19, Mstislav Izyaslavich fell ill, died, and was buried in Vladimir in Volyn' (figure 5).[56] Following his death, the

---

[49] According to the sources, he himself concluded a pact with the Polovtsy who came to negotiate on the left bank in the Pereyaslavl' lands. He sent his brother Mikhalko, however, to drive off the tribesmen who, having come to the river Ros' to negotiate peace, decided to pillage the Kievan land (s.a. 1169: Lav., cols. 357–61).

[50] The Hypatian chronicler introduces the account under the year 1171 and continues it under the year 1172 (Ipat., col. 547). Concerning the date, see Berezhkov, pp. 180–1.

[51] The town was in the Kievan land, evidently near the river Ros' (Barsov p. 125; compare Makhnovets', p. 558).

[52] Baum., V, 50.

[53] See s.a. 1172: Ipat., cols. 548–50; compare Makhnovets', pp. 297–8 and Gust., pp. 311–12. Concerning the date of Mstislav's retreat from Kiev, see Berezhkov, p. 182.

[54] In 1165 Vasil'ko's father Yaropolk had remarried and taken as his wife Maria, the sister of Oleg of Novgorod Severskiy. Oleg therewith became Vasil'ko's uncle (see above, pp. 108–9; Baum., IV, 31). Nevertheless, his family tie to his Monomashich uncle Mstislav dictated his political relationship with Svyatoslav of Chernigov.

[55] See s.a. 1171: Ipat., cols. 546–8. Concerning the date, see Berezhkov, pp. 181–2.

[56] See s.a. 1172: Ipat., col. 559. Concerning the date, see Berezhkov, pp. 183–4.

Figure 5   Cathedral of the Assumption, Vladimir in Volyn', where Mstislav
Izyaslavich was buried

Novgorodians expelled his son Roman and invited Andrey Bogolyubskiy
to be prince. On October 4 he sent Ryurik Rostislavich to rule Novgorod.[57]
Finally, that winter, the Polovtsy pillaged towns on the Kievan side of the
Dnepr. Gleb, gravely ill, was forced to send his younger brothers Mikhalko
and Vsevolod in pursuit.[58]

The death of Mstislav Izyaslavich terminated the political alliance that
had been centered on him. Accordingly, Svyatoslav of Chernigov lost a
powerful backer. In the meantime, the fortunes of Oleg's ally Andrey
Bogolyubskiy greatly improved when he obtained control of Novgorod.
By appointing Ryurik to the town, he strengthened his position further by
ingratiating himself with the Rostislavichi. Andrey's great military resources
in Suzdalia, his jurisdiction over Novgorod, his control over the princes of

[57] NPL, pp. 33, 221–2.
[58] See s.a. 1171: Lav., cols. 362–3. Concerning the date, see Berezhkov, pp. 76–7.

Murom and Ryazan', and his overlordship over Kiev now made him the most powerful prince in the land. Since Oleg of Novgorod Severskiy belonged to Andrey's alliance, his future looked more promising than that of Svyatoslav Vsevolodovich.

In 1170, Oleg's brother Igor' had a personal reason for rejoicing. On October 8, his son Vladimir, christened Peter, was born.[59] The boy's birth is the first allusion to Igor''s marriage. His wife, as we shall see, was Yaroslavna or the daughter of Yaroslav Osmomysl.[60] Vladimir's family tie with the dynasty of Galich would, as we shall see, play an important part in his political career. Indeed, disputes that would eventually implicate all of Igor''s sons in Galicia, dramatically reared their heads that very year.

Igor''s mother-in-law, Princess Olga, fled to the Poles with her son Vladimir. After eight months, her supporters in Galich persuaded her to return. They reported that they had taken her husband Yaroslav captive, had killed his henchmen, had burned his concubine Nastaska on a pyre, and had placed her son Oleg, Yaroslav's favourite, under lock and key. They had also made Yaroslav promise to treat Olga with due respect. "In this way, they were reconciled."[61] The chroniclers tell us little about Igor''s relations with his in-laws, but later events will show that he maintained ties with at least his wife's brother Vladimir.

The following year, 1171, the senior branch also grew in number. On June 24 a son was born to Yaroslav Vsevolodovich. He gave the child the princely name of Rostislav, but christened him Ivan.[62] The chroniclers neglect to reveal the identity of Yaroslav's wife, but the *Lyubetskiy sinodik* calls her Irene.[63] Assuming that Rostislav was their first-born, the couple married sometime in the autumn of the previous year.[64]

Earlier, on January 20, 1171, Gleb Yur'evich of Kiev died from his illness.[65] On February 15, the genealogically eldest prince from the House of Monomakh, Vladimir Mstislavich of Dorogobuzh, seized the

---

[59] See s.a. 1173: Ipat., col. 562; Gust., p. 313. Concerning the date, see Berezhkov, p. 187. Zotov suggests that Igor' had two sons named Vladimir (p. 276), but there is no chronicle evidence for this assertion.

[60] Basing their observations on the evidence of the *Slovo o polku Igoreve*, a number of historians have suggested that Yaroslavna's name was Evfrosinia and that she may have been Igor''s second wife (Baum., III, 16 and IV, 28; Zotov, p. 270; for a discussion of this problem, see M. D. Kazan, "Yaroslavna," *Entsiklopediya "Slova o Polku Igoreve"* [Sankt-Peterburg, 1995], vol. 5, pp. 295–7). The chronicles neither give Yaroslavna's name nor suggest that she was Igor''s second wife.

[61] See s.a. 1173: Ipat., col. 564; Gust., p. 313. Concerning the date, see Berezhkov, p. 188.

[62] See s.a. 1174: Ipat., col. 568. Concerning the date, see Berezhkov, p. 189.

[63] Zotov, pp. 267–8.

[64] Zotov suggested that Rostislav may have had an elder brother named Igor', who is mentioned only by Tatishchev (Tat. 4, pp. 326, 341–2; Tat. 3, pp. 166, 185; Zotov, pp. 40–1, 274). It has been argued elsewhere that this is an unlikely identification and that the Igor' in question, if he existed, was probably the son of Oleg Svyatoslavich ("Pitfalls," pp. 140, 142–5).

[65] See s.a. 1173: Ipat., cols. 563–4. Concerning the date, see Berezhkov, pp. 187–8.

town,[66] but Andrey Bogolyubskiy demanded that he abdicate because he had renounced his claim under oath. On May 10, Vladimir died. Although his demise left the Yur'evichi of Suzdalia next in line, Andrey decided not to give Kiev to another of his younger brothers. Perhaps Gleb's turbulent career made him reject that option. After the Yur'evichi, the next eligible candidate was Mstislav Izyaslavich's younger brother, Yaroslav, but Andrey rejected the hostile candidate outright. Instead, he chose Roman, the senior prince of the Rostislavichi, because the latter acknowledged him as their father. Roman occupied Kiev at the beginning of July.[67] The appointment boded well for Oleg of Novgorod Severskiy because he and Roman were brothers-in-law. It is noteworthy, however, that in giving Kiev to a Mono-mashich, Andrey ignored the claim of Svyatoslav, the senior prince of the Ol'govichi.

IGOR''s FIRST VICTORY AGAINST THE POLOVTSY

Around six months after Gleb's death, the Polovtsy renewed their raids along the river Ros'.[68] At the same time, they attacked towns belonging to the Ol'govichi. On the Feast of St. Peter,[69] Igor' Svyatoslavich led a campaign against the invaders. The chronicler does not identify his domain. To judge from earlier evidence, however, it was Putivl'. As we have seen, in 1159 Igor''s brother Oleg ruled Putivl', but in the following year he asked his father for Kursk.[70] In 1161, before his father died, Oleg was ensconced in Kursk while Igor' was living with his father in Chernigov.[71] Since Oleg preferred Kursk to Putivl', we may assume that after he took over control of Novgorod Severskiy, he retained Kursk as his patrimonial domain but gave Putivl' to Igor'.

Igor''s first reported campaign against the Polovtsy was a success. After crossing the river Vorskla, he learnt that Khans Kobyak and Konchak were devastating districts around Pereyaslavl'.[72] He crossed back over the river

---

[66] See s.a. 1173: Ipat., col. 566; compare s.a. 1171: NPL, pp. 34, 222. Concerning the date, see Berezhkov, p. 188.

[67] See s.a. 1174: Ipat., cols. 567–8. Concerning the date, see Berezhkov, p. 189.

[68] See s.a. 1174: Ipat., col. 568.

[69] This was probably the Feast of SS. Peter and Paul, which fell on June 29.

[70] See above, pp. 96–7.   [71] See above, pp. 103–4.

[72] Khan Konchak, mentioned here for the first time, lived until the beginning of the thirteenth century. He unified many of the Polovtsian tribes and, around 1184, seemingly achieved the peak of his power. His tribesmen lived in the basin of the river Donets. Concerning his career, see S. A. Pletneva, "Donskie polovtsy," *"Slovo o polku Igoreve" i ego vremya*, B. A. Rybakov (ed.) (M., 1985), pp. 265–79, her *Polovtsy*, pp. 156–68, and B. A. Rybakov, *"Slovo o polku Igoreve" i ego sovremenniki* (M., 1971), pp. 100–2.

at Ltava and rode to confront the raiders.[73] On July 20 his *druzhina* killed many of the nomads and took others captive.[74] To judge from the account, Igor' was the only prince on the expedition. Consequently his attacking force was small because it was made up primarily of his personal *druzhina*. In conducting his raid he followed the example of Oleg who, in 1166, campaigned against Kobyak on his own.[75] By defeating the two khans, he ingratiated himself with Vladimir Glebovich of Pereyaslavl', whose lands bore the brunt of the marauding, and with Roman of Kiev, who had the responsibility of overseeing the defense of Rus'.[76]

While returning from his victory via Pereyaslavl', Igor' visited the shrine of SS. Boris and Gleb to celebrate their feast. He arrived at Vyshgorod on the vigil. Igor''s visit was motivated, in part, by his devotion to the *strastoterptsy*. He therewith confirmed that the practice of visiting the shrine of St. Gleb, whom Svyatoslav Yaroslavich the progenitor of the dynasty had adopted as his patron, remained popular.[77]

After celebrating the feast of the two brothers on July 25, Igor' met with Roman, Ryurik, and Mstislav, exchanged gifts and returned home.[78] We have seen that the ritual of exchanging gifts was used to cement marriage contracts, political alliances, and personal ties.[79] In this instance it seemingly confirmed two such events. After Roman had occupied Kiev earlier in the month, the feast of the *strastoterptsy* was the first occasion on which Igor' had the opportunity to visit him. Their meeting was political in nature in that Igor' would have pledged allegiance to the new ruler of Kiev. Furthermore, as we have seen, Roman had married Igor''s sister. Consequently, the visit also gave Igor' an opportunity to firm up personal ties with his brother-in-law and the other Rostislavichi. We may assume that Svyatoslav of Chernigov had a similar meeting with Roman at which he pledged his allegiance.

[73] The so-called Zaloznyy put', or trade route from the Caspian, crossed the river Vorskla at the town of Ltava (see Makhnovets', p. 557 and his map).
[74] See s.a. 1174: Ipat., cols. 568–9; Makhnovets', p. 307; compare Gust., p. 314. Concerning the date, see Berezhkov, p. 189.
[75] See above, p. 111.
[76] Pletneva points out that this was the first occasion on which Konchak and his Donets Polovtsy waged an independent attack on the lands of Rus'. For this purpose, he formed an alliance with Kobyak of the Lukomorskie Polovtsy (*Polovtsy*, p. 157).
[77] *Dynasty*, pp. 76–9, 126–7.
[78] Concerning Igor''s visit to Vyshgorod, see s.a. 1174: Ipat., col. 569.
[79] We know a number of occasions on which princes exchanged gifts, namely, in 1147 when Svyatoslav Ol'govich met Yury Dolgorukiy at Moscow and concluded a marriage alliance (see above, p. 41), in 1159 when Rostislav met Svyatoslav Ol'govich at Moroviysk and negotiated a political agreement (see above, pp. 91–2), and in 1166 when Rostislav and Oleg exchanged gifts at Chichersk on a family visit (see above, p. 112).

Thus we see that the Hypatian Chronicle gives two reports of Polovtsian raids. The first, a terse entry recording a raid on the river Ros' basin, was probably written by a Kievan scribe. The second was probably recorded by Igor's chronicler. In making his report each scribe was influenced by his political and geographical orientation. Their combined information, however, tells us useful news about Polovtsian policy. Instead of negotiating a pact with Roman as they normally did with a new prince of Kiev, the tribesmen evidently decided to launch attacks on both sides of the Dnepr.

SVYATOSLAV BUILDS A CHURCH AND HARBORS A FUGITIVE

In the meantime Svyatoslav Vsevolodovich, who had successfully consolidated his rule, began realizing his ambitious building program. In 1173 he laid the foundation for the stone church of St. Michael in the prince's court in Chernigov.[80] The church was probably completed some three years later, but its location in the northeast corner of the *detinets* has not been determined.[81] Some historians have suggested that, in light of the church's dedication, St. Michael was Svyatoslav's patron.[82] Significantly, this is the first chronicle reference to church construction in Chernigov for some fifty years. Svyatoslav's grandfather, Oleg, and the latter's brother, David, were the last princes to found churches in the patrimonial capital.[83] In laying the foundation for his first church Svyatoslav, as we shall see, initiated an extensive building program.

Archaeological evidence reveals that during the last third of the twelfth century the prince of Chernigov increased the area of the *detinets* by a third. He filled in the ditch to the east of the Holy Saviour Cathedral and expanded the citadel to the river Strizhen'. He erected a new court in the expanded section, ordered a defensive wall to be constructed around the

---

[80] See s.a. 1174: Ipat., col. 571. Concerning the date, see Berezhkov, p. 190. For a description of the church, see Rappoport, p. 43.

[81] A number of investigators claim that the remains of the church have not been found. Among these are V. P. Kovalenko and P. A. Rappoport, "Pamyatniki drevnerusskoy arkhitektury v Chernigovo-Severskoy zemle," *Zograf* 18 (Beograd, 1987), p. 10; G. N. Logvin, *Chernigov, Novgorod-Severskiy, Glukhov, Putivl'* (M., 1980), p. 58. Among those who claim the church has been discovered are Belyaev, "Iz istorii zodchestva drevnego Chernigova," p. 4, and V. I. Mezentsev, "The Masonry Churches of Medieval Chernihiv," HUS 11, nr. 3/4 (1987), 379.

[82] Belyaev, "Iz istorii zodchestva drevnego Chernigova," p. 4. He bases his observation on the sphragistic evidence provided by Yanin. The latter observed that in 1181, Svyatoslav was prince of Novgorod for a period of time. During his stay there he probably issued seals. These, in Yanin's view, were ones with images of St. Michael and St. Cyril, the patron saints of Svyatoslav and his father Vsevolod (Yanin 1, pp. 105–6, 116, 203–4, 265, 306). Elsewhere it has been suggested that Vsevolod's baptismal name was George (*Dynasty*, p. 391).

[83] *Dynasty*, pp. 260–5, 301.

area, and built a ceremonial gate modeled on the Golden Gate of Kiev. It was capped with a small chapel. Although the chronicles do not reveal the identity of the prince who built the new court, it has been suggested, probably correctly, that the man was Svyatoslav.[84]

Although he avoided becoming implicated in the struggle for Kiev, he was drawn into the dynastic quarrel in Galicia. In that year, Vladimir Yaroslavich took his mother Olga and his wife Boleslava and fled from his father Yaroslav Osmomysl. He went to Yaroslav Izyaslavich in Lutsk, but Vladimir's father threatened to attack Yaroslav if he did not evict Vladimir. Yaroslav therefore sent him to Mikhalko Yur'evich in Torchesk, who was Olga's brother. Soon after, Svyatoslav Vsevolodovich, Vladimir's father-in-law, invited the fugitives to Chernigov with the intention of sending them to Andrey Bogolyubskiy. But, we are told, he did not.[85]

Svyatoslav offered sanctuary to his son-in-law, in part, because of their family tie. He considered providing safety for his daughter's family more important than the risk this entailed in antagonizing Yaroslav Osmomysl. Moreover, Svyatoslav's intention to send the fugitives to Suzdalia is the first hint the chronicler gives that Svyatoslav had become reconciled with Andrey Bogolyubskiy after the death of Mstislav Izyaslavich. Finally, in giving a helping hand, Svyatoslav once again demonstrated his penchant for offering sanctuary to fugitives. As we have seen, he had already provided asylum to Vladimir Mstislavich's mother and to Vasil'ko Yaropolchich of Mikhailov.

SVYATOSLAV MAKES A BID FOR KIEV

While Svyatoslav was concentrating on cultural and family affairs, Andrey Bogolyubskiy had difficulty in appointing his puppet to Kiev. At the beginning of 1173 he had ordered the Rostislavichi to hand over the three Kievans whom he accused of poisoning his brother Gleb.[86] Because they refused, he commanded Roman, David, and Mstislav to vacate Kiev, Vyshgorod, and Belgorod, and return to their Smolensk domains. Roman left Kiev and

---

[84] A. V. Kuza, V. P. Kovalenko, and A. P. Motsya, "Chernigov i Novgorod-Severskiy v epokhu 'Slova o polku Igoreve'," *Chernigov i ego okruga v IX–XIII vv.* (K., 1988), p. 63, and V. P. Kovalenko, "Itogi i zadachi izucheniya drevnego Chernigova," *Istoricheskoe kraevedenie v SSSR: Voprosy teorii i praktiki,* V. A. Kovalenko (ed.) (K., 1991), p. 206.

[85] See s.a. 1174: Ipat., col. 571; compare Gust., p. 314. Concerning the date, see Berezhkov, p. 190.

[86] The manner of Gleb's untimely death reflected that of his father Yury who died under questionable circumstances (see above, p. 82). Both lay ill for a number of days before their deaths, possibly owing to poison they had consumed. Since Andrey was aware of the hostility that the Kievans held towards his family, concern for his personal safety may have been one reason why he refused to occupy Kiev.

Andrey gave it to his own brother Mikhalko. The latter, however, handed it over to his younger brother Vsevolod and his nephew Yaropolk Rostislavich. On March 24, however, Roman's brothers retaliated, took Vsevolod and Yaropolk captive, and gave Kiev to Ryurik.[87]

After they had seized the town, the Rostislavichi consolidated their authority in the Kievan land. They marched against Mikhalko in Torchesk and offered him Pereyaslavl' in addition to Torchesk. In return, he deserted Andrey and Svyatoslav and joined the Rostislavichi. The latter also made a deal with Svyatoslav. They promised to release Vsevolod and his nephew Yaropolk Rostislavich if Svyatoslav would hand over to them Vladimir, whom they would return to Yaroslav Osmomysl in Galich. But the Rostislavichi reneged on their promise. Moreover, they expelled Yaropolk's brother Mstislav from Trepol' and he fled to Chernigov.[88]

The news that Mikhalko had deserted Andrey and Svyatoslav is the first concrete evidence that the two princes were allies. Indeed, in stating that Mikhalko deserted both, the chronicler speaks of the princes as co-equals. Svyatoslav's role in bartering on Andrey's behalf confirms this. He agreed to sacrifice his son-in-law to his fate with his father in Galich in order to free Andrey's brother and nephew. Svyatoslav assumed leadership of his allies in Rus' for good reasons: he was genealogically the most senior and politically the most powerful prince of the alliance in Rus'.

Andrey became enraged at the Rostislavichi for disobeying him. Svyatoslav and the Ol'govichi, we are told, were delighted with his fury. They sent messengers inciting him to wage war and promising to help. Andrey therefore commanded the Rostislavichi to abandon Rus'. The brothers resented being treated like subjects and declared their determination to defend their domains. They demonstrated their disdain for Andrey by cutting off his messenger's hair and beard.

Andrey's coalition, consisting of more than twenty princes and militias from many towns, was a formidable force but tenuous bonds held it together. It included participants who had been hostile to each other in the past, and who united in this endeavor for disparate reasons. The militias from the towns of Suzdalia were probably his most loyal troops. The auxiliaries from such towns as Novgorod, Murom, Ryazan', Smolensk, Polotsk, and Turov probably joined him primarily from fear of reprisals if they refused. The coalition also included his brothers Mikhalko and Vsevolod,

[87] See s.a. 1174: Ipat., cols. 569–71; Gust., p. 314; compare s.a. 1172: NPL, pp. 34, 222. Concerning the dates, see Berezhkov, pp. 189–90.
[88] See s.a. 1174: Ipat., cols. 571–2; Makhnovets', p. 308. According to the Gustinskiy Chronicle, Ryurik, while living in Kiev, sent Vladimir to his father in Galich, but Olga went to Moscow (*sic*) where she became a nun and took the name Evfrosinia (Gust., pp. 314–15). Concerning the date, see Berezhkov, p. 190.

and his nephews Mstislav and Yaropolk (the sons of his deceased brother Rostislav), all of whom he had evicted from Suzdalia. Consequently, their feelings towards Andrey must have been ambivalent. Their main reason for joining the attack would have been to find domains for themselves in the Kievan land.

The Ol′govichi also had a private agenda. They, like Andrey, wished to evict the Rostislavichi out of Kiev, but for a different reason. Andrey was angry with the brothers for their insubordination, for evicting his brother Vsevolod from Kiev, and for refusing to hand over Gleb's alleged murderers. The Ol′govichi, however, saw that Andrey had been unable to keep his underlings in Kiev and that the three Rostislavichi had little support from other princes for their usurpation. They therefore hoped to seize Kiev for themselves. There is evidence, albeit indirect, as we shall see, that Andrey concurred with Svyatoslav's intention to occupy the town.

The allies seized Kiev without a battle because the Rostislavichi abandoned the town. Ryurik went to Belgorod, Mstislav fortified himself in Vyshgorod with David's troops, and David rode to seek aid from Yaroslav Osmomysl in Galich. To judge from the information that the chronicler singles out only the Ol′govichi and the Monomashichi during the fighting, he clearly looks upon the campaign as a joint venture of the two dynasties. He makes it clear that Svyatoslav commanded not only the forces of the Ol′govichi, but that, with Andrey's assent, he was the commander-in-chief of the entire campaign. Andrey's brother Mikhalko led the contingents of the Monomashichi.

On September 8, Svyatoslav, accompanied by the Ol′govichi, Mikhalko and Vsevolod, their nephews the Rostislavichi, the Kievans, the Berendei, the forces of the Poros′e, and all the troops of Rus′, besieged Vyshgorod.[89] He ordered Igor′ Svyatoslavich and Vsevolod, later nicknamed "Big Nest" (*Bol′shoe Gnezdo*), to lead the junior Ol′govichi and Monomashichi against the town. Svyatoslav's choice of commanders shows that Igor′ and Vsevolod, though young, were already capable leaders. Both, as we shall see, would enjoy prominent careers.

Since Andrey conceded command of the campaign to Svyatoslav as his partner in the alliance, the two must have reached an agreement concerning the fates of the Rostislavichi and of Kiev after their victory. Andrey was determined to tame the Rostislavichi into submissive vassals who would acknowledge him as the senior prince in the House of Monomakh. He therefore insisted that they be evicted from their Kievan domains and relegated to less important towns in their patrimony of Smolensk.

---

[89] Concerning the date, see Berezhkov, p. 190.

Svyatoslav, who had his sights set on Kiev, assumed control of Kiev after Ryurik abandoned it. That is why Yaroslav of Lutsk, who brought reinforcements from Volyn' around November 10, offered to assist Svyatoslav and the Ol'govichi if they agreed to give him Kiev and to proclaim him the senior prince of Rus'.[90] But the Ol'govichi refused, Tatishchev explains, because they wanted to keep Kiev for Svyatoslav. When the Black Caps learnt that the Ol'govichi and Monomashichi intended to take the town for Svyatoslav, they exclaimed: "We have always pledged our allegiance to Vladimir Monomakh's clan, but now they are attempting to enthrone Svyatoslav. We do not want this." They therefore deserted.[91] The news that Andrey's brothers, who were also candidates for Kiev, expressed no surprise at the Black Caps' discovery supports their assertion. The princes had evidently been apprised of the plan. That is, Svyatoslav and Andrey had agreed before the campaign that Svyatoslav would rule Kiev.

The failure of the nine-week siege of Vyshgorod and the treachery of the Black Caps demoralized the allies. They feared that others would follow the example of the Black Caps who had recoiled at the prospect of placing an Ol'govich in Kiev. A general panic spread through their ranks and they fled. The Kievans also shared the Black Caps' frustration. They refused to enthrone Svyatoslav in Kiev and the Rostislavichi proclaimed Yaroslav of Lutsk to be the senior prince in Rus'.[92]

SVYATOSLAV DECLINES THE OFFER TO RULE KIEV

Svyatoslav, however, demanded that Yaroslav compensate him for his loss of Kiev. He reminded Yaroslav of the first pact that they had concluded. At that time, he pointed out, they had agreed that if Svyatoslav occupied Kiev he would give domains to Yaroslav, but if the latter occupied it he would give towns to Svyatoslav. Since Yaroslav had realized that objective, Svyatoslav demanded that he keep his promise.[93]

Svyatoslav and Yaroslav had probably formed their first pact in 1170, after the latter replaced his brother Mstislav Izyaslavich as senior prince of his family. Since Svyatoslav had been Mstislav's ally, he undoubtedly renewed the alliance with Mstislav's successor. That agreement was the first

[90] Concerning the date, see Berezhkov, p. 190. Yaroslav, as we have seen, was the younger brother of Mstislav Izyaslavich who died in August of 1170.

[91] Tat. 4, p. 283; compare Tat. 3, pp. 102–3.

[92] Concerning the attack on Kiev, see s.a. 1174: Ipat., cols. 572–8; Makhnovets', pp. 308–11; compare Mosk., p. 83. Tatishchev alone states that Yaroslav occupied Kiev on December 20 (Tat. 4, p. 284; Tat. 3, p. 103). In the light of this date, Makhnovets' suggests that Svyatoslav ruled Kiev from September 6 to December 18 or 19 (p. 309, n. 9).

[93] See s.a. 1174: Ipat., col. 578.

recorded occasion on which Svyatoslav expressed his intention to seek Kiev. As a result of that pact, Yaroslav asked Svyatoslav for Kiev after the latter took it from Ryurik. Svyatoslav rebuffed Yaroslav so he, in turn, denied Svyatoslav's request for Kievan towns some four months later. Moreover, Yaroslav argued that Svyatoslav had no right to "our patrimony." He claimed that Kiev was the inheritance of the Mstislavichi just as his great-grandfather Vladimir Monomakh had arranged with the Kievans. Svyatoslav objected, however, arguing that he had as much right to Kiev as Yaroslav because he also was descended from Yaroslav the Wise.

Svyatoslav attacked Yaroslav, occupied Kiev, and the townsmen enthroned him. This is confirmed by the report that he "sat on the throne of his grandfather and his father."[94] The most likely explanation for their about-turn was that they were disaffected with Yaroslav. On reoccupying Kiev, he gave credence to this observation by venting his anger against them for their lack of support. He also accused them of inviting Svyatoslav to replace him. Despite the citizens' backing, Svyatoslav decided not to rule Kiev. In September, when he had seized it from Ryurik, he had the support of Andrey's alliance. On this occasion, he had only his own forces. Moreover, his attack had caught Yaroslav's allies unprepared. Inevitably, Yaroslav would galvanize them into launching a counter-attack, one that Svyatoslav would find difficult to fend off. He therefore plundered Kiev for twelve days and withdrew. His seizure of Yaroslav's "countless wealth, wife, youngest son, and entire *druzhina*" suggests that his objectives were to avenge himself against Yaroslav and to coerce the latter into giving him domains in the Kievan land.

The Ol′govichi had evidently been united in attacking Yaroslav, but they had a falling out after their victory. Around January of 1174, when Yaroslav retaliated against Svyatoslav, we learn that Oleg of Novgorod Severskiy was pillaging Svyatoslav's lands. The latter therefore concluded peace with Yaroslav, put the torch to Oleg's domains, and returned to Chernigov.[95] Since Oleg evidently did not try to seize any of Svyatoslav's towns, his dispute was not over domains. Rather, he pillaged Svyatoslav's lands suggesting that he was venting his anger against Svyatoslav because the latter had wronged him. The event, which immediately preceded Oleg's rampage, was the attack of the Ol′govichi on Kiev. The most likely explanation for Oleg's discontent, therefore, was Svyatoslav's refusal to share with him an

---

[94] Once again, the chronicler uses the formula as an axiom rather than as a reflection of fact. Svyatoslav's grandfather, Oleg Svyatoslavich (d. 1115), never ruled Kiev. In using the formula, the chronicler wishes to signify Svyatoslav's official installation on the throne of Kiev.

[95] Concerning Svyatoslav's attack on Kiev, see s.a. 1174: Ipat., cols. 578–9; compare Makhnovets', p. 311; see s.a. 1175: Mosk., p. 83; Lav., cols. 366–7. Concerning the date, see Berezhkov, p. 190.

equitable amount of the booty that Svyatoslav had seized from Yaroslav.[96] But we are not told.

Antagonizing Oleg proved to be costly for Svyatoslav. Oleg's raid forced him to be reconciled with Yaroslav, who undoubtedly made him return the plundered wealth, drop his demand for Kievan towns, and hand back Yaroslav's family and *druzhina* without a ransom. What is more, Oleg devastated his domains before the two were pacified. The altercation shows that relations between the senior branch and the cadet branch were strained. Svyatoslav acted in a heavy-handed manner towards the junior branch in order to advance his own interests, but Oleg refused to tolerate unfair treatment from the senior prince.

But Svyatoslav's quest for Kiev would soon be put into abeyance because developments in Suzdalia changed the balance of power. Early in 1174, the Rostislavichi asked Andrey Bogolyubskiy to reinstate Roman in Kiev. Their request shows that, despite their recent falling out with him, they still acknowledged him to be the senior prince of the dynasty. It also reveals that they supported Yaroslav Izyaslavich out of expediency. If Roman could not control Kiev, they had preferred to have an ally from their own dynasty ruling it rather than an Ol'govich. Andrey remained loyal to Svyatoslav. We are told that he promised to give his answer to the brothers only after he received a reply from his allies in Rus'.[97] In other words, he refused to act without Svyatoslav's consent. Before Andrey could send his answer, however, his *boyars* murdered him on June 29.[98] His death removed the main obstacle to Roman's quest for Kiev, deprived Svyatoslav of his most powerful ally, and created a power vacuum in Suzdalia.[99]

RIVALRY FOR SUCCESSION IN SUZDALIA

Svyatoslav would play a salient role in the ensuing succession crisis in the northeast. Significantly, the four most eligible candidates – Andrey's two brothers Mikhalko and Vsevolod, and Andrey's two nephews, Mstislav

---

[96] As we learned from the princes' reaction to Mstislav's conduct on the campaign against the Polovtsy, when he allowed his troops to pillage the camps at night without informing his allies, princes were extremely critical of commanders who did not distribute equitably among all the participants the booty that they had taken on the campaign (see above, p. 115). As we shall see, in 1235 the Galician *boyars* were angry at Daniil's brother Vasil'ko for the same reason (see below, p. 333).

[97] Ipat., col. 580; compare s.a. 1175: Lav., col. 367.

[98] See s.a. 1175: Lav., col. 369; Ipat., col. 580. Concerning the date, see Berezhkov, pp. 78–9, 190–2.

[99] Concerning observations on Andrey's reign, see Hurwitz, *Prince Andrej Bogoljubskij*, pp. 20–2; *Emergence of Rus*, pp. 323–4, 350–1, 361–4; and J. Pelenski, "The Contest for the 'Kievan Succession' (1155–1175): The Religious–Ecclesiastical Dimension," in *The Contest for the Legacy of Kievan Rus'*, East European Monographs 377 (Boulder, 1998), pp. 21–43.

and Yaropolk – were refugees at his court. He had offered them sanctuary because of his alliance with Andrey and because of his senior status in Rus'. After Andrey's death, Svyatoslav became the undisputed senior prince and the most powerful prince of the Chernigov–Suzdalia alliance. As the protector of the junior Monomashichi, he was thus in a position to influence the selection of Andrey's successor.

Before Svyatoslav could dispatch candidates of his choice to Suzdalia, however, the people of Rostov, Suzdal', and Pereyaslavl' assembled at Vladimir on the Klyaz'ma to select a prince. Because Andrey's son Yury was in Novgorod and his brothers were in Rus', they asked Gleb Rostislavich of Ryazan' to join them in inviting his two brothers-in-law, Mstislav and Yaropolk, the sons of Andrey's eldest brother, Rostislav.[100] In doing so, the chronicler notes, the people broke their oaths to Yury Dolgorukiy because they selected his grandsons instead of his sons. Accordingly, as Tatishchev alone claims, it was probably Svyatoslav who persuaded the four Mono-mashichi to pledge loyalty to each other and to acknowledge the eldest, Mikhalko, as the senior prince.[101] The news that the princes took their oaths in the presence of the bishop of Chernigov bespeaks Svyatoslav's initiative in the ceremony. Despite his desire to assume a mediating role, however, Svyatoslav was soon forced to take sides.

After Mikhalko arrived in Vladimir on the Klyaz'ma, troops from Rostov, Murom, and Ryazan' besieged the town. Unable to repel the attack, its citizens reluctantly advised Mikhalko to flee to Chernigov.[102] The two Rostislavichi were therefore installed as princes: Mstislav sat in Rostov and Yaropolk sat in Vladimir.[103] On returning to Chernigov, Mikhalko un-doubtedly solicited Svyatoslav's help. Because the latter was an advocate of the lateral system of succession, he was predisposed to supporting Mikhalko, whom the other Monomashichi had acknowledged as their senior prince.

OLEG CHALLENGES SVYATOSLAV FOR DOMAINS

After the death of Andrey Bogolyubskiy, Svyatoslav faced a crisis at home. We are told that Oleg summoned his brothers-in-law, the Rostislavichi of Smolensk, to help him wage war against the Chernigov lands. Realizing that Svyatoslav had lost his most powerful ally in Andrey, Oleg consid-ered Svyatoslav's weakened position to be an opportune time for gaining

[100] Baum., VI, 1, 15–17.   [101] Tat. 4, p. 286; Tat. 3, pp. 107–8.
[102] See, for example, s.a. 1174: Erm., p. 50; s.a. 1175: Tver., col. 256.
[103] Concerning the succession dispute, see s.a. 1175: Ipat., cols. 595–8; compare Mosk., pp. 84–5; Lav., cols. 371–4.

concessions from him. The Rostislavichi also would not have attacked Svyatoslav if Andrey was alive because they were still waiting for Svyatoslav to
approve Andrey's reappointment of Roman to Kiev. After Andrey's death,
however, they would have jumped at the opportunity to retaliate against
Svyatoslav for having driven them out of Kiev. More importantly, by joining
Oleg they further undermined Svyatoslav's military potential and strengthened their own chances of regaining Kiev. Consequently, while Oleg and
his brothers attacked Starodub, which belonged to Svyatoslav's brother
Yaroslav, Yaroslav Izyaslavich and the Rostislavichi plundered Svyatoslav's
towns of Lutava and Moroviysk. After that, they concluded peace.

Oleg and his brothers failed to take Starodub. Since capturing the town
appeared to be his main objective, he was pressing his demand for more
domains. As we have seen, after the death of Oleg's father in 1164, Svyatoslav
had agreed to grant Oleg and his brothers additional towns. Oleg refused
to forgive Svyatoslav for reneging on that promise, but despite his repeated
attempts to seize additional domains, he failed. On this occasion, Svyatoslav
penalized Oleg by setting fire to the palisade of Novgorod Severskiy and
by killing many of his troops.[104] Thus, after ten years of arguing and of
going to war over promised towns, Svyatoslav finally forced Oleg to stop
his aggression.

The clergy also attempted to pacify the warring cousins. This is testified
to by the so-called "Sermon on princes" (*Slovo o knyaz'yakh*).[105] We do
not know in what year it was given, but it was probably preached in an
unidentified church in the Chernigov lands on May 2, the Feast of the
Translation of SS. Boris and Gleb.[106] The preacher, a bishop or an *igumen*,
was addressing princes embroiled in an internecine conflict. Rancor and
unforgivingness for a past offense fired their antagonism. He heaped shame
on them for their perjury, for their insubordination to their senior prince,
and for summoning pagans against their own kin. His aim was to stop the

[104] Concerning Oleg's attack, see s.a. 1175: Ipat., cols. 599–600; compare Gust., p. 316. Concerning the
      date, see Berezhkov, p. 193.
[105] For the texts and analysis of the sermon, see Kh. Loparev (ed.), "Slovo pokhvalnoe na prene-
      senie moshchey Svv. Borisa i Gleba," *Pamyatniki drevney pis'mennosti* 98 (Spb., 1894), pp. 1–30;
      P. V. Golubovsky, "Opyt priurocheniya drevne-russkoy propovedi 'Slovo o knyaz'yakh' k oprede-
      lennoy khronologicheskoy date," *Drevnosti*: Trudy Arkheograficheskoy Kommissii Imperatorskago
      Moskovskago archeologicheskago obshchestva, M. V. Dovnar-Zapol'sky (ed.) (M., 1899), vol. 1,
      vyp. 3, cols. 491–510; O. A. Lindeberg, "'Slovo o knyaz'yakh' (Problema sootnosheniya spiskov),"
      Literatura drevney Rusi: Istochnikovedenie (Sbornik nauchnykh trudov), D. S. Likhachev (ed.)
      (L., 1988), pp. 3–13; and P. Hollingsworth (trans. and intro.), *The Hagiography of Kievan Rus'*
      (Cambridge, Mass., 1992), pp. 219–28.
[106] One view has it that the sermon may have been delivered by Bishop Antony on May 2, 1175,
      in the St. Saviour Cathedral of Chernigov; see B. A. Rybakov, "Knyaz Svyatoslav Vsevolodovich
      (1125–1194)," *Materialy i issledovaniya po arkheologii drevnerusskikh gorodov*, vol. 1, N. N. Voronin
      (ed.), in *Materialy i issledovaniya po arkheologii SSSR* (M.-L., 1949), nr. 11, pp. 94, 95.

princes from fighting. If they refused they would suffer eternal damnation, but God would reward him who took the first step towards reconciliation. The preacher urged his listeners to imitate SS. Boris and Gleb, who had refused to raise a hand against their brother Svyatopolk, who deprived them not only of their domains but also of their lives. Moreover, he singled out David Svyatoslavich as an ideal. As prince of Chernigov he pardoned those who offended him and forgave those who broke their oaths. He never committed perjury, harmed no one, held no malice, and shunned war. He died a saint even though he had enjoyed worldly wealth, had a wife, and fathered children. As proof of David's sanctity, the preacher reminded the congregation of the favors God had bestowed on him at the time of his death.[107] Finally, the preacher encouraged his listeners to emulate David's son Svyatosha. The latter had renounced his princely position and had chosen to live the life of a monk in the Caves Monastery.[108]

With words such as these the prelate admonished Oleg and the princes of the cadet branch, it would seem, for their bellicosity. He exhorted them to live in the spirit of fraternal love that Yaroslav the Wise had advocated. Since, however, we do not know the year in which the speaker addressed the princes, we do not know if he played a decisive role in persuading Oleg to submit to Svyatoslav. Ultimately, Oleg was pacified, but his collaboration with the Rostislavichi rang a warning bell for Svyatoslav. The latter was patronizing the Yur'evichi of Suzdalia, but Oleg joined his brothers-in-law and thus divided the Ol'govichi in their alliances.

Despite their disaffection with Svyatoslav, the princes of the cadet branch also had reason to rejoice. Towards the end of 1174, a son was born to Oleg's brother Igor'. His parents gave him the princely name of Oleg but christened him Paul.[109] Since there was an interval of some four years between the births of their first son Vladimir,[110] and, evidently, the second son Oleg, it is possible that their daughter, whose name is not given but whose existence is revealed under the year 1190, was born in the interim.[111]

At the beginning of 1175 the Ol'govichi received the disturbing news that Roman Rostislavich had left Smolensk and joined his brothers in the Kievan land. Yaroslav Izyaslavich prudently withdrew to his patrimony in Lutsk allowing Roman to occupy Kiev.[112] It is noteworthy that from then

---

[107] Concerning David's death, see *Dynasty*, pp. 301–2. [108] *Dynasty*, pp. 252–4, 375–6, 398–9.
[109] See s.a. 1175: Ipat., col. 600; compare Gust., p. 316.
[110] Vladimir was born in 1170 (see above, p. 121).
[111] Concerning her marriage to David Ol'govich, see Ipat., col. 668, and below, p. 195.
[112] See s.a. 1175: Ipat., col. 600; Gust., p. 316; compare s.a. 1174: NPL, pp. 34, 223. Since the chronicler placed the entry at the end of the March year 1174, Roman probably occupied Kiev in January or February of 1175.

on up to the Tatar invasion, Kiev would be the bone of contention between
the Rostislavichi and the Ol'govichi.

For the immediate future, however, Suzdalian events preoccupied Svyatoslav. After Mstislav and Yaropolk were enthroned, we are told, they
sought to seize great wealth. The beleaguered townspeople therefore sent
messengers to Mikhalko inviting him to be their prince.[113] On May 21,
he and Vsevolod, accompanied by Svyatoslav's troops and eldest son,
Vladimir, left Chernigov. On reaching Moscow, troops from Vladimir on
the Klyaz'ma joined them. Vladimir commanded the vanguard force while
Mikhalko, grievously ill, directed the fighting from a stretcher. On June 15,
they won the day. Mstislav therefore fled to Novgorod,[114] and Yaropolk
escaped to Ryazan'. Mikhalko and Vsevolod gave many gifts to Vladimir
and then Mikhalko occupied Vladimir on the Klyaz'ma. After the victory,
we are told, Svyatoslav ordered his son Oleg to escort the wives of the two
Yur'evichi from Chernigov to Moscow.[115]

Ironically, whereas Andrey Bogolyubskiy had tried manipulating the appointment of the senior prince of Rus' in Kiev, Svyatoslav intervened in
the appointment of Andrey's own successor, the senior prince of Suzdalia.
Their tactics were significantly different. In sending his own underlings to
Kiev, Andrey had ignored the wishes of its citizens. Svyatoslav, however,
supported the prince that the people of Vladimir chose and the prince who,
according to seniority, was the rightful claimant. By helping the Yur'evichi
to win possession of their patrimonial domains, Svyatoslav indebted them
to him even more. In doing so, he took an important step towards restoring the balance of power that had existed before the death of Andrey
Bogolyubskiy.

After Oleg escorted Mikhalko and Vsevolod's wives to Moscow, he went
to his domain of Lopasna in the northeast corner of the Vyatichi lands.[116]
From there, he sent troops northeast to Sviril'sk and captured it because it

---

[113] See s.a. 1175: Ipat., cols. 598–9; s.a. 1176: Lav. cols. 374–5; Mosk., p. 85. Concerning the date, see
Berezhkov, p. 193.
[114] According to the Novgorod chronicler, after Mstislav had occupied Rostov, the Novgorodians had
expelled Andrey's son Yury, and Mstislav had appointed his son Svyatoslav to the town (NPL,
pp. 34, 223).
[115] See s.a. 1176: Ipat., cols. 600–2; compare Lav., cols. 375–9; Mosk., pp. 85–6. Concerning the date,
see Berezhkov, pp. 79, 193–4.
[116] Mentioned for the first time, Lopasna was located south of Moscow, on the south shore of the Oka,
where the river Lopasna flows into it (Nasonov, pp. 226–7; *Zemlya Vyatichey*, p. 149).

belonged to the Ol'govichi.[117] Gleb Rostislavich of Ryazan' sent his nephew, Yury's son, to repossess it, but Oleg defeated his brother-in-law.[118] The reference to Oleg's brother-in-law is noteworthy because, nine years earlier, in 1166, Oleg's wife, the daughter of Andrey Bogolyubskiy, had died.[119] Oleg therefore had remarried a Ryazan' princess on an undisclosed date. We do learn, however, that his father-in-law Yury was the younger brother of Gleb Rostislavich.[120] The entry also reveals that Svyatoslav had given to Oleg, his second eldest son, the district of Lopasna as his patrimony. Accordingly, he had probably given a domain in the Vyatichi lands to his eldest son, Vladimir.

SVYATOSLAV CAPTURES KIEV

In the middle of 1176 Svyatoslav Vsevolodovich used a family squabble among the Rostislavichi to make a bid for Kiev. In May, the chronicler reports, the Polovtsy attacked towns along the river Ros'.[121] Roman Rostislavich of Kiev sent his brother Ryurik and his two sons to confront the nomads. His brother David refused to go at first because he had quarreled with his brothers, but he joined them later. Consequently, the marauders inflicted an ignominious defeat on the four princes because they argued.[122] When Svyatoslav received the news, we are told, he rejoiced. Accusing David of being responsible for the defeat, he invoked a clause from the compact that he and Roman had concluded after the latter occupied Kiev. According to it, if a prince was guilty of an offense (the chronicler does not describe the offense) he was to forfeit his domain. Svyatoslav declared that David's transgression merited that punishment.[123] Roman, however, refused to penalize his brother so severely.

Svyatoslav therefore marched against Kiev. In addition to his dynasty's troops, he called upon his heretofore-unreported son-in-law from

---

[117] Sviril'sk is mentioned for the first time. Nasonov suggested that it was located northeast of Lopasna and north of Kolomna (Nasonov, p. 230). To date the site of the town remains undetermined (*Zemlya Vyatichey*, p. 150).

[118] See s.a. 1176: Ipat., cols. 602–3; Makhnovets', p. 321.   [119] See above, p. 109.

[120] Concerning the family of Oleg's wife, see Baum. 2, XIV, 10, 18, and 19. Compare Zotov who overlooked Oleg's second marriage (p. 272).

[121] Concerning the date, see Berezhkov, p. 194.   [122] Gust., p. 316.

[123] This is the first occasion on which the chronicler cites the clause, but it had evidently been incorporated into alliances in the past. The princes of Rus' seemingly enforced the same clause at Uvetichi in 1100, when they penalized David Igorevich of Vladimir in Volyn' for his offense against Vasil'ko Rostislavich of Terebovl'. Earlier, in 1096, after the princes had kissed the Holy Cross on their agreement at Lyubech, David had broken the agreement by blinding Vasil'ko. Later, at Uvetichi, the princes punished David for his crime by depriving him of his patrimonial domain and giving him a less important one (*Dynasty*, pp. 224–36).

the House of Monomakh. We are told that he instructed Mstislav
Vladimirovich of Dorogobuzh to break his alliance with the Rostislavichi
and to drive out Roman's sons from Trepol'.[124] As an aside we should note
that this is the only chronicle allusion to Svyatoslav's unidentified daughter
who married Mstislav of Dorogobuzh. Finally, the Black Caps, and, more
importantly, the Kievans also supported Svyatoslav. After he crossed the
Dnepr at Vitichev, Kievans came to inform him that Roman had fled to
Belgorod.

Svyatoslav occupied Kiev on July 22. Later, however, when Roman's
brother Mstislav brought reinforcements, he fled to Chernigov. Before leaving Kiev however, Svyatoslav summoned the Polovtsy, who, on learning that
he had fled, attacked Torchesk and took many inhabitants captive. Ultimately, it was their intervention that allegedly persuaded the Rostislavichi
to capitulate. According to the chronicler, they gave up Kiev to avoid devastating the land of Rus' and to avoid inflicting suffering on its Christian
inhabitants.[125]

Before Svyatoslav captured Kiev on July 22, the citizens of Rostov had
invited Mstislav Rostislavich to come from Novgorod and be their prince.
Meanwhile, on June 20, Mikhalko died in Vladimir on the Klyaz'ma and
the townsmen invited his brother Vsevolod, the new senior prince in the
House of Monomakh, to replace him. Mstislav attacked Vsevolod, but on
June 27 the latter defeated him.[126] After Vsevolod assumed sole power in
Suzdalia, Svyatoslav, as his ally, could call upon him for help. Svyatoslav's
reaffirmed alliance with Andrey Bogolyubskiy's youngest brother, therefore,
may also have influenced Roman to capitulate.

As was the custom on the accession of a new prince to Kiev, Roman and
his brothers promised Svyatoslav not to take Kiev from him and to help
him defend the lands of Rus'. At the same time, Svyatoslav agreed to hand
over Kiev to the Rostislavichi after his death. Although the chronicler does
not enunciate these terms, they are reflected in the subsequent actions of
the princes. Moreover, David and Ryurik retained control of Vyshgorod
and Belgorod. Thus, whereas the senior prince of one dynasty ruled Kiev,
princes of a potentially hostile dynasty ruled its two most powerful satellite
towns. The arrangement therefore curtailed Svyatoslav's freedom of action
by placing him under the constant scrutiny of the Rostislavichi. He was
the first prince of Kiev to rule under such debilitating conditions.

[124] Concerning Mstislav, see Zotov, p. 274, n. 25; Baum., V, 41; and see below, p. 159.
[125] See s.a. 1177: Ipat., cols. 603–5; Gust., pp. 316–17; compare Makhnovets', pp. 321–2. Concerning the dates, see Berezhkov, p. 194.
[126] See s.a. 1177: Lav., cols. 379–82; Mosk., pp. 87–8. Concerning the date, see Berezhkov, pp. 79–80.

On becoming prince of Kiev, Svyatoslav promoted his brother Yaroslav to Chernigov. By not turning over the town to his cousin Oleg, the senior prince of the cadet branch, he declared his intention to keep Chernigov in the hands of the senior branch in keeping with the practice of lateral succession. In this he differed from his father Vsevolod, who, after occupying Kiev in 1139, had handed over Chernigov to his eldest cousin, Vladimir Davidovich, rather than to his own brother Igor'.[127] Accordingly, Oleg was in line to occupy Chernigov only after Yaroslav's death.

Finally, after reporting Svyatoslav's seizure of Kiev, the compiler of the Hypatian Chronicle inserts an item of dynastic news. The son Svyatoslav was born to Igor' and his Galician wife. They christened him Adrian.[128] He is the last of their children whose birth is recorded. Roman was evidently also born during the 1170s, as was the couple's only daughter, whom the sources do not identify by name.[129]

SVYATOSLAV FORTIFIES HIS FRIENDSHIP WITH THE PRINCES OF SUZDALIA AND SMOLENSK

Disagreements with the princes of Ryazan', controversies in Novgorod, and Polovtsian attacks gave Svyatoslav the opportunity to strengthen ties with his allies. In the winter of 1177, after war broke out in Suzdalia, Svyatoslav sent his sons Oleg and Vladimir to help Vsevolod attack Gleb of Ryazan', who was harboring the two Rostislavichi. Svyatoslav demonstrated an active interest in the conflict for two reasons. As the senior prince of the Ol'govichi he had to honor the alliance he had formed with Vsevolod. As the senior prince of Rus' he sought to protect Vsevolod's rightful claim to Suzdalia. This was the first occasion on which the two princes joined forces. Significantly, the campaign found them acting from positions of unprecedented power. Svyatoslav was the prince of Kiev and Vsevolod the prince of Suzdalia. But the relationship between those positions was now reversed. Whereas Vsevolod's predecessor Andrey Bogolyubskiy had manipulated appointments to Kiev, Svyatoslav now assumed the dominant role in the Kiev–Suzdalia axis.

When Vsevolod's troops reached Kolomna, he learnt that Gleb was pillaging his lands so he turned back. On March 7 he routed the invaders and took Gleb, his son Roman, and Mstislav Rostislavich captive.[130] When

[127] *Dynasty*, pp. 352–5.   [128] See s.a. 1177: Ipat., col. 604; Gust., p. 317.
[129] Zotov, pp. 276–7; Baum., IV, 44–49; also see below, p. 238.
[130] Concerning the date, see Berezhkov, p. 194.

the citizens of Vladimir demanded that he blind the princes, Vsevolod attempted to mollify the mob by throwing the princes into a pit. He also ordered the inhabitants of Ryazan' to hand over Yaropolk Rostislavich, whom he incarcerated alongside his brother.

After Svyatoslav helped Vsevolod terminate Gleb's support of the Rostislavichi, Mstislav Rostislavich and his sister, Gleb's wife, asked him to mediate on behalf of the captives because they believed that he wielded the power to influence Vsevolod. Svyatoslav, for his part, conscientiously assumed his moral responsibility as prince of Kiev. He selected Bishop Porfiry of Chernigov and *Igumen* Efrem of the Eletskiy Monastery of the Mother of God, the two highest-ranking prelates from Chernigov, as his spokesmen.[131] Evidently, he did not send the metropolitan, who normally represented the prince of Kiev on such delegations, because the metropolitan's throne was vacant.[132]

Svyatoslav did not ask Vsevolod to return Gleb to Ryazan' from where the latter could continue waging war on Suzdalia. Rather, he requested that Vsevolod send the captive to Rus', where he would grant Gleb a domain. Svyatoslav's willingness to give Gleb sanctuary was in keeping with the compassion that he had shown in the past towards princes and princesses in dire straits. Gleb, however, rejected the offer of help saying that he preferred to die in Vladimir than to live in Rus'. On June 30, he died in the pit. His son Roman, however, pledged allegiance to Vsevolod and the latter allowed him to return to Ryazan'. Vsevolod may have acted leniently towards him owing to Svyatoslav's intervention and because Roman was Svyatoslav's son-in-law. Surprisingly, however, Vsevolod detained Svyatoslav's clerical mediators for two years. The seemingly hostile act was glaringly inconsistent with his friendship towards Svyatoslav. The chronicler, however, does not explain it, justify it, or condemn it.

Ultimately, the citizens of Vladimir got their way with the Rostislavichi. They rose in rebellion demanding that the brothers be blinded. On this occasion, Vsevolod failed to placate them. He had Mstislav and Yaropolk blinded and expelled from Suzdalia. They travelled to St. Gleb's church on the Smyadyn' hill in Smolensk where they allegedly regained their sight.[133]

[131] Efrem was evidently the *igumen* of the Eletskiy Monastery renowned for its Cathedral of the Assumption of the Mother of God (*Uspenskiy sobor*).
[132] One source, albeit a late one, reports that in 1177 the patriarch sent Metropolitan Konstantin to Kiev (Gust., p. 317). Since the bishop and the *igumen* were in Suzdalia before June 30, that is, before the date on which Gleb of Ryazan' who rejected Svyatoslav's invitation to move to Rus' died, Konstantin arrived in the summer at the earliest.
[133] Tatishchev contradicts the account of the miraculous cure. He reports that Vsevolod ordered his men to smear the brothers' eyes and faces with blood (in the second redaction he is more specific

From there they went to Novgorod, where the citizens installed Mstislav as prince and gave Torzhok (Novyy Torg) to Yaropolk.[134]

In April of 1178, Mstislav died and the Novgorodians invited his brother to replace him. Vsevolod, however, forced the townsmen to expel Yaropolk and to kiss the Holy Cross to him. Later, however, they summoned Roman Rostislavich from Smolensk and he came on February 18 of the following year.[135] To judge from this information Svyatoslav, unlike his father Vsevolod, expressed no interest in controlling Novgorod. Granted, he did not receive an invitation from the citizens, a prerequisite for any prince who hoped to successfully occupy the town. Perhaps even more importantly, he did not wish to antagonize Roman and the Rostislavichi whose support he solicited to fight the Polovtsy.

Later, in August of 1179, we learn that Khan Konchak and the "evil brood of the devil" attacked the lands of Pereyaslavl'. Meanwhile, Svyatoslav, accompanied by the Rostislavichi, was waiting for the Polovtsy south of Trepol', where they had arranged to conclude peace. On learning that the tribesmen were plundering the east bank, the princes rode beyond the river Sula to intercept them, but the nomads took a different route to their camps.[136] Since the princely allies came to Trepol' to meet the nomads three years after Svyatoslav occupied Kiev, we see that he enjoyed the loyalty of the Rostislavichi and we may assume that he had already negotiated an initial peace with the Polovtsy. This view is supported by the news that the raid on Pereyaslavl' was the first reported attack after 1176, when Svyatoslav seized Kiev. Moreover, the nomads' arrangement to meet the princes suggests that the two sides renegotiated their pacts regularly, probably annually. Konchak's attack therefore terminated a three-year period of peace.

MARRIAGES, DEATHS, AND ALLIANCES

As a rule, the Ol'govichi sought to arrange marriages with dynasties and foreign powers that would be of most political benefit to their sons when they reached maturity, especially those sons who were high on the ladder of seniority. Thus, we find that under the year 1179 the senior branch

and claims Vsevolod's men cut the skin under the eyebrows so that blood flowed over the eyes making it look as if the eyes were gouged out) and then showed the Rostislavichi to the people. That night, he ordered his men to escort the pair out of the town and see them off to Rus' (Tat. 4, p. 292; compare Tat. 3, p. 119).

[134] Concerning Vsevolod's rivalry with the Rostislavichi, see Mosk., pp. 88–9; Lav., cols. 383–6; Ipat., cols. 605–6; NPL, pp. 35, 224–5. Concerning the dates, see Berezhkov, pp. 79–80, 194–5.

[135] NPL, pp. 35–6, 225; Lav., cols. 386–7. Concerning the dates, see Berezhkov, pp. 80–1, 245–6.

[136] See s.a. 1178: Ipat., cols. 612–13; compare Gust., p. 317. Concerning the date, see Berezhkov, pp. 195, 199–200.

attempted to arrange three such marriages. First we are told that, during the fast of St. Philip on November 14, Svyatoslav brought a daughter of Casimir II "the Just" as wife for his son Vsevolod, who would become known as "the Red" (*Chermnyy*).[137] According to the *Lyubetskiy sinodik*, her name was Anastasia.[138] By selecting a Polish wife for his son, Svyatoslav maintained the ties with the Piast dynasty that his father had established.[139] This, as we shall see, would prove to be an important alliance for Vsevolod and for his son Mikhail.

Next, the chronicler reports that Vsevolod Yur'evich invited Vladimir, Svyatoslav's eldest son, to Suzdalia and gave to Vladimir his niece, the daughter of his deceased brother Mikhalko, as wife.[140] Vladimir returned to Chernigov, where he presented his wife to his father, who was living there.[141] It is unexpected to find Svyatoslav, the prince of Kiev, living in Chernigov with his brother Yaroslav. Svyatoslav evidently visited his patrimonial capital periodically to confer with his brother and, undoubtedly, to worship in the dynasty's churches, especially in the Church of St. Michael that he had built. Significantly, the confidence with which he absented himself from Kiev shows that he had successfully consolidated his rule in that town.

On November 8, Svyatoslav's brother Yaroslav gave his daughter as wife to Vladimir Glebovich of Pereyaslavl'.[142] The unnamed bride was evidently Yaroslav's only daughter. Vladimir Glebovich was Vsevolod's nephew. Consequently, the marriage was the second alliance that year which the senior branch formed with the dynasty of Suzdalia. The match was important to Yaroslav for an additional reason. Vladimir was his southern neighbor, whose lands were contiguous with those of Chernigov. Consequently, their new family bond would help them to collaborate more closely in defending their lands against the nomads.

The chronicler also records two deaths. First he reports that Svyatoslav's mother, Maria, died and was buried in the Church of St. Cyril in Kiev, which she herself had built.[143] Before her death she was professed into the

[137] See s.a. 1178: Ipat., col. 612; Gust., p. 317. Concerning the date, see Berezhkov, p. 200, n. 154.
[138] Zotov, pp. 44, 273. Concerning the confusion surrounding the true name of Vsevolod's wife, see *Mikhail*, pp. 9–10.
[139] Around 1141, Svyatoslav's sister Zvenislava had married Boleslav "the Tall" of Silesia (*Dynasty*, p. 383).
[140] According to the *Lyubetskiy sinodik*, her name was Evdokia, but some claim it was Elena and others Prebrana (Zotov, pp. 70, 272).
[141] See s.a. 1178: Ipat., col. 612; Gust., p. 317.   [142] See s.a. 1178: Ipat., col. 613; Gust., p. 317.
[143] Concerning the confusion surrounding the identities of the two wives, namely, that of Vsevolod Ol'govich, who died in 1179, and that of Vsevolod Svyatoslavich, who came from the Poles in the same year, see *Mikhail*, pp. 9–10.

skhima, the strictest monastic observance in the Orthodox Church.[144] As we have seen, under the year 1167 the chronicler reported that she was living in Glukhov.[145] It would seem, therefore, that after her son occupied Kiev, she joined him to reside in her former home, where she had lived with her husband, Vsevolod Ol'govich. She probably commissioned the building of the church in the Monastery of St. Cyril during the last three years of her life (figure 6).[146]

The Kievans' willingness to allow a member of the detested dynasty of Chernigov to be buried in Kiev was exceptional. Until then they had granted that right to no member of the dynasty. Significantly, she was a Monomashich by birth, and that dynastic affiliation probably persuaded the townspeople to allow Svyatoslav to bury her in her husband's monastery on the outskirts of Kiev. Indeed, Maria was the genealogically eldest member of the Monomashichi. She was a granddaughter of Monomakh himself and the last of Mstislav Vladimirovich's children to die.[147] She was an aunt to the Rostislavichi of Smolensk, to the Izyaslavichi of Volyn', and to the Vladimirovichi of Dorogobuzh. She was the eldest first cousin of Vsevolod of Suzdalia. As for the Ol'govichi, she was the matriarch of the senior branch and mother of the prince of Kiev. At the time of her death, therefore, Maria was the *grande dame* of Rus'.

Maria's death was a milestone in the dynastic histories of the Ol'govichi and the Monomashichi, but a second death was of greater political moment for the Ol'govichi. On January 16, 1180, Oleg Svyatoslavich died and his brother Igor' left Putivl' to succeed him in Novgorod Severskiy. Oleg was buried in that town in the Church of St. Michael that his grandfather, Oleg, had built.[148] Thus, the first senior prince of the cadet branch was the first Ol'govich to be buried in its capital.

The sources give few details concerning Oleg's personal life. The *Lyubetskiy sinodik*, for example, does not list his name because he never ruled Chernigov.[149] After his first wife, the daughter of Yury Dolgorukiy, died,

---

[144] See s.a. 1178: Ipat., col. 612; a number of chronicles identify her as Maria (Gust., p. 317; Maz., p. 65). Tatishchev alone claims that she adopted the *skhima* on August 6 (Tat. 4, p. 294; Tat. 3, p. 121).

[145] See above, p. 113.

[146] Concerning Maria's role in the building the Church of St. Cyril, see *Dynasty*, p. 390.

[147] Baum., V, 22.

[148] See s.a. 1178: Ipat., col. 613; Gust., p. 317. Archaeologists believe that they have discovered the remains of the church on the eastern part of the *detinets*, see P. A. Rappoport, "Iz istorii Kievo-chernigovskogo zodchestva XII v.," KSDPIIA 179 (1984), p. 61, and *Dynasty*, p. 257. According to one unlikely view, Oleg was buried in the Church of St. Michael in Chernigov (Makhnovets', p. 327).

[149] Zotov, pp. 41–2, 269.

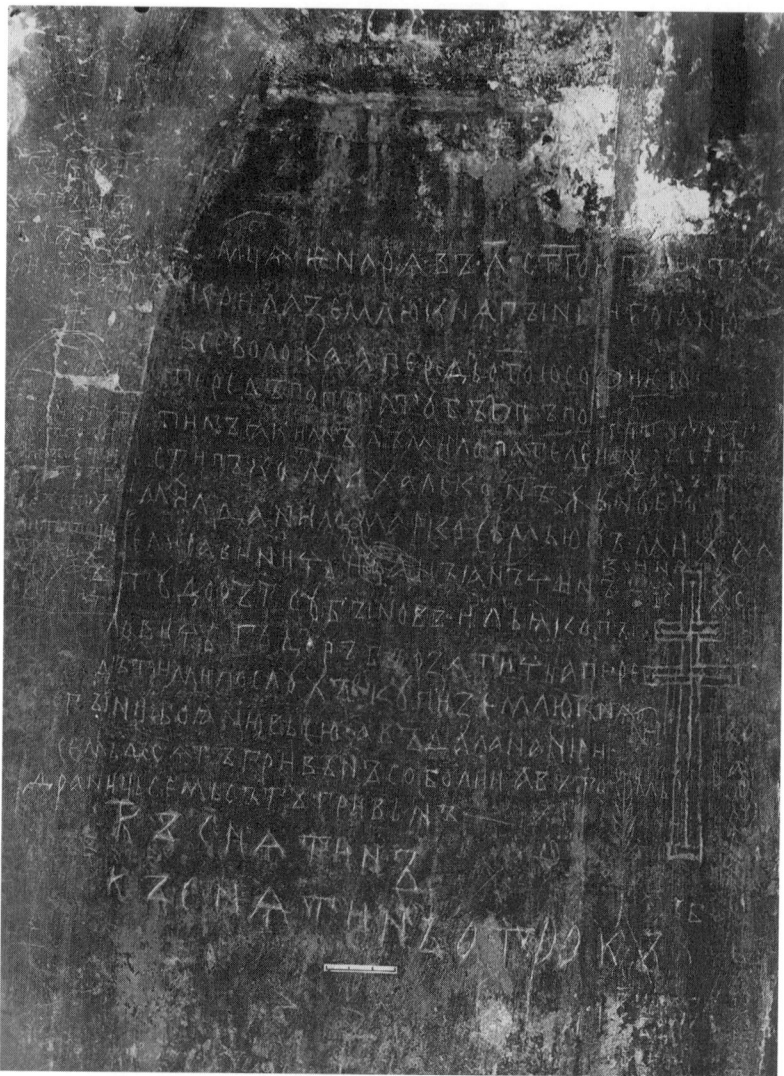

Figure 6   Graffito in St. Sofia Cathedral, Kiev, reporting Princess Maria's purchase of
Boyan's land, perhaps for the Monastery of St. Cyril

he married Agafia from the House of Smolensk, who most likely survived
him.[150] She probably spent her widowhood with her son Svyatoslav, who, as
we shall see, ruled Ryl'sk. He was fourteen years of age at the time of Oleg's

[150] Ipat., cols. 524–5; see above, p. 108.

death.[151] As the only son, he was the sole heir to his father's patrimonial domain in the Posem'e region. He also had the right to sit on the throne of his father in Novgorod Severskiy, but he was an *izgoi* for Chernigov. Although the chronicles tell us nothing about Oleg's cultural achievements, he evidently continued to patronize the family chronicle that his father Svyatoslav Ol'govich had initiated.[152]

Soon after Oleg's death, we are told, Svyatoslav Vsevolodovich summoned his brother Yaroslav, his cousin Igor' Svyatoslavich, and the latter's brother Vsevolod to Lyubech and concluded an agreement.[153] Since the princes met at Lyubech, it appears that the town had recovered its importance as the regional center despite the chronicler's earlier assertion that only dog herders lived there.[154] Furthermore, since Svyatoslav selected the venue, the town probably belonged to the senior branch. If this observation is correct, we may conclude that the lands between the Desna and the Dnepr, that is, the territory given to David at the Congress of Lyubech in 1097,[155] had passed into the hands of the senior branch after the demise of the Davidovichi.

Svyatoslav's main objective in assembling the senior generation of Ol'govichi was to secure Igor''s allegiance. After he became the senior prince of the cadet branch, Igor' had to kiss the Holy Cross to Svyatoslav, the senior prince of the dynasty and prince of Kiev. Svyatoslav, for his part, would have made his relatives promise to support his Polovtsian policy, to collaborate with the Rostislavichi, and to live at peace with Vsevolod of Suzdalia. The evidence that the Ol'govichi parted amicably bespeaks their unity of purpose.

As an aside we should note that, while the princes were at Lyubech, a devastating fire swept the hill of Kiev destroying many courts and damaging St. Sofia.[156] As prince of Kiev, Svyatoslav would have assumed responsibility for maintaining the metropolitan's cathedral, which he himself used for official functions. Given his enthusiasm for founding churches, he would not have shirked from the task of rebuilding St. Sofia.[157] Seven years earlier he had founded the Church of St. Michael in Chernigov and, in the years

[151] Svyatoslav was born in 1166 (Ipat., col. 526; see above, p. 109).
[152] Priselkov, *Istoriya russkogo letopisaniya*, p. 50.
[153] Ipat., col. 613; compare Gust., p. 317.
[154] See above, pp. 88–9.   [155] *Dynasty*, pp. 220–1.   [156] Ipat., cols. 613–14; Gust., p. 317.
[157] According to Rybakov, the observation that Svyatoslav oversaw the repairs of St. Sofia is supported by the evidence that the mosaics, which survived in the cathedral to the seventeenth century, were analogous to the ones found in the Church of the Annunciation that he had consecrated in 1186 ("Drevnosti Chernigova," p. 86; concerning the Church of the Annunciation, see below, pp. 281–4).

to come, as we shall see, he would commission more new churches there and in Kiev.[158]

SVYATOSLAV ANTAGONIZES HIS ALLIES OVER NOVGOROD, RYAZAN', AND KIEV

During the same year, 1180, Svyatoslav attained a level of military confidence that prompted him to chart an independent political course from his allies. First, we are told that he became involved in Novgorodian affairs. After Roman Rostislavich returned to Smolensk, the Novgorodians invited his brother Mstislav to replace him. On June 14 he died. For reasons not given, the townsmen chose not to invite another Rostislavich or Vsevolod of Suzdalia. Instead, they asked Svyatoslav to send a son. He dispatched Vladimir and they enthroned him on August 17.[159] Perhaps they turned to Svyatoslav because he had demonstrated that he was no man's lackey. Following the death of Andrey Bogolyubskiy, who had manipulated the appointment of princes to Kiev, Svyatoslav had seized it in his own name and successfully ruled it for over three years. He therewith proved to the satisfaction of the Novgorodians that he was the most powerful prince in Rus'. In this way he became the first senior prince of the Ol'govichi, since his father Vsevolod over forty years earlier, to rule the important commercial center. This control would not only bring financial benefits to his dynasty but would also strengthen his status in relation to his allies.

Svyatoslav's increased power, however, destroyed the equilibrium that he had sought to establish after Andrey Bogolyubskiy's death. By replacing the Rostislavichi in Novgorod he inevitably alienated them. His good fortune also strained his relations with Vsevolod of Suzdalia. The latter must have been chagrined to find Svyatoslav poaching in the town that he increasingly looked upon as his preserve. Svyatoslav, therefore, was in danger of becoming the odd man out. His predicament, however, seemingly did not worry him because, as we shall see, he initiated war against Vsevolod.

Second, we learn that Svyatoslav was already involved in Ryazan' affairs when he received the invitation to send his son to Novgorod. The problem arose in 1177 after Gleb died in Vsevolod's pit and his son Roman succeeded him as the senior prince. Before his death, Gleb had given each of his six sons a domain, thereby fragmenting the family's territorial holdings.[160] Roman attempted to consolidate his authority by seizing his brothers' patrimonies.

---

[158] Concerning the Church of St. Michael, see above, p. 124.
[159] NPL, pp. 36, 225–6. Concerning the date, see Berezhkov, p. 246.
[160] Concerning Gleb's sons, see Baum. 2, XIV, 11–17.

Vsevolod marched to assist the brothers, but Svyatoslav sent his son Gleb to help Roman. Why was Svyatoslav willing to help his son-in-law assert his supremacy at the cost of violating legitimate territorial bequests? And why was Svyatoslav willing to wage war against Vsevolod at the cost of breaking their alliance?

It was to Svyatoslav's advantage to have a strong centralized Ryazan' controlled by his son-in-law. Roman, as his ally, could challenge Vsevolod from the southeast. By forcing Vsevolod to direct his attention to the Ryazan' frontier, Svyatoslav evidently hoped to curb his expansionism towards the Baltic. Diverting him from Novgorod became even more important after the Novgorodians invited Svyatoslav to be their prince. Consequently, in challenging Vsevolod's overlordship over the princes of Ryazan', he launched his own expansionist policy. Instead of gaining the advantage, however, Svyatoslav lost ground: Vsevolod defeated Roman, took his son Gleb captive, and became his enemy.

Given his ambitious objective, it is surprising that Svyatoslav sent Gleb, a junior son, to help Roman. Indeed, this is the first occasion on which we learn that he had a fourth son. Svyatoslav evidently sent Gleb to give him experience in the field. Instead, his inexperience most likely led to his capture.[161] Svyatoslav was furious when he learnt that Vsevolod had bound his son in fetters. Unable or unwilling to retaliate against Vsevolod, he turned against the Rostislavichi. Nevertheless, his accusation – that they were thwarting his rule in Rus' at every turn – had a ring of truth.[162] After he assumed control of Novgorod in their place, they probably expressed their displeasure by obstructing his rule in Kiev.

Consequently, Svyatoslav's third course of independent action, this time against the Rostislavichi, was most unexpected. While David Rostislavich was travelling by boat along the Dnepr on a hunting excursion, we are told, Svyatoslav was hunting on the Chernigov side. After receiving the news of his son's capture, probably while he was hunting, Svyatoslav plotted with his wife. He insisted on avenging himself immediately by taking David captive and by driving out Ryurik from the Kievan land. After becoming the sole ruler in Rus' and thus increasing his military might, he intended to avenge himself against Vsevolod. He refused to consult his counselors,

[161] One late source claims that Gleb went to Vsevolod in good faith but the latter summoned him deceitfully (Gust., p. 317). Another late source claims that Gleb was captured while all his troops were inebriated (Nikon. 10, p. 7).

[162] Concerning the controversy, see Ipat., col. 614; compare Lav., cols. 387–8. Since the entry preceding this account in the Laurentian Chronicle reports the death of Mstislav Rostislavich in Novgorod on June 14, Vsevolod's attack on Ryazan' probably occurred after that date. Concerning the dates, see Berezhkov, p. 81.

however, because he believed that they would condemn his plan or even warn David. Significantly, his wife Maria conspired with him.[163] Since this is a rare reference to a wife's involvement in her husband's political machinations, it suggests that her conduct was extraordinary and that she encouraged her husband in his political ambitions. But he failed to capture David. Fearing to return to Kiev because he had declared his hostile intent against the Rostislavichi, he withdrew to Chernigov.

Svyatoslav, we are told, summoned his sons, the junior Ol'govichi, and his *druzhinniki* to a meeting. Thus, he sought their advice only after his scheme went awry. Surprisingly, the spokesman for the Ol'govichi was not the second in seniority, Yaroslav of Chernigov, but Igor'. The latter probably became the mouthpiece for the assembly because of his status as head of the cadet branch or, perhaps, because his chronicler recorded the event. Unfortunately for the investigator, the Hypatian chronicler has an incomplete text and reports Igor''s answer in a truncated form: "Father it is good to have peace, but as that did not come to pass, God grant us that you remain in good health." Despite the seeming irrelevance of Igor''s reply to Svyatoslav's question whether they should attack Smolensk or Kiev, it nevertheless reveals Igor''s sentiments. He advocated peace, but following Svyatoslav's unilateral declaration of war, he resigned himself to the inevitable conflict. Notwithstanding his implied criticism of Svyatoslav's conduct, he expressed his loyalty by wishing his cousin good health.

Tatishchev, who alone offers an expanded version of Igor''s statement, supports this observation:

Brother! It was good to have peace, and it would be better [for you] to be reconciled with Vsevolod over your son and for all [the princes] to defend the land of Rus' against the Polovtsy. If you wished to begin something [that is, a rivalry], however, you should have discussed it with us and with [your] senior *druzhina*. And now, if there is to be war, we should attack Smolensk and prevent Roman from seizing Kiev.[164]

After failing to abduct David, Svyatoslav's choice was to attack either Kiev, which Ryurik had occupied after he fled from it, or Smolensk, where Roman ruled. The chronicler does not report the decision of the Ol'govichi, but as we shall see, they attacked neither town. The most likely explanation for Svyatoslav's change of plan was Roman's death. It was the second in the dynasty that year and it further weakened the ranks of the Rostislavichi.

---

[163] She is given that name by the *Lyubetskiy sinodik* (Zotov, p. 267). Concerning their marriage, see *Dynasty*, p. 384.

[164] Tat. 4, p. 295; compare Tat. 3, p. 123.

David replaced Roman in Smolensk, but in doing so vacated Vyshgorod and reduced the presence of the Rostislavichi in the Kievan land. After that, Ryurik remained the main obstacle to Svyatoslav's autonomous rule in Rus'.[165]

SVYATOSLAV ATTACKS SUZDALIA

Despite failing to achieve the first part of his scheme, to capture David and to drive out Ryurik from the Kievan land, Svyatoslav assembled all his brothers and the Polovtsy to carry out the second part of his scheme, to avenge himself against Vsevolod and to free from captivity his son Gleb. Before setting out at the beginning of 1181 he addressed his brothers as follows:

I am older than [my brother] Yaroslav, and you Igor' are older than [your brother] Vsevolod. And now I have become a father to you all. I command you Igor' to stay here with Yaroslav and defend Chernigov and all our domains. I, however, will go with [your brother] Vsevolod to Suzdal' to find my son Gleb. Let it be between Vsevolod [Yur'evich] and us as God judges.[166]

In assuming the role of father of the dynasty, Svyatoslav alludes to the directive of Yaroslav the Wise, who appointed his eldest surviving son Izyaslav to be the father in his place.[167] In using Yaroslav as the fountainhead of his authority, Svyatoslav confirms that the Ol'govichi looked upon Yaroslav's so-called testament as the cornerstone of their political structure. Accordingly, as their father, Svyatoslav commanded Igor' and Yaroslav to remain behind and defend the dynastic capital against the Rostislavichi. Ordinarily, the commander-in-chief placed the next in seniority in charge of defending the capital. In this instance, however, Svyatoslav placed the responsibility on both branches by delegating the task to the two most senior princes after him in each branch. Moreover, by taking Igor''s brother Vsevolod with him, he declared that, in his view, the duty of freeing Gleb was a matter of dynastic honor, which both branches had to share.

The Ol'govichi also summoned auxiliaries. Vsevolod's nephew Yaropolk Rostislavich, now cured of his blindness, assisted Svyatoslav. In 1178, after the Novgorodians evicted him, he had become a fugitive once again. And, once again, Svyatoslav had welcomed him. On this occasion, both princes had grievances against Vsevolod. Svyatoslav sought to free his son and Yaropolk still hoped to displace his uncle from Suzdalia. The Polovtsy, who

---

[165] Concerning Svyatoslav's failed kidnapping attempt, see Ipat., cols. 614–18; compare Gust., p. 318.
[166] Ipat., col. 618.   [167] Dimnik, "Testament," pp. 374–5.

normally did not venture so far north, also joined the Ol'govichi. Finally,
Vladimir brought Novgorodian troops. The willingness of the townsmen
to fight against Vsevolod bespeaks their continued hostility towards him.
Svyatoslav's campaign turned into a farce. His son-in-law Roman of
Ryazan', who was responsible for the conflict which led to Gleb's capture,
changed allegiances and joined Vsevolod. Moreover, the latter made Svyatoslav look inept as a commander by deftly deflecting his every attempt to
initiate battle. The only military action the Ol'govichi engaged in was a
skirmish to defend their supply wagons. The onset of the spring thaw finally
forced Svyatoslav to withdraw ignominiously. Having failed to assuage his
craving for revenge, he set fire to Dmitrov as a token gesture of reprisal.[168]
Thus, after failing to kidnap David, he lost face yet again in failing to
free Gleb. Around March of 1181 he accompanied his son Vladimir to
Novgorod.[169]

SVYATOSLAV IN NOVGOROD

Svyatoslav's sojourn in Novgorod as senior prince of Chernigov was anoma-
lous. The Novgorod First Chronicle reports that the returning Novgorod
troops "took [*poyasha*] the prince (Svyatoslav) to Novgorod" and "Svyatoslav the great entered [*vnide*] Novgorod."[170] Although the meanings of
the words "took" and "entered" are ambiguous, they are probably formulaic terms signifying that the Novgorodians took Svyatoslav to become
their prince and he entered Novgorod as their ruler. The chronicle supports this rendering in its list of princes who ruled Novgorod. It reports
that Svyatoslav replaced his son Vladimir.[171]

No senior prince of Chernigov had ever occupied Novgorod while holding that office. Svyatoslav, however, acted from expediency. Before setting
off for Suzdalia he had abandoned Kiev, which Ryurik seized. Granted,
as senior prince of the Ol'govichi he could return to Chernigov, but this
meant evicting his brother Yaroslav. Consequently, Svyatoslav, who was

---

[168] According to a Novgorod source, however, Svyatoslav and the Novgorodians devastated the entire
Volga region. They set fire to all the towns and, later, the Novgorodians killed some 300 of Vsevolod's
men (NPL, pp. 36, 226).
[169] Concerning Svyatoslav's campaign, see Ipat. cols. 618–20; Mosk., pp. 89–90. Concerning the date,
see Berezhkov, p. 200.
[170] NPL, pp. 36, 226.
[171] NPL, p. 471. A number of lead seals found in Novgorod have been attributed to both Svyatoslav
(Yanin 1, pp. 106, 203–4; Yanin 3, pp. 46, 137–8) and to Vladimir (Yanin 1, p. 203; Yanin 3, pp. 46,
137). This evidence supports the observation that father and son ruled Novgorod for a period of
time.

without a domain, found it opportune to rule Novgorod. This not only enabled him to secure a domain but, undoubtedly, also to negotiate terms more favorable for the dynasty than his son had arranged. To judge from later information, he planned to remain in Novgorod for a short period of time, hand it over to his son, and then return to Kiev.

While Svyatoslav was in Novgorod his brother Yaroslav and Igor′ waged war on Drutsk. To judge from the chronicler's statement, they conceived the plan for the attack. On closer examination, however, we see that they had prearranged to meet Svyatoslav revealing that he had organized it. This is confirmed by the news that the Ol′govichi and Svyatoslav's brothers-in-law from Polotsk waited for him to arrive before they attacked. Consequently Svyatoslav probably sent instructions for the campaign from Novgorod. In the light of this sequence of events, the Ol′govichi launched the campaign sometime during the summer at the earliest. The chronicler, however, is tight-lipped about Svyatoslav's reason for besieging Drutsk.

As we have seen, before marching against Vsevolod, Svyatoslav had debated whether to attack Smolensk or Kiev. Surprisingly, he campaigned against Drutsk in the Polotsk lands instead. As we have seen, in 1158 Svyatoslav Ol′govich had helped Rogvolod Borisovich to reclaim his patrimony of Drutsk.[172] He had evidently remained faithful to the Ol′govichi. In 1181, however, David of Smolensk came to assist Rogvolod's son Gleb in Drutsk, showing that they had formed a pact. At that time, Gleb broke his ties with the Ol′govichi and with his own dynasty. Indeed, since Bryacheslav Vasil′kovich of Vitebsk and his brother Vseslav of Polotsk joined the Ol′govichi, they had probably asked their brother-in-law Svyatoslav to attack Gleb in an effort to bring him back into the fold. Consequently, Svyatoslav's reason for besieging Drutsk would have been to perform a favour for his in-laws.

Thus, following the fiasco in Suzdalia, Svyatoslav's stay in Novgorod and his attack on Drutsk were successful. Before leaving Novgorod, he secured his authority there. This is confirmed by the citizens' willingness to march with him against Drutsk and by their decision to install his son as prince.[173] At Drutsk, he also recouped some of his lost prestige as a military commander. He made David flee from the field of battle and by setting fire to the outer fortification of Drutsk, he evidently forced Gleb to capitulate.

From Drutsk, Svyatoslav travelled south to evict Ryurik from the Kievan land. The task seemed to be straightforward after he had neutralized David. Should the latter wish to ride to Ryurik's assistance, the princes of Polotsk

---

[172] See above, p. 85.   [173] See s.a. 1181: Mosk., p. 90.

could attack Smolensk. Therefore, when Ryurik learnt that Svyatoslav was marching on Kiev and that Igor′, accompanied by Khans Konchak and Kobyak, was waiting for him near Vyshgorod, he withdrew to Belgorod.[174]

SVYATOSLAV: CO-RULER WITH RYURIK

Even though Ryurik withdrew to Belgorod and Svyatoslav entered Kiev uncontested, his assumption of power was not a *fait accompli*. After Svyatoslav occupied the capital, the Polovtsy asked him to let Igor′ accompany them to Dolobsk.[175] When Ryurik learnt that Igor′ and the nomads were encamped on the other side of the Dnepr, he sent troops to attack them. They defeated the Polovtsy, killed Khan Konchak's brother Eltut, and took two of his sons captive. Igor′ and Konchak, however, escaped by boat to Chernigov.[176] The chronicler offers no explanation why the khans wanted Igor′ to join them. Since they were returning to their tents, however, they probably wished to fraternize with him before leaving Rus′. He evidently enjoyed a close friendship with them, especially with Konchak. The observation is confirmed by the news that the two fled together. The episode is, therefore, an important witness to the camaraderie that existed between them.

Ryurik's attack was a brilliant success. Since Igor′'s *druzhina* and the Polovtsy were vital to Svyatoslav's forces, their defeat undermined his military advantage and gave Ryurik the upper hand. This view is fortified by the news that Ryurik dictated unfavorable terms to Svyatoslav, and that the latter accepted them seemingly without demur. Because Svyatoslav was older, we are told, Ryurik ceded to him seniority in Rus′ and control of Kiev, but Ryurik took the entire Kievan land for himself.[177] Two princes had shared power over the Kievan domain in the past: the genealogically senior prince served as the figurehead while the younger one was the commander-in-chief of their joint forces.[178] Significantly, Ryurik's arrangement was different. Svyatoslav would not be just a figurehead. He would be the sole ruler of Kiev and also commander-in-chief. Ryurik would rule Belgorod and have jurisdiction over all the other towns in the Kievan land. Moreover, whereas

---

[174] Concerning the campaign on Drutsk, see s.a. 1180: Ipat., cols. 620–1; compare s.a. 1181: Mosk., p. 90.
[175] Dolobsk or Lake Dolobsk (*Dolobskoe ozero*) was located across the Dnepr from Kiev. Concerning its location, see Makhnovets′, p. 536.
[176] Concerning Ryurik's attack, see s.a. 1180: Ipat., cols. 621–3; Gust., p. 318.
[177] See s.a. 1180: Ipat., cols. 623–4; Gust., p. 318.
[178] An example of dual rule was that exercised by Vyacheslav Vladimirovich and his nephew Izyaslav Mstislavich (see above, p. 63).

in previous instances the co-rulers had come from the same dynasty, in this arrangement they came from rival dynasties. It is noteworthy, however, that the princes were cousins through Svyatoslav's mother.[179]

Ryurik's reason for negotiating a compromise, the chronicler claims, was to end spilling Christian blood. In addition to the alleged moral reason, however, he had practical ones. Namely, he probably believed that he lacked the necessary military power to strike a *coup de grâce* against Svyatoslav. Consequently, to judge from the results of the recent past, their battles would continue to end in stalemates. Ryurik also singled out Svyatoslav's seniority as a motive for relinquishing his claim to Kiev.[180] Svyatoslav was not only physically older but he also belonged to a more senior generation and to a more senior dynasty.[181] Ryurik's solution to his quest for political seniority in Rus', therefore, was to temporize. He waived his claim to Kiev but, as we shall see, he secured the right of succession after Svyatoslav's death. Meanwhile, as a duumvir he would keep one hand on the reins of supreme power and as heir apparent he secured a foothold on Kiev.

By accepting Ryurik's terms, Svyatoslav admitted his inability to defeat his rival. Moreover, by giving up control of the Kievan land he made an unprecedented concession. For the first time in the recorded history of Rus', the jurisdiction of the prince of Kiev was restricted solely to the capital. His authority therefore fell far short of that which his father Vsevolod had wielded. Just the same, because Svyatoslav had absolute control of Kiev, it cannot be said that the power of the prince of Kiev reached its lowest ebb with him. That had happened earlier when, for a few years, a number of princes had been puppets in the hands of Andrey Bogolyubskiy.

Despite Svyatoslav's diminished authority as prince of Kiev, the importance of the town itself did not wane. As the rivalry between Svyatoslav and Ryurik testifies, Kiev – the most important political, religious, cultural, and commercial center in the land – remained the bone of contention between the Ol'govichi and the Rostislavichi, the two most powerful dynasties in the south. The prestige that ruling Kiev bestowed on its prince surpassed that enjoyed by any other. It is therefore not surprising that Svyatoslav coveted

[179] For somewhat different interpretations of dual rule, see Rybakov, *Kievskaya Rus'*, p. 492 and Tolochko, *Drevnyaya Rus'*, pp. 216–17.
[180] His decision is reminiscent of Mstislav's action in 1024, when he ceded control of Kiev to his brother Yaroslav because the latter was his elder (Ipat., cols. 134–6; Lav., cols. 147–9. See also Dimnik, "Succession and Inheritance," pp. 112–13).
[181] Svyatoslav Vsevolodovich was descended from Svyatoslav (d. 1076) the second eldest son of Yaroslav the Wise, whereas Ryurik was descended from Svyatoslav's younger brother Vsevolod (d. 1093). Svyatoslav Vsevolodovich was also the grandson of Oleg (d. 1115), whereas Ryurik was the great-grandson of Monomakh (d. 1125), Oleg's cousin.

ruling the mother of all Rus' towns so much that he agreed to forgo control of the surrounding Kievan land if, by doing so, he became the senior prince of Rus'.

SVYATOSLAV AND VSEVOLOD RECONCILED

After concluding his pact with Ryurik, Svyatoslav used his sons to strengthen his ties with Vsevolod of Suzdalia and to secure his position in Kiev against Ryurik. At the beginning of 1182, it would seem, the Novgorodians expelled Svyatoslav's eldest son Vladimir and he returned to his father.[182] Svyatoslav's sons Gleb and Mstislav, however, had better luck. The chronicler reports that Vsevolod set Gleb free and re-established friendly relations with Svyatoslav. He also promised to give his wife's sister as wife to Svyatoslav's youngest son, Mstislav.[183]

Tatishchev gives a more detailed report. According to him, after Svyatoslav and Ryurik were reconciled, they asked Vsevolod to release Gleb. He welcomed their request, set Gleb free, and showered him with gifts. The three princes concluded peace and Svyatoslav dropped his claim to Novgorod.[184] According to this version of events, Vsevolod released Gleb, it would seem, because Svyatoslav promised not to seek control of Novgorod. Thus, by giving Vsevolod a free hand in appointing his lieutenants to the town, Svyatoslav reestablished friendly relations with the prince of Suzdalia. After that, the Novgorodians asked Svyatoslav's son Vladimir to return to his father.

Svyatoslav paid a high price for Gleb's release, but Vsevolod made his pill easier to swallow by concluding political and marriage alliances with him. Vsevolod's support was invaluable to Svyatoslav because it made his seniority more secure in relation to Ryurik. Moreover, Vsevolod's backing, in addition to that of the Ol'govichi and the Rostislavichi, gave him command of the most powerful force in the land. In order to maintain his supremacy, however, Svyatoslav had to keep his allies united.

He took steps to do so soon after. At the beginning of 1183, we are told, he arranged marriages for two of his sons. First, Gleb married Ryurik's daughter, whom the *Lyubetskiy sinodik* calls Anastasia.[185] Second, Mstislav, as had been arranged, married Vsevolod's sister-in-law Yasynya. The *Lyubetskiy*

---

[182] NPL, pp. 37, 227; N4, p. 172; compare the Hypatian Chronicle, which says Vladimir was expelled in the autumn (Ipat., col. 624).
[183] See s.a. 1180: Ipat., col. 624; compare Gust., p. 318.
[184] Tat. 4, p. 297; Tat. 3, p. 127.   [185] Zotov, p. 273.

sinodik gives her the Christian name Marfa.[186] Vsevolod was quick off the
mark to take advantage of his renewed friendship with Svyatoslav. Having
declared war on the Volga Bulgars, he asked Svyatoslav for assistance. The
latter complied by sending his eldest son, Vladimir.[187]

CHURCH AND DYNASTIC AFFAIRS

The year 1184 was very eventful in Church, dynastic, and political affairs.
Let us examine the Church and dynastic news first. In that year, the bishop
of Rostov died so Metropolitan Nikifor and Svyatoslav Vsevolodovich sent
Nikola, a Greek, to replace him. Vsevolod, however, challenged their choice
claiming that the right of selecting the candidate belonged to the people of
the appointee's see. It is not the purpose of this investigation to examine
the question of who had the right to select a bishop. For our purposes it
is noteworthy that after Vsevolod challenged Svyatoslav's choice, the latter
agreed with Vsevolod in order to avoid a confrontation.[188] Nevertheless,
even though the prince of Suzdalia presented his own candidate, it was
still the metropolitan and Svyatoslav who appointed him. Significantly, the
duumvir Ryurik did not share the authority that Svyatoslav exercised over
ecclesiastical matters.

Svyatoslav also initiated a building project soon after moving to Kiev. On
January 1, 1185, Metropolitan Nikifor, the bishop of Yur'ev, and the archi-
mandrite of the Caves Monastery, *Igumen* Vasily, consecrated the Church
of St. Vasily located on the great court. Although the chronicler states that
other bishops were present, only the hierarchy from the Kievan land officiated. Some fifty years had passed since the last church had been consecrated
on the great court,[189] and civic pride dictated that the event be an exclusively
Kievan affair.

After the ceremony Metropolitan Nikifor, the other bishops, the abbots,
the clergy, and the townspeople attended a feast which Svyatoslav, who built

---

[186] See s.a. 1182: Ipat., cols. 624–5. Concerning the date, see Berezhkov, p. 201. Concerning Marfa, see
Zotov, p. 274.
[187] See s.a. 1182: Ipat., cols. 625–6; compare s.a. 1183: Mosk., p. 90; s.a. 1184: Lav., cols. 389–90.
One source claims Vsevolod declared war in the winter, that is, early in 1183 (s.a. 1182: Gust.,
p. 318), while Tatishchev says the campaign took place in May and June (Tat. 4, pp. 298–9; Tat. 3,
pp. 128–30). Concerning the year, see Berezhkov, p. 201.
[188] See s.a. 1183: Ipat., cols. 629–30; Gust., p. 319; s.a. 1185: Lav., cols. 390–2. Concerning the date, see
Berezhkov, pp. 82, 201–2.
[189] See P. A. Rappoport, *Drevnerusskaya Arkhitektura* (Sankt-Peterburg, 1993), pp. 259–62 and P. P.
Tolochko, *Kiev i Kievskaya zemlya v epokhu feodal'noy razdroblennosti XII–XIII vekov* (K., 1980),
pp. 54–7.

the church, hosted.[190] The scribe expresses no interest in naming the other princes who attended. And yet, Ryurik and the Ol'govichi must have come to congratulate their senior prince on his achievement. The chronicler also tells us nothing about the church's appearance and how long it took to build it. If, however, we accept the rule of thumb that it took some three years to erect a brick church, Svyatoslav commissioned it around 1181, soon after occupying Kiev. Investigators are not agreed on its location, but it was probably the church which became known as the Trekhsvyatitel'skaya on the northeast corner of Vladimir's town, on the site known as Perun's Hill.[191]

What was Svyatoslav's motive for building a church on the great court? Why did he not choose a site in the Kopyrev suburb, where his great-great-grandfather Svyatoslav had built the Monastery of St. Simeon, or at Dorogozhichi, where his father had built the Monastery of St. Cyril? The most likely reason why he chose the citadel was that it provided his church with greater prominence. Since it was located in the heart of the renowned complex of structures boasting the Tithe Church and St. Michael the Golden-Domed, the reputations of the Church of St. Vasily and its patron were enhanced by their association with these jewels of early Rus' architecture.

The chronicler also fails to explain the intriguing question of why Svyatoslav dedicated the church to St. Vasily. We have seen that his patron was evidently St. Michael to whom he dedicated his first church in Chernigov.[192] We are therefore led to conclude, even though there appears to be no precedent for this, that he dedicated the church to another man's patron.[193] But whom did he wish to honor in this fashion? We know that three prominent men who were associated with Svyatoslav were identified with St. Vasily. They were: *Igumen* Vasily of the Caves Monastery; Svyatoslav's father-in-law Vasil'ko of Polotsk;[194] and Ryurik, whose patron was St. Vasily.[195]

---

[190] See s.a. 1183: Ipat., col. 634; Gust., p. 319; compare Makhnovets', pp. 334–5.

[191] See Rappoport, pp. 10–1; S. R. Kilievich, *Na gore starokievskoy* (K., 1982), p. 54, and Tolochko, *Kiev i Kievskaya zemlya*, pp. 54–5, nr. 8. Some historians argue that Ryurik built the Trekhsvyatitel'skaya Church in 1197 (e.g., K. N. Afanas'ev, *Postroenie arkhitekturnoy formy drevnerusskimi zodchimi* [M., 1961], p. 193). Also, see below, p. 155.

[192] See above, p. 124.

[193] The closest parallel is that found during the last quarter of the eleventh century between Svyatoslav's grandfather Oleg and the latter's uncle Vsevolod Yaroslavich. As has been suggested elsewhere, Vsevolod agreed to complete building the Church of SS. Boris and Gleb in Vyshgorod in return for Oleg's promise not to challenge Vsevolod's jurisdiction over Chernigov (M. Dimnik, "Oleg Svyatoslavich and his Patronage of the Cult of SS. Boris and Gleb," *Mediaeval Studies* 50 [Toronto, 1988], pp. 355–9, and *Dynasty*, pp. 166–7).

[194] Ipat., col. 313.

[195] Under the year 1197 we are told that Ryurik built the Church of St. Vasily after his own name (*vo imya svoe*) (Ipat., col. 707).

Igumen Vasily is mentioned in association with Svyatoslav for the first time at the consecration ceremony. In 1183 the monks of the Caves Monastery elected him as their *igumen*.[196] There is no evidence that Svyatoslav influenced the election. Consequently, we have no reason to believe that a special bond existed between the two. Nor do the chronicles report any special friendship, aside from the marriage tie, existing between Svyatoslav and his father-in-law. What is more, Vasil'ko was probably dead by this time.

This leaves Ryurik as the possible object of Svyatoslav's benefaction. We have seen that he negotiated a political pact with Ryurik concerning Kiev. Later, in 1183, he also established a personal bond with his co-ruler when his son Gleb married Ryurik's daughter. After that, the chroniclers almost always acknowledge their personal association by referring to Ryurik as Svyatoslav's *svat*, that is, the father of his daughter-in-law.[197] In the light of Ryurik's willingness to turn over control of Kiev and eagerness to cement the political pact with a marriage alliance, Svyatoslav most likely showed his gratitude by erecting a church in honor of Ryurik's patron saint.

Under the year 1197, Ryurik himself built a church of St. Vasily in Kiev.[198] Significantly, only one church dedicated to that saint, the so-called Trekhsvyatitel'skaya, has been identified. It has therefore been suggested that Ryurik merely repaired the church erected by Svyatoslav after it had been damaged, in 1196, by an earthquake.[199] If the churches built by Svyatoslav and Ryurik were one and the same, Ryurik's interest in Svyatoslav's church strongly suggests he had a special attachment to it.

Thus we see that, after the death of his father Vsevolod, Svyatoslav was the first prince of Kiev who had a propensity for building churches and who ruled for a sufficiently long period of time to contribute to the town's architectural splendour. In founding St. Vasily, he followed the examples of his relatives who had erected churches in the Kievan land. As we have seen, his father and mother had patronized the Monastery of St. Cyril at Dorogozhichi and his father had constructed the Church of St. George in Kanev. His grandfather, Oleg, had rebuilt the shrine to SS. Boris and Gleb in Vyshgorod begun by his father Svyatoslav. The latter had also

---

[196] See s.a. 1182: Ipat., cols. 626–8. Concerning the date, see Berezhkov, p. 201.

[197] See, for example, Ipat., cols. 628, 651, 652, and 659. Shakhmatov suggests that Ryurik's chronicler obtained a copy of Svyatoslav's chronicle at a later date and systematically inserted Ryurik's name alongside Svyatoslav's to make it appear as if Svyatoslav always made his decision after consultation with Ryurik (*Obozrenie*, p. 71). If this observation is correct, it confirms our argument that Ryurik, in particular, valued his family association with Svyatoslav, since his chronicler almost always identified him as Svyatoslav's *svat*.

[198] Ipat., col. 707.

[199] Concerning the earthquake, see below, p. 217 see also Rybakov, "Drevnosti Chernigova," p. 92.

founded the Monastery of St. Simeon in the Kopyrev suburb. Svyatoslav, however, was the only prince of the dynasty who could boast of having built a church in the most prestigious location in all of Rus': on the great court. His achievement shows that he established unprecedented good relations with the Kievans. Never before had the townsmen allowed a prince of their avowedly despised dynasty to build a church in the inner sanctum, as it were, of Kiev.

One item of information concerning the Ol'govichi under the year 1184 is of dynastic interest. We are told that Vladimir, after being driven out of Galich by his father Yaroslav Osmomysl, was living with Igor' in Putivl'. Ignoring the threat of Yaroslav's reprisals, Igor' harbored his brother-in-law for two years and, in the third, reconciled him with his father. After that, Igor' dispatched his son Svyatoslav, Ryurik's son-in-law (*zyat'*) we are told, to escort Vladimir home.[200] In sending his son to accompany Vladimir, Igor' reaffirmed his desire to foster friendship with his in-laws.

To judge from the news that Svyatoslav was Ryurik's son-in-law, Igor' had also negotiated a personal tie with the duumvir. Significantly, the boy would not marry until 1188.[201] Was calling him the son-in-law four years earlier therefore an anachronism? This seems unlikely since the chronicler probably recorded the entry in 1184 and knew about the betrothal at that time. Svyatoslav was only eight years of age in that year.[202] As was often the case, therefore, the fathers arranged the match before the children were of marriageable age.

SVYATOSLAV SENDS IGOR' IN PURSUIT OF THE POLOVTSY

All the while that the above-mentioned Church and dynastic events were taking place, the princes were on a war footing. The Polovtsy had dramatically escalated their incursions and confronting them became Svyatoslav's greatest challenge. On February 23, 1184, Khan Konchak with his Donets Polovtsy pillaged the Pereyaslavl' lands as far as Dmitrov.[203] Svyatoslav summoned his *svat* Ryurik and they rode against the raiders. At Ol'zhichi they met Yaroslav of Chernigov who advised them not to pursue the nomads

---

[200] See s.a. 1183: Ipat., cols. 633–4. It would appear that the entry was written after Vladimir returned to his father in Galich because we are told that he had come to Igor' when the latter was living in Putivl'. Since Igor' moved to Novgorod Severskiy after the death of his brother Oleg on January 16, 1180 (see above, p. 141), Vladimir came to Igor' before that date. As Vladimir stayed with Igor' for almost three years he probably returned to Galich some time in the early 1180s.

[201] See below, p. 189.   [202] He was born in 1176; concerning his birth, see above, p. 137.

[203] The town's exact location is not known, but it probably lay near the border of the Chernigov lands, namely, on the right bank of the river Romen not far from Glebl' (Makhnovets', p. 549; compare Barsov, p. 61).

but to organize a summer campaign. They heeded his counsel and returned home. Later, however, Svyatoslav sent his sons and his troops to Igor' ordering him to pursue the tribesmen. Ryurik, for his part, sent his troops under the command of Vladimir Glebovich of Pereyaslavl'.[204]

The account reveals that, although the duumvirs shared the obligation of supplying troops, Svyatoslav was the commander-in-chief with the responsibility of initiating campaigns in defense of Rus'. The chronicler further attests to Svyatoslav's superior status by giving him the place of prominence in relation to Ryurik. After Svyatoslav appointed Igor' to command all the troops of the Ol'govichi in his place, Ryurik also appointed Vladimir of Pereyaslavl' to lead his troops. More important, however, Svyatoslav had the authority to place Igor' in charge of the entire campaign.

Igor' asserted his authority even before his troops set out. He refused Vladimir of Pereyaslavl' permission to spearhead the attack. At first sight it is surprising that he turned down Vladimir's seemingly selfless offer to place himself at the forefront of the fighting. In addition to the glory that accrued to the prince leading the attack, however, there were additional benefits. Igor' and Vladimir quarreled, it has been observed, because the vanguard contingent would get the first chance to grab the booty.[205] Nevertheless, Vladimir made a fair request because Konchak had raided his towns and he wished to reclaim the pillaged property of his people.

After Igor' denied him his request, Vladimir compensated for his losses by pillaging the Seversk towns of the Ol'govichi.[206] Surprisingly, the chronicler did not condemn the prince for the misdeed. His silence suggests that he considered Igor''s rebuff unfair and Vladimir's vindictiveness justified. Moreover, as we shall see, after his defeat at the river Kayala in the following year, Igor' confessed that he had wronged the Christians of Rus' by attacking Vladimir's town of Glebov.[207] Because of Igor''s revenge, the chronicler had no cause to berate Vladimir because Igor' had balanced the scales. He probably did so on his way home from the river Khiriya, a tributary of the Vorskla, where he confronted the Polovtsy.

[204] Ipat., col. 628.
[205] V. G. Lyaskoronsky, "Severskie knyaz'ya i polovtsy pered nashestviem na Rus' mongolov," in *Sbornik statey v chest' Dmitriya Aleksandrovicha Korsakova: Istoriya – Istoriya literatury – Arkheologiya – Yazykovedenie – Filosofiya – Pedagogika* (Kazan', 1913), p. 285. As we shall see, after Igor''s initial victory at the river Syuurliy, he allowed the younger princes who formed the vanguard of his force to pursue the defeated nomads and to pillage their camps.
[206] Before the arrival of the Varangians in Rus', the tribe of Severyane occupied the territories along the middle and lower parts of the Desna. The domains of the Ol'govichi were therefore also known as "the land of the Severyane" (*Severskaya zemlya*) (*Dynasty*, p. 5).
[207] According to Makhnovets', Glebov was located on the right bank of the river Trubezh (p. 547). See below, p. 173.

After Vladimir rode off in a huff, the chronicler states enigmatically that Igor' sent the Kievan troops home and commanded his nephew Svyatoslav, Oleg's son, to escort them intact. Igor' presumably sent the men home as a precaution. After Vladimir withdrew Ryurik's forces from the campaign, Igor' evidently refused to take Svyatoslav's men into battle. It seems that he did not wish to leave Svyatoslav defenseless in Kiev while Ryurik had his *druzhina* at his side. Consequently, he went in pursuit of the Polovtsy with a greatly diminished force including his brother Vsevolod, Svyatoslav's son Vsevolod, a certain Andrey with Roman,[208] and some Black Caps.[209]

Svyatoslav placed Igor' in command because his brother Yaroslav had agreed to campaign with him in the summer. Igor', as the next in seniority, was therefore the obvious Ol'govich to lead the winter expedition. He had additional qualifications. Of the Chernigov domains, those of the cadet branch in the Posem'e region were the most vulnerable to Polovtsian raids. These not only gave Igor''s men greater expertise in fighting the nomads, but they prompted Igor' to form personal ties with several khans including Konchak. Indeed, it may have been his friendship with Igor' that dissuaded the khan from raiding the districts of the Ol'govichi on this occasion. Significantly, Igor''s commitment to defending the lands of Rus' overrode his friendship with the khan. Consequently, he pursued the raiders, found them at the river Khiriya, and took many captive.[210]

IGOR' AND YAROSLAV BOYCOTT SVYATOSLAV'S CAMPAIGN

That summer Svyatoslav launched a major campaign against the Polovtsy as his brother Yaroslav had advised him to do. The princes he and Ryurik conscripted were related to them either through blood or through marriage. Svyatoslav summoned the following: his sons Mstislav and Gleb; Vladimir of Pereyaslavl', who had been Ryurik's delegate for the winter campaign

---

[208] Since Andrey came with Roman, the two were evidently related in some way and Andrey was the elder. Makhnovets' claims they were Igor''s sons. Although, we learn later that Igor' had a son named Roman, the sources never mention an Andrey. Makhnovets' therefore suggests that Andrey was Igor''s son Svyatoslav to whom the chronicler refers by his baptismal name (Makhnovets', p. 332). According to the *Lyubetskiy sinodik*, however, Svyatoslav's baptismal name was Adrian (Zotov, p. 277). Although the chronicler could have mistakenly written the name Andrey for Adrian, he did not as a rule identify princes by their baptismal names. Indeed, as we have seen, under the same year he referred to Svyatoslav by his princely name when identifying him as Ryurik's son-in-law. It is unlikely, therefore, that Andrey and Roman were Ol'govichi. Perhaps they were *izgoi*, who, like Igor''s brother-in-law Vladimir, sought Igor''s hospitality and offered military service in return.
[209] Ipat., col. 629.
[210] Concerning the campaign, see s.a. 1183: Ipat., cols. 628–9; compare Gust., pp. 318–19. Concerning the dates, see Berezhkov, p. 201.

but was the son-in-law of Yaroslav of Chernigov; and Yaroslav Osmomysl, Igor′'s father-in-law. Mstislav of Goroden had Chernigov ties in that his sister had married Vladimir Davidovich (d. 1151).[211] Mstislav Vladimirovich of Dorogobuzh, as we have seen, had married one of Svyatoslav's daughters.[212] Ryurik's sons did not accompany him, but his nephews Mstislav Romanovich and Izyaslav Davidovich came.[213] Yaroslav and Gleb, princes from the House of Turov, were the brothers of Ryurik's wife Anna.[214] As for the princes of Lutsk, Vsevolod and Mstislav, the former had married Anna's sister.[215]

The chronicler's list of participants suggests that each duumvir summoned six princes. But the numerical balance was accidental. Svyatoslav's three eldest sons, Vladimir, Oleg, and Vsevolod, who were evidently living in the Vyatichi lands, failed to come.[216] Igor′ and the princes of the cadet branch also boycotted the expedition. But the most surprising absentee was Svyatoslav's brother Yaroslav who had suggested the summer campaign. He was seemingly the most inactive of the Ol′govichi from among the oldest generation. It is difficult to know whether he was shirking his military obligations or dutifully remaining behind to defend Chernigov.

Before condemning the Ol′govichi for truancy we must note that Yaroslav and Igor′ had sound reasons for not joining Svyatoslav. The campaign would take them on a long circuitous route from the Chernigov lands. In following the Dnepr deep into the steppe they would absent themselves for too long a period of time from their lands and leave their homes vulnerable to attack. They therefore proposed that Svyatoslav take the route across the Pereyaslavl′ lands and they would meet him at the river Sula. It was evidently the route that Igor′ had taken to the river Khiriya. That region was closer to the pastures of Konchak and the Donets tribes. Yaroslav and Igor′ believed Konchak's alliance to be a greater threat to them to judge from the news that Igor′ had routed them earlier in the year. Moreover, should a band invade the Posem′e region while the princes were

[211] Baum., VII, 4, 5.
[212] We have indirect chronicle evidence for the existence of Svyatoslav's unidentified daughter. Under the year 1177, the Hypatian chronicler tells us that Svyatoslav's brother Yaroslav and Svyatoslav's son Oleg sent messengers to Mstislav Vladimirovich "to his brother-in-law" (*zyat′*) indicating that Mstislav had married Oleg's sister (Ipat., col. 604). See also Zotov, p. 274 and Baum., V, 41.
[213] Baum., IX, 11 and 13.   [214] Baum., II, 24, 25, 27.   [215] Baum., XIV, 2, 3.
[216] Since Mstislav and Gleb did not have to come from the Chernigov side of the Dnepr, it appears that they were probably living with their father in Kiev. Svyatoslav could not give them any other towns in the Kievan land since he controlled only Kiev. Nevertheless, it is possible that as a gesture of good will Ryurik, who controlled the towns in the surrounding Kievan land, gave Svyatoslav's two youngest sons domains in the vicinity of Kiev. At a later date, as we shall see, Ryurik's son-in-law Gleb did rule a town in the Kievan land.

campaigning, they would be in a better position to intercept the marauders. Svyatoslav rejected their proposal because his and Ryurik's lands on the west bank were not in danger of attack from these nomads. They planned to raid Khan Kobyak's alliance of tribes in the region of the river Erel′, a left tributary of the Dnepr,[217] because the Dnepr tribes were the greatest threat to them.[218]

Whereas Igor′ willingly led a retaliatory campaign against Konchak earlier in the winter, he refused to march on an offensive expedition. Since Kobyak's bands had pillaged neither his nor Yaroslav's lands, he evidently harboured no special animosity towards the khan. But Igor′ may also have had a personal reason for not joining Svyatoslav's campaign. Kobyak's main victim had been Vladimir of Pereyaslavl′. Because of Igor′'s recent altercation with Vladimir, he was probably not eager to campaign on behalf of the Pereyaslavl′ lands. As the senior prince of Rus′, however, Svyatoslav had the duty of organizing all-Rus′ expeditions against any khans who devastated Rus′ lands. It mattered not if these lands belonged to the Ol′govichi or to the Monomashichi, if they were located on the left bank or on the right bank.

Svyatoslav led his allies along the west shore of the Dnepr and at "Inzhir′ brod" crossed over to the "warring side."[219] On July 30, the princes were victorious at the river Erel′. On the ideological level, the Christians of Rus′ inflicted a crushing defeat on the pagans. On the political level, the princes returned home basking in "great glory and honor." The booty that they seized included 7,000 Polovtsian captives, sixteen of their khans including Osoluk Burchevich,[220] Kobyak with two of his sons, large herds of animals, goods that the nomads had plundered, and Christians whom the Polovtsy had taken captive.

It should be noted, however, that in reporting this and other princely victories over the nomads, the chroniclers give ultimate credit to divine intervention. Thus, one reports that God inspired the hearts of Svyatoslav and Ryurik to march against the Polovtsy, implying that He assured them

[217] The chronicler explains that the Erel′ was called the Ugol (Ugla) by the Rus′. Today it is called the Orel′.

[218] Pletneva points out that the Polovtsy from the Don basin usually attacked the lands of Chernigov and that the Polovtsy from the Dnepr region normally attacked the lands of Pereyaslavl′ and Kiev ("Polovetskaya zemlya," p. 283 and her *Polovtsy*, p. 146).

[219] Investigators are not agreed on the location of the Inzhir′ brod ford. According to some it was on the Dnepr near the mouth of the river Sula (Murav′eva and Kuz′mina, *Imennoy i geograficheskiy ukazateli*, p. 85). Others claim it was on the Dnepr in the vicinity of the mouth of the river Vorskla (Rybakov, *"Slovo o polku Igoreve,"* p. 207). Others still place it on the river Erel′ near its mouth (Makhnovets′, p. 552).

[220] Concerning Osoluk, see below, p. 203.

victory. Later, Svyatoslav placed the campaign into the hands of Divine Providence. When the princes fought, God and His Holy Mother assisted them. The Polovtsy fled driven by the wrath of God and that of His Holy Mother. In granting the princes victory, God had mercy on the Christians of Rus′ and extolled the princes for their faith. The references to divine assistance reflected the beliefs of the princes and the Christians of Rus′ suffering at the hands of the pagans.[221]

IGOR′ CONDUCTS A SEPARATE RAID

Meanwhile, Igor′ had no intention of shirking his military obligations. His refusal to join Svyatoslav was counter-balanced by his resolve to fight tribesmen living closer to the Posem′e region. When he learnt that Svyatoslav's troops had departed, he summoned his relatives. Members of all three families of the cadet branch joined him: his eldest son Vladimir from Putivl′, his brother Vsevolod from Trubetsk, and Svyatoslav of Ryl′sk, the son of his deceased brother Oleg. In the light of Yaroslav's past and, as we shall see, future lack of participation on campaigns, Igor′ probably considered it pointless to call him. As for Svyatoslav's three eldest sons who had not arrived in time to join their father, it appears that Igor′ was also not prepared to wait for them.

He was unable to inform the campaigning Svyatoslav of his proposed raid, but even if he could have told Svyatoslav, he would not have considered it necessary to do so. First, his position of seniority in the cadet branch gave him a considerable degree of independence concerning military campaigns. Second, his initiative was in keeping with the behavior of the princes living on the "warring side" of the Dnepr. As has been noted, the towns of the Ol′govichi in the upper reaches of the Seym were especially vulnerable to nomadic raids. As a result, princes living in this frontier region frequently sallied forth in pursuit of marauders on their own initiative.[222] Thus, in leading his family against the nomads, Igor′ was exercising his prerogative.

His aim was to plunder Polovtsian camps because the nomads were preoccupied fighting Svyatoslav's forces and had left their tents unguarded.

---

[221] Concerning the campaign, see s.a. 1183: Ipat., cols. 630–3; s.a. 1185: Lav., cols. 394–6; Mosk., p. 91. Concerning the date, see Berezhkov, pp. 82, 202. In the second redaction of his work, Tatishchev gives a unique item of news. After the victory, Svyatoslav and Ryurik rewarded Vladimir for his valor by letting him take the Polovtsian princes whom he had captured. He later released them for a high ransom (Tat. 3, p. 132).

[222] In 1171, for example, Igor′ led a punitive campaign beyond the Vorskla in pursuit of nomads who had raided the Posem′e region. When he heard that Khans Kobyak and Konchak were raiding the Pereyaslavl′ lands, he turned back to confront them (see above, pp. 122–3).

Anticipating no opposition, Igor' was surprised to chance upon a Polovtsian raiding party of 400 strong around the river Merla south of the Khiriya. This was a fortuitous encounter. It gave his men an unexpected opportunity to win glory in battle. Although the confrontation diverted them from their original purpose, their victory over the would-be raiders was of greater benefit because it saved Christians from attack.[223] Igor' returned home content that the cadet branch had fulfilled its responsibility of protecting Rus'. Moreover, by pre-empting a Polovtsian raid, perhaps on the Posem'e, Igor' proved to Svyatoslav that his excuse for not going down the circuitous Dnepr route was justified.

In this way Igor' conducted yet another successful campaign. Moreover, he once again traveled across the Pereyaslavl' lands. He probably took the southeasterly route along the western edge of the so-called central-Russian plateau to the river Merla west of the Donets. This was the alternate course that he and Yaroslav had proposed to Svyatoslav. The evidence that Igor' followed it on both campaigns gives credence to his proposal that he was willing to accompany Svyatoslav provided the latter took the overland route.

KHAN KONCHAK ATTACKS RUS'

In 1185, "the cursed, godless, and thrice-damned Konchak" attacked Rus' with a large force. He wanted to set fire to the towns because he had an infidel with him who had a device for shooting living fire. After crossing the Khorol he stopped before reaching the Sula, which had a chain of outposts on its right bank.[224] He sent envoys to Yaroslav in Chernigov proposing peace. Perhaps, because Yaroslav stubbornly boycotted attacks against the Polovtsy, the khan contrived to secure the prince's neutrality, alienate him from Svyatoslav and Igor', and undermine the defenses of Rus'. Konchak judged his victim well because Yaroslav sent a certain Ol'stin Oleksich to negotiate.

On learning of Konchak's invasion, Svyatoslav and Ryurik quickly assembled a force. After crossing the river Khorol they spotted the enemy resting in a water meadow. They defeated the nomads, took many captive, but Konchak escaped. "God gave the victory to Svyatoslav and

---

[223] Concerning Igor''s campaign, see s.a. 1183: Ipat., col. 633; Makhnovets', p. 334; Gust., p. 319.

[224] The right bank of the river Sula is an escarpment, which served as a line of defense against nomadic attacks. It was fortified by a series of outposts like Romen, Kosnyatin, Luben, Lukoml', Goroshin, Rimov, and Zhelni (V. G. Lyaskoronsky, "K voprosu o Pereyaslavl'skikh Torkakh," Zh. M. N. P., chast' 358 [Spb., 1905], 298).

Ryurik on March 1 through the intercession of the holy martyrs Boris and Gleb."[225]

Yaroslav of Chernigov refused to join the campaign because he had sent Ol'stin to negotiate with Konchak and he did not wish to endanger the *boyar*. As a result, one chronicler observes, the princes were ashamed of Yaroslav because he refused to fight the nomads.[226] Igor', however, expressed an unbridled enthusiasm to attack Konchak. The chronicler claims that he was eager to campaign even against the advice of his *druzhinniki*. Granted, his zeal for fighting the enemy was consistent with his earlier conduct. Nevertheless, it is enigmatic if we take into account the news that, as we shall see, he had already negotiated a match for his son Vladimir with Konchak's daughter. It has therefore been suggested that, in reality, Igor' was unwilling to wage war against his future in-law. The report of his eagerness to do so was the chronicler's attempt at whitewashing the prince's true sentiments. Svyatoslav, it is argued, gave Igor' sufficient time to join the main force and the report that adverse weather conditions (soft snow with a thin crust of ice on top) prevented his departure was the chronicler's invention.[227] The argument is unconvincing in the light of Igor''s conduct before and after this event.[228]

Some seven weeks after Svyatoslav's victory over Konchak, he sent a certain Roman Nezdilovich and the Berendei to attack the nomads. On April 21, they pillaged many camps and captured much booty.[229] In imitation of the nomads who sent small raiding parties into the princes' domains, a Rus' contingent could also penetrate the Polovtsian pastures undetected, conduct a lightning strike, and return home safely. Roman's success shows that the princes favoured such daring ventures.

IGOR''S DEFEAT AT THE KAYALA

Next, the chronicles report Igor''s disastrous campaign of 1185, which has become immortalized through its literary rendering in "The Lay of Igor''s Campaign" (*Slovo o polku Igoreve*), an epic poem written by an anonymous bard.[230] We will not use the poem as a source for our investigation. Although

---

[225] See s.a. 1184: Ipat., cols. 634–6; Makhnovets', pp. 335–6. Concerning the date, see Berezhkov, p. 202.

[226] See s.a. 1185: Gust., p. 319.   [227] Rybakov, *"Slovo o polku Igoreve,"* pp. 214–15, 227.

[228] Ipat., cols. 636–7.   [229] Ipat., col. 637.

[230] The identity of the contemporary author is unknown. According to Hrushevsky, the work was written during Svyatoslav's reign in Kiev (*Istoriia*, vol. 2, p. 331, n. 8), while Rybakov claims it was composed around 1190 at Ryurik's court (*"Slovo o polku Igoreve,"* pp. 9–10).

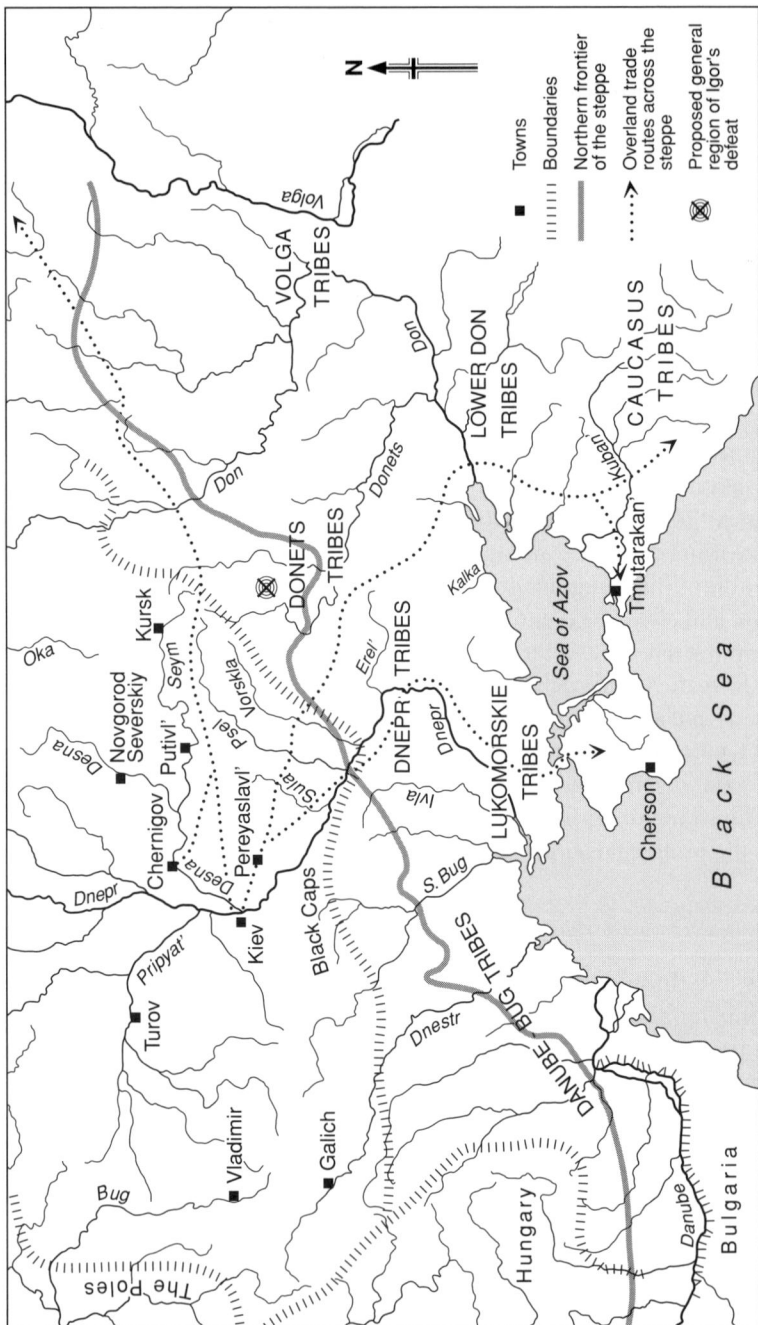

Map 3 Polovtsian tribes in the second half of the twelfth and the first half of the thirteenth century (adapted from S. A. Pletneva)

the literary work is based on the historical event and reflects the spirit of the age, researchers have pointed out that it offers no new evidence concerning the political history of the Ol'govichi. It merely repeats data found in the chronicles.[231]

The poem's greatest value to historical research is the evidence it offers concerning the chronology of events, the topography of the terrain, and specific details describing Igor''s military encounters. Investigators have used such details, along with those given by the chronicles, as signposts for determining the route of Igor''s march and the place of the massacre. Nevertheless, to date, no suggested site has been universally accepted as the definitive location of the defeat. But the proposal that Igor' campaigned in the upper reaches of the left bank of the river Donets is the most convincing (map 3).[232]

It is also not our purpose to do a textological study of the chronicle accounts. Others have established that the Hypatian account is the most detailed and based on eyewitness reports.[233] It will serve as our basic text. Investigators have also pointed out that a number of authors wrote different sections of the Hypatian account. The first section describing Igor''s campaign and capture came from Igor''s chronicler. Svyatoslav's Kievan scribe wrote the report of his intervention. Vladimir Glebovich's man described his prince's defense of Pereyaslavl'. Finally, the section describing Igor''s escape was, once again, the work of his author.[234]

The Laurentian Chronicle offers no cameos of individual princes; it presents a continuous narrative written by one author. His information is less reliable because he was unfamiliar with the events and with the geography of the south. He was also hostile to Igor'.[235] We will cite his

---

[231] See, for example, M. Yu. Braychevsky, "Chernigovskiy knyazheskiy dom i avtor 'Slova o polku Igoreve'," *Problemy arkheologii yuzhnoy Rusi*: Materialy istoriko-arkheologicheskogo seminara "Chernigov i ego okruga v IX–XIII vv.," Chernigov, 26–28 sentyabrya 1988 g., T. N. Telizhenko (ed.) (K., 1990), pp. 10–15, and A. A. Zimin, "Ipat'evskaya letopis' i 'Slovo o polku Igoreve'," *Istoriya SSSR*, nr. 6 (M., 1968), 43–64. Compare A. G. Kuz'min, who challenges Zimin's views ("Ipat'evskaya letopis' i 'Slovo o polku Igoreve' [Po povodu stat'i A. A. Zimina]," *Istoriya SSSR*, nr. 6 [M., 1968], 64–87).

[232] See Pyadyshev, "Pokhod Igorya," pp. 42–65; Pletneva, "Polovetskaya zemlya," p. 291. Some suggest that the Kayala was on the right bank of the Donets (for example, K. V. Kudryashov, *Pro Igorya Severskogo, pro Zemlyu russkuyu* [M. 1959], pp. 44–6; Getmanets, *Tayna reki Kayaly*, pp. 37–52, 101–11). Still others say that the battle was fought near one of the eastern tributaries of the Dnepr, namely, in the upper reaches of the river Orel' (for example, V. G. Fedorov, *Kto byl avtorom "Slova o polku Igoreve" i gde raspolozhena reka Kayala* [M., 1956], pp. 69–75, 172–3) and in the upper reaches of the river Samara (for example, Rybakov, *"Slovo o polku Igoreve,"* pp. 233–8, 245).

[233] See, for example, Shakhmatov, *Obozrenie*, pp. 69–74; M. D. Priselkov, *Istoriya russkogo letopisaniya*, pp. 46–52; Likhachev, *Russkie letopisi*, pp. 182–96; and Rybakov, *"Slovo o polku Igoreve,"* pp. 170–201.

[234] Zimin, "Ipat'evskaya letopis' i 'Slovo o polku Igoreve'," p. 49. Compare B. A. Rybakov, "Kievskaya letopisnaya povest' o pokhode Igorya v 1185 g.," *TODRL* 24 (L., 1969), 58–63.

[235] Concerning examples of errors in the Laurentian account, see Rybakov, *"Slovo o polku Igoreve,"* pp. 194–7, and Pyadyshev, "Pokhod Igorya," 48–9.

news only when it conflicts with or adds to the Hypatian account. Finally, Tatishchev has unique information. If it is not found in both redactions of his work, however, it will not be discussed in the main text. The purpose of our investigation is to present Igor''s campaign as reported by the chronicles. We will attempt to assess his relationships with the Polovtsy, the Ol'govichi, and the princes of Rus'.[236]

Thus, the Hypatian chronicler reports that two days after Easter, on Tuesday April 23, Igor' left Novgorod Severskiy.[237] He summoned his brother Vsevolod from Trubetsk (Trubchesk, Trubech), his nephew Svyatoslav Ol'govich from Ryl'sk, his son Vladimir from Putivl',[238] and Yaroslav of Chernigov. After gathering their men on hardy horses, the princes rode to the river Donets. On the evening of May 1, they witnessed an eclipse of the sun.[239] Igor''s men declared that it boded ill. He however replied that no one knew God's will but they would find out if they rode forth. After crossing the Donets and arriving at the river Oskol, Igor' waited for two days for Vsevolod, who was coming via Kursk.

The list of princes who participated on the campaign confirms that the sons of Oleg and Igor' inherited their fathers' domains. Oleg's patrimony of Ryl'sk went to his only son, Svyatoslav. After Igor' succeeded Oleg to Novgorod Severskiy, he gave his patrimony of Putivl' to his eldest son, Vladimir. We also learn that Igor''s brother, Vsevolod, ruled Trubetsk, located north of Novgorod Severskiy on the right bank of the Desna. The town is mentioned for the first time. Archaeological evidence reveals that it was founded around the middle of the twelfth century. Consequently, Vsevolod was probably its first prince.[240]

One view has it that Vsevolod's domain included Kursk.[241] There is no chronicle evidence for this assertion except that Vsevolod travelled via Kursk to join Igor'. Granted, since Vsevolod's two elder brothers, Oleg and Igor', were given Ryl'sk and Putivl', it is reasonable to assume that their father, Svyatoslav Ol'govich, may have given Kursk, the eastern-most town on the Seym, to his youngest son. Nevertheless, later evidence

---

[236] For a more detailed presentation of the chronicle texts, see M. Dimnik, "Igor''s Defeat at the Kayala: The Chronicle Evidence," *Mediaeval Studies* 63 (2001), 259–76.

[237] Berezhkov confirms that in 1185 the Tuesday after Easter fell on April 23 (p. 202).

[238] The more distant Laurentian chronicler claims that two of his sons accompanied Igor' (Lav., col. 397). No other source supports this claim.

[239] The Hypatian Chronicle does not record the date. See, however, s.a. 1185: NPL, pp. 37, 228; s.a. 1186: Lav., col. 396, and Berezhkov, pp. 82, 203, 246.

[240] P. A. Rappoport, "Trubchevsk," SA, nr. 4 (M., 1973), pp. 205, 207, 209, 216. See also A. V. Kuza, *Malye goroda Drevney Rusi* (M., 1989), pp. 81–2.

[241] Rybakov, "*Slovo o polku Igoreve*," p. 89.

suggests that Svyatoslav gave the adjoining districts of Ryl'sk and Kursk to Oleg, thereby making his eldest son's patrimony the most powerful in the family.[242]

Significantly, Igor' invited Yaroslav, a member of the senior branch, to join him. Surprisingly, he cooperated. He did not go in person or send his sons, Rostislav and Yaropolk, who were still too young.[243] Instead, he dispatched Ol'stin, his former envoy to Konchak, along with the Kovui of the Chernigov lands.[244] Yaroslav's action reveals that his negotiations with the khan had failed. His willingness to deploy troops also demonstrates that he concurred with Igor''s Polovtsian policy.

Why did Igor' assemble troops mainly from the cadet branch? There was the moral consideration. Having missed Svyatoslav's winter campaign, he undoubtedly wished to exonerate his family from the accusation that it was shirking its duty of defending Rus'. There was also the practical consideration. Igor' rode against Polovtsian camps located in the upper reaches of the river Donets. These tribes posed the greatest threat to the Seversk towns in the Posem'e so that the onus of keeping these nomads at bay fell on the cadet branch. Furthermore, a year earlier Svyatoslav had rejected Igor' and Yaroslav's invitation to march against the Polovtsy along their preferred overland route. It is therefore unlikely that, in 1185, he would have joined Igor' on a similar campaign.

According to the hostile Laurentian chronicler, Igor' had another motive for attacking the nomads: he wished to win glory in the battlefield and praise from the people of Rus'. Despite the scribe's desire to defame Igor', the Hypatian chronicler indirectly confirms the allegation. At the river Salnitsa, he reports, Igor' refused to return home for fear that the Ol'govichi would have to live in shame for avoiding battle. Later, before confronting the enemy at the river Syuurliy, Igor' reminded his troops that the moment they had sought, to do battle with the nomads, had come. In addition to peer pressure, the princes' quest for glory was also stoked by youth. In 1185, Igor' was thirty-four years of age.[245] At that young age he was older than the three princes who accompanied him. As we shall see, after Svyatoslav heard of their defeat he observed that the impetuosity of youth had driven Igor' and his comrades against the enemy.

---

[242] See Rybakov, however, who claims that, after Novgorod Severskiy, the second most important town for the cadet branch was Putivl' and not Ryl'sk ("*Slovo o polku Igoreve*," p. 89).

[243] Rostislav, the elder of the two, was born in 1174 (Ipat., col. 568).

[244] The Kovui were pagan auxiliaries fighting in the service of the Ol'govichi. They probably lived in the Zadesen'e (Rybakov, *Kievskaya Rus'*, p. 507; Zaytsev, p. 79).

[245] Igor' was born in 1151 (Ipat., col. 422).

Was Igor''s raid a reckless venture as some have argued?[246] The evidence of previous campaigns shows that his initiative was realistic. As he was leading his men into the steppe, Svyatoslav's *boyar* Roman was returning with the booty he had pillaged from Polovtsian camps. If the *boyar*'s small force could successfully raid enemy encampments, the contingents of the cadet branch supplemented by Chernigov auxiliaries were certainly adequate for the task.[247] Indeed, in the previous summer, Igor' had also successfully penetrated the Polovtsian steppe. Therefore, in 1185 his objective – to slip into Polovtsian steppe undetected, destroy a number of camps, perhaps engage an enemy band in a skirmish, and return home with the booty – had every chance of success.[248]

Igor''s successful military career also testifies to his responsible conduct. Over a year earlier, Svyatoslav had expressed unreserved confidence in his leadership by ordering him to lead the retaliatory force against Konchak. In 1185, Igor' demonstrated his organizational skills in the way he orchestrated his relatives to rendezvous with him in the field. It has also been suggested that he timed his attack to coincide with Roman's campaign. Since the latter probably raided tents to the east of the Vorskla thereby drawing tribesmen to defend that region, Igor' believed he would have a freer hand raiding the Donets camps.[249] As we shall see, he demonstrated great competence in the way he set up his battle formation before the encounter at the river Syuurliy. Finally, during the battle, the authority with which he held back two contingents to safeguard against a counter-attack, while allowing the others to pursue the Polovtsy, illustrated the discipline he wielded over his troops.

The chronicles describe the encounter at the river Syuurliy as follows. After the princes joined forces at the river Oskol, a band of Polovtsy spotted them and sent horsemen to warn the neighboring camps. While the tribesmen were gathering their forces, the band, acting as an advance guard, rode to confront the princes. When Igor' arrived at the river Salnitsa, his scouts informed him that they had spotted the enemy in battle array. They advised him either to attack quickly before the Polovtsian band received

---

[246] See, for example, Lyaskoronsky, "Severskie knyaz'ya i polovtsy," p. 287.

[247] It has been suggested that Igor''s force consisted of some 6,000–8,000 strong (Getmanets, *Tayna reki Kayaly*, pp. 59–60).

[248] Many investigators are of the opinion that Igor' planned his campaign to be executed quickly without a major military encounter on the frontiers of the Polovtsian steppe (for example, Pyadyshev, "Pokhod Igorya," pp. 45–7; Getmanets, *Tayna reki Kayaly*, pp. 5, 36, 51). Others suggest that his aim was also to establish safe passage for merchants along the trade routes (Lyaskoronsky, "Severskie knyaz'ya i polovtsy," pp. 287, 296; V. V. Mavrodin, "Chernigovskoe knyazhestvo," in *Ocherki istorii SSSR* [1953], vol. 1, p. 399).

[249] Pyadyshev, "Pokhod Igorya," pp. 60–1.

reinforcements or to withdraw. Igor′ and his brothers refused to return home without engaging the enemy in battle because, they argued, their peers would mock them for fearing to face death and heap shame upon them. The princes therefore resolved to strike. They rode all night. Early the following morning, on Friday, they spotted the enemy across the river Syuurliy.

Igor′ arranged his six contingents into three groups. He placed his own troops in the center of the main group with his brother Vsevolod to his right and his nephew Svyatoslav to his left. In the group in front he stationed his son Vladimir, Yaroslav's troops commanded by Ol′stin, and the Kovui. The third group, constituting archers from all the contingents, acted as the vanguard. Igor′ exhorted his men to battle by reminding them that this was the moment they had sought. Placing their hope in God they charged the enemy.

As Igor′'s forces came to the river Syuurliy, the enemy archers shot a volley of arrows at them and withdrew. Even before the princes crossed the river, the horsemen, who were at a greater distance from the river than their archers, also fled. Svyatoslav, Vladimir, Ol′stin, the Kovui, and their archers set off in pursuit. Igor′ and Vsevolod, however, advanced in formation at a steady pace. The pursuers caught the nomads, defeated them, looted their tents, and rejoined Igor′ that night (figure 7).

After all the contingents had reassembled, Igor′ told his men that God had inflicted defeat on the nomads and bestowed glory and honor on the men of Rus′. They had seen, however, how great a force the Polovtsy had already mustered and how all the tribes were still gathering against them. He therefore advised that they withdraw under the cover of darkness. But Svyatoslav pointed out that he had pursued the Polovtsy over a great distance and that his horses were too exhausted to set off immediately. Vsevolod agreed. Reluctantly, Igor′ ordered his troops to rest for the night but warned them that they were courting certain death.

The Laurentian chronicler then gloats on the futility of the high-mindedness that Igor′'s men allegedly expressed after their victory. In their euphoria, they boasted how they had already penetrated deeper into the steppe than Svyatoslav and Ryurik had done, and how they would outdo even their forefathers by following the nomads to the very shores of the Sea of Azov. The princes did not plan to occupy those territories and rule them as their forefathers had ruled Tmutarakan′. Instead, the chronicler claims, they proposed to exterminate the Polovtsy. Because of their elation and the exuberance of youth, the princes may well have expressed bravado in this manner.

Figure 7   Svyatoslav Ol'govich pursuing the fleeing Polovtsy

According to the Hypatian chronicler, however, Igor' and his brothers claimed to have achieved their objective at the river Syuurliy and wished to return home. Unfortunately for them, they had unwittingly stumbled upon a cluster of enemy encampments. They had evidently entered a region on the left bank of the Donets that no Rus' force had penetrated before.[250] Alarmed at the audacity of the princes to come to their very lairs, the Donets Polovtsy sounded a general alarm. A multitude of tribesmen living within a day's ride rallied in defense of their camps. Even khans who were Igor''s friends, including Konchak, rode out against him.

The true metal of Igor''s troops was now to be tested. For three days enemy archers shot arrows at them without engaging them in battle. Their objective was to prevent the princes from reaching the water (that is, the lake). As Saturday dawned horsemen emerged from every direction so that it seemed to Igor''s men that pine forests surrounded them. He exclaimed that they had drawn the entire Polovtsian land against them: Khans Konchak,

---

[250] It has been suggested that Igor' attacked Polovtsian pastures never before invaded by Rus' forces, and that he approached them from the rear, that is, from the direction of river Oskol in the northeast. This gave him the advantage of surprise (Pyadyshev, "Pokhod Igorya," pp. 52, 62).

Figure 8   The Polovtsy keeping the princes from the water

Koza (Kza), Burnovich, Toksobich, Kolobich, Etebich, and Ter'trobich. He
and his commanders dismounted to plot their strategy. Their only hope lay
in reaching the river Donets. If they fled, however, it meant deserting the
common soldiers (*chernye lyudi*) and, in so doing, sinning against God.²⁵¹
The princes therefore resolved to live or die with their men and, mounting
their steeds, rode against the enemy. In the intense heat men and horses
were overcome by thirst and fatigue. Finally, the Polovtsy allowed them
to approach the water, but as they were quenching their thirst the enemy
attacked. Pinning them against the lake the nomads forced them to fight
on foot (figure 8).

The Rus' forces defended themselves valiantly all day Saturday. Vsevolod,
we are told, fought until his hand became too numb to hold his weapon.
Igor' himself continued to fight heroically even after he was wounded in the
left arm. At dawn on Sunday, after the Kovui panicked and fled, he left the
protection of his troops and rode in pursuit of the deserters hoping to bring
them back. As he was returning to his men, the Polovtsy took him captive.
Despite the unflagging courage that the men of Rus' demonstrated, they
were denied the glory that they sought.

The Polovtsy, the chronicler reports, surrounded Igor''s forces like an
unyielding wall so that only fifteen of the Rus' men escaped and even fewer
of the Kovui. Many drowned in the lake. As for the princes, Vsevolod was

---

²⁵¹ Although some investigators suggest that the *chernye lyudi* were foot soldiers, circumstantial evidence
and the news that the campaign was a raid suggest that all of Igor''s troops were mounted. See
Getmanets, *Tayna reki Kayaly*, pp. 20–1, and Rybakov, *"Slovo o polku Igoreve,"* p. 225.

Figure 9   Vsevolod fighting on foot (left scene) and Igor''s capture (right scene)

seized by Roman the son of Koza, Svyatoslav was captured by a certain Eldechyuk, and Vladimir was led away by Khan Kopti. Igor' himself was seized by one called Chilbuk but later Konchak assumed responsibility for his *svat* Igor' because the latter was wounded (figure 9). "Our Lord unleashed his wrath against the Rus' forces on Sunday.[252] Instead of joy he brought weeping, and instead of happiness he brought grief at the river Kayala."[253]

At one fell swoop the Polovtsy decimated the military power of the cadet branch. The most important towns in the Seversk lands were the hardest hit: Novgorod Severskiy, Trubetsk, Ryl'sk, Putivl', and probably Kursk. The fear that Yaroslav and Igor' had expressed to Svyatoslav in the previous year about leaving their lands undefended in the face of nomadic incursions now became a reality. As Svyatoslav would later exclaim, Igor''s defeat "opened the gates into the land of Rus'."

The Polovtsian victory over the cadet branch was the most serious blow the nomads had ever inflicted on the princes. Not only did they massacre most of the family's fighting force, but by taking the princes captive the

---

[252] The defeat occurred on Sunday, May 12, 1185 (Berezhkov, p. 203; Getmanets, *Tayna reki Kayaly*, p. 35).
[253] Concerning the Hypatian account, see Ipat., cols. 637–44; Makhnovets', pp. 336–40.

nomads also left it leaderless. Any sons that Igor', Vsevolod, or Svyatoslav had left at home were too young to go into the field. The burden of protecting the Seversk towns therefore fell on the shoulders of the prince of Chernigov and his brother in Kiev. Yaroslav's track record against the Polovtsy, as we have seen, was poor. As for Svyatoslav, he was dedicated to defending the Dnepr frontiers rather than the Posem'e district.

Significantly, Igor' expressed no remorse for initiating the campaign. He believed that he had neither acted recklessly in leading the raid nor that he had been insubordinate to Svyatoslav. Since the chronicler refuses to criticize him it appears that Igor''s contemporaries also did not condemn him. Igor', however, assumed blame for the defeat and for the fate of his men. He confessed that he had caused much woe in Rus'. Above all, he regretted capturing Glebov in the Pereyaslavl' land.[254] The massacre, he proclaimed, was God's punishment for his sin. His moralizing is in keeping with the tradition which held that God gave victory to princes for their righteous living, but inflicted defeat on them for their sins. Igor''s self-deprecation also echoes the condemnation that the chronicler levied against his grandfather Oleg, whom he accused of sinning by bringing the pagans to kill the Christians of Rus'.[255]

Igor', as we have seen, had formed friendly ties with Konchak. Significantly, after he was taken captive, the khan referred to the prince as his *svat*. In this way we discover that the two had formed a marriage alliance. As we shall see, however, their children were not yet married. Therefore, by calling Igor' his *svat* in 1185 Konchak revealed that the two had arranged the match before that date.[256] The most likely time had been at their meeting at Dolobsk, four years earlier. According to the chronicler, that was the last occasion on which the two had fraternized.

After taking the Seversk princes captive, the Laurentian Chronicle reports, the Polovtsy conscripted a passing merchant to deliver their declaration of war to Svyatoslav. They challenged him and Ryurik to come and rescue their compatriots from the Polovtsian camps, but if they preferred, the Polovtsy would come to Rus' and set their tribesmen free.[257]

---

[254] The chronicler does not report Igor''s sack of Glebov. Presumably, he retaliated against Vladimir of Pereyaslavl' after the latter had pillaged his Seversk towns in the winter of 1184 (see above, p. 157).

[255] *Dynasty*, pp. 147–8, 189.

[256] This is the second instance in which the chronicler makes reference to a marriage tie even though the marriage had not yet taken place, but only been arranged. As we have seen, in 1184 he referred to Igor''s son Svyatoslav as Ryurik's son-in-law a number of years before the marriage took place (see above, p. 156.

[257] Concerning the Laurentian account, see s.a. 1186: Lav., cols. 397–9; compare, Mosk., pp. 91–2.

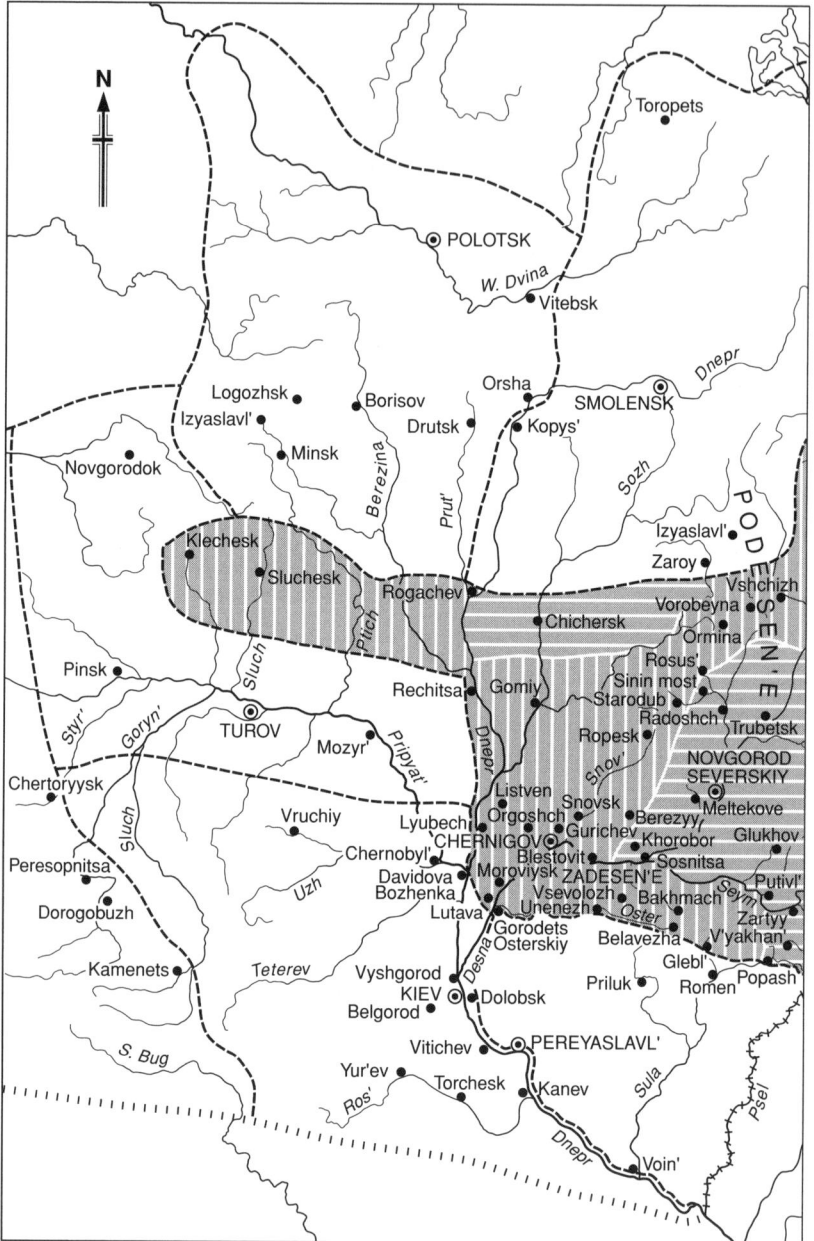

Map 4   A projected schema of the Ol'govichi domains during the reign of Svyatoslav
Vsevolodovich (d. 1194)

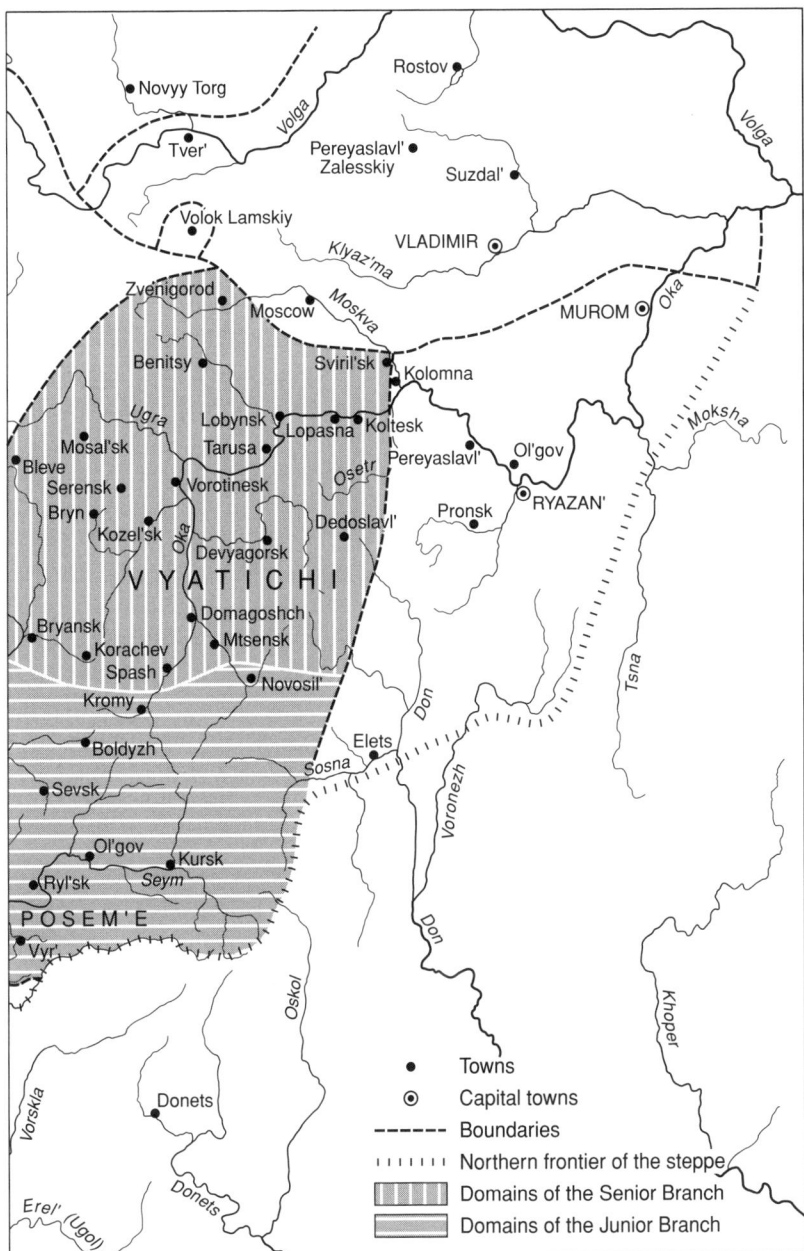

Map 4   (*cont.*)

Thus we learn that Svyatoslav was still holding Kobyak and his men captive.[258] Because of their victory the tribesmen were, as the chronicler puts it, "puffed up with confidence." Granted, they had weakened the military might of the Ol'govichi by annihilating Igor''s troops. Svyatoslav's alliance of princes, however, remained intact. The Polovtsy would have been foolish to underestimate its effectiveness.

While Igor' was campaigning, Svyatoslav was in his patrimony of Karachev marshaling troops for an expedition against the Don or Donets Polovtsy. It seems that he finally resolved to attack the tribes that Yaroslav and Igor' found troublesome. His conscription of the Vyatichi supports this. Until then, he had not used them against the nomads. Since his campaign was to benefit the Ol'govichi, however, he expected his subjects in Karachev and his sons who had domains among the Vyatichi, to help defend the Chernigov lands. The news that he intended to campaign all summer also suggests that he was organizing a major expedition. The ambitious scope of his attack is confirmed by the news that he summoned David of Smolensk, even though his lands were not in danger of attack and even though he had not sent troops against the nomads in the past.

On his return journey to Kiev, Svyatoslav travelled down the Desna. He stopped at Novgorod Severskiy, where he was distressed to discover that Igor' and his brothers had gone against the Polovtsy and concealed it from him. When he visited his brother in Chernigov, a survivor told him of the Polovtsian victory. Svyatoslav bewailed the loss of his brothers and the men of Rus'. God, he proclaimed, had helped him to vanquish many tribesmen the previous summer, but his brothers, unable to restrain the impetuosity of youth, "opened the gates into the land of Rus'."

We are not told what route Svyatoslav had taken to Karachev, but we know that all roads from Kiev to the forest land passed through the Seversk lands (map 4).[259] Significantly, on his return journey the only reason we learn of his stops at Novgorod Severskiy and Chernigov is because he received bad news there. We may assume, therefore, that he had encountered nothing out of the ordinary on his outward journey. Namely, he had seen no evidence of Igor''s mobilization for his campaign. Svyatoslav's accusation that Igor' concealed the expedition from him therefore may imply that Igor' had planned the raid before Svyatoslav passed through the Novgorod Severskiy lands en route to Karachev, but that Igor' refused to inform him.

---

[258] Relying on the report given by the *"Slovo o polku Igoreve,"* Pletneva believes that Kobyak was executed in Kiev ("Polovetskaya zemlya," p. 285 and *Polovtsy*, p. 147).

[259] For example, under the year 1146 we were told that Izyaslav Davidovich pursued Svyatoslav Ol'govich along the road from Putivl' to Sevsk and Boldyzh to Karachev (Ipat., col. 335).

As the commander-in-chief of all major offensives against the Polovtsy, Svyatoslav was angered by Igor''s deviousness and not by his raid as such. As noted above, the chronicler never condemns Igor' for leading the campaign: any attack against the nomads was laudable! More than likely, Igor' realized that if he informed Svyatoslav of his raid, the latter would insist that Igor' cancel it and join him in his summer campaign. In leading his attack, therefore, Igor' pre-empted Svyatoslav's initiative.

After learning of Igor''s defeat, Svyatoslav sent Vladimir and Oleg to the Posem'e region to serve as interim defenders of the Seversk towns. The information that he sent two sons suggests that he ordered them to occupy Ryl'sk and Putivl', which had recently lost their princes. Their main task would have been to close the "gates into the land of Rus'." It has been pointed out that one of the most frequently used gates, as it were, which the nomads used to cross the Seym was at Vyr', between Putivl' and Ryl'sk.[260]

Svyatoslav either received the Polovtsian declaration of war via the merchant they had sent or assumed that they would follow up their victory by attacking Rus'. He therefore summoned David of Smolensk to help defend Kiev. He also asked his brother Yaroslav for troops. On this occasion, he seemingly complied even though his *druzhina*, or part of it, had been massacred at the Kayala. He assembled a contingent and waited at Chernigov but we are not told if he joined Svyatoslav. The chronicler's silence suggests that he did not.[261] Despite Yaroslav's probable failure to help Svyatoslav, and despite David's return to Smolensk after his troops refused to defend any town other than Kiev, Svyatoslav's forces frightened Konchak into abandoning his attack on Pereyaslavl'.

According to the chronicler, the Polovtsy assembled their entire nation to march against Rus'. But the khans argued. Koza advocated a safe and ruthless course: to raid the towns of the defeated Seversk princes along the river Seym, where only widows and orphans remained. Besides, he remembered how, in 1167, Igor''s elder brother Oleg had raided his camp and taken his wife and children captive.[262] Konchak, however, proposed attacking the princes on the Kievan side because they had defeated Khan Kobyak. Konchak's friendship with Igor' and the consideration that his daughter was betrothed to Igor''s son must have also persuaded him to reject Koza's plan. Finally, he probably wished to avenge himself against Ryurik

---

[260] See Rybakov, *"Slovo o polku Igoreve,"* pp. 164, 261. Concerning routes used by the Polovtsy, see also Lyaskoronsky, "K voprosu o Pereyaslavl'skikh Torkakh," pp. 291–3.

[261] Rybakov is also of the opinion that Yaroslav did not send his troops to Svyatoslav's assistance (*Kievskaya Rus'*, p. 506).

[262] See above, p. 112.

for the massacre of his troops at Dolobsk. Because the khans obstinately stuck to their views, they split their horde into two.

Given his reduced force, Konchak aborted the plan to wage an all-out war against Svyatoslav.[263] Although the khans' disagreement spared the Kievan side from devastation, the left bank was less fortunate. In attempting to salvage the major campaign that had gone awry, Konchak followed Koza's example and pillaged. His main target was Pereyaslavl' but, failing to capture it, he razed the outpost of Rimov as a consolation prize.[264] Meanwhile, Koza attacked Igor''s patrimony of Putivl' but also failed to take it. Nevertheless, he set fire to its outer town, pillaged the district, and razed surrounding villages.[265] Despite the havoc that the nomads wreaked on the inhabitants of the left bank, their raids seemingly caused no lasting damage.[266]

Meanwhile, Igor' was spending his captivity in Konchak's camp. His captors appointed fifteen of their sons and five sons of nobles to guard him and to do his bidding. Moreover, some six servants were constantly at his beck and call. He was also free to ride wherever he chose and to hunt with hawks. Igor' expected his relatives to pay for his release, but the chronicles mention neither the cost of his ransom nor how long he remained with the nomads.[267] We are told only that he anticipated being a captive for a long time and that this was why he asked for a priest to be sent from Rus' to say the Divine Liturgy. Konchak granted his request. Thus, even though the chronicler condemns the khan as "cursed, godless, and thrice-damned," his concession to his *svat* Igor' reveals an unexpected tolerance for Christian practices.

As for Igor', his request for a priest demonstrates the ardor of his personal piety. He also expressed it in other ways. He sought the protection of his

---

[263] Compare Rybakov, who claims that Konchak did intend to attack Kiev (*"Slovo o polku Igoreve,"* p. 164; see also Lyaskoronsky, "K voprosu o Pereyaslavl'skikh Torkakh," 278–302).

[264] Rimov, one of the Rus' outposts on the right bank of the river Sula, was located near the trade route that merchants and nomads used to approach Kiev along the east bank of the Dnepr (Lyaskoronsky, "K voprosu o Pereyaslavl'skikh Torkakh," pp. 295–300).

[265] Tatishchev alone, and only in his second redaction, claims that Svyatoslav's son Oleg and his commander Tudor confronted Koza at the river Seym, where the Polovtsy suffered many casualties (Tat. 3, p. 138). If this encounter took place, one possible site for the battle was at the ford near the village of Chumakovo located southeast of Putivl' (V. V. Pryimak, "K izucheniyu okrugi drevnerusskikh gorodov srednego Poseym'ya," *Gomel'shchina: arkheologiya, istoriya, pamyatniki*: Tezisy Vtoroy Gomel'skoy oblastnoy nauchnoy konferentsii po istoricheskomu kraevedeniyu, 1991 g., O. A. Makushnikov and A. I. Drobushevsky (eds.) [Gomel', 1991], pp. 62–3).

[266] Concerning Svyatoslav's trip from Karachev, and Konchak and Koza's disagreement, see Ipat., cols. 644–9; Gust., p. 320; compare s.a. 1186: Lav., col. 399.

[267] Tatishchev states that Igor' expected to be in captivity for a long period of time because his people were unable to raise the 2,000 *griven* that the Polovtsy demanded for his ransom (Tat. 4, p. 305; Tat. 3, p. 138).

patron St. George by departing on the campaign on April 23, the saint's feast day.[268] Before escaping from captivity he prayed for God's assistance before the icon of Christ and the Holy Cross, which he kept in his tent. Igor´'s recourse to God and the saints was also in keeping with the moralizing sentiments that he expressed over his guilt after his defeat.

We are told that Lavr (Lavor), a Polovtsian by birth, offered to help Igor´ escape. At first, the prince mistrusted the man and held onto his youthful idealism. He had refused to flee from the field of battle in his quest for glory and now he refused to follow the road to dishonor by escaping from captivity in a cowardly manner. Igor´'s groom also encouraged him to run away. After the Polovtsy returned from Pereyaslavl´, Igor´'s well-wishers once again entreated him to abandon his ideal of glory and to flee. They warned him that they had overheard the Polovtsy plotting to kill all the captive princes. If they did, Igor´ would be denied his glory and lose his life.

In the end, the prince resolved to escape. But it was not easy to find an opportune moment because he was guarded day and night. Finally, one day at dusk, when his guards had become inebriated on koumiss, Igor´ sent his groom to tell Lavr to lead a horse across the river Tor and wait for him.[269] Towards nightfall, the groom informed Igor´ that Lavr was waiting. Full of fear and trepidation, he bowed to the icon of Christ, to the Holy Cross, and asked God's assistance. Hanging the icon and the Holy Cross around his neck he raised the tent flap and crawled out while the guards were entertaining themselves with games. After crossing over to the other side of the river, he rode away with Lavr. "God freed Igor´ on a Friday evening and he travelled eleven days to the town Donets."[270] From there he went to Novgorod Severskiy, where the citizens were overjoyed to see him. Even the unfriendly Laurentian chronicler rejoiced in Igor´'s escape:

> God did not abandon the righteous one to sinful hands. God watches over those who fear Him and heeds their prayer. They [the Polovtsy] sought him and could not find him. Just as Saul pursued David but God rescued him, in like manner God saved this one [Igor´] from pagan hands.[271]

Tatishchev offers unique information, which he may have borrowed from folklore tradition or from a now lost chronicle. When Igor´ was a

---

[268] In 1151, Igor´ received the baptismal name of George (Ipat., col. 422; see Rybakov, "*Slovo o polku Igoreve*," p. 228).

[269] The Tor is a western tributary of the Don south of the confluence of the latter and the Oskol.

[270] Donets was a Rus´ town located on the river Udy, a tributary of the river Donets. Today the site is located on the southern periphery of the city of Khar´kov (Getmanets, *Tayna reki Kayaly*, p. 64).

[271] Lav., cols. 399–400.

half-day's journey from Novgorod Severskiy, his horse stumbled and he fell
off injuring his leg. Unable to remount, he spent the night in the village of
St. Michael. Meanwhile, a local peasant hastened to Novgorod Severskiy
and reported Igor''s escape. At first the princess could not believe the good
news, but her anxiety overwhelmed her and she traveled at night to find
her husband. When she saw Igor' she fell into his arms and "they gazed
at each other through tears of joy." Early the next morning, they departed
for Novgorod Severskiy and a multitude of men, women, and children
came out to greet the prince. Later, Igor' rewarded Lavr and gave him the
daughter of *Tysyatskiy* Raduil as wife.[272]

We are not told when Igor' escaped, but he could not have been in
captivity for more than a few months. Since he was captured in the middle
of May, and to judge from the information that he was still a captive when
Konchak returned from the Pereyaslavl' campaign sometime in June, he
probably fled in the late summer at the latest.[273]

After arriving in Novgorod Severskiy, Igor' visited Yaroslav in Chernigov
and asked for military aid. His need of troops suggests that Vladimir and
Oleg had departed from Putivl' and Ryl'sk after Koza pillaged the region.
Yaroslav, we are told, was delighted to see Igor' and promised to send
reinforcements. Next, Igor' went to Svyatoslav in Kiev, who also rejoiced
at his escape and, to judge from the chronicler's silence, did not reprimand
Igor' for not advising him of the campaign. Surprisingly, Igor' did not ask
Svyatoslav for troops. Perhaps he believed that Svyatoslav had fulfilled his
duty earlier by sending his sons to defend the Posem'e or he asked for
another favor.

The onus of raising the ransoms for the three captive princes fell on
the cadet branch, in particular, on Igor'. He undoubtedly asked Svyatoslav
for assistance. As the senior prince of the dynasty, he was the wealthiest
Ol'govich and he had the responsibility of securing the freedom of any
captive dynast. Igor' also turned to Ryurik to judge from the information
that he visited his *svat* after leaving Svyatoslav. He probably asked the
Rostislavich for help because his nephew Svyatoslav, who was a captive, was
also Ryurik's nephew.[274] If Igor' requested the duumvirs to help pay for the
ransoms, we do not know their replies. The Polovtsy would, however, release

[272] Tat. 4, pp. 305–6; Tat. 3, p. 139; see L. I. Sazonova, "Letopisnyy rasskaz o pokhode Igorya Svyatoslavicha na polovtse v 1185 g. v obrabotke V. N. Tatishcheva," TODRL 25 (1970), 42, 45.
[273] Using as his source the "*Slovo o polku Igoreve*," which says that Igor' heard the nightingale sing
when he was fleeing, Rybakov claims that the prince escaped on Friday June 21. According to folk
tradition, the nightingale sings until June 29 ("*Slovo o polku Igoreve*," p. 271).
[274] Under the year 1165, the chronicler tells us that Ryurik's sister Agafia married Svyatoslav's father
Oleg (Ipat., cols. 524–5).

Igor''s brother and son in the not-too-distant future, but the chroniclers never tell us if Svyatoslav was set free.[275] On returning to Novgorod Severskiy, Igor' had to tackle three important tasks: negotiate the release of his kinsmen, renew the military resources of his family, and rebuild the fortifications in the Posem'e region. Above all, he had to close the gate which he had opened into Rus'. Accordingly, to judge from archaeological evidence, he reinforced the fortifications and founded new ones in the vicinity of Vyr'.[276] Although Igor''s catastrophic campaign had dire consequences for the cadet branch, it had a lesser impact on Rus' as a whole. In the final analysis, Koza's invasion of the Posem'e region and Konchak's attack on Pereyaslavl' amounted to no more than new raids, albeit more devastating than usual. Neither the duumvirs nor the Polovtsy gained the upper hand in their military encounters.

DOMESTIC AFFAIRS

Despite the dynasty's preoccupation with the Polovtsy, Svyatoslav's trip to Karachev reminds us that, between campaigns, the Ol'govichi were busy with their domestic duties. These included administering their domains, maintaining ties with other dynasties, overseeing Church affairs, and raising their families.

When Svyatoslav's grandson Mikhail, the son of Vsevolod Chermnyy, was a child, he suffered from a paralyzing illness. He gave much wealth to churches in unsuccessful attempts to obtain a cure. Finally, he heard of the miracle-worker Nikita living in the Monastery of St. Nicetas at Pereyaslavl' Zalesskiy in Suzdalia.[277] The prince, accompanied by *boyars*, rode to Pereyaslavl'. On the way the devil, disguised as a monk, thrice attempted to dissuade him from continuing his journey. But Mikhail remained constant through Nikita's prayerful intercession and arrived at the monk's pillar. He dispatched a *boyar* to tell the holy man of his ailment, and the stylite gave his staff to the man to take to the prince. Mikhail took hold of it, was cured, and walked to the miracle-worker's pillar for his blessing. Following his cure, we are told, he gave a generous benefaction

---

[275] Concerning Igor''s escape, see Ipat., cols. 649–51; compare Makhnovets', pp. 341–2.

[276] Morgunov points out that towards the end of the twelfth century, a strong fortification was constructed at Boyarskoe, southwest of Vyr' ("Letopisnyy gorod Popash," SA, nr. 1 [M., 1985], pp. 246, 248, and his "Letopisnyy gorod V'yakhan'," SA, nr. 2 [M., 1982], p. 244).

[277] See *Mikhail*, pp. 10–1, where Pereyaslavl' Zalesskiy in Suzdalia is incorrectly identified as the southern Pereyaslavl'.

to the monastery and ordered a stone cross to be erected, according to one source on May 16, 1186, on the spot where he was cured.[278]

This is the earliest chronicle reference to Mikhail. In 1179, as we have seen, Vsevolod Chermnyy married Anastasia, the daughter of Casimir II the Just.[279] They had three children, Mikhail and two daughters, but their births are not recorded. Even if Mikhail was the eldest, he would have been only some six years of age at the time of his cure. Consequently, his parents would have sent him to Pereyaslavl' Zalesskiy accompanied by *boyars*. In like manner, they probably made a donation to the monastery and erected the memorial cross after his cure. Although the event is reported only in late sources and embellished with pious details, the account has a ring of truth. Because the patrimonial domain of Mikhail's father was located in the northwestern part of the Vyatichi lands,[280] where Mikhail undoubtedly spent his childhood, the geographical proximity of his family to Suzdalia made such a trip plausible.

In 1186, Svyatoslav Vsevolodovich consecrated the Church of the Annunciation that he himself had built in Chernigov. Since the Feast of the Annunciation fell on March 25, he probably consecrated the building on that day.[281] It was the second church that he erected on the site of his new court in Chernigov. The first, as we have seen, had been that of St. Michael.[282] If, as some have suggested, he began building the Annunciation around 1183,[283] this means that he was building the church during the period of vigorous campaigning against the Polovtsy. In the light of this evidence, it would seem that after visiting Karachev in 1185, one reason why he stopped at Chernigov was to inspect the construction of the church. Moreover, as has been noted, on January 1 of that year he had already consecrated the Church of St. Vasily in Kiev. This means that he was building the two churches simultaneously. What is more, in 1180, after fire damaged the Cathedral of St. Sofia, he evidently assumed most of the cost for its repair.[284] His readiness to erect and repair three churches in the short period of some five years bespeaks not only his zeal for church building but also his ample funds to pay for the cost.

Archaeological evidence reveals that Svyatoslav built the Annunciation in the northeast corner of the citadel, on the right bank of the river Strizhen'.

[278] See s.a. 1186: "Kniga stepennaya tsarskogo rodosloviya," PSRL 21, chast' pervaya (Spb., 1908), pp. 248–9; compare Maz., p. 65; see also G. Lenhoff, "The Cult of Saint Nikita the Stylite in Pereyaslavl' and Among the Muscovite Elite," *Fonctions sociales et politiques du culte des saints dans les sociétés de rite grec et latin au Moyen Age et à l'époque moderne. Approche comparative*, M. Derwich and M. Dmitriev (eds.) (Wroclaw, 1999), p. 333.
[279] See above, p. 140.   [280] See below, p. 293.   [281] Ipat., col. 652; Makhnovets', p. 342.
[282] Concerning the Church of St. Michael built on the new court, see above, p. 124.
[283] See Rappoport, *Drevnerusskaya Arkhitektura*, p. 263.   [284] See above, p. 143.

The church was around 26 m wide and 34 m long.[285] It had three naves, three apses, six pillars, and probably five domes. It was lavishly decorated and boasted a number of innovative features. Its walls, for example, were constructed of red brick but the half-columns on the exterior pilasters were made of bright yellow brick. Moreover, Svyatoslav's builders resurrected architectural traditions of the eleventh century in reintroducing closed galleries with burial vaults on the north, west, and south sides. Carved white stone adorned the facades, and a white stone ciborium incised with intricate designs stood over the altar. In less public areas, the floor was covered with plain yellow, green, and cherry coloured slabs, but the central nave and the transept were decorated with mosaics.[286] The church was Svyatoslav's crowning achievement.

The evidence that other princes imitated its plan proves it was one of the most admired monuments in the land. Between the years 1185 and 1188 Vsevolod of Suzdalia expanded the Assumption Cathedral in Vladimir. He extended the three apses on the east side while on the remaining three sides he surrounded the building with galleries. Before his death in 1187, Yaroslav Osmomysl completed the grandiose Assumption Cathedral in Galich. It also had three naves and galleries on three sides. Towards the end of the twelfth century, David of Smolensk would add galleries to the Great Church built earlier by his father Rostislav on the river Smyadyn'. Significantly, from among the Annunciation and its three imitations, only Svyatoslav's church was built from start to finish according to its original plan.[287]

Even though Svyatoslav was no longer prince of Chernigov, he decided to build his masterpiece in the dynastic capital. Significantly, a prince had to obtain the approval of the local ruler to build a church in his domain.[288] Yaroslav of Chernigov obviously granted his brother that permission. Their cooperation confirms that they were on good terms during this period despite Yaroslav's collaboration with Igor' on Polovtsian policy.

What reasons prompted Svyatoslav to select Chernigov over Kiev as the site for his showpiece? The obvious answer is that he wished to enhance the prestige of his dynasty and its capital. This is supported by the news that

---

[285] Its exact dimensions cannot be determined because, in 1876, the eastern end of the church collapsed into the Strizhen' after the river eroded the bank under the apses (B. A. Rybakov, "Raskopki v Chernigove," KSIIMK 21 [M.-L., 1947], p. 41).

[286] The church no longer stands but its foundations were excavated in 1946 and 1947 by Rybakov (see his "Raskopki v Chernigove," pp. 40–2; Rappoport, pp. 43–4; Afanas'ev, *Postroenie arkhitekturnoy formy*, pp. 191–2; and Mezentsev, "The Masonry Churches of Medieval Chernihiv," pp. 379–80).

[287] Rybakov, "Raskopki v Chernigove," pp. 41–2 and his "Drevnosti Chernigova," pp. 90–3.

[288] See, for example, the difficulties Oleg Svyatoslavich had in obtaining permission from Svyatopolk Izyaslavich of Kiev to consecrate the Church of SS. Boris and Gleb in Vyshgorod (Dimnik, "Oleg Svyatoslavich," pp. 362–5).

he provided burial vaults in the church's galleries for the Ol'govichi. Just the same, it would not replace the Holy Saviour Cathedral as the repository for the princes who had ruled Chernigov.[289]

Bishop Porfiry would have officiated at the consecration along with Metropolitan Nikifor, who would have accompanied Svyatoslav from Kiev. They were probably joined by a third prelate, perhaps *Igumen* Efrem of the Eletskiy Monastery.[290] Other bishops, abbots, clergy, and monks would have also joined them. Moreover, Ryurik, the Ol'govichi, and neighboring princes would have brought their families to laud Svyatoslav's splendid achievement. The celebrations would have ended with a feast.

BISHOP PORFIRY'S PERFIDY

A month or so after the consecration ceremony in Chernigov, Bishop Porfiry travelled to Suzdalia to pacify Vsevolod with the Glebovichi. The Laurentian Chronicle reports that, in the previous year, the three eldest Glebovichi of Ryazan' (Roman, Igor', and Vladimir) quarreled with their brothers, Vsevolod and Svyatoslav of Pronsk, and plotted to kill them. The latter two turned to Vsevolod in Suzdalia for help and he sent the *druzhina* from Vladimir on the Klyaz'ma to help them. After Vsevolod Glebovich went to negotiate with Vsevolod in Suzdalia, his three elder brothers persuaded Svyatoslav to join them by giving him Pronsk. The princes of Ryazan' then seized the family and *boyars* of their brother Vsevolod and captured the *druzhina* from Vladimir on the Klyaz'ma. Vsevolod of Suzdalia was furious and prepared to attack Ryazan'.[291]

Porfiry travelled to Suzdalia to mediate on behalf of the Glebovichi because the Church in Ryazan' fell under the jurisdiction of the bishop of Chernigov.[292] Nevertheless, it was probably Svyatoslav and Yaroslav who sent him to Suzdalia. Svyatoslav, as the senior prince in Rus', saw it his duty to maintain peace in the land. Yaroslav, as Porfiry's secular superior, may have considered it his moral obligation to intervene. The two brothers

---

[289] Later, Yaroslav would be buried in St. Saviour (see below, p. 231).

[290] As we have seen, in 1185, at the consecration of the Church of St. Vasily, three prelates officiated at the ceremony (see above, p. 153). Efrem most likely qualified for that function. As noted above, his prominence in the Church of Chernigov was confirmed in 1177, when he accompanied Porfiry to Suzdalia as a mediator (see above, p. 138).

[291] See s.a. 1186: Lav., cols. 400–3; Mosk., pp. 92–3.

[292] Chernigov, Murom, and Ryazan' originally belonged to the patrimony that Yaroslav the Wise bequeathed to his son Svyatoslav. As has been shown elsewhere, Murom and Ryazan' were politically separated from the Chernigov domain in 1127, after Vsevolod Ol'govich usurped Chernigov from his uncle Yaroslav of Murom (*Dynasty*, pp. 319–20).

had other considerations. On the one hand, Svyatoslav's son, Vladimir, had married the niece of Vsevolod Yur'evich,[293] and his son, Mstislav, had married Vsevolod's sister-in-law.[294] Moreover, as we shall see, at the time that Porfiry visited Suzdalia, Yaroslav's son was betrothed to one of Vsevolod's daughters.[295] On the other hand, one of Svyatoslav's daughters was the wife of Roman Glebovich,[296] and his son Oleg had married Roman's cousin.[297] We may therefore assume that their personal ties also prompted the Ol'govichi to pacify their warring in-laws.

After listening to the pleas of Porfiry and Luka, his own bishop, Vsevolod sent them to negotiate peace. But Porfiry, the chronicler notes, did not merit the trust that the princes placed in him. He heaped dishonor on himself. When he and the mediators arrived at Ryazan', he addressed the Glebovichi in secret. The chronicler does not explain what Porfiry said but states: "Instead of acting like a man of God, he acted as a denouncer and a liar." To judge from those remarks, the bishop defamed Vsevolod. We are given no explanation for his misconduct. We may, however, find the cause of his vindictiveness in the manner in which Vsevolod had treated Porfiry in 1177, when he detained the bishop and *Igumen* Efrem for two years after they failed to negotiate the release of Gleb Rostislavich, the father of the Glebovichi.[298] Whatever Porfiry's reason for his betrayal, his scheme was discovered. Nevertheless, he seemingly succeeded in his plot because the Glebovichi and Vsevolod remained enemies.[299]

Porfiry's perfidious action did not jeopardize the friendly relationship between the Ol'govichi and Vsevolod. On July 11 his daughter Vseslava married Yaroslav's son Rostislav.[300] He was fifteen years of age.[301] In becoming the father-in-law of Vsevolod's daughter, Yaroslav forged an even closer family bond with the prince of Suzdalia than his brother Svyatoslav had done. That bond would serve Yaroslav well, as we shall see, after he became senior prince of the dynasty.

THREE PRINCELY DEATHS

In 1187, three princes died and their passing was significant, to a greater or lesser degree, for the Ol'govichi. First, when Vladimir Glebovich was returning with Svyatoslav and Ryurik from a campaign, he fell mortally

[293] See above, p. 140.   [294] See above, pp. 152–3.
[295] See below, n. 300.   [296] See Baum. 2, XIV, 11.
[297] Baum. 2, XIV, 19; see above, pp. 134–5.   [298] See above, p. 138.
[299] Concerning Porfiry's treachery, see s.a. 1187: Lav., cols. 404–5; Mosk, p. 94. Concerning the date, see Berezhkov, p. 83. See also Bagaley, *Istoriya Severskoy zemli*, pp. 285–6.
[300] See s.a. 1187: Lav., col. 405.   [301] He was born in 1171 (see above, p. 121).

ill and, on April 18, died in Pereyaslavl'.³⁰² As we have seen, his wife was
the daughter of Yaroslav of Chernigov and his sister had married Vsevolod
of Trubetsk. Aside from his animosity towards Igor', he evidently enjoyed
friendly relations with the Ol'govichi. He had also played an important role
in Svyatoslav's battles against the nomads. Because of the friendly relations
that existed between their dynasties, Svyatoslav had good reason to believe
that Vsevolod of Suzdalia would replace him with a prince willing to work
hand-in-glove with the Ol'govichi.

Second, in May, Mstislav, the son of David of Smolensk, died in
Vyshgorod.³⁰³ As we have seen, David himself had lived there before 1180
when Svyatoslav had seized Kiev. Mstislav's presence in the town therefore
corroborates the observation that, when Svyatoslav and Ryurik created the
duumvirate, Svyatoslav returned Vyshgorod to the Rostislavichi. In doing
so, he made not only a political concession but also a personal one. He
abjured direct control over his father's tomb and over the dynasty's shrine
of SS. Boris and Gleb. He would pay a price for his loss of jurisdiction. In
1191, David would transfer the wooden coffins of SS. Boris and Gleb from
Vyshgorod to the church that his father Rostislav had built in honor of the
two saints in the monastery on the Smyadyn' river west of Smolensk.³⁰⁴

Third, on October 1, Yaroslav Osmomysl died. He designated his
younger son Oleg, the son of his concubine Nataska, his successor in Galich.
To Vladimir, the son of princess Olga, who was the sister of Vsevolod of
Suzdalia, he gave Peremyshl'. Yaroslav also made Vladimir and the Gali-
cians promise not to take Galich from Oleg. After his death, however,
they deposed Oleg forcing him to seek help from Ryurik in Vruchiy.³⁰⁵
After that, Vladimir "sat on the throne of his grandfather and father" in
Galich.³⁰⁶ Yaroslav's deathbed allocations created a dilemma for Svyatoslav.
As the supreme mediator in Rus', he had to defend either Oleg, the des-
ignated prince of Galich, or Vladimir, the rightful heir to his father.³⁰⁷

---

³⁰² Ipat., cols. 652–3. According to the Laurentian Chronicle he died on March 18 (s.a. 1188: Lav., col. 406). Concerning the date, see Berezhkov, pp. 83, 203.
³⁰³ Ipat., cols. 654–5; Baum., IX, 12.
³⁰⁴ See "Prolozhnoe skazanie ob osvyashcheniy tserkvi sv. Borisa i Gleba i perenesenii ikh grobov iz Vyshgoroda na Smyadinu, v 1190/1 godu," in N. K. Nikol'sky, "Materialy dlya istorii drevne-russkoy dukhovnoy pis'mennosti," I–IV, *Izvestiya*, otdeleniya russkago yazyka i slovesnosti Imperatorskoy Akademii Nauk (Spb., 1903), tom 8, kn. 1, pp. 221–2; N. N. Voronin and P. A. Rappoport, *Zodchestvo Smolenska XII–XIII vv.* (L., 1979), p. 58; and Hollingsworth, *The Hagiography*, pp. 229–31.
³⁰⁵ Although Ryurik's patrimonial domain was Vruchiy, as co-ruler he lived in Belgorod.
³⁰⁶ Ipat., cols. 656–7; Gust., p. 321.
³⁰⁷ Custom dictated that in the absence of a more senior candidate, the eldest son (Vladimir) and not the favorite son (Oleg) succeeded his father. An analogous situation occurred in 1015, when Vladimir wished his favourite son Boris to succeed him instead of the eldest son Svyatopolk (see Dimnik, "Succession and Inheritance," pp. 108–10).

Svyatoslav's quandary was accentuated by family considerations. He was Vladimir's father-in-law,[308] and Vladimir's sister was married to Igor' of the cadet branch. Finally, the ease with which Vladimir overthrew Oleg suggested that the *boyars* backed him. The cards seemed to be stacked in Vladimir's favor, but Svyatoslav had to weigh the options carefully because his decision could put him on a collision course with Ryurik who was harboring Oleg. Of the three princely deaths, that of Yaroslav Osmomysl would be of the greatest importance for the Ol'govichi in the long term.

THE POLOVTSY RENEW THEIR INCURSIONS

More immediately, however, Svyatoslav and the Ol'govichi faced renewed Polovtsian attacks. In 1187 Konchak raided the river Ros' region. After that, we are told, enemy bands frequently pillaged along that river and in the Chernigov domain.[309] It is noteworthy that the nomads redirected their raids to the west bank. We may assume that after failing to launch a full-scale attack on Kiev following Igor''s defeat, Konchak resorted to directing lightning strikes against the duumvirs. At the same time, Koza and his allies, it would seem, increased their incursions into the Chernigov lands. Once again the main object of their attacks would have been the Posem'e region.

Towards the beginning of April, Svyatoslav, Ryurik, and Vladimir of Pereyaslavl', set out in pursuit of the Polovtsy who were pillaging the district of Tatinets, a ford on the Dnepr.[310] The Black Caps, however, warned the marauders of the approaching princes and they crossed to the east side of the Dnepr. Unable to pursue them because it was spring and the water had suddenly risen, the duumvirs returned home. Vladimir Glebovich, however, fell mortally ill and, as was noted above, died on returning to Pereyaslavl'.[311] As we have seen, in 1181, when Svyatoslav and Ryurik agreed to act as co-rulers, Svyatoslav got Kiev and Ryurik got the surrounding Kievan towns. In pillaging Tatinets, the nomads invaded Ryurik's districts. He therefore expressed a greater urgency for curbing their incursions.

The chronicler reflects Ryurik's personal concern when reporting his enthusiasm for Svyatoslav's decision to lead a campaign in the winter and his encouragement to Svyatoslav that he assemble all his brothers in Chernigov. The chronicler therewith implies that all the Ol'govichi participated in

[308] In 1166, Svyatoslav's daughter Boleslava had married Vladimir (see above, p. 109).
[309] Ipat., col. 653.
[310] Makhnovets' suggests that the ford was located on the Dnepr below the river Ros' (p. 571).
[311] See Ipat., cols. 652–3. Concerning Vladimir's death, see above, pp. 185–6.

the winter attack. This was not so. Although all the princes of the senior branch may have answered Svyatoslav's call to arms, the princes of
the cadet branch probably did not come at all. Igor''s brother Vsevolod,
his son Vladimir, and his nephew Svyatoslav were still being held captive. Not surprisingly, Igor' himself is not mentioned as participating. The
Seversk towns were still smarting from his defeat at the river Kayala, and
he needed to stay behind with the skeleton force and Yaroslav's auxiliaries
to defend his family's lands. Indeed, since the nomads increased their incursions into the Posem'e region in 1187, Igor' would have been irrespon-
sible to join Svyatoslav on a campaign taking him deep into the Dnepr
region.

Surprisingly, Yaroslav joined the expedition. Since Svyatoslav himself
travelled to Chernigov to assemble his dynasty's troops, we may assume
that he personally persuaded his younger brother to go as far as the river
Sneporod (Snoporod).[312] Nevertheless, after reaching the river and fulfilling his promise, Yaroslav insisted on returning home. Helping Ryurik to
make a pre-emptive strike against tribesmen who were attacking the Kievan
land, or helping Ryurik to retrieve the stolen goods were not his main
priorities. Instead, he demonstrated a genuine concern for his *druzhina*
and for the well-being of his own subjects whom he had left behind in
Chernigov.

Svyatoslav, for his part, declared his willingness to continue the cam-
paign, but refused to go on without his brother. He therewith antagonized
Ryurik. Perhaps fraternal loyalty motivated him to side with Yaroslav.[313]
But he may have had a political motive. As we have seen, after Yaroslav
Osmomysl died in the autumn, his son Oleg fled to Ryurik in Vruchiy.
Svyatoslav, however, had closer ties to Oleg's half-brother Vladimir, who
was his son-in-law. He, therefore, may have sided with Yaroslav as a warning
to Ryurik that, if he were pressed into choosing sides between a kinsman
and Ryurik, he would choose the kinsman. Ryurik, we are told, adamantly
insisted that the two Ol'govichi continue the campaign, but they refused.
Consequently, they quarreled and returned home without confronting the
nomads.[314] This was the first occasion since the creation of the duumvirate
that the two princes had a falling out.

---

[312] The Sneporod has been identified as the Samara, an eastern tributary of the Dnepr below the Erel'
(Ugol) (Murav'eva and Kuz'mina, *Imennoy i geograficheskiy ukazateli*, p. 101; Makhnovets', p. 568).

[313] As has been suggested above, the information that Yaroslav gave permission to Svyatoslav to
build the Church of the Annunciation in Chernigov shows that the brothers were on good terms
(see above, p. 183).

[314] Concerning the winter campaign, see Ipat., cols. 653–4; compare Gust., pp. 320–1.

MARRIAGE ALLIANCES AND FAMILY TIES

In light of the numerous Polovtsian raids on Rus' in 1187, it is surprising that the chronicler reports none in the following year. A number of princes took advantage of the respite to form marriage alliances. Thus, in 1188 Ryurik sent matchmakers to Suzdalia to collect Vsevolod's eight-year-old daughter, Verkhuslava, as a bride for his son Rostislav. She arrived in Belgorod on September 25 and, on the following morning, the couple was married. Ryurik lavished many gifts on his daughter-in-law and gave her the town of Bryagin. To celebrate the occasion he organized a feast the likes of which, we are told, the people of Rus' had never seen. Twenty princes attended.[315] Although not one of the princes is identified, there can be no doubt that a number of Ol'govichi came. Ryurik would have invited Svyatoslav, his *svat* and co-ruler. Svyatoslav's son Gleb, Ryurik's son-in-law, would have come with his wife. Finally, as we shall see, Igor' came with his family. The festivities helped to revive the friendly relations that had been strained during the winter campaign.

Ryurik did more to fortify his friendship with the Ol'govichi. During the same week that his son Rostislav got married, he gave away his daughter Yaroslava to Igor''s son Svyatoslav from Novgorod Severskiy.[316] The latter was twelve years of age.[317] Since Ryurik gave away his daughter while Igor' and his family were attending the festivities in Belgorod, Svyatoslav's marriage took place towards the end of October at the earliest. The alliance would stand Igor' and Ryurik in good stead when the two succeeded to positions of greater authority: Igor' was slated to replace Yaroslav in Chernigov, and Ryurik was the designated successor to Svyatoslav in Kiev.

Yaroslav was also given an opportunity to strengthen family ties with his in-laws in Suzdalia. Two years earlier, as we have seen, his eldest son Rostislav had married Vseslava the daughter of Vsevolod Yur'evich. Under the year 1188, the Laurentian Chronicle reports that Bishop Luka consecrated the Cathedral of the Assumption in Vladimir on August 14 in the presence of Vsevolod, his son Konstantin, and his son-in-law Rostislav Yaroslavich.[318] Despite the numerous prominent personages who must have attended the event, the chronicler singles out only three: Vsevolod, who paid for remodeling the cathedral his brother Andrey Bogolyubskiy had built, his eldest son

---

[315] See s.a. 1187: Ipat., col. 658; compare s.a. 1189: Lav., col. 407. Concerning the year, see Berezhkov, pp. 83–4, 203. Bryagin was evidently located on the river Braginka, a left tributary of the Pripyat' (Makhnovets', p. 542).
[316] See s.a. 1187: Ipat., col. 659.   [317] Svyatoslav was born in 1176; see above, p. 137.
[318] See s.a. 1189: Lav., col. 407. Concerning the date, see Berezhkov, pp. 83–4.

Konstantin, and his son-in-law Rostislav from Chernigov. The latter's presence suggests that Vsevolod had invited the Ol'govichi to the consecration to admire the church that he had renovated in imitation of Svyatoslav's Annunciation.[319] The chronicler therefore singled out the princeling because he was the only Ol'govich in attendance and added luster to the occasion owing to the great distance that he had traveled. Moreover, he was Vsevolod's most welcome guest: Rostislav would have brought his wife Vseslava to visit her parents.

The most dramatic news, however, was that Vladimir returned home from captivity with Konchak's daughter. At that time, we are told, Igor' had his son marry the child (that is, Konchak's daughter).[320] Vladimir was eighteen years of age,[321] but it is difficult to determine the age of the bride. As we have seen, in 1185 Igor' was already Konchak's *svat*. Consequently, the khan's daughter had been born before that year. If, as has been suggested, Igor' and the khan concluded the betrothal at Dolobsk in 1181,[322] she would have been at least seven years of age when she married. The marriage tie virtually assured the cadet branch that Konchak and his allies would continue their policy of non-aggression towards the Seversk lands.

Although the chronicler reports Vladimir's return to Rus' in the autumn of 1188, he does not mention if any other captives came home, notably, Vladimir's uncle Vsevolod of Trubetsk and his cousin Svyatoslav of Ryl'sk. Because Vladimir was released during an interval free from Polovtsian incursions, it is possible that the nomads agreed to a truce in order to conduct a general exchange of captives. If this was so, the other Seversk princes would have been among those repatriated.

After Igor''s son returned safely from captivity the duumvirs, it would seem, gave notice to the Polovtsy that they were renewing hostilities. That winter Svyatoslav and Ryurik ordered Roman Nezdilovich to lead a small force of Black Caps against the nomads. He successfully pillaged camps on the left bank, we are told, because the Polovtsy had gone to the Danube leaving their tents undefended.[323] Thus we see that, once again, the princes

[319] Concerning Vsevolod's imitation of Svyatoslav's church in Chernigov, see above, p. 183.
[320] See s.a. 1187: Ipat., col. 659; compare Gust., p. 321. Makhnovets' misinterprets this passage to mean that Vladimir married Konchak's daughter Svoboda, who by then had given birth to their child Izyaslav (Makhnovets', p. 346).
[321] As we have seen, he was born in 1170 (see above, p. 121).   [322] See above, p. 173.
[323] See s.a. 1187: Ipat., col. 659. The Polovtsy, whom the Greeks called Cumans, evidently rode to assist the brothers Theodore (Peter) and Asen, who, in 1185, rebelled against Emperor Isaac Angelus to create the Second Bulgarian Empire (J. V. A. Fine, Jr., *The Late Medieval Balkans* [Ann Arbor, 1987], pp. 10–12).

sent Roman to lead a lightning strike in imitation of the raid that he had conducted in 1185 with the Berendei.[324]

Although Svyatoslav and Ryurik renewed their cooperation against the Polovtsy at the end of 1188, at an unspecified time during the year relations between them had become seriously strained. The problem arose following the death of Yaroslav Osmomysl on October 1 in the previous year.[325] His demise precipitated a fierce rivalry during which a number of contestants challenged Oleg and Vladimir for their father's throne in Galich.

Vladimir, the chronicler reports, lived a dissolute life. He drank to excess, ignored his counsellors, forced himself on men's wives and daughters, and took to himself a priest's wife with whom he had two sons.[326] Roman Mstislavich of Vladimir in Volyn', whose daughter Fedora was married to Vladimir's elder son, urged the Galicians to evict Vladimir and make him their prince. But they failed either to expel Vladimir or to kill him. When, however, they threatened to kill his wife, Vladimir took her, his two sons, and his *druzhina*, and fled to King Béla III in Hungary.[327]

A late chronicle describes Vladimir's eviction differently. After Oleg, whom Vladimir had driven out of Galich, failed to solicit aid from Ryurik, he went to King Casimir II of the Poles. They marched against Vladimir and defeated him. After Vladimir fled to the Hungarians, Casimir appointed Oleg to Galich, but the townsmen poisoned him and invited Roman to be their prince.[328]

Soon after, Béla III marched against Roman intending to reinstate Vladimir. Roman fled to his patrimony of Vladimir in Volyn' where his brother Vsevolod of Bel'z, to whom he had given the town, refused him entry. He therefore went to the Poles and sent his wife Predslava, Ryurik's daughter, to her father. After the Poles refused to help Roman, he also rode to his father-in-law in Belgorod.[329]

Meanwhile, Béla III sent a message to Svyatoslav in Kiev inviting him to send his son and promising, enigmatically, to fulfill the pledge that he had made to Svyatoslav.[330] The latter, hoping the king would give his son Galich, despatched Gleb without informing Ryurik. When the latter learned of

---

[324] See above, p. 163.   [325] See above, p. 186.

[326] It would appear that Vladimir's wife Boleslava, Svyatoslav's daughter, died before he took the priest's wife to himself since there is no evidence that he repudiated Boleslava or that Svyatoslav objected to Vladimir's mistreatment of his daughter.

[327] Ipat., cols. 659–60.   [328] Gust., p. 321.   [329] Ipat., cols. 660–1; compare Gust., p. 321.

[330] The compiler of the Hypatian Chronicle placed this information under the year 1189.

these events, he sent men in pursuit of Gleb and quarreled with Svyatoslav for sending the son without informing him. After Svyatoslav explained that he had sent Gleb on private business and not to conspire against Ryurik, they were reconciled. We are not told the nature of the private business, but later evidence suggests that Svyatoslav had asked Béla III to arrange a marriage between Gleb's daughter and a prince of Byzantium. Since the girl was also Ryurik's granddaughter, Svyatoslav probably had little difficulty in mollifying Ryurik with his explanation.

Ryurik's anger at Svyatoslav for his separate dealings with Béla III gives us another insight into the nature of their political relationship. Believing his security to be threatened, Ryurik accused Svyatoslav of breaking their pact. In other words, in 1181 each had agreed not to enter into an agreement independently of the other. This appears to have been the clause that Ryurik believed Svyatoslav violated to judge from the latter's assurance that he had not sent Gleb to Béla III to conspire against Ryurik. To prove his innocence, Svyatoslav agreed to attack the Hungarians with Ryurik. He thus proved that he was willing to wage war against the king in order to keep the duumvirate intact.

Ryurik rode with his brothers, that is, with all his allies. Svyatoslav, however, rode with his sons: Vladimir, Oleg, Vsevolod, and Mstislav. Gleb was visiting the king in Galich. Svyatoslav's comrades-in-arms, significantly, did not include his brother Yaroslav and the princes of the cadet branch. Perhaps Yaroslav did not join his brother because, as was his wont, he refused to travel such a long distance from his domain. The cadet branch, as has been suggested, was still recovering from Igor''s defeat.

Just the same, another reason for their absence comes to mind: Svyatoslav did not invite them. If he was interested in appropriating the Galician lands solely for his family, as he first led Ryurik to believe, he would not have invited Igor' because the latter could be an embarrassment. If challenged for his expansionist policy into Galicia, Svyatoslav could argue that he had a right to those lands owing to his marital ties with Yaroslav Osmomysl's dynasty: he was Vladimir's father-in-law. Igor', however, could also present a cogent claim by pointing out that he was Vladimir's brother-in-law. What is more, his sons were Yaroslav Osmomysl's grandsons. If, therefore, Svyatoslav refused to invite Yaroslav and Igor', he did so because he did not wish to share Galician lands with them.

En route to Galich, however, Svyatoslav expressed his true intentions. He wanted Ryurik to take all of Galicia and in exchange to hand over the Kievan land to him. Svyatoslav's readiness to cede Galich confirms that controlling it was not his main objective. He wished to use it as a bargaining chip to gain possession of the Kievan land. By becoming the sole ruler of Kiev and the Kievan land he would terminate the duumvirate! In other words, he attempted to make the prince of Kiev the undisputed single most powerful ruler in Rus' once again. Ryurik, however, refused to part with his Kievan possessions, above all, with his patrimony of Vruchiy. Instead, he proposed that they partition Galicia. Failing to reach an agreement, we are told, they returned home.[331]

Meanwhile, instead of handing over Galich to Vladimir as he had promised, Béla III gave it to his son Andrew. He took the hapless Vladimir and his wife back to Hungary and incarcerated them. At the same time, Roman solicited military aid from his father-in-law Ryurik in Belgorod and renewed his bid for Galich. Andrew's troops, however, repelled his attack. Ryurik therefore, helped Roman to drive out his brother Vsevolod from Vladimir in Volyn' and return to his patrimony.[332]

After expelling Vladimir, murdering Oleg, and losing Roman, the Galicians searched for another prince. They invited Rostislav the son of Ivan Berladnik.[333] On arriving in Galicia, however, he discovered that not all the people supported him. When he came face to face with the Hungarian and Galician forces, the latter betrayed him. He was wounded in the battle and the Hungarians took him captive. Later, they poured poison into his wounds and killed him. After that, the Hungarians intensified their atrocities: they abused local women and stabled their horses in Orthodox churches. "The Galicians were much aggrieved and regretted having expelled their prince."[334]

Thus we see that the rivalry for Galich attracted a number of princely claimants. By the end of the year, however, not one of them had succeeded in his objective. Nevertheless, the dynasties that would vie for control of Galich over the next fifty years had declared their intent. These included the Mstislavichi of Volyn', the Rostislavichi of Smolensk, and the Ol'govichi of Chernigov. Svyatoslav, the first Ol'govich to show an interest in controlling Galicia, would not be the last.

VSEVOLOD OF SUZDALIA DEFENDS VLADIMIR YAROSLAVICH IN GALICH

In 1189, peace finally returned to Galicia. Vladimir Yaroslavich escaped from the Hungarians and solicited military aid from Casimir II of the

---

[331] Concerning the duumvirs' campaign, see s.a. 1189: Ipat., cols. 662–3.
[332] See s.a. 1188: Ipat., cols. 661–2; compare Gust., pp. 321–2.
[333] Baum., III, 12–14; see above, p. 29.
[334] See s.a. 1189: Ipat., cols. 663–5; compare Gust., p. 322. For the dates concerning the rivalry over Galich, see Berezhkov, pp. 204–5.

Poles. When he arrived in Galicia, the *boyars* welcomed him and drove out Prince Andrew. After occupying Galich in the early part of August, Vladimir requested his uncle Vsevolod in Suzdalia to support his rule and, in return, promised to be Vsevolod's loyal vassal. The latter therefore demanded that all the princes pledge not to challenge his nephew. They agreed.[335]

The princes directly affected were Svyatoslav, Ryurik, and Roman. Vsevolod's relationship with the latter two, who were also Monomashichi, was different from his association with the Ol'govich. The Monomashichi had ties on three levels: political, personal, and dynastic. First, they all belonged to the same alliance of which Ryurik was notionally the head as a duumvir. That association between Ryurik and Roman, however, would be imperiled if they both continued to seek control of Galich. Vsevolod's heavy-handed intervention therefore deterred them from becoming involved in a military confrontation. Second, Ryurik enjoyed personal ties with the other two Monomashichi. His son Rostislav had married Vsevolod's daughter Verkhuslava and his daughter Predslava had married Roman. These ties undoubtedly served as mollifying factors.

Finally, all three belonged to the House of Monomakh. Roman and Ryurik were descended from Monomakh's eldest son, Mstislav, while Vsevolod was descended from Monomakh's youngest son, Yury Dolgorukiy. Significantly, they belonged to different generations: Vsevolod, as Yury's son, belonged to the second generation after Monomakh; Ryurik, as Mstislav's grandson, belonged to the third generation after Monomakh; and Roman, as Mstislav's great-grandson, belonged to the fourth generation after Monomakh. Vsevolod, therefore, was genealogically the eldest.[336] Accordingly, he assumed the role of the father as Yaroslav the Wise stipulated in his so-called "Testament". Vsevolod, as we shall see, would place much weight on the moral authority that his genealogical seniority gave him.

The relationship between Vsevolod and Svyatoslav was different. On the personal level, as we have seen, their families enjoyed a number of marital ties. On the political level, they were allies. They were also equals in that they were both senior princes of their dynasties. Svyatoslav, however, was more. He was the prince of Kiev to whom Vsevolod, according to the directive of Yaroslav the Wise, owed allegiance. Therefore, in forbidding Svyatoslav to attack Galich, Vsevolod challenged his political superior. Svyatoslav's reaction must have been ambivalent. On the one hand, since his mandate as prince of Kiev was to protect the rights of individual princes, it was

---

[335] See s.a. 1190: Ipat., cols. 666–7. Concerning the date, see Berezhkov, p. 205.
[336] Baum., V, 7, 16, 47; VI, 1, 14; IX, 6.

his moral obligation to support Vsevolod's dictate. On the other hand, he realized that other princes might interpret his compliance with Vsevolod's decree as a sign of weakness. It undermined his moral authority as prince of Kiev and bolstered Vsevolod's prestige.

Despite their political tug of war, the two remained friends. We learn that towards the end of the year, Vsevolod sent his spiritual father Ioann to Svyatoslav and to Metropolitan Nikifor to have him appointed bishop. Ioann was consecrated on January 23, 1190 and went to Rostov.[337] It is noteworthy that Vsevolod sent Ioann to both Svyatoslav and Nikifor. The latter, as the highest-ranking ecclesiastic in the land, had the authority to appoint the bishop in the name of the Church. Svyatoslav had a comparable political authority. Significantly, by sending Ioann to Svyatoslav, Vsevolod acknowledged him to be the ultimate political authority in the land that approved the appointment of bishops. By doing so, Vsevolod once again confirmed that Ryurik, the other duumvir, did not share Svyatoslav's authority over all-Rus' Church affairs.

THE FIRST INTRA-DYNASTIC MARRIAGE IN THE DYNASTY

The year 1190 witnessed the first marriage between the senior branch and the cadet branch. We are told that Svyatoslav married his grandson David Ol'govich to the daughter of Igor' Svyatoslavich.[338] The identity of Igor''s daughter is not revealed. David, however, was the son of Svyatoslav's second son, Oleg. He was evidently the most senior princeling of the youngest generation of Ol'govichi.[339] Svyatoslav must therefore have looked upon David's marriage as an especially important one since the youth had a good chance of becoming the senior prince one day.

In the light of this consideration, it is surprising that Svyatoslav opted for an intra-dynastic marriage rather than selecting a bride from the House of Monomakh. Clearly, he and Igor' believed that a marriage between their families was preferable. In uniting the senior families of both branches with a personal tie, they consolidated the internal organization of the dynasty. Because the two branches were now related through a marriage bond in addition to blood ties, the Ol'govichi could work in closer cooperation against rival dynasties and against external enemies like the Polovtsy.

---

[337] See s.a. 1190: Lav., col. 408. Concerning the date, see Berezhkov, p. 84.
[338] Ipat., col. 668. Concerning the date, see Berezhkov, p. 206. Baum., IV, 49, 50.
[339] Svyatoslav's eldest son Vladimir evidently had no sons, and the only other princeling in David's generation mentioned to date has been Mikhail, Vsevolod Chermnyy's son. The sources have not reported the births of any princesses in David's generation.

THE KHAN KUNTUVDEY AFFAIR

In the summer Svyatoslav and his *svat* Ryurik pacified the land of Rus′,
we are told, and forced the Polovtsy to accept their terms. The chronicler
last spoke of the nomads two years earlier, under 1188, when Svyatoslav
and Ryurik sent Roman Nezdilovich to pillage their camps. Perhaps it was
because of such punitive strikes that the tribesmen agreed to negotiate
peace. Although the chronicler does not identify the khans who formed
the pact, Konchak and Koza must have been among them. The chronicler
tells us that, following the agreement, the duumvirs considered themselves
to be so safe from attack that they organized a hunting trip to the very
threshold of the Polovtsian steppe. They traveled by boat down the Dnepr
to the mouth of the river Tesmen′, south of the river Ros′.[340]
     The period of peace ended in the autumn. Svyatoslav, we are told, took
Khan Kuntuvdey of Torchesk captive because others had levied slanderous
accusations against him. Later, Svyatoslav released him because Ryurik interceded on his behalf. As the ruler of Torchesk in the Poros′e, Kuntuvdey
was Ryurik′s man. His compatriots were evidently jealous of his good fortune in ruling Torchesk and plotted against him. Surprisingly, they accused
him before Svyatoslav and not Ryurik. Since he acted upon the false charge,
it probably dealt with the safety of Rus′. An offense such as collaborating
with the Polovtsy would have given Svyatoslav, the commander-in-chief,
the right to punish his co-ruler′s subordinate. Indeed, since Ryurik did not
challenge Svyatoslav′s judgment, he also believed that the alleged crime fell
within Svyatoslav′s jurisdiction. Nevertheless, Ryurik convinced him of the
khan′s innocence and the treachery of the accusers. Svyatoslav concluded
a pact with Kuntuvdey in an attempt to reestablish peace between them.
     But Kuntuvdey refused to ignore the shame that he had suffered. He
rode to the Polovtsy and persuaded Khan Toglyy to break his pact with
Svyatoslav and to help him obtain revenge.[341] They attacked towns along
the Ros′ controlled by the Black Caps who had maligned Kuntuvdey. On
learning that Ryurik′s son Rostislav had come to Torchesk, however, the
nomads withdrew. After that, we are told, Kuntuvdey and the Polovtsy
frequently raided the Poros′e region.[342] Significantly, the Black Caps were
Ryurik′s vassals so that, in avenging himself on the culprits, Kuntuvdey

---

[340] Ipat., col. 668. Concerning the date, see Berezhkov, p. 206. The Tesmen′, today known as Tyasmin,
     is located on the right bank of the Dnepr between the Sula and the Psel (Makhnovets′, p. 571).
[341] According to Pletneva, Toglyy became the most prominent khan among the Lukomorskie Polovtsy
     after Kobyak′s death (*Polovsty*, p. 147).
[342] Ipat., cols. 668–9.

also attacked his protector. Thus, even though Ryurik had secured the khan's release, his attacks on the Poros'e towns punished Ryurik rather than Svyatoslav.

After sending his son Rostislav to Torchesk because he knew Kuntuvdey would attack the Poros'e region, Ryurik alerted Svyatoslav to the danger. He advised that the two of them should not leave Rus' undefended while they went away, the one to Vruchiy and the other to Chernigov, to look after private affairs. Since Ryurik had sent his son to Torchesk, he suggested that Svyatoslav also send his son to the Poros'e. Svyatoslav promised to send Gleb but did not because, we are told, he was involved in a controversy with the Rostislavichi.

Thus we see that, after releasing Kuntuvdey, Svyatoslav faced two problems: the threat of the khan's revenge and the dispute with Ryurik. The latter outweighed the former to judge from the news that, because of the argument, Svyatoslav broke his word to send his son Gleb to the Poros'e. He therewith strained his relationship with Ryurik further. The latter could accuse him of shirking his responsibility for overseeing the defense of Rus'. Despite Ryurik's insistence that he take measures to defend the Poros'e region, Svyatoslav considered his meeting with the Ol'govichi to be of greater urgency.

SVYATOSLAV'S DISAGREEMENT WITH RYURIK

Svyatoslav, the chronicler reports enigmatically, had a disagreement with Ryurik, David, and the Smolensk land. In the autumn, therefore, he summoned his brothers to help him determine how he could avoid violating his oath. Since this was the first plenary council of the Ol'govichi that he called after occupying Kiev, the crisis was obviously of major importance to him. Because Ryurik served as the spokesman for the Rostislavichi, he evidently had the greatest interest in the dispute in his dynasty. He drew his *svat* Vsevolod of Suzdalia into the controversy to gain additional backing.

Ryurik reminded Svyatoslav that, after he had occupied Kiev in 1181, he had pledged to abide by the same terms that Ryurik's brother Roman had ruled. As long as Svyatoslav honored that agreement he would remain their brother. If, however, he would cite the ancient dispute with Ryurik's father, Rostislav, he would be violating their pact and the Rostislavichi would not accept that. Ryurik's declaration implies that Roman's terms of rule had resolved in favor of the Rostislavichi a dispute that the Ol'govichi and the Rostislavichi had had during the reign of Ryurik's father Rostislav. That is, the Ol'govichi had presented demands to Rostislav that they later renounced when Roman occupied Kiev. Ryurik insisted that Svyatoslav not revive those forsworn demands. To judge from the chronicler's vague references to the dispute, it seemingly had its origin during Rostislav's reign. An examination of the sources suggests that the controversy reared its head in 1188, when the princes marched against Béla III. At that time Svyatoslav asked Ryurik to give him the Kievan land in exchange for Galicia. But Ryurik refused to part with his patrimony.[343] In this entry the chronicler, for the first time, alluded to Vruchiy, famed for its rich slate deposits, as Ryurik's patrimony.[344] Nevertheless, some twenty years earlier, in 1168, the chronicler had already reported that Ryurik ruled that town.[345] Since his father Rostislav had died as prince of Kiev a year earlier,[346] the latter had undoubtedly carved out Vruchiy from the Kievan land as Ryurik's inheritance. This was a highly irregular allocation. As prince of Kiev, Rostislav had the authority to grant temporary control of Kievan towns to his allies, but not as patrimonies. To judge from Ryurik's comments to Svyatoslav in 1190, the Ol'govichi had unsuccessfully challenged Rostislav over that irregular allocation. In other words, they had disputed Ryurik's right to rule Vruchiy as his patrimony. According to tradition, after Rostislav's death, Ryurik would lose the town and the new prince of Kiev would give it to a man of his choice.

After Rostislav's death, Andrey Bogolyubskiy had appointed his puppets to Kiev. Ryurik's brother Roman was his appointee from 1171 to 1173,[347] and, after Andrey's death, Roman ruled again, but independently, from 1175 to 1176.[348] During one of those two periods, probably the second, he reallotted Vruchiy to Ryurik as his patrimony. At that time the Ol'govichi had evidently pledged to abide by his decision. In 1181, Svyatoslav, as Roman's successor, assumed similar authority over the Kievan land. Ryurik's victory over the Polovtsy at Dolobsk, however, enabled him to force Svyatoslav to reallot Vruchiy to him according to Roman's previous agreement. In giving all the remaining Kievan towns to Ryurik, Svyatoslav had made a separate deal.

In the autumn of 1190, if our interpretation is correct, Svyatoslav sought to find a means of seizing control of Vruchiy without breaking his pledge to

---

[343] See above, pp. 192–3.

[344] Local craftsmen produced luxury slate goods and exported them not only to Kiev, Chernigov, and other towns in Rus', but also to the Poles and to the Volga Bulgars (V. T. Pashuto, *Ocherki po istorii Galitsko-Volynskoy Rusi* [M., 1950], pp. 165–6). Concerning the manufacture of slate goods in Kiev, see Miller, "The Kievan Principality," pp. 218–19.

[345] See above, p. 114.   [346] See above, p. 112.

[347] Concerning his rule in 1171, see above, p. 122; concerning his eviction in 1173, see above, p. 125.

[348] Concerning his rule in 1175, see above, p. 133; concerning his abdication in 1176, see above, pp. 135–6.

Ryurik. Thus, for the second time he attempted to deprive his co-ruler of his patrimony. If he succeeded, however, he would not only weaken Ryurik's power as a duumvir but also score a victory against his dynasty. David would have to compensate Ryurik for his loss of Vruchiy with a domain from Smolensk. In carving up the dynastic lands, he would decrease his own territorial base and that of the other Rostislavichi. Svyatoslav's victory would also strengthen his position in relation to Vsevolod of Suzdalia because the latter would have failed to defend Ryurik's claim. Vsevolod, therefore, had little choice but to challenge Svyatoslav once again, just as he had done when he had forbidden Svyatoslav to attack Vladimir in Galich.

The chronicler offers no explanation why Svyatoslav tried changing his agreement with Ryurik. The initiative, it would appear, was his. As we shall see, he would die in four years' time. It could therefore be argued that pride motivated him to secure absolute power over the Kievan land before his death. But why should he seek to strengthen his position at Ryurik's expense? Future events will show that, according to their agreement of 1181, Ryurik was Svyatoslav's designated successor to Kiev. After Svyatoslav died all the Kievan land, including Vruchiy, would fall into Ryurik's hands.

This raises the pivotal question: was Svyatoslav wavering in his resolve to hand over Kiev to Ryurik? Did he summon all the Ol'govichi because he wished to designate his brother Yaroslav to succeed him just as his father Vsevolod had designated his brother Igor'?[349] If that were the case, Svyatoslav assembled the Ol'govichi not merely to decide whether or not to evict Ryurik from Vruchiy. More importantly, after designating Yaroslav his successor, he would have made all the Ol'govichi swear allegiance to him. Later events will show that there may be some truth in these observations.

Svyatoslav's plans came to naught. Ryurik's envoys gave him the document containing the terms which Ryurik, David, and Vsevolod wanted him to accept. He refused, procrastinated, argued with the envoys, and dismissed them. Later, we are told, he recalled them and kissed the Holy Cross.[350] The threat of a full-scale war undoubtedly persuaded him to capitulate. By submitting to the Rostislavichi, however, he relegated the Ol'govichi to a place of secondary importance in Rus' after his death.

Having strained his relations with Ryurik through his disagreement, Svyatoslav hurried back to Kiev. Earlier in the winter, it would seem, the Black Caps had appealed to Rostislav in Torchesk for help because the Polovtsy were raiding their towns. His father Ryurik in Vruchiy was too

---

[349] *Dynasty*, pp. 404–11.
[350] Concerning Svyatoslav's meeting with the Ol'govichi, see Ipat., cols. 669–70; compare Makhnovets', p. 350.

far away they claimed, and they dared not ask Svyatoslav because they had deceived him in denouncing Kuntuvdey. Rostislav therefore led the Black Caps against the marauders and captured some 600 tribesmen. Later in the winter, the Polovtsy returned to pillage, but when they learned that Svyatoslav was waiting for them at Khan Kuldyur's town, they fled beyond the Ros'. In the light of Svyatoslav's ire against the Black Caps, the news that he came to the Poros'e region is noteworthy. It shows that, on returning from Chernigov, he resumed his responsibilities of defending Rus'. Undoubtedly, his main motive for doing so was to placate Ryurik after their recent dispute.

Svyatoslav ingratiated himself further by bringing his son Gleb who ruled Kanev. Since Ryurik had jurisdiction over all the Kievan land, he had obviously appointed his son-in-law to that domain. Consequently, when Ryurik had warned Svyatoslav of Kuntuvdey's threat, he had probably advised Svyatoslav to send Gleb to Kanev just as he had sent his son Rostislav to Torchesk. Svyatoslav, however, honored his pledge to send Gleb only after he and Ryurik had been reconciled. Meanwhile, after Svyatoslav departed from Khan Kuldyur's town, Kuntuvdey returned with the tribesmen. Gleb therefore came from Kanev and killed many, but Kuntuvdey escaped.[351]

THE OL'GOVICHI RENEW THEIR RAIDS ON THE POLOVTSY

At the same time, the nomads were also pillaging the lands of the Ol'govichi on the east bank of the Dnepr. As we have seen, after Konchak raided the river Ros' region in 1187, the chronicler reported that enemy bands frequently pillaged the Poros'e district and the Chernigov lands.[352] Five years later, in 1192, the Ol'govichi finally retaliated by waging two campaigns against the nomads. The first was crowned with success. We are told that Igor' and his brothers marched against the Polovtsy, captured many cattle and horses, and returned home.[353] Significantly, this was the first expedition that Igor' organized following his defeat seven years earlier.

The success of the first raid undoubtedly prompted the second larger expedition which included princes from both branches. Svyatoslav of Kiev sent three sons: Vsevolod, Vladimir, and Mstislav. His youngest delegate was his grandson David, Oleg's son and Igor''s son-in-law. Yaroslav of Chernigov sent his son Rostislav. The two eldest princes of the cadet branch, Igor' and Vsevolod, went in person. Vsevolod's presence is noteworthy

[351] Ipat., cols. 670–3; compare Makhnovets', pp. 350–1.
[352] See above, p. 187.   [353] Ipat., col. 673.

because it testifies to his return from captivity. Significantly, by placing Igor′ in command, Svyatoslav demonstrated his complete confidence in Igor′'s leadership despite his defeat at the Kayala.

Three Ol′govichi did not join the campaign. The first was Svyatoslav's son Gleb, who probably absented himself because, as we have seen, his father had ordered him to stay in Kanev and defend the Ros′ frontier. Indeed, Svyatoslav probably remained in Kiev for the same reason. Igor′'s son Vladimir also did not come. Since he ruled Putivl′ in the Posem′e region, Igor′ most likely ordered him to remain there to defend his domain. The third absentee was Igor′'s nephew Svyatoslav of Ryl′sk. As we have seen, he was one of the princes taken captive at the Kayala, but his return to Rus′ has not been reported. It is noteworthy, however, that his domain was also in the Posem′e region. Consequently, if he had been released he, like Vladimir, remained behind to defend his patrimony.

The purpose of the second campaign, like that of the first, was to plunder Polovtsian camps. Because of the raids that Koza and his tribesmen had conducted on the Posem′e district, the Ol′govichi undoubtedly attacked camps belonging to his people. The second campaign, however, was different in two respects. First, it was more ambitious. Relying on their greater numbers, the Ol′govichi ventured deeper into the steppe, past Kursk into the upper reaches of the river Oskol. This was evidently as far east as they had ever campaigned except for the raid in 1185, when Igor′ led his troops into that region. To be sure, it appears that in 1192 he revisited the site of his defeat with the intention of avenging the Seversk princes. But the nomads refused to be surprised a second time. After their scouts warned them of the approaching Ol′govichi, they once again assembled in great numbers and awaited the princes. Igor′ had also learned his lesson at the Kayala. On seeing that he was outnumbered, he resolutely ordered his troops to steal away under the cover of darkness.[354]

Second, the composition of the second campaign was different. Although the cadet branch suffered most from the attacks that the tribesmen from the Oskol region directed at its domains, Svyatoslav sent his sons to assist the Seversk princes. In doing so, he deviated from the policy that he had espoused some seven years earlier. At that time, he had insisted that Igor′ and Yaroslav accompany him on expeditions down the Dnepr, but he refused to campaign southeast of Kursk. The collaboration of the two branches in 1192 reflects a change in his policy, one that he and Igor′ probably negotiated two years earlier when they formed their marriage alliance. The presence

---

[354] Ipat., col. 673; compare Gust., p. 323.

on the campaign of David, Svyatoslav's grandson and Igor''s son-in-law, supports this view. Although the chronicler fails to explain why Svyatoslav changed his mind, Igor''s defeat at the Kayala may have finally convinced him of the seriousness of the Polovtsian threat from the Donets basin.

THE DUUMVIRS FAIL TO NEGOTIATE PEACE WITH THE NOMADS

The remainder of the year 1192 was peaceful, but the princes remained on a war footing. Svyatoslav and his *svat* Ryurik summoned their brothers and rode to Kanev, where they stationed their troops for the entire summer. In this manner, they protected Rus' from the pagans.[355] Presumably, the brothers who accompanied Svyatoslav and Ryurik were princes and Black Caps from the Kievan land. It is unlikely that any Ol'govichi came from the right bank. Svyatoslav's son Gleb, who ruled Kanev, would have been the only exception. Noting the princes' determination to stem the tide of their attacks, the nomads refused to let Kuntuvdey cajole them into making foolhardy raids.

The coda to the Kuntuvdey affair came in the winter: Ryurik bribed the Polovtsy into handing over the gadfly. He acknowledged the khan's original innocence by reinstating him as a vassal. Nevertheless, he did not reappoint Kuntuvdey to Torchesk. He demoted the khan, in part for his attacks on the Poros'e towns, by giving him the less important town of Dveren, on the river Ros'.[356] Ryurik therewith also appeased the Black Caps who had objected to Kuntuvdey's rule in Torchesk.

In 1193, Polovtsian affairs once again occupied the lion's share of the chronicler's report. Ryurik, we are told, had concluded peace with the Lukomorskie Polovtsy.[357] They, evidently, had joined Kuntuvdey in attacking the river Ros' region. Consequently, in the summer, Svyatoslav suggested that the duumvirs negotiate peace with all the Polovtsy, especially the Burchevichi.[358] In addition to securing peace for the people of Rus', however, Svyatoslav probably had a personal desire for ending Polovtsian raids. He was some seventy years of age and he must have found participating on campaigns ever more difficult.[359]

Svyatoslav's stated desire to negotiate peace with all the Polovtsy is misleading. It is unlikely that the Burchevichi represented all the tribes east of

[355] Ipat., col. 673.   [356] Ipat., col. 674. For the location of Dveren, see Makhnovets', p. 548.
[357] These tribesmen probably lived at the mouth of the river Dnepr and along the shores of the Black Sea and the Sea of Azov (Pletneva, "Polovetskaya zemlya," p. 286).
[358] Pletneva points out that the Burchevichi lived along the east bank of the Dnepr ("Polovetskaya zemlya," pp. 286–8).
[359] Svyatoslav was probably born in the early 1120s (*Dynasty*, pp. 313–14).

the Dnepr since Konchak and Koza were not invited to the negotiations. Nevertheless, it is noteworthy that Svyatoslav singled out Osoluk and Izay of the Burchevichi.[360] Evidently, he believed them to be the most troublesome along the Dnepr. Indeed, Osoluk was among the khans whom Svyatoslav and Ryurik had taken captive in 1184 at the river Erel'.[361] It would seem, therefore, that the Burchevichi and the Lukomortsy were the tribes against whom Svyatoslav and Ryurik had been waging their campaigns along the Dnepr region. Svyatoslav wished to conclude peace with them because they were of the greatest danger to the duumvirs. He evidently did not propose negotiating a pact with the nomads in the Donets basin against whom Igor' was waging war.

The duumvirs came to Kanev and the Burchevichi came to the other side of the Dnepr. Osoluk and Izay, however, never intended to conclude peace. They antagonized the princes by demanding that the latter come to them. The princes retorted that neither their grandfathers nor their fathers had ever gone to the Polovtsy, but invited the tribesmen to come to them. Moreover, the news that the khans refused to set free Black Caps whom they were holding captive shows that they had come in bad faith. Indeed, it is surprising why they came at all unless they hoped to gain some advantage through deceit. If so, the duumvirs pre-empted their treachery by refusing to go to them. They preferred to wage war than to lose face.

The willful action of the khans to undermine Svyatoslav's peace initiative was predictable. What was surprising was Svyatoslav's refusal to be reconciled with khans Yakush (Akush) and Toglyy (Itoglyy) of the Lukomortsy, who had come in goodwill.[362] He declared that he could not conclude peace with only half of the enemy.[363] As we have seen, when Ryurik concluded peace with the Lukomortsy he had showered them with gifts. Was this the price he paid for Kuntuvdey's return or was it appeasement through bribery? If the latter was the case, then Svyatoslav probably believed it pointless to pay off the same nomads yet again knowing that the nomads on the east bank were still bent on pillaging.

After the failed negotiations, Ryurik advised Svyatoslav to launch a winter campaign, probably against the Burchevichi. Svyatoslav rejected the proposal perhaps, as has been suggested, because his advancing years made

[360] Concerning these khans, see Pletneva, *Polovtsy*, pp. 147–51.　　[361] See above, p. 160.
[362] Concerning these khans, see Pletneva, *Polovtsy*, pp. 147–51.
[363] Concerning the negotiations, see Ipat., cols. 675–6. The late Gustinskiy Chronicle says that Svyatoslav and Ryurik did not conclude peace with the nomads because Svyatoslav always opposed Ryurik's good advice (p. 323). This is the only chronicle reference suggesting that constant discord existed between Svyatoslav and Ryurik.

it difficult for him to endure the rigors of a winter campaign. But he could not admit such a weakness to Ryurik; it would jeopardize his status as commander-in-chief. By claiming that he had to oversee the business of his patrimony owing to a bad harvest, however, he saved face and stifled Ryurik's proposal. Nevertheless, when the latter declared his intention to lead an expedition against the Lithuanians, Svyatoslav accused him of neglecting his duty. He pointed out that the Poros'e district belonged to Ryurik and it was his obligation to defend it. At the end of the sparring, Svyatoslav asserted his superior rank and dissuaded Ryurik from conducting his private campaign.[364]

Despite Svyatoslav's claim that he had to visit his domain in the winter, he had not yet departed in December. Earlier in the year, we are told, the archbishop of Novgorod had died and the townsmen chose a certain Martury to replace him. Prominent Novgorodians escorted him to Kiev, where Svyatoslav and Metropolitan Nikifor welcomed them. Martury was consecrated on December 10.[365] Granted, his appointment required Svyatoslav's approval. In this instance, however, he may have attended the ceremony more out of self-interest than from duty. Hosting the Novgorodian magnates would give him the opportunity to negotiate commercial arrangements for Kiev and the Ol'govichi. Establishing friendly relations with the new archbishop was also important because he was one of the most powerful personages in Novgorod. Such considerations undoubtedly persuaded Svyatoslav to delay his departure for Karachev.

That winter the Polovtsy renewed their attacks on the Poros'e. A delegation of Black Caps rode to Ryurik's son Rostislav who was hunting at Chernobyl' and asked him to lead them against the nomads.[366] Succumbing to promises of booty and glory, he agreed to lead the raid without informing his father. As the Black Caps pointed out, Ryurik would have objected because he was preparing to wage war against the Lithuanians and did not want his son to organize a separate attack. Rostislav rode to Torchesk, summoned his cousin Mstislav from Trepol',[367] and set out for the steppe.

A parallel can be drawn between his raid and the one Igor' had led eight years earlier. In 1185 Igor' had also campaigned in quest of booty and glory

---

[364] Ipat., cols. 676.   [365] NPL, pp. 231–2.
[366] Chernobyl', near the confluence of the rivers Pripyat' and the Usha, was in the Kievan land and may have belonged to Ryurik's patrimony of Vruchiy.
[367] Mstislav was the son of Ryurik's younger brother Mstislav and later became known as "the Bold" (*Udaloy*) (Baum., IX, 24; Rapov, p. 182). As prince of Trepol', he would have been among Ryurik's brothers who joined him on his Polovtsian campaigns.

without telling his senior prince. Although the circumstances of the two attacks were similar, the immediate outcomes were different: Rostislav was victorious. He returned to Torchesk on Christmas Day with much booty. Despite his short-term success, however, the long-term consequences, like those of Igor''s failure, were damaging for Rus'.

Svyatoslav remonstrated with Ryurik over Rostislav's raid declaring that even though the latter had renewed war with the Polovtsy, Ryurik was still planning to abandon his lands to conduct a private campaign. After Svyatoslav alerted him to the immediate danger, Ryurik canceled his campaign. In light of the friction that existed between the two, Ryurik's compliance with Svyatoslav's summons stabilized their relationship. Perhaps Ryurik changed his plans because Svyatoslav promised to do the same. Even though, in the autumn, he had excused himself from organizing a winter expedition, after Christmas he joined Ryurik at Vasiliev, where they stood guard against the expected attacks. He realized that, whereas conducting an offensive campaign into the steppe was an option, defending the frontiers of Rus' was an obligation.

Svyatoslav was unable to depart for Karachev until around the end of February at the earliest. In light of his prior warning to Ryurik that they should not vacate the lands of Rus' at the same time, it is surprising that they did exactly that. After standing guard at Vasiliev during January and February of 1194, Svyatoslav went to Karachev and Ryurik returned to Vruchiy.[368] We may assume that they left the field because their supplies had run out, winter had taken its toll on their troops, and they had to look after their patrimonial domains. Their withdrawal was the signal to the Polovtsy to renew their raids. As we have seen, the Burchevichi, who had rejected peace at Kanev, had returned to their camps as bellicose as before. The Lukomortsy, who had come seeking peace were first rebuffed by Svyatoslav and later attacked by Rostislav.

SVYATOSLAV'S DEATH

The year 1194 was momentous for Rus'. It witnessed Svyatoslav's death, the accession of Ryurik to Kiev, and the start of Vsevolod's active interference in the affairs of Rus'. The events of interest to us begin with Svyatoslav's visit to Karachev. While there, he summoned the senior members of the two branches: his brother Yaroslav from Chernigov, his cousin Igor' from Novgorod Severskiy, and the latter's brother Vsevolod from Trubetsk. They

---

[368] Concerning Rostislav's campaign and Svyatoslav's response, see Ipat., cols. 676–9.

met to organize a campaign against the princes of Ryazan', whom they accused of seizing one of their domains. In 1175, the chroniclers had reported a similar dispute. At that time Svyatoslav's son Oleg recaptured Sviril'sk from his Ryazan' in-laws.[369] In 1194 the domain in question was evidently contiguous with the Ryazan' territories, in the northeast corner of the Vyatichi lands. Since it allegedly belonged to Svyatoslav's family, the proposed attack was Svyatoslav's private business.

Svyatoslav, however, refused to initiate war without the backing of Vsevolod of Suzdalia. If the Ol'govichi attacked Ryazan' without his consent, he would undoubtedly look upon their aggression as an incursion into his sphere of influence. Consequently, after he objected to the attack, the Ol'govichi abandoned it. Nevertheless, it is impossible to know whether they aborted the attack owing to Vsevolod's refusal to march with them or to the ailment that immobilized Svyatoslav. Whatever the real reason for their decision, the Ol'govichi were forced to defer their claim to the unidentified domain. Svyatoslav, we are told, departed from Karachev by sledge because an open sore had formed on his foot. On reaching the river Desna, he continued the journey by raft.[370]

His journey to Kiev took him some three months. He left his patrimony on April 23 and arrived in Kiev some time before Friday, July 22. Since his route down the Desna took him through Novgorod Severskiy and Chernigov, he undoubtedly stopped for respite with Igor' and Yaroslav. His stay at the dynastic capital would have been especially poignant because he would have visited the tombs of his ancestors in the Holy Saviour Cathedral. He must have also taken the opportunity to worship in the churches of St. Michael and the Annunciation that he had built. His visits to the churches in Chernigov are suggested by the information that, after he returned to Kiev, he traveled to his family's shrine in Vyshgorod and to his father's monastery at Dorogozhichi. Moreover, the chronicler's remark that Svyatoslav wished to pray at his father's tomb in Vyshgorod, as was his wont, implies that he habitually visited the family monuments.

Svyatoslav had a deep devotion to SS. Boris and Gleb. When living in Kiev he had the habit of going to Vyshgorod to venerate at their shrine. Since the anniversary of his father's death was only eight days after their feast, he normally took advantage of the visit to pray at his father's tomb located in a nearby vault. To enter the vault, however, he had to obtain the key from an attendant priest. That latter, the chronicler reports tongue-in-cheek, was absent. The cleric could not have picked a more inopportune time to be

[369] See above, pp. 134–5.   [370] Ipat., col. 679.

truant, namely, at the moment when the most important personage who could possibly have visited the tomb came: the eldest son of the deceased prince, the senior prince of the Ol'govichi, and the prince of Kiev. What is more, he came from his sickbed.

Svyatoslav demonstrated his devotion to the *strastoterptsy* again the next day, Saturday, by attending his last liturgy in their church at his father's monastery of St. Cyril. This is the first reference to the Church of SS. Boris and Gleb at Dorogozhichi. Since the chronicler neglected to report its construction, it was most likely a chapel attached to the Church of St. Cyril.[371] Because Vsevolod founded the monastery after 1139 when he became prince of Kiev, either he or his son Svyatoslav built the chapel.[372] Vsevolod demonstrated a special devotion to the martyrs by being buried next to their shrine in Vyshgorod. Svyatoslav had a special attachment to his father's monastery since he chose to be buried in it. He may have therefore contributed to its splendor by building a church dedicated to the brothers. Since he attended his last liturgy in that chapel and wished to visit it on the saints' feast, he demonstrated not only his devotion to the *strastoterptsy* but also a personal attachment to the chapel. Although we do not know the identity of the chapel's patron, the reference to its existence reveals that it was the most recent church that the Ol'govichi had built in honor of their patron St. Gleb.[373]

Sunday, July 24, was the Feast of SS. Boris and Gleb, but Svyatoslav was too ill to leave his new court so he celebrated the feast there. The passing reference to his new court suggests that he had built it. But we are not told when he did so or where it was located. Since he found the distance from it to the Church of SS. Boris and Gleb too great, it is safe to assume that the court was not at Dorogozhichi. He therefore probably built it near the patrimonial Monastery of St. Simeon in the Kopyrev *konets* or on the great court in the heart of the citadel. As we have seen, he was sensitive to the prestige attached to the office of prince of Kiev. The evidence that he was the only Ol'govich to build a church, St. Vasily, on the great court, supports this. It is therefore likely that, for the same reason, he built his new court near the Church of St. Vasily.[374] From there, he had to travel some 6 km

---

[371] This observation is based on the information that no remains of a church have been found on the premises of the monastery which could be identified with the Church of SS. Boris and Gleb (Rappoport, *Drevnerusskaya Arkhitektura*, pp. 259–62, 280).

[372] Concerning the Church of St. Cyril, see *Dynasty*, pp. 389–94.

[373] The two earlier ones, as has been noted elsewhere, were in Chernigov and Vyshgorod (*Dynasty*, pp. 262–4, 276–82).

[374] Concerning his reasons for building St. Vasily in the great court, see above, p. 154. According to Braychevsky, however, the new court was located in the Kopyrev *konets* ("Chernigovskiy knyazheskiy dom i avtor 'Slova o polku Igoreve'," p. 15).

to the monastery. Significantly, the residence in Kiev was the second new court Svyatoslav built. The first had been in Chernigov.

On Monday morning, Svyatoslav received word that Greek matchmakers were coming to collect his granddaughter, Gleb's daughter Evfimia, as bride for the emperor's son. Despite his flagging strength, he was determined to conclude an alliance with an unidentified emperor's son, evidently a Greek.[375] The chronicles have not reported any communications between Kiev and Constantinople in recent years. The last recorded contact was around 1163, when Bishop Leon of Suzdalia visited the emperor in the presence of envoys from Kiev, Chernigov, Suzdal', and Pereyaslavl'.[376] Because Gleb was not yet married at that time, negotiating a betrothal for his daughter had not been on the agenda. The only ties with the Greeks that the chroniclers allude to with any regularity are the arrivals of metropolitans. Despite the silence of the sources, therefore, the coming of Greek matchmakers in 1194 shows that Svyatoslav remained in contact with the imperial court. This is the first instance since the early 1080s, when Svyatoslav's grandfather Oleg had married Feofania Muzalon, that the chronicler reports a marriage alliance between the Ol'govichi and the Greeks.[377]

In 1188, as has been suggested, arranging a marriage alliance with the Greeks may have been the private business that Svyatoslav was conducting with Béla III.[378] If so, Svyatoslav initiated the process because the king agreed to fulfill the promise that he had made to the prince. His pledge, presumably, was to act as matchmaker. Béla III had excellent credentials to act as a broker with the Greeks. He had spent his early years in Constantinople under the patronage of Manuel I Comnenus (d. 1180) and was for a time betrothed to the emperor's daughter Mary. More importantly, his daughter Margaret (Margit) had married the current emperor, Isaac II Angelus (1185–95). Béla III, therefore, was the emperor's father-in-law.[379]

---

[375] Only the late Gustinskiy Chronicle identifies the emperor's son as a Greek (p. 324). A number of investigators suggest the imperial family in question belonged to the Angelus Dynasty. If this was so, the emperor was Isaac II and the son betrothed to Evfimia was his son, the future Emperor Alexius IV (Zotov, p. 280; Makhnovets', pp. 354, 524; Murav'eva and Kuz'mina, *Imennoy i geograficheskiy ukazateli*, p. 6). This claim, however, is not confirmed by the sources. Indeed, according to one view, there is no documentary evidence that the marriage ever took place (A. Kazhdan, "Rus'–Byzantine Princely Marriages in the Eleventh and Twelfth Centuries," HUS 12/13, 1988/1989 Proceedings of the International Congress Commemorating the Millennium of Christianity in Rus'–Ukraine [1990], 424).

[376] See above, p. 103. In 1186, the Novgorod chroniclers reported simply that Alexius II, the son of Manuel I Comnenus, came to Novgorod (NPL, pp. 38, 228). If he stopped at Svyatoslav's court in Kiev, no chronicler found the visit noteworthy enough to report.

[377] Concerning Feofania, see *Dynasty*, pp. 160–1.   [378] See above, pp. 191–2.

[379] Concerning Béla's engagement to Mary and the marriage of Béla's daughter Margaret to Isaac II, see F. Makk, *The Árpáds and the Comneni*, Political Relations between Hungary and Byzantium in the 12th Century (Budapest, 1989), pp. 86, 120.

What is more, the evidence that, in 1188, Svyatoslav sent his son Gleb to negotiate with Béla III suggests that Gleb had a vested interest in the matter. This would have been the case if the private business were the betrothal of his daughter Evfimia. Gleb concluded the arrangement with the king to judge from the arrival of the Greek delegation to Kiev. Svyatoslav's private business was therefore a success at least to the point of the matchmakers coming to collect the bride, who, at that time, was some eleven years of age.[380] We are not told, however, if the Greeks honored their commitment following Svyatoslav's death. If they did, the personal tie with the imperial family was a great boon to the Ol'govichi. It was just such a union that Vladimir the Christianizer of Rus' had demanded as part of the price for accepting Christianity from Byzantium.

Svyatoslav's ailments finally sapped his energy and impeded his speech. On gaining consciousness, he asked his wife, whom the *Lyubetskiy sinodik* calls Maria,[381] on what day the Feast of the Holy Maccabees fell. The chronicler interjects that the feast, which fell on August 1, was the day on which his father had died. Maria told him Monday, and he replied that he would not live to see it. Next, he told her that he wished to be tonsured as a monk. At that time he adopted a monastic name which the sources do not give us. Since he was buried in the Monastery of St. Cyril, its *igumen* probably performed the ritual.

Svyatoslav's last official act was to summon Ryurik. This news confirms that he had pledged to designate Ryurik as his successor. Since Yaroslav of Chernigov did not challenge the succession, his acquiescence confirms that he and the Ol'govichi supported his brother's designation of Ryurik. The peaceful transition of power was therefore auspicious for the future relations between the Ol'govichi and the Rostislavichi.

Svyatoslav died during the last week of July; the chronicler does not record the date. Nevertheless, since he was alive on Monday, July 25, he died on or after that date, but before August 1, the Feast of the Maccabees.[382] In addition to his wife, his brother Yaroslav may have come to the funeral. Ryurik was undoubtedly present. According to one source, he was laid to rest in the Church of St. Cyril that his father had built.[383] Consequently,

---

[380] Gleb married Ryurik's daughter in 1183 (see above, p. 152).   [381] Zotov, p. 267.

[382] According to Berezhkov, Svyatoslav died on July 25 (p. 207). Others adopt the date July 27 given by Tatishchev (Tat. 4, p. 317; Tat. 3, p. 156; Rapov, p. 111; Makhnovets', p. 354).

[383] See s.a. 1195: Lav., col. 412 and elsewhere. The late Gustinskiy Chronicle alone says that Svyatoslav was buried in the Church of St. Cyril that his mother had built (p. 324). As has been suggested elsewhere, Maria either completed building the Church of St. Cyril which her husband had founded, or, what is most likely, she built one of the adjacent chapels in which she was later buried (see *Dynasty*, p. 390).

the *igumen* of the Monastery of St. Cyril and Metropolitan Nikifor most likely officiated at the liturgy.

The location of Svyatoslav's interment was unique. He chose to be buried near his mother Maria in his father's monastery at Dorogozhichi. As has been noted elsewhere, Vsevolod had prepared the Church of St. Cyril as a repository for his family by providing it with burial niches.[384] Svyatoslav's preference for Kiev over Chernigov is understandable in that, as prince of Kiev, it was his prerogative to be interred in the capital of Rus'. His interment, however, was not in keeping with those of his ancestors. His great-grandfather, Svyatoslav, had spurned burial in Kiev and had chosen the Holy Saviour Cathedral in Chernigov. His father, Vsevolod, had preferred Vyshgorod to Kiev. And, the Ol'govichi had transferred to Chernigov the body of Svyatoslav's murdered uncle Igor', which had been interred in the family's Monastery of St. Simeon in Kiev.

Perhaps, however, it was not a question of the princes of Chernigov not choosing Kiev for their resting place, but of the Kievans refusing to give them permission to be buried in their town. Svyatoslav (d. 1076) and Vsevolod (d. 1146) had usurped Kiev and forcibly imposed their wills on the townsmen. Igor' had been designated prince of Kiev against the wishes of many citizens who eventually murdered him. Svyatoslav was the only Ol'govich whom the Kievans themselves chose as their prince. The consideration that his mother had belonged to their favorite dynasty, the House of Monomakh, would have helped to sway their opinion in his favor. Consequently, it was because they liked him that they probably permitted him to be interred in their town.

These observations appear to be corroborated by Svyatoslav's chronicler, perhaps a monk at the Monastery of St. Cyril.[385] He reports that Svyatoslav was a wise ruler who observed God's precepts, cherished bodily purity, loved the monks and the priests, and gave alms to the poor.[386] Chroniclers were often critical of princes.[387] Consequently, the commonplace praises of Svyatoslav should not be discarded as fatuous. The consideration that he received little bad press as prince of Kiev is also a useful monitor of his popularity. Furthermore, the evidence that Svyatoslav worked successfully with Ryurik for some thirteen years, that he faithfully defended the Kievan land, that he patronized culture and chronicle writing,[388] and that

---

[384] *Dynasty*, p. 392.　　[385] See Shchapov, *Gosudarstvo i tserkov'*, p. 137.
[386] Concerning the account of Svyatoslav's death, see Ipat., cols. 679–81; compare Gust., p. 324 and s.a. 1195: Lav., col. 412. Concerning the dates, see Berezhkov, pp. 206–7.
[387] See, for example, a chronicler's evaluation of the life of Svyatoslav's father (*Dynasty*, pp. 411–12).
[388] There is evidence in the chronicles that Svyatoslav kept a chronicle as prince of Kiev, but that he evidently did not keep one as prince of Chernigov (Priselkov, *Istoriya russkogo letopisaniya*, pp. 48, 50–1).

he sponsored building projects in Kiev in addition to Chernigov, were all
actions that helped to endear him to the Kievans. Indeed, their willingness
to accept him as prince in preference to Ryurik confirms that he was the
more popular of the two.

According to the Hypatian chronicler, the Kievans welcomed Ryurik
with the customary pageantry. He venerated the icons of the Holy Saviour
and the Mother of God in St. Sofia and then "sat on the throne of his
grandfather and his father."[389] The implication is that he was acclaimed
by the townsmen and enthroned by the metropolitan. The Laurentian
chronicler, however, claims that Vsevolod of Suzdalia sent his men to enthrone Ryurik.[390] The southern chronicler undoubtedly made no reference
to Vsevolod's delegation because the Kievans believed the Suzdalians had
no business telling them whom to appoint as prince. Vsevolod's chronicler, however, wished to record the authority that his prince, the patriarch
of the Monomashichi, allegedly wielded over the dynasty. Nevertheless, it
would have been impossible for Vsevolod's men to reach Kiev as quickly
as Ryurik arrived from Belgorod. The northerners therefore came after
Ryurik's installation and merely registered Vsevolod's approval. Whatever
the chronology, the chronicler's claim alerts us to Vsevolod's intention to
play an active role in Ryurik's rule.

An incident, which occurred before Svyatoslav's death, supports the observation that Vsevolod proposed to monitor southern affairs closely. At the
beginning of 1194, he sent his *tivun* Georgy to fortify the patrimonial citadel
at Gorodets on the river Oster.[391] Vsevolod's father, Yury Dolgorukiy, had
abandoned it in 1152, after Izyaslav Mstislavich had dug up its walls.[392] By
refounding his family's southern outpost, Vsevolod demonstrated his interest in the impending political transfer of power in Rus', namely that Ryurik
would succeed Svyatoslav. Vsevolod could use Gorodets as an observation
post to watch Ryurik's activities.

Svyatoslav's death changed the order of seniority among the Ol'govichi.
His only brother, Yaroslav of Chernigov, became the new senior prince of
the senior branch and, concomitantly, senior prince of the dynasty. His
first cousin, Igor', remained the senior prince of the cadet branch but now
also became the second in seniority in the entire dynasty. The genealogical
reshuffle made Svyatoslav's sons – Vladimir, Oleg, Vsevolod, Gleb, and
Mstislav – answerable to their uncle Yaroslav and then to Igor'. Even though
the latter belonged to the cadet branch, he was ahead of Svyatoslav's sons
in precedence because he belonged to the older generation.

[389] Ipat., col. 681.   [390] See s.a. 1195: Lav., col. 412.
[391] See s.a. 1195: Lav., col. 412. Concerning the date, see Berezhkov, p. 85.
[392] See above, p. 70.

Svyatoslav's death also affected the territorial holdings of the Ol'govichi. Most important, they lost Kiev. Ryurik also removed Svyatoslav's son Gleb, his son-in-law, from Kanev. Although the Ol'govichi were all relegated to the Chernigov side of the Dnepr, as we shall see they retained control of their Dregovichi districts north of the Pripyat'. In the Chernigov lands, Yaroslav would have appropriated all the domains that Svyatoslav had controlled in his capacity as senior prince. At the same time Svyatoslav's personal patrimony of Karachev also fell vacant. Since he, as the eldest son, had received it from his father Vsevolod, and since Vsevolod, as the eldest son, had received it from his father Oleg, Svyatoslav probably bequeathed it to his eldest son Vladimir.

After Svyatoslav resolved his territorial squabbles with Oleg Svyatoslavich in 1174, he had successfully unified the dynasty. Under his leadership the Ol'govichi had adopted his policies towards other dynasties and maintained a relatively cohesive strategy towards the Polovtsy. One of Yaroslav's most important challenges would be to preserve that dynastic harmony. Fortunately for the Ol'govichi, he and Igor' had worked in concord in the past and there was reason to believe they would do so in the future.

It should also be noted that, while Svyatoslav ruled Kiev, the Ol'govichi enjoyed a position of nominal if not real supremacy over the Rostislavichi. After Ryurik occupied the town they became his subordinates and had to pledge allegiance to him as their new commander-in-chief. Moreover, the duumvirs had established an equilibrium in their all-Rus' policies because they had addressed the interests of the Ol'govichi and the Rostislavichi. Without Svyatoslav to counter-balance Ryurik, the latter would inevitably favor the interests of the Rostislavichi. What is more, he enjoyed greater power than Svyatoslav had held because he ruled Kiev and the Kievan land. Since the Ol'govichi had not challenged Ryurik's succession, however, he had good reason to be conciliatory. His personal tie with his son-in-law Gleb would also stimulate him in that direction. In the light of these considerations, the future looked promising for the Ol'govichi.

VSEVOLOD CHALLENGES RYURIK'S ALLOCATION OF TOWNS

While Ryurik was ensconcing himself in Kiev and demanding the usual oaths of allegiance from the other princes of Rus', Yaroslav asserted his authority over the Ol'govichi in the same manner. The calm lasted until the following summer. At that time, trouble reared its head for the Ol'govichi not through any action on their part, but because the Monomashichi quarreled among themselves.

On May 17, 1195, the chronicler reports, David of Smolensk came to Kiev after Ryurik invited him to help allocate domains in the Kievan land to the princes in Monomakh's dynasty. Thus we see that the Rostislavichi, like the Ol'govichi, held that genealogical seniority dictated political relationships. Accordingly, Ryurik and his son Rostislav held feasts in David's honor out of deference to his seniority among the Rostislavichi. But Ryurik demonstrated his subordination in an even more important way. Although, as prince of Kiev, he controlled all the Kievan domains, he refused to allocate them without his elder brother's approval. David had no jurisdiction over the Kievan towns, but he had direct authority over Ryurik. The arrangement reflected Andrey Bogolyubskiy's appointment of his younger brothers to the capital of Rus'.

In the light of the Suzdalian chronicler's earlier report that it was Vsevolod's men who enthroned Ryurik in Kiev, it is noteworthy that Ryurik did not consult Vsevolod in making his allocations. He considered the job to be a prerogative of the Rostislavichi rather than a dynastic affair requiring Vsevolod's blessing. He therefore gave Vyshgorod to David and appointed his son Rostislav to Belgorod. All the other recipients were Monomashichi; the Ol'govichi, including Ryurik's son-in-law Gleb, were excluded.[393]

After Vsevolod learnt of the allocations, the chronicler continues, he reminded Ryurik that the Rostislavichi had acknowledged him to be the senior prince in Monomakh's dynasty.[394] Despite this, Ryurik had snubbed him by not giving him domains. Vsevolod therefore declared that those to whom Ryurik had allotted lands could help him defend Rus'. He was vexed because Ryurik had given the best towns – Torchesk, Trepol', Korsun', Boguslavl', and Kanev – to his son-in-law Roman, and Vsevolod wanted these for himself. He therefore threatened to wage war. When Roman learnt of Vsevolod's indignation, he agreed to relinquish the towns in exchange for comparable domains or a suitable payment in *kuny*. Ryurik therefore gave Vsevolod the five towns and they were reconciled. Vsevolod, in turn, handed over Torchesk to his son-in-law Rostislav and sent his men to administer the other four towns.

Vsevolod's stated pretext for challenging Ryurik was his wounded pride, but he had another reason for making his demand. By acquiring the five

---

[393] Ipat., cols. 681–2. Concerning the date, see Berezhkov, p. 207.
[394] The chronicler does not tell us on what occasion all the Monomashichi, above all, the Rostislavichi and Roman, acknowledged Vsevolod as their senior prince. This, however, may have occurred in 1189, when Vsevolod demanded that all the princes of Rus' pledge not to evict his nephew Vladimir Yaroslavich from Galich (see above, pp. 193–4). This is supported by the news that when Svyatoslav and Ryurik quarreled in the following year, Ryurik turned to Vsevolod for his assistance (see above, p. 197).

towns, he strengthened his grip on the prince of Kiev. Indeed, he turned the tables on Ryurik. Just as the latter had curtailed Svyatoslav's rule in Kiev by controlling the surrounding Kievan land, Vsevolod could now curb Ryurik's authority through his control of the five outposts. As a result, Ryurik's power in Kiev was significantly diminished. Whereas Svyatoslav had ruled jointly with Ryurik, he had been the senior partner. Ryurik, however, had to rule under the shadow of two overlords: David, the senior prince of the Rostislavichi, and Vsevolod, the senior prince of all the Monomashichi.

On learning that his brother-in-law Rostislav had received Torchesk, Roman became furious. He accused Ryurik of contriving to give the domain to Rostislav from the very start. Ryurik, however, reminded Roman that he had given Torchesk to Roman in preference to everyone else, and that it was because of his favoritism of Roman that Vsevolod had challenged him. Ryurik also reminded him that he had willingly relinquished the five towns to Vsevolod. After that, the latter could do with them as he wished. He warned Roman that they could not afford to alienate Vsevolod because all the princes in Monomakh's dynasty recognized him as their senior prince.

THE MONOMASHICHI MAKE AN UNREASONABLE DEMAND ON YAROSLAV

Roman refused to be mollified and conspired against his father-in-law. He turned to Yaroslav of Chernigov and the Ol'govichi, who agreed to join him. Thus, about a year after Svyatoslav's death, his brother declared his intent to make a bid for Kiev. When Ryurik learnt how his son-in-law had persuaded Yaroslav to seize Kiev, he informed Vsevolod that Roman and the Ol'govichi were planning to wage war on all the Monomashichi. He declared that, as senior prince, Vsevolod should organize the defense of Rus' and of the dynasty. Ryurik also denounced Roman. Fearing retribution, the latter rode to the Poles where he was wounded in battle. He therefore asked Ryurik for clemency. Metropolitan Nikifor reconciled the two, and Ryurik gave him the town of Polonyy, southwest of Kamenets, and a district on the river Ros'.[395]

Thus we see that Roman turned an in-house squabble of the Monomashichi into an inter-dynastic conflict by implicating the Ol'govichi. They were the only dynasty other than the Monomashichi who had a claim to Kiev. The most surprising news was Yaroslav's admission that he

---

[395] Concerning the controversy over Ryurik's allocation of domains, see Ipat., cols. 683–8; compare s.a. 1196: Mosk., pp. 96–7. For the location of Polonyy, see Makhnovets', p. 565.

wished to rule Kiev. Moreover, the backing that the Ol'govichi gave him reveals that they were opposed to Ryurik's rule. Indeed, their unanimous response to Roman's proposal suggests that they had concurred unwillingly with Svyatoslav's designation of Ryurik as his successor. Their action reinforces our contention that, at their congress in 1190, one of the topics that the Ol'govichi probably debated was Ryurik's succession to Kiev.[396]

Roman had good reason for believing that Yaroslav would be amenable to his offer. He had demonstrated hostility towards Ryurik by refusing to pledge allegiance to him. At least, the chronicler does not report that Yaroslav broke his pledge to Ryurik by kissing the Holy Cross to Roman, which he probably would have reported had that been the case. Significantly, Yaroslav's alliance was a dismal failure. After he declared his hostile intent against Ryurik, Roman deserted him. As a result, Yaroslav found himself on a war footing against an allegedly united House of Monomakh.

Yaroslav's failed bid for Kiev alerted Ryurik to the threat that the Ol'govichi posed to his rule. In the autumn, therefore, after he conferred with Vsevolod and David, the three commanded Yaroslav and the Ol'govichi to promise not to seize their patrimonies of Kiev and Smolensk from them, their children, or any other member of the House of Monomakh. Kiev was not necessary for the Ol'govichi. Their demand, they declared, was in keeping with the allocations that Yaroslav the Wise had made when he gave Chernigov to their forefather Svyatoslav (d. 1076). Significantly, in insisting that the Ol'govichi confine themselves to the east bank of the Dnepr, the Monomashichi cited Yaroslav as their authority. Their argument, therefore, was groundless. Yaroslav had given Monomakh's father Vsevolod the patrimony of Pereyaslavl' which, like Chernigov, was on the left bank of the Dnepr. Consequently, the Ol'govichi could use the argument of the Monomashichi against them by pointing out that they also had no need of Kiev.

Their demand that the Ol'govichi renounce their right to rule Kiev forever was even more contentious. With it they attempted to realize their long-standing dream of making the capital of Rus' their dynasty's hereditary possession. As has been suggested elsewhere, in 1097 at the Congress of Lyubech, Svyatopolk of Kiev and Monomakh had demoted the princes of Chernigov to a rung below Monomakh on the ladder of succession to Kiev so that he would have the prior claim.[397] Before his death, he persuaded the Kievans to treat the town as the patrimony of his eldest son

[396] See above, p. 199.   [397] *Dynasty*, pp. 216–18.

Mstislav.[398] Some seventy years later, Monomakh's heirs tried once again to deny the Ol'govichi their right of succession. Significantly, even according to Monomakh's plan, the Rostislavichi had no immediate claim to Kiev. Vsevolod had the prior right.

Yaroslav agreed to honor the first demand: the Ol'govichi would not attempt taking Kiev from Ryurik or Vsevolod. In this, they merely acknowledged the status quo. Ryurik already controlled Kiev and the forces of the Monomashichi were superior to theirs. They refused, however, to abjure the claims of future generations of Ol'govichi. Instead, after the deaths of Ryurik and Vsevolod, the question of Kiev would revert to the hands of God. That is, the two dynasties would have to fight for the town. They based their argument on the consideration that, as the descendants of Yaroslav the Wise, they and the Monomashichi both had the right to rule the capital of Rus'.[399]

In fighting for Kiev, the two dynasties showed that it remained the most coveted political, ecclesiastical, commercial, and cultural center in Rus'. Moreover, as long as the Ol'govichi successfully competed for it, they maintained a political equilibrium between the two dynasties. Should they abandon their claim, they would probably suffer the same fate that had befallen the descendants of Izyaslav Yaroslavich of Turov (d. 1078) or the princes of Ryazan'. They would be relegated to a political backwater.

Ryurik undoubtedly initiated the demand of the Monomashichi because he had the most to lose if Yaroslav occupied Kiev. He would be evicted from the town; he would forfeit political seniority in Rus'; and he would probably lose Vruchiy. Moreover, having had his knuckles wrapped by Vsevolod over his allocation of domains to Roman, he acknowledged Vsevolod's seniority by asking him to spearhead the challenge to Yaroslav. Vsevolod also grasped at the opportunity to assert his authority by promising to lead an attack against the Ol'govichi in the winter.

Yaroslav sought to dissuade Vsevolod from attacking Chernigov and sent *Igumen* Dionisy to ask for peace.[400] Significantly, Yaroslav did not send Bishop Porfiry if he was still alive. In 1186, when he had visited Vsevolod to negotiate peace on behalf of the princes of Ryazan', he had betrayed Vsevolod.[401] In the light of his treachery, Porfiry's presence in the

---

[398] *Dynasty*, pp. 305–8, 324–32.

[399] According to a late source, Yaroslav argued that from the days of their forefathers the Ol'govichi and the Monomashichi both had the right to rule Kiev according to the ladder system of succession depending on to whom God chose to give it (Nikon. 10, pp. 26–7).

[400] *Igumen* Dionisy was probably the head of the most prestigious monastic institution in Chernigov, the Eletskiy Monastery. Concerning the Eletskiy Monastery, see *Dynasty*, pp. 111–13.

[401] See above, p. 185.

delegation of 1196 would have jeopardized the mission. The *igumen*, however, persuaded Vsevolod to cancel his attack by informing him that the Ol'govichi submitted to all his demands. There was perhaps another reason why Vsevolod would have been amenable to Yaroslav's plea. By sending the *igumen* to him Yaroslav, like all the Monomashichi, acknowledged him to be the senior prince in the House of Monomakh. Believing the Ol'govichi, we are told, Vsevolod canceled the campaign.

His threat to march against the Ol'govichi was not just a sabre-rattling tactic. The Novgorod chronicler tells us that when Vsevolod canceled the campaign, the Novgorodian troops had already set out.[402] Vsevolod demonstrated his determination to attack in other ways. It was the first time he assembled a force consisting of all the Monomashichi; it was the first attack he organized against the Rus' lands; and it was the first campaign he planned to lead against the Ol'govichi in person. In some ways, his expedition was reminiscent of Andrey Bogolyubskiy's campaign of 1169, when his coalition attacked Kiev. In both instances, the prince of Suzdalia wished to secure control of Kiev for his candidate. There was, however, one important difference. On this occasion, the object of attack was to be Chernigov. Unlike his elder brother Andrey, Vsevolod intended to win Kiev as a prize and not to pillage it.

While *Igumen* Dionisy was negotiating peace with Vsevolod, Yaroslav arranged a separate pact. He asked Ryurik not to attack the Chernigov lands before they decided with Vsevolod and David either to conclude peace or go to war. After conceding to Yaroslav's request, Ryurik disbanded his troops and let the Polovtsy return to their camps. He himself went to Vruchiy.[403] His action suggests that he and Yaroslav did not wish to wage war in the winter because they had to make the rounds of their domains.

THE OL'GOVICHI ATTACK VITEBSK

On Tuesday, March 12, 1196, an earthquake struck the Kievan land. It shook churches in Kiev to their very foundations.[404] The tremors terrified the people and some fell helplessly to the ground. The abbots proclaimed that God was manifesting his might as a warning to Christians to abandon their sinful ways. Others declared that the earthquake was an omen presaging the

---

[402] NPL, pp. 42, 234–5.
[403] Concerning the demand of the Monomashichi, see Ipat., cols. 688–90; s.a. 1196: Mosk., p. 97. Concerning the dating of these events, see Berezhkov, p. 207.
[404] It has been suggested that one of the stone churches damaged in the earthquake was that of St. Vasily, which Svyatoslav had built (see above, p. 155).

fall of many, much bloodshed, and great strife. The chronicler concludes: "All these things came to pass."[405]

At the beginning of winter when the two formed their truce, it appears, Ryurik had promised to give Vitebsk to Yaroslav. As we have seen, before forming his pact with Ryurik, Yaroslav had sent *Igumen* Dionisy to Vsevolod promising not to challenge the Rostislavichi for control of Kiev. He would have made the same pledge to Ryurik when they concluded their separate pact. In exchange for renouncing his claim to Kiev during Ryurik's lifetime, Yaroslav undoubtedly demanded that Ryurik compensate him. Ryurik evidently promised to give him Vitebsk, a domain that the Rostislavichi controlled, but one that was neither part of their patrimonial domain nor part of the Kievan land.

Even so, David and not Ryurik had the authority to allocate Vitebsk. As the senior prince, he had jurisdiction over domains controlled by the dynasty of Smolensk. Consequently, when Ryurik sent his messengers to David informing him that he had promised Vitebsk to Yaroslav, he would have asked David to confirm the allocation. This would explain why Yaroslav challenged David rather than Ryurik after the prince of Vitebsk refused to hand over the town to Yaroslav. It appeared to the latter that David had refused to approve Ryurik's allocation.

In the winter, therefore, during the Great Fast which began on March 4, Yaroslav and his brothers broke the oath that they had made to Ryurik promising not to attack before concluding their negotiations. Not waiting for the envoys to return from Vsevolod and David, he sent troops to attack David's son-in-law in Vitebsk.[406] The Gustinskiy chronicler retorts that the Ol'govichi "were always destroying the land of Rus' ... [and] lacking in truth."[407] His accusation reflects the stigma that the Ol'govichi inherited from their grandfather Oleg the "Son of Bitter Glory" (*Goreslavich*), whom earlier chroniclers had condemned for bringing the pagans to kill the Christians of Rus'.[408] To be fair to Yaroslav, however, he may have launched the attack inadvertently. If we can take at face value Ryurik's later declaration that his messenger had not yet reached David before Yaroslav waged war,

[405] See s.a. 1195: Ipat., col. 690. Concerning the date, see Berezhkov, p. 207.
[406] At this point, the Hypatian account is unclear against whom Yaroslav sent his nephews. The text could be interpreted to read "against his [Yaroslav's] son-in-law David" or "against David's son-in-law" (Ipat., col. 691). The Laurentian chronicler, who had a better understanding than his southern counterpart of the marital ties between the northern princes, says that David sent his nephew Mstislav "to help his [David's] son-in-law at Vitebsk" (s.a. 1197: Lav., col. 413). Later in the account the Hypatian chronicler confirms this report when he states that Yaroslav accused David of guilt because he was trying to help his son-in-law in Vitebsk (Ipat., col. 693).
[407] Gust., p. 325.   [408] *Dynasty*, pp. 290–1.

it would appear that Yaroslav should be condemned for impatience rather than for perfidy.

Yaroslav sent two of his nephews to accomplish the task. He appointed Oleg, the second in seniority among Svyatoslav's sons, as commander-in-chief. Vladimir was older, but he is never again mentioned as participating in campaigns. It would appear, therefore, that he had withdrawn from the political arena, perhaps owing to poor health. Consequently, Oleg must have been accompanied by one of his younger brothers, namely Vsevolod, Gleb, or Mstislav.

Before reaching Vitebsk, the Ol'govichi pillaged the lands of Smolensk. David retaliated by sending his nephew Mstislav Romanovich, the Smolensk militia, and other troops to confront the invaders. The two sides clashed on the very Tuesday that the earthquake struck the Kievan land. Mstislav defeated Oleg's troops and his son David fell in the fray. His demise was noteworthy because he was Igor''s son-in-law and the eldest prince in the youngest generation of the senior branch. Meanwhile, the Smolensk militia marched against the princes of Polotsk who had come to Oleg's assistance. But the townsmen fled without engaging in battle. On seeing that Oleg and his troops had been routed, the Polotsk forces hurried to his aid and defeated Mstislav's men. When the latter, who had left the battlefield to pursue Oleg, returned, the Polotsk princes took him captive. Later, Boris of Drutsk handed over Mstislav into Oleg's custody.

The princes of Polotsk are rarely reported as participating in the rivalries of the southern princes, but when they are mentioned they are invariably allies of the Ol'govichi. This is not surprising because, as we have seen, Svyatoslav Vsevolodovich had married a princess of Polotsk. She was the mother of Oleg and his unidentified brother who were leading the campaign. Since the chronicler reports that a number of Polotsk princes helped the Ol'govichi, it may be that they had a vested interest in the conflict. Vitebsk had once belonged to them.[409] Indeed, its present prince, David's son-in-law Vasil'ko Bryacheslavich, belonged to the dynasty of Polotsk.[410] As the ruler of Vitebsk, however, he had sworn allegiance to David. Consequently, the two Svyatoslavichi probably did not intended to keep Vitebsk for the Ol'govichi. After seizing it, they undoubtedly proposed to return it to their Polotsk relatives.

---

[409] In 1021, Yaroslav the Wise had given Vitebsk to his nephew Bryacheslav Izyaslavich of Polotsk (Baum., I, 20; N5, p. 113; Nasonov, p. 86). In 1165, however, Vitebsk belonged to the princes of Smolensk since David occupied the town in that year (Ipat., col. 525; L. V. Alekseev, "Polotskaya zemlya," *Drevnerusskie knyazhestva X–XIII vv.*, L. G. Beskrovny [ed.] [Moscow, 1975], pp. 232–3).

[410] Baum., VIII, 41; IX, 15.

Meanwhile, Oleg sent word to Yaroslav in Chernigov that he had defeated David's forces and captured Mstislav. Moreover, vanquished Smolensk militiamen had told him that the people of Smolensk were unhappy with David. He therefore advised Yaroslav to assemble the brothers and come to win honor for the dynasty. The Ol'govichi rejoiced at Oleg's missive. They immediately set out for Smolensk, but Ryurik sent messengers from Vruchiy to intercept Yaroslav with the following challenge:

If you have set out to kill my brother and revel at the prospect, you have broken your agreement and your pledge on the Holy Cross. Here are the very documents on which you made your oath. If you march against Smolensk, I shall attack Chernigov and God and the Holy Cross will determine our fates.

After hearing Ryurik's threat, Yaroslav returned to Chernigov. He sent messengers to Ryurik exculpating himself from guilt and placing the blame on David because the latter was helping his son-in-law keep Vitebsk. "This is the way in which Yaroslav and Ryurik quarreled, and they were not reconciled."[411]

Thus we see that, at first, Yaroslav initiated rivalry with David for the benefit of the princes of Polotsk even though it would further strain his fragile relationship with the Rostislavichi. After Oleg informed him that the citizens of Smolensk would act as a fifth column against David, however, Yaroslav decided to challenge the Rostislavichi themselves. He therewith turned a territorial squabble into an inter-dynastic war. By attacking David, he would have broken the oath the Ol'govichi had pledged to Vsevolod not to challenge David and Ryurik for control of Smolensk and Kiev. The seriousness of Yaroslav's intent is confirmed by his rare personal presence on a campaign, by the participation of both branches, and by Ryurik's claim that Yaroslav wished to kill David.

After Ryurik defused the crisis with the Ol'govichi, he sought to spur on Vsevolod into attacking Chernigov. Ryurik reminded him that he had agreed to march against that town at Christmas, but had not because he had trusted the Ol'govichi to keep their promise. Taking advantage of Vsevolod's inaction, Yaroslav had attacked Smolensk and sullied the dynasty's honor by taking Mstislav captive. Ryurik entreated Vsevolod to avenge the insult to their dynasty by freeing Mstislav. One of the most unforgivable offenses a dynasty could commit against another was to take one of its members captive. As we have seen, the Ol'govichi themselves had attempted to free

[411] Concerning the campaign against Vitebsk, see Ipat., cols. 690–4; compare Makhnovets', pp. 358–60. Concerning the date, see Berezhkov p. 207.

captured relatives in the past. In 1180, Svyatoslav had endeavored unsuc-cessfully to free his son Gleb from Vsevolod in Suzdalia. In 1147 Svyatoslav Ol'govich's attempts to free his brother Igor' from the clutches of Izyaslav Mstislavich had ended in disaster.

Vsevolod responded by instructing Ryurik to initiate attacks and promised to bring reinforcements. Ryurik therefore led raids against the Chernigov lands, but waited in vain all summer for Vsevolod. Meanwhile, Yaroslav sent envoys to Ryurik demanding to know why he was pillaging the domains of the Ol'govichi. He pointed out that he had no argument with Ryurik and no intention of seizing Kiev. He also offered to release Mstislav and underscored his good will by waiving the ransom usually demanded for a captive's release. The Ol'govichi bore no grudge against Mstislav for his part in the battle since he had been merely following his commander-in-chief's orders. Moreover, he was also related to them: his mother was Igor''s sister. Yaroslav's willingness to release Mstislav therefore suggests that, de-spite Ryurik's cynicism, he was truly seeking a *rapprochement*. In return, he asked Ryurik to reconcile him with David and Vsevolod.

Nothing came of Yaroslav's offer because the two princes mistrusted each other. In attacking Vitebsk, Yaroslav had broken his promise to Vsevolod and violated his truce with Ryurik. Because of Yaroslav's al-leged perfidy, Ryurik refused to believe his promises to release Mstislav and to drop his claim to Kiev. If Yaroslav truly wished to restore ami-cable relations, Ryurik demanded that Yaroslav allow his messengers to travel through the Chernigov lands to Vsevolod and David. But Yaroslav blocked the roads because he, in turn, mistrusted Ryurik. His misgivings imply that, during their rivalry, Ryurik, in Yaroslav's eyes, had also failed in his integrity. As a result, they waged war throughout the summer and into the autumn.[412]

THE DEATH OF VSEVOLOD "FIERCE AUROCHS"

During the hostilities, the Ol'govichi lost one of their foremost fighters. In May, Igor''s brother Vsevolod Svyatoslavich died. He was one of the unfortunates of whom the elders spoke when they declared that the earth-quake on March 12 presaged the fall of many. We are not told the cause of his death. Because of his reputation for military prowess, however, he may

---

[412] Ipat., cols. 694–6. Concerning the date, see Berezhkov, p. 207.

have died defending his domains against the Polovtsy whom Ryurik had unleashed onto the Chernigov lands.

The bishop of Chernigov, presumably Porfiry, officiated at the funeral in the Church of the Mother of God. As we have seen, two churches in Chernigov were dedicated to the Mother of God: the Assumption at the Eletskiy Monastery,[413] and the Annunciation that Svyatoslav had consecrated ten years earlier. Since the latter had provided his church with burial vaults, Vsevolod was probably one of the first princes to be interred in it. The prince who may have been buried there before him, at least the only one whose death the chronicles report following the erection of the church, was Oleg's son David, who was killed on the very day of the earthquake. The news that Vsevolod was not buried in Trubetsk, his patrimony, suggests that there was no suitable church in that town.

Vsevolod's wife, perhaps named Olga, was the daughter of Gleb, prince of Pereyaslavl', and the granddaughter of Yury Dolgorukiy.[414] As has been suggested, Vsevolod was probably the first prince of Trubetsk.[415] Under the year 1232, as we shall see, the Novgorod chronicler speaks of a certain Svyatoslav of Trubetsk.[416] It is possible that the princeling was Vsevolod's son. After Vsevolod's death, however, his heirs became *izgoi* and were debarred from ruling Novgorod Severskiy because he had not ruled it. Moreover, his demise decreased the number of princes in the eldest generation of the dynasty to two: Yaroslav of Chernigov in the senior branch, and Igor' of Novgorod Severskiy in the cadet branch.

Vsevolod, it could be argued, had been a model prince. He had won renown at the battle of the Kayala, where Igor' observed him hewing down the Polovtsy with unequaled courage. Indeed, after his death the chronicler declared that Vsevolod surpassed all the Ol'govichi in daring, bearing, and stature. Unmatched in good works and valor, he was a friend to all.[417] The brief eulogy reflects the sobriquet "Fierce Aurochs" (*Yar ture*) with which the unknown author of the *Slovo o polku Igoreve* dubbed him.[418] Despite Vsevolod's military fame, his genealogical minority prohibited him from achieving the highest rank in the dynasty or, for that matter, even in the cadet branch. Significantly, he refused to use his military prowess for personal gain. Instead, he demonstrated a compliant respect for his elders' rights and faithfully adhered to the political bounds within which his birth had placed him in the lateral system of succession.

[413] *Dynasty*, pp. 261–4.   [414] Zotov, p. 271.   [415] See above, p. 166.
[416] NPL, p. 280; Zotov, pp. 277–8.   [417] Concerning Vsevolod's death, see Ipat., col. 696.
[418] Concerning Vsevolod's sobriquet, see "The Lay of Igor''s Campaign," p. 65.

YAROSLAV'S AGREEMENTS WITH VSEVOLOD, NOVGOROD,
AND RYAZAN'

Vsevolod's death did not affect the hostilities between the Ol'govichi and Rostislavichi. In the autumn, however, there was an important development. As we have seen, after Roman of Volyn' had drawn the Ol'govichi into conflict with Ryurik, he was forced to conclude a truce with Ryurik after being wounded in battle. But his heart was not in the reconciliation. In the autumn of 1196, presumably after his wounds had healed, he broke his pledge to his father-in-law and came to Yaroslav's aid.

He ordered his lieutenants to use Polonyy, which Ryurik had given him, as their base for raiding the domains belonging to Ryurik's brother David and son Rostislav.[419] Ryurik retaliated by sending his nephew Mstislav to Vladimir Yaroslavich of Galich instructing him to join Mstislav in attacking Roman's lands.[420] Ryurik himself could not campaign against his son-in-law, we are told, because he rode to join Vsevolod and David, who were pillaging the domains of the Ol'govichi. Accordingly, Vladimir and Mstislav razed Roman's district around Peremil', while Rostislav and his force attacked Roman's district near Kamenets.[421] Thus, by raiding the domains of the Rostislavichi, Roman forced Ryurik to divert some of his troops from the Chernigov lands.

In the meantime, Vsevolod, accompanied by the princes of Ryazan', Murom, and the Polovtsy, worked his way south towards Chernigov. On entering the Vyatichi lands, he would have devastated towns such as Koltesk, Lopasna, and Lobynsk. From there he probably went southwest towards Karachev to meet David, who undoubtedly came from Smolensk via the upper reaches of the Desna. Along the way, he would have pillaged towns such as Ormina, Vorobeyna, and Vshchizh. Since no Ol'govichi are reported defending these domains, they had probably joined Yaroslav.

Meanwhile, Yaroslav placed his nephews Oleg and Gleb in charge of defending Chernigov against Ryurik, but ordered his remaining two nephews, Vsevolod and Mstislav, to accompany him against Vsevolod and David.

---

[419] As we have seen, David's domain was Vyshgorod and Rostislav ruled Belgorod. Nevertheless, they probably had additional domains in the Kievan land. We know that Rostislav received Torchesk from his father-in-law Vsevolod after Roman returned the town to Ryurik. Furthermore, since, in 1195, Ryurik originally gave Roman five towns, we may assume that he also gave his son and his elder brother David more than just one town. Concerning the domains of other Rostislavichi in the Kievan land, see below, p. 277.

[420] Since the Ol'govichi were holding his nephew Mstislav Romanovich captive, the Mstislav in question was Mstislav Mstislavich "the Bold," who, in 1193, was prince of Trepol' (see Baum., IX, 24).

[421] Ipat., cols. 696–8.

Yaroslav put Oleg in command of the patrimonial capital because he was the eldest active prince in Svyatoslav's family and thus, in effect, the second in command in the senior branch.[422] In appointing Gleb to join Oleg, however, Yaroslav undoubtedly hoped that Ryurik would abandon his siege of Chernigov on discovering that his son-in-law was defending it.

The news that the Polovtsy came to assist the Ol'govichi is noteworthy. The chroniclers have reported no nomadic attacks on Rus' after Svyatoslav's death. Since it was customary for the tribes to renew their peace pacts with a new prince of Kiev, it is most likely that, despite the chronicler's silence, Ryurik concluded such agreements with the nomads. This is supported by the information that Yaroslav accused him of using the tribesmen, probably the Lukomortsy, to pillage the lands of the Ol'govichi. In like manner, nomads, probably from the Donets basin, joined Yaroslav's camp. Among them would have been the in-laws of Igor's son Vladimir, who had married Konchak's daughter.

Yaroslav sent messengers to Vsevolod, whom he called *svat*, proposing peace. The reference to their family tie was clearly meant to dispose Vsevolod more favorably to the offer by reminding him that Yaroslav was the father-in-law of his daughter. At the same time, Yaroslav condemned him for devastating the patrimony of the Ol'govichi and for seizing their grain. That is, he had deprived the Vyatichi of the harvest which the princes of the senior branch would normally have collected as tribute. Yaroslav also challenged Vsevolod. He declared his willingness to abide by Vsevolod's terms only if they were equitable. He rejected the demand that the Ol'govichi promise never again to seize Kiev. Yaroslav warned Vsevolod that the Ol'govichi were determined to fight for their right. His statements reveal that he genuinely wished to be reconciled, but they also show that he rejected the outrageous proposal of the Rostislavichi.

Vsevolod consulted David and the princes of Ryazan' how to be pacified with the Ol'govichi. But they urged him to attack. David pointed out that Vsevolod had promised Ryurik and David to join them at Chernigov, where they would conclude an agreement with the Ol'govichi according to terms that all three Monomashichi would accept. What is more, Vsevolod had promised Ryurik to attack the Ol'govichi before the spring, but Ryurik had waited in vain. Indeed, it was owing to Vsevolod's breach of promise that Ryurik had fought the Ol'govichi on his own all summer. And now Vsevolod advocated peace without consulting Ryurik who would reject a settlement. Despite David's objections, Vsevolod sent envoys to negotiate

---

[422] Concerning Oleg's elder brother Vladimir, see above, p. 219.

peace with Yaroslav. Since he had neither incurred losses nor was threatened in any way by the Ol'govichi, he sought a reconciliation. Perhaps he was also influenced by the consideration that the Ol'govichi had helped him to win the throne of Vladimir.

Significantly, he modified the terms of the Rostislavichi to reflect his own priorities. First, he demanded that Yaroslav release his *svat* Mstislav.[423] The chronicler's reference to the family tie suggests that Vsevolod's personal relationship with Mstislav was more important to him than, as Ryurik argued, the restoration of family honor.[424] Second, Vsevolod demanded that the Ol'govichi expel his nephew Yaropolk Rostislavich from Chernigov.[425] As we have seen, after Andrey Bogolyubskiy died in 1174, Yaropolk had occupied Vladimir for a short period of time.[426] He therefore remained a claimant to the town and, with the backing of the Ol'govichi, posed a threat to Vsevolod's rule. To prevent this danger from materializing, Vsevolod required that the Ol'govichi cease proffering safe haven to his eldest nephew. This demand, as Ryurik later pointed out, benefited only Vsevolod.

Third, Vsevolod demanded that Yaroslav break his alliance with Roman. Vsevolod himself had no argument with Roman even though it was because the latter had originally received the five towns from Ryurik that Vsevolod had complained. Rather, with this stipulation Vsevolod seemingly appeased Ryurik. But even in this instance, personal interests guided Vsevolod more than a desire to help the Rostislavichi. He made only a perfunctory effort at forcing Yaroslav to terminate his friendship with Roman. Fortunately for Yaroslav, the demand that would have debilitated him most was of least interest to Vsevolod. To be sure, the latter saw advantages to keeping the alliance between Yaroslav and Roman intact. It would keep their threat against Ryurik alive. In this way, the latter would remain dependent on Vsevolod's backing and, accordingly, find it necessary to acknowledge Vsevolod's supremacy in the House of Monomakh.

Yaroslav refused to break his pact with Roman, but he agreed to release Mstislav and to evict Yaropolk. Content with Yaroslav's reply, Vsevolod sent his men to seal the agreement. The proceedings began on a personal note. His envoys inquired about Vsevolod's domain and his children. The chronicler does not identify the domain, but it was probably Gorodets Osterskiy. As for his children, we have seen that in 1186 Vsevolod's daughter Vseslava

---

[423] One of Mstislav's daughters married Vsevolod's eldest son Konstantin (Baum., IX, 28).
[424] According to Vsevolod's chronicler, the prince's main objective for marching south was to obtain the release of his *svat* Mstislav and to secure Kiev for Ryurik (Lav., col. 413).
[425] Yaropolk was the son of Vsevolod's eldest brother Rostislav (Baum., VI, 16; Rapov, pp. 165–6).
[426] See above, p. 131.

had married Yaroslav's son Rostislav.[427] Vsevolod was seemingly interested in obtaining news of his daughter and her family before imposing political terms on his *svat*. Indeed, his daughter's presence among the Ol'govichi may have been part of the reason why he had procrastinated over half a year before riding against them and, when he finally did, why he negotiated peace rather than waged war.

Vsevolod modified his demands from the ones that he and the Rostislavichi had made a year earlier. As before, he forbade Yaroslav to seize Kiev from Ryurik and to take Smolensk from David. Significantly, he dropped the clause demanding that the Ol'govichi renounce their claim to Kiev in the name of future Ol'govichi. Prohibiting Yaroslav from evicting Ryurik was understandable since Yaroslav had expressed a desire to usurp Kiev. The requirement that the Ol'govichi not seize Smolensk, however, is problematic. We have no evidence that they ever attempted to appropriate the town. We get only a hint that this may have been Yaroslav's intention when, following Oleg's victory over Vitebsk, he prepared to lead all the Ol'govichi against David. Since Ryurik accused him of planning to kill his brother, Yaroslav possibly intended to appropriate Smolensk at that time.[428]

Yaroslav and the Ol'govichi agreed to Vsevolod's terms. In accepting them, Yaroslav admitted that they were sensible. He also demonstrated that, despite the chronicler's accusations of perfidy, he wished to conclude a just settlement. Nevertheless, the agreement had weaknesses. Yaroslav might argue that he did not consider himself bound by an oath which he had taken under duress. Moreover, the Rostislavichi remained discontented. David had kissed the Holy Cross, it is true, but Vsevolod probably pressured him into accepting the agreement. Most seriously, however, Ryurik remained on a war footing with Yaroslav.

The latter also concluded pacts that had nothing to do with the dispute he had with the Monomashichi. First, he sealed an agreement with the princes of Ryazan'. Their unexplained grievance may have been the territorial dispute that had flared up during Svyatoslav's last visit to Karachev. At that time, as we have seen, he had asked Vsevolod to join the Ol'govichi against the princes of Ryazan'.[429] Vsevolod had refused, and the issue remained unresolved. In 1196, the princes of Ryazan' probably took advantage of Vsevolod's conflict with Yaroslav to press their demand on the new prince of Chernigov. Given Yaroslav's vulnerability in the face of Vsevolod's

[427] See above, p. 185.
[428] V. I Sergeevich held this view (*Veche i knyaz'. Russkoe gosudarstvennoe ustroystvo i upravlenie vo vremena knyazey Ryurikovichey* [M., 1867], p. 215).
[429] See above, pp. 205–6.

superior forces, he probably capitulated. Moreover, as we shall see, at this time Yaroslav may have granted the princes of Ryazan' permission to establish an independent bishopric.[430]

Second, the princes granted the Novgorodians the freedom to select their prince from whichever dynasty they chose.[431] It is noteworthy that Vsevolod, David, and Yaroslav, the senior princes of the dynasties that sent princes to Novgorod, jointly issued a decree regulating appointments to Novgorod. In effect, they acted as a dynastic summit. Ryurik's presence was not necessary because he was not a senior prince. It would seem that the decree was meant to curb the increasing control that the prince of Suzdalia was asserting over the town in making princely appointments. Surprisingly, in agreeing to give the citizens a free hand in choosing their prince, Vsevolod curtailed his own initiative in the town. He also conceded that Yaroslav and David shared with him the authority for passing the important ruling. His compliance suggests that his power over the town and the two senior princes was not as great as his chronicler purported it to be.

After concluding the agreement, Vsevolod returned to Vladimir on October 6. Meanwhile, he informed Ryurik that he had concluded peace. Ryurik was furious. He reminded Vsevolod that when he had demanded a district in Rus', Ryurik had given him the best towns even though he had to take them from his brothers and son-in-law. As a result, Roman had rebelled against him. Roman had also forced him to take up arms against the Ol'govichi because they had tried to usurp Kiev. Although Vsevolod had pledged to treat Ryurik's enemies as his own, he had done nothing to curb Roman. Moreover, at about that time, Roman began repudiating his wife, Ryurik's daughter, and threatening to confine her to a monastery.[432] Finally, Vsevolod had pledged to ride to Ryurik's assistance, but failed to come in the winter and in the summer. When he did arrive in the autumn, he excluded Ryurik from the negotiations and concluded a private pact permitting Roman to stay allied with Yaroslav. In short, Vsevolod had broken every promise that he had made. After venting his rage, Ryurik confiscated all the towns that he had given to Vsevolod in the Kievan land and returned them to his brothers.[433]

[430] See below, pp. 230–1.
[431] NPL, pp. 42–3, 235–6. Compare Fennell, who suggests that the Novgorodians received this privilege in 1136 (*Crisis*, p. 18).
[432] Lav., cols. 412–13.
[433] Concerning Vsevolod's campaign against Chernigov, see Ipat., cols. 698–702; see also s.a. 1197: Lav., col. 413. Concerning the date, see Berezhkov, pp. 85, 208.

Accordingly, his relations with the prince of Suzdalia had come full circle. At first, he had unintentionally antagonized Vsevolod by failing to allocate towns to him in the Kievan land; later he intentionally alienated Vsevolod by confiscating those very towns. His vindictiveness made him turn a blind eye to the consequences. That is, his estrangement from Vsevolod turned the coalition between Yaroslav and Roman into a serious threat to his authority.

One hundred years earlier, in 1096, the progenitors of the Ol'govichi and the Monomashichi, Oleg Svyatoslavich and Vladimir Monomakh, had engaged in an inter-dynastic rivalry. At that time, the princes of Rus' resolved the dispute at a council in Lyubech, where Oleg was allowed to keep his hereditary domain.[434] In 1196, Oleg and Monomakh's descendants engaged in a new rivalry. The Monomashichi attempted to deny the Ol'govichi their right to rule the capital of Rus'. Once again, the princes negotiated a settlement at a council of princes. On this occasion they confirmed the right of Oleg's descendants to rule Kiev. Whereas at Lyubech the princes of the so-called "inner circle" from the dynasties of Turov, Chernigov and Pereyaslavl' had been the main agents of the agreement, in 1196 the senior princes of Chernigov, Suzdalia, and Smolensk negotiated the settlement. Thus, at the end of the twelfth century a new "inner circle," as it were, determined the balance of power in Rus'.

THE OL'GOVICHI IN NOVGOROD

The princes of Chernigov never turned down an invitation to rule Novgorod even though, during the twelfth century, they were often invited as compromise candidates. Inevitably, the appointments were short.[435] In 1196, we are told, Vsevolod was determined to maintain a firm grip on the town and refused to grant its citizens their request to replace his appointee Yaroslav Vladimirovich with his son or some other prince. Failing to have their way, they used their recently confirmed right to invite a prince of their own choice. On November 26 they evicted Vsevolod's man and sent a delegation to Yaroslav in Chernigov, who promised to give them his younger son Yaropolk.[436] The Novgorodians were a sound monitor of the balance of power in the land. They invariably chose a prince from what they considered to be the most powerful family. Having failed to obtain an acceptable

---

[434] *Dynasty*, pp. 194–223.
[435] The last time they had controlled Novgorod was for some two years, from 1180 to 1182, when both Svyatoslav and his son Vladimir ruled for a time (see above, pp. 144, 152).
[436] NPL, pp. 43, 236; Ipat., col. 702. Concerning the date, see Berezhkov, p. 208.

appointee from their preferred prince in Suzdalia, they turned to Yaroslav; in their opinion, the Ol'govichi were the next most powerful dynasty.

It is reasonable to assume that, when they passed the decree giving the Novgorodians a free hand in selecting their prince, Vsevolod and David had agreed, tacitly at any rate, that should the Novgorodians select an Ol'govich, they would not object. Nevertheless, Yaroslav's failure to send his son all winter suggests that the Ol'govichi faced obstacles. According to a number of late chronicles, Yaroslav could not send his son because the Ol'govichi were embroiled in a conflict with Monomakh's dynasty.[437] Since Yaroslav had been reconciled with Vsevolod, the princes of Monomakh's dynasty who prevented Yaroslav from sending his son must have been the two Rostislavichi. Nevertheless, early in 1197 they were pacified to judge from the news that Yaroslav's younger son finally arrived in Novgorod at the end of March.

It is noteworthy that Yaroslav did not send his elder son Rostislav but Yaropolk, who is identified by name for the first time. One possible explanation for his choice is that he took Rostislav's personal association with Vsevolod into consideration. Since the latter was Rostislav's father-in-law, Yaroslav may not have wished to risk straining that relationship by sending Rostislav on such a potentially volatile posting.

After six months the Novgorodians expelled Yaropolk and recalled Yaroslav Vladimirovich.[438] Indeed, the Ol'govichi were not given a realistic chance of establishing prolonged rule in the town because most of the citizens supported Vsevolod. Their dispute, after all, had been over which of Vsevolod's lieutenants was the most desirable, one of his sons, Yaroslav Vladimirovich, or some other puppet. They turned to Yaroslav in Chernigov only as an expedient. The pro-Vsevolod faction hoped that by bringing an Ol'govich to Novgorod it would coerce Vsevolod into sending a Suzdalian candidate that the townsmen approved. Instead, Vsevolod got his way and reappointed Yaroslav Vladimirovich.[439] Just the same, Yaroslav's readiness to accommodate the Novgorodians alerted Vsevolod to the threat that the Ol'govichi posed to his authority in that town.

[437] Mosk., p. 98; Nikon. 10, p. 28.
[438] Although Yaropolk's sojourn in Novgorod was brief, a number of lead seals that were found there have been attributed to him (Yanin 1, p. 205; Yanin 3, pp. 47, 139).
[439] Concerning Yaroslav's appointment of Yaropolk, see NPL, pp. 43, 236. Concerning the date, see Berezhkov, p. 247. Tatishchev claims that Vsevolod gave the Novgorodians an ultimatum to expel Yaropolk within two months and to take back his appointee as prince (Tat. 4, p. 325; Tat. 3, pp. 164–5). This is a plausible explanation but no chronicle substantiates it. If true, Vsevolod, one of the three princes who granted the Novgorodians the right to choose whichever prince they wished, refused to let them exercise that right.

IMPORTANT POLITICAL AND ECCLESIASTICAL DEVELOPMENTS

While Yaropolk was in Novgorod, the relationship of the Ol'govichi to the Rostislavichi changed. On April 23, David died and his nephew Mstislav Romanovich succeeded him in Smolensk.[440] More importantly, Ryurik replaced David as senior prince. He therewith assumed control over all his nephews including the new prince of Smolensk. His combined offices as head of the Rostislavichi and prince of Kiev therefore placed him at the zenith of his power.

In 1197, another important event probably took place, but the informa-tion is found only in Tatishchev. We are told that the princes of Ryazan' resolved to create an autonomous eparchy. They sent *Igumen* Arseny to the metropolitan, who appointed him bishop of Ryazan'.[441] It is hazardous to take Tatishchev's account on its own, but his information is corroborated by chronicle reports. As we have seen, Ryazan' was under the ecclesias-tical jurisdiction of Chernigov up to at least 1186, when the princes of Ryazan' asked Bishop Porfiry to intercede on their behalf with Vsevolod of Suzdalia.[442] Later, under 1207, the chronicler alludes to Ryazan' as an autonomous bishopric when he refers to Bishop Arseny of Ryazan',[443] the very man whom Tatishchev identifies as the town's first bishop. It appears, therefore, that between 1186 and 1207 Ryazan' obtained its own bishop. Tatishchev alone provides a specific date for the event.

The request of the princes of Ryazan' was an obvious one. Distance pre-vented the bishop of Chernigov from effectively ministering to the Church in Ryazan'. Indeed, serving the Ol'govichi and the princes of Ryazan', who were under the thumb of the prince of Suzdalia, could prove to be an impossible task as Bishop Porfiry had learned. In the light of these consider-ations, we may ask three questions. Was Ryazan's request for independence influenced by Porfiry's scandalous behavior? Since Vsevolod was especially incensed at the bishop, did he pressure the princes into making the request? Was autocephaly one of the issues Yaroslav agreed to in 1196, when he con-cluded a separate agreement with the princes of Ryazan'? Circumstantial evidence suggests that we may answer all three questions in the affirmative. Assuming that the princes of Ryazan' successfully negotiated for their own

---

[440] Ipat. cols. 702–6. Concerning the date, see Berezhkov, p. 208.
[441] Tat. 4, p. 326; Tat. 3, p. 166. Tatishchev places this unique information under the year 1198. Since, however, the other entries he places under this year report events from both 1197 and 1198, we may assume that Ryazan' got its own bishop in 1197, at the earliest, or in 1198.
[442] See above, pp. 184–5.
[443] Lav., col. 432. See also, A. G. Kuz'min, *Ryazanskoe letopisanie* (M., 1965), pp. 127–8.

bishop in the autumn of 1196, the following year was evidently the first convenient opportunity for them to act on the agreement. Although we may never ascertain the events that led to the separation, it appears that around 1197 the dynasty of Chernigov lost its last formal hold on its distant relatives in Ryazan'.[444]

YAROSLAV'S DEATH

On an unspecified date in 1198, Yaroslav Vsevolodovich of Chernigov died. The bishop, the abbots, and Yaroslav's nephews escorted his body with due ceremony and laid it to rest in the Cathedral of St. Saviour. He was succeeded on the throne of Chernigov by Igor' Svyatoslavich.[445] Yaroslav was fifty-nine years of age when he died. He was the only Ol'govich with the distinction of having been born in Kiev.[446] Although, as we have seen, his brother Svyatoslav and their mother Maria were buried in the Monastery of St. Cyril, Yaroslav was not laid to rest in what was purportedly their family mausoleum. Given his recent rivalry with Ryurik, the latter might well have refused permission for him to be buried in Kiev. Moreover, unlike his brother, Yaroslav did not die as prince of Kiev so that he could not claim the right to be interred in that town. As a prince who had ruled Chernigov, however, he merited the right of being laid to rest in the Cathedral of St. Saviour alongside his grandfather, Oleg, the progenitor of the Ol'govichi, and his great-grandfather, Svyatoslav, the founder of the dynasty.

As is frequently the case even with important Ol'govichi, the sources tell us little about Yaroslav's personal life. According to the *Lyubetskiy sinodik*, he became a monk before his death and took the name Vasily. The same source reports that his wife's name was Irene.[447] Their sons were Rostislav and Yaropolk. The former's wife was the daughter of Vsevolod of Suzdalia, but if the latter had married before his father's death, the sources do not say. Yaroslav's only daughter had married Vladimir Glebovich of Pereyaslavl', who had died in 1187.

Yaroslav was one of the few Ol'govichi whom the accident of birth and good fortune allowed to climb to the pinnacle of power within the dynasty. The accident of birth placed him on the second rung of seniority in his generation. As we have seen, he began his political career unassumingly by ruling the provincial domain of Ropesk.[448] He remained there for some

[444] In 1127, as has been noted elsewhere, the princes of Murom and Ryazan' became politically independent of Chernigov (*Dynasty*, pp. 319–20).
[445] Ipat., cols. 707–8; Gust., p. 326. Concerning the date, see Berezhkov, p. 209.
[446] Ipat. col. 306; *Dynasty*, p. 361.   [447] Zotov, pp. 267–8.   [448] See above, p. 87.

twenty years. His good fortune was to have his succession to Chernigov accelerated because, in 1176, Svyatoslav occupied Kiev.[449] Consequently, he did not have to wait for his brother to die before succeeding him to Chernigov. Finally, by outliving his brother, he also assumed seniority in the dynasty for four years.

Hostile chroniclers condemned Yaroslav for acting perfidiously. But a close look at his career contradicts that accusation. He was loyal to his subjects to the point of locking horns with his brother Svyatoslav in their defense. He refused to participate on campaigns that would take him too far afield from his lands, leaving them vulnerable to attack. Although he lived in the shadow of his elder brother most of his life, he demonstrated resolute leadership in defending the rights of his dynasty after Svyatoslav's death. In his controversy with the Monomashichi he successfully protected his dynasty's right to lay claim to Kiev. If he broke pledges they were ones that he had made either under duress or ones that jeopardized the rights of his dynasty. After kissing the Holy Cross to Vsevolod, in the autumn of 1196, he demonstrated his integrity by remaining faithful to his promises by never again attacking the Rostislavichi.

IGOR' AS SENIOR PRINCE

After Yaroslav's death, the dynasty executed a smooth transition of power thus testifying to the moral discipline of its princes. Two important criteria for the transfer of seniority were the generation to which a prince belonged and the branch (senior or cadet) to which he belonged. On the one hand, all the eligible candidates for seniority in the oldest generation had to die before seniority passed to a member of the next generation. On the other hand, princes of the senior branch had precedence over those of the cadet branch. Following Yaroslav's death, no prince of the oldest generation in the senior branch was still alive. Seniority therefore passed to the next eligible prince in the oldest generation in the cadet branch. That was Igor'. He was also eligible according to a third criterion. His father Svyatoslav had ruled Chernigov and this gave him the formulaic right to sit on the throne of his father. His promotion from Novgorod Severskiy to Chernigov was of special significance. This was the first occasion, indeed the only occasion, on which the eldest member of the cadet branch became senior prince of the dynasty and prince of Chernigov.

---

[449] See above, p. 137.

It is difficult to determine who succeeded Igor' to Novgorod Severskiy. With the rise of two branches of Ol'govichi in Igor''s generation, it became practicable for the senior prince of each branch to rule one of the two dynastic capitals. Thus, the senior prince of the senior branch ruled Chernigov, and the senior prince of the cadet branch ruled Novgorod Severskiy. In 1198, however, Igor''s promotion to seniority enabled him to jump the breach between the two branches and to occupy Chernigov. By doing so, he denied the eldest prince of the senior branch that position. The closest parallel is found in the case of Igor''s father Svyatoslav Ol'govich, the progenitor of the cadet branch. In 1157, when he occupied Chernigov, his nephew Svyatoslav Vsevolodovich, the eldest prince of the senior branch, occupied Novgorod Severskiy.[450] If Igor' followed his father's example, as was likely the case, Novgorod Severskiy went to the senior branch. This meant that Vladimir Svyatoslavich was the rightful claimant to the town.

During Igor''s reign Novgorod Severskiy enjoyed the status of the second most powerful town in the Chernigov land (map 5). Named after the tribe of Severyane who inhabited the region, it was located on the high right bank of the Desna. After the Congress of Lyubech in 1097, it became the patrimonial capital of Oleg Svyatoslavich.[451] He built a residence, erected the Church of St. Michael, and expanded the town's fortifications (figure 10). After the Davidovichi became extinct during the middle of the twelfth century, it became, in effect, the capital of the cadet branch. By that time, the town's suburbs had been fortified with palisades and made accessible by such entrances as the Kursk Gate, the Chernigov Gate, and the Water Gate. The fortified area was more than twice the size of similar areas in Putivl', Trubetsk, Vshchizh, Lyubech, and Gomiy. During the middle of the century, the Monastery of the Transfiguration of the Holy Saviour (*Spasskiy monastyr'*) was built some 4 km downstream from the *detinets*. Igor' evidently adorned it with its first stone church.[452] Since he and his elder brother Oleg kept chronicles, the town received much publicity during their reigns. After Igor' moved to Chernigov, however, chronicle references to it virtually ceased.[453]

---

[450] See above, p. 83.
[451] Concerning Oleg's acquisition of Novgorod Severskiy, see *Dynasty*, pp. 219–21.
[452] See below, p. 239.
[453] A. V. Kuza, "Novgorod-Severskiy – stol'nyy gorod Igorya Svyatoslavicha," *Novgorodu-Severskomu – 1000 let* (Tezisy dokladov oblastnoy nauchno-prakticheskoy konferentsii [may 1989 g.]), A. B. Kovalenko *et al.* (eds.) (Chernigov and Novgorod-Severskiy, 1989), pp. 20–3, and his *Malye goroda*, pp. 77–9. See also V. P. Kovalenko and A. P. Motsya, "Novgorod-Severskiy v X–XIII vv.," *Novgorodu-Severskomu – 1000 let* (Tezisy dokladov oblastnoy nauchno-prakticheskoy konferentsii [may 1989 g.]), A. B. Kovalenko *et al.* (eds.) (Chernigov and Novgorod-Severskiy, 1989), pp. 25–9.

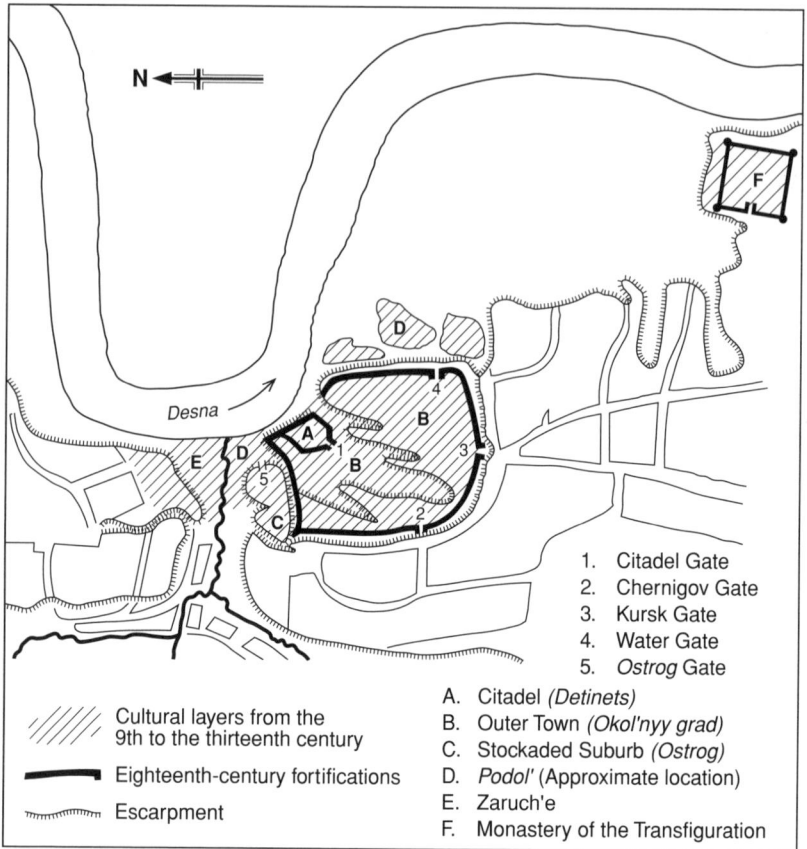

Map 5   Novgorod Severskiy in the twelfth and thirteenth century (adapted from
A. L. Kazakov and V. Kovalenko)

On becoming prince of Chernigov, one of Igor''s first tasks was to renew the alliances that Yaroslav had concluded. Accordingly, since he had
been party to Yaroslav's pact with Roman, Igor' would have confirmed
the commitment of the Ol'govichi to him. He also endorsed the alliances
Yaroslav had made with Vsevolod and the Rostislavichi. Since he and all
the Ol'govichi had agreed not to take Kiev from Ryurik, they remained
bound by that pledge. After David died, however, the clause prohibiting
them from seizing Smolensk from him had become defunct. Igor' therefore
would have concluded a similar agreement with David's successor Mstislav
Romanovich. Finally, Igor' undoubtedly confirmed his dynasty's alliances
with the Donets Polovtsy.

Figure 10   The citadel of Novgorod Severskiy on the river Desna viewed
from the north

The chronicles report a death under 1198, which was of immediate interest to Igor' and the Ol'govichi. Yaroslav Mstislavich, the nephew of
Vsevolod of Suzdalia, died in Pereyaslavl'.[454] His demise is noteworthy
because Pereyaslavl', Chernigov's southern neighbour, was under the jurisdiction of the prince of Suzdalia. Significantly, Yaroslav had posed no
threat to the Ol'govichi during their recent confrontation with Vsevolod.
Following the debilitating Polovtsian attacks on Pereyaslavl' during the
1180s, its manpower resources were probably still too weak for it to become
involved in inter-princely conflicts. Besides, the threat of nomadic attacks
on Pereyaslavl' remained. Although Vsevolod was unable to count on receiving military aid from the patrimonial domain of the Monomashichi in
the south, he did not ignore it. A year earlier he had sent a certain Paul to
serve as the town's bishop.[455] After Yaroslav's death, however, Vsevolod did
not send anyone immediately to replace him.

   Under the year 1198 the Gustinskiy Chronicle reports the death of
Vladimir Yaroslavich of Galich.[456] Igor' and the Ol'govichi would have
noted his demise with even greater interest. Both branches had marriage
ties with him. He was related to the senior branch through his marriage

---

[454] See s.a. 1199: Lav., col. 415; Mosk., p. 99. Concerning the date, see Berezhkov p. 86. Concerning
      Yaroslav, see also Baum., VI, 27.
[455] See s.a. 1198: Lav., col. 414. Concerning the date, see Berezhkov, p. 86.
[456] See s.a. 1199: Gust., p. 326. Under the year 1199, the late Gustinskiy Chronicle reports the death
      of Yaroslav Mstislavich and other events which the Laurentian Chronicle puts under the year
      1199, but which occurred in 1198 (Berezhkov, p. 209). This suggests that the events the Gustin-
      skiy Chronicle reports under the year 1199 also occurred in the year 1198. Tatishchev, the only
      other source to report Vladimir's death, places it under the year 1197 (Tat. 4, p. 325; Tat. 3,
      p. 165).

to Boleslava, the daughter of Svyatoslav Vsevolodovich. And his sister had married Igor'.[457]

Vladimir's death changed the balance of power in Rus'. As has been noted, he had been politically ineffectual and lived a debauched life.[458] Nevertheless, the protection that his uncle Vsevolod of Suzdalia gave him ensured political stability in Galicia. This ended with his death. Even though he had two sons, the chronicles never mention them again.[459] His death therefore created a political vacuum that a number of claimants were eager to fill. Roman, as we have seen, had already challenged Vladimir for control of Galich. Ryurik could now claim that, after the dynasty of Galicia became defunct, the territory reverted to the jurisdiction of the prince of Kiev. The princes of the two branches of Ol'govichi could argue that their marriage ties with Osmomysl's dynasty gave them the right to rule Galich. The last claimant was the king of Hungary who had already made a bid for the domain ten years earlier.

After Vladimir's death, however, Roman was the quickest off the mark. He rode to Leszek, king of Little Poland, promising to be at his beck and call if the king helped him to win Galich. When its citizens refused to welcome Roman, Leszek besieged the town. After capturing it, he forced them to accept Roman as prince. The latter kissed the Holy Cross to the king and to the townsmen, promising to be subservient to the former and to live in peace with the latter. "Roman, however, kept neither promise."[460]

The next two years were evidently uneventful for Igor' and the Ol'govichi. Nevertheless, in 1200 two noteworthy events occurred. First, we are told that at the beginning of August, Vsevolod of Suzdalia sent his son Yaroslav to Pereyaslavl'.[461] The information that Vsevolod sent a son ten years of age rather than an experienced but more distant relative is noteworthy.[462] Now that his sons were coming of age he decided to assert more direct control over the patrimonial domain in imitation of his father Yury Dolgorukiy, who had ruled the town through his sons. Indeed, as

[457] Baum., III, 17; IV, 28.
[458] According to Tatishchev, Vladimir either drank himself to death or was poisoned (Tat. 4, p. 325; Tat. 3, p. 165).
[459] Baum., III, 20, 21; see above, p. 191.
[460] See s.a. 1199: Gust., p. 326. Tatishchev writes that the Galicians asked Ryurik for his son Rostislav, but failing to receive word from him and on learning that the Hungarians were on their way, agreed to take Roman as their prince (Tat. 4, p. 325; Tat. 3, p. 165).
[461] See s.a. 1201: Lav., col. 416. The Laurentian chronicler gives the date, wrongly, as August 10, but other sources give it, correctly, as August 3 (for example, s.a. 1200: TL, p. 284; s.a. 1201: L'vov, p. 141; Tver., col. 290). Concerning the year, see Berezhkov, p. 86.
[462] Yaroslav, whose baptismal name was Fedor, was born on February 8, 1190 (Lav., col. 408; Vosk., p. 101; Rapov, pp. 170–1). Concerning the year, see Berezhkov, p. 84.

has been noted elsewhere, in the past the Monomashichi had used their patrimonial capital as a stepping-stone to Kiev.[463] We have no evidence that Vsevolod had designs on the capital of Rus'. Nevertheless, since he himself had ruled Kiev, this made his sons eligible to sit on the throne of their father. Vsevolod's appointment of a son to Pereyaslavl' may have therefore sounded warning bells to the Ol'govichi and the Rostislavichi.

Second, we are told that Vladimir, the eldest son of Svyatoslav Vsevolodovich, died in the autumn.[464] He was probably interred in the Church of the Annunciation that his father had built. Since his parents married in 1143, he was probably in his mid-fifties when he died.[465] His baptismal name, according to the *Lyubetskiy sinodik*, was Boris.[466] In 1179, as we have seen, he married Evdokia the daughter of Mikhalko, the elder brother of Vsevolod of Suzdalia.[467] If they had sons, they became *izgoi* after Vladimir's death. In 1198, after Igor' had succeeded Yaroslav in Chernigov, Vladimir probably occupied Novgorod Severskiy. At that time he also became the senior prince of the senior branch. Consequently, Vladimir's passing was important. It advanced each of his brothers – Oleg, Vsevolod, Gleb, and Mstislav – up a rung on the ladder of succession. Oleg became the new senior prince of the senior branch and second in precedence in the entire dynasty after Igor'. It was also his turn to rule Novgorod Severskiy.

IGOR''S DEATH

In 1201, according to most chronicles, Igor' Svyatoslavich the prince of Chernigov died.[468] He was the last prince of the fourth generation. It is ironic that the chroniclers made only a passing reference to the death of

---

[463] *Dynasty*, pp. 324–6.

[464] See s.a. 1201: Gust., p. 327; compare Lav., col. 416. See also Baum., IV, 32; Rapov, pp. 117–18. A number of sources give Vladimir's patronymic as Vsevolodovich (for example, Mosk., p. 100; L'vov, p. 142; Erm., p. 58). Given this information, it has been suggested that Vladimir was the son of Vsevolod Ol'govich (d. 1146) and the brother of Svyatoslav and Yaroslav (Zotov, pp. 70–2, 268). This is improbable. If the prince in question was Vladimir Vsevolodovich he, and not Igor', would have replaced Yaroslav in Chernigov in 1198, because he would have been higher in seniority than Igor'. Moreover, in light of the abundance of information concerning Svyatoslav and Yaroslav for the previous two decades, it is unlikely that the chroniclers would have completely ignored a third brother if he existed. Concerning the year, see Berezhkov, p. 86.

[465] *Dynasty*, p. 384.   [466] Zotov, p. 272.   [467] See above, p. 140.

[468] See s.a. 1202: Lav., col. 417. The Laurentian Chronicle does not give Igor''s patronymic, but most other sources do (for example, Gust., p. 327; Mosk., p. 100). A number of historians claim Igor' died in 1202 (for example, Zotov, p. 270; Baum., IV, 28; Rapov, pp. 112–13). Concerning the problem of dating, see Berezhkov, pp. 86–7. Most chronicles place the news of Igor''s death as the first entry for the year. From this we may assume that he probably died in the spring.

the prince whose fated campaign at the Kayala was the inspiration for the most celebrated epic of Rus'. More than likely, his chronicler did write an encomium but it was lost. This is implied by the evidence that the Hypatian Chronicle, the most likely source to have included a report of Igor'␣'s rule in Chernigov, has a lacuna for the years 1199–1204 which included his term as senior prince.[469]

As the prince of Chernigov, Igor' merited burial in the Cathedral of St. Saviour. He was fifty years of age when he died. He received the name Yury at baptism,[470] but we are not told if he took the monastic tonsure before his death. He and his wife, the daughter of Yaroslav Osmomysl,[471] had at least five children. Their widowed daughter married the hapless David Ol'govich of the senior branch.[472] Their eldest son, Vladimir, was born in 1170,[473] and some four years later Oleg was born, but he evidently died at an early age.[474] In 1176 Svyatoslav was born.[475] As we shall see, the couple also had a son named Roman. All the children, it appears, were born in Igor'␣'s patrimonial domain of Putivl', where he lived over twenty years. In 1180 he moved to Novgorod Severskiy, where he ruled for eighteen years as senior prince of the cadet branch.

Investigators claim to have found tangible evidence of his administrative and cultural activities. They suggest that a lead seal found near Pskov belonged to Igor'. It has the images of St. George (Yury) and St. Nicholas on the obverse and reverse. St. George was Igor'␣'s patron and St. Nicholas was the patron of his father Svyatoslav.[476] Researchers cannot verify that he owned this particular seal, but there is little doubt that he used similar seals with images of the two saints. Igor' evidently inherited his father's Greek-made silver ceremonial cup with the figure of St. Nicholas embossed at the bottom of the bowl. He asserted his ownership of the cup by having

[469] Concerning the compilation of the Hypatian Chronicle and the relevant hiatus, see Makhnovets', pp. vi–viii; Berezhkov, pp. 209–11; O. P. Likhacheva, "Letopis' Ipatevskaya," SKKDR, 235–41.
[470] Concerning Igor'␣'s birth, see above, p. 63.
[471] See above, p. 121.   [472] See above, p. 195.   [473] See above, p. 121.
[474] See above, p. 133.   [475] See above, p. 137.
[476] In 1983, the seal was found on the left bank of the river Velikaya near the sixteenth-century Church of St. Clement. The authors draw the association between Pskov and Igor' because a copy of the "Slovo o polku Igoreve" was made in Pskov evidently at the Spaso-Mirozhskiy Monastery. The original text had perhaps been sent to Pskov by Igor', who attached his seal to it. They concede, however, that the questions whether Igor' ever ruled Pskov, and whether his alleged seal was attached to the document of the "Slovo o polku Igoreve," remain unanswered (V. D. Beletsky and S. V. Beletsky, "Pechat' knyazya Igorya," Drevnosti Slavyan i Rusi, B. A. Timoshchuk [ed.] [M., 1988], pp. 105–10). Although there is no proof whatsoever that an Ol'govich ever ruled Pskov, the evidence that a text of the "Slovo o polku Igoreve" reached the town may suggest that ties existed between monasteries in Pskov and Chernigov.

his Christian name Prince George (*K'nyazhya Gyur'eva*) inscribed on it.[477] Basing their observations on archaeological evidence, a number of investigators proposed that Igor' built the Cathedral of St. Saviour in the Monastery of the Transfiguration outside of Novgorod Severskiy.[478] It has also been suggested that he founded the stone church in Putivl'.[479] Finally, some claim that Igor''s chronicler recorded much of the information that has come down to us concerning his family.[480]

To judge from circumstantial evidence, Igor''s reign in Chernigov was uneventful. The Monomashichi made no special demands on him and the Polovtsy stayed their attacks on the Chernigov lands. Moreover, he himself expressed no desire to rule Kiev. The reason for his seeming lack of interest was, in part, his faithfulness to his pledge. As we have seen, the Ol'govichi had promised not to usurp Kiev from Ryurik.

Igor' was the last member of his generation of Ol'govichi. Three princes out of five in that generation attained the prestigious position of seniority in the dynasty. The eldest of the three, Svyatoslav, also climbed to the pinnacle of political power in Rus' by ruling Kiev. Although Igor' did not achieve such distinction, chronicle evidence reveals that he had an enviably successful military career. His brothers in the cadet branch showed him every respect as their senior prince and followed him into battle without demur. Moreover, Svyatoslav of Kiev had the utmost confidence in his leadership skills and routinely asked him to command expeditions against the Polovtsy. Consequently, Igor' led many campaigns from among which the chronicles report only one defeat. Despite his successes, popular tradition remembers him as the vanquished prince over whom Yaroslavna sang her lament in the *Slovo o polku Igoreve*.

After Igor''s death, the office of senior prince passed to the fifth generation and to the senior branch. Accordingly, Oleg Svyatoslavich occupied

---

[477] See Kovalenko, "Chasha kniazia Ihoria," pp. 142–51. Concerning his father's ceremonial cup, see above, pp. 104–5.

[478] Investigators point out that there is no trustworthy evidence for ascertaining the date on which the cathedral was built. The architectural forms and the construction techniques, however, led them to date its foundation to the first third of the thirteenth century (A. V. Kuza, V. P. Kovalenko and A. P. Motsya, "Novgorod-Severskiy: Nekotorye itogi i perspetivy issledovaniy," *Na Yugo-Vostoke Drevney Rusi: Istoriko-arkheologicheskie issledovaniya*, A. D. Pryakhin *et al.* [eds.] [Voronezh, 1996], pp. 17–19; and L. N. Bol'shakov, V. P. Kovalenko, and P. A. Rappoport, "Novye dannye o pamyatnikakh drevnego zodchestva Chernigova i Novgoroda-Severskogo," KSIA 195 [M., 1989], 51–3).

[479] Yu. S. Aseev, "Arkhitektura severn'oho pridniprov'ia ta Galits'ko-Volyns'kykh zemel' u XII–XIII stolittiakh," in vol. 1, *Mystetstvo naidavnishykh chasiv ta epokhy Kyivs'koi Rusi*, in series *Istoriia Ukrains'koho Mystetstva*, 6 vols. (Kyiv, 1966), pp. 213–14; see below, p. 284.

[480] Priselkov, *Istoriya russkogo letopisaniya*, pp. 48–52; Likhachev, *Russkie letopisi*, pp. 182–4, 186–96; Shakhmatov, *Obozrenie*, p. 72.

Chernigov. His transfer, presumably from Novgorod Severskiy, left the capital of the cadet branch vacant. According to the ladder system of succession it should have passed to the new senior prince in the cadet branch, Igor′'s eldest nephew Svyatoslav Ol′govich. As we have seen, however, the chronicles have not mentioned him since 1185, when the Polovtsy took him captive.

3

The fifth generation: 1201–1223

After Svyatoslav Vsevolodovich died in Kiev in 1194, Ryurik Rostislavich, with the backing of the dynasties of Smolensk and Suzdalia, sought to secure for the Rostislavichi the sole right of succession to Kiev. Because he failed to deprive the Ol'govichi of their right to supremacy in Rus', the princes of both dynasties remained claimants to Kiev. By the beginning of the thirteenth century, princely seniority in the dynasty of Chernigov had passed to the senior branch of Ol'govichi. This constituted the four youngest sons of Svyatoslav Vsevolodovich who were all eligible to occupy the office of senior prince. Ryurik could also expect them to make a bid for Kiev where they had the right to sit on the throne of their father.

THE REIGN OF OLEG SVYATOSLAVICH IN CHERNIGOV

As we have seen, some three years before Igor''s death his brother-in-law Vladimir had died in Galich. Roman Mstislavich of Vladimir in Volyn' quickly seized the town and soon after began wreaking havoc on domains belonging to Ryurik of Kiev and other princes. He refused to forgive his father-in-law for taking his five towns in order to give them to Vsevolod of Suzdalia.[1] In 1201, therefore, Ryurik summoned the Ol'govichi to campaign against Roman. In 1196, as has been noted, Yaroslav of Chernigov had refused to break his alliance with Roman. Five years later Oleg, on becoming prince of Chernigov, changed that policy. He decided to cooperate with Ryurik just as his father Svyatoslav had done when the two had been co-rulers. Oleg, however, would never attain a position of superiority over Ryurik. Instead, he pledged loyalty to the prince of Kiev and answered the latter's call to attack Roman.

The latter pre-empted their attack by rallying the troops of Galich and Vladimir in Volyn'. The Monomashichi, the Black Caps, and all the towns

[1] See. s.a. 1200: Gust., p. 326; see above, pp. 213–14.

241

in Rus' also joined him. The desertion of Ryurik's allies suggests that they were predisposed to abandoning him. The observation is supported by Tatishchev, who alone reports that Ryurik suffered much at Roman's hands. He was not given a moment's peace because he drank to excess and lived a profligate life. He devoted little attention to administering his lands, and his officials caused much grief. As a result, even the Kievans held him in little esteem.[2] Consequently, they opened the gates of the *podol'* to Roman.

He forced Ryurik and the Ol'govichi to capitulate. One late source states that Ryurik and Oleg agreed to accept his authority, while another declares that Ryurik promised to renounce his claim to Kiev.[3] After that, Roman let Ryurik withdraw to Vruchiy and the Ol'govichi to return to Chernigov. Ironically, therefore, the Ol'govichi found themselves supporting their erstwhile foe Ryurik in opposition to the now powerful alliance centered on Roman. In this way Oleg, the new senior prince of the dynasty, began his rule on an unpropitious note.

The most damaging to Ryurik was Vsevolod's support of Roman. A late chronicle claims that, before his attack, Roman had sent word to Vsevolod apprising the latter of his intention to evict Ryurik.[4] Moreover, Roman deferred to Vsevolod on the appointment of a replacement for Ryurik.[5] This is confirmed by the report that both Vsevolod and Roman gave Kiev to Ingvar' Yaroslavich of Lutsk.[6] By seeking Vsevolod's approval, Roman acknowledged his status as senior prince of the House of Monomakh.

In the winter of 1202, we are told, many people of Rus' witnessed omens. One night the sky turned dark red and began to flow. It seemed as if blood streamed over the land, the houses, and the snow. Others saw a shower of stars come plummeting to the ground. They were convinced that they were witnessing the end of the world. "Such signs appeared in the sky, the stars,

[2] Tat. 4, p. 341; Tat. 3, pp. 184–5; M. Dimnik, "The Place of Ryurik Rostislavich's Death: Kiev or Chernigov?," *Mediaeval Studies* 44 (1982), 381.

[3] Gust., p. 328; Tver., col. 291.

[4] See s.a. 1201: Nikon. 10, p. 34. See also s.a. 1202: Tat. 4, p. 327; Tat. 3, p. 167.

[5] As we shall see, on February 16, 1203, when Roman confronted Ryurik at Vruchiy, he advised him to send a petition to Vsevolod to reinstate him in Kiev and Roman would support his request (see below, pp. 246–7).

[6] See s.a. 1202: Lav., cols. 417–18; Gust., pp. 327–8; Mosk., p. 160. Concerning the date, see Berezhkov, pp. 86–7. Roman was Ingvar's senior cousin. His father Mstislav had been the elder brother of Ingvar's father Yaroslav. Although Ingvar' had a claim to Kiev because his father had ruled the town, Roman had a prior claim. Vsevolod of Suzdalia and Ryurik, however, had prior claims to Roman. Not wishing to usurp Kiev for himself, Roman gave it to his junior relative in imitation of Andrey Bogolyubskiy and David of Smolensk, who had appointed their younger brothers to Kiev. Since Ingvar' was not in immediate line to rule Kiev, Roman probably appointed him as a stopgap measure.

the sun, the moon, and elsewhere not to foretell good but to portend evil. They foreshadowed wars, famine, and death."[7]

On January 2, 1203 Ryurik and the Ol'govichi captured Kiev.[8] He therewith avenged himself against the Kievans for opening the gates to Roman. The Ol'govichi, however, had no immediate grievances against the townsmen. They joined Ryurik because of their promise to help him rule Kiev. But by assisting him they incurred the Kievans' wrath and antagonized Roman. They probably consoled themselves with the thoughts that, in the short term, they won Ryurik's gratitude and enriched their towns with Kievan booty. And in the long term, any policy that helped to keep the families of the Monomashichi at odds was to their advantage.

The entire Polovtsian land also participated in the slaughter. The chronicler identifies two khans: Konchak and Daniil Kobyakovich.[9] In 1184, as we have seen, Svyatoslav and Ryurik had taken Kobyak and two of his sons captive at the river Erel'.[10] Daniil, perhaps one of the two sons, therefore brought tribesmen from the east bank of the Dnepr. His ally Konchak was the father-in-law of Igor'′s son Vladimir of Putivl'. He undoubtedly summoned the khan from the Donets basin. Ryurik would have called the Lukomortsy from the right bank since he had used them as auxiliaries in the past. The tribesmen cut down old monks and nuns, elderly priests, the blind, the lame, the deaf, and the infirm. But the younger monks and nuns, priests and their wives, the Kievans and their children, they carried off to their camps. The chronicler declares that the evil inflicted on Kiev was unparalleled since the inception of Christianity in Rus'. In his view, Ryurik's devastation exceeded that caused by all previous attacks, including the one organized by Andrey Bogolyubskiy.[11]

Ryurik must have ordered his men to set fire to the *podol'*, where the townsmen had betrayed him. On the *detinets*, his forces plundered the Cathedral of St. Sofia, the Tithe Church, and all the monasteries. They stripped many icons of their adornments, and others they carried off along with holy crosses, sacred vessels, and books. We are also told that they seized the garments of the blessed first princes that the latter had hung in churches in their memory. From this we learn that the early princes

[7] See s.a. 1203: Lav., col. 419. Berezhkov observes that the winter phenomenon probably refers to the Aurora Borealis, and the second sign was a shower of Leonids observed earlier on October 18, 1202 (Berezhkov, p. 87).

[8] Lav., col. 418. The Novgorod chronicler says the attackers captured Kiev on January 1, on the Feast of St. Basil (NPL, pp. 45, 240). Only one source explains that Ryurik and the Ol'govichi attacked Kiev on January 1, but captured it on January 2 (Tver., col. 292). Concerning the date, see Berezhkov, pp. 87, 247.

[9] NPL, pp. 45, 240; Gust., p. 328.   [10] See above, p. 160.   [11] See above, pp. 118–19.

hung their apparel in churches, evidently over their thrones in imitation of the Greek tradition.[12] Since the looters stole the garments from the Tithe Church and St. Sofia, those of St. Vladimir would have been kept in the former which he had built, and those of Yaroslav the Wise would have been kept in St. Sofia which he had built.[13]

In imitation of the practices followed in St. Sofia and the Tithe Church, the Ol'govichi and Rostislavichi would hang the garments over the thrones in their own cathedrals.[14] Their dynastic capitals would thus become the new repositories of the venerated garments of the two Christianizers of Rus'. Nevertheless, their motive for stealing the garments may not have been simply to acquire "relics." Had this been the case, Andrey Bogolyub-skiy's company of princes would have plundered them in 1169, when they desecrated those churches. It is possible that Oleg and Ryurik appropriated the apparel hoping that their dynasties would profit ideologically from their association with the symbols of divinely transmitted authority.

The removal of the sacramentals from Kiev meant that a claimant in-stalled in St. Sofia would find it more difficult to argue that he was invested on the throne of Yaroslav the Wise according to the tradition of divinely transmitted authority. This, his rivals could argue, made his claim disputed.

[12] The garments of the blessed first princes reflected the Byzantine political ideology of the divine transmission of power to the emperor. According to popular belief, Constantine the Great received his authority directly from God. In a vision on the Milvian Bridge, Christ appeared to him before the battle promising him victory if he fought under the sign of the Holy Cross. Doing as he was bidden and wearing garments given to him by an angel, Constantine was victorious. He adopted Christianity as the state religion and became the first Christian emperor. After that his garments assumed a mystical significance and, according to the angel's directive, were hung in the church above his throne, where they became symbols of the emperor's supremacy in the Christian world. After his death, they were used as ritual clothing during ceremonials such as the enthronement of a new emperor. Some seven centuries later in Rus', Metropolitan Hilarion gave his famous "Sermon on Law and Grace" in which he spoke of St. Vladimir as the "new Constantine" (A. M. Moldovan, *"Slovo o zakone i blagodati" Ilariona* [K., 1984], pp. 96–7). During the middle of the eleventh century the concept of the blessed first princes took root in Rus' and their garments, like those of Constantine, became symbols of divinely transmitted authority (A. P. Tolochko, "'Porty blazhennykh pervykh knyazey': k voprosu o vizantiyskikh politicheskikh teoriyakh na Rusi," *Yuzhnaya Rus' i Vizantiya*, L. L. Vashchenko [ed.] [K., 1991], pp. 36–40).

[13] Evidently, the garments and weapons of SS. Boris and Gleb were not among those seized since they were kept in their mausoleum in Vyshgorod. Indeed, Andrey Bogolyubskiy probably took these to Suzdalia in 1155, when he moved from Vyshgorod. Since he took the famous icon of the Mother of God with him at that time (Ipat., col. 482) he probably took other religious artifacts including at least some of the garments and weapons of the two saints. This is supported by the news that, in 1175 when his *boyars* attacked him, he attempted to defend himself with the sword of St. Boris (Ipat., cols. 586–7).

[14] According to chronicle evidence, various dynasties observed the practice of hanging princely gar-ments in churches. In addition to Kiev, Chernigov, and Smolensk the practice is reported as existing in Suzdalia (s.a. 1185: Lav., chast' 2, col. 392; s.a. 1237: Lav., chast' 2, col. 463; Tolochko, "Porty," pp. 35, 38–9) and in Ryazan' (Tolochko, "Porty," p. 39).

Significantly, by 1203, the Ol'govichi and the Rostislavichi had become the main claimants. In seizing the apparel, therefore, it would seem that Ryurik and Oleg intended to use the divine association of the garments as underpinning for their pretensions to Kiev. By hanging the attire in their cathedrals, they could argue that, when their senior prince was enthroned, his investment was confirmed under the aura of the sacred garments. Consequently, as a senior prince with divinely transmitted authority, he also had a valid claim to Kiev. In this way, the Ol'govichi and the Rostislavichi seemingly sought to appropriate to their dynasties the right of succession to the capital of Rus'.

The princes did not loot Kiev randomly. Not wishing to jeopardize the flow of trade to Rus', they spared the lives of the foreign merchants and let them keep half of their wares.[15] By not attacking the traders, Ryurik also saved the buildings in which they had sought sanctuary. Moreover, the princes would not have allowed their men to plunder the churches of St. Vasily and St. Michael at Vydubichi patronized by Ryurik,[16] and the monasteries of St. Cyril and St. Simeon belonging to the Ol'govichi.

The chronicler, presumably a monk, is uncharacteristically lenient on the perpetrators of the greatest evil that ever befell Kiev. The people, he declares, brought God's punishment on themselves "for their sins." These included betraying Ryurik. The author would have his reader believe that the attack was justified on moral grounds. This is a rare occasion on which the descendants of Oleg *Goreslavich* escaped the reproach of the chronicler. Even more surprisingly, he does not condemn the Polovtsy. Instead of calling them cursed, godless, or thrice damned, he refers to them simply as foreigners. They, like the princes, were God's instruments of justice.

Owing to a happenstance, we learn the names of two princes who were present during the sack of Kiev. Rostislav Yaroslavich captured Mstislav Vladimirovich of Dorogobuzh who had probably come to Kiev to celebrate the Christmas season.[17] Since Rostislav took part in the siege, and he was one of the lowest-ranking princes in the senior branch, we may assume that most if not all of the Ol'govichi participated. Moreover, the chance remark,

---

[15] NPL, pp. 45, 240. According to another interpretation, the princes took all the merchants' goods and divided them with the Polovtsy (A. P. Novosel'tsev and V. T. Pashuto, "Vneshnyaya torgovlya Drevney Rusi [do serediny XIII v.]," *Istoriya SSSR* 1 [M., 1967], p. 103).

[16] In 1197, Ryurik consecrated a church he built or rebuilt in honor of St. Vasily (s.a. 1198: Ipat., col. 707; see above, p. 155). In the same year, he reinforced the supporting wall beneath the church of St. Michael at Vydubichi (s.a. 1199: Ipat., cols. 708–9).

[17] Since Ingvar''s father Yaroslav and Mstislav were cousins (Baum., V, 39, 41; XIV, 1), and since Ingvar' and Mstislav controlled the neighboring lands of Lutsk and Dorogobuzh before Ingvar' occupied Kiev, it is most likely that they were friends and that Mstislav came to Kiev to celebrate Christmas with his relative.

that Rostislav took the captive to his domain of Snovsk, reveals the identity of his patrimony.[18] Since he had received it from his father Yaroslav, we may assume that it formed part of the patrimony that the latter had inherited from his father Vsevolod.[19]

Ryurik had no intention of occupying Kiev. He did not wish to face Roman's vengeance or to live with the hostile townsmen. But he could not leave Kiev without a prince for fear that it would return into Roman's hands. Accordingly, Oleg's younger brother Vsevolod Chermnyy occupied the town.[20] Ryurik evidently appointed his ally to Kiev until he could settle his dispute with Roman and be reinstated.

His appointment of an Ol'govich is intriguing. He could not place a Monomashich in Kiev because all the princelings with domains in Rus' had defected to Roman. From among the Ol'govichi, Vsevolod was the logical choice because he was second in seniority. It is also unlikely that Oleg would have abandoned Chernigov for an ephemeral posting. Moreover, Ryurik would not have the senior prince of the Ol'govichi occupy Kiev because Oleg would have posed a threat to his own claim. Ironically, Ryurik, who some seven years earlier had waged war against Yaroslav because he wanted the Ol'govichi to renounce their claim to Kiev forever, was now compelled to ask an Ol'govich to serve as his lieutenant.

Since Roman's raids had provoked Ryurik and the Ol'govichi to despoil Kiev, he took it upon himself to restore peace. He therefore asked Vsevolod to be pacified with the Ol'govichi. Vsevolod sent men to Chernigov and, on February 6, 1203, Oleg and the Ol'govichi kissed the Holy Cross. At a later date, they sent messengers to Suzdalia and Vsevolod kissed the Holy Cross.[21] On February 16, after Roman also concluded peace with the Ol'govichi, he

[18] Concerning the sack of Kiev, see s.a. 1203: Lav., cols. 418–19; Gust., p. 328; NPL, pp. 45, 240; Tver., col. 292; see also s.a. 1202: Mosk., p. 100.

[19] In 1155, we learn that Svyatoslav Ol'govich had refused to return Snovsk to his nephew Svyatoslav Vsevolodovich even though it evidently had formed part of the latter's familial domain (see above, p. 77). This suggests that Snovsk had been part of the patrimony that his father Vsevolod had bequeathed to his two sons, Svyatoslav and Yaroslav. We may assume therefore, that sometime after 1155 Yaroslav reclaimed Snovsk and other territories along the Snov' as his patrimony.

[20] N4, p. 180; N5, p. 180. Fennell, who believes that only the N4 gives this information, suggests it is an error and that Vsevolod's name was taken from a later entry (*Crisis*, p. 41, n. 28).

[21] It is not known when the Ol'govichi formed their treaty with Vsevolod because the Hypatian Chronicle has no information for the years 1199 to 1205, and the text in the Laurentian Chronicle for the years 1203 to 1205 is corrupt (Lav., cols. 418–21; see Berezhkov, p. 87). Since, however, sources using the March year place the entry at the beginning of the year 1203 (for example, Mosk., pp. 100–1; Erm., p. 58), and sources using the Ultra-March year place the entry at the beginning of the year 1204 (for example, Lav. [*Radzivilovskiy spisok {R}* and *Rukopis' b. Moskovskoy Dukhovnoy Akademii {A}*], col. 420; L'vov, p. 143; Tver., col. 293) this suggests that Roman, Vsevolod, and the Ol'govichi were negotiating around March of 1203. Moreover, under the year 1205, R and A

marched against Ryurik in Vruchiy. The latter submitted to Roman and to Vsevolod promising to sever relations with the Ol′govichi and the Polovtsy. After that, Roman also advised him to ask Vsevolod to reinstate him in Kiev and promised to support his request. Consequently, Vsevolod forgave Ryurik for the evil that he had wrought on Kiev and reappointed him to the town.[22]

Roman's desire to appease Ryurik is understandable. He himself did not wish to rule Kiev because that meant forfeiting Galich. More importantly, because he had no immediate claim to Kiev, Vsevolod would probably not approve his rule. Moreover, the longer Ryurik was denied Kiev the longer he would devastate its lands with the Ol′govichi and the Polovtsy. Roman also considered it injudicious to let the Ol′govichi take Kiev even though he had promised to assist Yaroslav a number of years earlier. Ryurik would challenge any Ol′govich who occupied the capital. Consequently, after Roman failed to neutralize his father-in-law by appointing Ingvar′ to Kiev, the next best thing was to reinstate Ryurik as an impotent figurehead. He achieved this by forcing Ryurik to sever ties with the Ol′govichi and the Polovtsy. By forcing Ryurik to submit to Vsevolod and to himself, he also ensured that Ryurik would be under their thumbs.

That winter, we are told, Ryurik, Roman, and other princes attacked the Polovtsy and took many captives. Oleg and the Ol′govichi did not join the expedition. This is not surprising since Ryurik and Roman marched against the nomads on the west bank of the Dnepr. As we have seen, Yaroslav and Igor′ had objected to campaigning so far from their domains because it meant leaving them vulnerable to attack. The new generation of Ol′govichi evidently adopted their policy. Moreover, the main purpose of the campaign, it would seem, was for the Monomashichi to avenge themselves against the Polovtsy for their role in sacking Kiev.

After the expedition, we are told, Ryurik, Roman, and the other princes met at Trepol′ to allocate domains in accordance with the services that each had rendered in the defense of Rus′. But they quarreled. Roman seized Ryurik, sent him to Kiev, and had him tonsured as a monk. He also forced Ryurik's wife and daughter (his own wife whom he had repudiated) to become nuns. Ryurik's sons Rostislav and Vladimir, however, he took with him to Galich.

repeat the information they gave under 1204, but add that the Ol′govichi kissed the Holy Cross on February 6 (Lav., col. 421). If the princes kissed the cross on February 6, 1203, Vsevolod probably kissed the Holy Cross after the envoys sent by the Ol′govichi reached him some time in March.

[22] See s.a. 1203: Lav., col. 419; s.a. 1202: Mosk., p. 100.

Roman undoubtedly objected to Ryurik's allocations just as he had done
some nine years earlier after relinquishing control of the five towns. Significantly, he refused to wage war against Ryurik because that course of
action had failed to achieve the desired result in the past. He also refrained
from resorting to the Byzantine practice of blinding his rival in the manner
that, in 1177, Vsevolod had blinded his nephews Mstislav and Yaropolk.[23]
Moreover, he rejected murder, the expedient that the Kievans had used in
1147 to remove Igor'. Instead, he followed the precedent set by the brothers
Izyaslav, Svyatoslav, and Vsevolod in 1059, when they removed their uncle
Sudislav from the political arena by forcing him to become a monk.[24]

Roman therewith evicted his father-in-law from Kiev the second time.
On the first occasion he had appointed Ingvar' to serve as his lieutenant,
but in 1204 he chose no one to rule Kiev.[25] This created a succession crisis.
Vsevolod and Roman were the two eldest Monomashichi eligible to replace
Ryurik. Vsevolod, the dynasty's senior prince, refused to leave Suzdalia, and
Roman, the next eligible candidate, refused to abandon Galich. Vsevolod
therefore adopted an irregular measure: he appointed his son-in-law,
Rostislav, to replace his father.[26] Significantly, on taking monastic vows
Ryurik renounced all his political rights so that, to all intents and purposes,
he had died. The Ol'govichi could therefore claim that his tonsure released
them from the pledge that they had made in 1196 not to seize Kiev during
his lifetime.

During the same winter that the Monomashichi attacked the Polovtsy,
Oleg and the Ol'govichi defeated 1,700 Lithuanians.[27] This, perhaps, was
the main reason why the Ol'govichi failed to help Ryurik and Roman: they
waged their own campaign. This is the first reported battle between the
Ol'govichi and the Lithuanians. It has been suggested, plausibly, that the
Ol'govichi attacked the Lithuanians in order to help the princes of Polotsk.[28]
As we have seen, the Ol'govichi had personal and political ties with that

---

[23] See above, p. 138.   [24] *Dynasty*, pp. 44–5.
[25] In both redactions of his *Istoriya Rossiyskaya*, Tatishchev claims that after Roman had Ryurik tonsured
he submitted to all the princes a proposal for reforming the system of succession to Kiev (s.a. 1203:
Tat. 4, pp. 328–9; Tat. 3, pp. 169–70). O. P. Tolochko shows convincingly that Tatishchev invented
Roman's proposal for his own political purposes ("Roman Mstyslavič's Constitutional Project of
1203: Authentic Document or Falsification?," HUS 18, nr. 3/4 [1994], 249–74).
[26] Concerning Ryurik's deposition, see s.a. 1203: Mosk., p. 101; s.a. 1204: Gust., pp. 328–9; L'vov,
p. 143. Copies R and A of the Laurentian Chronicle misplace the information under s.a. 1205
(Lav., cols. 420–1).
[27] See s.a. 1203: Mosk., p. 101; s.a. 1204: Gust., p. 328; s.a. 1205: Lav., col. 421.
[28] Tatishchev expresses this view only in the second redaction of his *Istoriya Rossiyskaya* (Tat. 3,
p. 170) and not in the more reliable first redaction (Tat. 4, p. 329). Consequently, the observation was probably not in the original text but reflected his own view.

dynasty. Oleg of Chernigov exemplified this well: his mother was a princess
of Polotsk and, in 1196, he had become indebted to the princes of Polotsk
for saving him from the forces of Smolensk.[29] Nevertheless, the possibility
remains that the Ol'govichi attacked the Lithuanians in defense of their
Dregovichi domains.

   Under the year 1204, a number of chronicles state that Oleg Svyatoslavich
of Chernigov died,[30] while others add that his son died with him.[31] It is
intriguing to discover that a son died with Oleg. As we have seen, in 1196
his son David fell at his side while fighting the princes of Smolensk. Eight
years later, the unidentified son who died was therefore a different offspring.
Surprisingly, historians have ignored this information and failed to attribute
a second son to Oleg.[32] Moreover, the news that father and son died together
bespeaks an untimely death: they probably fell in battle. Most recently, the
Ol'govichi had attacked the Lithuanians. Because of their overwhelming
victory on that occasion, Oleg may have led his brothers against those same
tribes a second time. If he and his son fell in battle, this suggests that the
princes suffered a defeat which the local chronicler was reticent to record.

   Oleg was in his late fifties when he died.[33] According to the *Lyubetskiy
sinodik*, his baptismal name was Feodosy.[34]After his wife, the daughter of
Andrey Bogolyubskiy, died in 1166,[35] he remarried. We know this because,
in 1175, he defeated his brother-in-law, an unnamed son of Yury Rostislavich
of Ryazan'.[36] The *Lyubetskiy sinodik* calls his wife Evfrosinia, but we are not
told if she was his first or second wife.[37]

VSEVOLOD CHERMNYY FORMS A PACT WITH MSTISLAV
OF SMOLENSK

The chroniclers do not identify Oleg's successor at the time of his death,
but later evidence confirms that his brother Vsevolod Chermnyy replaced
him. We have not been told the location of Vsevolod's patrimony, but we
may assume that, with the demise of Oleg's family, he appropriated his
brother's domains along with the territories Oleg himself had taken from
his elder brother, Vladimir. Thus, with the extinction of the lines of his
two elder brothers, Vsevolod's family became the senior line of the senior
branch and, because of its territorial acquisitions, the most powerful.

[29] See above, p. 219.   [30] Mosk., p. 104; L'vov, p. 144; Tver., cols. 300–1.
[31] TL, p. 287; Vlad., p. 80; Sim., p. 39.
[32] According to Tatishchev, Oleg may have had a third son named Ingor (see below, p. 269).
[33] *Dynasty*, pp. 384–6.   [34] Zotov, p. 272.   [35] See above, p. 109.
[36] See above, pp. 134–5.   [37] Zotov, p. 272.

One of his first tasks was to confirm the treaties concluded by his prede-cessor. This meant renegotiating peace with Vsevolod of Suzdalia, Roman of Galich, the princes of Polotsk, and the Polovtsy. Above all, he had to pledge loyalty to Rostislav in Kiev. According to the promises that the Ol'govichi had made not to evict Ryurik, Vsevolod's three predecessors Yaroslav, Igor', and Oleg had not attacked Kiev. Vsevolod, however, could argue that he was not bound by that pledge after Ryurik became a monk. Indeed, in the previous year he had ruled Kiev as Ryurik's substitute. Did that sojourn whet his desire to occupy the capital of Rus' in his own name?

Unfortunately for Vsevolod, at the beginning of 1205, the Monomashichi enjoyed supremacy. Vsevolod Yur'evich of Suzdalia, who became known as Vsevolod "Big Nest" (*Bol'shoe Gnezdo*),[38] not only asserted his con-trol over Novgorod,[39] but as the senior prince of the Monomashichi also commanded the loyalty of Rostislav Ryurikovich of Kiev, Mstislav Romanovich of Smolensk, and Roman Mstislavich of Galich. Since the united Monomashichi presented such a formidable opposition to the Ol'govichi, Vsevolod Chermnyy seemingly had little hope of seizing Kiev. Nevertheless, chronicle information suggests that he began scheming for Kiev as soon as he became senior prince.

On March 2, 1205, the wife of Vsevolod Bol'shoe Gnezdo entered the Monastery of the Mother of God in Vladimir where she died some two weeks later. Her death is of interest for two reasons. First, we are told that Mstislav Romanovich sent the bishop of Smolensk and a certain *Igumen* Mikhail to the funeral. Some sources claim that their mission was to ne-gotiate peace, others say that it was to beg Vsevolod's pardon, while still others claim that Mstislav wished to ask Vsevolod for forgiveness for form-ing a treaty with the Ol'govichi.[40] This report is most enigmatic in light of the earlier information that Roman had reconciled the Ol'govichi with Vsevolod Bol'shoe Gnezdo. Accordingly, it is surprising that Mstislav, a Monomashich, would have offended Vsevolod of Suzdalia by negotiating a treaty with Vsevolod Chermnyy. The inference is that, in concluding their pact, the two conspired against the prince of Suzdalia in some way.

In all likelihood, Vsevolod Bol'shoe Gnezdo offended Mstislav by giv-ing Kiev to Ryurik's son Rostislav. According to seniority among the

---

[38] He acquired the sobriquet because he had some twelve children (Baum., X). Historians also refer to him as Vsevolod III (for example, *Crisis, passim*).

[39] In March of 1205, he sent his eldest son, Konstantin, to rule Novgorod in place of his younger son, Svyatoslav (NPL, pp. 49–50, 246; s.a. 1206: Lav., col. 421). Concerning the date, see Berezhkov, pp. 88, 254.

[40] See s.a. 1206: Lav., cols. 424–5; s.a. 1205: Mosk., p. 104; L'vov, p. 144; Tver., col. 302; TL, pp. 290–1; Sim. p. 41. Concerning the dating, see Berezhkov, pp. 88, 254.

Rostislavichi, Mstislav was the next in precedence after Ryurik and in line to rule Kiev. In appointing Ryurik's son to the post, Vsevolod bypassed Mstislav. The latter undoubtedly looked upon this violation of genealogical precedence as a slight. Accordingly, the most drastic action he and the Ol'govichi might have plotted was to evict Rostislav from Kiev. Vsevolod, however, received word of their scheme and forced Mstislav to recant. In allegedly concurring with Mstislav, Vsevolod Chermnyy demonstrated a hostile inclination towards the policy of his namesake in Suzdalia.

Second, we are told that among the company of relatives who escorted Vsevolod's ailing wife Maria to the monastery was her daughter Vseslava, who had come to visit her mother and father.[41] Tatishchev alone adds that Maria, wishing to spend her last days by herself, requested everyone to depart from the monastery except Vseslava. The latter remained at her side until she died.[42] Vseslava, as we have seen, was the wife of Rostislav Yaroslavich of Snovsk, a first cousin of Vsevolod Chermnyy.[43] It has also been noted that, in 1188, she had probably accompanied her husband to Vladimir for the consecration of the Cathedral of the Assumption.[44] Although, in 1205, the chronicler does not mention Rostislav, more than likely they visited her parents together once again. Since the couple were favorites at Vsevolod's court, it is not unreasonable to assume that his fondness for his daughter and son-in-law influenced him to adopt a more lenient disposition towards the Ol'govichi and their pact with Mstislav of Smolensk.

VSEVOLOD CHERMNYY AND RYURIK FAIL TO CAPTURE GALICH

On June 19, 1205, Roman of Galich died fighting the Poles. Two sons survived him: Daniil aged four and Vasil'ko aged two. The Galicians, we are told, pledged allegiance to Daniil.[45] Nevertheless, the passing of Roman created a power vacuum that Daniil was too young to fill. During the period of his minority, rival *boyar* factions would inevitably rip the domain apart. Moreover, it was unlikely that neighboring rulers would watch disinterestedly while Galician magnates manipulated the princeling. Daniil's rule was vulnerable for another reason. He had no dynastic claim to Galich. Roman's patrimonial domain, and consequently that of Daniil, was Vladimir in Volyn'. Granted, Daniil's claim to Galich was justified on the grounds that he had the right to sit on the throne of his father, but this right was unlikely to deter ruthless rivals.

[41] See s.a. 1205: L'vov, p. 144; compare Tver., cols. 301–2; s.a. 1206: Lav., col. 424.
[42] Tat. 4, p. 331, Tat. 3, p. 174.   [43] See above, p. 185.   [44] See above, pp. 189–90.
[45] See s.a. 1206: Lav., col. 425; s.a. 1205: Mosk., p. 104. Concerning the date, see Berezhkov, p. 88.

Ryurik, we are told, threw off the monk's habit and reinstated himself in Kiev. Meanwhile, the Ol'govichi marched to Kiev, met Ryurik, and made a pact to attack Galich.⁴⁶ Their agreement was similar to the one that Ryurik had made with Vsevolod's father Svyatoslav in 1188, when they had marched against Galich. At that time, Svyatoslav had proposed that Ryurik take Galich and give the Kievan land with Vruchiy to Svyatoslav.⁴⁷ In 1205, the chronicler does not explain how Vsevolod and Ryurik planned to divide the spoils. Nevertheless, since he cryptically states that the Ol'govichi achieved nothing and returned home humiliated, they had seemingly hoped to take the town for themselves. Because the two sides had struck the deal before setting off on the campaign, the Ol'govichi had presumably promised Ryurik that, in exchange for Galich, they would support his rule in Kiev.

The support of the Ol'govichi was of the utmost importance for Ryurik. By backing him they promised not to seek Kiev for themselves and agreed to help him fight any challengers. His occupation of Kiev was precarious for two reasons. By deposing his son, Ryurik acted against the wishes of Vsevolod Bol'shoe Gnezdo. And by defrocking himself, his right to rule Kiev became a moot point. In Rus', a monk had never renounced his vows to assume political office.⁴⁸ Granted, Ryurik could argue that, just as princes coerced into making pledges might not consider themselves morally bound to honor them, he had been forced to take the tonsure and did not believe himself bound to remain in vows after the constraint was removed. Just the same, his challengers could use the monastic argument against him. He therefore needed military aid to confront rivals, and Vsevolod Chermnyy agreed to give it.

Ryurik paid Vsevolod for his support by giving him Belgorod. Vsevolod, in turn, handed it over to his brother Gleb.⁴⁹ Significantly, Ryurik did not give the Ol'govichi the town of Vyshgorod, where their grandfather Vsevolod was buried and which held the family shrine to SS. Boris and Gleb. Even though the Ol'govichi were his allies, Ryurik still believed it necessary to take precautions against them. He therefore gave Vyshgorod to his son Rostislav who drove out Yaroslav Vladimirovich. Granted, in expelling Yaroslav, Ryurik once again antagonized Vsevolod Bol'shoe Gnezdo, who

---

⁴⁶ See Mosk., p. 104; Tver., col. 303; s.a. 1206: Lav., cols. 425–6.   ⁴⁷ See above, pp. 192–3.
⁴⁸ Nevertheless, this was done on occasion in the Byzantine Empire. According to S. Runciman, "where the vows were forced unwillingly on victims whom popular sentiment could regard as wronged, there might be a return, though only among the highest; occasionally an Emperor or an Empress came back to the world and the Palace" (*The Emperor Romanus Lecapenus and his Reign* [Cambridge, 1929; reprinted 1995], p. 26). This, for example, had been the case with Empress Zoe Carbopsina in the tenth century (*Emperor Romanus Lecapenus*, pp. 49, 52).
⁴⁹ Mosk., p. 104; s.a. 1206: Lav., col. 426.

had appointed his brother-in-law to that town.[50] But more importantly, his son in Vyshgorod could act as the first line of defense against the prince of Chernigov should the latter decide to attack Kiev.

Vsevolod Chermnyy's decision to appoint his brother Gleb to Belgorod was predictable. Gleb was the next in precedence after him. From political considerations, therefore, Gleb was the obvious person to award with the lucrative post. But he was also the logical choice for another reason. He was Ryurik's son-in-law and he could use the family association to influence Ryurik's policies towards the Ol'govichi.

THE IGOREVICHI OCCUPY GALICH

Vsevolod Chermnyy's failure to capture Galich did not deter him from trying again. In the early summer of 1206, it would seem, he assembled all the Ol'govichi for a *snem* in Chernigov presumably to organize a second campaign. In telling us that Vsevolod came with his brothers and Vladimir Igorevich came with his brothers, the chronicler distinguishes between the senior branch and the cadet branch, thus indicating that the division was important. Vsevolod also invited the in-laws of the Ol'govichi to join the campaign. Mstislav Romanovich, whose mother had been Igor''s sister, came from Smolensk. Vladimir's brothers-in-law were undoubtedly among the Polovtsian khans who joined the campaign. Vsevolod Chermnyy's Polish in-laws also brought troops.[51] Although his grandfather Vsevolod Ol'govich had maintained military ties with the Poles,[52] Vsevolod Chermnyy was the first senior prince to seek their assistance in sixty years. His action was noteworthy for another reason. His grandfather had been prince of Kiev when he had asked the Poles for help,[53] and his father Svyatoslav, who arranged Vsevolod's marriage, had also been prince of Kiev at that time. Vsevolod Chermnyy, however, was only prince of Chernigov. Thus, he was the first Ol'govich whose political interests in that office ranged so far west that they warranted implicating the Poles.

We are not told why Vsevolod called the general assembly of Ol'govichi. Since his declared objective was to appropriate Galich for the dynasty, however, he would have asked all the princes to pledge their support. Undoubtedly, another purpose of the meeting was to determine to whom he would allot Galician towns. The meeting ended in concord since both branches set out under his command. Significantly, at Kiev, Ryurik joined

---

[50] Baum., V, 42.   [51] His wife Anastasia was the daughter of Casimir II (see above, p. 140).
[52] *Dynasty*, pp. 383–5, 405–7.   [53] *Dynasty*, pp. 405–7.

them with his troops. Although Vsevolod's objective was outright appropriation, Ryurik's support gave his action legitimacy. As has been noted, the lands of an extinct dynasty reverted to the jurisdiction of the prince of Kiev. Accordingly, Ryurik had the right to take away Galich from the Romanovichi and give it to the prince of his choice.

When the Galicians and Daniil heard how large a force had assembled against them, they asked the king of Hungary for help. Even so, Daniil fled to his patrimony of Vladimir in Volyn'. Meanwhile, King Andrew II crossed the mountains and, on learning that the Poles were marching against Daniil, went to confront them. He also sent messengers to Yaroslav Vsevolodovich in Pereyaslavl' inviting him to rule Galich. The king evidently hoped to draw Yaroslav's father, Vsevolod Bol'shoe Gnezdo, into the conflict. As we have seen, the latter had already intervened in Galician affairs when he had forbidden other princes to take Galich from his nephew Vladimir Yaroslavich.[54] If Yaroslav occupied Galich, the Ol'govichi could not challenge his rule without antagonizing his father. Fortunately for the Ol'govichi, the townsmen took matters into their own hands before Yaroslav arrived in Galich.

On learning that the Hungarians stood poised for battle near Vladimir in Volyn', the Ol'govichi dared not attack Galich. For many days neither side made a move. Finally, after the king negotiated peace with the Poles and returned home, the Ol'govichi also withdrew. When the Galicians learnt that the king had deserted them, they feared that the Ol'govichi might attack them while they had no prince. They therefore sent word in secret to Vladimir Igorevich asking him to rule Galich.

We are told that two disgruntled tutors of Daniil and Vasil'ko persuaded the townsmen to ask the Igorevichi for help. We can guess at least one of the arguments they used: Igor''s sons had a claim to Galich because of their blood ties to the extinct dynasty. They were the grandsons of Yaroslav Osmomysl through their mother. In getting the support of the citizens, Vladimir obtained perhaps the most important requirement for successfully occupying Galich. On receiving their invitation, we are told, he stole away at night from his brothers, rode to Galich, and occupied it. His brother Roman went to Zvenigorod. Meanwhile, Yaroslav, who was riding to Galich, learnt that Vladimir had already entered the town so he returned to Pereyaslavl'.

The news that the Galicians and Vladimir acted covertly is noteworthy. The townsmen considered it necessary to send for Vladimir in secret in

---

[54] See above, pp. 193–4.

order to avoid revealing their intention to Vsevolod. Vladimir stole away
at night for the same reason. His refusal to inform his senior prince of
the Galicians' invitation means that he acted contrary to the plan that
the Ol'govichi had adopted at the *snem* in Chernigov. In other words,
Vsevolod proposed to give Galich to another prince. As we shall see, after
seizing control of Pereyaslavl', he gave it to his son. In this, he imitated
his grandfather Vsevolod Ol'govich who, after asserting his rule in Kiev,
sought to strengthen his personal authority rather than that of his brothers.
Thus, after seizing Turov, he gave it to his son Svyatoslav and not to one
of his brothers.[55] In the same way it seems that, before Vladimir thwarted
Vsevolod's bid for Galich, the latter had intended to appoint his son to
the town. Knowing Vsevolod's plan, Vladimir withdrew secretly from the
camp lest Vsevolod discover his purpose and stop him.

The Galicians also gave domains to Vladimir's brothers. Roman occupied Zvenigorod and, as we shall see, Svyatoslav also got a town. This was
the largest exodus of princes from the Chernigov lands that the dynasty had
ever witnessed. The sources do not report the fate of Novgorod Severskiy
and the Posem'e towns after the Igorevichi vacated them. To judge from
later evidence, Vladimir and his brothers retained the right to return to
their patrimonies from Galicia.[56] It is less certain, however, who controlled
the districts in their absence. To judge from an earlier example of an absentee prince, Vsevolod probably administered the vacated towns of the
Igorevichi.[57] This consideration undoubtedly made him more amenable to
Vladimir's usurpation of Galich even though the latter had frustrated his
plan for the town.

VSEVOLOD CHERMNYY EVICTS RYURIK FROM KIEV

After Vsevolod Chermnyy failed to take Galich the second time, the chronicler reports that he placed his hope in his military might, seized Kiev, sent
his *posadniki* to all the Kievan towns, and forced Ryurik to withdraw to
Vruchiy. In this way he initiated a rivalry for Kiev between the two that
would end only with Ryurik's death. In doing so, he evidently violated two
oaths: first, the one that he had taken in 1196, when all the Ol'govichi had
pledged with Yaroslav not to usurp Kiev from Ryurik;[58] and second, the one

---

[55] *Dynasty*, pp. 366–8.   [56] See below, p. 263.
[57] In 1141, Vsevolod Ol'govich of Kiev had refused to return to his brother Svyatoslav the domains
in the Chernigov lands that Svyatoslav had controlled before moving to Novgorod (*Dynasty*,
pp. 369–70).
[58] See above, p. 226.

that he had made to Ryurik before their first campaign against Galich. The alleged declaration of the Ol'govichi that it was not fitting for a monk to rule,[59] however, implies that they believed their pledges were not binding because Ryurik's status as a monk made him an ineligible candidate for Kiev. Seizing the opportunity that the anomaly of his tonsure presented, Vsevolod Chermnyy made a bid for supreme power in Rus'.

It is unlikely that Vsevolod discussed attacking Kiev at the *snem* in Chernigov. Had he declared his intention at that time, any opportunist could have sold the information to Ryurik. More than likely, Vsevolod decided on this course of action after he failed to take Galich for his son. Taking advantage of the large force at his disposal, he snatched Kiev from Ryurik. As the senior prince of the dynasty, and because his father Svyatoslav had ruled Kiev, Vsevolod was a rightful claimant.

The chronicler's observation that Vsevolod placed his hope in his military might suggests that most of the troops that accompanied him to Galicia supported his usurpation of Kiev. Indeed, we have already seen that Ryurik was unpopular with the Kievans and the princelings of Rus'. Since they had deserted him in 1201, Vsevolod presumably had little difficulty in soliciting their support on this occasion.[60] This is testified to by the news that Ryurik's son Rostislav returned to Vyshgorod and his nephew Mstislav of Smolensk sat in Belgorod. Since Vsevolod had to authorize the appointments, the two Rostislavichi were obviously numbered among his allies.

It is unlikely that Mstislav relinquished control of Smolensk to rule the second most important town in the Kievan land. Presumably, he ruled Belgorod in addition to Smolensk. This arrangement reflected the one between Svyatoslav and Ryurik when the latter had controlled Belgorod in addition to his patrimony of Vruchiy. Mstislav and Rostislav must also have insisted that Vsevolod allow Rostislav to remain in Vyshgorod. In this way, the two Rostislavichi flanked Kiev and monitored Vsevolod's actions. Moreover, since Mstislav evidently imitated Ryurik's arrangement with Svyatoslav, he most likely asked Vsevolod to designate him the successor to Kiev. The chronicler does not confirm these observations, but there can be no doubt that Vsevolod made generous concessions to the Rostislavichi to win their support.

Vsevolod, however, evicted Yaroslav from Pereyaslavl' and he returned to his father in Suzdalia on September 22. He posed a threat to Vsevolod's control over the patrimonies of the Igorevichi because he was a rival for Galich. Although the Galicians who had invited him failed to install him,

[59] Tip., p. 85; Pisk., p. 81.   [60] See above, p. 241–2.

there was no guarantee that they would not try again. If they succeeded in expelling the Igorevichi, the latter would demand that Vsevolod return their patrimonies in the Posem'e. To obviate that possibility, it was imperative for him to remove Yaroslav from the reach of the Galicians. After expelling him, he also took an important step to strengthen his family's power in Rus'. Although Mstislav was next in line for a major domain after his elder brother Gleb occupied Chernigov following Vsevolod's seizure of Kiev, Vsevolod bypassed Mstislav and gave Pereyaslavl' to his son Mikhail.[61]

Vsevolod's success was impressive. In addition to his patrimony, he controlled Kiev, the domains of the Igorevichi, and probably the Dregovichi lands. Indeed, given his personal holdings and the allegiance he commanded from the princes of Chernigov, Pereyaslavl', Galicia, Smolensk, Turov, Pinsk, and Polotsk, his authority was greater than his father's had ever been. Notionally, he was even more powerful than the prince of Suzdalia. There was, however, an important difference between the power bases of the two men. Vsevolod Bol'shoe Gnezdo was firmly ensconced in his domain, while Vsevolod Chermnyy still had to prove his ability to fend off rivals for Kiev.

RIVALRIES FOR KIEV AND VLADIMIR IN VOLYN'

The erstwhile monk was determined to regain control of Kiev. Consequently, soon after Vsevolod occupied the town, Ryurik expelled him with relative ease. This is not surprising because the troops that had helped Vsevolod to capture Kiev had returned home and his retinue on its own was no match for all the Rostislavichi. His failure to barricade himself in Kiev also suggests that the townsmen deserted him. As was often the case, one faction probably supported Vsevolod and another favored Ryurik. The latter most likely opened the town gates to the attackers. Finally, Vsevolod must have realized that it was futile to resist after learning that the two Rostislavichi, Mstislav and Rostislav, whom he expected to bring reinforcements, had joined Ryurik. Vsevolod's first occupation of Kiev, therefore, was short-lived.

Ryurik ordered Vsevolod's son to vacate Pereyaslavl'. Mikhail, like his father, had only a small retinue at his disposal. Moreover, the townsmen were hostile to him because he had replaced their rightful prince, Yaroslav.

---

[61] Concerning the campaign against Galich, see Lav., cols. 426–8; Mosk., pp. 104–5. Compare the Hypatian and Gustinskiy chronicles, which have corrupt texts (Gust., p. 329; s.a. 1202: Ipat., col. 718). Only a late chronicle identifies Vsevolod's son as Mikhail (Nikon. 10, p. 51; see also, Tat. 4, p. 333 and Tat. 3, p. 176). Concerning the date, see Berezhkov, pp. 99–100.

This left him with no choice but to withdraw to his father in Chernigov. Not surprisingly, Ryurik refused to return Pereyaslavl' to the hostile Vsevolod Bol'shoe Gnezdo, but appointed his younger son Vladimir to the town.[62]

Vsevolod, however, refused to give up. At the beginning of 1207, he marched against Kiev, but this time his attacking force constituted only his brothers Gleb and Mstislav with their sons. The Polovtsy came in the main to pillage. Moreover, on this occasion Vsevolod did not have the advantage of surprise. Having discovered his appetite for Kiev, Ryurik was prepared for the attack and successfully kept the besiegers outside the walls. They pillaged around Kiev for three weeks but, we are told, accomplished nothing and withdrew.[63]

While Vsevolod was attempting to seize Kiev from Ryurik, the Igorevichi initiated an expansionist policy. With Galician support, Vladimir of Galich sent troops against the Romanovichi in Vladimir of Volyn' forcing Roman's wife to flee to the Poles with her sons, Daniil and Vasil'ko. Vladimir's objective, it would seem, was to secure his family's rule in Galich. Just as Vsevolod Chermnyy had evicted Yaroslav from Pereyaslavl' because the latter was a rival to the Igorevichi for Galich, the Igorevichi themselves removed Daniil from his patrimony because he presented a threat to their rule. Vladimir's action, however, differed from Vsevolod's in one important detail. He appointed his brother Svyatoslav rather than his son to Vladimir in Volyn'.[64] He therewith showed that he was not seeking to increase his personal power, but that he wished to strengthen the power of the Igorevichi as a family.

The Igorevichi drove Roman's family into exile, but they underestimated the ambition of Roman's nephew, Aleksandr of Belz.[65] Being Daniil's younger cousin, he was next in line to succeed Daniil's brother Vasil'ko. Taking advantage of his cousins' absence, he asserted his own claim to Vladimir with help from Leszek (Lestko) of Cracow, king of Little Poland. By expelling the Romanovichi, the Igorevichi had also antagonized the people of Vladimir. The latter therefore betrayed Svyatoslav by opening the gates to Aleksandr and Leszek. Thus, Svyatoslav not only lost his newly acquired domain to Aleksandr but also was taken captive by Leszek.[66] Nevertheless, his fate was not as adverse as might first appear. According to Polish

[62] Concerning Ryurik's occupation of Kiev, see Lav., col. 428; Mosk., p. 105.

[63] Lav., col. 428; Mosk., p. 105.

[64] See s.a. 1206: Lav., col. 428; Mosk., p. 105; Gust., p. 330; compare s.a. 1202: Ipat., col. 718. Concerning the date, see Berezhkov, p. 99.

[65] Concerning Aleksandr, see Baum., XIII, 1.

[66] Concerning the attack on Vladimir in Volyn', see Gust., p. 330; compare s.a. 1204: Ipat., col. 720.

sources, he and Leszek became friends, formed an alliance, and sealed their pact with a personal bond. Svyatoslav's daughter, Agafia, married Leszek's brother Conrad of Mazovia.[67]

On February 28, 1207, there was an eclipse of the sun. On seeing the omen, the chronicler reports, many pious people beseeched God to turn it into good.[68] But their prayers were not answered. The inhabitants of the Kievan land became the victims of renewed internecine strife.

Some time in the summer of 1207, Vsevolod assembled his brothers, his nephews, the Polovtsy, and the Svyatopolchichi of Turov and Pinsk. This is the first recorded occasion in over twenty years on which the Svyatopolchichi accompanied the Ol'govichi into battle.[69] Despite the hiatus in their military cooperation, the two dynasties must have remained in regular contact because they had political interests in common. The Dregovichi lands of the Ol'govichi bordered on Turov and Pinsk. Just the same, the Ol'govichi evidently never formed marriage alliances with the Svyatopolchichi as Ryurik had done. Significantly, the Svyatopolchichi did not consider their personal tie with Ryurik sufficiently strong to dictate their political relationship. Since Turov bordered on Vruchiy, they may have quarreled with Ryurik and agreed to help Vsevolod to seize Kiev on the understanding that he would give them a favorable judgment in the dispute. We are not told. Also noteworthy is the news that Vladimir of Galich came to Vsevolod's aid. This confirms that Vsevolod held no ill will towards the Igorevichi for occupying Galicia.

Instead of approaching Kiev via Vyshgorod as he probably had done in the winter, Vsevolod came via Trepol'. His plan was to disable Kiev's southern outposts and deprive Ryurik of their military assistance. Moreover, the attack evidently caught Ryurik unprepared. Outnumbered and outmaneuvered, he fled to Vruchiy even before the Ol'govichi reached Kiev. On hearing of his flight and that Mstislav Romanovich had barricaded himself in Belgorod, Vsevolod besieged that outpost forcing Mstislav to flee to Smolensk. Next, he attacked Ryurik's nephew Mstislav Mstislavich "the Bold" (*Udaloy*) in Torchesk.[70] The latter put up such a valiant resistance, however, that Vsevolod unleashed the Polovtsy onto his lands. To stop their atrocities, Mstislav capitulated. In the light of Ryurik's flight and Vsevolod's victories over Trepol', Belgorod, and Torchesk, the Kievans opened their

---

[67] A. Szymczakowa, "Księżniczki Ruskie w Polsce XIII wieku," *Acta Universitatis Lodzensis*, Zeszyty Naukowe Uniwersytetu Łódzkiego, Nauki Humanistyczno-społeczne, Folia Historica, Seria I, zeszyt 29 (1978), pp. 32–6; B. Włodarski, *Polska i Ruś 1194–1340* (Warszawa, 1966), p. 44.
[68] Lav., col. 428. Concerning the date of the eclipse, see Berezhkov, p. 99.
[69] See above, p. 159.   [70] Baum., IX, 24.

gates. In this way, "Vsevolod Chermnyy occupied Kiev after inflicting much grief on the land of Rus'."[71]

Vsevolod Chermnyy's success in Rus' goaded Vsevolod Bol'shoe Gnezdo into retaliating. On hearing that the Ol'govichi and the pagans were devastating Rus', the chronicler reports, he declared: "Let God decide my fate with them. I shall march against Chernigov." He maintained that the land of Rus' was the patrimony of his dynasty as much as it was of the Ol'govichi. He therewith admitted, contrary to his claim to Yaroslav over a decade earlier, that the Ol'govichi had a right to the Kievan right bank. At the same time, however, he intimated that the Ol'govichi had taken territories to which the Monomashichi, and he in particular, had a right. Since Vsevolod of Suzdalia and Ryurik were at odds in 1207, his intent was not to defend Ryurik's claim to Kiev as he had done in 1196, when Yaroslav ruled Chernigov. The news that he set out to attack Chernigov and not to evict Vsevolod Chermnyy is significant. It shows that he did not wage war because the Ol'govich had seized Kiev.

He was angry because, he proclaimed, Vsevolod Chermnyy "expelled my son Yaroslav from Pereyaslavl' in disgrace and brought great shame on me."[72] Thus, he wished to avenge Yaroslav's eviction and to recapture Pereyaslavl'. The chronicles do not report what happened to Pereyaslavl' after Vsevolod Chermnyy occupied Kiev the second time. Circumstantial evidence suggests, however, that he evicted Ryurik's son Vladimir and appointed an Ol'govich to rule it. Such action would have prompted Vsevolod Bol'shoe Gnezdo to declare war. After all, it had been Vsevolod Chermnyy who had kicked out Yaroslav from that town in the first place.

Vsevolod Bol'shoe Gnezdo was wont to procrastinate in launching campaigns against the Ol'govichi, but on this occasion he acted swiftly. He summoned his eldest son Konstantin from Novgorod, Roman of Ryazan' with his brothers, and David of Murom. On August 19 he set out for the river Oka to meet the princes of Ryazan'. After the latter arrived, two of the princelings accused their uncles of conspiring with the Ol'govichi against Vsevolod. On satisfying himself that the accused were guilty, he took them captive on September 22 and carted them off to Vladimir on the Klyaz'ma. Thus, on learning that his own authority was imperiled, he decided that subjugating his traitorous neighbors was more important than regaining his lost domain in Rus'.

---

[71] Lav., col. 429; Mosk., p. 106.   [72] Nikon. 10, p. 54.

The chroniclers are unanimous in stating that Vsevolod convinced himself that the princes of Ryazan' had formed a pact with the Ol'govichi. If he was correct, as was likely the case, the alliance reveals that despite the general absence of chronicle references to contacts between Chernigov and Ryazan', these existed. Interestingly enough, the last reported political dealings between the two dynasties had been in 1196, when the two sides were reconciled in the company of Vsevolod Bol'shoe Gnezdo himself.[73] We are not told at what later date they formed a pact against him, but they probably did so before Vsevolod Chermnyy seized Pereyaslavl'.

To judge from the alliances that he had formed, Vsevolod Chermnyy could call upon more troops than any other prince. In addition to the backing of his relatives from Chernigov and Galicia, he could summon the Polovtsy and the Poles. Moreover, he negotiated pacts with the princes of Turov, Pinsk, and Ryazan'. He undoubtedly maintained friendly ties with his mother's dynasty in Polotsk. After occupying Kiev in 1207, he also asserted his authority over the Rostislavichi who ruled its outposts. Finally, he controlled Pereyaslavl'. Accordingly, aside from the Romanovichi and their relatives in Volyn', Vsevolod was allied to most of the princes west of the Dnepr and to most of those south of the Oka on the east bank. Vsevolod of Suzdalia, however, took decisive steps to terminate his pact with the princes of Ryazan'.

Thanks to the punitive measures Vsevolod Bol'shoe Gnezdo took against the traitors, we obtain two useful items of news. First, we are told that he marched against Pronsk, where Vsevolod Chermnyy's son-in-law *Kir* Mikhail was prince.[74] From this we learn that *Kir* Mikhail had married a daughter of Vsevolod Chermnyy. The latter may have arranged this, the most recent match between the two dynasties, when he concluded his alliances with the princes of Ryazan'. As we have seen, Vsevolod's elder brother Oleg had also taken a wife from Ryazan'.[75] More importantly, one of Vsevolod's unidentified sisters had married Roman who, in 1207, was the senior prince of the Ryazan' dynasty.[76] Second, *Kir* Mikhail's readiness to flee to his father-in-law in Chernigov for safety and, indeed, the marital ties between the two dynasties, reveal that the princes of the two lands maintained close family relations. Consequently, the personal bonds would also have predisposed the two dynasties to form an alliance against Vsevolod of Suzdalia.

Although *Kir* Mikhail was the only prince of Ryazan' who did not join the campaign against his father-in-law, his concern that his uncles had been

---

[73] See above, p. 226. [74] Concerning *Kir* Mikhail, see Baum. 2, XIV, 28.
[75] See above, p. 135. [76] Baum. 2, XIV, 11; Zotov, p. 274.

taken captive confirms that he belonged to their camp. Vsevolod Bol'shoe Gnezdo had no doubts about his treachery. On October 18 Vsevolod captured Pronsk and took *Kir* Mikhail's wife captive. By carrying off the daughter of Vsevolod Chermnyy, whose name may have been Vera,[77] he added a personal dimension to the conflict. He could now use the princess as a bargaining chip for pressing his demands on the prince of Kiev. After devastating the lands of Ryazan', we are told, Vsevolod returned home without attacking Chernigov.[78]

According to the chronicle, when Ryurik learnt that Vsevolod of Suzdalia was devastating Ryazan' and that he intended to attack Chernigov, he rode post-haste to Kiev, drove out Vsevolod for the second time, and occupied the town.[79] Tatishchev claims that Ryurik scored such an easy victory because he assembled his troops and summoned the Polovtsy in secret so that nobody was aware of his preparations. When he heard that the nomads were near Kiev, he quickly left Vruchiy, met the tribesmen, and attacked Vsevolod. The latter failed to organize an effective resistance because he had dispatched most of his troops to defend Chernigov. Although the element of surprise and Vsevolod's lack of troops were important factors for his defeat, there was probably a third one. The townsmen, realizing that Ryurik would unleash the nomads on their lands if they refused to welcome him, probably opened the gates.

If Tatishchev's information is correct, Vsevolod fled from Kiev with his wife and children.[80] According to the chronicles, he had two daughters and a son.[81] One daughter, as we have seen, had married *Kir* Mikhail and lived in Pronsk. This meant that two children accompanied Vsevolod from Kiev: Mikhail and, as we shall see, Agafia, whom the chronicles have not yet mentioned. If Mikhail was with his father in Kiev, the latter had not sent him to Pereyaslavl'. Presumably, therefore, Vsevolod had appointed another Ol'govich to that town. Indirect evidence supports this observation. According to the Gustinskiy Chronicle, Ryurik attacked Kiev "with his sons."[82] This suggests that Vsevolod had evicted Rostislav and Vladimir from Vyshgorod and Pereyaslavl', where they had ruled while their father had been prince of Kiev.

---

[77] Tatishchev alone claims, and only in his second redaction, that the name of Vsevolod's daughter was Vera (Tat. 3, p. 180).

[78] Concerning Vsevolod's campaign, see Lav., cols. 429–32; compare Vosk., pp. 114–15; L'vov, pp. 145–6. Concerning the dates, see Berezhkov, p. 100.

[79] Lav., cols. 432–3; Mosk., p. 106.

[80] Concerning Ryurik's attack on Kiev, see s.a. 1208: Tat. 4, p. 337; Tat. 3, p. 181; compare Nikon. 10, p. 59.

[81] Baum., IV, 51–3.   [82] See s.a. 1208: Gust., p. 330.

Vsevolod retaliated some five months after losing Kiev. The attack, which he launched in late February of 1208, resembled his failed attempt in the winter before.[83] His force was inadequate. Nevertheless, his main purpose may not have been to capture Kiev but to vent his frustration against the townsmen. After all, Vsevolod was unable to use the element of surprise because Ryurik was expecting an attack. Although the chronicler claims that the Ol'govichi accomplished nothing, they must have derived some satisfaction from pillaging the environs of Kiev.[84]

RIVALRIES FOR GALICH

Vladimir Igorevich of Galich failed to join Vsevolod Chermnyy on his attack against Kiev because at that time Galicia was witnessing dramatic political upheavals. As we have seen, at the beginning of 1207 Vladimir had forced the Romanovichi to flee from Vladimir in Volyn' to the Poles.[85] Leszek kept Vasil'ko at his side but sent Daniil to Andrew II of Hungary requesting him to reinstate the princeling in Galich. Nevertheless, at the beginning of 1208 Vladimir was still in Galich because he had bribed the Hungarians and the Poles not to attack him.[86] To his distress, however, he discovered that Daniil was not his only rival for Galich.

In that year, Vladimir and Roman quarreled. The latter rode to the Hungarians and with their help defeated his elder brother. He therefore occupied Galich forcing Vladimir to flee to Putivl'.[87] As was frequently the case, the dispute was probably over domains. Since the Poles were holding their brother Svyatoslav captive, Vladimir, as the senior prince of the cadet branch, probably appropriated his brother's domain. Roman may have considered Vladimir's action to be inequitable and demanded a fair share of Svyatoslav's lands. We are not told.

Significantly, after losing Galich, Vladimir fled to his patrimony. His action is proof that the Igorevichi retained the right to return to their domains in the Posem'e after moving to Galicia. His flight to Putivl', however, raises an important question. Why did he not go to Novgorod Severskiy,

---

[83] See above, p. 258.
[84] Lav. col. 434; Mosk., p. 107. Concerning the date, see Berezhkov, p. 100.
[85] See above, p. 258.   [86] See s.a. 1203: Ipat., col. 719; Perfecky, p. 19.
[87] See s.a. 1203: Ipat., cols. 719–20. The dating in the Hypatian Chronicle for the first half of the thirteenth century is unreliable. In some instances, as is the case here, it is as many as five years off the mark. Most sources place the information of Roman's revolt under the March year 1208 or Ultra-March year 1209 (see s.a. 1208: Mosk., p. 107; L'vov, p. 146; and s.a. 1209: Gust., p. 330 which alone identifies Putivl' as Vladimir's patrimony). Therefore, the earliest possible date for the conflict was March of 1208 and the latest possible date was February of 1209.

where he had probably been living before moving to Galicia? The most likely explanation is that a prince of the senior branch, probably Vsevolod's brother Mstislav, had occupied it.[88]

Following the news that Roman occupied Galich, the dating in the sources becomes extremely unreliable. It is especially difficult to determine the correct order of events between the years 1208 and 1215 because different chronicle traditions give conflicting dates for developments in Galicia and Rus'. Keeping in mind the chronological hurdles that we must overcome, it appears that events in southern Rus' unfolded in the following manner.

On September 4, Ryurik's son Rostislav occupied Galich and the townsmen drove out Roman Igorevich. In the autumn, the Galicians expelled Rostislav and installed Roman with his brother.[89] Although all the sources place the news of Roman's eviction under the year 1210, other evidence refutes this date. Tatishchev alone states that Ryurik sent Rostislav to Galich after persuading the king of Hungary to prevail upon the Galicians to evict Roman.[90] This is probably correct. As we have seen, Roman had occupied Galich with Hungarian aid and the concurrence of the townsmen. Rostislav, a minor prince, could not evict Roman without similar backing. His father's status as prince of Kiev placed him in an ideal position to negotiate a deal with Andrew II. It also made Rostislav's candidacy more desirable to the Galicians. Since the chronicles confirm that Rostislav expelled Roman with the help of the townsmen, we may assume that the king intervened on Rostislav's behalf. As we shall see, under the year 1208 Ryurik died. Consequently, Rostislav occupied Galich in that year before his father's death.

The Galicians, however, expelled Rostislav that same autumn. We are not told the reason for their change of heart, but Ryurik's death undoubtedly prompted the townsmen to evict his son. They enthroned Roman and an unidentified brother. Since Roman had usurped power from Vladimir, it is unlikely that the latter was reinstated. If he had returned to Galicia, his senior rank would have entitled him to govern the capital. We may assume, therefore, that Roman ruled with his younger brother Svyatoslav who had returned from captivity. Thus, by the end of 1208, Roman and Svyatoslav were reinstated in Galicia while their eldest brother, Vladimir, monitored their success from Putivl'.

---

[88] Concerning Novgorod Severskiy, see below, p. 304.

[89] See s.a. 1210: Mosk., p. 108; Erm., p. 62; L'vov, p. 146; Tver., col. 308; compare Nikon., which alone gives the date of Roman's expulsion (Nikon. 10, p. 60). The Hypatian and the Gustinskiy chronicles do not give this information.

[90] See s.a. 1210: Tat. 4, p. 340; compare Tat. 3, pp. 182–3.

While the Igorevichi were having difficulty keeping control of Galicia, Vsevolod Chermnyy had a stroke of good fortune. Under the year 1208, two obscure chronicles give valuable news: "In that year Ryurik prince of Kiev died and Vsevolod Chermnyy occupied Kiev."[91] As we have seen, since Ryurik evidently helped his son Rostislav to occupy Galich on September 4, he probably died soon after that date before Rostislav was evicted that autumn. As for Vsevolod, he had captured Kiev on two previous occasions. This, however, was the first time that he occupied it without having to evict Ryurik. After he became the only claimant to the capital of Rus', his primary objective was to consolidate his rule. Following the example of his father Svyatoslav, who had handed over Chernigov to his brother Yaroslav after occupying Kiev, Vsevolod also gave Chernigov to Gleb. Mstislav, the youngest brother, probably got Novgorod Severskiy.

Vsevolod realized that his rule in Kiev was not yet guaranteed. Rostislavichi support remained questionable. From Ryurik the mantle of seniority had passed to his nephew Mstislav Romanovich of Smolensk. As we have seen, the latter had been Vsevolod's ally in the past, but more recently, Vsevolod had evicted him from Belgorod. It remained to be seen how Mstislav would respond to Vsevolod's seizure of Kiev. The latter's greatest challenge, however, was to win the approval of his namesake in Suzdalia. The most serious stumbling block to their reconciliation remained the dispute over Pereyaslavl'.

Despite these considerations, Vsevolod faced no immediate challenge. Indeed, he found himself in the eye of the storm, so to speak. During the years 1208 and 1209, the princes of Ryazan', and the Igorevichi of Galicia suffered unspeakable atrocities. Most chronicles report how Vsevolod Bol'shoe Gnezdo razed the towns of Ryazan' and took the inhabitants captive while asserting his control over the region.[92] The upheaval in Galicia was of greater concern to the Ol'govichi. If the Galicians had taken Ryurik's death as the cue for evicting his son Rostislav, the king of Hungary took their rebellion as the excuse for attacking them. In 1209, after Andrew II learnt of the "lawlessness and revolt" of the Galicians, he dispatched Palatine

---

91 Tip., p. 85; Pisk., p. 81. Tatishchev says he died in 1211 in Kiev (Tat. 4, p. 341; Tat. 3, p. 184). According to others he died in Chernigov in 1215 (for example, Lav., col. 438; Mosk., p. 110) or in 1216 (for example, TL, p. 301). Still another source gives 1219 as the date (Gust., p. 334). For an examination of the problem, see Dimnik, "The Place of Ryurik Rostislavich's Death," pp. 371–93. Compare J. Fennell, who makes the unlikely suggestion that Ryurik died in 1215 in Chernigov as a prisoner of the Ol'govichi ("The Last Years of Riurik Rostislavich," *Essays in Honor of A. A. Zimin*, D. C. Waugh [ed.] [Columbus, Ohio, 1985], p. 163). According to another view the original account probably said that Ryurik died as a monk (*v chernech' stve*) rather than in Chernigov (*v Chernigove*) (O. P. Tolochko, "Shche raz pro mistse smerti Riuryka Rostyslavycha," *Sviatyi kniaz'*, pp. 75–6).
92 Lav., col. 434; Mosk., p. 107.

Benedict Bor against Galich.[93] The latter took Roman Igorevich captive while he was washing in the bathhouse and carted him off to Hungary. After occupying Galich, Benedict, "the Antichrist" and "a lecher," tormented the people. He and his men also gave vent to their lust by defiling married women, nuns, and the wives of priests.[94]

The king sent troops to Galicia purportedly to quell the anarchy, but his henchman's conduct spoke otherwise. After he had formed his pact with Ryurik and the Galicians, Andrew II had expected the townspeople to support Ryurik's son Rostislav in Galich. They, however, betrayed him by reinstating two Igorevichi and therewith incurred his wrath. Thus, after taking Roman captive, Andrew II refused to appoint a prince to Galich even though he could have sent Daniil, who was a ward at his court. The atrocities the Hungarian troops inflicted on the Galicians suggest that the king wished to avenge himself on them for breaking their promise.

Sometime in the early part of 1210, it seems, Roman escaped from Hungary. He evidently returned to the Posem'e just like his brother Svyatoslav had done after escaping from Galicia. Significantly, Vsevolod Chermnyy did not challenge their return to their patrimonies. This is suggested by the news that, after the Galicians sent messengers to Vladimir in Putivl' admitting that they had sinned against the Igorevichi and begging him to save them from the tormentor,[95] all three brothers set out against Benedict. Their joint action also reveals that Vladimir and Roman had been reconciled.

The Igorevichi drove out Benedict from Galicia and evidently returned to the same towns that they had ruled before their quarrel. Vladimir occupied Galich and Roman took Zvenigorod. Svyatoslav, we are told for the first time, got Peremyshl'. Vladimir also gave his elder son Izyaslav the town of Terebovl' but commissioned the younger Vsevolod with the delicate task of placating Andrew II. According to the Hypatian account, Vladimir sent the king many gifts hoping to bribe him into allowing the Igorevichi to stay in Galicia.[96] The Gustinskiy Chronicle, however, claims that Vladimir

[93] Makhnovets', p. 371.
[94] See s.a. 1205: Ipat., cols. 721–2; compare s.a. 1210: Gust., p. 331. The Gustinskiy Chronicle uses the Ultra-March year system of dating for the years 1207 to 1209. It is therefore reasonable to assume that the information concerning Benedict's seizure of Galich, which it has under the year 1210, is also reported according to the Ultra-March year. Compare Makhnovets', who suggests that the correct date is 1208 (p. 371), and Perfecky, who suggests the correct date is 1210 (p. 20).
[95] The chronicler reports that the Galicians had already invited Mstislav Yaroslavich of Peresopnitsa (Baum., XIV, 2) to drive out Benedict, but he failed (see s.a. 1206: Ipat., col. 722; s.a. 1210: Gust., p. 331).
[96] See s.a. 1206: Ipat., cols. 722–3. Although the Hypatian Chronicle gives wrong dates for these events, it places Benedict's occupation of Galich under 1205 and Roman's escape under 1206. This suggests the events occurred in two different years, namely in 1209 and 1210. See also s.a. 1210: Gust., p. 331.

asked the king to hand over Daniil. But the king refused because he wanted Daniil to marry his daughter.[97] Thus, Vladimir's attempt to secure his rule against any future claims of the Romanovich failed.

VSEVOLOD CHERMNYY CONSOLIDATES HIS RULE IN KIEV

After occupying Kiev, Vsevolod Chermnyy waited for two years before proffering an olive branch to his namesake in Suzdalia. His procrastination is understandable. The prince of Suzdalia was furious at the Ol'govichi because he held them responsible for the treacherous conduct of the princes of Ryazan'. As has been noted, he wreaked havoc on their lands after taking them captive. So long as he demonstrated such hostility towards the allies of the Ol'govichi, Vsevolod Chermnyy considered the time to be inopportune for a *rapprochement*.

Two years later, however, he evidently believed that his enemy's fury had subsided sufficiently to make a proposal of peace. He was also more confident of his own position. Nobody had challenged his rule in Kiev and the Igorevichi had been reinstated in Galicia. Moreover, Vsevolod Chermnyy had a personal reason for not delaying longer. As we have seen, the capture of a family member was looked upon as an affront to dynastic honor.[98] Consequently, Vsevolod Bol'shoe Gnezdo's stubborn refusal to release Vera must have helped to incite her father in Kiev to action.

During the winter of 1210, therefore, Vsevolod and all the Ol'govichi sent Metropolitan Matfey to Vsevolod in Suzdalia requesting peace. The chronicler states that they submitted to him in all matters. In 1207, as we have seen, he had declared war on the Ol'govichi because Vsevolod Chermnyy had seized Pereyaslavl'. As part of the peace settlement, therefore, he undoubtedly demanded that the Ol'govichi relinquish control of that domain. He would also have insisted that they repudiate their alliance with the princes of Ryazan'. Fortunately for the Ol'govichi, having to terminate that agreement was not a great loss. Since its main purpose had been to unite the two dynasties against Vsevolod of Suzdalia, the *rapprochement* between the two Vsevolods nullified that need. Kiev was not a problem. Vsevolod of Suzdalia had not objected when Vsevolod Chermnyy had occupied it while Ryurik was alive, and he did not object now that Ryurik was dead. Indeed, he probably preferred Vsevolod Chermnyy's rule. The

Compare Perfecky, who says Roman escaped in 1211 (p. 20) and Makhnovets', who gives the year as 1209 (p. 371).
[97] See s.a. 1210: Gust., p. 311; compare s.a. 1206: Ipat., col. 723.
[98] See under 1196, when Ryurik appealed to Vsevolod of Suzdalia to avenge a similar insult to their dynasty (see above, pp. 220–1).

pact therefore defused any threat that the Rostislavichi may have posed if they had not yet pledged allegiance to the Ol'govich.[99]

After Vsevolod Chermnyy submitted in all matters, the prince of Suzdalia released his daughter and her female Ryazan' compatriots. Nevertheless, he stubbornly kept the princes of Ryazan' in chains and refused to forgive them. He further mollified the Ol'govichi by betrothing his son Yury to Agafia,[100] the second daughter of Vsevolod Chermnyy.[101] They were married in the following year, on April 10, 1211, in the Cathedral of the Mother of God in Vladimir. Bishop Ioann officiated while Vsevolod attended with all his court.[102]

Although Tatishchev gives erroneous data, he also reports seemingly correct information. In 1210 around Christmas, after Vsevolod of Suzdalia negotiated peace, he betrothed his son Yury to the daughter of Vsevolod Chermnyy. He sent his eldest son Konstantin with his wife and entourage to collect the bride. After entertaining the visitors in Kiev, Vsevolod Chermnyy sent his daughter to Suzdalia accompanied by his nephew Ingor Ol'govich (Tatishchev calls him Ingor Yaroslavich), by his son Mikhail (Tatishchev says his son-in-law Mikhail of Pronsk), their wives, the bishop of Chernigov, and *boyars* with their wives. Vsevolod showered his daughter with gold, silver, pearls, and fine garments. He also sent many gifts to his son-in-law: horses, precious objects, weapons, and rich apparel. After leaving Kiev on April 8, 1211, the bridal party stopped at Chernigov, where Gleb Svyatoslavich (Tatishchev calls him Ryurik Ol'govich) welcomed the bride and held a feast in her honor. On the third day, he and his wife escorted her out of the town and sent his son to accompany her as far as Kolomna. She arrived in Vladimir on Saturday April 28. The next day Bishop Ioann officiated at her marriage to Yury in the Monastery of the Mother of God. The celebrations lasted eight days. Among those who attended were the princes of Ryazan' (this is unlikely since Vsevolod Bol'shoe Gnezdo was holding them captive) and David of Murom. Vsevolod gave his daughter-in-law gold, silver, pearls, fine garments, as well as the town of Yur'ev. After presenting gifts

[99] Fennell's interpretation of the peace agreement is significantly different (*Crisis*, p. 33).
[100] The chronicles do not give the bride's name but historians generally agree that she was called Agafia; see, for example, Zotov, p. 280; Murav'eva and Kuz'mina, *Imennoy i geograficheskiy ukazateli*, p. 5; Index to Lav., p. 541; Index to NPL, p. 567; compare Baum., who calls her Agatha (IV, 52). It has also been suggested that Agafia was her monastic name (Makhnovets', p. 394, n. 6; Index to Lav., p. 541). This is unlikely since she died with members of her family in the Cathedral of the Assumption to which the Tatars set fire while storming Vladimir (see below, p. 344).
[101] Concerning Metropolitan Matfey's mission, see Lav., col. 435; Mosk., p. 108. Concerning the date, see Berezhkov, p. 103. Tatishchev alone reports that the metropolitan arranged the betrothal with Vsevolod Bol'shoe Gnezdo (Tat. 4, p. 341; Tat. 3, p. 185).
[102] Lav., col. 435; Mosk., p. 108. Concerning the date, see Berezhkov, p. 103.

to the matchmakers and the *boyars* whom Vsevolod Chermnyy had sent, Tatishchev concludes, he saw them off.[103]

If our evaluation of Tatishchev's account is correct, we learn useful information. First, we discover the existence of Ingor (Igor'), a third son of Vsevolod's elder brother, Oleg.[104] Since the latter had ruled Chernigov, his son Ingor was also eligible to rule it. Ingor was also ahead of Vsevolod's son Mikhail in genealogical seniority. As we shall see, however, Ingor would never rule Chernigov and that is perhaps why the chronicles do not mention him. Second, we learn that Mikhail and his wife accompanied Agafia. Thus, Tatishchev alone tells us that Mikhail had married before the spring of 1211. Third, Vsevolod sent the bishop of Chernigov rather than the metropolitan to escort the bride. The highest-ranking prelate in the land, it appears, had no special affiliation with the Ol'govichi. Consequently, Vsevolod sent ecclesiastical and secular representatives with dynastic loyalties to attend the marriage. Finally, because of the dynastic nature of Tatishchev's information, it appears that he obtained it from a chronicle written at the court of Vsevolod Chermnyy.[105]

The latter was the first of the five brothers to form a marriage tie with Vsevolod of Suzdalia.[106] Moreover, by 1211 he had arranged matches for his two daughters, but no source reports the marriage of his son Mikhail. Only the Hypatian Chronicle might have an allusion to it. Under the year 1211, it begins its account with the phrase that appears to be out of context: "while Vsevolod Svyatoslavich was ruling in Kiev, he had a great love for Roman's children."[107]

Aside from this reference, the sources do not report a close friendship between Vsevolod Chermnyy and Roman Mstislavich. As we have seen, in 1204, the year before Roman's death, Vsevolod had become prince of Chernigov. Although he may have established his fondness for Roman's children before that date, he was in a better position to do so after becoming prince of Chernigov. Moreover, in light of the chronicler's claim that Vsevolod had great love for Roman's children after he became prince of Kiev in 1208, we may assume that he pursued the peregrinations of Roman's second wife and his brood as she traveled from Vladimir in Volyn' to the Poles and to the Hungarians. The only children whom the chronicles have

[103] See s.a. 1211 and 1212: Tat. 4, pp. 341–2; Tat. 3, p. 185.
[104] Concerning Oleg's first two sons, see above, p. 249.
[105] For a more detailed examination of Tatishchev's account, see "Pitfalls," pp. 137–53.
[106] The last marriage alliance that the Ol'govichi had arranged with Vsevolod Bol'shoe Gnezdo was in 1186, when the latter's daughter Vseslava married Rostislav Yaroslavich, the cousin of Vsevolod Chermnyy (see above, p. 185).
[107] See s.a. 1211: Ipat., col. 729.

mentioned to date have been Roman's sons, Daniil and Vasil'ko. Other evidence reveals, however, that he also had three daughters with his first wife, Ryurik's daughter.[108]

Because the relations between Vsevolod and Roman are poorly documented, how are we to interpret the chronicler's enigmatic statement? A closer examination of the entry shows that it is incomplete. The chronicler seemingly made the observation apropos an event that he had just reported, but the text of which was lost. Indeed, the remark has the appearance of a coda, as it were, punctuating the news that Vsevolod had either performed a special favor for Roman's children, or confirmed his friendship with them. Let us see if we can find evidence to substantiate this view.

Some twenty-seven years later, in 1238, the chronicler reports that Mikhail's wife was the sister of Daniil and Vasil'ko.[109] According to the *Lyubetskiy sinodik*, her name was Elena.[110] Evidence from other sources helps to determine the approximate date of their marriage. Feodula, their eldest daughter, was born in 1212, to judge from the Life (*Zhitie*) of St. Evfrosinia, the name that she adopted on becoming a nun.[111] Tatishchev, as we have seen, reported that in April of 1211 Mikhail's wife accompanied him to Suzdalia. Accordingly, they had probably married a year or two before that while Mikhail's father ruled Kiev and during which time he also arranged the marriages of his daughters. It would seem likely, therefore, that Vsevolod's chronicler recorded Mikhail's marriage, but his closing remark concerning Vsevolod's love for Roman's children is all that has survived.

THE HANGINGS

The year 1211 was propitious for Vsevolod Chermnyy but catastrophic for his relatives in Galicia. According to the chronicler, the Igorevichi conspired to do away with the Galician *boyars* and, as chance presented itself, killed some 500 of them. In persuading the citizens of Peremyshl' to rebel against Svyatoslav Igorevich, the *boyar* Volodislav Kormil'chich accused the princes of murdering their fathers and brothers, of plundering their estates, of handing over their daughters to marry slaves, and of giving their patrimonies to outsiders from the Chernigov lands. Because of these outrages, we are

[108] Baum., XI, 1–5.
[109] Ipat., cols. 782–3. Mikhail's wife was probably the daughter of Roman and his first wife, Ryurik's daughter Predslava whom Roman repudiated (Baum., XI, 2).
[110] Zotov, p. 25; *Mikhail*, pp. 11–12.
[111] Filaret, Archbishop of Chernigov, *Russkie svyatiye*, third edition (Spb., 1882), vol. 3, pp. 120–1; Baum., XII, 3; see also *Mikhail*, pp. 11, 23; see below, p. 305.

told, some *boyars* fled to Hungary and beseeched Andrew II to let them have Daniil and to help them seize Galich. Another albeit late source tells the story differently. It claims that the Galicians conceived a hatred for their master Roman and his brothers and plotted to kill him. Failing to poison him and to hunt him down, they sent in secret to the Hungarians for help.[112] The king answered their plea by dispatching a great force with Daniil.

To judge from the two seemingly conflicting reports, neither gives an objective rendering of events. Let us therefore attempt to find the truth by peeling away the biases. Since the chronicler gives the names of several victims, there is no doubt that the Igorevichi executed certain *boyars*. The chronicler's contention that they killed 500 of them, however, is probably an exaggeration. We may therefore accept as fact that the Igorevichi, aided and abetted by their *druzhinniki*, adopted a policy of eliminating *boyar* families from Galicia. Since they never acted so mercilessly in their patrimonies in the Posem'e, why did they resort to such alleged cruelty in Galicia?

The loyalty that the citizens in the towns showed towards the Igorevichi is proof that they had friends among the *boyars*, merchants, and townsfolk. The people of Peremyshl', for example, defended Svyatoslav until Volodislav persuaded them to take him captive. The Zvenigorodians demonstrated their loyalty to Roman by preventing the enemy from taking their town and by refusing to capitulate to Daniil for as long as Roman was free. Circumstantial evidence also reveals that Izyaslav was liked in Terebovl'. At the river Nezda, a tributary of the Seret, he fought off his pursuers but lost his packhorses. Since Terebovl' lay on the river Nezda, we may assume that on fleeing from Galich, he rode east to Terebovl' to collect his family and to load his valuables onto packhorses before going to the Posem'e. Because the citizens allowed him to depart without hindrance, they did not support Daniil. The loyalty of these Galicians therefore demonstrates that many were content with the Igorevichi and that the latter did not embark on a campaign of wholesale slaughter of *boyars*.

It would have been senseless for the princes to antagonize all the magnates because they intended to make Galicia their permanent home. Rather, because a faction championed Daniil's return, the Igorevichi undoubtedly removed the hostile *boyars* from their domains and replaced them with Chernigov *druzhinniki* and loyal Galicians. Accordingly, to secure their hold over Galician towns, the Igorevichi would have directed their aggression against Daniil's supporters.

[112] See s.a. 1212: Nikon. 10, p. 63.

Significantly, Daniil's attacking forces were made up mostly of non-Galicians. Except for the Galician *boyars* who organized the revolt, the troops backing them constituted the Hungarians, the Poles, and the Mono-mashichi of Volyn'. From among the latter, Vasil'ko of Belz sent reinforcements to his brother Daniil, Mstislav Yaroslavich came with auxiliaries from Peresopnitsa,[113] Aleksandr Vsevolodovich and his brother Vsevolod brought troops from Vladimir in Volyn',[114] and Ingvar' Yaroslavich sent his son with the militias of Lutsk, Dorogobuzh, and Shumsk.[115]

Although their common objective was to enthrone Daniil in Galich, they had disparate motives. The Galician *boyars* wished to regain the privileges that they had lost under the Igorevichi. The Hungarians and the Poles hoped to profit from Daniil's rule in Galich. The Monomashichi, alarmed by the expansionism of the Igorevichi into Vladimir in Volyn', sought to drive out the brothers from Galicia for their own safety. Moreover, Daniil was the senior prince of the dynasty of Volyn' and required the support of all the local Monomashichi. Finally, since he was the rightful prince of Vladimir, this was of special importance to his cousin Aleksandr. By helping Daniil to occupy Galich, Aleksandr could remain in Vladimir.

The strategy of Daniil's forces was to capture the towns ruled by the three Igorevichi: Svyatoslav, Roman, and Vladimir. The latter's son, Izyaslav, held Terebovl' but the attackers evidently considered him to be insufficiently important to merit a detour off the eviction route. Not surprisingly, Izyaslav, whose mother was Konchak's daughter, was dispatched to bring the Polovtsy. After the nomads routed the Hungarians besieging Zvenigorod, Roman rode out to seek help from Kiev. While passing by the hostile town of Shumsk, enemy soldiers captured him and handed him over to Daniil. After Vladimir learned that his two brothers had been taken captive, he fled from Galich with Izyaslav. The chronicles tell us nothing about his second son, Vsevolod, whom he had sent to Hungary in the previous year. Most likely, the king threw him into prison just as he had earlier incarcerated Roman.

After that, the *boyars* of Vladimir and Galich, along with the Hungarians, installed Daniil on the throne in the Church of the Mother of God. The Hungarians proposed to take the three princes that they had taken captive – Roman, Svyatoslav, and Rostislav – to the king. But the Galicians bribed the commanders to turn over the captives to them. In September, we are told, the Galicians hanged the princes.[116]

[113] Baum., XIV, 2.   [114] Baum., XIII, 1–2.   [115] Baum., XIV, 1.
[116] Concerning the deposition of the Igorevichi, see s.a. 1208: Ipat., cols. 723–7; compare s.a. 1211: Gust., pp. 331–2. Historians are not agreed in which year the Igorevichi were hanged. Rybakov says it happened in 1208 (*Kievskaya Rus'*, p. 508), Makhnovets' says the year was 1210 (p. 373), others

Rostislav is mentioned here for the first time.[117] Significantly, under the year 1210, when the chronicles reported seemingly all the Igorevichi who received domains in Galicia, Rostislav was not included. This inconsistency in the accounts has led historians to disagree concerning his identity. Since he was not placed on the list in 1210, some argue that he was not an Igorevich.[118] Most, however, believe that he was the brother of Vladimir, Roman, and Svyatoslav.[119] Which view is correct?

Because the chronicles give conflicting reports about the three princes, let us examine the information in the order of the chronicles' reliability. The contemporary Hypatian Chronicle states: "the captured princes were Roman, Svyatoslav, Rostislav."[120] It does not mention their relationship. The Gustinskiy Chronicle, although younger, seemingly drew its information from the Hypatian Chronicle. It reports that "the Igorevichi, they were Roman, Svyatoslav, and Rostislav."[121] It, therefore, identifies the three as Igorevichi.

The Novgorod chronicler, much further removed from the events but evidently also a contemporary, states that, in the following year, Vsevolod Chermnyy accused the Rostislavichi of hanging "two of my brothers in Galich."[122] Historians have puzzled over this phrase because all the other sources speak of three Igorevichi. Significantly, the Igorevichi were not Vsevolod's brothers by blood. Therefore, he used the term "brothers" in the sense of allies because they had sworn allegiance to him as senior prince. But why does he identify only two of the Igorevichi, presumably Roman and Svyatoslav, as his allies? Significantly, they both belonged to his generation and both had sworn allegiance on their own behalf and, it seems, on behalf of their sons. This suggests that Rostislav had not sworn allegiance because he was still too young to do so and his father would have done it for him. In other words, Vsevolod was not claiming that only two Igorevichi

give the year as 1211 (Baum., IV, 45, 47, 48; Perfecky, pp. 21–2; Pashuto, *Ocherki*, p. 198) and Zotov believes it was 1212 (pp. 276–7). As we shall see, following the hangings in September, Vsevolod Chermnyy evicted the Rostislavichi from Rus′ for their alleged complicity with the Galicians. The Rostislavichi sought help from Mstislav of Novgorod, who attacked Vsevolod in Kiev in June of 1212 (s.a. 1214: NPL, pp. 53, 251–2; concerning the date, see Berezhkov, p. 257). Since the September in question occurred before June of 1212, the latest possible date for the hangings was September 1211. The Igorevichi, as we have seen, had returned to Galicia some time in 1210. Accordingly, the hangings occurred in 1211. This is supported by the chronicles that use the March-year system of dating and place the hangings under the year 1211 (for example, Mosk., p. 108; Vosk., p. 117; L′vov, p. 147; Erm., p. 63; Tver., col. 310).

[117] See Pashuto, who claims that only two princes were hanged (*Ocherki*, p. 198).
[118] *Istoriia*, vol. 3, p. 509; Solov′ev, *Istoriya Rossii drevneyshikh vremen* (M., 1962), kn. 1, vol. 2, Genealogical Table nr. 3, p. 737.
[119] See, for example, Zotov, p. 277; Baum., IV, 48; Perfecky, Table I; Pashuto, *Ocherki*, p. 194; Rapov, p. 120; Makhnovets′, p. 373.
[120] Ipat., col. 727.   [121] Gust., p. 332.   [122] NPL, pp. 53, 251; see below, p. 276.

were hanged, but rather, that only two of the ones hanged had special ties with him: they had become his brothers by forming moral and political relationships on the Holy Cross.

The majority of the chronicles reflect the latest and the least reliable chronicle tradition. They use the phrase: "three Igorevichi, Roman with his brothers."[123] This is the first time the chronicles call Roman's companions his brothers. Because Svyatoslav was Roman's brother through blood, this implies that Rostislav was also born of the same father. Since, however, the older chronicles do not identify Svyatoslav and Rostislav as Roman's brothers, the description is suspect. Indeed, as we have seen, the Novgorod chronicler implied that one of the three princes, namely Rostislav, was not of the same generation as the other two. In the light of this evidence, who was Rostislav?

Let us first establish the little we know about the prince. Since Daniil's allies attacked the towns of only the three eldest Igorevichi (Vladimir, Roman, and Svyatoslav), Rostislav was not a major political figure. Because the chronicles seemingly list the Igorevichi who were hanged in the order of seniority, Rostislav was the youngest. Moreover, as he was not one of the Igorevichi who acquired a domain in 1210, he was of less importance than Izyaslav Vladimirovich. Furthermore, since he did not rule a town, it means that he was probably living with his father in one of the three towns that Daniil's alliance attacked. Because, however, the Galicians believed that he merited hanging, it appears that he actively opposed them.

Circumstantial evidence supports the testimony of most sources that Rostislav was an Igorevich. For example, there is no written evidence that the prince of any other family ruled in Galicia. What is more, as we have just seen, under 1210 the chroniclers listed the three eldest Igorevichi along with Vladimir's two sons. There is no reason to believe that the list was exhaustive. Indeed, a closer look at the list reveals that the chronicler was selective in giving the names of princes. He enumerated only the eldest Igorevichi and, more specifically, those who acquired domains and one, Vsevolod, who was old enough to carry out a political assignment. Presumably, Vladimir's brothers also had sons. From this we may conclude that, since the list was selective, other junior Igorevichi were not named because they were not politically active.

If Rostislav was still a minor, why was he treated as a military captive and executed? As we have seen, the Hungarians attacked only three towns. After the inhabitants of Peremyshl' surrendered, they took Svyatoslav captive.

[123] See, for example, Mosk., p. 108; Vosk., p. 117; L'vov, p. 147; Erm., p. 63; Tver., col. 310.

Although his wife and children were seized with him, there was no other prince who, in the chronicler's opinion, merited being identified by name. Later, the chronicler reports that Vladimir fled with his son Izyaslav from Galich. To judge from this news, no other prince accompanied them. Consequently, it is reasonable to conclude that Rostislav was not the son of either Svyatoslav or Vladimir.

Roman's case was different. When the Polovtsy came to his assistance and routed the Hungarians, he left Zvenigorod to seek help. As was the practice, he would have appointed a lieutenant to oversee the defense of the town in his absence. Although the acting commander was undoubtedly a veteran *boyar*, the official commander-in-chief would have been a prince. Roman's eldest son, even though still a minor, was the obvious candidate.[124] Accordingly, he probably fell into the Hungarians' hands when they captured Zvenigorod. The Galicians would have ranked him with the Igorevichi of the senior generation and executed him because he had assumed official command similar to his father and his uncle Svyatoslav. Because of the paucity of information, however, it is impossible to confirm Rostislav's identity.

The Galician *boyars* demonstrated unprecedented arrogance in venting their spleen on the Igorevichi. As we have seen, they had demonstrated disdain for princely authority in the past when, in 1170, they had forced Yaroslav Osmomysl to submit to their will and burned his concubine on a pyre.[125] In hanging the Igorevichi, however, they imitated the Kievans, who, in 1147, had murdered Igor'. They therewith committed the ultimate crime against the princely status.

After they lost Galicia, the Igorevichi did not die out but they ceased being a political force. If the information of a late chronicle is true, Roman and Svyatoslav's wives and children were executed with them.[126] Consequently, the Igorevichi were reduced to one family, that of Vladimir. He and his son Izyaslav returned to their patrimonies in the Posem'e region and, as we shall see, Izyaslav continued to play a part in the political life of Rus'. The chronicles, however, never again mention Vladimir. Presumably, he died in Putivl'.[127]

---

[124] According to chronicle evidence, a princeling who was still a youth could officially command the defense of a town. As we shall see, this was the case in 1238, when Vasil'ko, who was only twelve years of age, defended Kozel'sk against the Tatars (see below, pp. 345–6).

[125] Ipat., col. 564; see above, p. 121.   [126] Nikon. 10, p. 63.

[127] Vladimir was in his early forties when he disappears from the chronicles. The site of his burial is not given, but he was probably interred in or beside the Church of the Ascension in Putivl' which is reported as existing in 1146 (Ipat., col. 334). His grandfather Svyatoslav Ol'govich evidently had built it.

276 *The Dynasty of Chernigov*

The loss of Galicia depleted the territorial holdings of the dynasty by reducing them to the lands of Kiev and Chernigov. Nevertheless, in appropriating the patrimonies of the two executed Igorevichi, Vsevolod Chermnyy increased his personal holdings. Moreover, even though he lost direct control over the Galician princes with the eviction of the Igorevichi, his influence in Galich did not disappear. As we have seen, the Hypatian chronicler reported that he was fond of Roman's children. Presumably, he remained on friendly terms with Daniil. What is more, he was the father-in-law of Daniil's sister and could use that tie to advantage.

VSEVOLOD CHERMNYY'S REVENGE AND DEATH

Vsevolod Chermnyy's authority was not undermined by the hangings in Galich but they were an unforgivable insult to the dynasty. If, as the Ol'govichi had declared in the past, the capture of one of their number called for requital, the ignominious murder of three of their princes called for unmitigated reprisals. The job of executing these fell on Vsevolod as the head of the dynasty. This placed him in a quandary. Although the *boyars* of Galicia were his avowed enemies, their prince was his friend.

At the beginning of 1212 Vsevolod waged war against the Rostislavichi. He kicked them out of Rus' saying: "you hanged two of my brothers like villains in Galich and insulted all of us [that is, the Ol'govichi]. There is no place for you in the land of Rus'."[128] Surprisingly, he unleashed his wrath neither against the Galicians, who had perpetrated the outrage, nor against Daniil, who had replaced the Igorevichi. He was undoubtedly swayed in his decision by practical and personal considerations. Attacking the Galicians could entail serious losses for his dynasty because the *boyars* would inevitably call the Hungarians, the Poles, and the Monomashichi of Volyn' to help them. As has been noted, his special affection for the Romanovichi probably dissuaded him from attacking Daniil.

Instead, Vsevolod accused the minor Rostislavichi ruling insignificant domains in the Kievan land of killing his brothers. His accusation is unexpected since the sources did not report that the Rostislavichi participated in the Hungarians' attacks on the Igorevichi. Did Vsevolod condemn them simply because of their dynastic association with the real culprits, the Monomashichi of Volyn'? Did they have the misfortune of becoming the victims of his vengeance because he needed scapegoats and they were the most

[128] See s.a. 1214: NPL, pp. 53, 251; compare s.a. 1213: Gust., p. 333. Concerning the date, see Berezhkov, p. 257.

vulnerable since their towns fell under his jurisdiction? Or, is there evidence that the Rostislavichi were implicated in the atrocity?

As we have seen, whenever Ryurik had occupied Kiev, he had given towns in the Kievan land to Rostislavichi. Because they were still there in 1212, Vsevolod probably concluded an agreement with Mstislav Romanovich of Smolensk allowing his kinsmen to retain Kievan towns. We are not told where these were located. In 1196, however, when Roman had helped Yaroslav of Chernigov by pillaging the lands of the Rostislavichi in Rus', he had used Polonyy as his base, the town Ryurik had given him on the western frontier of the Kievan land.[129] While some of the Rostislavichi ruled towns close to Kiev and in the Poros'e region, others would have been given domains in the western Kievan land adjoining Volyn'. Furthermore, as we shall see, in June of 1212, when Mstislav Romanovich would attempt to reinstate the expelled princelings, Ingvar' Yaroslavich of Lutsk came to help. His willingness to assist the victims of Vsevolod's vengeance suggests that he was in some way responsible for their expulsion. It appears, therefore, that a political bond existed between the Rostislavichi of Rus' and the Monomashichi of Volyn'. Accordingly, the latter may well have invited the Rostislavichi to join Daniil's alliance against the Igorevichi.

Vsevolod made a dramatic show of avenging his dynasty, but he probably also had a covert motive for evicting the Rostislavichi. By seizing their domains, he asserted his control over more Kievan territories. His action reflected the expansionist policy that his father Svyatoslav had attempted to implement in the late 1180s, when he sought to acquire Ryurik's Kievan land.[130] In 1212, Vsevolod appeared to achieve part of his father's objective. In doing so, however, he provoked the Rostislavichi. Their Kievan domains, they believed, were their patrimonies because their grandfather Rostislav had given them to their fathers. They therefore looked upon their eviction as a violation of their hereditary rights. Realizing that his action was a declaration of war, Vsevolod no doubt expected Vsevolod of Suzdalia to help him.

He was disappointed almost immediately. On April 13, Vsevolod Bol'shoe Gnezdo died and was succeeded in Vladimir by his son Yury. Therewith Vsevolod Chermnyy lost his most powerful ally. Yury's support was much weaker. Unlike Vsevolod, who had controlled his sons with a strong paternal hand, Yury's elder brother Konstantin of Rostov challenged Yury's control of Vladimir.[131] Moreover, Vsevolod had imposed his will over all the Monomashichi, in part, by the threat of his military might

---

[129] See above, p. 223.   [130] See above, pp. 192–3.

[131] See Lav., cols. 436–7; compare Mosk., p. 109. In 1211, Vsevolod had summoned his eldest son Konstantin from Rostov intending to bequeath Vladimir on the Klyaz'ma to him and Rostov to

and, in part, by the moral authority that he wielded as the senior prince of the dynasty. Yury's manpower resources were smaller than his father's had been because, before his death, Vsevolod had divided the territories of Suzdalia among his six sons. Yury also lacked the moral authority his father had enjoyed as senior prince. He was only second in precedence after his brother Konstantin. Finally, Vsevolod's passing released the Rostislavichi from their oaths of allegiance to him as senior prince of the Monomashichi. They owed no such loyalty to Yury.

Some two months after Vsevolod's death, therefore, the Rostislavichi launched a major offensive against Vsevolod Chermnyy to reclaim their lands. In addition to the troops that Mstislav Romanovich mustered from the Smolensk domains, Mstislav Mstislavich Udaloy set out on June 8, with the Novgorodian militia. Mstislav of Smolensk also summoned the Monomashichi of Volyn', who had demonstrated their hostility towards the Ol'govichi when they had attacked the Igorevichi. Consequently, Ingvar' Yaroslavich of Lutsk joined them.

The attackers' route southward is noteworthy. The news that they pillaged many districts belonging to the Ol'govichi beginning with Rechitsa shows that they came down the right bank of the Dnepr.[132] Because they did not cross over to the left bank but nevertheless pillaged the lands of the Ol'govichi, we learn that the princes of Chernigov controlled a strip along the right bank. It evidently stretched from Rechitsa in the north to the region of Davydova bozhenka, at the confluence of the Pripyat' and the Dnepr, in the south.

Vsevolod Chermnyy and his brothers confronted the attackers at Vyshgorod. Perhaps he believed it to be too risky to remain in Kiev and to rely on the townsmen's support. He evidently wished to prevent the Rostislavichi from capturing the outpost before laying siege to Kiev, the tactic he himself had used in 1207, when he had driven out Ryurik.[133] We are not told to which relative Vsevolod had given Vyshgorod. We know, however, that one brother, Gleb, was in Chernigov and the other, Mstislav, probably ruled Novgorod Severskiy. The news that the Rostislavichi captured Vsevolod's

Yury. Konstantin refused to visit his father and demanded that Vsevolod give him both Vladimir and Rostov. Vsevolod summoned Konstantin a second time, but the latter still refused to come. Vsevolod therefore assembled the *boyars* from all the towns and districts, Bishop Ioann, abbots, priests, merchants, courtiers, and all the people and made them pledge allegiance to Yury. He bequeathed Vladimir to Yury and he entrusted all of Yury's brothers to his care. When Konstantin learnt this he became angry at his brothers, but especially at Yury (Mosk., p. 108).

[132] Mentioned for the first time, Rechitsa was located on the right bank of the Dnepr, west of Gomiy (Nasonov, pp. 60, 229).

[133] See above, p. 259.

cousins, Rostislav Yaroslavich and his brother Yaropolk, and occupied Vyshgorod, suggests that one of them probably ruled that town. Since they were the next in seniority in the senior branch after Mstislav, Vsevolod most likely gave Vyshgorod to the elder Rostislav.

As the Rostislavichi pillaged the towns of the Ol'govichi on their march to Kiev, their slow approach allowed the beleaguered inhabitants to warn Vsevolod of the advancing enemy. Accordingly, he had time to summon reinforcements. The chronicler's observation that, after his defeat, he fled across the Dnepr with his brothers confirms that more princes than just the two Yaroslavichi, who were taken captive, came to his aid. He was probably accompanied by his *druzhinniki*, loyal Kievans, friendly Black Caps, and his son Mikhail. Gleb would have remained in Chernigov, but Mstislav may have come from Novgorod Severskiy. It is unlikely that the Igorevichi came from the Posem'e since their numbers had dwindled after the Galician *débâcle*. The easy victory of the Rostislavichi suggests that they greatly outnumbered the Ol'govichi.

Vsevolod fled from Kiev for the third time and sought safety in Chernigov. Although the Rostislavichi pursued him, they failed to capture the well-defended citadel. After some two weeks they succeeded only in setting fire to the outer town and in pillaging surrounding villages. Their objective, when they had set out from Smolensk, had been to win back their Kievan patrimonies. We have no evidence that they changed their intent after Vsevolod fled from Kiev. Indeed, their pursuit of the Ol'govich suggests that they remained constant in their resolve. As they pressed their attack, however, Vsevolod died.

His passing probably expedited an armistice between Mstislav of Smolensk and Gleb. The dispute over the domains of the Rostislavichi also became a non-issue because Gleb was not the prince of Kiev and therefore was unable to change a ruling his brother had made in that capacity. The main question now became control of Kiev. Even though he was the new senior prince of the Ol'govichi, Gleb could not make a bid for Kiev because the Rostislavichi had him under siege and they held Kiev.

After the Rostislavichi defeated the Ol'govichi at Vyshgorod, we are told that Ingvar' Yaroslavich occupied Kiev and Mstislav Romanovich got Vyshgorod. The Rostislavichi evidently enthroned Ingvar' before pursuing Vsevolod to Chernigov. His appointment confirms that, at that point, Mstislav had no intention of occupying Kiev. Presumably, Ingvar' was selected to serve as the caretaker prince, so to speak, until Vsevolod returned. He was chosen for two reasons: he was the most senior of the Monomashichi present and his father had ruled Kiev. After Vsevolod Chermnyy died, however, Ingvar''s status as caretaker prince ceased because the throne became vacant. Taking advantage of the opportunity that presented itself, the Rostislavichi forced Ingvar' to return to Lutsk and gave Kiev to their senior prince, Mstislav.[134]

The latter would have demanded that Gleb and the Ol'govichi acknowledge his rule in Kiev and that Gleb renounce any claim to the town during his lifetime. He also would have evicted from the Kievan land all the Ol'govichi, such as the two Yaroslavichi and perhaps Mikhail, to whom Vsevolod had given towns. Consequently, the pendulum of power swung away from the Ol'govichi once again. The Rostislavichi not only regained their patrimonies in Rus', but also seized the capital. In avenging themselves for the deaths of the Igorevichi, therefore, the Ol'govichi paid a great price: they lost Kiev and Vsevolod lost his life.

In reporting Vsevolod's death the chronicles merely state that he died after arriving in Chernigov. Mstislav Mstislavich, as we have seen, set out from Novgorod on June 8. After that, the Rostislavichi pillaged Chernigov towns along the Dnepr, captured Vyshgorod, occupied Kiev, and besieged Chernigov for two weeks. Since the hostilities probably lasted throughout the summer, Vsevolod would have died sometime in August of 1212 before Gleb capitulated. It has been suggested that he died of grief.[135] This is unlikely. He was too hardened a campaigner to die of a broken heart. Since, however, he was in his early fifties at the most, his passing was untimely. It is possible, therefore, that he died from a mortal blow that he received while defending Chernigov.

As the former prince of Chernigov he was interred inside the Cathedral of St. Saviour. In addition to being the dynasty's mausoleum, after 1203 it also housed the venerated garments of the blessed first princes of Rus'. Consequently, as the first senior prince of the dynasty to have been installed after his brother Oleg placed the garments in the cathedral, Vsevolod had the distinction of being the first Ol'govich to have been confirmed in office under the aura of the sacramentals that symbolized the divine transmission of power.[136]

AN EVALUATION OF VSEVOLOD'S REIGN

Even though he was one of the most successful senior princes of the dynasty, the chroniclers tell us almost nothing about him as an individual.

---

[134] Concerning the campaign of the Rostislavichi against Vsevolod Chermnyy, see s.a. 1212: Mosk., p. 109; compare s.a. 1213: Gust., p. 333; s.a. 1214: NPL, pp. 53, 251–2. Concerning the date, see Berezhkov, p. 257.

[135] Ekzemplyarsky, "Chernigovskie knyaz'ya," p. 239.   [136] See above, pp. 243–5.

We know, however, that his nickname was "the Red" (*Chermnyy*) suggesting that he had red hair. According to the *Lyubetskiy sinodik*, his baptismal name was Daniil,[137] and he married Anastasia the daughter of Casimir II of the Poles.[138] She and their son Mikhail probably attended his funeral, but their two daughters, Agafia and Vera, lived in distant Suzdalia and Pronsk. Vsevolod's chronicle, traces of which have survived,[139] undoubtedly contained a eulogy. In it the scribe would have described the prince's personal qualities, his cultural achievements, his love of the Church, and his charity to monastic institutions and the poor.

Moreover, had his chronicle come down to us, we may have learned the names of the churches he built. Svyatoslav (1076), Oleg (1115), and after him every Ol'govich who ruled Kiev, erected churches in at least two towns.[140] Since Vsevolod's political ambitions were in keeping with those of his ancestors, it is not surprising to discover that he probably imitated them in church building as well. Archaeologists have uncovered the remains of a church in the Kopyrev *konets* of Kiev constructed towards the end of the twelfth or the beginning of the thirteenth century.[141] As prince of Kiev, Vsevolod controlled the *artel'* or team of builders that erected churches in Kiev. If the unidentified structure was put up during his rule, he granted the artisans permission to build it. What is more, given his dynasty's association with the Kopyrev *konets*, he may well have commissioned its construction.

Architectural and circumstantial evidence also suggest that he initiated building projects in Chernigov. In 1211, an *artel'* moved to that town from Kiev. Until then, the group had worked under Ryurik's patronage erecting such churches as St. Vasily in Kiev and St. Vasily in Vruchiy. Before that, Vsevolod's father Svyatoslav had commissioned the team to build the Church of the Annunciation in Chernigov.[142] Since the *artel'* worked under

---

[137] Zotov, p. 273.   [138] See above, p. 140.

[139] See above, p. 269; see also Rybakov, "*Slovo o polku Igoreve*," pp. 199–201.

[140] Concerning the building projects of Vsevolod's great-great grandfather Svyatoslav (d. 1176), see *Dynasty*, pp. 101–4, 111–16, 120–2. Vsevolod's great grandfather Oleg (d. 1115) never ruled Kiev but he rebuilt the Church of SS. Boris and Gleb in Vyshgorod and probably built churches in Tmutarakan' and Chernigov (*Dynasty*, pp. 260–5, 419–21). Concerning the projects of Vsevolod's grandfather Vsevolod Ol'govich (d. 1146), see *Dynasty*, pp. 389–97. For the projects of Vsevolod's father Svyatoslav (d. 1194), see above, pp. 182, 207–8.

[141] P. P. Tolochko and Yu. S. Aseev, "Novyy pamyatnik arkhitektury drevnego Kieva," *Drevne-russkoe iskusstvo*, Khudozhestvennaya kul'tura domongol'skoy Rusi (M., 1972), pp. 80–7.

[142] Rappoport, *Drevnerusskaya Arkhitektura*, p. 95. Rappoport observed that the transfer of *artel's* from one town to another was associated with dynastic alliances or with the transfer of princes themselves. Thus, Chernigov master craftsmen moved to Kiev around 1139 when Vsevolod Ol'govich occupied Kiev. In like manner, during the 1170s and 1180s Kievan builders constructed churches in Chernigov because they were sent there from Kiev by Svyatoslav, the father of Vsevolod Chermnyy ("Stroitel'nye arteli Drevney Rusi i ikh zakazchiki," SA, nr. 4 [M., 1985], pp. 85–6).

the direct patronage of the prince of Kiev, it is clear that, in 1211, Vsevolod Chermnyy sent it to Chernigov.[143]

Between 1211 and 1214 it built the Church of St. Paraskeva Pyatnitsa (figure 11).[144] The identification marks of patrons and craftsmen on its bricks reveal that at least two princes helped to pay for the church.[145] The identities of these two patrons readily come to mind. The one was Vsevolod, who sent the *artel'* to Chernigov, and the other was Gleb, who ruled the town. A comparison of the Church of St. Paraskeva with that of St. Vasily in Vruchiy (figure 12) reveals that the same master builder constructed both.[146] Thus, it is ironic that Ryurik and Vsevolod, who were bitter enemies towards the ends of their lives, used the same craftsmen for erecting their churches.

Of the various buildings that the Ol'govichi hired the Kievan *artel'* to erect, the Church of St. Paraskeva was the masterpiece. It was an outstanding example of the new style of architecture that appeared in Rus' towards the end of the twelfth century.[147] Unlike the Church of the Annunciation that Vsevolod's father had built on the *detinets*, it stood in the market square. Its location suggests that it was a parish church and not a showpiece built for a prince's glorification.[148] Indeed, the patrons' marks on its bricks reveal that tradesmen and merchants also paid for it.

Archaeological evidence reveals that the *artel'* also beautified the *detinets*. It built a small masonry church,[149] a gate next to the Cathedral of St. Saviour, a second gate for the new prince's court,[150] and the unidentified

---

[143] It has been suggested, wrongly in our opinion, that Ryurik Rostislavich was the prince responsible for the building projects in Chernigov at the beginning of the thirteenth century when he was resident in Chernigov (Kovalenko and Rappoport, "Pamyatniki drevnerusskoy arkhitektury," p. 10). As has been shown above, Ryurik never lived in Chernigov and died in 1208 in Kiev (see above, p. 265).

[144] Rappoport, *Drevnerusskaya Arkhitektura*, p. 263; Rappoport, pp. 44–5.

[145] N. V. Kholostenko, "Arkhitekturno-arkheologicheskie issledovaniya Pyatnitskoy tserkvi v g. Chernigove (1953–1954 gg.)," SA, nr. 26 (M.-L., 1956), pp. 286–8; Rybakov, "Drevnosti Chernigova," pp. 89–90.

[146] Rappoport, *Drevnerusskaya Arkhitektura*, p. 95; Kholostenko, "Arkhitekturno-arkheologicheskie issledovaniya Pyatnitskoy tserkvi," p. 292.

[147] Mezentsev, "The Masonry Churches of Medieval Chernihiv," pp. 380–3.

[148] Kholostenko, "Arkhitekturno-arkheologicheskie issledovaniya Pyatnitskoy tserkvi," p. 291.

[149] Its remains were discovered in 1956 and erroneously believed to be those of the Church of St. Michael built in 1174 by Svyatoslav Vsevolodovich. Architectural evidence reveals that the church was built at the beginning of the thirteenth century, and that the remains of St. Michael have not yet been found. In 1981 and 1984, some 100 m to the southwest of the church discovered in 1956, archaeologists discovered the remains of yet another medieval brick structure that has not yet been identified (Kovalenko and Rappoport, "Pamyatniki drevnerusskoy arkhitektury," p. 10).

[150] Bol'shakov, Kovalenko, and Rappoport, "Novye dannye o pamyatnikakh drevnego zodchestva," pp. 55–6; Kovalenko and Rappoport, "Pamyatniki drevnerusskoy arkhitektury," p. 10.

Figure 11   The reconstructed Church of St. Paraskeva Pyatnitsa, Chernigov

Figure 12   The reconstructed Church of St. Vasily, Vruchiy

structure found under the Church of St. Catherine.[151] Moreover, it erected
a church similar to that of St. Paraskeva in the Severskiy Monastery, an institution that the chronicles never mention.[152] In transplanting the *artel'* to
Chernigov, Vsevolod also enabled other Ol'govichi to conscript its services.
A number of unidentified princes commissioned it to construct churches
in Novgorod Severskiy, Putivl', Trubetsk, and Vshchizh.[153]

Vsevolod's political accomplishments were also significant. Following
the death of his father Svyatoslav in 1194, he was the first senior prince to
make a bid for Kiev. He did so because he had the requisite seniority, he
had the necessary manpower, and he was not constrained by any pledges
that he had made to rival challengers.

[151] Bol'shakov, Kovalenko, and Rappoport, "Novye dannye o pamyatnikakh drevnego zodchestva,"
pp. 53–4.
[152] The remains of the church were discovered in the early 1980s. The Severskiy Monastery was
located on the Severyanskaya ulitsa (L. N. Bol'shakov and V. P. Kovalenko, "Novyy pamyatnik
Drevnerusskogo zodchestva v Chernigove," *Pamyatniki Kul'tury Novye Otkrytiya*, Ezhegodnik 1988
[M., 1989], pp. 541–3; Bol'shakov, Kovalenko, and Rappoport, "Novye dannye o pamyatnikakh
drevnego zodchestva," pp. 54–5).
[153] Rappoport, pp. 47–9 and his "Arkhitektura," *Drevnyaya Rus', Gorod, zamok, selo*, B. A. Kolchin (gen.
ed.), in series *Arkheologiya SSSR*, B. A. Rybakov (gen. ed.) (M., 1985), p. 163; V. P. Kovalenko and
P. A. Rappoport, "Etapy razvitiya drevnerusskoy arkhitektury Chernigovo-Severskoy zemli," *Russia
Mediaevalis* 7, 1 (München, 1992), pp. 53–4. Concerning the church in Putivl', see Bohusevych,
"Rozkopky v Putyvl's'komu kremli," pp. 165–71.

How did Vsevolod's successes as prince of Kiev compare with those of his predecessors? As it has been shown elsewhere, at the zenith of his power Vsevolod's great-great grandfather, Svyatoslav Yaroslavich (d. 1076), controlled most of Rus'. In addition to Chernigov which included Tmutarakan', Murom, and Ryazan', he asserted his rule over Kiev, Novgorod, Smolensk, the Beloozero region, Turov, and Vladimir in Volyn'.[154] Vsevolod's grandfather, Vsevolod Ol'govich (d. 1146), usurped Chernigov and Kiev. Moreover, he appointed his lieutenants to Novgorod, Turov, and Vladimir in Volyn'. In addition, he commanded the loyalty of the princes of Galicia and Polotsk, and could summon forces from the Poles and the Polovtsy.[155] Vsevolod Chermnyy never matched the successes of these two ancestors.

Compared to his father's sojourn in Kiev that lasted almost thirteen years, Vsevolod Chermnyy's stay of just over three years was short. Nevertheless, he controlled Kiev unchallenged for almost as long a period of time as his most eminent predecessor, Svyatoslav Yaroslavich. Even though the latter had ruled Kiev for just under four years (1073–76), he had greater power than any of his descendants were ever to hold. The duration of a prince's stay in Kiev, therefore, is not a fair measure of his political success. Accordingly, it can be shown that even though Vsevolod Chermnyy's stay in Kiev was only a third as long as that of his father, it was more successful.

Svyatoslav's greatest achievement, as we have seen, was to rule Kiev, but he did not control the Kievan land. Vsevolod Chermnyy attained greater power. At the peak of his career, from 1208 to 1212, he ruled Kiev and the Kievan land. He also scored two unprecedented victories. In 1206, he asserted control over Galicia through the Igorevichi and in the same year appointed his son to Pereyaslavl'. Consequently, while he was senior prince, the Ol'govichi for the first time established their rule over lands stretching from Galicia through Kiev and Pereyaslavl' to Chernigov. This control made him, notionally at any rate, the most powerful prince in Rus'. He lost Pereyaslavl' almost immediately, however, and after five years the Igorevichi lost Galicia. Despite these losses, Vsevolod's power before his death was still greater than that of his father had been.

How successful was Vsevolod in terms of his own goals? Acquiring Galicia was his boldest venture: he evidently hoped to add it permanently to the dynasty's possessions. His inability to do so was his greatest failure. It is unlikely that he had the same objective for Pereyaslavl'. His goal there, most likely, was to control it for as long as was necessary to keep out Yaroslav

<hr />

[154] *Dynasty*, pp. 131–2.   [155] *Dynasty*, pp. 414–15.

Vsevolodovich from Rus' because he was a rival to the Igorevichi in Galich. As for Kiev, we have no evidence that he wished to appropriate it for the Ol'govichi and hand it over to his brother Gleb in the manner that his grandfather Vsevolod had designated Igor' his successor. Instead, Vsevolod probably made a pact with Mstislav of Smolensk to the effect that the latter would support his rule in Kiev and Mstislav would succeed him. In the light of his objectives, therefore, Vsevolod's greatest success was to rule Kiev until his death.

Vsevolod has been described as a "typical representative of the restless and insidious Ol'govichi" whose "excessive lust for power" led to his downfall.[156] Is this a fair evaluation? A look at the balance sheet of his career shows that he was similar to a number of his relatives but different from others. On the one hand, he was unlike his three immediate predecessors, Oleg, Igor', and Yaroslav, who made no effort to seize Kiev but contented themselves with ruling Chernigov. On the other hand, he resembled his great-great-grandfather Svyatoslav, his grandfather Vsevolod, and his father Svyatoslav, who all took Kiev by force. He was more ambitious than his father, however, but not as Machiavellian as his grandfather. Did this make him a typical representative of the Ol'govichi? Perhaps it is more accurate to say that he was typical of the handful of senior princes who seized control of Kiev in the name of the dynasty.

Was Vsevolod restless? His rivalries with Ryurik seemingly justified this description. But was such behavior exceptional? If being restless meant championing his dynasty's right to rule Kiev, then the prince of any dynasty who repeatedly attempted to assert his dynasty's claim could be deemed restless. Ryurik was by far the outstanding example from among Vsevolod's contemporaries. He sought to seize Kiev for a longer period of time, antagonized more rivals, and was evicted on the greatest number of occasions. It could be argued, therefore, that restlessness was a trait of princes who vied for control of Kiev, no matter to which dynasty they belonged.

Was Vsevolod insidious? The available evidence speaks against this. Unlike his grandfather, he did not usurp Chernigov but attained seniority according to the natural order of genealogical progression. Moreover, he never used deceit to achieve his ends. In 1206, when he attacked Galich, he had the backing of all the Ol'govichi and many Monomashichi. After Ryurik defrocked himself, Vsevolod and other princes believed that he was unacceptable as a ruler so that Vsevolod had the right to evict him from Kiev. After the Igorevichi pre-empted his bid for Galich he refused to

[156] Ekzemplyarsky, "Chernigovskie knyaz'ya," pp. 238, 239.

avenge himself. Significantly, on failing to reclaim Kiev after Ryurik drove him out the second time, he curbed his ambition until his rival's death. Vsevolod's equanimity bespeaks qualities of constraint and fair play that are conspicuously lacking in an insidious person.

Did Vsevolod's excessive lust for power lead to his downfall? The accusation presumably refers to his eviction of the Rostislavichi from Rus' which led to his defeat. This, his seemingly most ruthless measure, pales before the acts of some allegedly righteous Monomashichi. Adopting an unprecedented course of action in Rus', Roman forced Ryurik to renounce the throne of Kiev and incarcerated him in a monastery. Vsevolod of Suzdalia blinded Mstislav and Yaropolk because they threatened his rule. Moreover, he devastated the lands of Ryazan', took the princes, princesses, and Bishop Arseny captive, and kept many in chains until his death. Vsevolod Chermnyy, it is true, died during a war which he had precipitated under the guise of satisfying his dynasty's honor, but also with the aim of seizing more land. Roman, however, also fell in battle in pursuit of territorial aggrandizement. Therefore, to accuse Vsevolod of behaving in a manner beyond the bounds of "normal" princely conduct is to profess a myopic view of inter-princely relations in Rus'.

A TIME OF TEMPORIZING

Following the dynamic career of Vsevolod Chermnyy, the Ol'govichi faced a period of political doldrums. They had to wait for one of their number with the required genealogical seniority, the necessary personal prowess, and military resources to emerge at the optimum time to seize the capital of Rus'. The current generation had had its chance and was not likely to get another. When Gleb capitulated to Mstislav Romanovich, he committed himself and his brother Mstislav to playing second fiddle to the Rostislavichi.

In 1215 Gleb Svyatoslavich, who had succeeded Vsevolod Chermnyy to Chernigov, married his daughter to Vladimir, the brother of Yury of Vladimir.[157] This was a useful alliance because two years earlier Yury had appointed Vladimir to Pereyaslavl'.[158] In this way Gleb established a personal tie with the second dynasty that controlled a domain adjacent to Chernigov. Since his wife was a daughter of Ryurik Rostislavich, he already had a family bond with the Rostislavichi who ruled Kiev and Smolensk.[159] Unfortunately for Gleb, the alliance with his southern neighbor suffered a

---

[157] Lav., col. 438; Mosk., p. 110. In 1194, as we have seen, Gleb's daughter Evfimia was taken away as a bride for a Greek prince (see above, p. 208).
[158] Lav., col. 438.　　[159] Concerning Gleb's marriage to Ryurik's daughter, see above, p. 152.

severe blow later in the year. The Polovtsy attacked Pereyaslavl' and took
Vladimir captive when he rode out to confront them.[160]
For the past two decades the princes of Rus' had frequently summoned
the nomads to their aid. In 1203, as we have seen, Ryurik and the Ol'govichi
used them to sack Kiev. Later, Vsevolod Chermnyy and Ryurik employed
them in their battles against each other. In 1211, Izyaslav Vladimirovich summoned them to fight the Galicians.[161] Four years later, however, the Polovtsian attack on Pereyaslavl' was only the second recorded in five years.[162]
There may have been others that the chronicler did not report, but he considered this one worth noting because the nomads defeated Vladimir. His
capture and the decimation of his troops alerted Gleb and the Ol'govichi
to the danger of possible Polovtsian attacks on their Zadesen'e and Posem'e
regions.

The year 1216 witnessed an important upheaval in Suzdalia which indirectly implicated the Ol'govichi. On March 1 the Rostislavichi, including Mstislav Mstislavich Udaloy of Novgorod and Vladimir Ryurikovich
of Smolensk, joined Konstantin of Rostov against his brother Yaroslav because the latter had challenged Mstislav Udaloy for Novgorod. Yaroslav was
joined by Yury of Vladimir, their brothers, and the troops from Suzdalia.
On April 21, the two sides clashed at the river Lipitsa near Yur'ev Pol'skiy.
Konstantin won the day, deposed Yury, and assumed the office of senior
prince.

Their family ties evidently dictated Konstantin and Yury's alliances.
Konstantin had married the daughter of Mstislav Romanovich of Kiev
so he sided with the Rostislavichi.[163] Yury's marriage to Agafia, the daughter of Vsevolod Chermnyy, inclined him towards the Ol'govichi. Despite
his defeat, it appears that the Ol'govichi faced no serious danger. Gleb's
personal tie with the Rostislavichi may have helped to curb their vindictiveness. As has been noted, through his marriage to Ryurik Rostislavich's
daughter, Gleb was the brother-in-law of Vladimir of Smolensk.

After the battle, soldiers from Smolensk found a copy of the pact that
Yury and Yaroslav had drawn up in anticipation of their victory. It stated
how they would partition the lands of Rus' with their allies. In addition
to keeping Vladimir, Yury proposed to appropriate Konstantin's Rostov.

---

[160] Lav., col. 438; Mosk., p. 110.
[161] To judge from the silence of the chronicles, after the death of Svyatoslav Vsevolodovich, in 1194, the
Ol'govichi conducted no campaigns against the Polovtsy. In 1201, however, Roman led a successful
raid against them (s.a. 1202: Lav., col. 418) and, in 1204, he and Ryurik joined forces against the
tribesmen (see above, p. 277).
[162] The earlier attack was in 1210 (Lav., col. 435.)   [163] Baum., X, 1.

Yaroslav intended to seize Novgorod from Mstislav Udaloy. Svyatoslav, their younger brother, would take Smolensk from Vladimir Ryurikovich. The Vsevolodovichi would also occupy Galich. Significantly, they planned to evict Mstislav Romanovich from Kiev and give it to the Ol'govichi. Their scheme, however, came to naught.[164]

Although the victors might have inferred from Yury's plan for Gleb's occupation of Kiev that the latter had been privy to the scheme, there is no evidence that Yury advised Gleb of the plan. Indeed, since the Ol'govichi did not attack Kiev while Yury was fighting the Rostislavichi, they seemingly were not party to his plot to evict Mstislav. In their view, it seems, the battle at the Lipitsa was an in-house quarrel of the Monomashichi: Konstantin and Yury fought for supremacy in Suzdalia, and Yaroslav fought Mstislav Udaloy for control of Novgorod. Since the Ol'govichi were drawn into it seemingly against their will, Konstantin and the Rostislavichi demanded no compensation from them. Significantly, on September 11, 1217, Konstantin designated Yury his successor and gave him Suzdal'.[165] After their *rapprochement*, Konstantin would also have reestablished amicable relations with the Ol'govichi.

The year 1217 witnessed an unprecedented atrocity. In his greed to gain control of all the Ryazan' lands, we are told, Gleb Vladimirovich plotted with his brother Konstantin to kill their cousins and their younger brother. On July 20, therefore, he invited them to a feast and butchered them.[166] One of the six murdered princes was *Kir* Mikhail who had married Vsevolod Chermnyy's daughter Vera. Their son Vsevolod escaped the massacre and succeeded his father in Pronsk.[167] After that, the Ol'govichi continued to have friendly relations with Ingvar', the new prince of Ryazan'.

In the following year, the balance of power shifted once again in Suzdalia, but on this occasion peacefully. On February 2, 1218, Konstantin died and his brother Yury succeeded him.[168] The Ol'govichi would have welcomed the transfer of power since their in-law was once again back at the helm among the Vsevolodovichi. It remained to be seen, however, if Yury would renew the expansionist policy that he had failed to implement two years earlier.

In the same year, Galicia became the focus of princely rivalry. Mstislav Udaloy and his cousin Vladimir Ryurikovich set off for Galich, captured

[164] Ak. sp., cols. 492–502; Sof. 1, pp. 193–201; N4, pp. 186–97; compare Mosk., pp. 111–14; NPL, pp. 55–7, 254–7. For a more detailed discussion of the battle on the Lipitsa river, see *Crisis*, pp. 48–9.
[165] Ak. sp., cols. 439–40; Mosk., p. 115.   [166] Lav., cols. 440–1; Mosk., p. 115.
[167] Baum. 2, XIV, 40.   [168] Lav., cols. 442–4; Mosk., p. 116.

it, and took Kalman, the son of Andrew II, captive.[169] Mstislav strengthened his grip on the town by giving his daughter Anna in marriage to Daniil Romanovich, another claimant for Galich. In 1219, following a misunderstanding between Mstislav, Daniil, and Leszek of Cracow, the latter summoned the Hungarians who ousted Mstislav and reinstated Kalman. In defending his claim, Mstislav was supported by all the princes of Rus' and Chernigov.[170] Later, in the winter of 1220, he and his allies once again attacked Kálmán but, after a futile siege, withdrew.[171]

The news that, in 1219, Gleb and the Ol'govichi helped Mstislav Udaloy to defend Galich suggests that they assisted him in all his battles with the Hungarians. Their collaboration therefore ran counter to the spirit of Yury's partition plan in which the Ol'govichi had been the enemies of the Rostislavichi. This evidence confirms that, after Yury became senior prince of Vladimir for the second time, he and the Ol'govichi dropped whatever ambitions they may have had against the Rostislavichi.

The cooperation of the Ol'govichi with the Rostislavichi tells us more. In 1206, when the Vsevolod Chermnyy had aspired to seize Galich for his family, the Rostislavichi had served as his auxiliaries. Over a decade later, the reversed roles of the two dynasties testify to their changed fortunes. The chronicler's failure to identify any of the Ol'govichi by name, even Gleb their senior prince, further confirms the subordinate status to which they had fallen. Nevertheless, it is possible that part of the reason why the Rostislavichi enjoyed places of prominence in the accounts was that their chronicle was used by the authors of later compilations whereas the chronicle of the Ol'govichi was either ignored or lost.

Under the year 1220 we find a trace of such a chronicle. The Chernigov tenor of the news leaves little doubt that it was written by a scribe working for the prince of that town. In the winter, we are told, the Lithuanians pillaged the lands of the Ol'govichi. Mstislav Svyatoslavich set out in pursuit from Chernigov, caught the raiders, killed them all, and retrieved the plundered goods.[172] We are not told what territory the Lithuanians pillaged. It is unlikely, however, that they crossed the Dnepr to the east bank. Since the marauders probably made lightning strikes, the Dnepr would have presented too great an obstacle to cross quickly with booty, prisoners, and

---

[169] See s.a. 1219: NPL, pp. 59, 260–1; Mosk., p. 116. Concerning the date, see Berezhkov, p. 260.

[170] See s.a. 1213: Ipat., cols. 732–5; Perfecky, pp. 24–6; Makhnovets', pp. 375–7. The chronology of events in this chronicle is chaotic for the beginning of the thirteenth century. The investigator must rely, in large part, on the sequence of events as other chronicles describe them even though their reports are not as detailed.

[171] Mosk., p. 118; L'vov, p. 151.

[172] Mosk., pp. 117–18; L'vov, p. 151; Erm., p. 68; compare s.a. 1221: Gust., p. 334.

livestock. Accordingly, the area they most likely attacked lay between their lands and the rivers Dnepr and Pripyat'. That is, they would have pillaged Dregovichi settlements or districts that the Rostislavichi had plundered in 1212, when they had marched south via Rechitsa to Vyshgorod.[173]

The main reason why the chronicler reported the event was undoubtedly to extol Mstislav. This may well have been the first campaign that he commanded as prince of Chernigov and he therefore directed his scribe to record the victory. The news that Mstislav was commander-in-chief is proof that Gleb had died and that Mstislav had replaced him as senior prince. Gleb was last mentioned under 1215, when his daughter had married Vladimir of Pereyaslavl'. Consequently, Gleb died between that event and 1220. According to the *Lyubetskiy sinodik*, his baptismal name was Pakhomy and his wife's name was Anastasia.[174] Two daughters, Vladimir's wife and Evfimia, who had married a Greek prince, survived him.[175] The son Mstislav has not yet been mentioned by the chronicles.

MSTISLAV SVYATOSLAVICH AS SENIOR PRINCE

Mstislav Svyatoslavich was not an exceptional ruler and he would not distinguish himself by seizing the capital of Rus' for his dynasty. His reign, however, would be memorable because he and other Ol'govichi, along with most of their troops, would fall victim to the Tatar lance. Before that catastrophe, however, Mstislav served the prince of Kiev as a loyal ally.

In 1221, according to a number of chronicles, Mstislav Udaloy took Prince Kálmán captive and seized Galich.[176] Although Tatishchev is the only source to report that Mstislav of Chernigov participated in the campaign, circumstantial evidence supports his claim.[177] As we have seen, the Ol'govichi had assisted Mstislav Udaloy in his battles for Galich in the three previous years. It is therefore likely that, in 1221, they helped him again. Their participation shows that they remained loyal to Mstislav Romanovich of Kiev in helping his dynasty assert its expansionist policy.

In the following year, unease spread over the land as harbingers of evil days to come manifested themselves. Many forests and swamps caught fire in the dry summer. They produced so much smoke it was impossible to see any distance. It was as if a low fog hovered over the land making it

---

[173] See above, p. 278.   [174] Zotov, p. 273.
[175] See above, p. 208.   [176] Lav., col. 445; Mosk., p. 118.
[177] Tat. 4, pp. 359–60; Tat. 3, pp. 210–12. Since Tatishchev reports Mstislav's presence in both redactions, it is likely that he did not fabricate the information.

impossible for birds to fly. They fell helplessly to the ground and died.[178]
A comet also appeared portending ruin. "It foreshadowed the invasion of
the godless Tatars, who, until then, were unknown in Rus'."[179]

In the spring of 1223, the Tatars arrived on the frontiers of Rus'.[180] The
Hypatian Chronicle account, which drew information from a Chernigov
source, will serve as the basis for our investigation.[181] We are told that an
unknown enemy, "the godless Moabites called the Tatars," attacked the
Polovtsy. Unable to withstand the onslaught, they fled to Rus' warning the
princes that if they refused to send aid the same fate would befall them.[182]
All the princes assembled in Kiev and agreed that it was better to confront
the Tatars on foreign soil than to wait for them to attack.

At that time, Mstislav Romanovich ruled Kiev, Mstislav Svyatoslavich
had Kozel'sk and Chernigov, and Mstislav Mstislavich Udaloy was in
Galich. They were the main elders in Rus'. The only elder who failed
to come was Yury Vsevolodovich of Suzdalia. The junior princes were
as follows: Daniil Romanovich of Volyn', Mikhail the son of Vsevolod
Chermnyy, Vsevolod the son of Mstislav Romanovich of Kiev, and others.
In 1097 all the princes of Rus' had met in council to consolidate their defense against an earlier threat from the steppe, the Polovtsy.[183] In 1223, an
all-Rus' assembly of princes once again bespoke their unity of purpose.

The chronicler singles out two Ol'govichi. The first was Mstislav the
senior prince. We learn for the first time that he owned Kozel'sk on the
river Zhizdra, a tributary of the Oka in the Vyatichi lands. As we have
seen, the latter had been the patrimony of his great-grandfather Oleg, who

---

[178] See s.a. 1223: Lav., col. 447; Mosk., p. 121.

[179] Gust., p. 334; compare s.a. 1223: Lav., col. 447; Mosk., p. 121. Concerning the comet that appeared
in the autumn of 1222 and reached its perihelion on September 15, see Berezhkov, p. 107.

[180] During the middle of the twelfth century, the Tatars defeated the neighboring tribe of Mongols and
became one of the leading tribes in Mongolia. Since the future emperor Chingis Khan was born
to a Mongol tribe, all the tribes became known as the Mongols after he united them. In Western
Europe, the term Tatars (in the form Tartars) was used generically to identify all the Mongol
invaders, but the inhabitants of Rus' kept the name Tatars (*Tatary*). For a detailed explanation,
see G. Vernadsky, *The Mongols and Russia* (New Haven, 1953), pp. 11–12. Concerning the Tatar
conquests before coming to Rus', see *Crisis*, pp. 63–4.

[181] Four extant accounts reflect the original descriptions of the invasion. The Laurentian Chronicle is
the most removed from the event. The Novgorod First Chronicle is more accurate and uses a Kievan
source. The Hypatian Chronicle uses Chernigov and Volynian–Galician sources. The Sofiyskiy First
Chronicle draws from all the above but also from a non-extant chronicle from Smolensk (J. Fennell,
"The Tatar Invasion of 1223: Source Problems," FOG, Band 27 [Berlin, 1980], pp. 18–31, and his
Crisis, pp. 64–5).

[182] According to the Novgorod account, Khan Kotyan, the father-in-law of Mstislav Udaloy, came to
Galich bearing gifts of "horses and camels and buffaloes and girls" for his son-in-law and the other
princes of Rus' hoping to persuade them to help the Polovtsy against the Tatars (s.a. 1224: NPL,
pp. 62, 265).

[183] *Dynasty*, pp. 207–23.

bequeathed it to his son Vsevolod. Mstislav's father Svyatoslav was the first to divide up the Vyatichi lands among several sons. Thus, Mstislav's brother Oleg got the district around Lopasna,[184] and Vsevolod Chermnyy received the region of Bryn on the river Bryn that flows into the Zhizdra.[185] Gleb and Vladimir's domains have not been reported. Since Karachev was their father's patrimony, however, he probably bequeathed it to Vladimir as his eldest son. Mstislav's patrimony clearly was Kozel'sk, which he kept after occupying Chernigov.

The second Ol'govich, Mikhail, attended the meeting as Mstislav's successor. His status as second in seniority is revealing. According to the system of lateral succession, seniority passed from Mstislav to the next family in the senior branch, the Yaroslavichi, Rostislav and Yaropolk. Since Mikhail bypassed them, they had died. Moreover, Igor''s sons from the cadet branch who also had prior claims to Mikhail were dead. Finally, since seniority passed from Mstislav to his nephews' generation, among whom Mikhail was not the eldest, we learn that his elder cousins, the sons of Vladimir and Oleg, were either dead or *izgoi*.[186] Because of his status as the second in seniority, Mikhail probably occupied Novgorod Severskiy when Mstislav moved to Chernigov. Moreover, after the death of his father who had evidently received the district of Bryn as his patrimony, it had passed on to Mikhail as his inheritance.

THE KALKA BATTLE

The princes of Rus' set out against the Tatars in April. At the Varangian Island (that is, Zarub) on the right bank of the Dnepr, the Polovtsy met them.[187] Troops from Kiev, Smolensk, Galicia, Volyn', and all the Ol'govichi also came. In addition to Mstislav and Mikhail, the chroniclers single out Oleg of Kursk, two unidentified princes from Putivl' and Trubetsk, and Mstislav's son. The total response of the Ol'govichi to the alarm bells

---

[184] See above, pp. 134–5.

[185] For a description of the archaeological site, see *Zemlya Vyatichey*, p. 153. In 1229, Bryn was evidently part of Mikhail's patrimony (NPL, pp. 67–8; 274; *Mikhail*, p. 25; see below, p. 311), therefore, the same region had probably been the patrimony of his father, Vsevolod Chermnyy.

[186] According to Tatishchev, in 1211 a prince named Ingor' (Igor'), allegedly the son of Mikhail's uncle Oleg, may have been ahead of Mikhail in seniority ("Pitfalls," pp. 143–5). Because of the silence of the chronicles, however, he must have died before 1223.

[187] According to the Novgorod account, when the princes arrived at Zarub they met Tatar envoys who attempted to convince them that the Polovtsy were their common enemies. The princes refused to believe them and killed the envoys. The Tatars allegedly sent a second delegation repeating their peaceful intent. On this occasion, the princes let the envoys depart (NPL, pp. 62, 265–6; Mosk., p. 119).

from Kiev is further attested to by Mikhail's presence. Before departing
on a campaign, the senior prince normally left his immediate subordinate
behind to defend Chernigov. Since Mstislav considered it more important
to take Mikhail with him, we may conclude that he ordered all the princes
of fighting age to join him. In 1184 Yaroslav of Chernigov and Igor' of
Novgorod Severskiy had refused to march down the Dnepr against the
Polovtsy because it would have taken them too far from their domains.
In 1223, after the Tatars had removed the Polovtsian threat, the Ol'govichi
agreed to leave their domains and travel to the furthest limits to confront
the new enemy.

The chronicler singles out three towns from the cadet branch: Kursk,
Putivl', and Trubetsk. In 1185, as we have seen, Igor''s younger brother,
Vsevolod, had ruled Trubetsk. Since the chronicle reports that in 1223 the
local prince commanded the town's troops, he was probably an unidentified
son of Vsevolod.[188] In 1211, when Igor''s son Vladimir had fled from Galich,
he returned to Putivl'. Since Vladimir's son Izyaslav escaped with him, the
latter inherited the town from his father. The prince of Putivl' who fought
the Tatars, therefore, was probably Izyaslav. Igor''s eldest brother, Oleg, had
received Kursk and Ryl'sk from his father.[189] In 1185, as we have seen, his
son Svyatoslav had ruled Ryl'sk when he had accompanied Igor' against
the Polovtsy. Accordingly, in 1223 Oleg of Kursk may have been the son of
Svyatoslav of Ryl'sk. From this information, we see that all three families
of the cadet branch sent troops.

Because the chronicler singles out towns owned by the cadet branch, it
would appear that he had a special interest in reporting the activities of
their princes. That is, the information bespeaks a chronicler working for
the Ol'govichi. Additional evidence supports this view. Oleg of Kursk is
the only prince from among all the Ol'govichi singled out for his bravery.
Granted, it is possible that his valor merited special mention. Just the
same, because of the scribe's interest in the cadet branch in general, and his
favoritism of Oleg in particular, he probably singled out the prince because
he was Oleg's chronicler. In like manner, Daniil's scribe drew the reader's
attention to his prince's exploits.[190]

---

[188] Under the year 1232, the chronicles speak of a Svyatoslav of Trubetsk. Perhaps it was he who
participated in the Kalka battle (see below, p. 326).
[189] In 1160, Svyatoslav gave Kursk to his son Oleg (see above, p. 122) and, in 1164, at the time of
Svyatoslav's death, Oleg was prince of Kursk (see above, p. 103).
[190] Fennell points out, probably correctly, that the report of the Kalka battle was based on a Chernigov
source whose account was embellished by information from a Galician–Volynian source ("The
Tatar Invasion of 1223," pp. 23–6). According to another view, however, the account was written

After crossing the Dnepr, Mstislav of Kiev, Mstislav of Chernigov, and the other princes encountered a band of Tatars. Their bowmen routed the enemy and, after pursuing them deeper into the prairie, cut them down and captured their herds. The princes rode further, and on the eighth day some of their men confronted a Tatar vanguard at the river Kalka.[191] They engaged the enemy in battle, but the latter crossed the river to fight on the other side. Mstislav Udaloy ordered Daniil to cross the river as the vanguard and he followed to reconnoiter. On spotting the Tatars, he returned post-haste to his troops and ordered them to prepare for battle. Mstislav of Kiev and Mstislav of Chernigov, however, were unaware of his actions. Mstislav Udaloy, we are told, refused to inform them out of envy because there was a great rivalry between them. Despite individual feats of bravery and a few initial successes, the princes were overcome. "Never before had they suffered such a devastating defeat."[192]

Thus we learn that the outward show of unanimity hid discord. Mstislav Udaloy refused to coordinate his attack with the other two Mstislavs and this contributed to their defeat. We are told neither the nature of the dispute nor when it arose, but a number of possibilities can be suggested. Mstislav of Kiev was the commander-in-chief. Since Mstislav Udaloy acted independently of the other two, and because of his fiery spirit that his nickname "the Bold" reflected, he may have been envious of his cousin's position as supreme commander and wished to assume that role himself. Or he disagreed with his cousin's strategy. Finally, he may have wished to assume a role in battle different from the one that his cousin assigned to him.[193] If one or more of these reasons were the cause of the dispute, it probably arose before the princes set out on the campaign. For the purposes of our investigation, however, it is important to note that the Ol′govichi cooperated with the prince of Kiev.

A number of sources report that, even though Mstislav of Kiev witnessed the calamity that befell his comrades-in-arms, he held his ground. He had taken up a position on a rocky knoll overlooking the river Kalka and, having fortified himself with a stockade, continued fighting a hopeless rearguard

solely in Galicia-Volyn′ (M. B. Sverdlov, "K voprosu o letopisnykh istochnikakh 'Povesti o bitve na Kalke'," *Vestnik Leningradskogo Universiteta*, nr. 2, Seria Istorii, Yazyka i Literatury, vyp. 1 [L., 1963], p. 143).

[191] The river Kalka was probably a tributary of the Kalmius that flows into the Sea of Azov west of the Don (Barsov, p. 87; Makhnovets′, p. 553; *Crisis*, p. 66).

[192] See s.a. 1224: Ipat., cols. 740–5; Perfecky, pp. 28–30; Makhnovets′, pp. 379–81.

[193] In the past, comrades-in-arms had become enemies over personal disputes in the field. In 1184, for example, Igor′ and Vladimir Glebovich became bitter rivals because the former refused to allow the latter to assume the vanguard position against the Polovtsy (see above, p. 157).

action for three days. Although the main force of Tatars pursued the fleeing princes to the Dnepr, they assigned two commanders to attack Mstislav. His son-in-law Andrew and a certain Aleksandr, prince of Dubrovitsa, remained at his side.[194] Unfortunately for Mstislav, a band of his allies from the steppe betrayed him. The Tatars therefore broke through the stockade and took the three princes captive. Covering them with boards, the victors feasted on top of the princes until they expired.[195] Six other princes fell in battle: Svyatoslav of Kanev,[196] Izyaslav Ingvarevich,[197] Svyatoslav of Shumsk,[198] and a certain Yury Nesvezhskiy.[199] The Tatars inflicted this evil, we are told, on May 31.[200]

The most important casualty for the Ol'govichi was their senior prince Mstislav Svyatoslavich of Chernigov, the last prince of the fifth generation in the dynasty. According to the *Lyubetskiy sinodik*, his baptismal name was Panteleymon and his wife's Christian name was Marfa.[201] Her secular name, as we have seen, was Yasynya.[202] In 1223 the couple had been married for forty years so that Mstislav was probably in his mid-fifties when he died. Mstislav's only reported son was also killed in the battle. This is the only occasion on which the chronicles mention him. Judging from the length of time that his parents had been married, he was in his late thirties. According to the *Lyubetskiy sinodik*, his Christian name was Dmitry and his wife was Mamelfa.[203] We do not know if they had children. The chroniclers also

---

[194] Andrew's identity is not known and investigators are not agreed on Aleksandr's identity. Some say he was Aleksandr Vsevolodich (s.a. 1225: Gust., p. 335; NPL, p. 567), some suggests he was the son of Gleb of Turov (Baum., II, 31; Makhnovets', p. 381, n. 10), while others, without giving his patronymic, suggest he belonged to the dynasty of Turov (Mosk., p. 401).

[195] According to Mongol tradition, the blood of a prince could be shed only in battle. Otherwise, he was to be killed without shedding blood as, for example, by suffocation, by strangulation, or by having his back broken (D. Ostrowski, *Muscovy and the Mongols: Cross-Cultural Influences on the Steppe Frontier, 1304–1589* [Cambridge, 1998], pp. 24–5).

[196] One source calls him Svyatoslav Ol'govich (Gust., p. 335). According to another view, he may have been Svyatoslav Ryurikovich (Makhnovets', p. 381, n. 10), and still another view has it that he may have been the son of Rostislav Ryurikovich (Rapov, p. 196). In all likelihood, he was a minor prince from the dynasty of Rostislavichi.

[197] He was probably the son of Ingvar' Yaroslavich of Lutsk (Baum., XIV, 8).

[198] He was probably Izyaslav's brother (Makhnovets', p. 381, n. 10; Rapov, p. 196). It is less likely that he was, as others suggest, Svyatoslav Ryurikovich (Gust., p. 335; NPL, p. 590).

[199] The town Nesvezh was located north of Klechesk in the Polotsk lands. It would appear, therefore, that Yury belonged to the Polotsk dynasty.

[200] See s.a. 1224: NPL, pp. 63, 267; s.a. 1223: Mosk., pp. 120–1. Concerning the date, see Berezhkov, pp. 106–7, 317–18.

[201] Zotov, pp. 69–70; 273–4.   [202] See above, pp. 152–3.

[203] Zotov, pp. 89–90, 281. Tatishchev gives him the princely name of Vasil'ko (Tat. 4, p. 364; Tat. 3, p. 218). The Gustinskiy Chronicle calls him Yury (that is, George). The compiler, however, conflated the phrase "Mstislav of Chernigov with his son, George Nesvezh'skiy" (NPL, pp. 63, 267) to read as "Mstislav Svyatoslavich of Chernigov and his son George" (Gust., p. 335).

fail to reveal his patrimony. In keeping with tradition, however, Mstislav would have given his son a portion of his own patrimony in the region of Kozel'sk. His body, like that of his father, was left to the mercy of prairie scavengers.

According to the Suzdalian chronicler, when the princes of Rus' were marshaling their troops, they asked Yury in Vladimir to send men. He dispatched his nephew Vasil'ko Konstantinovich, who, on arriving at Chernigov, learnt of the defeat and returned home.[204] Although Yury sent his nephew in a gesture of support, it was a fruitless military exercise. It may, however, have achieved another purpose. As we have seen, Vasil'ko's father Konstantin had been allied to the Rostislavichi. Yury, however, had formed a pact with the Ol'govichi and also wished Vasil'ko to establish closer ties with them. This is suggested by the news that, four years later, he would have Vasil'ko marry Mikhail's daughter.[205] Plans for a marriage may have been percolating in Yury's mind when he sent his nephew south via Chernigov. Since Vasil'ko was in the town when the first survivors returned from the river Kalka, Mikhail was probably among their number because he would have returned as quickly as possible to be installed as senior prince. If Vasil'ko was there for the ceremony, he would have met his future wife at that time. The chronicles do not confirm this.

Indeed, they do not even tell us that Mikhail, who was some forty years of age, replaced Mstislav as prince of Chernigov. Nevertheless, later evidence reveals that after his uncle's demise he sat on the throne of his father and grandfather in St. Saviour Cathedral. Under the array of garments once worn by his predecessors and the blessed first princes of Rus', the bishop of Chernigov installed him as the new senior prince. The ceremony probably took place around June 16, that is, about the time that Vladimir Ryurikovich of Smolensk, who also escaped from the battle, occupied the throne of Kiev.[206]

Thus, the death of Mstislav Romanovich of Kiev also brought about a change of leadership among the Rostislavichi, but in this case it affected the very summit of power in Rus'.[207] The simultaneous change of senior princes among the Ol'govichi and the Rostislavichi could have created havoc if the two dynasties had been at odds. Fortunately for Rus', this was one of those

[204] Lav., cols. 446–7; Mosk., p. 121.
[205] Baum., XII, 2; see below, p. 305.   [206] Tver., col. 343.
[207] Among the Rostislavichi only the sons of Roman and Ryurik were eligible to occupy Kiev because their fathers had ruled it before them. The deceased Mstislav Romanovich had no younger brothers. Since Vladimir's elder brother Rostislav had died in 1218 (Mosk., p. 115; L'vov, p. 150; Erm., p. 67), Vladimir, as Ryurik's only surviving son, succeeded his senior cousin.

periods of inter-dynastic history when the princes were living at peace and
the process of succession was functioning smoothly.

In addition to the deaths of two princes, the Ol'govichi had suffered im-
mense losses of manpower. The chronicler states that the Tatars killed more
fighting men than had ever before been slaughtered at one fell swoop. We
have no way of establishing the number of casualties because the chronicles
give only conventional estimates. One says 10,000 Kievans perished while
another claims that one in ten escaped with his life.[208] Since both branches
of the Ol'govichi sent troops, the number that was killed must have been
staggering. Nevertheless, the Tatars evidently ravaged no Chernigov towns.
They pursued the defeated horsemen to the west bank of the Dnepr as
far as Novgorod Svyatopolch south of Kiev.[209] There, they massacred the
inhabitants and devastated the surrounding region.[210] The Arab historian
Ibn al-Athir (1160–1233) seemingly corroborates this when he reports that
the Tatars ravaged much of Rus' as they cut down the fleeing men. At that
time, he notes enigmatically, many merchants and wealthy men of Rus'
gathered their most valued goods, sailed down the Dnepr, and crossed the
Black Sea to the Muslim lands.[211]

The Polovtsy were less fortunate. The Tatars destroyed them as a military
power.[212] After that, they no longer posed a serious threat to Rus'. On the
few occasions when the chroniclers mention them again, they are allies of
the princes.[213] As welcome as this development was to the Ol'govichi and
to other princely families, the Tatars would give them a relatively short
period of peace. Unfortunately for the princes, they underestimated the
invincible power of the new enemy and the catastrophe that awaited them.
The Ol'govichi returned to their old ways as if the scourge of God, having
cleansed the Christians of Rus' for their offenses, had vanished never to
return. Even the chroniclers, after expressing their initial shock over the
unprecedented massacre at the river Kalka, slowly forgot the Tatars.

[208] Lav., cols. 446–7; NPL, pp. 63, 267; *Crisis*, p. 66.
[209] Novgorod Svyatopolch or Svyatopolch-grad (Vitichev) was located south of Trepol' (Ipat., col. 745; Tolochko, *Kiev i Kievskaya zemlya*, p. 142; *Crisis*, p. 66).
[210] To judge from archaeological evidence, the Tatars devastated many towns and villages around Novgorod Svyatopolch after they crossed the Dnepr (V. I. Dovzhenok, "Drevnerusskie gorodishcha na srednem Dnepre," SA, nr. 4 [M., 1967], p. 261). They evidently destroyed no towns on the east bank.
[211] V. G. Tizengauzen, *Sbornik materialov, otnosyashchikhsya k istorii Zolotoy Ordy* (Spb., 1884), vol. 1, pp. 26–7.
[212] Pletneva, "Polovetskaya zemlya," pp. 299–30.
[213] For example, under the years 1225 and 1228 Khan Kotyan is mentioned (Ipat., cols. 746, 753), and, in 1235, the Polovtsy came to help the princes (Ipat., cols. 772–4).

4

The sixth generation: 1223–1246

The defeat at the Kalka battle had important consequences for the Ol'govichi. Mstislav Svyatoslavich's premature death, as we have seen, advanced Mikhail Vsevolodovich to the office of senior prince. Significantly, he could expect little opposition to his policies from the other Ol'govichi because all his cousins who had prior claims to Chernigov had died. What is more, because princes of his generation from the senior and cadet branches had predeceased him and had no heirs, Mikhail, in his capacity as senior prince, assumed control over a number of their domains. This accumulation of territories made him the largest landowner in the land. In the light of his vast resources and having inherited a politically unified dynasty, his potential for making a successful bid for Kiev looked exceedingly promising.

Nevertheless, for the time being, Mikhail decided to live in concord with the Rostislavichi in the manner that his uncles had done for the past eleven years following the death of his father Vsevolod Chermnyy. His decision was not surprising since, following the defeat at the river Kalka, the Ol'govichi were licking their wounds and in too great a disarray to launch an offensive. Family ties may also have dissuaded him from challenging Vladimir Ryurikovich in Kiev. The latter's sister Predslava had married Roman of Volyn'.[1] Since Mikhail had married their daughter, this made Vladimir the uncle of Mikhail's wife. Moreover, as the new senior prince, Mikhail still had to assert his authority over the Chernigov lands. Finally, one of his main tasks was to conclude new alliances with the princes of the other dynasties. The most important of these were the three Rostislavichi: Mstislav Davidovich of Smolensk,[2] Vladimir Ryurikovich of Kiev, and Mstislav Mstislavich Udaloy of Galich. He also had to form agreements with his two brothers-in-law: Daniil Romanovich of Vladimir in Volyn' and Yury Vsevolodovich of Vladimir in Suzdalia.

---

[1] Baum., IX, 20.   [2] Baum., IX, 16.

MIKHAIL BECOMES YURY'S AGENT IN NOVGOROD

Mikhail's deliberations with Yury unexpectedly involved him in Novgorodian affairs in an unprecedented manner. From the beginning of the thirteenth century the northern emporium had been the object of rivalry between two dynasties of Monomashichi, the one in Suzdalia and the one in
Smolensk. Vsevolod Bol'shoe Gnezdo held the upper hand until a few years
before his death in 1212, when Mstislav Udaloy wrested control from him.
After some ten years, as we have seen, Mstislav moved to Galich and, in 1221,
the faction supporting the dynasty of Suzdalia reasserted its dominance.[3]
But even though the townsmen acknowledged Yury as their overlord, they
challenged his appointment of princes. In 1224, the Novgorodians and Yury
reached an impasse.

Yury's son Vsevolod, we are told, fled from Novgorod for the second
time.[4] He waited for his father at Torzhok.[5] Yury came with his brother
Yaroslav of Pereyaslavl' Zalesskiy, Vasil'ko Konstantinovich of Rostov, and
his brother-in-law Mikhail of Chernigov. The Novgorodians asked Yury
to send back his son and to vacate Torzhok. He, however, did neither
and threatened to attack. In response, they confirmed their loyalty to him
but made a pact to die in defense of the Cathedral of St. Sofia. Yury,
therefore, proposed that they accept Mikhail as prince. They agreed and,
in March of 1225, Mikhail occupied Novgorod. Nevertheless, we are told,
Yury demanded the sum of 7,000 *novuyu* as a fine from the citizens and
confiscated their goods.[6]

We are not told why Mikhail was visiting Yury. It is unlikely that the latter
summoned him for the purpose of marching against Novgorod. The prince
of Vladimir had never before asked the prince of Chernigov to campaign
against that town. Besides, because of the great distance between their
domains, such collaboration would have to be arranged well in advance.

---

[3] For the background to the political rivalries in Novgorod, see V. L. Yanin, *Novgorodskie posadniki*
(M., 1962), pp. 124–33; *Crisis*, pp. 51–8, 69–70.
[4] In 1222, Yury had sent his son Vsevolod to Novgorod but the latter fled secretly at night in the
winter (NPL, pp. 60–1, 262–3). Yury then appointed his brother Yaroslav, who arrived in 1223, but
towards the end of the year returned to his domain in Pereyaslavl' Zalesskiy (NPL, pp. 61, 263).
The Novgorodians therefore asked Yury to send his son Vsevolod once again and he arrived at the
beginning of 1224 (NPL, pp. 61, 264).
[5] Torzhok (Novyy Torg) was a border town of Novgorod located on its southeast trade route to the
Volga river. It was the most important center of commerce between Novgorod and the lands of
Suzdalia.
[6] NPL, pp. 63–4, 267–8. Concerning the date, see Berezhkov, pp. 268–9. *Novaya* was a unit of currency,
see *Mikhail*, p. 17. Concerning Mikhail's involvement in Novgorodian politics, see also Yanin,
Novgorodskie posadniki, pp. 133–9, and *Mikhail*, pp. 15–51.

His son's flight and Yury's swift retaliation, however, bespeak actions taken on the spur of the moment. What is more, had Mikhail responded to a call for help, he would have taken a more direct route to Novgorod rather than the circuitous one via Suzdalia. It appears, therefore, that he was already in Vladimir when Yury learnt of Vsevolod's flight, and his presence there means that he had come for different business. Since this was evidently his first visit to Suzdalia after becoming senior prince, the obvious purpose for his meeting with Yury was to conclude a new agreement.[7]

Mikhail's occupation of Novgorod was a significant departure from customary practice. No prince of Chernigov had ever abandoned the dynastic capital to rule that town.[8] A senior prince considered ruling Kiev to be the only promotion. Indeed, had Mikhail looked upon the appointment to Novgorod as an improvement of his political status, he would have treated the town as his main domain. This was not the case. As we shall see, he went to Novgorod with the intention of returning to Chernigov. Moreover, he acted as Yury's appointee and not as an autonomous ruler. The Novgorodians confirmed this in acknowledging Yury to be their prince.

Mikhail and Yury's collaboration bespoke an extraordinary degree of trust in each other. Yury was confident that Mikhail would not try asserting his authority over Novgorod. Mikhail, for his part, was seemingly motivated to help because of his personal friendship for his brother-in-law. Nevertheless, later evidence shows that he was also driven by self-interest. In going to Novgorod he ingratiated himself with Yury by honoring their newly formed alliance. What is more, Yury became indebted to him for his service. Finally, control of the wealthy trading center would allow Mikhail to initiate new commercial exchanges between it and Chernigov.

To judge from the chronicler's declaration that Mikhail made life easy for the Novgorodians, he was more accommodating than the Vsevolodovichi who had sought to assert their dominance over the townspeople. He also demonstrated his talents as a mediator by pacifying them. The chronicler does not tell us what measures he implemented to alleviate their burdens. We do know, however, that one of his most important tasks was to recover the Novgorodians' wares that Yury had confiscated at Torzhok and in his own domain.

Mikhail may also have been instrumental in implementing a transfer of jurisdiction. It appears that Yury washed his hands of any future dealings

---

[7] Elsewhere it has been wrongly suggested that Yury summoned Mikhail in order to march against Novgorod (*Mikhail*, p. 17).

[8] As we have seen above, in 1181 Svyatoslav Vsevolodovich of Kiev ruled Novgorod for a few months, but at that time he had lost control of Kiev (see above, pp. 148–9).

with the Novgorodians. This is suggested by the news that after Mikhail departed from Novgorod, the *veche* sent its request for a prince to Yaroslav in Pereyaslavl' Zalesskiy. Significantly, between the years 1221 and 1224 it had always asked Yury for a prince. In bypassing him, the Novgorodians deviated from their traditional practice suggesting that their relationship to the two brothers had altered. Since the chronicler reported this change after Mikhail returned from Yury with the confiscated goods, Mikhail may have persuaded him to hand over the affairs of Novgorod to his younger brother. The chronicles do not report this development, but later events support it.[9]

Mikhail had come to Novgorod as Yury's man, but after Yury handed over Novgorod's affairs to Yaroslav, he believed it expedient to leave. Besides, he had successfully fulfilled the assignment Yury had given him. He had placated the Novgorodians and reconciled them with Yury. What is more, Mikhail was eager to return to Chernigov, which he had occupied two years earlier, but ruled for only a year before being drawn into northern affairs. He had been away from his patrimony for over a year, which was the longest period of time that any prince of Chernigov had absented himself.

Before departing from Novgorod, he invited the townsmen to send merchants to Chernigov and declared that their lands and his would be as one.[10] His attempt to increase the flow of trade between Novgorod and Chernigov confirms that his willingness to help the Novgorodians was also motivated by the benefits he could secure for his own people. Even though he disappointed the Novgorodians by abandoning them, he could rest assured that, given his popularity, he had made powerful friends. Accordingly, we may assume that the townsmen responded positively to his request to send merchants.[11]

DYNASTIC CRISIS AND MARRIAGE ALLIANCES

About a year after Mikhail returned to Chernigov, it appears, he became involved in a dynastic dispute. During the winter of 1226, the chronicler reports, Yury and his nephews, Konstantin's sons Vasil'ko and Vsevolod, came to help Mikhail against Oleg of Kursk. Yury undoubtedly answered Mikhail's summons for help because of their alliance and because he owed his brother-in-law a favor. Nevertheless, Yury's willingness not only to help

---

[9] For a more detailed examination of this transfer of jurisdiction over Novgorod, see *Mikhail*, pp. 34–7.
[10] Concerning Mikhail's stay in Novgorod, see NPL, pp. 64, 268–9; Mosk., pp. 121–2.
[11] See also, *Mikhail*, pp. 15–22.

Mikhail in an intra-dynastic dispute, but also to do so in person, was unprecedented. His father Vsevolod Bol'shoe Gnezdo had never sent military aid to a prince of Chernigov even though, as we have seen, the Ol'govichi had given him sanctuary and helped him win Suzdalia. Instead, on the few occasions when Vsevolod had marched or intended to march into the Chernigov lands, he had planned to attack the Ol'govichi.[12] The new senior princes of Chernigov and Suzdalia were charting a friendlier course.

Oleg of Kursk, like Mikhail, had escaped from the Kayala massacre. As has been suggested, he was probably the eldest son of Svyatoslav Ol'govich of Ryl'sk and thus the senior prince of the cadet branch.[13] Svyatoslav's father Oleg Svyatoslavich had died in 1180 as prince of Novgorod Severskiy.[14] Since the chronicles do not mention Svyatoslav after 1185, we have only circumstantial evidence to suggest that he returned from captivity and that he also occupied the throne of his father in Novgorod Severskiy.

The chroniclers fail to reveal the nature of Oleg's complaint. They imply, however, that, being convinced in the justice of his claim, he prepared to wage war on Mikhail. The evidence that this was the first occasion in over fifty years on which two Ol'govichi quarreled highlights his discontent.[15] Traditionally, the most acrimonious rivalries between princes arose either over their rights of succession or over their claims to domains. Since Mikhail was the rightful senior prince, it is unlikely that Oleg challenged him for control of Chernigov. Had he wished to usurp power, he could have done so while Mikhail was preoccupied in Novgorod. It is more than likely, therefore, that the bone of contention was another domain.[16]

The available evidence suggests that it was Novgorod Severskiy. In 1226, Oleg was prince of Kursk, but two years later, as we shall see, he evidently ruled Novgorod Severskiy.[17] It is noteworthy that the chroniclers accuse neither Mikhail nor Oleg of wrongdoing.[18] This suggests that each had

---

[12] For example, in 1196 Vsevolod attacked Yaroslav of Chernigov (see above, p. 223), and in 1207 he set out against Vsevolod Chermnyy but diverted his attack against Ryazan' (see above, p. 260).

[13] See above, p. 294. See also, M. Dimnik, "Russian Princes and their Identities in the First Half of the Thirteenth Century," *Mediaeval Studies* 40 (1978), 158–65, and *Mikhail*, pp. 56–8.

[14] See above, p. 141.

[15] The last time that two Ol'govichi had been pitted against each other was in 1174, when Mikhail's grandfather Svyatoslav Vsevolodovich of Chernigov and Oleg's grandfather Oleg Svyatoslavich pillaged each other's domains (Lav., col. 367); see above, pp. 129–30.

[16] Tatishchev alone, and only in his first redaction, claims that the princes quarreled over a domain (Tat. 4, p. 365; Dimnik, "Russian Princes," p. 164).

[17] This observation is based on Tatishchev's identification and on circumstantial evidence (Tat. 4, p. 366; Tat. 3, p. 221). See also Dimnik, "Russian Princes," pp. 163–4, and see below p. 308.

[18] In reporting that Yury went to help Mikhail against Oleg, the Laurentian chronicler implies that Mikhail was in the right. According to Tatishchev, however, the metropolitan accused Mikhail of picking a quarrel unfairly (Tat. 4, p. 365; Dimnik, "Russian Princes," p. 164).

a just cause. Significantly, Oleg had a rightful claim to the town only if his father Svyatoslav Ol′govich had ruled it. Consequently, this allusion to Svyatoslav is tenuous evidence that he returned from captivity and assumed the office of senior prince in the cadet branch.

We are not told on what grounds both Mikhail and Oleg had a claim to Novgorod Severskiy, but let us reconstruct a possible scenario. According to the normal order of succession, Svyatoslav Ol′govich would have been succeeded in the town by Igor′'s son Vladimir, and the latter by his brothers. After they all had ruled in turn, succession would have gone to Svyatoslav's son Oleg of Kursk. In 1206, however, Vladimir and his brothers relinquished their claim to Novgorod Severskiy by moving to Galich. Control of the town therefore reverted to the senior prince of the dynasty, Vsevolod Chermnyy.[19] After that, the senior branch used the town as a stepping-stone to Chernigov. Accordingly, Mikhail ruled it while his uncle Mstislav was in Chernigov. After Mikhail occupied Chernigov, he probably gave it to his son. By that time, all the Igorevichi had died, including Vladimir, who had returned to Putivl′ but had forfeited his right to Novgorod Severskiy. Significantly, in the cadet branch, Oleg of Kursk still had a claim to the town because he had the right to sit on the throne of his father. Mikhail challenged Oleg's claim and both were prepared to wage war. If, therefore, Novgorod Severskiy was the bone of contention in 1226, the news that two years later Oleg ruled it reveals that Mikhail yielded in the dispute.

In addition to Yury, Metropolitan Kirill also helped to reconcile Mikhail with Oleg. In light of the chronicler's remark that the prelate was present "by the grace of God," that is, fortuitously, the original purpose for which Vladimir Ryurikovich of Kiev had sent him to Chernigov was not to reconcile the two Ol′govichi. Since the Greek had arrived in Rus′ three years earlier,[20] Vladimir probably encouraged him to make general visitations of the eparchies under his jurisdiction.[21]

Although Yury's primary objective was to bring Mikhail military aid, later evidence suggests that he had an additional motive for visiting his brother-in-law and for bringing his nephews to Chernigov. Within the next two years, as we shall see, Vasil′ko and Vsevolod would marry Mikhail and Oleg's daughters. Thus, after pacifying the fathers, Yury undoubtedly arranged marriage alliances with them.

---

[19] See above, pp. 255, 263–4.
[20] Metropolitan Matfey died on August 19, 1220 (Lav., col. 445). Some three and a half years later, on January 6, 1224, Kirill was installed as his successor (Lav. col. 447). Concerning the date, see Berezhkov, pp. 106–7.
[21] Concerning Yury's visit to Chernigov, see Lav., col. 448; see s.a. 1227: Mosk., p. 122.

Before those matches were realized, however, Mikhail attempted to marry off one of his daughters to a princeling in Suzdalia. The chronicles do not report the failed marriage, but the Life (*Zhitie*) of St. Evfrosinia tells us that he had a daughter named Feodula. In 1227 she was betrothed to a certain Mina Ivanovich who died before she arrived in Suzdal'. Instead of returning to Chernigov, Feodula entered the convent dedicated to the Deposition of the Precious Robe of the Mother of God at Blachernae (*Rizpolozhenskiy monastyr'*). She adopted the religious name of Evfrosinia and remained there until 1250, when she died.[22]

That winter, we are told, Mikhail married his daughter Maria to Yury's nephew Vasil'ko Konstantinovich. The ceremony took place in the Church of the Annunciation and, on February 12, 1228, the couple arrived in Rostov.[23] Contrary to custom, the couple were married in the bride's town.[24] This is confirmed by the news that the marriage ceremony took place in the Cathedral of the Annunciation. No such church existed in Vladimir, but as we have seen, in 1186 Mikhail's grandfather Svyatoslav Vsevolodovich had built the Cathedral of the Annunciation in Chernigov.[25]

The marriage alliance was important for Mikhail because with it he formed a personal tie with the senior family of Suzdalia. Vasil'ko was the son of Yury's elder brother, Konstantin. Since the latter had been the senior prince and the prince of Vladimir, Vasil'ko was eligible to occupy both offices. The match also strengthened Mikhail's bond with Yury. The latter's own friendship with the Konstantinovichi, and the importance he placed on their association with the Ol'govichi, is reflected in the tasks he assigned to them. In 1223 he dispatched Vasil'ko via Chernigov against the Tatars; in 1227 he brought both Vasil'ko and Vsevolod to help Mikhail; and in the same year he sent Vsevolod to govern Pereyaslavl' which abutted on the lands of the Ol'govichi.[26]

---

[22] V. T. Georgievsky, "Zhitie pr. Evfrosinii Suzdal'skoy s miniatyurami po spisku XVII v." *Trudy Vladimirskoy uchenoy arkhivnoy komisii* (Vladimir, 1899), bk. 1, pp. 73–172; Barsukov, cols. 179–81; Golubinsky, *Istoriya kanonizatsii svyatykh*, pp. 115, 549; and Filaret, *Russkie svyatiye*, vol. 3, pp. 120–5. Concerning her cult, see P. Bushkovitch, *Religion and Society in Russia: The Sixteenth and Seventeenth Centuries* (Oxford, 1992), p. 98.

[23] Lav., col. 450. Maria's name is not given under the year 1227, but it is given under the years 1238 and 1271 (Ak. sp., cols. 520, 525; Zotov, pp. 286–7).

[24] According to Tatishchev, Yury sent Vasil'ko to the princes of Smolensk, Chernigov, and to other princes to select a bride. Vasil'ko fell in love with Maria the daughter of Yury's brother-in-law Mikhail. He did not, however, take the bride to Suzdalia as was the custom. Instead, Yury sent his son with a company of Suzdalian notables and, on January 10, the marriage took place in Chernigov (Tat. 4, p. 366; Tat. 3, p. 221). Mikhail's daughter Feodula, as we have just seen, traveled to Suzdalia to be married as did Mikhail's sister Agafia (see above, pp. 268–9).

[25] See above, p. 182.   [26] Lav., col. 450; Mosk., p. 122.

Sometime in 1228 the Ol'govichi concluded another marriage alliance
with the princes of Suzdalia. Oleg Svyatoslavich of Novgorod Severskiy gave
his daughter in marriage to Vsevolod Konstantinovich.[27] Just as Mikhail
of the senior branch had formed a family tie with the Konstantinovichi,
Oleg of the cadet branch also arranged a match with them. Moreover,
the marriage with Vsevolod established a personal link with the prince of
Pereyaslavl'. As we have seen, two previous princes of that domain had
married Chernigov princesses.[28] The Ol'govichi were evidently still eager
to establish family ties with their southern neighbor to facilitate closer
cooperation against any potential enemy from the steppe.

MIKHAIL AND VLADIMIR OF KIEV AT ODDS WITH
DANIIL OF VOLYN'

While Mikhail was strengthening his family ties with Yury, he was also mon-
itoring the rivalries of the Rostislavichi and Daniil Romanovich over Galich.
He however, refrained from becoming involved in their wars even though
Daniil was his brother-in-law. Eventually, Daniil and Mstislav Udaloy of
Galich joined forces against the Hungarians and the Poles in an effort
to keep the foreign powers out of Galich. Daniil also initiated an expansionist policy with Mstislav's backing. In 1227, it appears, he took Lutsk
from Yaroslav Ingvarevich and captured Chertoryysk from Rostislav Svyatopolchich of Pinsk.[29] Moreover, he took the latter's sons, Vladimir and
Michael, captive.[30]

The situation changed in 1228 when Mstislav Udaloy fell ill on his way
to Kiev and died.[31] His death disrupted the balance of power in Galicia
and Volyn'. As Daniil's father-in-law, he had helped to keep at bay would-
be challengers to his son-in-law's authority. His passing therefore deprived
Daniil of his strongest defender. Mstislav had also wielded control over
Galich, first as its prince and later as the father-in-law of Prince Andrew of
Hungary to whom he had given the town. Before his death, however, he had
attempted to take it back from Andrew and give it to Daniil.[32] His change

---

[27] Mosk., p. 122; Tver., col. 347. Yury sent Vsevolod to Pereyaslavl' in 1227, and he arrived on September
15 (Lav., col. 450; Mosk., p. 122). Only Tatishchev calls Oleg Svyatoslavich prince of Novgorod
Severskiy (see s.a. 1227: Tat. 4, p. 366; Tat. 3, p. 221), but circumstantial evidence supports this
identification.
[28] In 1179, Yaroslav of Chernigov arranged for his daughter to marry Vladimir Glebovich (see above,
p. 140). In 1215, the daughter of Gleb of Chernigov married Vladimir Vsevolodovich (see above,
p. 287).
[29] Baum., II, 30.
[30] Ipat., cols. 745–52; Perfecky, pp. 30–4. Concerning the princes of Pinsk, see Baum., p. 14.
[31] Mosk., p. 122; Lav., col. 450; Tver., col. 347.
[32] Ipat., col. 752.

of heart bolstered Daniil's determination to seize Galich. Mstislav's death also deprived the Rostislavichi of their military clout in Galicia and Volyn'. His sobriquet "the Bold" bespeaks the respect that he had commanded among the princes.³³ It remained to be seen, therefore, whether they would sit idly by and watch Daniil and Andrew fight for Galich, or if they also would attempt to assert their influence in the southwest.

The chronicler alludes to mounting tension between the princes. He states enigmatically that Metropolitan Kirill came in the hope of restoring peace, but failed.³⁴ Since Daniil's chronicler wrote the report, and since he tells us that Kirill came but does not tell us to which town, we may assume that the metropolitan visited the chronicler's town of Vladimir and that he approached the chronicler's patron, Daniil. He also neglects to identify the prince with whom Daniil was at loggerheads. Nevertheless, he immediately announces that Rostislav Svyatopolchich of Pinsk continued slandering Daniil because the latter was holding his sons captive.³⁵ Finally, the chronicler does not report to whom Rostislav slandered Daniil, but subsequent information makes it clear that it was to Vladimir Ryurikovich of Kiev.

Vladimir, we are told, summoned Mikhail and all the princes and attacked Daniil in Kamenets. The town, located on the boundary between the lands of Kiev and Volyn', was a strongly fortified Romanovichi outpost.³⁶ For example, in 1196, when Ryurik was embroiled in a controversy with Roman, he dispatched his son Rostislav, the elder brother of Vladimir of Kiev, to attack Kamenets.³⁷ Later, in the years 1210 and 1211, Roman's widow took her sons, Daniil and Vasil'ko, to Kamenets for safety.³⁸ In 1228, Daniil's presence in the town also testifies to its importance as a regional center.

The town's ability to withstand Vladimir's siege is all the more impressive because he allegedly attacked with all his allies. He was accompanied by his senior prince, Mstislav Davidovich of Smolensk and all the minor Rostislavichi, especially those ruling towns in the Kievan land bordering on Volyn'.³⁹ He also summoned his relatives from Turov and Pinsk. His father

---

³³ *Mikhail*, pp. 58–9.   ³⁴ Ipat., col. 753.

³⁵ Ipat., col. 753. As we have seen, in 1227 Daniil had taken Rostislav's sons Vladimir and Michael captive when he seized Chertoryysk.

³⁶ Although historians are not agreed on the location of the Kamenets in question, it was probably located in the vicinity of the river Khomora, a tributary of the Slutch (M. Dimnik, "Kamenec," *Russia Mediaevalis* 4 [München, 1979], pp. 26–9; see also Ya. P. Dashkevich, "Kamenets – eshche raz," *Russia Mediaevalis* 5, 1 [München, 1984], pp. 7–8, and Makhnovets', p. 553).

³⁷ Ipat., col. 698.   ³⁸ Ipat., cols. 728–9.

³⁹ Although the Hypatian chronicler does not identify the prince of Smolensk, under the year 1230 a number of chronicles report the death of Mstislav Davidovich as prince of Smolensk (Mosk., p. 125; Erm., p. 73).

Ryurik, as has been noted, had married Anna of Turov. This made the princes of Turov and Pinsk Vladimir's cousins.[40] Rostislav of Pinsk would have reinforced Vladimir's call to arms by encouraging his relatives to help him free his sons.[41]

The Ol'govichi also came in force. Two copies of the Hypatian Chronicle assert that Mikhail was accompanied by "all the princes," that is, by Ol'govichi from both branches.[42] No princes or towns from the senior branch are singled out, but we are told that troops from Kursk and Novgorod Severskiy, towns of the cadet branch, joined Mikhail. The association of Kursk with Novgorod Severskiy could be interpreted to mean that they were ruled by the same prince. Since Kursk was Oleg's patrimony, this would mean that he took over control of Novgorod Severskiy following his reconciliation with Mikhail. At that time he would have handed over control of Kursk to a son. By naming the two towns the chronicler may have wished to stress that even Oleg, who had challenged Mikhail, now accompanied the latter with his troops.

Vladimir also summoned Kotyan who had been related to Mstislav Udaloy and had helped the Rostislavichi in the past.[43] But Daniil won the khan over to his side. Since they were both in-laws of the deceased Mstislav, Daniil being his son-in-law and Kotyan being his father-in-law, their family tie must have been a binding force. Consequently, Kotyan deserted Vladimir without joining the attack. His tribesmen, however, had come to pillage and would not be denied. They therefore added carnage to treachery by plundering the lands of Andrew in Galicia as they returned to the steppe. Thus, even though the Hungarian prince did not join the siege of Kamenets, he paid a price for his alliance with Vladimir and Mikhail. We know neither when the three formed their pact nor the terms of their agreement.[44] It undoubtedly included military and commercial clauses. For the moment, however, it is important to note that Vladimir and Mikhail's support of Andrew was a direct challenge to Daniil's expansionism.

Mikhail's cooperation with Vladimir is noteworthy. In pledging allegiance to the prince of Kiev and therewith joining ranks with the

[40] Baum., II, 27.
[41] The Gustinskiy chronicler alone mentions Rostislav of Pinsk (s.a. 1232: Gust., p. 336).
[42] The *Khlebnikovskiy spisok* and the *Pogodinskiy spisok* have the phrase "*a Mikhail s vsemi knyazi*" (Ipat., col. 753, var. 16).
[43] Kotyan was the leader of the Durut tribe probably living in the steppe along the Dnepr river (Pletneva, "Polovetskaya zemlya," p. 299). This was the fourth and last occasion on which the chronicles speak of him. They mentioned him under the years 1202, 1224, and 1226 (Ipat., cols. 717, 747; NPL, pp. 62, 265).
[44] In forming an alliance with the Hungarians, Mikhail was acting in the tradition of his grandfather Svyatoslav, who had formed an agreement with the King Béla III (see above, p. 191).

Rostislavichi, he drove a wedge between two dynasties of Monomashichi. He also reversed the political alignment that had existed in 1212, when his father fought the Rostislavichi for control of their Kievan domains. Furthermore, Mikhail changed his father's policy towards the Romanovichi. As we have seen, Vsevolod Chermnyy had expressed great affection for Roman's children.[45] For reasons unexplained, Mikhail was hostile towards his brother-in-law.

Vladimir, however, expressed two grievances against Daniil. The latter's father Roman had tarnished his family's honor by forcing his father Ryurik to become a monk. Vladimir sought retribution for that insult. The chronicler veiled Vladimir's second pretext for attacking Daniil in his enigmatic remark that "Vladimir had a great fear in his heart." By examining the events of the preceding year, we can expose that fear. As we have seen, Daniil had seized the towns of Lutsk and Chertoryysk in a bid to increase his power. Of even greater moment had been Mstislav Udaloy's declaration before his death that he intended to give Galich to Daniil. The latter's expansionist ambitions alarmed Vladimir. If Daniil added Galicia to his growing Volyn' domains, his military resources would rival those of the prince of Kiev himself.

Mikhail had the same apprehensions as Vladimir plus a private ambition. As we have seen, in 1206 his father had attempted to acquire Galich for the Ol'govichi, but the execution of the Igorevichi had put paid to his plans. Although the chronicles have as yet given us no hint that Mikhail shared his father's ambition for Galich, we shall see it surface in the not too distant future. Consequently, it is most likely that, in 1228, his expansionist plan was already germinating. If, as was likely the case, Galich was the hub of the controversy, Vladimir and Mikhail attacked Daniil hoping to make him abandon that quest. Besides, Vladimir and Mikhail were Prince Andrew's allies and their pact with him undoubtedly demanded that they help the Hungarian keep Galich.

Mikhail and Vladimir failed to take Kamenets. The defenses of the town, Daniil's political dexterity, and Daniil's Polish allies proved to be more than a match for them. Daniil's victory enabled him to increase his control over his acquisitions and to demand undisclosed concessions from the vanquished princes. Undoubtedly, he would have reiterated his claim to Galich and demanded that they promise not to obstruct him. Mikhail therefore gained nothing by attacking his brother-in-law, and Vladimir failed to assuage the great fear in his heart.[46]

[45] See above, p. 269.
[46] Concerning the attack on Kamenets, see Ipat., cols. 753–4. See also *Mikhail*, pp. 59–63.

MIKHAIL RETURNS TO NOVGOROD AS ITS PRINCE

Meanwhile, there was political unrest in Novgorod. In the summer of 1228, the chronicler reports, Yaroslav Vsevolodovich departed from the town leaving his sons Fedor and Aleksandr as the nominal rulers. In December, it appears, the common people marched to the archbishop's court, evicted Arseny and reinstated Antony.[47] They also rose up in arms against *tysyatskiy* Vyacheslav and appointed Boris Negochevich in his place. After removing Yaroslav's lieutenants, the Novgorodians invited him to return according to a new agreement. They insisted that he abide by all their terms and by all the laws of Yaroslav.[48] He also had to cancel the *zabozhnits'e* (a special tax levied on churches which also served as warehouses),[49] and to stop appointing his judges in the Novgorodian lands. He could, they declared, either accept their offer or leave. On February 20, 1229, therefore, Yaroslav's sons fled to their father in Pereyaslavl' Zalesskiy.

The Novgorodians rebelled against Yaroslav's officials because, in their view, the latter had advised him to implement policies detrimental to the people. The *veche* therefore evicted the undesirables from office and attempted to reduce the power of the prince by increasing that of the *posadnik* and the *tysyatskiy*. But Yaroslav rejected the terms designed to curb his authority. He knew that Novgorod was unable to resist enemy attacks or to launch expansionist campaigns against neighboring tribes without a prince's leadership. Significantly, after 1217, when Mstislav Udaloy departed from Novgorod, the princes of Suzdalia had become the undisputed rulers of the northern emporium. Consequently, when Novgorod needed a prince again, the *veche*, in Yaroslav's opinion, would have to ask him for help since, as we have seen, Yury had turned over command of Novgorod to him. At that time, he would dictate his own terms.

But Yaroslav miscalculated. His rebuff prompted the Novgorodians to pursue an option they had ignored for over three decades. They bypassed the Vsevolodovichi and the Rostislavichi and turned to the Ol'govichi. Just

---

[47] Novgorod, located on the river Volkhov a few miles north of Lake Il'men', was divided by the river into two sides, the market side on the east bank and the Sofia side on the west bank. The first contained Yaroslav's court while the second held the Cathedral of St. Sofia and the archbishop's court. A defensive wall protected the Sofia side. The whole town was divided into five suburbs (*kontsy*): two were on the east side of the river (the *Plotnitskiy konets* and the *Slavenskiy konets*), and three were on the west side of the river (the *Nerevskiy konets*, the *Zagorodskiy konets,* and the *Goncharskiy* or *Lyudin konets*).

[48] When the Novgorodians referred to all the laws of Yaroslav they evidently had in mind the "Rus'sian" law (*Russkaya pravda*) promulgated by Yaroslav the Wise (see M. N. Tikhomirov, *Drevnyaya Rus'* [M., 1975], pp. 221–2).

[49] *Mikhail*, pp. 24–5.

as the impasse in 1224 had prompted Yury to send Mikhail to Novgorod as mediator, the stalemate four years later induced the Novgorodians themselves to ask Mikhail to be their prince. When their envoys reached the lands of Smolensk, however, Mstislav Davidovich blocked all the routes because Yaroslav had instructed him to do so. Despite the obstacles, the Novgorodians got word to Mikhail while he and his son, Rostislav,[50] were visiting Bryn in the Vyatichi lands.[51]

Mstislav Davidovich's willingness to help Yaroslav is, at first glance, surprising because a year earlier the Rostislavichi had been allied with the Ol'govichi against Daniil. We are not told what power Yaroslav, who was not the senior prince of the Vsevolodovichi, wielded over the senior prince of the Rostislavichi. What is more, in 1216, at the Lipitsa battle, he had been an enemy of the Rostislavichi. His cooperation with Mstislav therefore suggests that the two had made a pact to help each other against any prince who sought to undermine their influence in Novgorod. They failed to stop the messengers, but their obstruction made Mikhail painfully aware of the serious obstacles that he would face in ruling Novgorod. One was the great distance between Chernigov and Novgorod, and the other was the opposition of Yaroslav and Mstislav.[52]

Mikhail set out for Novgorod upon receiving the invitation. Although he had declined the Novgorodians' pleas to remain with them in 1225, his change of heart is understandable. At that time, he had been Yury's agent, but now the citizens invited him to rule in his own name. He therefore decided that the time was right to initiate his own policy in Novgorod. On April 8, 1229 he arrived at Torzhok.[53]

Mikhail was willing to risk war with Yaroslav because he saw the growing strength of the Monomashichi as a threat to the Ol'govichi. In 1228, as we have seen, he and Vladimir had agreed not to challenge Daniil's claim to Galich. Meanwhile, Yaroslav was asserting his control over Novgorod, and the Rostislavichi were ensconced in Kiev. Accordingly, princes of the three dynasties of Monomashichi laid claims to lands abutting their patrimonial domains. Mikhail was the odd man out because he found no adjacent domain to appropriate. When, therefore, the Novgorodians asked him to be their prince, they offered him the opportunity to redress the imbalance.

After Mikhail arrived in Novgorod around the beginning of May, discontented *boyars* instigated dissent among the Vsevolodovichi in Suzdalia.

---

[50] This is the first time that the chronicles mention Mikhail's son. They do not give his name, but under the following year we learn that it is Rostislav (NPL, pp. 68, 275).

[51] Concerning Bryn, see above, p. 293. [52] See also *Mikhail*, pp. 26–9; *Crisis*, pp. 71–3.

[53] NPL, pp. 66–8, 272–4; see also *Mikhail*, pp. 23–5.

They convinced Yaroslav that Yury had helped Mikhail replace him in Novgorod.[54] Given Yury's initiative in sending Mikhail to the town in 1224, Yaroslav readily believed the lies. Moreover, he had an additional reason for being irked with Yury's purported meddling. As has been noted, four years earlier Yury had turned over Novgorodian affairs to Yaroslav while he continued to oversee the dealings of the Vsevolodovichi with the Volga Bulgars and the princes of Rus'.[55] Consequently, when Yaroslav heard the lies claiming that his brother had helped Mikhail to occupy Novgorod, he took exception to Yury's alleged breach of their agreement. On September 7, Yury finally exonerated himself of any complicity in Mikhail's appointment,[56] but he did so by declaring his solidarity with Yaroslav. For the first time, therefore, Mikhail and Yury became enemies.

Significantly, in 1229, Mikhail was not the citizens' first choice. Just as in 1224 they had accepted him as a compromise because they had rejected Yury's son, five years later they invited him because Yaroslav had refused to accept their terms. On the second occasion, however, his role was significantly different. He did not come as Yury's lieutenant, but on his own authority. This independence enabled him to implement changes of his own choosing rather than ones dictated by Yury. The Novgorodians believed Mikhail would pass legislation in their favor because, during his first stay, he had demonstrated his goodwill. He justified their trust in him by pledging to govern according to their will, according to the laws of Yaroslav, and not to coerce them.

In 1226, when Yaroslav had replaced Mikhail in Novgorod, he had assumed authority according to his own terms.[57] Three years later, Mikhail and the townsmen introduced measures to weaken his power. The *veche* appointed Vnezd Vodovik as the new *posadnik* who supported the changes. The Novgorodians also removed Yaroslav's other administrators. Contrary to the popular practice of killing the deposed officials, throwing them off the bridge, and pillaging their courts, the citizens acted with moderation. They punished *Posadnik* Ivan Dimitrievich by giving him the less important town of Torzhok. After levying heavy fines on Yaroslav's supporters, they also adopted the fair-minded measure of using the money for the benefit of the entire community by paying for the construction of a new bridge.[58] The citizens' forbearance was in keeping with the policy of temperance that the

---

[54] Tatishchev claims Yaroslav accused Yury of helping Mikhail occupy Novgorod, but only in his second redaction (Tat. 3, p. 224).

[55] Concerning this arrangement between Yury and Yaroslav, see *Mikhail*, pp. 34–8.

[56] Lav., cols. 451–2; Mosk., p. 123.   [57] L'vov, p. 154; Tver., col. 345.

[58] It has been suggested that later, between 1230 and 1235, Yaroslav passed the so-called "Statute of Yaroslav concerning bridges" in an attempt to free his supporters from the fines that Mikhail's officials imposed on them and to transfer the burden of the cost to all the Novgorodians

veche had demanded of Mikhail when it had instructed him not to coerce Novgorod. By not taking oppressive punitive action against Yaroslav's men, Mikhail acted in a spirit of humaneness.

His pro-Novgorod legislation included granting the town officials some of the prince's power. Yaroslav, for example, had refused to stop sending his judges to the countryside to adjudicate fines from the peasants. Mikhail helped the *boyars* to make life easier for their people by permitting them to appoint their own judges. Unlike Yaroslav, he also promised to uphold all the laws of Yaroslav the Wise. What is more, since he had agreed to rule by all the Novgorodians' terms, he abrogated the church tax (*zabozhnits'e*) which Yaroslav had refused to abolish. He therewith endeared himself to the merchants.

Another of Mikhail's tasks was to alleviate the burden of the commoners. Accordingly, he placed a moratorium on the payment of tribute for five years on those peasants who had fled to other lands and agreed to return to their Novgorodian homes. The chronicler does not explain why the peasants had fled, but the reason was undoubtedly an exorbitant tax levied on them by Yaroslav. This is suggested by the news that Mikhail also improved the lot of peasants who had remained on their Novgorodian allotments during Yaroslav's rule. He instructed them to pay the lighter tribute imposed on them by earlier princes, that is, by princes who had ruled Novgorod before Yaroslav.[59] Mikhail's willingness to lessen the tax burden of the common people was a stark contrast to Yaroslav's money-grubbing practice.

He also oversaw the appointment of a new archbishop. While Yaroslav had been in Novgorod, he had refused to remove Antony from office. Even though the bishop was ineffectual owing to a handicap, he remained useful to Yaroslav as his man.[60] It was therefore imperative for Mikhail to replace the infirm cleric. On his directive, the people selected three candidates, prepared three lots, and Mikhail's son Rostislav drew one. The choice fell on Spiridon, a monk from the Yur'ev Monastery. By appointing Spiridon, the Novgorodians assured the Church's cooperation with Mikhail and his supporters.

(Ya. N. Shchapov, *Drevnerusskie knyazheskie ustavy: XI–XV vv.* [M., 1976], pp. 149–52 and L. V. Cherepnin, *Russkie feodal'nye arkhivy XIV–XV vv.* [M.-L., 1948], part 1, p. 254).

[59] For an examination of the different views historians hold on Mikhail's legislation concerning the peasants, see I. Ya. Froyanov, "O sobytiyakh 1227–1230 gg. v Novgorode," *Novgorodskiy istoricheskiy sbornik* 2 (12) (L., 1984), 105–8, and his *Myatezhniy Novgorod. Ocherki istorii gosudarstvennosti, sotsial'noy i politicheskoy bor'by kontsa IX – nachala XIII stoletiya* (Spb., 1992), pp. 272–5.

[60] In 1215, when Yaroslav came to Novgorod for the first time, Antony welcomed him to the town (NPL, pp. 53, 252). In 1225, after reporting that Yaroslav replaced Mikhail in Novgorod, the chronicler immediately states that Antony returned to Novgorod from Peremyshl' (NPL, pp. 64, 269), indicating that Yaroslav summoned the bishop back to Novgorod.

Mikhail also took on the task of retrieving the Novgorodian outpost of Volok (Volok Lam'skiy) and other districts that Yaroslav had seized.[61] His assignment was not unlike the one in 1225, when he had recovered Novgorodian goods from Yury. Whereas he had used his personal tie with Yury to negotiate that settlement, he had no such hold over Yaroslav. The latter refused to return the territories or to conclude peace declaring, in effect, that he would have no truck with the Novgorodians. Mikhail's failure to retrieve the domains was the only Novgorodian demand which he seemingly failed to fulfill.

In 1225, when Mikhail had departed from Novgorod he had cut off all political ties with the town. Four years later, his departure was markedly different. Having set the house in order, he designated his son Rostislav to remain as his lieutenant.[62] Before departing, however, he promised to revise Novgorod's laws and, should he fail, to recall his son to Chernigov. To judge from the account, Mikhail spoke only of administrative matters, but he must have committed himself to carrying out military obligations as well. Leading campaigns on behalf of Novgorod was one of the prince's most important duties.

It is unlikely that solely humane considerations motivated Mikhail to help the Novgorodians. One reason why he passed popular legislation was, undoubtedly, to derive personal benefits. It has been suggested that Vnezd Vodovik and his supporters repaid Mikhail for his concessions with sums of money.[63] What is more, on returning to Chernigov, Mikhail took with him prominent Novgorodians including Gleb, the son of the new *posadnik*.[64] As we have seen, in 1225 when he had departed from the town he had asked the Novgorodians to send merchants to Chernigov. It is reasonable to assume that, four years later, the grandees who accompanied him came, in part, to set up new business ventures. Moreover, in the light of Yaroslav's refusal to be pacified with Novgorod and because of the latent support that he enjoyed there, Mikhail probably used the Novgorodians, especially Gleb,

---

[61] Volok Lam'skiy (Volokolamsk), one of Novgorod's vassal towns, was located on the river Lama on the borders between the Novgorod, Suzdal', and Smolensk lands. Concerning the importance of Volok Lam'skiy, see A. A. Zimin, "Novgorod i Volokolamsk v XI–XV vekakh," *Novgorodskiy istoricheskiy sbornik* 10 (Novgorod, 1961), 99–101.

[62] Appointing a princeling to rule in his place was the usual practice for a prince who intended to maintain control of Novgorod from his patrimonial domain. For example, in 1228 Yaroslav departed for Pereyaslavl' and appointed his sons Fedor and Aleksandr to remain in Novgorod (NPL, pp. 66, 272).

[63] N. Rozhkov, "Politicheskie partii v Velikom Novgorode XII–XVI vv.," *Istoricheskie i sotsiologicheskie ocherki, sbornik statey* (M., 1906), pt. 2, p. 50.

[64] Concerning Mikhail's rule in Novgorod, see NPL, pp. 68, 274–5; Ak. sp., col. 511. Concerning the dates, see Berezhkov, p. 269. See also *Mikhail*, pp. 29–33.

as collateral. Their presence at his court would ensure that, should the need arise, Vnezd Vodovik would make a special effort to protect Rostislav and the Chernigov officials in Novgorod from Yaroslav's faction.

After spending some three months in Novgorod, Mikhail returned home to the Ol'govichi. In referring to the latter, the chronicler's use of the plural form "brothers" is evidence that several princes were living in the Chernigov lands. Chronicle information reveals six. These included Mikhail's cousin Mstislav Glebovich, who, as second in seniority, probably commanded the Ol'govichi during Mikhail's absence.[65] The other known prince of the senior branch was Vasil'ko of Kozel'sk whom the chronicles have not yet mentioned.[66] Oleg Svyatoslavich of the cadet branch ruled Novgorod Severskiy. Izyaslav Vladimirovich, who had escaped from Galich in 1211, was probably in Putivl'.[67] Svyatoslav of Trubetsk, whom we will meet soon, was evidently a descendant of Vsevolod "Fierce Aurochs."[68] Finally, in 1228 as we have seen, an unnamed prince of Kursk, perhaps Oleg's son, had participated in the campaign against Kamenets.

In December, the monk Spiridon left Novgorod to present himself to Metropolitan Kirill who consecrated him archbishop on February 24.[69] As Spiridon's political superior, Mikhail would have attended the ceremony in Kiev. On his return journey to Novgorod, Spiridon undoubtedly traveled via Chernigov, where Mikhail and the visiting Novgorodians would have honored him.

MIKHAIL ANTAGONIZES YAROSLAV OVER NOVGOROD

On May 3, 1230, during the liturgy in the Cathedral of the Mother of God in Vladimir, tremors shook the church. The icons swayed on the walls and the candelabra rattled on the floor as the worshipers stood transfixed. The earthquake was most severe in the south. In Kiev, the Church of the Assumption in the Caves Monastery split into four while Metropolitan Kirill was celebrating the liturgy. In the nearby refectory, stones plummeted from the ceiling crushing tables and benches. Tremors shook the entire land at the same hour damaging many churches. "An earthquake forebodes ill and not good. God sent it as a warning for Christians to repent."[70]

---

[65] See s.a. 1237: Ipat., col. 782.   [66] See s.a. 1237: Ipat., cols. 780–1 and see below, pp. 345–6.
[67] See above, p. 271.   [68] See s.a. 1232: NPL, p. 280 and see below, p. 326.
[69] NPL, pp. 68–9, 275–6. Concerning the dates, see Berezhkov, p. 270.
[70] Lav., col. 454; Mosk., p. 124; NPL, pp. 69, 275–6; Tver., col. 354. Tatishchev alone reports that the earthquake also hit all the Seversk lands, that is, the Chernigov lands (Tat. 4, p. 369; Tat. 3, p. 226).

The people of Rus' witnessed additional signs. On May 10, the sun rose earlier than usual. It had the shape of a triangle and, after a short while, it changed into a star, then it disappeared. Later, at the usual time, it rose again in its normal shape. Four days later the Kievans witnessed a frightening phenomenon. The sun took on the appearance of the moon and its two halves assumed the shapes of red, green, and blue columns. What is more, a huge ball of fire like a great cloud plummeted from the sky across the river Lybed' south of Kiev. The citizens watched in terror believing they would perish. "The all-merciful Lord directed the menacing fire to fly over the town into the Dnepr, where it dissipated. In this way God saved the people."[71]

In hindsight, the Novgorodians believed that the earthquake and the celestial signs had heralded the catastrophic famine that devastated their town in the autumn. In Suzdalia, Kiev, and Chernigov the people declared the phenomena to be harbingers of the famine that struck Smolensk that year. In the long term, however, they believed the signs foreshadowed the princely strife and the Tatar invasion that were to make the 1230s the most horrendous decade the people of Rus' had ever witnessed.

Despite the damage caused by the earthquake, Mikhail did not remain in Chernigov for long to supervise the rebuilding. He evidently escorted Spiridon to Novgorod. This is suggested by the news that, after the archbishop returned home on May 19, Mikhail invited him to conduct the ritual hair-cutting ceremony (*postrig*) on Rostislav in the Cathedral of St. Sofia. After that, Mikhail installed his son on the throne and returned to Chernigov.[72] Before departing, as we shall see, he promised the Novgorodians to return with troops by September 14.

Rostislav is the first Ol'govich who is reported undergoing a *postrig*.[73] The Vsevolodovichi of Suzdalia were the only other princes who, according to the chronicles, followed the practice.[74] Mikhail considered the ceremony to be extremely important to judge from the news that he visited Novgorod

---

[71] Lav., cols. 454–5; Mosk., p. 124.

[72] NPL, pp. 69, 276. Tatishchev alone reports that Mikhail ordered the *postrig* soon after Spiridon returned to Novgorod. He also claims that Rostislav was seven years of age at that time (Tat. 4, p. 369; Tat. 3, p. 226).

[73] The ceremony, a carry-over from paganism, initiated a princeling into public life. At the age of four or five a youth had his locks cut for the first time and was placed on a horse in the presence of the bishop, the *boyars*, and the townspeople. His father celebrated the event by holding sumptuous feasts and bestowing gifts on his guests (Karamzin, *Istoriya gosudarstva Rossiiskago*, vol. 3, pp. 154–5).

[74] Before 1230, the chronicles report only three hair-cutting ceremonies. In 1192, Yury Vsevolodovich had his hair cut (Lav., col. 409); two years later his brother Yaroslav underwent the same ceremony (Lav., col. 411); and, in 1212, two of the Konstantinovichi brothers, Vasil'ko and Vsevolod, had the *postrig* (Lav., col. 437).

expressly for that purpose. The *postrig* conferred on Rostislav the official status of prince and the prerogatives becoming that office. Until then he had been a minor, but after the ceremony he ruled Novgorod as a fully fledged prince. Thereafter Rostislav, in keeping with his father's policy, continued to pass legislation favoring the Novgorodians.[75] The latter, however, by accepting him in his new capacity, distanced themselves even further from Yaroslav.

On an unspecified date after the *postrig*, a delegation from Rus' went to Suzdalia with the task of preventing war between Mikhail and Yaroslav. It is noteworthy that, two years after attacking Daniil in Kamenets, Vladimir and Mikhail collaborated once again, but on this occasion to secure peace. Granted, Vladimir's duty as prince of Kiev required him to maintain concord among princes according to the mandate of Yaroslav the Wise. Nevertheless, he also had personal reasons for preserving harmony. A conflict between the Ol'govichi and the Vsevolodovich would place him in the embarrassing position of having to choose between two allies. Vladimir and Mikhail had an additional reason for preventing war. Daniil's expansionist ambitions in the southwest threatened both. If they were to become distracted in a conflict with the Vsevolodovichi, it would provide Daniil with an opportunity to make inroads into Galicia. Finally, Mikhail had a personal motive for not fighting Yaroslav. If the latter could be persuaded to back down from a confrontation, the reconciliation would strengthen Mikhail's hold over Novgorod.[76]

The two princes sent three prelates on the peace mission to Yury, to his brothers Yaroslav and Svyatoslav, and to the Konstantinovichi. Although Vladimir purportedly sent Metropolitan Kirill, the latter would also have acted in his own name as the highest Church official in Rus'. He had conducted such missions in the past. In 1226, as we have seen, he had helped to pacify Mikhail with Oleg, and two years later, he had failed to reconcile Daniil and Rostislav of Pinsk. Mikhail sent Bishop Porfiry, who, mentioned here for the first time, would remain bishop of Chernigov for most of Mikhail's term as senior prince. The third delegate *Igumen* Petr Akerovich, whose Monastery of the Holy Saviour at Berestovo in Kiev was a foundation of the Monomashichi, had close ties with the princes of

---

[75] Archaeologists have discovered a number of lead seals which they believe were used either by Mikhail or by Rostislav (Yanin 1, p. 208; Yanin 3, pp. 48, 142). Similarly, they have identified a princely sign of the Ol'govichi, which they believe either Mikhail or Rostislav used (A. A. Molchanov, "Ob atributsii lichno-rodovykh znakov knyazey Ryurikovichey X–XIII vv.," *Vspomogatel'nye istoricheskie distsipliny*, 16 [1985], pp. 70–1, 78–9).

[76] See also *Mikhail*, pp. 64–6.

Suzdalia.⁷⁷ Vladimir and Mikhail counted on him to follow Yury's example in asserting moral pressure on Yaroslav to be pacified.⁷⁸

Yury undoubtedly favored peace. War with the Ol'govichi would destroy the spirit of friendship that had reigned between the two dynasties since 1210, and he did not wish to take up arms against his brother-in-law. His hands, however, were tied by his oath to Yaroslav. As we have seen, he had ceded control of Novgorod to his brother. Moreover, when he and Yaroslav had been reconciled in the previous year, Yury had reaffirmed his support for Yaroslav's policy in Novgorod. Consequently, he would become embroiled in the conflict against his will should Yaroslav go to war.

Yaroslav accused Mikhail of wrongdoing but the chroniclers do not explain his grievance. They state only that Mikhail broke the oath that he had made to Yaroslav at some undisclosed date. In 1229, as we have seen, he had sent men to Yaroslav demanding that the latter return Volok. Since Yaroslav refused to negotiate on that occasion, it is unlikely that the princes concluded a pact at that time or after that date. Mikhail therefore made his promise around 1225, that is, towards the end of his first stay in Novgorod. As has been suggested, at the time that Mikhail had retrieved the Novgorodians' wares from Yury, the latter had handed over the running of the town to Yaroslav. On assuming jurisdiction over Novgorod, Yaroslav had undoubtedly required Mikhail to agree to an arrangement stipulating the limits of his involvement in the town.

In 1229, Mikhail had probably antagonized Yaroslav by occupying Novgorod in his own name.⁷⁹ He had also undermined the authority of the prince with pro-Novgorodian legislation. Mikhail had angered Yaroslav further by demanding that the latter return Volok Lam'skiy. He had then appointed his son, albeit a minor, as his lieutenant. Nevertheless, it seems that the official installment of Rostislav, in 1230, was the last straw. The evidence that Yaroslav reached the limit of his endurance after the hair-cutting ceremony supports this. On that occasion, Mikhail must have agreed to serve the Novgorodians in a manner that Yaroslav construed as a violation

---

⁷⁷ Yury Dolgorukiy, the grandfather to Yury and Yaroslav, was buried there (Ipat., col. 489). In 1185, their father Vsevolod demanded that the metropolitan consecrate *Igumen* Luka of Holy Saviour as bishop of Rostov (Ipat., cols. 629–30).

⁷⁸ According to Pashuto, one reason why Peter Akerovich spoke on Mikhail's behalf was because his monastery of the Holy Saviour owned the village of Holy Saviour near Chernigov (*Ocherki*, p. 58; see s.a. 1160: Ipat., col. 507). This observation is probably wrong. It is improbable that an institution of the Monomashichi in Kiev would own lands in the environs of Chernigov, the capital of the Ol'govichi. More than likely the institution that owned the village was Holy Saviour Cathedral in Chernigov.

⁷⁹ Yaroslav may have developed a resentment towards Mikhail as early as 1206, after Vsevolod Chermnyy evicted him from Pereyaslavl' and gave the town to Mikhail (see above, pp. 256–7).

of Mikhail's oath to him. Significantly, as we shall see, Mikhail, for the first time, promised to bring troops to Novgorod. His military intervention would greatly undermine Yaroslav's hold over the Novgorodians because the latter would no longer have to depend on Yaroslav's troops. Observing with increasing consternation how Mikhail was strengthening his hold over Novgorod, Yaroslav finally resolved to stop his meddling with force.

Fortunately for Mikhail, the moral authority of the three prelates and the entreaties of Yury persuaded Yaroslav to be pacified.[80] He seemingly resigned himself to Mikhail's continued presence in Novgorod. It is unthinkable, however, that he backed down without demanding concessions. We are not told what these were. We shall see, however, that later in the year Mikhail failed to bring troops to Novgorod by September 14 as he had promised. It is possible, that Mikhail had to break that promise to the townsmen as the price for peace with Yaroslav.

The autumn brought new hardships on the people of Rus' just as, according to many, the celestial portents and the earthquake had augured. On September 14 a frost destroyed the crops in the Novgorod district causing a great famine. Many starved to death. Archbishop Spiridon ordered a pit to be dug in which they buried 3,030 of the dead. Two additional pits were dug, but even they could not hold the great number of victims. The disaster struck the entire land of Rus' except the Kievan region. Chernigov is not singled out, but Smolensk lost more than 30,000 inhabitants in two years.[81] Novgorodians opposed to Mikhail's rule took advantage of the calamity to foment unrest. Stepan Tverdislavich quarreled with Mikhail's man, *Posadnik* Vodovik.[82] He incited the townsmen to plunder Vodovik's court. The latter had two of the ringleaders killed and then forced the rival *boyars* to swear oaths of allegiance. In this way, the pro-Mikhail faction reasserted its control on November 6.[83]

A month later, on December 8, Rostislav and *Posadnik* Vodovik visited Torzhok. The next day the Novgorodians looted Vodovik's court and those of his supporters. On hearing of the reprisals, the *posadnik* and his brothers, including *Tysyatskiy* Boris Negochevich, fled to Chernigov. The Novgorodians then made Stepan Tverdislavich their *posadnik*. They also forced Rostislav to flee to his father on the feeble pretext that Mikhail had not kept his promise to wage war on their behalf. They complained that he had promised to bring troops by September 14, but it was already December 6 and he had not come. It is difficult to imagine how the Novgorodians

[80] Concerning the peace delegation, see Lav., cols. 455–6; Mosk., p. 125; see also *Mikhail*, pp. 39–41.
[81] NPL, pp. 69–71; 277, 279–80. Concerning the famine in Smolensk, see Mosk., p. 125.
[82] NPL, pp. 60, 261–2.   [83] NPL, pp. 69, 276.

expected Mikhail to lead them on a campaign at a time when famine was decimating the population of Novgorod. Nevertheless, because Mikhail broke his pledge, they considered themselves released from their oath to him and free to invite another prince. In this way Yaroslav's supporters evicted the Ol'govichi from Novgorod, as it turned out, for the last time.

They summoned Yaroslav and he came on December 30. On this occasion, he promised to abide by all the laws of Yaroslav the Wise and by all the terms of the Novgorodians.[84] He therewith accepted the arrangement that the townsmen had concluded with Mikhail.[85] In other words, he agreed to rule according to all the terms that he had rejected a year earlier. Significantly, it was the pro-Yaroslav faction and not Mikhail's backers that forced him to accept the crippling terms. By capitulating, however, he successfully reasserted his authority over the town and his henchmen secured control of the leading administrative posts.[86]

Meanwhile, a core of dissenters found refuge with Mikhail. Thus, even though the Ol'govichi lost Novgorod, the conflict between Mikhail and Yaroslav's partisans remained unresolved. We are not told whether Mikhail hoped to reassert his claim to Novgorod, but as long as he harbored the town's malcontents Yaroslav considered him to be a threat. To secure his hegemony over Novgorod, therefore, Yaroslav had to eliminate Vodovik's cadre and to stop Mikhail from giving it support.[87]

THE *SNEM* OF 1231 AND MIKHAIL'S ATTACK ON KIEV

In the meantime, Mikhail himself seemingly distanced himself from Novgorodian politics and became increasingly involved in Kievan affairs. On March 25, 1231, Vasil'ko Konstantinovich of Rostov sent his spiritual father Kirill to Kiev. On April 6, Metropolitan Kirill,[88] Porfiry of Chernigov, and other bishops consecrated Kirill as bishop. Porfiry probably officiated because he ranked next after the metropolitan. In addition to eight abbots and archimandrites from Kievan monasteries, *Igumen* Ioann from the

---

[84] Concerning Rostislav's eviction from Novgorod, see NPL, pp. 69–70, 276–8; see also *Mikhail*, pp. 41–3.

[85] Historians have suggested that on his return to Novgorod in 1230, Yaroslav drew up a new agreement according to which princes would rule (for example, Yanin, *Novgorodskie posadniki*, p. 136; Cherepnin, *Russkie feodal'nye arkhivy*, pp. 239–54). In light of Mikhail's legislation in Novgorod in 1229, Yaroslav's so-called "new agreement" of 1230 was probably new for the Vsevolodovichi of Suzdalia. It was not new for the Novgorodians because they had already agreed to it with Mikhail in the previous year (*Mikhail*, pp. 44–5).

[86] The strength of Yaroslav's control over Novgorod after 1230 is illustrated by the uninterrupted term of office *Posadnik* Stepan Tverdislavich enjoyed until his death in 1243 (NPL, pp. 79, 297–8).

[87] See also *Mikhail*, pp. 43–5; *Crisis*, pp. 71–3.

[88] Metropolitan Kirill died two years later, in 1233 (NPL, pp. 72, 282).

Monastery of the Holy Martyrs in Chernigov also attended. His monastery, mentioned here for the first time, was evidently affiliated with the Church of SS. Gleb and Boris which David Svyatoslavich (d. 1123) had built.[89] Mikhail would have expressed a special interest in meeting Kirill because the latter was to be the bishop of his daughter Maria in Rostov.

In addition to Vladimir and his son Rostislav in whose presence the consecration took place, we are told that many princes were in Kiev attending a *snem*. Evidently, Vladimir organized the meeting to coincide with the religious ceremony. The chronicler gives the names of only the most important attendees: Mikhail of Chernigov and his son Rostislav; Rostislav Mstislavich the prince of Smolensk; Mstislav Glebovich the next in seniority after Mikhail among the Ol'govichi; Yaroslav Ingvarevich of Lutsk in Volyn'; Izyaslav Vladimirovich, who was now probably the senior prince of the cadet branch;[90] and Rostislav Borisovich of Polotsk.[91] Since Mikhail's name is placed immediately after Vladimir's, his contemporaries clearly considered him to be the second most important prince at the congress.

The list of names contains a heavy concentration of Rostislavichi and Ol'govichi. Yaroslav of Lutsk and Rostislav of Polotsk are the exceptions. The latter may have been present as an observer in that, having escorted the bishop of Polotsk to Kiev, he was invited to attend the *snem*. Or, he may have been invited because his dynasty was traditionally allied to the Ol'govichi. The chronicler concedes, however, that he did not mention by name many of the attendees, presumably, because they were less important. Not surprisingly, the dynasties that sent no princes were those from distant Suzdalia and Ryazan'. Remarkably, however, the Romanovichi were absent. Since Daniil was the head of his dynasty, the chronicler did not omit him because he was insignificant. We may conclude that his name was excluded from the list because Vladimir had not invited him.

Vladimir's reasons for convoking the council are not given. We have seen that princes met at irregular intervals to address a crisis. Eight years

---

[89] *Dynasty*, pp. 262–5, 301–2. In 1883, D. Ia. Samokvasov discovered a communal burial site with eight skulls and bones piled in an orderly fashion near the Church of SS. Gleb and Boris. This was evidently the common grave of the monastery whose monks adopted the Byzantine burial practice (V. Ia. Rudenok, "D. Ia. Samokvasov ta arkheolohichne vyvchennia Borysohlibs'koho monastyria u Chernihovi," *Slov'iany i Rus' u naukovii spadshchyni D. Ia. Samokvasova*. Materialy istoryko-arkheolohichnoho seminaru, prysviachenoho 150-richchiu vid dnia narodzhennia D. Ia. Samokvasova [14–16 veresnya 1993 r., m. Novgorod-Sivers'kyi] [Chernihiv, 1993], p. 96).

[90] As we have seen, in 1226 the senior prince of the cadet branch had been Oleg Svyatoslavich of Kursk (see above, p. 303). Two years later, the troops of Kursk and Novgorod Severskiy, presumably under his command, accompanied Mikhail against Daniil in Kamenets (see above, p. 308). Since Oleg did not attend the *snem* in Kiev, he was more than likely dead at that time.

[91] See *Mikhail*, pp. 66–7; for a detailed examination of the princes who attended the *snem*, see Dimnik, "Russian Princes," pp. 165–80.

earlier, for example, they had assembled to march against the Tatars. In
1231, however, there is no evidence to suggest that they debated how to
confront the invaders should they return. If the Tatars had been a concern,
Daniil would surely have come to the deliberations. Consequently, the
crisis was internal. One view has it that the princes met to discuss Mikhail's
controversy with Yaroslav and that they resolved the conflict.[92] This was
not so. As we shall see, Yaroslav would attack Mikhail later in the year.
Besides, their conflict over Novgorod was a private squabble that in no way
threatened the princes of southern Rus'.

Daniil's absence from the *snem* is an important clue. In 1228, as we have
seen, Vladimir and Mikhail had challenged his expansionism. Yaroslav of
Lutsk had echoed their anxiety because, in 1227, Daniil had seized his
domain and given him Peremil' and Mezhibozh'e in exchange.[93] Three
years later, Daniil captured Galich.[94] His growing strength was of grave
concern to the Rostislavichi, the Ol'govichi, and the princes of Volyn'.
Formulating a joint strategy against him, therefore, must have been high
on their agenda. It would explain why Vladimir refused to invite him to
the council.

Vladimir also had personal reasons for convoking the *snem*. Some two
months earlier, Mstislav Davidovich the prince of Smolensk had died.[95]
Since he had been the senior prince of the Rostislavichi, his mantle fell
on Vladimir's shoulders. In light of his promotion, Vladimir would have
insisted that all the princes form alliances with him in his new capacity.
He may also have considered such reassurance necessary because the power
of the Rostislavichi had waned significantly since 1223, when he had occupied Kiev. At the Kalka battle the Rostislavichi had suffered great losses
of manpower. Four years later, they had lost their renowned commander, Mstislav Udaloy. After Kalka, the Lithuanians had also pillaged the
lands of the Rostislavichi on at least four occasions.[96] Moreover, at the
beginning of 1231 a famine killed over 30,000 citizens of Smolensk. Finally,
a succession crisis split the dynasty asunder. After the death of Mstislav
Davidovich, his son Rostislav usurped power from his cousins, the sons
of Mstislav Romanovich.[97] As the senior prince, Vladimir had to set his
house in order. More importantly, as prince of Kiev he had to convince the

[92] *Istoriia*, vol. 2, p. 245.   [93] Ipat., cols. 751, 753; Perfecky, pp. 33–4.
[94] Ipat., col. 758–61; Perfecky, pp. 36–8.
[95] Most chronicles place this information as the last entry under 1230 suggesting the prince died around February of 1231 (Mosk., p. 125; Ak. sp., col. 512).
[96] NPL, s.a. 1223, pp. 61, 263; s.a. 1224, pp. 61, 264; s.a. 1225, pp. 64, 269; s.a. 1229, pp. 68, 275.
[97] The chronicles do not record the dynastic rivalry, however, P. V. Golubovsky is undoubtedly correct in asserting that the conflict, which arose between the descendants of Mstislav Romanovich and

other princes that the Rostislavichi remained a powerful force and that his control of Kiev remained secure. Accordingly, he would have asked all the princes at the *snem* to confirm their oaths of loyalty to him.

We are not told whether the princes reached a consensus of opinion concerning Daniil or renewed their pledges of allegiance to Vladimir. The chronicler does report, however, that after the ceremony in St. Sophia, all the princes went to the Caves Monastery for a feast.[98] He thereby implies that they parted amicably. Nevertheless, in the past, public manifestations of amity had been illusory. In 1072, at the translation of the relics of SS. Boris and Gleb, Izyaslav, Svyatoslav, and Vsevolod had declared their brotherly love. The following year, however, Svyatoslav and Vsevolod evicted Izyaslav from Kiev.[99] In 1231, therefore, the genuineness of the brotherly love that the princes expressed in Kiev remained to be tested.[100]

That brotherly love was short-lived. In the same year, Vladimir and Mikhail, who had lived in harmony for some seven years after the Kalka battle, came to blows for unexplained reasons. We are simply told that Vladimir sent an appeal for help to his brother Daniil because Mikhail was waging war against him. Perhaps Mikhail learned that the other princes were wavering in their loyalties to Vladimir. Perhaps he decided that the crisis among the Rostislavichi seriously weakened Vladimir's power in Kiev. Or, perhaps, the latter antagonized Mikhail. The chronicler reports that, in asking Daniil for help, Vladimir called him "brother," a term connoting ally. This suggests that Vladimir had also asked Daniil to pledge allegiance to him and that Daniil had done so after the *snem*. Mikhail would have treated Vladimir's reconciliation with Daniil as treachery. Whatever his reasons for waging war, Mikhail was the first to challenge his wife's uncle as prince of Kiev.

His initiative paid no dividends. We are told that Daniil came and pacified the two princes.[101] Nevertheless, Mikhail had declared his hand.

Mstislav Davidovich split the dynasty into two camps (*Istoriya Smolenskoy zemli do nachala xv st.* [K., 1895], p. 171). Concerning the two Mstislavs, see Baum., IX, 11, 16. Concerning Rostislav the son of Mstislav Davidovich, see Baum. 2, XVII, 2.

[98] Concerning the consecration and the *snem*, see Lav., cols. 456–7. Concerning the date, see Berezhkov, p. 108.

[99] *Dynasty*, pp. 76–81.　　[100] See also, *Mikhail*, pp. 66–9.

[101] Ipat., col. 766. Although the chronicler does not give the exact date, Mikhail must have declared war on Vladimir in the summer or autumn of 1231, after the *snem*. We are told that, after Daniil pacified the two rivals, he was still with Vladimir in Kiev when he learned that Prince Andrew of Hungary was attacking his lands. Daniil went out to confront Andrew and after the battle went to Torchesk, where he spent Holy Saturday in the spring of 1232 (Ipat., col. 770; see also *Mikhail*, pp. 69–70). Others suggest that Mikhail attacked Vladimir in the winter of 1232 (Perfecky, p. 40; Makhnovets', pp. 388–9).

After the *snem*, he decided that the time for temporizing had ended. He believed that the Ol'govichi were once again powerful enough to make a bid for Kiev. By repudiating his alliance with Vladimir, he revived the struggle for supremacy between the Ol'govichi and the Rostislavichi that had lain dormant since 1212, when the latter had driven out his father from Kiev. Moreover, in waging war against Vladimir, Mikhail forced him to throw in his lot with Daniil. Mikhail's change of policy therefore made him the odd man out.

MIKHAIL RELINQUISHES NOVGOROD TO YAROSLAV

Whereas Mikhail's rivalry with the Monomashichi in Rus' had only begun to simmer, he discovered that his conflict with Yaroslav over Novgorod had reached boiling point. In the autumn of 1231, Yaroslav attacked the northwest district of the Vyatichi lands. He set fire to Serensk,[102] but when he besieged Mosal'sk to the northwest on the river Mozhayka,[103] he failed to take it. Two years earlier, as we have seen, the Novgorodian messengers had found Mikhail visiting his patrimony in the region of Bryn. Serensk and Mosal'sk were located a short distance to the north of Bryn, suggesting that the two towns also belonged to Mikhail. Although the chronicles do not give the names of any other settlements in the district, archaeologists have discovered the remains of Meshchovsk and Serpeysk, which were probably part of Mikhail's domain.[104]

Since Yaroslav seemingly made Serensk the main object of his attack, it was most likely the administrative center of Mikhail's patrimony. Archaeologists have unearthed many artifacts from diverse trades, which show that Serensk was a wealthy town. It was noted for its blacksmiths who specialized in making agricultural implements. Silversmiths and jewellers produced copper and silver luxury goods. Glass ornaments such as bracelets and beads were also made locally and exported to Kiev.[105] An exchange of goods with other towns in Rus' was made easy because Serensk was conveniently

[102] Serensk was located on the high right bank of the river Serena, a tributary of the Zhizdra (*Zemlya Vyatichey*, p. 139).
[103] The remains of the medieval *detinets* of Mosal'sk are located in the present-day town of Mosal'ska (*Zemlya Vyatichey*, pp. 153–4).
[104] The two settlements, located between Serensk and Mosal'sk, were evidently not large enough to merit being mentioned by the chronicler. Archaeological evidence reveals, however, that they existed in the twelfth and thirteenth century (*Zemlya Vyatichey*, p. 155).
[105] *Zemlya Vyatichey*, pp. 139–41; T. N. Nikol'skaya, "Liteynye formochki drevnerusskogo Serenska," *Kul'tura srednevekovoy Rusi* (L., 1974), pp. 40–6; V. P. Kovalenko, "Votchinnye mastera-yuveliry v gorodakh Chernigovo-Severskoy zemli," *Slavyanskaya arkheologiya, 1990, Rannesrednevekovyy gorod i ego okruga* (Materialy po arkheologii Rossii), vyp. 2 (M., 1995), pp. 80–1.

located. It lay on the Volga–Oka trade route that brought merchandise such as ceramics from Iran and Central Asia. Amphorae for wine found in Serensk reveal that its people also conducted trade with the Black Sea region. The wine and Kievan manufactured goods came to it along the Kiev–Suzdalia route which wends its way east from Kiev to Putivl' then north to Sevsk, Boldyzh, Karachev, Serensk, Lobynsk, and Moscow.[106]

The objective of Yaroslav's raid was obvious. Novgorod remained the main bone of contention between the two princes. After Vodovik and his cronies fled to Chernigov, Yaroslav broke his peace with Mikhail because, in his view, Vodovik had revived the quarrel. He attacked Mikhail's patrimony with the intention of striking him where he would feel the damage most and forcing him to stop supporting the malcontents. The presence of the Novgorodian militia among Yaroslav's troops shows that the *veche* was also eager to stop Mikhail from backing the refugees.

Significantly, Yury and the Konstantinovichi helped Yaroslav. For the first time, therefore, Vasil'ko of Rostov waged war against his father-in-law. His action assumed a special poignancy when we discover that, earlier in the summer, Mikhail's first grandson, Boris, was born to his daughter Maria. Later evidence will show that Maria and her sons were especially fond of Mikhail.[107] On this occasion, however, Vasil'ko's political obligations to his uncle in Novgorod outweighed his personal tie with his father-in-law. This was not the case with Yury. He rode only as far as the border of the Chernigov lands where his loyalty to his brother-in-law prevailed and he returned to Vladimir.[108] Yaroslav's campaign may have resembled a Polovtsian raid, but it served to register his displeasure. By refusing to conclude peace, he also signaled to Mikhail that he was prepared to pursue his objective with force until Mikhail expelled the Novgorodian fugitives from his lands.[109]

Towards the end of 1231, Vnezd Vodovik died in Chernigov.[110] His death, in addition to Yaroslav's raid, gave Mikhail compelling reasons for severing

[106] *Zemlya Vyatichey*, pp. 285–6.
[107] Boris was born on July 24, the Feast of SS. Boris and Gleb (Lav., col. 457). As we shall see, in 1246 Boris accompanied Mikhail to Saray and was present at his death (NPL, p. 301; *Mikhail*, pp. 130, 134). Maria and her sons Boris and Gleb dedicated a feast and built a church in his honor and evidently commissioned a narrative account of his martyrdom (*Mikhail*, pp. 141–2, 152).
[108] Yury pitched camp at an unidentified location, which the chronicler calls Upolozekh, and then returned home (Lav., col. 459). The reference may be to the Poloz'e (Polozh'e, Poluzh'e) district along the river Luzha, a tributary of the Protva that flows into the Oka. It is located approximately halfway between Moscow and Serensk. During the first half of the thirteenth century the northern boundary of the Chernigov lands was evidently located just to the south of it.
[109] For Yaroslav's attack, see NPL, pp. 71, 280; compare s.a. 1232: Lav., col. 459. Concerning the dating, see Berezhkov, p. 108; see also *Mikhail*, pp. 45–7.
[110] NPL, pp. 71, 280. Vodovik probably died during the winter, that is, in January or February of 1232.

his support of the fugitives. On being deprived of its leader, the faction's chances of regaining power in Novgorod were greatly reduced. Moreover, Mikhail had been bound to support Vodovik owing to their mutual oaths. The *posadnik's* death therefore released him from that obligation. We are not told if he evicted the Novgorodians from Chernigov, but their act of desperation shows that he abandoned them. Before Easter of 1232, *Tysyatskiy* Boris Negochevich and his band left Chernigov. On their way north they persuaded Svyatoslav of Trubetsk, who is mentioned only on this occasion, to go with them and, presumably, to help them oust Yaroslav from Novgorod.[111] He accompanied them to the south of Lake Il'men' from where he returned to Rus' after discovering that they had deceived him.[112] Mikhail therefore mollified Yaroslav by severing his ties with the refugees. After that he was free to devote his complete attention to affairs in southern Rus'.

MIKHAIL CAPTURES KIEV

In 1232 Mikhail and the princes of Rus' received ominous news. The Tatars had invaded the Volga Bulgars but had withdrawn to their winter camps before attacking the Bulgarian capital.[113] Despite being warned of the danger, the princes of Rus' were too preoccupied with their rivalries to organize any united action against the approaching enemy.[114] At that time, the chronicler notes, "many uprisings, great conspiracies, and countless wars" engulfed Rus'.[115]

Since at least 1228 Mikhail had been allied with Andrew II and his actions suggest that his salient obligation towards the king was to let the Hungarians rule Galich. He would also have promised to help the king keep out Daniil from that town and to refrain from occupying it himself. The agreement, however, did not impinge upon his ambitions for Kiev. Accordingly, in 1231 he had attacked Vladimir Ryurikovich but, after Daniil pacified the two, Mikhail agreed to leave Vladimir in peace.

---

[111] Trubetsk, as we have seen, belonged to the most junior family of the cadet branch (see above, p. 166).
[112] NPL, pp. 71–2, 280–1; *Mikhail*, pp. 47–8.   [113] Lav., col. 459.
[114] Tatishchev alone reports that the Bulgars sent messengers to Yury in Suzdalia asking him for reinforcements against a powerful and unknown nation whose language they had never heard before. Yury deliberated with his brothers, but on learning that the Tatars came in great force he refused to send troops. Meanwhile, the Tatars devastated much of the Bulgarian land (Tat. 4, p. 370; Tat. 3, p. 227).
[115] Ipat., col. 762.

Two years later, Daniil summoned Khan Kotyan and Izyaslav Vladimirovich of the Ol'govichi.[116] They rode to Kiev, where Daniil insisted that Vladimir and Izyaslav swear oaths of loyalty. But before they encountered the Hungarians, Izyaslav pillaged Daniil's town of Tikhoml' and deserted him.[117] In doing so, he renewed the Ol'govichi aggression against the two Monomashichi. After that, "unfaithful" Galicians and all the princes of Bolokhov invaded Daniil's lands.[118] They besieged Kamenets, and withdrew. Troops sent by Vladimir pursued and captured the princes of Bolokhov, and handed them over to Daniil. Mikhail and Izyaslav, we are told, threatened to attack Daniil if he refused to release their brothers.[119] Later, Prince Andrew's untimely death in the winter of 1233 forced the Hungarians to vacate Galich.[120] Daniil therewith occupied it unchallenged. In 1234, therefore, Vladimir sent his son Rostislav to Daniil to strengthen their alliance. Despite their renewed pact, however, Mikhail and Izyaslav continued waging war against Vladimir forcing him to ask Daniil for help.

Vladimir's growing vulnerability probably encouraged Mikhail to intensify his aggression. In addition to the famine in Smolensk and the Lithuanian attacks against its lands, the Rostislavichi had experienced a new dynastic upheaval. In 1232, the legitimate claimant, Roman's grandson Svyatoslav Mstislavich, finally seized control of Smolensk. After achieving his objective, however, he mercilessly slaughtered many of the townspeople.[121] We are not told if Vladimir became involved in the rivalry, but this devastation further depleted the manpower resources and undermined the political effectiveness of the Rostislavichi.

Why did Mikhail attack Vladimir? Although the chroniclers fail to explain, archaeological evidence reveals that at this time trade was flourishing

[116] Historians are divided over Izyaslav's identity. It has been argued elsewhere that he was Izyaslav Vladimirovich of the cadet branch who attended the *snem* in 1231 (Dimnik, "Russian Princes," pp. 170–7). Others claim he was Izyaslav Mstislavich, a grandson of Roman Rostislavich (Pashuto, *Ocherki*, p. 214; Perfecky, p. 41; Makhnovets', p. 390).

[117] Ipat., cols. 770–1; *Mikhail*, pp. 71–2.

[118] The Bolokhov lands were located in the southwest corner of the Kievan land, bordering on the lands of Volyn' and Galicia. More specifically, the region lay to the north and east of Mezhibozh'e located on the upper reaches of the Southern Bug river (see *Mikhail*, pp. 117–18; P. A. Rappoport, "Goroda Bolokhovskoy zemli," KSIIMK 57 [M., 1955], 52–9). The association of the Ol'govichi with the Bolokhov district went back to at least 1146 when Mikhail's grandfather Svyatoslav Vsevolodovich had received five towns in the Bolokhov lands as his domain (see above, p. 29).

[119] Ipat., cols. 774–5. The chronicler misplaces this entry under the year 1235. Concerning the correct year, see *Mikhail*, p. 99, n. 18.

[120] See s.a. 1234: Ipat., col. 771; *Mikhail*, pp. 96–7.

[121] Svyatoslav Mstislavich seized control of Smolensk on July 24 with the help of Polotsk forces (NPL, pp. 72, 281). Concerning Svyatoslav Mstislavich, see Baum., IX, 29.

in Rus'. Chernigov and Kiev had commercial ties with Galicia, Hungary, and Western Europe. As we shall see, the Galicians supplied the two towns with much of their salt.[122] Hungary not only sent its horses and other goods to Rus', but also served as the conduit for luxury items coming from Western Europe.[123] From the second half of the twelfth century, Chernigov and Kiev conducted trade with Lower Lotharingia, the Rhine region, Westphalia, and Lower Saxony. This is attested to by the hoard of gold and silver objects discovered in 1957 and in 1958 in the western suburb of Chernigov. Among the items was a golden ciborium lid from the third quarter of the twelfth century created by goldsmiths in the region of the river Maas in Lower Lotharingia.[124] Significantly, during this period Chernigov not only rivaled Kiev in trade, crafts, and architectural projects, but evidently, also surpassed it in size. It has been estimated that, at the beginning of the thirteenth century, Chernigov occupied a territory covering some 400–450 hectares, whereas Kiev had an area of some 360–380 hectares.[125]

Did Vladimir, encouraged by Daniil, disrupt the flow of western goods passing through the Kievan land to Chernigov? As a counter-measure, did Mikhail attempt to pressure Vladimir into renewing their alliance and into reactivating the commercial and military arrangements they had enjoyed in 1228, when they had opposed Daniil? Or, did Mikhail launch an independent expansionist policy in quest of Kiev and of hegemony over Rus'? The sources do not tell us. Whatever his objectives, he seemingly failed because Vladimir remained staunchly allied to Daniil. The latter therefore rode to Vladimir's assistance. Unable to withstand their combined forces, Mikhail lifted his siege of Kiev and withdrew. But the two Monomashichi pursued him to Chernigov.[126]

Twenty-three years earlier Mikhail's father, Vsevolod Chermnyy, died while the Rostislavichi besieged Chernigov. At that time, the attackers failed to capture the citadel but pillaged the countryside until the prince of Chernigov, Vsevolod's brother Gleb, capitulated. In 1235, Vladimir and Daniil repeated that tactic. They plundered the environs and set fire to the outer town hoping to make Mikhail submit. He, however, came out of

---

[122] See below, p. 362.
[123] Concerning trade between Rus' and Hungary, and concerning Western European goods passing through Hungary to Rus', see Novosel'tsev and Pashuto, "Vneshnyaya torgovlya Drevney Rusi," pp. 86–7.
[124] V. P. Darkevich and I. I. Edomakha, "Pamyatnik zapadnoevropeyskoy torevtiki XII veka," SA, nr. 3 (M., 1964), pp. 247–55; V. P. Darkevich, "K istorii torgovykh svyazey Drevney Rusi," KSIA 138 (1974), pp. 99, 101.
[125] Mezentsev, *Drevniy Chernigov*, p. 150, and his "The Territorial and Demographic Development of Medieval Kiev," pp. 161–9.
[126] Ipat., col. 772.

the citadel and, after tricking Daniil,[127] slaughtered many Galicians forcing them to withdrew to the Kievan land.[128]

Mikhail waited until Izyaslav Vladimirovich brought the Polovtsy and then rode in pursuit.[129] Daniil's troops, however, were war-weary because they had been pillaging the Chernigov lands for over four months, from January 6 to May 14. The two sides clashed near Torchesk where, after "the godless Grigory Vasil'evich and the Molibogovich *boyars* betrayed them," Vladimir and Daniil were defeated. Vladimir and many *boyars* were also taken captive. Meanwhile, Mikhail's allies took Kiev and the Polovtsy, we are told, inflicted great evil on the Kievans. Defeating Vladimir and Daniil was Mikhail's greatest military victory until then, and capturing Kiev was his crowning achievement. It was the first time since 1212, when the Rostislavichi drove out his father, that an Ol'govich captured the capital of Rus'.

His victory asserted the supremacy of the Ol'govichi over southern Rus' and bolstered his prestige to an unprecedented height. He also humiliated Vladimir by allowing the nomads to carry him off for ransom. Moreover, by neutralizing Vladimir, he assured himself free reign in appointing his puppet to the throne. He deputed Izyaslav Mstislavich, a Rostislavich, to the job.[130] He evidently did so on the understanding that Izyaslav would step down after Vladimir returned from captivity.[131] In designating Vladimir as his lieutenant in Kiev, Mikhail imitated Andrey Bogolyubskiy. In 1171, as we have seen, the latter had appointed Roman Rostislavich, the then senior prince of the Rostislavichi, to Kiev. Nevertheless, in selecting a prince from a different dynasty to serve as his lieutenant in Kiev, Mikhail adopted an unprecedented measure for a prince of Chernigov.

[127] Tatishchev alone describes Mikhail's trick. He promised Daniil many gifts if he would desert Vladimir and pacify the latter. Daniil agreed and attempted to persuade Vladimir to lift the siege. Meanwhile, Mikhail sallied out of Chernigov at night, caught Daniil's troops by surprise, and killed many of them. Daniil barely escaped (Tat. 4, p. 372; Tat. 3, pp. 229–30).

[128] NPL, pp. 73–4, 284; compare the Hypatian Chronicle, which has spurious information and incorporates details from 1239, when the Tatars attacked Mstislav Glebovich in Chernigov (Ipat., col. 772). See M. Dimnik, "The Siege of Chernigov in 1235," *Mediaeval Studies* 41 (1979), 387–403; *Mikhail*, pp. 72–3.

[129] Many sources state, wrongly, that the Izyaslav who went to collect the Polovtsy was Izyaslav Mstislavich, the grandson of Roman, a Rostislavich (for example, Mosk., p. 126; Ak. sp., col. 513; Erm., p. 74; L'vov, p. 156). As it has been shown elsewhere, the Izyaslav who fetched the Polovtsy was Izyaslav Vladimirovich, an Ol'govich (Dimnik, "Russian Princes," pp. 172–6).

[130] Mosk., p. 126; Ak. sp., col. 513; L'vov, p. 156; Erm., p. 74; see Dimnik, "Russian Princes," pp. 172–6; Baum., IX, 32. Izyaslav Mstislavich was a legitimate claimant to Kiev because his father Mstislav had died at Kalka in 1224 as prince of Kiev (Baum., IX, 32).

[131] As we shall see, after Vladimir returned from captivity, Izyaslav handed over Kiev to him without a fight according, it would appear, to a prearranged agreement (M. Dimnik, "The Struggle for Control over Kiev in 1235 and 1236," *Canadian Slavonic Papers* 21, nr. 1 [1979], 31–7).

Before turning over Kiev to Izyaslav Mstislavich, however, Mikhail evidently made the Germans in Kiev pay redemption-fees for their goods.[132]
At first glance his treatment of the foreigners is puzzling. In 1225, as we have
seen, he had sought to promote trade when he instructed the Novgorodians to send foreign merchants to Chernigov. Ordinarily, merchants who
visited Kiev would also visit Chernigov. Why then did he take punitive
action against welcome traders? The Novgorod chronicler alludes to the
answer. Since he alone reports that Mikhail fined the Germans it was probably only they, who traveled north and reported their fate to the chronicler,
who suffered such ill fortune. This implies that Mikhail did not fine all the
merchants in Kiev but only those who came via Novgorod, where Yaroslav
was prince. After occupying Novgorod in 1231, Yaroslav undoubtedly severed the commercial ties with Chernigov that the Novgorodians had initiated at Mikhail's behest. Instead, he promoted trade with the Rostislavichi
in Smolensk and Kiev. By demanding redemption-fees from the
Germans, Mikhail took advantage of his seizure of Kiev to create mischief
for Yaroslav.

At the same time, we may assume, he took steps to improve the terms
of trade for the Ol'govichi. Just as ten years earlier he had requested the
Novgorodians to send merchants to Chernigov, in 1235 he undoubtedly
strengthened commercial ties between Kiev and Chernigov. Ten years later,
the Franciscan monk John de Plano Carpini passed through Kiev on his
way to the Tatars. He traveled with merchants from Bratislava to Kiev,
where he met others from Constantinople, Genoa, Venice, Pisa, and Acre
in Palestine. After he departed from Kiev, other traders arrived including
men from the Poles and Austria.[133] If such active trade existed in Kiev after
the Tatars razed it, we may assume that, in 1235, even greater numbers
of merchants traveled along the well-trodden routes through the Kievan
land.

By seizing Kiev, Mikhail eliminated the obstacles that Vladimir's control
of the town had posed. After Vladimir had formed his pact with Daniil,
the Kievan domain had became a buffer zone between Chernigov and
Galich. Mikhail was prevented from marching freely against Daniil because Vladimir could either attack him as he passed through the Kievan
domain, or invade the Chernigov lands in Mikhail's absence. Vladimir
could likewise impose debilitating tariffs on Chernigov merchants using

---

[132] Concerning Mikhail's capture of Kiev and occupation of Galich, see Ipat., cols. 773–4; NPL,
pp. 74, 284–5.
[133] Vernadsky, *The Mongols*, pp. 62–4; C. Dawson (ed.), *The Mongol Mission* (New York, 1955),
pp. 70–1; *Mikhail*, pp. 76–7.

Kievan routes, or obstruct foreign caravans passing through his lands to Chernigov. In capturing Kiev, Mikhail removed these obstacles. Nevertheless, it is perplexing to discover that after capturing Kiev, he chose not to rule the mother of all Rus' towns in person.

The chroniclers do not explain Mikhail's reasons for turning over control of Kiev to a lieutenant. They also fail to provide a complete picture of the events that transpired during the summer and autumn of that year. Above all, they neglect to answer two important questions. For how long a period of time did Mikhail remained in Kiev after he captured it? And, did he himself rule Kiev before appointing a Rostislavich as his puppet? We can glean partial answers by scrutinizing two events.

At an undisclosed date after Daniil returned to Galich from his defeat at Torchesk, its *boyars* rebelled. They forced him to take a startling course of action: he fled to Hungary. This was a seemingly foolhardy act because Andrew II was his arch-rival for Galich. Daniil's conduct becomes understandable only after we discover that, on September 21, 1235, the king had died.[134] Daniil therefore must have traveled to Hungary after hearing of his enemy's demise. Indeed, a Hungarian source reports that, on October 14, Daniil attended the coronation of Andrew's son and successor Béla IV.[135]

We must remember that Mikhail had pledged to abide by the oath that he had made to Andrew II. According to it, he had agreed to defend the king's claim to Galich, and the king's agent had been his son, Andrew. Following the latter's death in 1233, Daniil had occupied Galich therewith placing increased pressure on Mikhail to help the king regain control of it. Two years later, Andrew II's death terminated their agreement. Mikhail therefore had to renew it with the new king. Daniil, however, contacted Béla IV first, and the evidence that he attended the coronation suggests that the new king had changed his policy towards Daniil. Mikhail therefore saw Andrew II's death and the vacant throne in Galich as an ideal opportunity for seizing the town. Control of Galich in addition to Kiev would enable him to regulate all trade passing through those lands to Chernigov. We may therefore reconstruct Mikhail's activity for 1235 as follows. Sometime in June he evicted Vladimir from Kiev and replaced him as prince. Towards the end of September, after Andrew II died and Daniil had fled from Galich, Mikhail appointed Izyaslav Mstislavich to rule Kiev in his place and he occupied Galich.

[134] B. Hóman, *Geschichte des Ungarischen Mittelalters* (Berlin, 1943), vol. 2, p. 105.
[135] According to the account, Daniil was at the coronation of Béla IV on Sunday, the eve of the ides of October (S. Katona [ed.], *Historia critica regum Hungariae stirpis Arpadianae ex fide domesticorum et externorum scriptorum* [Posonii et Cassoviae, 1783], vol. 5, p. 754).

As we shall see, Mikhail would be a popular ruler in Galich who enjoyed the loyalty of most *boyars* so that his brother-in-law Daniil would be unable to depose him. Significantly, Mikhail did not hand over the town to Izyaslav Vladimirovich of the Igorevichi even though the latter had a claim to it. Izyaslav's grandmother, as we have seen, had belonged to the town's defunct dynasty. What is more, because Izyaslav's father Vladimir had ruled Galich, Izyaslav had the right to sit on the throne of his father. Instead of handing over the town to the cadet branch, however, Mikhail occupied it in person. The chronicler does not tell us his plans for the town. Perhaps he was going to use his earlier sojourn in Novgorod as the model, but with an important difference. As we have seen, he had remained in Novgorod only long enough to consolidate his power and then he had appointed his son Rostislav as his lieutenant. Mikhail had not planned to make Novgorod a possession of the Ol'govichi because the town traditionally did not have its own dynasty. In Galich, however, the local dynasty had died out over thirty-five years earlier. We may assume, therefore, that he intended to follow the example of his father, Vsevolod Chermnyy who, in 1206, had attempted to take Galich for his own family.

Mikhail's chances of achieving his objective were good. He had effectively neutralized Vladimir, whose presence in Kiev now depended on his goodwill. Daniil, it is true, remained at large and, after losing Vladimir's support, seemingly gained the backing of Béla IV. Even so, their alliance presented no immediate danger. The newly crowned king had to consolidate his control at home.[136] As for Daniil, his manpower had been greatly depleted in the battles with the Ol'govichi and the Polovtsy. His military weakness was exposed that winter when he returned from Hungary without Hungarian auxiliaries and hopelessly strove to regain Galich. He and Vasil'ko were unable even to reach the town. An important reason for their failure was probably the stiff opposition they met along the way from the local *boyars* who threw in their lot with Mikhail.

The *boyars* had been fickle in the past, but for the time being their support gave Mikhail the advantage. As we have seen, when Daniil had fled to Galich

[136] Hungary experienced great internal unrest during the reign of Andrew II. In 1222, for example, the nobles restricted the king's authority with a Golden Bull. Surprisingly, the leader of the nobility was the king's own son and future king, Béla IV. Andrew's death provided an excellent opportunity for revitalizing the government and the office of monarch. Béla IV therefore attempted to restore some of the king's former power (C. A. Macartney, *Hungary, A Short History* [Edinburgh, 1962], pp. 26, 31–2).

from Torchesk, he had found the magnates in a rebellious mood. The pro-Ol'govichi faction was able to present effective opposition for at least two reasons: he had suffered great losses of manpower outside Chernigov, and at Torchesk the Polovtsy had taken captive his commander Miroslav and many other *boyars*. By eliminating or temporarily removing Daniil's partisans, the Ol'govichi strengthened the position of their supporters, or the "unfaithful Galicians" as the Hypatian chronicler calls them.[137] The immediate reason for their revolt against the Romanovichi, however, had been the greedy conduct of Daniil's brother, Vasil'ko. On returning to Vladimir in Volyn' from the Chernigov lands, he had refused to divide the booty with the Galicians.[138]

Two *boyars* were especially active in fomenting opposition to Daniil. Grigory Vasil'evich, as we have seen, had betrayed Vladimir and Daniil at Torchesk. Later, he would become the major-domo (*dvorskiy*) to Mikhail's son Rostislav and defend Galich against Daniil.[139] In 1241, he would be one of the two malefactors who would create untold havoc throughout Galicia during Daniil's absence.[140] The second ringleader was Dobroslav Sud'ich, who also conspired against Daniil because Vasil'ko absconded with the spoils. After Daniil returned to Galich from Torchesk, Dobroslav and a *boyar* named Zbyslav prompted a certain Boris of Mezhibozh'e to tell the prince that Izyaslav Vladimirovich was leading the Polovtsy against his patrimony. Daniil treated the news as a lie, believing that the *boyars* were attempting to lure him out of Galich.[141] The chronicler does not state which prince Dobroslav favored, but it was Mikhail. This is confirmed by the news that, after the Tatar invasion, he assumed the role of prince for a time and allotted Galician territories to *boyars* from Chernigov rather than

---

[137] The Hypatian chronicler names a number of *boyars* who opposed Daniil in the late 1220s and early 1230s and were probably among the "unfaithful Galicians" who supported Mikhail. They were: (1) Sudislav, who backed Prince Andrew until the latter's death in the winter of 1233 (Ipat., col. 771); in 1228 when Mikhail attacked Daniil, Sudislav was with Prince Andrew in Galich and, we are told, they were at peace with Mikhail (Ipat., col. 753); (2) Zhiroslav who, in 1226, fled to Mikhail's ally Izyaslav Vladimirovich (Ipat., cols. 747–50); (3) the Molibogovich family which plotted to kill Daniil in 1230 (Ipat., cols. 762–3); in 1235 the family betrayed Daniil at Torchesk (Ipat., col. 774); (4) Filip, who plotted to kill Daniil with the Molibogovich family (Ipat., col. 762); (5) Klimyata from Golyye Gory who, in 1231, deserted Daniil (Ipat., col. 765); (6) the Arbuzovich family whom Daniil attacked in 1232 (Ipat., col. 770); as we shall see, the following also conspired against Daniil: (7) Grigory Vasil'evich; (8) Dobroslav Sud'ich; (9) Zbyslav; and (10) Boris of Mezhibozh'e. Finally (11), the princes of Bolokhov were Daniil's enemies (Ipat., cols. 767, 774; see also, Pashuto, *Ocherki*, pp. 142–7).
[138] Ipat., col. 774.
[139] Ipat., cols. 777–8. The *dvorskiy* managed the prince's household and landed estates and took part in administrative and judicial activities.
[140] Ipat., cols. 789–91; *Mikhail*, p. 116.   [141] Ipat., col. 774.

from Galicia.[142] Thus, with the help of a local fifth column, as it were, Mikhail had a good chance of securing his hold over Galich.

In the meantime, his comrade-in-arms, Izyaslav Vladimirovich, also seized one of Daniil's towns. As we have seen, in 1233 the "unfaithful Galicians" and the princes of Bolokhov had retaliated against Daniil by attacking Kamenets. To judge from the news that in 1233 the town belonged to Daniil and that, as we shall see, in 1240, the next time it is mentioned it was Izyaslav's Kamenets, the change of ownership occurred between those years. The most likely occasion was in 1235, after the Ol'govichi routed Daniil at Torchesk. As we have seen, after Daniil had fled to Galich, Dobroslav attempted to convince him that Izyaslav was marching against his patrimony. Daniil treated the information as a lie, but there was probably an element of truth in Dobroslav's allegation. Izyaslav did march against Daniil's domain, but instead of attacking Vladimir in Volyn' he captured Kamenets. Since Mikhail had taken Galich as the prize for defeating Daniil, Izyaslav evidently took Kamenets as a prize for his part in the victory (map 6).[143]

The roles between Mikhail and Daniil were now reversed. The former became the defender of Galich and the latter the challenger. Mikhail succeeded in keeping his brother-in-law at bay for the next three years by protecting his position in Galich and by taking the war to Volyn'. In the spring of 1236, he attacked Daniil. In addition to his own retinue, he was probably accompanied by his son Rostislav, Galician *boyars*, the princes of Bolokhov, and troops from the Kievan land. He also sent Izyaslav to bring the Polovtsy. Finally, he summoned Conrad of Mazovia.[144] If he had formed his initial pact with his uncle after becoming prince of Chernigov, he undoubtedly reaffirmed it after occupying Galich because Polish backing would be vital to his control of that town. This was the first occasion on which Mikhail and Conrad collaborated in a military venture. What is more, in joining his nephew, Conrad broke off friendly ties with Daniil.[145]

The chronicler does not give Mikhail's reasons for attacking Daniil. Since, however, he was consolidating his rule in Galicia, he presumably wished to do more than merely plunder Daniil's lands. For the latter exercise, the Poles and Polovtsy were superfluous. The size of his attacking force

[142] Ipat., cols. 789–90; *Mikhail*, pp. 115–16.   [143] Dimnik, "Kamenec," pp. 30–3; *Mikhail*, 100–1.
[144] When Mikhail was informed of Kiev's capitulation in the winter of 1240, he fled to Conrad prince of Mazovia (Ipat., cols. 783–4). After the Tatars passed through the Polish lands, Mikhail "left his uncle" and returned to Kiev (Ipat., col. 788). Conrad therefore was the son of Casimir II the brother of Mikhail's mother (W. Dworzaczek, *Genealogia: Tablice* [Warsaw, 1959], table 3).
[145] In 1229, for example, Daniil and Vasil'ko rode to Conrad's assistance (Ipat., cols. 754, 757). Later in the year, the Poles assisted Daniil against the Hungarians (Ipat., col. 761).

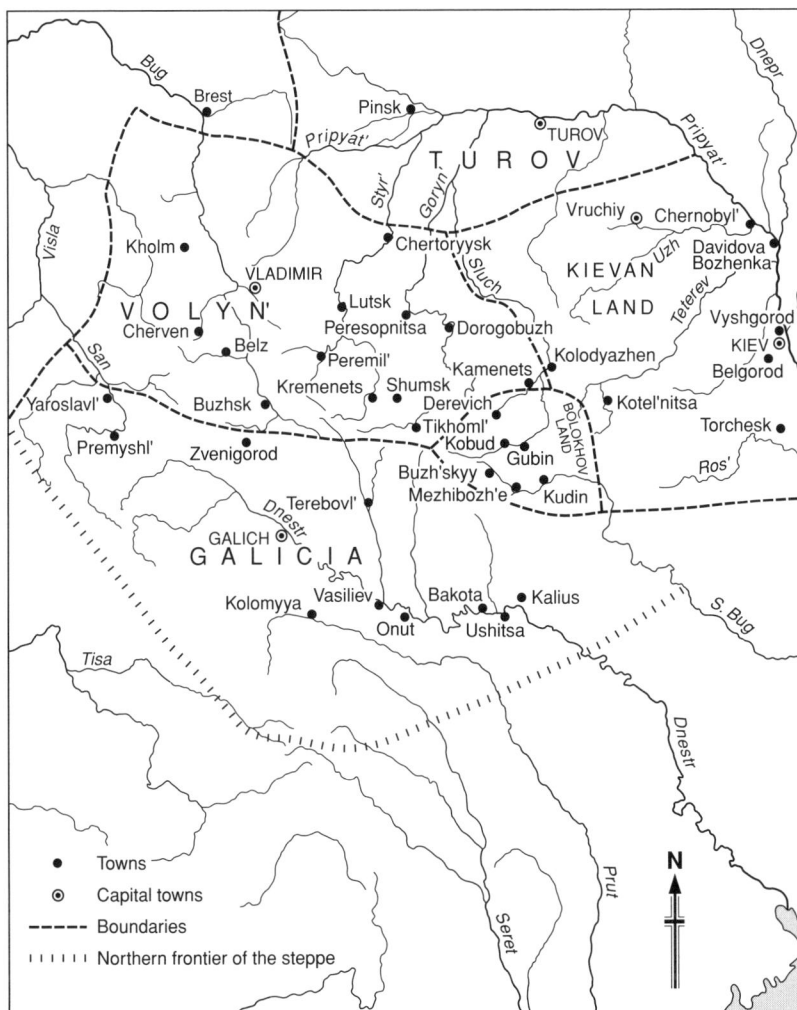

Map 6   The lands of Galicia and Volyn' during the second half of the twelfth
and the first half of the thirteenth century

suggests that he had a more demanding goal in mind, namely, to capture
Daniil's capital of Vladimir. It is unlikely, however, that he wished to evict
his brother-in-law permanently. The town was Daniil's patrimony and taking it away from him could escalate their personal rivalry into a dynastic
conflict bringing other Monomashichi to Daniil's aid. Mikhail probably

intended to capture Vladimir and use it as a lever for making Daniil abandon his claim to Galich. Thanks, in the main, to the treachery of the Polovtsy, Mikhail failed. Just as they had deserted him and Vladimir in 1228, when they had attacked Daniil in Kamenets, on this occasion Polovtsian perfidy once again saved Daniil from additional losses. The nomads plundered the Galician lands forcing Mikhail to abandon his campaign.[146]

At the beginning of the summer, Daniil and Vasil'ko rallied their troops to march against Mikhail and his son Rostislav. But their objective to drive him out of Galich was too ambitious. He barricaded himself in the town with his retinue, the local militia, and a contingent of Hungarians. The Romanovichi also had little hope of capturing the town without partisan support from among the townsmen who could open the gates to them. Dissuaded from taking Galich, they sought to assuage their frustration by seizing its northern outpost of Zvenigorod. Its citizens, who had been zealous supporters of the Igorevichi in the past, repelled the attack.[147]

Surprisingly, Mikhail had Hungarians at his disposal. This meant that, even though Daniil had participated in the king's coronation ceremony a year earlier, Béla IV had not forsaken the Ol'govichi. He renewed his father's pact with Mikhail on some unspecified date between October 1235 and the beginning of summer in the following year. Béla IV's pact differed from that of his father in two ways. To judge from the news that he did not challenge Mikhail's rule, the king seemingly relinquished his claim to Galich. He also agreed to give Mikhail military aid. This was the first occasion on which the Hungarians and the Ol'govichi joined forces. Indeed, Mikhail had probably asked both, Béla IV and Conrad, to send troops for his attack against Daniil. Thus we see that on becoming prince of Galich, Mikhail strengthened his military resources by persuading the Hungarians and the Poles to assist him against his brother-in-law.

Rostislav is mentioned here for the first time after 1230, when he had fled from Novgorod. Since Mikhail had his son at his side in Galich, he evidently had not given Rostislav another town as, in 1210, Vladimir Igorevich had given his son Izyaslav the town of Terebovl'.[148] It appears, therefore, that

---

[146] Ipat., col. 775. The dating for this account is supported by the Gustinskiy Chronicle which places it under the year 1236 (Gust., p. 338). The Hypatian Chronicle has several entries concerning encounters between the Ol'govichi and the Romanovichi under the year 1235, but its dating is unreliable. Since it has no information for southwest Rus' under the years 1236 and 1237, and since the information under 1238 is for the year 1239 and later, the accounts under 1235 may describe events that occurred as late as 1238.

[147] In 1206, Roman Igorevich occupied Zvenigorod (see above, p. 254) and the townsmen became his loyal subjects. In 1211, they fought valiantly in support of Roman against the pro-Daniil *boyars* and the Hungarians (see above, p. 272).

[148] See above, p. 266.

Mikhail intended to follow a policy for Galich that was similar to the one he had used in Novgorod. Namely, he was keeping his son at his side with the intention of making Rostislav prince of Galich after he returned to Kiev. This observation, as we shall see, is supported by later evidence.

After failing to take Galich when the Hungarians were present, Daniil tried again after they had departed. Having to rely solely on his own resources, Mikhail attempted to placate his brother-in-law by giving him Peremyshl'. This was an important commercial center on the trade route from Central Europe to Kiev. Obtaining the town appealed to Daniil for the added reason that its inhabitants had supported him in the past. As we have seen, in 1211, when Svyatoslav Igorevich had been its prince, Daniil's supporter Volodislav had persuaded the citizens to rebel against Svyatoslav.[149] Granted, Mikhail's peace offering enabled Daniil to secure a foothold in Galicia, but their truce that autumn also freed Mikhail to face a greater challenge in Kiev.[150]

MIKHAIL RETURNS TO KIEV

As we have seen, in the autumn of 1235, Mikhail had appointed Izyaslav Mstislavich to act as interim ruler in Kiev. His tenure was short-lived. After the Polovtsy released Vladimir Ryurikovich some time towards the end of the year, he replaced Izyaslav.[151] The news, that he occupied Kiev without the aid of his *druzhina* and without opposition from Izyaslav or the Kievans, supports our contention that Mikhail had pre-arranged his return in the autumn before departing for Galich. Vladimir therefore acted as Mikhail's lieutenant. The Vsevolodovichi of Suzdalia, however, were unhappy with the power that Mikhail had acquired. Consequently, Yury and Daniil formed a pact, forced Vladimir to vacate Kiev, and appointed Yury's brother Yaroslav to the town.[152]

---

[149] See above, pp. 270–1.

[150] Concerning Daniil's attacks on Galich, see Ipat., col. 776. The Gustinskiy Chronicle, which alone in addition to the Hypatian Chronicle reports Daniil's second attack against Mikhail and the latter's allocation of Peremyshl' to him, places the entry under 1236 (Gust., p. 338). A number of investigators suggest that Daniil led both attacks in 1237 (Perfecky, p. 44; Makhnovets', p. 392). Elsewhere it was wrongly suggested that the two entries refer to the same attack (*Mikhail*, p. 103).

[151] NPL, pp. 74, 284–5; Mosk., p. 126; N4, p. 214. Since the chronicles give the news of Vladimir's capture and release under 1235, both events evidently happened in the same year (see also Hrushevsky, *Ocherk*, pp. 285–6 and Pashuto, *Ocherki*, p. 220).

[152] Karamzin, who apparently was quoting a source now lost, provided this information (*Istoriya gosudarstva Rossiyskago*, vol. 3, pp. 312–13). The Vsevolodovichi used strong-arm tactics against the Rostislavichi before and after this event. As we have seen, in 1229 Yaroslav instructed the prince of Smolensk to stop Novgorod messengers from reaching Mikhail. Later, in 1239, Yaroslav meddled in the internal government of Smolensk by appointing its prince (Lav., col. 469).

The chronicles do not state explicitly that Daniil and the Vsevolodovichi joined forces. We are, however, given evidence which suggests that they formed an alliance after 1235, when Mikhail captured Kiev. Four years later, as we shall see, Daniil would ask Yaroslav for a favor which the latter would grant.[153] This supports the view that they had concluded an agreement at an earlier date. Daniil's willingness to join forces with the Vsevolodovichi is understandable. He had to find new allies after Mikhail neutralized Vladimir, won over Conrad of Mazovia, and concluded an alliance with Béla IV.

Although Yury had no quarrel with Mikhail, Yaroslav had crossed swords with him over Novgorod. Most recently, he had tasted Mikhail's spleen when the latter had fined the Germans in Kiev. Since Yaroslav had lost the most through Mikhail's meddling in Novgorod's business, and given the news that he occupied Kiev with prominent Novgorodians, it appears that Novgorodian affairs were once again the bugbear. Consequently, it was probably Yaroslav who, by reminding Yury of the pledge that he had made to help Yaroslav in his Novgorodian policy, pressured his brother into forming a pact with Daniil and into giving him Kiev. Mikhail's threat to Daniil and to Yaroslav therefore forced the two dynasties of Monomashichi to join forces.

Their pact alienated them not only from the Ol'govichi but also from the Rostislavichi. Vladimir, whom Mikhail had coerced into becoming his ally in 1235, and placated by letting him stay in Kiev, was drawn into an even closer partnership with Mikhail. What is more, by challenging Mikhail's rule in Rus', the Vsevolodovichi introduced a new dimension to their political policy. This was the first occasion after Andrew Bogolyubskiy that the princes of Suzdalia deemed it vital to their interests to make a bid for control of the capital of Rus'.

Around March of 1236 Yaroslav arrived in Kiev.[154] His unchallenged occupation of the town was facilitated, in part, by Vladimir's inability to oppose Daniil and Yury and, in part, by the timing of his takeover. He came when Mikhail was preoccupied fighting Daniil. Yaroslav was also a

---

[153] In 1239, Yaroslav captured Mikhail's wife and *boyars* at Kamenets. Daniil asked Yaroslav to release his sister, Mikhail's wife, and send her to him because Mikhail was planning evil against both of them (Ipat., cols. 782–3; Dimnik, "Kamenec," pp. 31–2; Dimnik, "Russian Princes," pp. 180–4; see below, p. 349).

[154] NPL, pp. 74, 285; Mosk., p. 126. According to the most reliable chronicles, Yaroslav entered Kiev without a fight. This is supported by the information that he obtained no military assistance from any of the other Vsevolodovichi but traveled south with only a small group of prominent Novgorodians and a hundred men from Torzhok. The force was far too small to besiege the most powerful town of Rus' (Dimnik, "The Struggle for Control over Kiev," pp. 36–7).

rightful claimant to Kiev according to the custom that a son had the right to sit on the throne of his father.[155] Even so, he seemingly had little chance of consolidating his rule. His supply lines from Novgorod and Suzdalia passed through the hostile lands of the Ol'govichi. Realizing this, Daniil and Yury's main purpose for appointing him to Kiev may have been to obtain bartering power against Mikhail. They would return Kiev to him if he handed over Galich to Daniil and promised not to obstruct Kievan trade with Novgorod. One of Yaroslav's main objectives would have been to revive the commercial arrangements that Novgorod had enjoyed with Kiev before Mikhail seized the town from Vladimir.

Yaroslav failed to consolidate his rule and returned to Suzdalia. The Kievans were hostile to him and had accepted him only because Vladimir had fled and he was foisted on them by two powerful princes. One reason for his unpopularity was that he was the scion of a detested dynasty. The Kievans had demonstrated their animosity towards his grandfather, Yury Dolgorukiy, by poisoning him, and had also killed his uncle Gleb. Moreover, they had despised his uncle Andrey Bogolyubskiy for sacking Kiev. Even earlier, he had antagonized them by stealing from Vyshgorod the sword of St. Boris and their cherished icon of the Mother of God that had been brought from Constantinople.[156] Finally, the townsmen opposed Yaroslav because he was more interested in championing Novgorod's interests than theirs. Even though Yaroslav failed to assert his authority, the ease with which he replaced Vladimir was a warning to Mikhail. He realized that if he wished to rule Kiev he had to do so in person.

Mikhail therefore came to Kiev after appointing Rostislav to rule Galich.[157] Like Yaroslav, he entered Kiev uncontested, but his position was much stronger. He controlled two of the domains adjacent to the Kievan land: the patrimony of the Ol'govichi to the northeast and the Galician territories to the southwest. Moreover, Vladimir and the Rostislavichi, his seemingly loyal but ineffectual allies, controlled Vruchiy and Smolensk. Most important, however, Mikhail had the advantage over Yaroslav in that he had concluded an agreement with the Kievans a year earlier. The evidence

---

[155] In 1173, Yaroslav's father Vsevolod Bol'shoe Gnezdo had ruled Kiev (Ipat., col. 570; see above, pp. 125–6).

[156] Under 1155, the chronicler reports that Andrey left Vyshgorod against the will of his father Yury Dolgorukiy and took the icon (Ipat., col. 482). In 1174, when his murderers attacked him, Andrey had in his possession the sword of St. Boris (Ipat., cols. 586–7). He undoubtedly had stolen it along with the icon, since the sword had probably been hanging near the saint's tomb in the Church of SS. Boris and Gleb in Vyshgorod.

[157] Ipat., col. 777. For a detailed examination of the confused reports on the chronology of these events see Dimnik, "The Struggle for Control over Kiev," pp. 32–40.

that the citizens had accepted Izyaslav Mstislavich and then Vladimir as his puppets shows that they respected his military might. Still smarting from the Polovtsian onslaught, the Kievans realized that they could incur new reprisals should they antagonize him.

Mikhail's occupation of Kiev was an important victory over the princes of Volyn' and Suzdalia. Aside from his temporary sojourn in Kiev in 1235, this was the first occasion on which an Ol'govich occupied the town since 1212, when the Rostislavichi had driven out his father. Granted, Mikhail's hold of Kiev still had to stand the test of time, but at first sight his achievement surpassed that of his father. Whereas the latter had controlled Galich through the Igorevichi, he held it through his son. Unfortunately for Mikhail, however, he had been compelled to leave Galich before he had forced Daniil to drop his claim to it.

Nevertheless, Mikhail did not find defending his interests in Galicia an obstacle to ruling Kiev. Soon after occupying the latter, he and Rostislav attacked Peremyshl' and took it back from Daniil. After that, "the Ol'govichi and Daniil alternated between being at peace and going to war."[158] As we have seen, Mikhail had given Peremyshl' to Daniil as payment for lifting his second siege of Galich. He may have used Daniil's complicity with the Vsevolodovichi in driving out Vladimir from Kiev as the pretext for repossessing it. Significantly, the evidence that Mikhail left Kiev with his *druzhina* for extended campaigns against Daniil, and that neither the Vsevolodovichi nor Daniil challenged his rule there in his absence, proves that they considered such a venture to be futile. More importantly, it showed that the Kievans wished to keep him as prince.

While Mikhail was at war with one brother-in-law in Galicia, the other in Suzdalia learnt that the "godless Tatars" had arrived virtually at his doorstep. In the autumn, they attacked the Bulgars, set fire to their capital, and took the entire land captive.[159] Despite the dire warnings, Yury considered it unnecessary for the safety of his lands to join forces with the other princes like Mstislav Romanovich of Kiev had done twelve years earlier. If he believed it needless to take precautions against an invasion, the princes of Rus', who were a greater distance away, had even less urgency to do so. With reasoning such as this, it would appear, they lulled themselves into

---

[158] Ipat., col. 777; Gust., p. 338. The Hypatian chronicler places this information incorrectly under the year 1235. The Gustinskiy chronicler has it, probably correctly, as the last entry under the year 1236. This suggests that the event occurred towards the end of that year or the beginning of 1237. See also *Mikhail*, p. 104 and Perfecky, p. 45. According to another view, these events occurred in 1238 (Makhnovets', p. 392).

[159] Lav., col. 460; NPL, pp. 74, 285.

a false sense of security. Accordingly, the Ol'govichi and the Romanovichi continued their internecine rivalries.

MIKHAIL'S SON ROSTISLAV LOSES GALICH

Rostislav, who replaced his father Mikhail as prince of Galich, retained the loyalty of the Galician *boyars* but, unfortunately for the Ol'govichi, he was not as capable a military commander as his father. The chronicler explains that, after Daniil and Mikhail had concluded a truce in the autumn of 1236, Daniil sent Prince Mendog and the Lithuanians against Conrad of Mazovia.[160] Daniil evidently wished to repay Conrad for the damage he, as Mikhail's ally, had inflicted on Volyn'. After the Lithuanians pillaged Conrad's lands he in turn, it seems, asked Rostislav, as Mikhail's successor in Galich, to help him retaliate against the Lithuanians. Accordingly, around 1237 Rostislav rode against them but committed a serious blunder: he took all the *boyars* and horsemen with him. Only a skeleton force remained behind to defend Galich.

The people of Galich therefore summoned Daniil from Kholm and installed him as prince. First, it is noteworthy that it was the townspeople who betrayed Rostislav. All the *boyars* from Galicia, it seems, demonstrated their loyalty by going on the campaign with him. After Mikhail had occupied Galich in 1235, the *boyars* evidently posed no threat to him or to his son. This is remarkable because during the first three decades of the thirteenth century the *boyars* had been the instigators of seemingly every intrigue in Galicia. Rival factions had consistently conspired against the incumbent prince. To judge from Mikhail's conciliatory conduct in Novgorod towards its citizens, he may have adopted a similar policy of appeasement to win over the Galician magnates.

Second, Bishop Artemy and the major-domo, Grigory Vasil'evich, whom Rostislav had left in charge of the town, remained loyal and refused Daniil entry. They evidently commanded troops that were not made up of the townspeople. This is supported by the news that the citizens had to greet Daniil outside the town because the defending force stopped them from opening the gates to him. We may therefore assume that Rostislav left the two men in charge of a foreign contingent. The chronicler seemingly confirms this when he reports that, after Artemy and Grigory capitulated, Daniil announced his occupation of the town by hanging his standard on the German Gate. It evidently served as the entrance to the foreign

---

[160] Ipat., col. 776.

quarter of the European merchants and troops. The latter were probably Hungarians to judge from the information that, in 1236, Hungarian soldiers had helped Mikhail defend the town against Daniil.

This was the first reported occasion on which Rostislav led a campaign independently of his father. Thus we see that Mikhail had weaned his son from depending on his backing and had given Rostislav free rein in Galician affairs. The latter therefore launched his own initiatives with the Poles, the Lithuanians, and the Hungarians. After losing Galich he demonstrated his independence yet again by fleeing to Béla IV.

Rostislav's loss of Galich was a serious blow to the Ol'govichi, but it is difficult to know how effectively Daniil asserted his authority over it. We learn nothing about the fates of Peremyshl' and Zvenigorod which pro-Ol'govichi officials had administered. Did they remain loyal to Rostislav or follow the example of Galich and desert him? Granted, the chronicler asserts that all the *boyars* of Galicia submitted to Daniil. We cannot, however, take his word at face value. Daniil had seized Galich and if they refused to pledge allegiance he would take punitive measures against them. Because they were motivated by expediency, their loyalty was notoriously fickle.[161]

THE TATARS INVADE RYAZAN' AND SUZDALIA

In the autumn of 1236, as we have seen, the "godless Tatars" had eliminated the Bulgars as a fighting force. Having therewith removed the last major enemy east of the Volga, they forged relentlessly westward. They launched a two-pronged invasion of Rus'. First, they attacked Ryazan' and Suzdalia in the east and northeast.

In the winter of 1237, we are told, Khan Baty, the son of Chingis Khan's eldest son Juchi,[162] came to the frontiers of Ryazan'.[163] He sent a sorceress

---

[161] See s.a. 1235: Ipat., cols. 777–8; compare s.a. 1237: Gust., p. 338. As has already been noted, under the year 1235, the Hypatian chronicler includes information for southwest Rus' covering a number of years. Since its information under 1238 is for the year 1239 and later, the accounts under 1235 evidently describe events that occurred from that year up to 1238. Since the news of Rostislav's campaign is the last entry under 1235, it presumably occurred closer to the year 1238. The Gustinskiy Chronicle, the only other source to give the information of Rostislav's flight to Hungary, places it under the year 1237. Consequently, Rostislav probably fled some time in 1237 or 1238. See also *Mikhail*, pp. 105–7.

[162] Baty was the nominal head of the Western campaign sent out by his uncle Great Khan Ogedey, who succeeded Chingis Khan. Baty was accompanied by seven cousins, all grandsons of Chingis Khan, including two future great khans, Guyuk and Mongke. Subetey (Subutay), one of the best Tatar generals, was made commander-in-chief of the entire operation (Vernadsky, *The Mongols*, p. 49; *Crisis*, p. 77; A. N. Nasonov, *Mongoly i Rus'* [M.-L., 1940], p. 9).

[163] Three chronicle traditions report the first wave of the invasion. The Laurentian Chronicle, based on a chronicle written at Yury's court, reports events in Suzdalia. The Novgorod First Chronicle reports events as given by a now lost Ryazan' source and as seen by the Novgorod chronicler.

and two men to the princes of Ryazan', Murom, and Pronsk exacting a
tithe of everything. They spurned the demand and sent messengers to Yury
in Vladimir requesting that he either send troops or come in person. But
he ignored their plea because he intended to organize his own defense.
The Tatars devastated Ryazan'. On December 21, they butchered Prince
Yury Ingvarevich, his wife, many inhabitants, and took others captive. After
putting the torch to churches and surrounding villages, they advanced north
towards Kolomna.[164]

The Ol'govichi were not directly affected by the invasion of Ryazan', but a
seventeenth-century chronicle compilation, evidently citing a lost Ryazan'
source, refers to Mikhail. It reports that, during the invasion, a certain
grandee of Ryazan' named Eupaty Lvovich Kolovrat and Prince Ingvar'
Ingvarevich (Ingor Igorevich) were visiting Mikhail in Chernigov.[165] On
learning of the catastrophe that had befallen his lands, Eupaty pursued
Baty to Suzdalia with a force of 1,700 men. He cut down many Tatars with
extraordinary feats of valor before the nomads finally killed him with siege
machinery. Impressed with his bravery, Baty commanded Eupaty's men to
carry away his body for burial. On January 11, Ingvar' interred Eupaty in
Ryazan'.[166]

It has been suggested that when Yury Ingvarevich of Ryazan' sent messengers to seek help from Yury in Vladimir, the delegation was led by
Roman Ingvarevich, Ingvar''s elder brother.[167] It is possible, therefore, that
Yury of Ryazan' had sent Ingvar' to Chernigov for the same reason. If this
was the case, we learn that Mikhail, like his brother-in-law in Vladimir,
sent no troops to the beleaguered princes. The account also provides a rare

The Hypatian Chronicle reflects a southern source (John Fennell, "The Tale of Baty's Invasion of
North-East Rus' and its Reflexion in the Chronicles of the Thirteenth–Fifteenth Centuries," *Russia
Mediaevalis* 3 [München, 1977], pp. 41–78).

[164] Mosk., pp. 126–7; Ak. sp., cols. 514–15; Lav., col. 460; s.a. 1238: NPL, pp. 74–5, 286–7. Concerning
the date, see Berezhkov, pp. 109–10. For a summary of Tatar conquests prior to their arrival at
Ryazan', see L. V. Cherepnin, "Mongolo-Tatary na Rusi (XIII v.)," *Tataro-Mongoly v Azii i Evrope*,
S. L. Tikhvinsky (ed.) (M., 1970), pp. 183–5; J. L. I. Fennell, "Russia on the Eve of the Tatar
Invasion," *Oxford Slavonic Papers*, 14 (1981), 1–13; *Crisis*, pp. 76–7.

[165] Ingvar' was the nephew of Yury Ingvarevich, the prince of Ryazan' killed by the Tatars (Baum. 2,
XIV, 34).

[166] Maz., pp. 69–70. A lyrical presentation of these events is given by the "military tale" (*voinskaya
povest'*) "The Tale of the Capture of Ryazan' by Baty" ("Povest' o razorenii Ryazani Batyem," in V. P.
Adrianova-Peretts [ed.], *Voinskie povesti drevney Rusi* [M.-L., 1949], pp. 9–19, and in J. Fennell and
D. Obolensky [eds.], "Povest' o razorenii Ryazani Batyem," *A Historical Russian Reader* [Oxford,
1969], pp. 76–85). The earliest version of the *voinskaya povest'* was probably written soon after the
events and incorporated into the now lost Ryazan' Chronicle (John Fennell and Anthony Stokes,
Early Russian Literature [London, 1974], pp. 88–97).

[167] Baum, 2, XIV, 33. After Ryazan' fell, Yury of Vladimir dispatched his son Vsevolod and Roman
Ingvarevich of Ryazan' to confront the Tatars. This suggests that Roman was with Yury in Vladimir
when the invaders pillaged the lands of Ryazan'. His reason for visiting Yury, presumably, had been
to solicit reinforcements (A. L. Mongayt, *Ryazanskaya zemlya* [M., 1961], p. 358).

reference to the ties that existed between Chernigov and Ryazan'. These are confirmed by the military tale (*voinskaya povest'*) recounting the fall of Ryazan'. It alludes to regular commercial relations between the two lands. After the Tatars took the town, we are told, they plundered the treasures of the inhabitants including the wealth of their relatives from Kiev and Chernigov.[168] Some of this wealth probably reached Ryazan' along the trade route connecting Kiev and the Bulgars.[169]

The Ryazan' chronicler's report is of interest for another reason. It is the only account which tells us that, in December 1237, Mikhail was in Chernigov. Since we learn of his presence there by chance, we may assume that he visited his patrimonial capital on other occasions. The chronicles undoubtedly fail to record those sojourns because they had no political significance. Whatever his reason for visiting Chernigov, his absence from Kiev is important. It shows that his rule there was secure allowing him to leave the capital of Rus' for protracted periods of time.

As the Tatars forged ahead, Yury appointed two of his sons to defend Vladimir, while he and his nephews, Vasil'ko, Vsevolod, and Vladimir, rode to the river Sit' northwest of Rostov to wait for his brothers Yaroslav and Svyatoslav. On February 7, the Tatars broke down the gates of Vladimir forcing the princes' families to seek sanctuary in Assumption Cathedral. Baty set fire to the building and all inside it perished including Yury's wife Agafia (Mikhail's sister). The Tatars slaughtered the people and plundered the churches of their treasures, including the garments of the blessed first princes (figure 13).[170] After razing Vladimir, Baty sent a force in pursuit of Yury.[171] On March 4, at the river Sit', the Tatars routed Yury's troops, killed him, and took Vasil'ko captive.[172]

Significantly, Yaroslav failed to arrive from Novgorod because relations between the brothers were strained. A late source notes that the princes were defeated because they disagreed with each other.[173] The Novgorod chronicler, probably a partisan of Yaroslav's camp, is more damning of Yury. He suggests that the prince died owing to his cowardly conduct.[174] As for

---

[168] Adrianova-Peretts, *Voinskie povesti*, pp. 12, 289–90.

[169] Kiev, Chernigov, Ryazan', and the Bulgars were connected by the Dnepr, Desna, Oka, and Volga water route. The main caravan route from Kiev to the Bulgars passed to the south of the Chernigov lands and to the south of Ryazan' (A. P. Motsya, "Obshchie zakonomernosti torgovo-ekonomicheskikh vzaimootnosheniy Kieva i Bulgara v IX–XIII vv.," *Put' iz Bulgara v Kiev*, A. Kh. Khalikov [gen. ed.] [Kazan', 1992], pp. 10–11; Kovalenko and Sytyy, "Torgovo-ekonomicheskie vzaimosvyazi," pp. 55–61). See above, p. 50.

[170] See above, pp. 243–5.   [171] Lav., cols. 460–4; Mosk., pp. 127–8; Ipat., cols. 779–80.

[172] Lav., cols. 464–5; L'vov, pp. 156–7.   [173] Gust., p. 338.

[174] NPL, pp. 76, 288. According to the so-called *Chudovskoe zhitie*, a sixteenth-century redaction of the Life of Mikhail written by Pakhomy the Serb, Yury was proud, envious, miserly, unmerciful, lusted after power, indulged in drunkenness and debauchery, and "in truth, lived like a beast."

Figure 13   A mock-up of the Tatar siege of Vladimir on the Klyaz'ma

Vasil'ko, the Tatars tried to entice him into capitulating to their terms and into fighting for them. After he refused to betray his allies and his Christian faith, they killed him.[175] We are not told why the Tatars sought to proselytize Vasil'ko, but their action suggests that it was their practice to spare those who joined them. Thus we see that Mikhail's brother-in-law Yury and son-in-law Vasil'ko died under circumstances which the chroniclers considered noteworthy. The one fell under a cloud and the other, according to many, died a martyr.[176]

The Tatars continued their march westward until they came to within 100 *versty* of Novgorod.[177] There they turned south. In the Vyatichi lands they came upon the town of Kozel'sk which they decided to take by force because its inhabitants refused to be cajoled into submission. But the townspeople

The princes were defeated at the Sit', the author claims, because Yury was a coward at heart (N. Serebryansky, *Drevne-russkie knyazheskiya zhitiya [Obzor redaktsiy i teksty]* [M., 1915], Texts, pp. 81–2; *Mikhail*, pp. 37–8).
[175] Lav., cols. 465–7; s.a. 1238: Mosk., pp. 128–9.
[176] It has been suggested that the original story of Vasil'ko's death was recorded in the chronicle that his widow Maria, Mikhail's daughter, commissioned to be written at her court in Rostov (Likhachev, *Russkie letopisi*, pp. 283–4; John Fennell, "The Tale of the Death of Vasil'ko Konstantinovich: A Study of the Sources," *Osteuropa in Geschichte und Gegenwart. Festschrift für Gunther Stökl zum 60. Geburtstag* [Vienna, 1977], pp. 34–46).
[177] NPL, pp. 76–7, 288–9. *Versta*, a measure of length, is about 1.1 km or 0.66 mile.

resolved to fight to the death for their twelve-year-old prince, Vasil'ko. Accordingly, after the Tatars scaled one of the ramparts, the defenders refused to capitulate even though they had to resort to fighting with knives. In desperation, they made a sortie, destroyed the Tatars' catapults, and killed 4,000 attackers before they themselves fell under the lance. Baty vented his rage on the town by slaughtering all its inhabitants, down to infants at the breast. They failed to find Vasil'ko in the carnage, "and some claimed that he had drowned in a pool of blood." Following the town's valiant defense, the Tatars dared not speak its name. They called it Evil Town because they had struggled seven weeks to crush it and had lost three sons of Tatar generals. From Kozel'sk, we are told, Baty withdrew to the Polovtsian steppe.[178]

Of all the towns that the Tatars destroyed, Kozel'sk was the only reported casualty of the Ol'govichi. Archaeological evidence reveals, however, that the horde left other towns levelled in its wake. Mikhail's domains of Mosal'sk and Serensk located to the north of Kozel'sk,[179] and Vshchizh situated to the southwest, suffered the same fate.[180] Boldyzh,[181] Domagoshch, Karachev, Kromy, and other settlements to the south were also devastated.[182] Whereas their destruction was not memorable, Kozel'sk fought heroically. The resistance of the citizens illustrated their determination to oppose subjugation, and Baty's persistence reflected his fear of losing face to a paltry provincial town. In the end, the Tatars conquered, but the moral victory went to the townspeople. Living up to their resolve they won "earthly glory in this world and heavenly garlands from Christ our God in the next."[183]

The identity of prince Vasil'ko is problematic because his patronymic is not given. Although he was the ruler of Kozel'sk in 1238, fifteen years earlier the town had belonged to Mstislav Svyatoslavich of Chernigov.[184] Since he had received it as his patrimony from his father Svyatoslav, he would have handed it on to his son. But the latter was not Vasil'ko. The twelve-year-old youth was born in 1226, three years after Mstislav had been killed at

---

[178] Ipat., cols. 780–1; s.a. 1238: Mosk., p. 130. Two sources say Vasil'ko was twelve years of age (N4, pp. 221–2; N5, pp. 213–14). Concerning the capture of Kozel'sk, see also Rashid ad-Din, *The Successors of Genghis Khan*, J. A. Boyle (trans.) (New York and London, 1971), p. 60.

[179] Archaeological evidence shows that Serensk, which Yaroslav attacked in the winter of 1231 (see above, pp. 324–5), was pillaged by the Tatars seven years later (see T. N. Nikol'skaya, "Voennoe delo v gorodakh zemli Vyatichey [Po materialam drevnerusskogo Serenska]," KSIA 139 [M., 1974], p. 35, and her "K istoricheskoy geografii zemli Vyatichey," p. 162).

[180] Rybakov, "Raskopki vo Vshchizhe v 1948–1949," p. 38. The Tatars evidently destroyed the masonry church that had been erected only a few decades earlier (Rybakov, "Vshchizh – udel'nyy gorod XII veka," p. 58; see also Kuza, *Malye goroda*, p. 83).

[181] Nikol'skaya, *Slobodka*, pp. 5–6; *Zemlya Vyatichey*, p. 164.

[182] V. P. Kovalenko, "Chernihovo-sivers'ka zemlia v seredyni XIII st.," *Sviatyi kniaz'*, p. 38.

[183] Ipat., col. 781; Mosk., p. 130.   [184] See above, p. 292.

the Kalka. Vasil'ko, therefore, was probably Mstislav's grandson. Mstislav's eldest son Dmitry was not Vasil'ko's father either because he also died at the Kalka.[185] Therefore, Vasil'ko's father must have been an unidentified son of Mstislav, who, in 1238, either ruled a more important town than Kozel'sk or was dead.[186]

On the first phase of their invasion, the Tatars left a trail of carnage through the lands of Ryazan', Suzdalia, the eastern Novgorod region,[187] the eastern Smolensk territories,[188] and the Vyatichi lands. It is impossible to estimate the extent of their destruction, but in the eyes of the survivors it was cataclysmic. The populations of the devastated regions were decimated, numerous towns were razed (fourteen were reported destroyed in Suzdalia), and princely families butchered. The dynasties of Ryazan' and Suzdalia lost their senior princes who were replaced by their surviving relatives. Thus, Yury's brother Yaroslav, who had failed to bring troops to the Sit', came quickly enough when summoned to occupy his brother's vacant throne in Vladimir.[189] As the survivors of the northeastern lands set about burying their dead and rebuilding their homes, the people of Rus' awaited a similar fate. Meanwhile, the Tatars rested.

MIKHAIL SEEKS SANCTUARY IN KAMENETS

Alarm bells pealed early in 1239 as Baty's forces approached the towns of southern Rus'. The second phase of the invasion had begun. On March 3, one contingent took Pereyaslavl' and set fire to it. The attackers massacred its inhabitants, destroyed the Church of the Archangel Michael, and killed Bishop Simeon.[190] From Pereyaslavl' would the invaders cross the Desna to attack Chernigov or would they cross the Dnepr to attack Kiev? In either case, the Ol'govichi were the target.

---

[185] See above, p. 296.

[186] The chronicles do not speak of Mstislav's younger sons, but according to the *Eletskiy sinodik* and the *Severskiy sinodik,* he had three sons in addition to the Dmitry, who was killed at Kalka. They were Andrey, Ioann, and Gavriil (Zotov, pp. 69–70, 281).

[187] Concerning the invasion of Ryazan', Suzdal', and regions of Novgorod, see also *Crisis*, pp. 78–81, and Vernadsky, *The Mongols*, pp. 50–2.

[188] According to folk tradition, Smolensk was besieged by the Tatars but successfully defended by a certain Merkury of Smolensk (M. Skripil', *Russkie povesti xv–xvi vekov* [M.-L., 1958], pp. 106–7, 276–8, 441–5; L. T. Beletsky, "Literaturnaya istoriya povesti o Merkurii Smolenskom," *Sbornik otdeleniya russkago yazyka i slovesnosti Rossiiskoy Akademii nauk* 99, nr. 8 [P., 1922], 55–7). Smolensk may not have suffered a direct attack, but the Tatars passed through its territories on the way from the Novgorod to the Vyatichi lands.

[189] Lav., col. 467; Nikon. 10, p. 113.

[190] Ipat., cols. 781–2; Gust., p. 338. The Pskov chronicles give the date (s.a. 1230: Pskov, vol. 2, p. 79; compare Pskov, vol. 1, p. 11; see also Av., col. 51).

Not long after Pereyaslavl' fell, it would appear, Mikhail went to Kamenets which, since 1235, had belonged to Izyaslav Vladimirovich of the cadet branch.[191] Pereyaslavl's fate seemingly propelled him into action. Because a similar destiny probably awaited Kiev, he removed his family from the town. The personal nature of his trip is confirmed by the news that he traveled with his wife. Presumably, his *boyars* also brought their families. Our contention that Mikhail organized a general evacuation of his retinue from Kiev is supported by the news that he sought sanctuary in the strongest citadel in the westernmost part of the Kievan land. Unfortunately for Mikhail, his heavily laden caravan attracted attention as it traveled through the countryside so that even Yaroslav in Suzdalia got word of its destination.

He besieged Kamenets, captured Mikhail's wife, many of his *boyars*, and seized much booty.[192] His foray was uncharacteristic for a prince of Vladimir who, as a rule, avoided leading expeditions into the Kievan land. Indeed, a prince of Suzdalia had not dispatched his troops to the west bank since 1169, when Andrey Bogolyubskiy had sent his forces to sack Kiev. What is more, because of the chaos reigning in Suzdalia, it is surprising that Yaroslav not only organized an offensive campaign but also participated in person. Significantly, he attacked Mikhail when he was most vulnerable. He had arrived in Kamenets in a state of alarm seeking a safe haven and was not expecting any trouble from another prince. Although Yaroslav had the advantage of surprise, he failed to achieve his main objective because Mikhail escaped and returned to Kiev.[193]

Yaroslav's aim to take captive a rival prince had precedent. In 1180, as we have seen, Mikhail's grandfather Svyatoslav had attempted to capture David Rostislavich while the latter was on a hunting expedition.[194] We are not told why Yaroslav tried to seize Mikhail, but he may well have been driven by his deep-seated desire for revenge. Mikhail had successfully crossed swords with him on a number of occasions. As we have seen, he had passed anti-Yaroslav measures in Novgorod. Yaroslav had retaliated by attacking Mikhail's patrimony. The latter responded by levying punitive measures against German merchants who had come to Kiev via Novgorod.

[191] Concerning the date of their visit to Kamenets, see Dimnik, "Russian Princes," p. 181, n. 8. Concerning Izyaslav's ownership of the town, see above, p. 334.
[192] The sources do not give Yaroslav's patronymic, therefore historians disagree concerning his identity. They generally argue that he was either Yaroslav Vsevolodovich of Suzdalia or Yaroslav Ingvarovich of Lutsk. For a detailed examination of the question, see Dimnik, "Russian Princes," pp. 180–4. According to one view, Yaroslav captured Mikhail's wife while Mikhail was fleeing to the Hungarians (Solov'ev, *Istoriya Rossii* [M., 1963], kn. 2, vol. 3, pp. 143–4). There is, however, no chronicle evidence to suggest that Mikhail fled to the Hungarians after leaving his wife and *boyars* at Kamenets.
[193] Only a sixteenth-century chronicle reports that Mikhail escaped (Vlad., p. 90).
[194] See above, pp. 145–6.

The Vsevolodovichi then retaliated by appointing Yaroslav to Kiev only to see Mikhail replace him. What is more, Mikhail was probably the cause of the bad blood that had existed between Yaroslav and Yury, and that had prompted Yaroslav to abandon his brother at the river Sit'. In 1239, therefore, without Yury to restrain him, Yaroslav attacked his foe, revealing that after Yury's death his animosity seemingly became even more inflamed.[195]

Yaroslav failed to capture Mikhail but his raid bore fruit nonetheless. He could obtain ransoms for the captives and keep their wealth. He also achieved useful political results. When Daniil learnt that his sister, Mikhail's wife, was being held captive, he asked Yaroslav to send her to him. Daniil argued that he, like Yaroslav, was Mikhail's enemy because the latter was plotting against both of them. Yaroslav therefore sent the princess to her brother.[196] In this way, as we shall see, Daniil gained an important advantage over Mikhail for their future dealings and, concomitantly, became indebted to Yaroslav. Consequently, in keeping with the pact that his brother Yury had concluded with Daniil in 1236, Yaroslav demonstrated his willingness to work hand-in-glove with Daniil against Mikhail. Unfortunately for Rus', the princes' hostility to Mikhail made Baty's conquest of Rus' even easier.

THE TATARS RAZE CHERNIGOV

In the autumn of 1239, the Tatar horde advanced against Chernigov along the northern shore of the river Seym. Glukhov, north of Putivl', capitulated.[197] Presumably, the invaders also captured Kursk, Ryl'sk, and Putivl'.[198] On reaching the Desna, they advanced towards Chernigov. When Mstislav Glebovich heard that the Tatars were attacking the town, he came with his troops to confront them. The nomads, we are told, used catapults that hurled stones the distance of a bowshot and a half. Each stone was so heavy it took four strong men to lift it (figure 14).[199] Mstislav barely escaped,

---

[195] For a slightly different interpretation, see *Crisis*, p. 100.

[196] Lav., col. 469; compare s.a. 1238: Ipat., cols. 782–3.

[197] As we shall see, after attacking Chernigov the Tatars returned to the steppe via Glukhov where they rested. Since they did not attack the town on their return from Chernigov, they had evidently occupied it earlier when they had advanced against Chernigov.

[198] In 1246, as we shall see, a certain Doman of Putivl' was at Baty's court (see below, p. 369). Since a native of Putivl' defected to the Tatars, it is reasonable to assume that he did so after the invaders captured the town. Moreover, archaeological information reveals that the Tatars sacked the town (Rappoport, p. 47; O. V. Sukhobokov, "Nekotorye itogi archeologicheskikh issledovaniy v Putivle," *Arkheologiya slavyanskogo Yugo-Vostoka*, A. G. D'yachenko [gen. ed.] [Voronezh, 1991], p. 71; Kuza, *Malye goroda*, p. 81).

[199] Concerning Tatar war machines, see W. Świętosławski, *Arms and Armour of the Nomads of the Great Steppe in the Times of the Mongol Expansion (12th–14th Centuries)*, M. Abramowicz (trans.) (Łódź, 1999), pp. 67–71.

Figure 14   Stones allegedly used by the Tatars in besieging Chernigov

but many of his men were killed.[200] After Chernigov fell on October 18,[201] the Tatars pillaged the towns in the surrounding countryside.[202] East of the river Snov' they besieged Khorobor, Sosnitsa,[203] and Snovsk; they also attacked other towns along the Desna basin.[204] Archaeological evidence reveals that they took Blestovit and Novgorod Severskiy.[205] To the west of Chernigov, the towns of Orgoshch, Listven, Gomiy, and Lyubech evidently fell victim to the Tatar lance.[206]

[200] One late source reports that Mstislav escaped (Nikon. 10, pp. 114–15). Compare Lav., col. 469 which states that the princes of Chernigov fled to Hungary. The reference is to Rostislav's flight from Galich in 1237 and, as we shall see, to Mikhail's flight from Kiev in the winter of 1239. There is no evidence that Mstislav Glebovich fled to the Hungarians (see *Mikhail*, pp. 84–5).

[201] Concerning the date, see Pskov, vol. 1, p. 12; Pskov, vol. 2, p. 79, and Av., col. 51.

[202] For a more detailed examination, see Dimnik, "The Siege of Chernigov," p. 399.

[203] Concerning Sosnitsa, see V. P. Kovalenko and O. V. Shekun, "Litopysna Sosnytsia," *Mynule Sosnytsi ta ii okolyts*, O. B. Kovalenko (gen. ed.) (Chernihiv, 1990), pp. 9–13.

[204] The information concerning the towns pillaged along the Desna is given by a corrupt account in the Hypatian Chronicle (see s.a. 1234: Ipat., col. 772).

[205] Concerning the history of Novgorod Severskiy, see Kuza, *Malye goroda*, pp. 77–9.

[206] Concerning Lyubech and Orgoshch, see Kuza, *Malye goroda*, pp. 79–81. It has been suggested that three hoards of precious items found in Lyubech were buried in 1239, during Mengu Khan's invasion of Chernigov (V. P. Kovalenko, "Maisternia iuvelira XIII st. na dytyntsi Liubecha," *Starozhytnosti Rusi-Ukrainy*, L. L. Vashchenko [ed.] [K., 1994], p. 139). Concerning Gomiy, see O. A. Makushnikov, "Osnovnye etapy razvitiya letopisnogo Gomiya (do serediny XIII v.)," *Problemy arkheologii Yuzhnoy Rusi*, T. Telizhenko (ed.) (K., 1990), p. 61.

Mstislav was not in Chernigov at the time of the attack because he came to confront the Tatars after they besieged the town. The chronicles never tell us that he ruled Chernigov, but his seniority merited him that post. Moreover, the evidence that the onus of defending the town fell on his shoulders supports this. We are also not told where he was when he was summoned against the Tatars. Since, however, he had to be informed of the attack, it appears that his patrimony was not located east of Chernigov along the path of the approaching enemy. Proof that the invaders had not attacked his domain is the news that he came with all his troops. This also suggests that his patrimony was not in the Zadesen'e region, which the Tatars probably ravaged when they had attacked Pereyaslavl'.²⁰⁷ Finally, his town must have been located sufficiently close to Chernigov to enable him to come to the latter's defense while the attack was in progress. Accordingly, his domain probably lay west of the Snov' and Desna rivers.

The chroniclers use commonplaces to describe the damage that the Tatars inflicted on Chernigov: they set fire to it, they butchered its people, and they desecrated its churches and monasteries. We may assume that in the outskirts of the town the latter included the Eletskiy Monastery with its Assumption Church, the Caves Monastery adjoining the Church of St. Elias,²⁰⁸ and the Severskiy Monastery.²⁰⁹ On the citadel, the Monastery and the Church of SS. Gleb and Boris and the adjacent St. Saviour Cathedral were gutted by fire.²¹⁰ The churches of the Annunciation and St. Michael also fell victim to desecration, as did Paraskevaya Pyatnitsa in the market square.

The chronicler offers few details concerning the damage that the invaders inflicted on the inhabitants (figure 15).²¹¹ Indeed, he gives only one specific

²⁰⁷ Since, according to archaeological evidence, the Tatars ravaged Bélaya Vezha (Kovalenko and Sytyy, "Letopisnaya Bélavezha," p. 65), they probably devastated most of the Zadesen'e region at the same time.
²⁰⁸ Archaeologists have established that the Caves Monastery continued to function until the thirteenth century (V. Ia. Rudenok, "Novovidkrytyi pidzemnyi khram v Antonievykh pecherakh v Cherni-hovi," *Chernihivs'ka starovyna*, Zbirnyk naukovykh prats', prysviachenyi 1300 – littiu Chernihova, P. P. Tolochko [gen. ed.] [Chernihiv, 1992], pp. 42–9).
²⁰⁹ Concerning the latter, see above, p. 284.
²¹⁰ Concerning the misfortunes which befell the St. Saviour Cathedral after it was devastated by fire in 1239, see M. E. Markov, "O dostopamyatnostyakh Chernigova," *Chteniya*, nr. 1 (M., 1847), pp. 14–17.
²¹¹ In 1957 and 1958 workers unearthed a hoard of gold and silver objects in the western suburb of Chernigov, which in the twelfth and thirteenth century was located near the road leading from Chernigov to Lyubech. The hoard was evidently buried in a prince's country estate before the Tatars set fire to it (V. P. Darkevich and I. I. Edomakha, "Pamyatnik zapadnoevropeyskoy torevtiki XII veka," *SA*, nr. 3 [M., 1964], pp. 247–55). In 1985, another hoard, the largest to date, was discovered in a jeweler's shop on the *detinets*. It comprised various silver ornaments including three large silver cups (Kovalenko, "Votchinnye mastera-yuveliry v gorodakh Chernigovo-Severskoy zemli," pp. 72–3).

Figure 15   A hoard found in the prince's court in Chernigov was probably buried during
the Tatar siege of the town

item of information: the invaders took Bishop Porfiry captive and withdrew
to Glukhov.²¹² Surprisingly, they spared his life unlike that of the bishop
of Pereyaslavl'. We are not told why they acted with clemency. Most likely,
they took the bishop, as they had taken Vasil'ko from the river Sit', with
the intention of cajoling him into collaborating. The evidence that they
released him suggests that they succeeded. From Glukhov they rode to their
camps.²¹³

Before departing from the town, however, the Tatars sent messengers to
Kiev proposing peace. If Porfiry agreed to cooperate with them, he may well
have been one of their envoys. They were pacified, we are told, with Mstislav
Glebovich of Chernigov, Vladimir Ryurikovich of the Rostislavichi,²¹⁴ and

²¹² Only one source identifies Porfiry by name (Vlad., p. 89).
²¹³ Concerning the Tatar attack on Chernigov, see Ipat., col. 782; Mosk., p. 130; Sof. 1, pp. 218–19;
N4, pp. 222–3. The Hypatian Chronicle misplaced information of the Tatar siege of Chernigov in
1239 into the account reporting Vladimir and Daniil's attack on Chernigov in 1235. For a detailed
examination of the transposed information, see Dimnik, "The Siege of Chernigov," pp. 387–403.
²¹⁴ Since his father Ryurik never ruled Smolensk, Vladimir was not eligible to rule the dynasty's capital
town. After the Vsevolodovichi and Daniil deprived him of Kiev, therefore, he probably returned

Daniil Romanovich of Volyn'.[215] Although the chronicles say that the Tatars sent their messengers to Kiev, there is no evidence that the three princes were in that town. Most likely, the delegation approached Mikhail in Kiev, but after he refused to submit it went to the other princes separately. The chronicler probably made only a passing reference to their capitulation in an effort to underplay the nature of their commitments. Namely, the Tatars would have made the same overtures to the three princes that they had made to the ones in Ryazan' two years earlier. They would have promised not to attack if the princes agreed to pay a tithe in everything. Moreover, since the three accepted Baty's terms they, unlike Vasil'ko, must have submitted to his authority and agreed to campaign with him. As we shall see, most of the princes on the west bank either capitulated to the conquerors in the hope of saving their lives or fled in search of safety.

MIKHAIL'S ODYSSEY

By the autumn of 1239 Mikhail himself had not yet faced the fury of the horde, but his patrimony had been pillaged, his dynastic capital had been razed, and Chernigov towns lay in ruins. As the right bank braced itself for the inevitable onslaught, he resolved to resist the enemy. During the first half of 1240, we are told, Baty sent Khan Mongke to reconnoiter Kiev.[216] When his messengers came to Mikhail for the second time seeking to coax him into submitting, he defied the khan by putting his envoys to death.[217]

In executing the messengers, Mikhail imitated Mstislav Romanovich, who, in 1223, had killed the Tatar envoys before confronting the enemy at the river Kalka.[218] Mikhail, however, was unable to follow Mstislav's example of uniting the princes against the invaders. To be sure, by 1240 almost all the princes of the east bank had been rendered militarily impotent. The lands of Chernigov, Pereyaslavl', Ryazan', and Suzdalia lay in ruins. Only Yaroslav's *druzhina* remained intact, but he was Mikhail's avowed enemy. The healthy lands of Rus' lay on the west bank: Kiev, Galicia, Volyn', Vruchiy, Turov,

---

to his father's patrimony of Vruchiy northwest of Kiev. Compare a late source which says, wrongly, that he died as prince of Smolensk ("Rodoslovnaya kniga," VOIDR, bk. 10 [M., 1851], p. 13).

[215] Sof. 1, p. 219; N4, p. 223. Compare Fennell, who suggests that the reference to the Tatars making peace with the three princes is misplaced (*Crisis*, p. 82, n. 101).

[216] The chroniclers refer to Mongke as Mengu Khan. He was the son of Tuluy and grandson of Chingis Khan. He, unlike Baty, became great khan at a later date (Vernadsky, *The Mongols*, pp. 49, 425).

[217] A number of sources say that this was the second time on which the Tatars sent envoys to Mikhail (s.a. 1240: Gust., p. 339; s.a. 1246: Mosk., p. 136). The first time, presumably, was after Chernigov fell when they sent envoys to Kiev and negotiated a settlement with Mstislav, Daniil, and Vladimir.

[218] NPL, pp. 62, 265.

and Polotsk. Mikhail's prospects of soliciting aid from these regions were also slim. Owing to their pacts with the Tatars, his nearest neighbors the Romanovichi and the Rostislavichi would refuse to march against their new overlords. Therefore, the forces in Rus' on whom Mikhail could still rely were his own *druzhina* and the Kievan militia. The only other allies to whom he could turn for aid were the Hungarians and the Poles. He therefore fled to Hungary.[219]

He was the most important prince to flee in the face of the Tatar menace. Some of his contemporaries undoubtedly looked upon his action as cowardly. Nevertheless, his decision was justified. From the capture of the seemingly impregnable Chernigov, he had learned that it would be futile to fortify himself against Tatar siege machinery. From Yury's defeat in Suzdalia, he had learnt that princes who challenged the enemy in the open field with inadequate forces were butchered mercilessly. He was also not made of the same metal as Eupaty Kolovrat, whose valor had catapulted him into a suicidal pursuit of the Tatars. Mikhail strove to survive, but not at the cost of kowtowing to Baty. In an act of desperation, it seems, he placed the defense of Kiev into the hands of his commander, and rode to seek aid from Béla IV. In this he imitated the Polovtsy who, in 1223 after the Tatars had decimated their tribes, had fled to Rus' warning the princes that if they did not send assistance, the same fate would befall them.

In the chaos that preceded the invasion of the west bank, minor princelings and *boyars* took advantage of the opportunities that presented themselves to seize power. With half of Rus' already at the mercy of the horde, and despite the inevitable destruction that awaited Kiev, the vacant throne beckoned to upstarts. Rostislav Mstislavich, the grandson of David of Smolensk, answered the call.[220] The Rostislavichi, as we have seen, had ruled Kiev on a number of occasions. Most recently Vladimir Ryurikovich had controlled it from 1223 until 1235, when Mikhail had deposed him. By 1240 Vladimir was dead.[221] Rostislav therefore seized Kiev for the Rostislavichi. He had no claim to the town because his father had never ruled it, but an explanation can be found for his reckless action. In 1231 he had usurped Smolensk. Eight years later, however, Yaroslav of Suzdalia deposed him and gave it to Vsevolod Mstislavich, a grandson of Roman.[222] Out of frustration, it would appear, Rostislav seized Kiev.

[219] See s.a. 1237: Ipat., col. 782.
[220] Rostislav, the son of Mstislav Davidovich (Baum. 2, XVII, 2), usurped Smolensk in 1231 (see above, p. 322; see also Dimnik, "Russian Princes," pp. 166–8, and *Mikhail*, p. 87).
[221] According to the Pskov chronicles, he died in 1239 (Pskov, vol. 1, p. 12; Pskov, vol. 2, p. 79).
[222] Mosk., p. 130; L'vov, p. 158; Erm., p. 77; see also Baum., IX, 33.

Daniil objected to the usurpation even though he also had no claim to Kiev. As we have seen, his father had evicted Vladimir's father Ryurik from Kiev on two occasions, in 1201 and 1204, but he himself had never occupied it.[223] Following his father's example of meddling in Kievan affairs, Daniil evicted Rostislav. He, like Mikhail, had no desire to rule it on the eve of the Tatar attack, but he deemed it necessary to evict Rostislav who had no claim to the town. Moreover, in 1236 he had helped the Vsevolodovichi to evict Vladimir from Kiev. In keeping with that policy, he deposed the upstart Rostislav therewith expressing his determination to keep the Rostislavichi out of the capital of Rus'. What is more, by placing his commander Dmitry in charge of the town, Daniil obtained a greater advantage over Mikhail. In addition to holding the latter's wife captive, he now controlled Mikhail's domain. The two trump cards, as it were, gave him the upper hand in any future dealings he would have with his brother-in-law.[224]

Meanwhile, Mikhail had arrived in Hungary where he attempted to arrange a marriage for his son Rostislav with the king's daughter. According to the chronicles, he was the first Ol'govich to try forming a family bond with the Hungarian dynasty. He was motivated, we may assume, by the immediate need to defend his domain. As part of the marriage contract, he would have asked Béla IV to give him military aid.[225] In the light of Mikhail's plight, the king saw no advantage to forming such an alliance and evicted the two Ol'govichi from Hungary.

In Mazovia, Mikhail received a warm welcome from his uncle Conrad. Even so, his refugee status compelled him to take drastic action. Chernigov lay devastated, and Galich and Kiev were both in Daniil's hands. What is more, even if he could find sanctuary in Rus', he had to travel through his brother-in-law's domain of Volyn'. The situation looked hopeless. He therefore decided that the expedient course of action was to seek reconciliation. Having no bargaining power, Mikhail placed himself at Daniil's mercy.

He sent envoys to his brother-in-law admitting that he had sinned against him on many occasions by waging war and by reneging on his promises. He pledged never again to antagonize Daniil and forswore making any future attempts on Galich. Overlooking his misdeeds, Daniil invited him to Volyn', returned his wife, and relinquished control of Kiev. To Mikhail's

[223] See above, pp. 241–2, 247.
[224] Concerning Mikhail's flight to Hungary, see Mosk., p. 131; Gust., p. 339; N4, pp. 225–6; *Mikhail*, pp. 86–8.
[225] Compare Tolochko, who argues that Mikhail fled from Kiev because he feared the Tatars and had no intention of soliciting military aid from Béla IV (*Drevnyaya Rus'*, p. 173).

son Rostislav he gave Lutsk, evidently, in compensation for taking away Galich.[226] In the face of the Tatar attack, however, Mikhail did not return to Kiev but allowed Daniil's man Dmitry to remain there. The Romanovichi therefore let Mikhail and his entourage stay in their lands.[227]

After that, Daniil traveled to Hungary hoping to marry his son Lev to the king's daughter. He probably believed that he had a better chance of success than Mikhail had had because he was negotiating from a position of power. Whereas Mikhail had been a refugee when he visited the king, Daniil controlled Volyn' and Galicia. Moreover, he probably assured the king that his domains were safe from attack. This is suggested by the evidence that his departure from Volyn', unlike Mikhail's from Kiev, lacked urgency. The obvious explanation for his seeming unconcern for the invaders is that in 1239, when he had submitted to the Tatars, they had given him assurances of immunity. This is supported by the evidence given at a later date, when we learn that he deemed it needless to fortify the towns of Galicia against the Tatars.[228] Despite Daniil's optimism, Béla IV rejected his request.[229]

THE FALL OF KIEV AND THE AFTERMATH

Meanwhile, the Tatars sacked Kiev. Towards the end of 1240, the chroniclers report, Baty encircled Kiev with his troops.[230] He set up catapults opposite the Polish Gate and hurled projectiles day and night until the wall was breached. The townspeople retreated into the fortification around the Church of the Tithe, and the next morning they sought sanctuary in the church itself. They clambered onto the balconies, but the walls collapsed under their weight and crushed them.[231] Kiev fell on December 6.[232] One chronicler notes that Baty spared the wounded commander Dmitry and, on

[226] Although this was the first occasion on which an Ol'govich got Lutsk, there was precedent for a prince of Chernigov ruling the town. In 1099, Svyatopolk Izyaslavich of Kiev had given Lutsk to his son-in-law Svyatoslav (Svyatosha) Davidovich (Lav., col. 272; *Dynasty*, p. 231).
[227] See s.a. 1238: Ipat., cols. 783–4.
[228] In 1245, the Galicians expressed regret for not having fortified their lands (Ipat., cols. 805–6).
[229] Ipat., cols. 785–6, 787.
[230] A late source reports that Baty commanded an army of "six times one hundred thousand" (Gust., p. 339).
[231] According to one view, the stone walls of the church did not collapse owing to the weight of the people, but because of the destruction caused by Tatar siege machinery. It has also been suggested that the fugitives attempted to escape by digging a tunnel under the church to the side of the hill on which it stood (M. K. Karger, "Kiev i mongol'skoe zavoevanie," SA, nr. 11 [M.-L., 1949], 72–7, 88–90).
[232] Most sources give the date December 6 for the capture of Kiev. According to other sources, the Tatars came to Kiev on September 5, besieged it for ten weeks and four days, and captured it on Monday, November 19 (for example, Av., col. 51). For a discussion of these dates, see Berezhkov, pp. 110–11.

his advice, set off for Hungary.[233] After the khan placed his official in Kiev, another chronicler has it, he marched against Daniil's town of Vladimir in Volyn'.[234] Thus, after Kiev fell, Baty divided his invading army into two divisions.

By placing his administrator in Kiev, Baty in effect imposed Tatar over-lordship over the land. To all intents and purposes, the capture of the mother of all Rus' towns terminated the existing political order. The system adopted in the days of Ryurik in the ninth century and modified over the genera-tions by Svyatoslav (d. 972), Vladimir (d. 1015), Yaroslav the Wise (d. 1054), the princes at the congress of Lyubech (1097), and Vladimir Monomakh (d. 1125), had been uprooted. Inter-dynastic relationships evolving slowly within the framework of lateral succession had been the hallmark of the old order. In the future, the traditional princely allegiances to the senior prince of the dynasty and to the prince of Kiev would be replaced by subservience to the foreign overlords. But first, in order to complete the subjugation of Rus', the Tatars had to capture Daniil's lands.

He had miscalculated in trusting Baty. After taking Kiev, the latter razed two towns located near the border of Kiev and Volyn': Kolodyazhen on the river Sluch' and Kamenets which belonged to the Ol'govich, Izyaslav Vladimirovich.[235] When the Tatars arrived in Volyn' they captured Daniil's capital of Vladimir. To the south, Galich fell after a short siege, as did many other towns.[236] Daniil learnt of the disaster from refugees whom he encountered on his return journey from Hungary. He therefore fled to the Poles, where Conrad's son Boleslav offered him sanctuary.[237] Thus, after giving Daniil temporary superiority over Mikhail by razing Chernigov and by forcing Mikhail to abandon Kiev, the Tatars nullified Daniil's advantage by ravaging his domains. The political rivalry between the brothers-in-law was thus put in abeyance.

On learning Kiev's fate, Mikhail withdrew from Volyn' and for the sec-ond time imposed himself on Conrad's good graces. When, however, the

---

[233] Gust., p. 339. According to the account, the khan did not kill Dmitry because of his bravery. More than likely, Baty spared his life because he agreed to provide strategic information to the Tatars as they passed through southwest Rus' (*Mikhail*, pp. 109–12).

[234] Ipat., cols. 784–5; Mosk., pp. 131–2; Lav., col. 470 and elsewhere. A number of sources say Baty put his commander in charge of Kiev (Nikon. 10, p. 117; Maz., p. 71).

[235] The chronicler refers to Kamenets as "Izyaslav's Kamenets" (*Kamentsyu Izyaslavlyu*). Concerning the identification of this town, see Dimnik, "Kamenec," pp. 25–34; compare Dashkevich, "Kamenets – eshche raz," pp. 7–19.

[236] Ipat., col. 786.

[237] Ipat., cols. 787–8. As we have seen, in 1236 Daniil had sent Prince Mendog and the Lithuanians to attack Conrad's lands (see above, p. 341). To judge from the evidence that, in 1241, Daniil did not seek sanctuary with Conrad, the two were probably still at odds.

Tatars also threatened Mazovia, he traveled west to Breslau (Wroslaw) in Silesia. As his caravan pressed northwest, it came to Środa, where, seeing the heavily laden packhorses, the local inhabitants attacked Mikhail's train. They plundered his goods and killed a number of his people including his granddaughter.

The reference to Mikhail's granddaughter is noteworthy. We are not told which of Mikhail's children was her parent. Circumstantial evidence, however, excludes the three we have already met: Rostislav was not yet married, Maria was living in Rostov, and Feodula was a nun in Suzdal'. Mikhail therefore had another offspring who begot the granddaughter. We may assume that the unidentified parent was a son because a daughter would have moved to her husband's home, just as Maria and Feodula had done. The allusion to another son is important because it reveals that Mikhail had sons whom the chronicles have not yet mentioned. This reference therefore gives credence to the unique news in the Ermolinskiy Chronicle which, after reporting Mikhail's death, names four sons who survived him: Roman, Mstislav, Simeon, and Yury.[238] Presumably, one of them fathered the girl killed in Silesia.[239] Moreover, since the chronicler mentions the child only because of her misfortune, Mikhail may have had other grandchildren who are not mentioned because no ill befell them.

Meanwhile, the Tatars invaded Silesia and attacked the local duke, Henry II the Pious.[240] After the invaders had passed through Volyn' and the Polish lands, Mikhail returned to Mazovia.[241] Some time in the spring of 1241, he considered it safe to go home.[242] He stopped at the devastated town of Vladimir in Volyn', rode northeast to Pinsk, and then traveled down the river Pripyat' to Kiev. Unable to return to his court on the citadel because Baty's official had presumably occupied it, he took up residence on an island near the *podol'*. Significantly, Baty's man did not challenge his arrival thereby indicating that, for the time being, the Tatars were willing to let refugee princes return to their ravaged towns without obstruction.

---

[238] Erm., pp. 81–2. The Ermolinskiy Chronicle gives the names of only those sons who remained in Rus'. Rostislav is not on the list because, as we shall see, he moved to Hungary.

[239] The child's death later became the subject of a local legend describing the death of a Tatar princess (A. V. Florovsky, *Chekhi i vostochnye slavyane* [Prague, 1935], vol. 1, pp. 207–8).

[240] On April 9, 1241, the Tatars routed Henry II at the battle at Liegnitz near Breslau. A second Tatar force moved against Béla IV and, on April 11, 1241, crushed the Hungarians at Mohi near the confluence of the rivers Tisa and Sajo (Ipat., cols. 786–7). Concerning Baty's campaign in the West, see Vernadsky, *The Mongols*, pp. 52–8.

[241] See s.a. 1238: Ipat., col. 784.

[242] The Tatars were gone from Rus' by early April of 1241 since, as we have seen, they crushed Henry II and Béla IV early in that month. For a discussion of why the Tatars overran Rus' with such ease, see *Crisis*, pp. 84–6.

At the same time, Mikhail gave Chernigov to his son Rostislav. This news is surprising because, in 1239, his younger cousin Mstislav Glebovich had defended it. The chronicle does not report why Mikhail replaced the rightful ruler with his own son. As has been suggested elsewhere, he may have repudiated Mstislav because, contrary to his wishes, Mstislav had formed a pact with the enemy.[243] But there may have been another reason why he did not return to Chernigov. Although the chronicles fail to tell us, he may have died following his pact with the Tatars. The possibility of his demise is implied by the silence of the chronicles, which never mention him again. Assuming, therefore, that Rostislav was the rightful ruler of Chernigov, his appointment gives us useful dynastic information. It tells us that all of Mikhail's younger cousins, who were ahead of Rostislav in seniority, were dead.[244] Accordingly, only members of Mikhail's family retained the right to occupy the office of senior prince.

At that time, Rostislav, the son of Vladimir Ryurikovich the former prince of Kiev, also returned from abroad. As he passed through Volyn' he visited Daniil in Kholm. By doing so he confirmed his fidelity and proved that he was not plotting against Daniil with Mikhail. The latter, the chronicler retorts, failed to express his gratitude to Daniil for his magnanimity. Instead of visiting his brother-in-law in person, he merely sent a messenger.[245]

Although other princelings passed through Volyn' on their way home, the chronicler singles out only Rostislav.[246] Because the latter had recently succeeded his father Vladimir as head of the Ryurikovichi and prince of Vruchiy,[247] Daniil wished to know if he had adopted his father's policy of collaborating with the Ol'govichi. The marriage alliances between the two dynasties testified to the long-standing friendship that existed between them.[248] Also troublesome for Daniil was the hatred that the Ryurikovichi harbored against him because of his father's mischief. As we have seen, Roman had not only repudiated his wife Predslava, one of Rostislav's aunts,[249]

<hr>

[243] *Mikhail*, pp. 114–15.
[244] These were the sons of Mikhail's uncles Gleb and Mstislav. His uncle Gleb evidently had only one son, Mstislav. His uncle Mstislav, it appears, had at least two sons: Dmitry was killed with him in 1223 at the Kalka river (see above, p. 296); and a second son may have been the father of the twelve-year-old Vasil'ko of Kozel'sk who was killed by the Tatars (see above, pp. 346–7).
[245] Concerning Mikhail's travels, see s.a. 1240: Ipat., cols. 788–9.
[246] Later, we learn that the princes of Bolokhov were in Boleslav's domain of Mazovia at the same time that Daniil and Vasil'ko were staying with him. The Romanovichi saved the princes from Boleslav's aggression so that, like Mikhail, they were indebted to the Romanovichi (see below, p. 362).
[247] Elsewhere it was wrongly suggested that Rostislav was the prince of Pinsk (*Mikhail*, p. 114).
[248] Two of Rostislav's aunts married Ol'govichi. In 1182, Anastasia married Gleb Svyatoslavich of the senior branch (Ipat., cols. 624–5; Zotov, p. 273; Baum., IX, 19), and in 1187 Yaroslava married Svyatoslav Igorevich of the cadet branch (Ipat., col. 659; Zotov, p. 277; Baum., IX, 21).
[249] Baum., IX, 20.

but had also forced Rostislav's grandfather Ryurik to become a monk. By visiting Kholm, therefore, Rostislav assured Daniil that he did not harbor hostility against him, and was not collaborating with Mikhail as his father had done. The confirmation was important to Daniil because Rostislav had replaced his father Vladimir as a claimant to Kiev.

In the same year that Mikhail returned to Kiev, one chronicle gives us unique news. It states that in 1241 the Tatars killed Mstislav of Ryl'sk.[250] His identity is uncertain because we do not know his patronymic. We are safe in assuming, however, that he was not Mstislav Glebovich. Ryl'sk belonged to the cadet branch. Since, according to lateral succession, the town would have been passed on from prince to prince in the same family, Mstislav of Ryl'sk evidently belonged to the senior line of the cadet branch. He was most likely a younger brother or a son of Oleg of Kursk who, in 1226, had challenged Mikhail. The death of the unidentified prince once again testifies to the possible existence of still other princelings whom the sources fail to mention.

We are not told if the Tatars killed Mstislav in battle or if they executed him for insubordination. His death reveals, however, that Baty left contingents behind to perform mopping up operations. Thus, if the Tatars had not captured Ryl'sk two years earlier on their way to Chernigov, they undoubtedly did so when they killed Mstislav. The reference to his death therefore gives us news of Baty's consolidation tactics. During this exercise, his rearguards systematically secured the Tatars' grip over the conquered towns.

ROSTISLAV FIGHTS FOR CONTROL OF GALICIA

The Tatars wreaked unprecedented havoc,[251] but the people of Rus' were resilient. They had weathered nomadic incursions before, and they believed that they could do so again. In the past, forays from the Pechenegs and Polovtsy had been transitory because the nomads withdrew to the steppe with their booty without attempting to assert their hold over the regions they had pillaged. The Ol'govichi evidently believed that the Tatars would do the same. Ignoring the mopping up exercises of the conquerors and the officials they were appointing to the captured towns, the princes attempted to resume the pace of political life that they had lived before the invasion.

---

[250] Lav., col. 470.

[251] Concerning estimates of the damage the Tatars inflicted on Rus', see *Crisis*, pp. 86–90; J. Martin, *Medieval Russia 980–1584* (Cambridge, 1995), pp. 145–7; Ostrowski, *Muscovy and the Mongols*, pp. 108–10; Charles J. Halperin, *Russia and the Golden Horde* (Bloomington, 1985), pp. 75–6, 120–1.

The Gustinskiy chronicler observes wryly that "the princes slandered each other, quarreled over deserted territories, and destroyed whatever lands the Tatars had failed to devastate."[252] Despite the chronicler's accusation, no source reports that Mikhail engaged in any rivalries following his return to Kiev. Nevertheless, he evidently deputed Rostislav in Chernigov to conduct all of the family's military ventures. The Hypatian chronicler monitored these carefully. *Boyar* greed gave Rostislav the pretext for reviving his quest for Galicia. Taking advantage of the chaos in that region, local magnates acknowledged Daniil as their prince, but appropriated authority to themselves. Two pro-Ol'govichi ringleaders got the upper hand. Dobroslav Sud'ich assumed princely powers and strengthened the faction of the Ol'govichi by giving Galician domains to *boyars* from Chernigov. After capturing Bakota on the river Dnestr south of Galich, he also appropriated the surrounding Poniz'e district.[253] Meanwhile, Grigory Vasil'evich, Rostislav's former major-domo in Galich, attempted to seize Peremyshl'.[254] Eventually, the two quarreled and asked Daniil to arbitrate. After they rejected his ruling, and on learning that they intended to give his lands to Rostislav, Daniil took them captive.[255]

In 1241, after discovering that Daniil had recaptured Bakota, Rostislav marshalled the princes of Bolokhov and the remainder of the Galicians, and besieged the regional capital of the Poniz'e.[256] Chancellor (*Pechatnik*) Kirill, whom Daniil had sent to restore order, commanded the town. When Rostislav attempted to cajole him into capitulating, the *Pechatnik* berated the prince. He reminded Rostislav how the Romanovichi had welcomed him and his father to Volyn' after Béla IV had evicted them. He pointed

---

[252] See s.a. 1242: Gust., p. 340.

[253] The Poniz'e comprised the southern periphery of Galicia. It included the towns Kalius, Ushitsa, Bakota, Onut, Vasiliev, and Kolomyya, which served as outposts against the incursions of the nomads. Although officially part of Galicia, the towns did not have a strong affiliation with its central authority. In the twelfth century, the region was called the Galician borderland (*Galichskaya ukrayna*), but in the thirteenth century it became known as the Poniz'e (P. A. Rappoport, "Voennoe zodchestvo zapadnorusskikh zemel' X–XIV vv.," *Materialy i issledovaniya po arkheologii SSSR*, nr. 140 [L., 1967], p. 177).

[254] In 1236, Mikhail attempted to placate Daniil by giving him Peremyshl', probably because its inhabitants had supported Daniil in the past (see above, p. 337).

[255] Ipat., cols. 789–91. The chronicler places this information under the year 1240. The *boyars* probably appropriated control of the Galician districts after the Tatars passed through these regions at the beginning of 1241 while Daniil was a refugee in Poland. Concerning Dobroslav and Grigory, see *Mikhail*, pp. 115–16, and see above, pp. 333–4.

[256] As we have seen, in 1233 the princes of Bolokhov were allied to the Ol'govichi when Mikhail and Izyaslav Vladimirovich called the princes their brothers (see above, p. 327 and *Mikhail*, pp. 98–9, 118–19). The remainder of the Galicians presumably constituted friends of the Ol'govichi who had worked in cahoots with Dobroslav and Grigory against Daniil.

out that the brothers had shown their esteem for Mikhail by returning Kiev to him and by giving Lutsk to Rostislav. What is more, they had freed Rostislav's mother from Yaroslav's clutches. But Rostislav was not swayed by Kirill's admonition. The latter therefore sallied out of Bakota with his infantry and Rostislav withdrew to Chernigov.

On learning that the princes of Bolokhov had joined Rostislav, Daniil attacked their domains in the southwest corner of the Kievan land. He put their towns to the torch and leveled their earthen walls.[257] Kirill also came from Bakota and set fire to their fields. The Tatars, we are told, had spared their crops because they wanted their farmers to supply them with wheat and millet. Daniil was incensed at the princes for placing their hope in the invaders and for forgetting his favor to them in Mazovia. At that time, after the princes of Bolokhov had fled from the Tatars to the Poles, Boleslav had challenged them because they were not allies of the Romanovichi. Daniil intended to defend them with force but found it unnecessary after Vasil'ko paid for their safety. Despite this act of friendship, the ungrateful princes of Bolokhov helped Rostislav attack Bakota. Daniil therefore made them pay for their treachery by demolishing their towns.[258]

Bakota and the surrounding Poniz'e district were desirable to Rostislav because they were important purveyors of salt. We are told that during the last decade of the eleventh century, when the local princes prohibited merchants from leaving Galicia, they cut off the salt supply to all of Rus'.[259] The importance of the Galician salt trade is confirmed by the size of its caravans. In 1164, when the river Dnestr overflowed, it claimed the lives of over 300 men who were bringing salt from Udech, a town located to the north of Galich.[260] The commodity was especially vital to the local prince who used it for remunerating his troops. Daniil relied on controlling the town of Kolomyya, west of Bakota, for that very reason.[261] By seizing the Poniz'e district, therefore, Rostislav hoped to deprive Daniil of this valued resource. He not only failed but also gave notice to his uncle that he was renewing his fight for Galicia.

Rostislav redirected his attack against the more important towns of Galich and Peremyshl'. He had strong support from the local *boyars*,

[257] Concerning the towns that Daniil razed, see *Mikhail*, p. 117. They were located to the north and east of the town of Mezhibozh'e on the upper reaches of the Southern Bug (P. A. Rappoport, "Goroda Bolokhovskoy zemli," KSIIMK 57 [M., 1955], 52–9).
[258] Ipat., cols. 791–3.
[259] D. Abramovich, *Kievo-pecherskiy Paterik* (K., 1930), pp. 151–2; Heppell, *The "Paterik,"* pp. 171–2.
[260] Ipat., col. 524.
[261] Ipat., cols. 789–90. Concerning the Galician salt trade, see *Mikhail*, p. 117.

including Volodislav.[262] The scope of his influence is attested to by the news that he persuaded the inhabitants of Pechera Domamira to join Rostislav's camp and cajoled the townsmen of Galich itself into capitulating without a fight. In gratitude, Rostislav made him *tysyatskiy*. Although Rostislav evidently lost the backing of the Bolokhov princes after Daniil razed their towns, the remainder of the so-called "unfaithful Galicians" most likely accompanied him against Galich. Their number probably included the commander of the town called Shchekotov where, as we shall see, Rostislav would later seek sanctuary. The people of Bakota and Kalius also rejoined Rostislav's camp. This, as we shall see, is implied by the chronicler's comment that after Daniil evicted Rostislav from Galich, he had to go and reassert his authority over the towns in the Poniz'e district.

After occupying Galich, Rostislav also made Konstantin of Ryazan' the ruler of Peremyshl', where he and the local bishop incited sedition against Daniil.[263] The prince was probably Konstantin Vladimirovich who, in 1217, made a bid for power with his elder brother, Gleb, by treacherously murdering five cousins and their youngest brother. The conspiracy failed and the villains fled to the Polovtsy.[264] To judge from Konstantin's presence in Peremyshl', he left the nomads and sought his fortune with the Ol'govichi. The news that Rostislav gave him Peremyshl', a town second in importance only to Galich, suggests that he considered the refugee to be one of his staunchest allies.

Daniil and Vasil'ko retaliated by marching against Galich. Unable to withstand their attack, Rostislav fled with his supporters, including Bishop Artemy.[265] Later, Daniil also dispatched his men to capture the bishop and Konstantin in Peremyshl'.[266] Thus we see that the bishops of the only two eparchies in Galicia supported Rostislav.[267] This implies that during the early 1240s Daniil may have pursued an anti-Galician Church policy.

---

[262] Volodislav vacillated in his loyalty between Daniil and Rostislav. Under the year 1229, the chronicler reports that he fought for Daniil (Ipat., col. 759), but under the year 1231, he calls Volodislav a traitor to Daniil on one occasion (Ipat., col. 764) and on another reports that Daniil placed Volodislav in command of his forces (Ipat., col. 766). At the beginning of 1242, the chronicler again accuses Volodislav of being unfaithful for helping Rostislav (Ipat., col. 793). At a later date, as we shall see, Daniil executed the *boyar* for his treachery.

[263] Ipat., cols. 793–4.

[264] Concerning the princely murders of 1217, see above, p. 289. Although it cannot be proven that Rostislav's ally was Konstantin Vladimirovich, circumstantial evidence supports this identification (Baum. 2, XIV, 31). Elsewhere it was wrongly suggested that Konstantin fled to Chernigov after surviving the Tatar invasion (*Mikhail*, p. 120).

[265] As we have seen, in 1237 the bishop had supported the prince when he and the major-domo Grigory Vasil'evich defended Galich on Rostislav's behalf (see above, pp. 341–2).

[266] Ipat., cols. 793–4.

[267] Concerning the two eparchies, see *Mikhail*, p. 120, n. 89.

Indeed, in 1242, after Baty withdrew from Hungary, the chronicler notes that Daniil was in Kholm with Metropolitan Kirill.[268] Because the latter sought safety with Daniil rather than with Mikhail, who as prince of Kiev was the metropolitan's secular superior, it appears that Kirill, like Daniil, may have been hostile to the Ol'govichi. Although the chronicler does not tell us if Daniil and Kirill were scheming against the Church in Galicia, the opposition of the two bishops suggests that Daniil was hostile to them. Significantly, the bishops' preference for the Ol'govichi also shows that the latter promoted a Church policy for Galicia that was more acceptable to the local prelates.[269]

Meanwhile, Rostislav sought sanctuary in Shchekotov. The Romanovichi pursued him, but on learning that the Tatars had left Hungary and were returning via Galicia, they abandoned the chase.[270] Instead, Daniil went to Bakota and Kalius to restore order.[271] Although the returning conquerors unwittingly saved Rostislav from Daniil's wrath, he soon fell victim to their lance. As they passed through Galicia, they routed his force at a location which the chronicler identifies as a small pine forest, probably near Shchekotov. He therefore fled to the Hungarians.

ROSTISLAV DESERTS HIS FATHER

On this occasion Rostislav had much better luck with the king. Béla IV, who had returned home from Dalmatia after May in 1242,[272] approved

---

[268] Ipat., col. 794. It has been suggested that Metropolitan Kirill had been Daniil's former *pechatnik* who, in 1241, defended Bakota against Rostislav (J. G. Fuhrmann, "Metropolitan Cyril II [1242–1281] and the Politics of Accommodation," JBfGOE, Neue Folge, Band 24 [Wiesbaden, 1976], pp. 161–3, and G. Stökl, "Kanzler und Metropolit," *Studien zur Geschichte Osteuropas*, III. Teil, Gedenkenband für Heinrich Felix Schmid in Wiener Archiv für Geschichte des Slawentums und Osteuropas V [Graz-Köln, 1966], pp. 156–73). It is not relevant to our investigation to examine this problem. It can be noted, however, that the only occasion on which Daniil seemingly had the authority to select a candidate for the metropolitan's office was in 1240, when he was the *de facto* prince of Kiev. Consequently, the news that *Pechatnik* Kirill defended Bakota in 1241 argues against the contention that he and Metropolitan Kirill were one and the same person. See also Makary, *Istoriya russkoy tserkvi v period mongol'skiy* (Spb., 1886; Slavica-Reprint nr. 16, The Hague, 1968), vol. 4, bk. 1, pp. 7–8, 309–10, and Shchapov, *Gosudarstvo i tserkov' Drevney Rusi X–XIII vv.*, pp. 204–6.

[269] See also *Mikhail*, pp. 120–1.

[270] On December 11, 1241, Great Khan Ogedey died in Mongolia. On receiving the news in the spring of 1242, Baty withdrew from Hungary probably because he wished to be in a position to influence the choice of the new great khan (Vernadsky, *The Mongols*, pp. 57–8; B. Spuler, *Die Goldene Horde. Die Mongolen in Russland 1223–1502* [Wiesbaden, 1965], p. 24; C. A. Macartney, *Hungary, A Short History* [Edinburgh, 1962], pp. 32–3). Accordingly, Rostislav probably occupied Galich and fled from the Romanovichi during the spring or summer of 1242.

[271] Kalius was located east of Bakota at the mouth of the river Kalyus, a tributary of the Dnestr (Makhnovets', p. 553).

[272] The king sought safety from the Tatars in the environs of Split (Z. J. Kosztolnyik, *Hungary in the Thirteenth Century*, East European Monographs 439 [Boulder, 1996], p. 185).

Rostislav's marriage to his daughter Anna.[273] Although Rostislav and his father had unsuccessfully sought to form an alliance with the king two years earlier when they had been fugitives in Hungary, he had a change of heart after the Tatars devastated his lands. On learning that Béla IV had given his daughter in marriage to Rostislav, Mikhail believed that his efforts to form an alliance with the Árpád dynasty had finally been realized. He therefore rode to Hungary expecting to negotiate the commercial, cultural, and political agreements that normally accompanied such an alliance. One of his main objectives, undoubtedly, was to establish closer collaboration over Galicia.

His hopes were dashed. To stop his lands from being invaded again, the king sought to organize a new defensive system by creating client states to the south and east of Hungary.[274] In his search for a vassal whom he could appoint to Galicia, he chose Rostislav and won his loyalty by giving him a wife of royal blood. In other words, rather than forming a marriage alliance with Rostislav as the representative of the Ol'govichi, Béla IV concluded a personal pact with the prince. The two therefore rebuffed Mikhail when he came to the king's court. Mikhail, greatly angered by his son, returned empty-handed to Chernigov.[275] Rostislav, for his part, severed all ties with his dynasty. He lived out his life in the kingdom of Hungary, where his father-in-law granted him various titles and lands.[276]

Rostislav's defection was a severe blow to the Ol'govichi. In addition to the personal loss that he inflicted on his father, he also altered the order of succession within the dynasty because he had been the heir apparent. His betrayal also deprived the Ol'govichi of their most valued agent in Galicia. He had received strong support from many peasants and magnates who, as we shall see, continued to back him after he joined Béla IV. Finally, in renouncing his family, Rostislav robbed his father of the much-sought-after alliance with Béla IV. Understandably, the Ol'govichi disowned him. They

[273] See s.a. 1243: Ipat., col. 794; Makhnovets', p. 400; Kosztolnyik, *Hungary*, p. 200. The date of the marriage has not been preserved.
[274] Macartney, *Hungary*, pp. 33–4. To reflect his alleged control over the neighboring client states, Béla IV assumed the title "King of Hungary, Dalmatia, Croatia, Bosnia (Rama), Serbia, Galicia, Vladimir (Lodomeria), and Cumania" (G. Fejer [ed.], *Codex diplomaticus Hungariae ecclesiasticus ac civilis* [Budae, 1829], bk. 4, vol. 1, p. 577).
[275] Ipat., col. 795. The chronicler misplaces the information under the year 1245 (*Mikhail*, pp. 122–3).
[276] Rostislav became the Ban of all Slavonia, the Ban of Machva, and the Lord of Bosnia (Florovsky, *Chekhi i vostochnye slavyane*, pp. 240–3; E. Hosch, "Russische Fürsten im Donauraum des 13. Jahrhunderts," *Münchner Zeitschrift für Balkankunde*, Band 2 [München, 1979], pp. 97–107; and J. V. A. Fine, Jr., *The Late Medieval Balkans* [Ann Arbor, 1987], pp. 171–5).

demonstrated their outrage by excising his name from their genealogical charts.[277]

Acting as the king's agent Rostislav made two unsuccessful attacks on Galicia. Sometime in 1244 he led a Hungarian force against Peremyshl' where he also conscripted numerous local peasants as infantrymen. Daniil, however, marshalled his troops and routed the attackers making Rostislav flee to Hungary.[278] In the following year, he recruited many Hungarians and Poles and launched an attack against Yaroslavl' north of Peremyshl'. On August 17, 1245 Daniil, with Polovtsian help, annihilated the enemy. He executed many of the captured Hungarians, including their commander and Volodislav Yur'evich, who had remained loyal to Rostislav.[279] The latter, however, escaped to Hungary.[280]

With his resounding victory and his merciless execution of prisoners, Daniil emphatically demonstrated that he was determined to use extreme measures to keep out the Hungarians from Galicia. By executing the *bo-yar* ringleader Volodislav, he effectively eliminated Galician support for Rostislav. By decimating the Hungarian troops, he forced Béla IV to stop supporting his son-in-law's bid for Galich. Instead of uselessly sacrificing more men, the king decided to recoup his manpower losses.[281] Conse-quently, after his defeat at Yaroslavl', Rostislav never returned to Galicia. At long last, Daniil became the undisputed ruler of Galich.

BATY MAKES ALL PRINCES OF RUS' SUBMIT TO HIM

After returning through Galicia, Volyn', and the Kievan land, Baty led his forces to the mouth of the river Volga, where he set up his headquarters at Saray, some 100 km north of Astrakhan'. From there the Kipchak Khanate, or the Golden Horde as it came to be known, subjugated Rus' under the so-called "Tatar Yoke."[282] After appointing his officials to the towns that he had conquered, he commanded all the princes to visit Saray and pay him homage. He made each one walk between two fires and bow to a statue. After completing this ritual the vassal was allowed to kowtow to the khan. Many of the princes obeyed his directive "for the glory and the honor."[283]

---

[277] See the list of Mikhail's sons in the Ermolinskiy Chronicle (PSRL 23, p. 81) and the *Lyubestkiy sinodik* (Zotov, pp. 194–5); see also *Mikhail*, p. 123.

[278] See s.a. 1245: Ipat., col. 797.

[279] In 1242, as we have seen, Volodislav had helped Rostislav to capture Galich (see above, pp. 362–3).

[280] Ipat., cols. 800–5. The chronicler misplaces this lengthy account under the year 1249 (*Mikhail*, pp. 124–5; compare s.a. 1243: Gust., p. 340).

[281] Historians believe that the Tatar invasion followed by plague and starvation cost Hungary almost half its population (Macartney, *Hungary*, p. 33).

[282] Vernadsky, *The Mongols*, p. 60; *Crisis*, p. 84.   [283] See s.a. 1239; Maz., p. 71.

Yaroslav Vsevolodovich of Suzdalia was the first to respond to the summons. At the beginning of 1243, he traveled to Saray, where Baty appointed him senior prince in Rus'.[284] After returning to Suzdalia in the same year, he sent his commander Dmitry Eikovich to rule Kiev.[285] Accordingly, some time during the second part of that year, Mikhail abandoned his court on the island below Kiev and returned to Chernigov.

Yaroslav was the first to rule Kiev and to become the senior prince of Rus' by Tatar mandate. His appointment terminated the traditional system of succession to Kiev. Significantly, in making his appointee as the senior prince of Rus' the prince of Kiev, Baty acknowledged it to be the most important town in the land. Moreover, since Yaroslav considered it necessary to send his lieutenant to Kiev, he also believed that ruling the mother of all Rus' towns was a vital component of his seniority. He probably refused to occupy it in person, however, because in 1236 the Kievans had rejected him and they would probably do so again. Significantly, he sent a *boyar* rather than a prince as his deputy. He undoubtedly did so out of spite to belittle Mikhail's status since he had been the last autonomous prince of Kiev. We have seen that he harbored great animosity towards Mikhail over their past rivalries. Indeed, his hatred may have prompted Baty to select him as Mikhail's replacement. After all, the khan also had a score to settle with the Ol'govich. The latter had committed the unforgivable crime of killing Tatar envoys. Thus, in toadying up to Baty, Yaroslav was able to achieve his greatest revenge by replacing Mikhail in Kiev.[286]

Mikhail's course of action became clear. On the one hand, attempting to seize Kiev from Yaroslav, who enjoyed Baty's protection, was out of the question. On the other hand, Rostislav's desertion had put paid to his Galician policy. Even though he had younger sons who could champion his interests, he could not compete with both Béla IV and Daniil for control of Galich. What is more, they had the advantage in that their lands lay adjacent to Galicia. Mikhail therefore had to satisfy himself with ruling Chernigov. But even there his authority was insecure. Like all the other princes of Rus', he had to obtain Baty's patent (*yarlyk*) to rule his patrimony.

---

[284] See s.a. 1242: NPL, pp. 79, 297; s.a. 1243: Lav., col. 470; Mosk., p. 136. Concerning the date, see Berezhkov, p. 271.

[285] See s.a. 1243: Gust., p. 340. When Daniil passed through Kiev two years later, in 1245, he reported that the town was controlled by Yaroslav's *boyar* Dmitry Eikovich (see s.a. 1250: Ipat., col. 806; *Mikhail*, pp. 125–6).

[286] The active roles that Yaroslav's unnamed son and his henchman Sangor played in greeting princes who arrived in Saray is strong evidence that Yaroslav had won special favor with Baty. Accordingly, he may have influenced some of the khan's decisions concerning the princes of Rus' (see below, p. 370).

The trip to Saray was a humiliating proposition. It meant kowtowing to Baty and acknowledging his overlordship. More importantly, the visit held personal danger. Mikhail had to place himself at the mercy of the khan who might well demand recompense for his offense. Nevertheless, he would be foolish to attempt evading Tatar justice by closeting himself in Chernigov. In his own time, the khan would vent his anger by dispatching a punitive force against the defiant prince. Mikhail had no choice but to go. For unexplained reasons, however, he dallied for two more years.

While Mikhail sat obstinately in Chernigov, other princes journeyed submissively to the Golden Horde. After Yaroslav's initial visit in 1243, his brothers and nephews, including Mikhail's grandsons Boris and Gleb of Rostov, followed suit.[287] Oleg Ingvarevich of Ryazan' visited not only Saray, but was also compelled to make the arduous trek to the Great Khan's capital of Karakorum in Mongolia.[288] As we shall see, a number of Ol'govichi also visited Saray.

Even though his brother-in-law Daniil had successfully driven out Rostislav and the Hungarians from Galicia, he soon discovered that control over his newly acquired domain remained insecure. Moguchey, one of the Tatar commanders in the region, ordered him to hand over Galich. But Daniil refused to part with it and, on October 26, 1245, he rode to place his petition before Baty.[289] The khan gave him the *yarlyk* to rule Galicia in addition to Volyn'.[290] Consequently, Daniil's patent put paid to any thoughts that Mikhail may still have had about ruling that town. Once again it was the Tatar overlord who settled the dispute between him and his rival, and once again Baty's decision went against Mikhail. Daniil and Yaroslav held patents for Galich and Kiev; Mikhail, however, held only his patrimony of Chernigov for which Baty had not yet granted him a *yarlyk*.

By the end of 1245, therefore, only Mikhail from among the three senior princes had not yet kowtowed to the conqueror. Although Daniil had fulfilled his obligation, Baty had expressed his displeasure by demanding to know why he had dallied so long in coming.[291] In light of his veiled threat to Daniil, how long would the khan tolerate Mikhail's tardiness?

MIKHAIL'S DEATH

In the end, Mikhail went in time to pre-empt a Tatar punitive strike against his domain. He therewith saved Chernigov from carnage but hastened his

---

[287] Lav., cols. 470–1; Ak. sp., col. 523; Mosk., p. 136. Also, see *Crisis*, p. 99.
[288] N4, p. 228. Concerning Oleg's identity, see Baum. 2, XIV, 38.   [289] *Mikhail*, pp. 125–6, n. 105.
[290] Ipat., s.a. 1250: cols. 805–8; compare s.a. 1244: Gust., pp. 340–1.   [291] Ipat., col. 807.

own demise. He set off in the summer of 1246, perhaps in response to the khan's personal summons. Three types of accounts reporting his visit have survived. The first are chronicle entries that give either a brief factual report or a longer narrative account frequently embellished with pious interpolations. The second are reports of contemporary non-Rus′ visitors to Saray. The third are expanded religious narratives that treat Mikhail's death as martyrdom. Their purpose was to edify the Orthodox faithful with the prince's Christian fortitude rather than to present a factual description of his death. The religious narratives will be used only as supplementary sources for our investigation.[292]

Almost all the chronicles report Mikhail's death, but they repeat, in the main, the information given by the Hypatian Chronicle and the Laurentian Chronicle. They recount how Mikhail went to the Golden Horde with his grandson, Boris Vasil′kovich of Rostov, to obtain a *yarlyk*. When they arrived at Saray, Baty sent messengers to Mikhail's camp instructing him to worship according to the laws of the Tatars by bowing to the fires and the idols. Mikhail agreed to bow to the khan because God had placed him into Baty's hands for his sins. But he insulted the Tatar by refusing to obey his impious command to worship idols. Enraged by the prince's retort, Baty ordered that he be put to death. On September 20, 1246, Mikhail was slaughtered by the godless Doman of Putivl′, and Fedor his *boyar* was killed after him.[293] Thus, "the two men received the crown of martyrdom."[294]

The *Komissionnyy spisok* of the Novgorod First Chronicle, the oldest chronicle reporting Mikhail's death, contains a number of additional details. Before the journey, Mikhail went to his priest, Ivan, to obtain his blessing. At Saray, shamans ordered the prince to observe the customary purification ritual and to worship an idol. As a symbolic gesture of his resolve to cast off the honors of this world, Mikhail flung his cloak at the tempters. After the Tatars killed him and Fedor, the apostate Doman cut off their

---

[292] A religious account of Mikhail's death is popularly called a Life (*Zhitie*). Concerning these accounts, see Barsukov, cols. 372–9; N. Serebryansky, *Drevne-russkiya knyazheskiya zhitiya (Obzor redaktsiy i teksty)* (M., 1915), pp. 108–41; Makary, Mitropolit Vserossiyskiy, *Velikiya Minei Chetii*, September 14–24 (Spb., 1869), cols. 1298–1305, 1308–36; *Mikhail*, pp. 151–4; and L. A. Dmitriev, "Skazanie o ubienii v orde knyazya Mikhaila Chernigovskogo i ego boyarina Feodora," *SKKDR*, pp. 412–16. The most recent facsimile edition is V. I. Sinyukov, *et al.* (eds.), *Skazanie o knyaze Mikhaile chernigovskom i o ego boyarine Feodore* (M., 1988). A unique account reporting Mikhail's death is the Life (*Zhitie*) of St. Evfrosinia, Mikhail's daughter Feodula, who became a nun in Suzdalia (Georgievsky, "Zhitie pr. Evfrosinii Suzdal′skoy," pp. 116–18).

[293] Putivl′, as we have seen, was under the jurisdiction of the cadet branch of Ol′govichi. Doman, a native of Putivl′, evidently defected to the Tatars in 1239, when they sacked his town.

[294] See s.a. 1245: Ipat., col. 795; s.a. 1246: Lav., col. 471. Concerning the date of Mikhail's execution, see *Mikhail*, pp. 132–3, n. 7.

heads. The executioners then threw their bodies to the dogs. As a sign of divine favor, their bodies remained unmolested and pillars of fire hovered over them.[295]

The Franciscan friar John de Plano Carpini, whom Pope Innocent IV sent to Mongolia in the hope of converting the Tatars, also left an account of Mikhail's death.[296] The Tatars, he writes, made an idol of their first emperor Chingis Khan, placed it by the khan's tent, and bowed to it at noon as to a god. They did not, as a rule, compel anyone else to worship the idol and therewith force him to deny his faith "with the exception of Michael." They made him walk between two fires and demanded that he bow to the idol. Mikhail agreed to pay homage to Baty, but refused to worship the image of a dead man because it was against Christian belief. Because Mikhail remained adamant, Baty sent the son of Yaroslav Vsevolodovich with the ultimatum that Mikhail either worship the idol or suffer death.[297] The prince kept his faith and Baty kept his word. He ordered his bodyguard to kick Mikhail's heart with his heels until the prince expired. The *boyar* Fedor remained faithfully at the prince's side exhorting him to persevere. A Tatar cut off Mikhail's head with a knife and later also beheaded Fedor.[298]

From the accounts it is evident that, after the invasion, Mikhail continued to maintain close ties with his daughter Maria in Rostov. The news that her son Boris, rather than one of Mikhail's own sons living in the Chernigov lands, accompanied him bespeaks the close bond that existed between him and his daughter's family.[299] Boris evidently played a prominent role in his grandfather's last journey. Perhaps it was he who finally convinced Mikhail

[295] NPL, pp. 298–303. A number of chronicles, which have the narrative account, give the name of Mikhail's priest as Ivan and call Doman a Severyanin, that is, a man from the land of the Severyane in the Chernigov lands (Sof. 1, pp. 230–5; Mosk., pp. 136–9).

[296] The friar departed from Lyons, France, in April of 1245, and arrived at Saray in April of 1246. In November of 1246, he departed from Karakorum and, on arriving at Saray, learnt of Mikhail's death (Vernadsky, *The Mongols*, pp. 62–4).

[297] When Daniil arrived at the khan's court a certain Sangor, Yaroslav Vsevolodovich's man, met him (Ipat., col. 807). The friar also reports that on arriving in Saray he met a son of Yaroslav Vsevolodovich accompanied by a certain Sangor (Dawson, *The Mongol Mission*, p. 70). The same son of Yaroslav apparently presented Baty's ultimatum to Mikhail. Because of the active role that Yaroslav's son and henchman Sangor played as Baty's agents in greeting princes from Rus' and, in particular, because of the role Yaroslav's son played in presenting the khan's final threat to Mikhail, Nasonov suggested that Yaroslav was implicated in Mikhail's execution (*Mongoly i Rus'*, pp. 26–8). Whether this was the case or not, Yaroslav never learned of Mikhail's execution because, as we shall see, he died ten days after Mikhail on his way back from distant Karakorum.

[298] Dawson, *The Mongol Mission*, pp. 9–10; B. Spuler, *History of the Mongols, Based on Eastern and Western Accounts of the Thirteenth and Fourteenth Centuries*, Helga and Stuart Drummond (trans.) (London, 1972), pp. 72–3; *Mikhail*, pp. 133–4.

[299] It has been pointed out that Maria's close ties to her family in Chernigov are reflected in the entries she had recorded in her chronicle concerning Chernigov's fate and that of the Ol'govichi (Likhachev, *Russkie letopisi*, p. 284).

to visit the Golden Horde by pointing out that all the princes of Suzdalia who had gone had returned safely. The active involvement of Boris in his grandfather's visit is confirmed by the role he played in attempting to save Mikhail's life. After Baty's courtier Eldega failed to cajole Mikhail into bowing to the idol, Boris also endeavored unsuccessfully to change his mind.[300]

Mikhail flouted the khan's command and paid the ultimate price. Ironically, Yaroslav of Suzdalia, who had been the first to obey Baty's summons and, in 1245, had set out a second time to Saray, also fell victim to the Tatars. Members of the Great Khan's court poisoned him at Karakorum.[301] Almost all the chronicles report Yaroslav's demise briefly, as an important event, but one having only political importance. Mikhail's death received much wider publicity. But this was so not because he was the senior prince of his dynasty, a prince of Kiev, and one of the three major princes in the land. Yaroslav held the same credentials. Mikhail's death had special relevance for the Christians of Rus′ because he had died a martyr.

Mikhail was not the first prince of the dynasty to be canonized. Svyatoslav Davidovich (d. 1143), who became known as Svyatosha after entering the Caves Monastery in Kiev, probably held that honor.[302] Mikhail was also not the first prince of the dynasty to be sanctified for dying a violent death. In 1147, as we have seen, Igor′ Ol′govich had become a passion-sufferer (*strastoterpets*) after the Kievans murdered him.[303] Mikhail, however, was the first prince of the dynasty to become a martyr according to the commonly understood meaning of the word: he underwent the penalty of death for persistence in his Christian faith. The chronicle narrative accounts show that the people of Rus′ acknowledged Mikhail and Fedor, who later became known as The Passion-Sufferers of Chernigov and The Miracle-Workers of Chernigov, as martyrs immediately after their deaths.[304] Accordingly, when their bodies were brought to Chernigov from Saray, they were entombed in a side-chapel dedicated to them in the St. Saviour Cathedral.[305]

[300] See, for example, NPL, pp. 300–1; Mosk., pp. 137–8.
[301] The Tatars killed Yaroslav Vsevolodovich on his return journey from Karakorum. He died, on September 30, 1246, ten days after Mikhail (Lav., col. 471; Mosk., p. 139). According to John de Plano Carpini, Great Khan Ogedey's widow poisoned him in Karakorum (Dawson, *The Mongol Mission*, pp. 58, 65). For a discussion as to why the Tatars killed Yaroslav, see Vernadsky, *The Mongols*, pp. 142–3, and *Crisis*, pp. 100–1.
[302] *Dynasty*, pp. 252–4, 398.   [303] See above, pp. 47–8.
[304] NPL, p. 303; Sof. 1, p. 235; Mosk., p. 139.
[305] Filaret, Archbishop of Chernigov (Gumilevsky, D. G.), *Istoriko-statisticheskoe opisanie Chernigovskoy eparkhii* (Chernigov, 1861–74), vol. 5, pp. 4–5, 10. P. Khavsky maintained that the relics were first taken to Vladimir in Suzdalia and then transferred to Chernigov (*Istoricheskoe issledovanie o rodosloviyakh svyatago muchenika knyazya chernigovskago Mikhaila i rossiyskikh velikikh knyazey opochivayushchikh v Moskovskom Arkhangelskom sobore* [M., 1862], p. 51).

Figure 16   The Church of SS. Mikhail and Fedor, Chernigov

Mikhail's religious renown ultimately outshone his political importance, but in 1246, it was the latter that led to his demise (figures 16, 17).[306] Baty had several reasons for executing him. First, as the senior prince of Rus' and prince of Kiev he had been, in the khan's eyes, the most powerful ruler in Rus' at the time of the invasion. Second, he had killed Tatar envoys. Third, he was the last of the three most powerful senior princes to submit to the Golden Horde.[307] Since Baty had ample political reason for executing Mikhail, why did he use Mikhail's refusal to apostatize as the pretext for killing him? According to the friar, the Tatars never forced anyone to renounce his faith; Mikhail was the exception. The khan therefore had a special motive for singling out Mikhail. It appears that he wished to disgrace the Ol'govich by making him capitulate totally. Since, as the senior prince of Rus' he had been the highest-ranking exponent of the Orthodox faith, Baty evidently resolved not only to depose him politically but also to discredit him morally. In the end, by refusing to renounce his Christian faith, Mikhail scored the moral victory.

[306] Concerning the cult of Mikhail and Fedor, see *Mikhail*, pp. 140–55.
[307] It has been suggested that Baty suspected Mikhail's loyalty because he had been a refugee in the West and his son married a Hungarian princess (Dawson, *The Mongol Mission*, p. 10). These were unlikely reasons for Baty's ill treatment of Mikhail. Daniil, as we have seen, also had close ties with the Hungarians and the Poles, and Baty received him warmly.

Figure 17   Fresco of St. Mikhail in the central nave of the present-day Cathedral
of St. Vladimir, Kiev

He was, arguably, the most successful Ol'govich since the reign of his great-grandfather, Vsevolod Ol'govich (d. 1146). As we shall see, within the lands of Chernigov, he established his control over greater territories than his father or grandfather had ruled.[308] The balance sheet also shows that he asserted his authority over more domains outside the Chernigov lands than his father or grandfather had controlled. Granted, he never ruled them simultaneously, and he failed to assert his jurisdiction permanently over Novgorod and Galich. Because of the great distances that separated Chernigov from the two towns, because of the powerful hostile factions in the two towns, and because of the tenacity of Daniil and Yaroslav in pursuing their claims to the two towns, asserting permanent jurisdiction over them proved impossible for Mikhail. Significantly, however, he was the last autonomous senior prince of Kiev, where he was deposed not by a more powerful prince but by the invincible Tatars.

Mikhail recorded other important successes. Except for Oleg's rebellion in 1226, no Ol'govich challenged his authority within the dynasty. As the senior prince, he united the Ol'govichi into a military power rivaling the Monomashichi of Suzdalia, Smolensk, and Volyn'. In inter-dynastic relations, his marriage ties with the Vsevolodovichi enabled him to maintain friendly relations with Yury of Suzdalia. He also negotiated commercial treaties and political alliances with the Poles and the Hungarians. As senior prince he would also have promoted culture and maintained the churches and monasteries that his ancestors had built in Chernigov and Kiev. Although we have no record that he founded monasteries or erected churches, we may assume that, at the least, he built churches for the inhabitants of his patrimony in the districts of Serensk, Mosal'sk, and Bryn.

Mikhail was the last prince in the sixth generation of the dynasty. His death signaled the demise of the House of Chernigov as an autonomous power. After executing him, as we shall see, the Tatars gave Chernigov to one of his sons who became their pawn. Significantly, because Yaroslav of Suzdalia had obtained a *yarlyk,* Baty's blessing gave life to his dynasty and enabled his domain to become a center of power under the Mongol Yoke. It would draw Mikhail's descendants into its orbit.[309]

MIKHAIL'S FAMILY

The Tatar invasion sounded the death knell for the political fortunes of the Ol'govichi, but it did not eradicate the dynasty. Having satisfied his

---

[308] See below, pp. 379–80.   [309] See also *Mikhail*, pp. 136–9.

need for vengeance against Mikhail, Baty took no further punitive action against his family. Thus, Mikhail's wife Elena evidently survived him and promoted his cult. His daughter Maria played a prominent role in Suzdalia to judge from the evidence that the chronicles mention her on seven occasions before reporting her death, on December 9, 1271, in Rostov.[310] Moreover, she and her sons, Boris and Gleb, inaugurated the Feast of the Miracle-Workers of Chernigov, on September 20, and built a church in their honor.[311] She also recorded her father's martyrdom in the chronicle that she kept at her court.[312] Her sister Feodula, as we have seen, had become the nun Evfrosinia, who died on September 25, 1250 in Suzdal' and was canonized.[313] According to her Life (*Zhitie*), she sent books to Mikhail in Saray to help him defend the Orthodox precepts.[314] She also advanced his cult to judge from a seventeenth-century account which reports the existence of a wooden chapel in Suzdal' dedicated to the Miracle-Workers of Chernigov.[315]

In addition to Rostislav, who defected to Hungary and disappeared from the history books of Rus', four sons survived Mikhail.[316] Only the Ermolinskiy Chronicle gives their names and domains:

The sons of Grand Prince Mikhail of Chernigov were: Grand Prince Roman of Chernigov, who was childless and left no heirs; the second was Mstislav of Karachev and Zvenigorod; the third was Simeon of Glukhov and Novosil'; the fourth was Yury of Bryansk and Torusa.[317]

The *Lyubetskiy sinodik* seemingly corroborates this information.[318] Writing in the second half of the nineteenth century, Archbishop Filaret of Chernigov observed that in his day many branches stemming from Mikhail flourished. He listed nine: the Boryatinskie, the Gorchakovy, the

---

[310] She is mentioned under the years 1227, 1231, 1237, 1238, 1249, 1258, 1259, and 1271 (Zotov, pp. 286–7). Concerning her death, see Ak. sp., col. 525.

[311] Serebryansky, *Drevne-russkie knyazheskie zhitiya*, Texts, p. 51 and p. 111; see also *Mikhail*, pp. 141–2.

[312] Concerning Maria's chronicle, see Likhachev, *Russkie letopisi*, pp. 282–5.

[313] Barsukov, cols. 179–80; Filaret, *Russkie svyatye*, vol. 3, pp. 120–5; S. Pavlenko, *Kniaz' Mykhailo Chernihivs'kyi ta ioho vyklyk ordi* (Chernihiv, 1996), p. 60.

[314] Georgievsky, "Zhitie pr. Evfrosinii Suzdal'skoy," pp. 116–18; *Mikhail*, p. 151.

[315] "Arkhivnye materialy (opisi, gramoty, ukazy, i pr.), – prilozhenie k opisaniyu Rizpolozhenskago monastyrya," *Trudy Vladimirskoy uchenoy arkhivnoy komissii*, bk. 2 (Vladimir, 1900), p. 7.

[316] Rostislav had two sons and four daughters (Baum., XII, 6–11; compare Zotov, pp. 289–90), but not one came to live in Rus' (see above, p. 365).

[317] Erm., p. 81; see above, p. 358.

[318] Basing his order of seniority on lists given by later sources, Zotov identifies the brothers in the following order: Roman "the Old" (*Staryy*) prince of Chernigov and Bryansk; Simeon prince of Glukhov and Novosil'; Mstislav prince of Karachev; and Yury prince of Torusa (Zotov, pp. 285–6).

Dolgorukie, the Eletskie, the Zvenigorodskie, the Kol'tsovy-Mosal'skie, the Obolenskie, the Odoevskie, and the Shcherbatovy.[319]

Mikhail's wife most likely persuaded him to name their second son, Roman, after her father, Roman Mstislavich of Vladimir in Volyn'. The *Lyubetskiy sinodik* gives him the sobriquet "the Old" (*Staryy*).[320] Since he died after 1288,[321] he was probably in his early seventies at that time.[322] His wife's name, according to the same source, was Anna.[323] The Ermolinskiy Chronicle claims that they had no offspring, but other chronicles testify to the existence of six children. Under the year 1264, the Hypatian Chronicle reports that Roman of Bryansk sent his eldest son, Mikhail, to escort Olga, one of Mikhail's four sisters, to her betrothed, Vsevolod Vasil'kovich of Volyn'.[324] Ten years later the same chronicler states that Khan Mangu Temir ordered a number of princes, including Roman of Debryansk (i.e. Bryansk) and his son Oleg, to campaign against the Lithuanians.[325] Thus we also learn that Roman's patrimony was Bryansk. Located on the river Desna at the mouth of the river Bolva, it controlled the water routes from Chernigov to Smolensk and across the Vyatichi lands to Suzdalia.

Significantly, the *Lyubetskiy sinodik* and the Ermolinskiy Chronicle identify Roman as the prince of Chernigov. In the light of Baty's directive that only those princes who submitted to him would receive a *yarlyk*, Roman obviously visited the khan after his father's execution. The chronicles do not report his visit, but John de Plano Carpini alludes to it. He recounts how, in 1246 or 1247 when he was returning from the Golden Horde, he met a certain Prince Roman who was travelling to Saray.[326] If, as is most likely the

---

[319] Filaret, *Russkie svyatiye*, vol. 3, p. 101, and V. V. Krasheninnikov, "Potomki Mikhaila Vsevolodovicha chernigovskogo i bryanskiy kray," *Sviatyi kniaz'*, pp. 33–6.

[320] Zotov, pp. 82–6, 196–201, 285.

[321] In 1288, according to an account of the foundation of the Uspenskiy Svenskiy Monastery in Bryansk, when Roman was living in that town he became blind and was cured through the intervention of an icon of the Mother of God. In thanksgiving for his cure, he founded the Uspenskiy Monastery near the Desna, where the river Svin' flows into it. According to some accounts, the Tatars killed him at the Golden Horde (Zotov, pp. 84, 197–8).

[322] As we have seen, Mikhail married not long before 1212 (see above, pp. 269–70, and *Mikhail*, p. 11). Since Roman evidently had three elder siblings (Rostislav, Maria, and Feodula), he would have been born around 1215 at the earliest. If he died after 1288, he would have been over 70 years of age.

[323] Zotov, p. 82. According to the account of the Uspenskiy Svenskiy Monastery, however, Roman's wife was named Anastasia. Perhaps, as Zotov suggests, Anastasia was the name of Roman's second wife (Zotov, p. 85).

[324] Ipat., cols. 861–2; Zotov, pp. 290–1.

[325] Ipat., col. 872. Concerning Oleg, see Zotov, pp. 83–6, 291.

[326] Dawson, *The Mongol Mission*, p. 71; John de Plano Carpini, *Istoriya Mongalov*, A. I. Malein (ed. and trans.) (Spb., 1911), pp. 61–2. As Zotov points out, the only other prince in Rus' with the name Roman was Daniil's son, who, according to the chronicles, remained at home at that time (Zotov, pp. 197–8).

case, this reference was to Roman Mikhaylovich, Baty gave him the *yarlyk* not only for his patrimonial domain of Bryansk, but if the information of the Ermolinskiy Chronicle is correct, also for Chernigov.[327] Surprisingly, other chronicles never refer to Roman as the prince of Chernigov but call him the prince of Bryansk.[328] Available evidence suggests that, even though he held the *yarlyk* for Chernigov, the town was probably occupied by Baty's official (*baskak*),[329] who requisitioned it for himself.[330] Roman's physical association with the patrimonial capital was undoubtedly limited to the visits he made to the *baskak*. He was therefore merely the titular prince of Chernigov. Unlike his father Mikhail, he lacked the power to initiate campaigns and to allocate domains to junior Ol'govichi.[331] Nevertheless, Roman was probably instrumental in having the bishop of Chernigov transferred to Bryansk.[332]

With Roman's submission, the last of the major dynasties of Rus' formally acknowledged Baty as its overlord. He seemingly allowed the Ol'govichi to follow the customary practices of succession and territorial allocations. This is supported by the news that he let Roman, Mikhail's eldest son in Rus', replace his father as prince of Chernigov in keeping with the system of lateral succession. Baty also let Mikhail's sons remain in the regional centers that he had given to them as patrimonies.[333]

---

[327] See Zotov who wrongly suggests that a certain Vsevolod Yaropolchich, reported in the *Lyubetskiy sinodik* but not mentioned by the chronicles, preceded him as prince of Chernigov from 1246 to 1263 (Zotov, pp. 80, 281). According to Zotov, Vsevolod was the son of Yaropolk Yaroslavich of the senior branch (Baum., IV, 41). Since Yaropolk never ruled Chernigov, his son was debarred from ruling the town.

[328] See, for example, s.a. 1263: Ipat., col. 860; s.a. 1264: Ipat., cols. 861–2; s.a. 1274: Ipat., col. 872; and s.a. 1285: Lav., col. 482.

[329] A Ryazan' charter of 1257 reports that Baty appointed a certain Ivan Shayn the commander of Chernigov (see Halperin, *Russia and the Golden Horde*, p. 34).

[330] This is suggested by a similar case in Kursk. We are told that, in 1283, Akhmat the *baskak* of the Kursk principality became involved in a dispute with two princes, Oleg of Ryl'sk and Vorgol and his relative Svyatoslav of Lipetsk (Mosk., p. 154). Since neither of the two seemingly most powerful princes in the district lived in Kursk, the most important town in the principality, this suggests that the *baskak* requisitioned the town for himself (see below, p. 382).

[331] Concerning Roman, see V. V. Mavrodin, "Levoberezhnaya Ukraina pod vlast'yu Tataro-mongolov," *Uchenye zapiski*, nr. 32, Seriya istoricheskikh nauk, vyp. 2 (L., 1939), pp. 52–3, and G. P. Polyakov, "Knyaz' Roman Mikhaylovich bryanskiy," *Sviatyi kniaz'*, pp. 28–33.

[332] Nasonov, *Mongoly i Rus*, p. 28; Makary, *Istoriya russkoy tserkvi*, vol. 4, bk. 1, p. 108. Concerning Roman's measures to make Bryansk the new episcopal see of the Chernigov lands, see V. N. Gur'yanov and G. P. Polyakov, "Novye issledovaniya drevnego Bryanska," *Rol' rannikh mis'kykh tsentriv v stanovlenni Kyivs'koi Rusi*, Materialy pol'ovoho istoryko-arkheolohichnoho seminaru. Serpen' 1993 r., s. Zelenyi Hai Sums'koho r-nu Sums'koi obl., O. P. Motsia (gen. ed.) (Sumy, 1993), pp. 27–8.

[333] To judge from the testimony of genealogical books, when Roman's sons came of age he gave them districts from his patrimony. Mikhail therefore became prince of Bryansk and the progenitor of the Osovetskie princes, named after the town of Osovik in the Bryansk region (Zotov, pp. 290–1). Oleg evidently renounced his inheritance to become a monk (Zotov, pp. 82–6, 291).

We know much less about Mikhail's third son, Mstislav. The *Lyubetskiy sinodik* fails to give his baptismal name and that of his wife. According to the Ermolinskiy Chronicle, the couple had two sons, Tit and Andrey (Ondreyan).[334] Mstislav's patrimonial domain was Karachev, but he also controlled Zvenigorod.[335] The two towns probably marked the southern and northern limits of his domain. This is supported by the information that Mstislav's grandson Ivan, the son of Tit, later ruled Kozel'sk located between Karachev and Zvenigorod.[336] The location of Ivan's domain also suggests, indirectly, that Mstislav allocated towns within his patrimony to his two sons.

We have only snippets of information about Simeon. His baptismal name and the identity of his wife are unknown. Although the Ermolinskiy Chronicle does not list Simeon's sons, other sources name three: Mikhail, Aleksandr, and Vsevolod.[337] Simeon was prince of Glukhov and Novosil'. The latter was a town south of Mtsensk on the river Zusha in the southeast frontier of the Vyatichi lands. Evidently, the Tatars did not raze Novosil' after they withdrew from Kozel'sk. Significantly, Simeon was the only son to whom Mikhail gave a town, Glukhov, in the Posem'e district of the cadet branch.

Details concerning Yury's life are also sparse. As Mikhail's youngest son, he was born around 1220. He and his unidentified wife had several children, but their number is disputed. The most extensive list claims the couple had six sons. They were: Simeon of Torusa and Kanin, who fathered the Kaninskie and Spasskie princes; Vsevolod of Torusa, who fathered the Mezetskie and Baryatinskie princes; Mikhail of Myshaga (Myshega), who fathered the Myshetskie princes; Ivan "the Elder" of Torusa, who had no children; Konstantin of Obolensk, who fathered the Obolenskie princes; Ivan "the Younger" of Volkon, who fathered the Volkonskie princes. Their

---

[334] Erm., pp. 81–2.
[335] Zvenigorod was located on the high left bank of the river Moskva west of Moscow. The written sources mention it for the first time in the 1330s when it formed part of the Moscow domain. The chronicles never identify Zvenigorod as belonging to the Vyatichi lands of the Ol'govichi. Nevertheless, archaeologists have established not only that the town existed as early as the eleventh century, but also that princely stamps found on pots in that town from the twelfth century resemble those of the princes of Chernigov. B. A. Rybakov therefore suggested that Zvenigorod was the northeasternmost point in the lands of Chernigov on the border with Suzdalia ("Raskopki v Zvenigorode [1943–1945 gg.]," *Materialy i issledovaniya po arkheologii SSSR*, nr. 12 [M.-L., 1949], p. 125; *Zemlya Vyatichey*, pp. 155–7). The *Lyubetskiy sinodik* supports this conclusion when it reports that Mstislav's second son Andrey also ruled Zvenigorod (Zotov, p. 292.)
[336] Erm., p. 82.
[337] Mikhail ruled Glukhov, Aleksandr ruled Novosil', and Vsevolod ruled Usty, a town located northeast of Bryansk (Zotov, pp. 286, 291).

one daughter, Ksenia, married Yaroslav Yaroslavich of Tver'.[338] Although the Ermolinskiy Chronicle identifies Yury as prince of Bryansk and Torusa, a town located in the northeast corner of the Vyatichi lands,[339] the available evidence suggests he ruled only Torusa.[340]

The domains Mikhail allotted to his sons reveal the breadth of his territorial holdings. He evidently gave Roman his own patrimony including Bryn, Serensk, and Mosal'sk. To Mstislav he gave Karachev. Earlier, it had belonged to Mikhail's grandfather Svyatoslav, who had bequeathed it to one of Mikhail's uncles.[341] As has been noted, Mstislav's grandson Ivan inherited Kozel'sk, indicating that Mikhail had given the town to Mstislav as part of his Karachev allotment. Accordingly, Mikhail must have appropriated Kozel'sk in 1238, after its princeling Vasil'ko fell victim to the Tatar lance.[342] Novosil' in the southeast corner of the Vyatichi lands had probably been part of the Karachev domain when the latter had belonged to Mikhail's grandfather. Mikhail, however, made it part of Simeon's Glukhov patrimony. To Yury he gave Torusa, the district that his uncle Oleg had ruled in the northeast corner of the Vyatichi lands.[343]

Thus we see that, in addition to the patrimony of his father, Vsevolod Chermnyy, Mikhail owned Vyatichi domains that had formerly belonged to his uncles Vladimir, Oleg, and Mstislav. If his uncle Gleb inherited a domain in the Vyatichi lands, he bequeathed it to his son Mstislav, who defended Chernigov against the Tatars. In addition to the Vyatichi lands that belonged to the senior branch, Mikhail also asserted his jurisdiction over territories in the Posem'e region that belonged to the cadet branch. The evidence that he gave Glukhov to Simeon confirms this. Since he evidently gave his sons all the Vyatichi lands, his personal holdings must have been located between the rivers Snov' and the Dnepr, in the Zadesen'e region, and in the Novgorod Severskiy lands. This information reveals that while Mikhail was pursuing his expansionist policy in Novgorod, Galicia, and Kiev, he was also consolidating his control over Chernigov domains. He evidently began accumulating these soon after becoming prince of

---

[338] Zotov, pp. 293–5.
[339] Torusa lies at the confluence of the rivers Tarusa and Oka, south of Lobynsk located at the confluence of the rivers Protva and Oka.
[340] See Zotov, p. 286. Since the Ermolinskiy Chronicle made an error in claiming that Roman had no children, it evidently made another error in calling Yury prince of Bryansk. Because he did not allocate Bryansk to one of his sons, he most likely did not rule it himself. This is supported by the observation, as has been noted, that either Mikhail or Oleg succeeded their father Roman to the town. According to the system of lateral succession, Yury could occupy Bryansk only if both of Roman's sons predeceased their father and if Yury outlived his three elder brothers.
[341] See above, p. 212.   [342] See above, pp. 345–6.   [343] See above, pp. 134–5.

Chernigov to judge from the information that, in 1226, Oleg had challenged him in a territorial dispute.[344]

Mikhail's allocation of domains to his sons gives us additional news. We learn that Bryansk, Zvenigorod, Novosil', and Torusa had become new regional centers. The transformation of these towns into administrative seats signifies that during Mikhail's reign the axes of commerce, industry, and politics shifted in the Chernigov lands.[345] It also bespeaks a growth in the wealth of the Ol'govichi on the eve of the invasion.[346]

DESCENDANTS OF OTHER FAMILIES

In addition to making sporadic references to Mikhail's descendants, the chroniclers infrequently mention scions from other families of the dynasty. Thus, under the year 1261 they report that Vasil'ko of Vladimir in Volyn' gave away his daughter Olga as wife to Andrey Vsevolodovich of Chernigov.[347] Since Roman of Bryansk had the *yarlyk* for Chernigov, the chronicler's identification of Andrey as a prince of Chernigov merely signified that he was an Ol'govich. He evidently belonged to the generation of Mikhail's grandchildren because, as we have seen, three years later Mikhail's granddaughter Olga married Vasil'ko's son. Andrey's father was a certain Vsevolod,[348] but as Mikhail had no son by that name Andrey was not his grandson. Since the chronicles do not report the existence of any Vsevolod belonging to the generation of Mikhail's sons, the lack of information brings the search for Andrey's father to a dead end.

We are also on uncertain ground when it comes to identifying Ol'govichi of the cadet branch descended from the brothers Oleg, Igor', and Vsevolod.

[344] See above, pp. 303–4.
[345] During the second half of the fifteenth century, for example, Bryn and Bryansk are reported as being on the trade route that ran from Moscow to the Crimean Peninsula through Kaluga, Bryn, Bryansk, Novgorod Severskiy, and Putivl'. It has been suggested that the route was there for a period of time before the surviving sources report its existence (Ostrowski, *Muscovy and the Mongols*, p. 112, and J. Martin, *Treasure of the Land of Darkness* [Cambridge, 1986], pp. 146, 148). Consequently, commerce between Suzdalia and Crimea probably passed through these Chernigov lands during the reigns of Mikhail and Roman.
[346] Concerning the growth of wealth and commerce during the twelfth and early thirteenth century in Chernigov and Rus' in general, see D. B. Miller, "Monumental Building and its Patrons as Indicators of Economic and Political Trends in Rus', 900–1262," *Jahrbücher für Geschichte Osteuropas* 38, H. 3 (1990), pp. 337, 341, 345, and Darkevich, "K istorii torgovykh svyazey Drevney Rusi," p. 102.
[347] Ipat., col. 848.
[348] The *Lyubetskiy sinodik* speaks of a certain "Lavrenty [in baptism] Vsevolod Yaropolchich" whom Zotov identifies as the son of Yaropolk Yaroslavich of the junior line in the senior branch of Ol'govichi. He suggests that Vsevolod succeeded Mikhail to Chernigov from 1246 to 1263. Andrey, according to Zotov, was his son and married Vasil'ko's daughter (Zotov, pp. 281, 287). The chronicles do not support Zotov's assertions. Moreover, if Yaropolk Yaroslavich was Vsevolod's father, neither was eligible to rule Chernigov because Yaropolk was an *izgoi*.

News of the princes in the Posem'e region comes to us in dribs and drabs. Two chronicles give an item of information that they evidently culled from a now lost Chernigov source. In 1246, in the same year that the Tatars killed Mikhail, Baty executed a certain Andrey Mstislavich.[349] John de Plano Carpini confirms this:

During our stay [at the Golden Horde]…it happened that Andrew, Duke of Cherneglone,[350] which is in Russia, was accused before Bati of taking Tartar horses out of the country and selling them elsewhere; and although the charge was not proved he was put to death. Hearing this, his younger brother came with the widow of the slain man to the chief Bati to petition him not to take away their territory from them.[351]

Thus the friar identifies Andrey as an Ol'govich. The chronicles, however, give us insufficient information to determine the identity of his father.

Andrey could have belonged either to the senior branch or to the cadet branch because each had a prince named Mstislav who could have fathered him. In the senior branch, Mstislav Glebovich was Mikhail's cousin. And, as we have seen, in 1241 the Tatars had killed Mstislav of Ryl'sk.[352] Since we cannot determine the identity of Andrey's father from this sparse chronicle information, let us seek help from circumstantial evidence. Because Andrey was accused of rustling Tatar horses, the location of his domain was probably a relevant factor. Ryl'sk on the frontier of the steppe was more conducive to such activity than the Zadesen'e or the districts west of the river Snov', where Mstislav Glebovich probably had his domain.[353] Moreover, if Ryl'sk was ruled first by Mstislav and later, after the Tatars killed him for an unexplained reason, by Andrey, it is possible that both were killed for the same alleged misdeed. Consequently, circumstantial evidence points to Mstislav of Ryl'sk as Andrey's father. If the identification is correct, Andrey belonged to the senior line of the cadet branch.

The friar's account enables us to make a number of additional observations. After Andrey's death, his brother asked Baty to grant him the patent for Andrey's domain. In giving the unnamed brother the *yarlyk*, Baty adhered to the system of lateral succession: he authorized a younger brother to succeed an elder one to his domain. The younger brother's request also implies that Andrey himself had received a patent from the khan on a visit

[349] See s.a. 1245: Av., col. 52; s.a. 1246: Rog., col. 31.
[350] Although the Franciscan friar uses the name "Cherneglone" to identify the town, there is no doubt that the reference is to Chernigov. Since Mikhail was prince of Chernigov until his death in 1246, however, the friar's identification of Andrey as a duke (that is, a prince) of Chernigov simply means that Andrey belonged to the dynasty of Chernigov.
[351] Dawson, *The Mongol Mission*, pp. 10–11; Carpini, *Istoriya Mongalov*, p. 9.
[352] See above, p. 360.   [353] See above, p. 351.

earlier to the one on which he was executed. What is more, since Andrey had already visited Baty between the year 1242, when the latter occupied Saray, and 1246, when the khan killed him, we may assume that other Ol'govichi also traveled to the khan before Mikhail set out on his fateful trek. Unlike the latter, they complied more quickly with Baty's directive to submit to him. Finally, the suggestion that Andrey's younger brother succeeded him to Ryl'sk is supported by the news that the family of that town was flourishing in 1283, when the chronicles once again mention a prince of Ryl'sk.

In that year, Oleg, prince of Ryl'sk and Vorgol, and his relative Svyatoslav of Lipetsk (Lipovichsk) rebelled against Akhmat, the *baskak* of the principality of Kursk.[354] The princes took opposing sides: the one sought support from Khan Nogay and the other from Khan Telebuga. In the following year, Oleg returned from Khan Telebuga with Tatar troops and killed Svyatoslav. In retaliation, the latter's brother Aleksandr,[355] who succeeded him at Lipetsk, killed Oleg and two of his sons, David and Semen.[356]

The controversy, which led to the most brutal recorded slaughter of princes in the dynasty's history, provides useful family information. Oleg was politically senior to Svyatoslav, judging from the evidence that he ruled two domains. Moreover, both were more centrally located than Svyatoslav's frontier allotment, and one of them was the important town of Ryl'sk. Since Oleg ruled a domain associated with the cadet branch, and because he and Svyatoslav were related, both presumably belonged to the senior line. The identification is supported by the location of their patrimonies in the Posem'e region. As has been suggested, Kursk and Ryl'sk belonged to the senior family of the cadet branch, and, by the year 1223, Kursk had replaced Ryl'sk as the more important town of the two.[357] The Tatars continued to look upon Kursk as the capital of the region in light of the evidence that the *baskak* used it as his capital. The existence of the heretofore-unknown patrimonies of Vorgol and Lipetsk shows that the princes found it necessary to break up Kursk and Ryl'sk into smaller domains because of a plenitude of princes.

---

[354] Concerning Oleg and Svyatoslav, see Zotov, pp. 288–9. Vorgol or Vorgola was located on the river Vorgol, a tributary of the Sosna, northeast of Kursk. Lipetsk is located northeast of Kursk, on the river Voronezh, north of the town Voronezh. Svyatoslav's Lipetsk domain lay to the east of Oleg's Vorgol district and served as the frontier between the Kursk and Ryazan' lands (Barsov, pp. 40, 113).

[355] Zotov, p. 289.

[356] Mosk., pp. 154–6; TL, pp. 340–3; Nikon. 10, p. 165. See also Halperin, *Russia and the Golden Horde*, p. 36, and Mavrodin, "Levoberezhnaya Ukraina," pp. 56–61.

[357] See above, p. 294.

Proof of a relative abundance of Ol'govichi in the Posem'e region is provided by the list of participants in the conflict with Akhmat. Even after the family lines were pruned of Svyatoslav, Oleg, and two of his sons, there was no shortage of princelings. Since Aleksandr killed only two of Oleg's sons, an unspecified number evidently escaped his vengeance. Towards the end of the thirteenth century, therefore, the known Ol'govichi in the Posem'e region constituted at least Oleg's remaining sons, Svyatoslav's heirs, and his brother Aleksandr with his family. They belonged to the senior line of the cadet branch descended from Oleg Svyatoslavich (d. 1180).

In 1235, as we have seen, Izyaslav Vladimirovich of Putivl' had helped Mikhail defeat Daniil and Vladimir at Torchesk. At that time he seized Kamenets.[358] Twenty years later, an unidentified Izyaslav attacked Galich and attempted to disrupt Daniil's salt works in the Poniz'e.[359] His futile effort reflected the tactics Rostislav had used against Daniil after the Tatars had passed through Rus'. Since Izyaslav Vladimirovich had assisted Mikhail against Daniil in the 1230s, it was more than likely he who, in 1255, made a last unsuccessful attempt on behalf of the Ol'govichi to win control of the Galician lands.[360] His action shows that, as the head of the Putivl' family descended from Igor', he had abandoned his patrimony on the river Seym and sought his fortune on the west bank of the Dnepr. We are not told who occupied Putivl'. As we have seen, however, Mikhail appropriated Glukhov north of Putivl' for his son Simeon. Since the Tatars had devastated Putivl', it is possible that Mikhail incorporated it into Simeon's patrimony of Glukhov.

We have no chronicle information concerning the existence of princes descended from the youngest of the three brothers, Vsevolod "Fierce Aurochs," who, in 1185, distinguished himself for his valor on Igor''s fateful campaign against the Polovtsy.

---

[358] See above, p. 334.   [359] Ipat., cols. 829–30.
[360] See also Zotov, p. 282. Others suggest the prince was Izyaslav Mstislavich of Smolensk (Perfecky, p. 69; Makhnovets', pp. 413–14).

Conclusion

In conclusion, we have seen that, following Igor''s murder, the Ol'govichi and the Davidovichi became embroiled in an acrimonious conflict. The Davidovichi attempted to deprive the Ol'govichi of their patrimonial domains and to eradicate them as a political force. Svyatoslav Ol'govich resolutely resisted them and obtained help from Yury Dolgorukiy of Suzdalia. His alliance with Yury was a reversal of the policy that his brother Vsevolod had followed. The latter had backed the Mstislavichi, his brothers-in-law. The Davidovichi not only failed to eliminate the Ol'govichi as powerful rivals, but they themselves died out as a family. The Ol'govichi therewith became the sole rulers of the Chernigov lands. After Igor''s death, however, they bifurcated into two branches, the senior and the cadet. Although Chernigov remained the capital of the entire dynasty, it also became, in effect, the capital of the senior branch, while Novgorod Severskiy became, in effect, the capital of the cadet branch.

Following Svyatoslav's example, later senior princes of Chernigov preferred to form alliances with the dynasty of Suzdalia rather than with the Mstislavichi of Volyn' or Smolensk. Thus, Svyatoslav Vsevolodovich joined forces with Andrey Bogolyubskiy to evict Ryurik Rostislavich from Kiev. Moreover, Andrey supported Svyatoslav's bid for Kiev. He thereby not only acknowledged Svyatoslav's claim but also tacitly admitted that his attempts at controlling Kiev through puppets had failed. In the meantime, Svyatoslav gave Andrey's brothers and nephews sanctuary in the Chernigov lands and, following Andrey's murder, helped his brothers to fight for their inheritance. Vsevolod Bol'shoe Gnezdo ultimately won control of Vladimir on the Klyaz'ma and became indebted to Svyatoslav for his victory. Later, Svyatoslav's son, Vsevolod Chermnyy, also concluded an alliance with Vsevolod Bol'shoe Gnezdo, and on the eve of the Tatar invasion their sons, Mikhail and Yury, were close friends. On occasion, the Ol'govichi and the princes of Suzdalia pursued conflicting policies, but on the whole, they lived in friendship for the hundred years following the death of Vsevolod Ol'govich.

Svyatoslav Vsevolodovich's relationship with Ryurik Rostislavich was unique. At first, the two were rivals for Kiev, but in 1181, they agreed to a *modus vivendi* by forming a partnership to rule Kiev and the Kievan land. No such arrangement had existed before them or would exist after them. Granted, princes had exercised dual rule in the past: Oleg and his brother David had shared control of Chernigov; the Davidovichi, Vladimir and Izyaslav, seemingly ruled Chernigov together; and later Izyaslav Mstislavich and his uncle Vyacheslav Vladimirovich were co-rulers of Kiev. These arrangements, however, were made between princes of the same dynasty, whereas Svyatoslav and Ryurik belonged to rival dynasties. Their partnership, therefore, signified a high-water mark in the collaboration between the Ol'govichi and the Rostislavichi.

Svyatoslav was the senior partner of the duumvirate and one of the dominant political figures of Rus' in his day. He maintained diplomatic relations with foreign powers like the Hungarians and the Poles. He was also the last Ol'govich to arrange a marriage alliance with the imperial family in Constantinople. Nevertheless, Ryurik's presence in Belgorod and control of the surrounding Kievan towns impinged on Svyatoslav's jurisdiction. As prince of Kiev he had less power than his father Vsevolod Ol'govich had wielded, and less authority than his son Vsevolod Chermnyy and his grandson Mikhail would command. Svyatoslav's greatest responsibility as commander-in-chief was to defend Rus' against the Polovtsy. He conducted numerous successful offensive and defensive campaigns against them. Although he enjoyed the loyalty of both branches of the Ol'govichi, his brother Yaroslav of Chernigov and his cousin Igor' of Novgorod Severskiy refused to participate on the offensive expeditions that he led against the nomads in the Dnepr river basin. Instead, they campaigned against the Donets river tribesmen who pillaged their Posem'e and Zadesen'e lands. Despite the nomadic incursions, Svyatoslav's reign enjoyed a period of inter-dynastic stability, which allowed princes to engage in cultural activities. Svyatoslav himself was one the greatest patrons of building in the dynasty. He erected two new courts and founded three churches rivaling those of his father and grandfather.

After Svyatoslav's death, Ryurik attempted to make the Rostislavichi the only claimants to Kiev by depriving the Ol'govichi of their right to rule the capital. Svyatoslav's brother Yaroslav refused to capitulate, thereby forcing Ryurik to seek help from Vsevolod Bol'shoe Gnezdo. The latter, undoubtedly swayed by the determination of the Ol'govichi to fight for their right and by the help that they had given him to secure his rule in Suzdalia, refused to deprive them of their claim to Kiev in perpetuity.

Moreover, he probably objected to giving the Rostislavichi a preferential claim ahead of his own family. He therefore mitigated the demands of the Rostislavichi by allowing Yaroslav to promise merely not to challenge Ryurik's rule in Kiev. Yaroslav's stalwart defense of his dynasty's rights was a milestone in its history. Had he capitulated, he would have jeopardized any future claims of the Ol'govichi to Kiev.

Igor's defeat at the hands of Konchak and the Donets Polovtsy fueled the imagination of an unknown bard to write the epic poem "*Slovo o polku Igoreve.*" The popular memory of Rus' associated Igor's name with that disaster. Significantly, however, he led a number of successful raids against the Donets tribes, which complemented Svyatoslav's campaigns against the Dnepr nomads. Moreover, his occupation of Chernigov, although virtually ignored by the chronicles, was important. It confirmed that the Ol'govichi adhered faithfully to the lateral system of succession. When his turn came according to the order of genealogical seniority, Igor', even though he belonged to the cadet branch, occupied Chernigov. Following his death, no other member of the cadet branch reached the top rung of the dynasty's genealogical ladder. Consequently, after Igor', the most important town that the senior prince of the cadet branch would rule was Novgorod Severskiy.

During the sack of Kiev in 1203, Ryurik and Oleg Svyatoslavich plundered the sacred garments of the blessed first Christian princes of Rus'. Their objective, undoubtedly, was to adorn their own cathedrals with the sacramentals, so to speak. By hanging the robes in their throne rooms, however, Ryurik and Oleg may have also hoped to buttress their dynasties' claims to the capital of Rus'. They could argue that the Rostislavichi and the Ol'govichi had secured the exclusive right to Kiev because, on being enthroned under the aura of the mantles, their senior princes had the right of succession to Kiev transmitted to them. The chronicles, however, do not confirm this.

After his grandfather Vsevolod Ol'govich, Vsevolod Chermnyy was one of the most successful Ol'govichi up to his day. Unlike all the senior princes before him, he sought control of Galich. The only senior prince who had considered capturing the town had been his father Svyatoslav, but he had proposed to give it to Ryurik. Vsevolod Chermnyy asserted his jurisdiction over Galich through the Igorevichi who occupied it for a number of years. He also controlled Pereyaslavl' for a short time through his son Mikhail. His personal seizure of Kiev, however, was the most successful. His rivalry for the town with Ryurik threw the two men into conflict from 1206 to 1208. After Ryurik's death, which contrary to many historians occurred in 1208, Vsevolod Chermnyy took Kiev uncontested and obtained support for his rule from Vsevolod Bol'shoe Gnezdo.

He was only the third Ol'govich after his grandfather and father to occupy Kiev. Although history books overlook his career, it could be argued that he attained greater power than his father. Granted, he did not rule Kiev for as long a period of time as Svyatoslav had ruled it. Nevertheless, he asserted his authority over Galich and Pereyaslavl', something his father had not done and, unlike his father, he was the autonomous ruler of both Kiev and the Kievan land. Vsevolod was also a worthy successor to his father and grandfather as a patron of church building. The chronicles fail to record his projects or those of other Ol'govichi living at the turn of the thirteenth century. But archaeological evidence testifies to vigorous architectural activity during this period when, according to most historians, the fortunes of the dynasty were at low ebb.

At the turn of the thirteenth century, the relatively high mortality rate among the princes in the senior branch significantly reduced the number of eligible candidates for Chernigov. Svyatoslav had five sons and his younger brother Yaroslav had two. Yaroslav's sons, Rostislav and Yaropolk, died before their turn came to rule Chernigov. Their sons therefore became debarred. Svyatoslav's eldest son Vladimir also died before occupying the capital. His second son Oleg ruled Chernigov, but his sons evidently died during his lifetime. Svyatoslav's youngest son Mstislav, and one of his sons, fell at the Kalka battle, but a second son whom the chroniclers never mention evidently survived Mstislav. In this way three families of the senior branch became *izgoi* or politically defunct. This meant that Vsevolod Chermnyy and his younger brother Gleb were left with the enviable task of providing claimants for Chernigov. Significantly, it also meant that the two princes, but above all Vsevolod Chermnyy, would have appropriated many of the domains of their deceased relatives.

The number of princes in the cadet branch also declined. Svyatoslav Ol'govich, the progenitor of the branch, left three sons: Oleg, Igor', and Vsevolod. Oleg's son Svyatoslav was captured in 1185 at the Kayala. After that the chronicles never mention him again, but circumstantial evidence suggests he returned home. Although his family survived, it lived in obscurity. The *boyars* of Galich hanged three of Igor''s heirs but Vladimir and his son Izyaslav escaped. The latter became Mikhail's ally and eventually appropriated Daniil's Kamenets therewith abandoning his Posem'e domain. Vsevolod probably had a son, but he became an *izgoi* because Vsevolod failed to occupy Novgorod Severskiy.

Mikhail was one of the most ambitious senior princes of the dynasty. No Ol'govich, indeed, no other prince of Novgorod improved the lot of the Novgorodians more than he did. He alleviated their tax burden and granted their *boyars* greater political freedom from the prince. By placating the townsmen he was also able to negotiate favorable trade agreements with them for the Ol'govichi. Archaeological evidence reveals that Chernigov towns enjoyed an unprecedented degree of prosperity during this period, suggesting that promoting trade was a priority for Mikhail. Commercial interests, in part, also motivated him to seize control of Galich and Kiev because they were channels through which goods from the Rhine valley and Hungary passed to Chernigov.

On the eve of the invasion, Mikhail was one of the most powerful princes in Rus'. His success was greater than his father's had been in that for a time he administered Novgorod, controlled Galich, and successfully ruled Kiev. Granted, he has been accused of ineffective leadership because he failed to unite the princes of Rus' against the invaders. In his defense it must be pointed out that this was an impossible task. Some princes were determined to confront the enemy on their own, others fled in the face of the invincible Tatars, while others still were hostile to Mikhail. His rivalry with Yaroslav over Novgorod was the most acrimonious. The latter took his vindictiveness to Saray, where he persuaded Baty to give him Kiev realizing full well that he could not rule it in person because the Kievans were hostile to him. But by soliciting the *yarlyk*, Yaroslav achieved what he had failed to do with his own resources: he deprived Mikhail of the capital of Rus'.

* * *

A number of more general observations can also be made. We have seen that marriage alliances were part and parcel of the political process in Rus'. Princes of different dynasties would be more inclined to become allies if they already shared a family bond, as was the case between Vsevolod Ol'govich and the Mstislavichi. Princes also cemented political alliances with marriage ties. Thus, marriages of the Ol'govichi from generation to generation reflected a frequent political association with the dynasty of Suzdalia. As a rule of thumb, it would seem, a prince attempted to anticipate which of his sons had a good chance of becoming senior prince according to the system of lateral succession. Consequently, he sought to find a bride for such a son either from a powerful dynasty or from one that had similar political interests as his own. The son's in-laws, it was hoped, would become his political allies when he attained seniority. Occasionally, however, such personal ties failed to generate the desired political collaboration. One notable example was Mikhail's marriage to Daniil's sister, which did not prevent the brothers-in-law from becoming bitter rivals.

The princes of Chernigov had close ties with the Church. They had a special love for SS. Boris and Gleb and, in particular, for St. Gleb, who was the patron saint of the dynasty. Igor' Svyatoslavich demonstrated this devotion when, on one occasion after returning from a campaign, he made a special trip to Vyshgorod to visit the shrine of the two *strastoterptsy*. In like manner, Svyatoslav Vsevolodovich expressed his attachment to the two brothers before his death. What is more, the princes of Chernigov themselves were honored with saints. David's son Svyatosha was canonized because of his saintly life as a monk. Igor' Ol'govich, like SS. Boris and Gleb, was a victim of a succession struggle and earned the status of *strastoterpets*. Mikhail became a martyr in the full sense of the word, because he died in defense of the Christian faith. The three princes became objects of religious cults and their shrines became places of pilgrimage.

A number of the Ol'govichi took an active part in the administration of the Church. Those who became princes of Kiev shared the responsibility with the metropolitan of appointing bishops. In Chernigov, the princes became involved in disputes over ecclesiastical appointments and over religious practices. Svyatoslav Ol'govich strongly opposed the selection of Metropolitan Klim, but evidently supported Leon's so-called heresy. Svyatoslav Vsevolodovich, however, championed traditional fasting practices and evicted Bishop Antony from Chernigov because the latter kept pestering him to adopt the more stringent observances. The princes also adorned their towns with churches and monasteries. Vsevolod Ol'govich, his son Svyatoslav, and his son Vsevolod Chermnyy were avid patrons of ecclesiastical building projects in imitation of their ancestors Svyatoslav Yaroslavich and Oleg Svyatoslavich.

The Ol'govichi were a highly disciplined dynasty and diligently observed the genealogical practice of succession. Unlike Monomakh's descendants, two or more Ol'govichi never challenged each other for Kiev. They adhered to the principle of succession advocated by Yaroslav the Wise that only the senior prince of the dynasty was the rightful claimant to the capital of Rus'. In like manner, the senior and cadet branches faithfully followed the system of genealogical succession to the dynastic capital of Chernigov. The notable exception was Oleg Svyatoslavich, who, in 1164, briefly challenged Svyatoslav Vsevolodovich, but after negotiating an agreement, submitted to him. The princes of Chernigov also evoked loyal support from their subjects. The chronicles report no *boyar* rebellions against them similar to the one in Galich, where the magnates killed the concubine of Yaroslav Osmomysl, or the one in Suzdalia, where the *boyars* murdered Andrey Bogolyubskiy.

Although the princes of Chernigov did not fight over succession claims, they squabbled viciously over domains. As we have seen, Svyatoslav Ol'govich valiantly fought to keep his patrimonial lands from falling into the hands of the Davidovichi, but later he refused to hand over towns to his nephew Svyatoslav Vsevolodovich. The latter in turn withheld domains from Oleg Svyatoslavich, and Mikhail evidently attempted to retain control of lands that Oleg of Kursk claimed as his. Such rivalries frequently arose after a senior prince appropriated the towns of an offender and the latter was determined to retrieve them, or after a new senior prince refused to hand over his predecessor's domains to the latter's son. At other times, if the senior prince occupied Chernigov or Kiev with the assistance of junior princes, the latter argued over the towns they should receive in payment for services rendered.

Special problems arose in the 1160s after the Davidovichi died out. The senior prince of the Ol'govichi, Svyatoslav Ol'govich, appropriated their lands and undoubtedly retained as many as possible for himself and his sons. His action inevitably displeased his relatives who considered themselves unfairly denied. A similar situation arose after the Igorevichi had moved from their patrimonies to Galicia. The senior prince, Vsevolod Chermnyy, evidently appropriated their towns in the Posem'e region, but his brothers would have demanded a share of the spoils. After the Galicians rebeled against the Igorevichi, the two survivors, Vladimir and his son Izyaslav, returned to the Posem'e undoubtedly hoping to reoccupy their former lands. Vsevolod Chermnyy, it seems, did not hand back their domains, or all of them, because Izyaslav seemingly became a soldier of fortune. The exodus of the Igorevichi from the Posem'e region therefore increased the territorial holdings of the princes from the senior branch, notably those of Vsevolod Chermnyy and his son Mikhail.

We have seen that the proposed order of succession to Kiev, which Yaroslav the Wise established for the three families of the inner circle, failed. As a result of Monomakh's scheming, above all, the princes of Chernigov and the Izyaslavichi of Turov became *izgoi*. This left Monomakh's descendants as the only rightful claimants, but they fought among themselves. The Mstislavichi, the heirs of his eldest son Mstislav, argued that they had the right to rule Kiev according to the pact that Monomakh had made with the Kievans. They rejected the claims of their uncles, the Monomashichi (Mstislav's younger brothers), who maintained that they had a prior claim according to the system of genealogical seniority advocated by Yaroslav the Wise. After the Mstislavichi usurped power from their uncles, peaceful succession to Kiev, on the whole, ceased. The militarily strongest pretender from the two camps usually won the day. On occasion, an acknowledged claimant would forgo his bid for Kiev if his dynasty was militarily too weak or if he himself was incapable of taking up the challenge.

The system of succession envisioned by Yaroslav the Wise might have been doomed from the start, as some have argued, but it had a rebirth in a modified form. Vsevolod Ol'govich, whose strongest claim to the capital of Rus' was that he was the senior prince of the dynasty of Chernigov, was the first non-Monomashich to usurp Kiev. He therewith entitled his descendants to rule it by giving them the right to sit on the throne of their father. Thus, tempered by time, Yaroslav's inner circle evolved into one forged by political and genealogical realities. By the middle of the twelfth century it constituted three families once again: the senior branch of the Ol'govichi, the descendants of Mstislav Vladimirovich in Volyn' and in Smolensk, and the family of his younger brother Yury Dolgorukiy in Suzdalia.

Eventually, the princes of Suzdalia realized that their prospects of ruling Kiev were unrealistic. The fates of Yury Dolgorukiy and his son Gleb, whom the Kievans murdered, and the distances between Suzdalia and Kiev convinced them that it was foolhardy for their senior prince to occupy Kiev in person. As Yaroslav the Wise foresaw, only a prince whose domain abutted on Kiev had a realistic chance of ruling the capital of Rus' because he could receive military aid quickly from his patrimony. In the meantime, the Mstislavichi of Volyn' also relinquished their right to rule Kiev because they preferred Galich. This left only the Rostislavichi of Smolensk as claimants from the House of Monomakh. Granted, the princes of Suzdalia (Andrey Bogolyubskiy and his brother Vsevolod Bol'shoe Gnezdo) and the princes of Volyn' (Roman and his son Daniil) kept a watchful eye on Kiev and at times manipulated its ruler.

After the Rostislavichi and the senior branch of Ol'govichi emerged as the only viable contenders for Kiev, Ryurik attempted to deprive Yaroslav and the Ol'govichi of their right to succession in perpetuity. Vsevolod Bol'shoe Gnezdo, however, defended the claim of the Ol'govichi. In 1216, his sons Yury and Yaroslav echoed his policy in their pre-battle manifesto at Lipitsa, where they proposed to give Kiev to the Ol'govichi and deprive the Rostislavichi of all their domains. Nothing came of the scheme because Yury was too weak to implement it. Later, in 1237, he joined forces with Daniil of Volyn' against Mikhail of Chernigov and they unsuccessfully tried to deprive him of Kiev. In the meantime, following an internal political upheaval and the decimation of their population by famine, the power of the Rostislavichi waned. They became, in effect, the vassals of the prince of Suzdalia. When the Tatars captured Kiev, therefore, Mikhail was the acknowledged ruler of the capital of Rus'. In the eyes of the majority of the Kievans, he was the most powerful prince in the land.

Thus we have seen that the princes of Chernigov were one of the most important dynasties in the twelfth and the first half of the thirteenth century. During the reign of Vsevolod Ol'govich they held supreme power in Rus'. Following Igor''s death the fortunes of the Ol'govichi plummeted as they fought for survival against the Davidovichi. During that rivalry, however, the Davidovichi ruled Kiev for short periods of time. Following their demise, the Ol'govichi attained supremacy under Svyatoslav Vsevolodovich's leadership. His fourteen-year reign in Kiev, albeit as co-ruler with Ryurik, lasted longer than that of Vladimir Monomakh. His son Vsevolod Chermnyy occupied Kiev for only four years, but his authority there was absolute and for a time he also controlled Galicia and Pereyaslavl'. Mikhail, the last senior prince, had even wider-reaching powers. For brief periods of time he became prince of Novgorod and of Galich, and he was the last prince of Rus' to rule Kiev under the traditional system of genealogical seniority. No rival deposed him from the capital of Rus'. That deed was executed by the invincible Tatars. In the light of our investigation, therefore, it is erroneous to contend that the dynasty of Chernigov was of secondary importance in Rus'.

The history of the dynasty as an autonomous political entity also ends on a high moral note. Chroniclers accused Oleg Svyatoslavich, the progenitor of the Ol'govichi, of bringing the pagan Polovtsy to butcher the Christians of Rus'. Paradoxically, the descendants of the very Christians whom Oleg's pagan allies had slaughtered, venerated Mikhail for winning the crown of martyrdom in defense of the Christian faith. It could be argued, therefore, that Mikhail exonerated his vilified ancestor.

Genealogical tables

Table 1 *The first princes of Rus'*

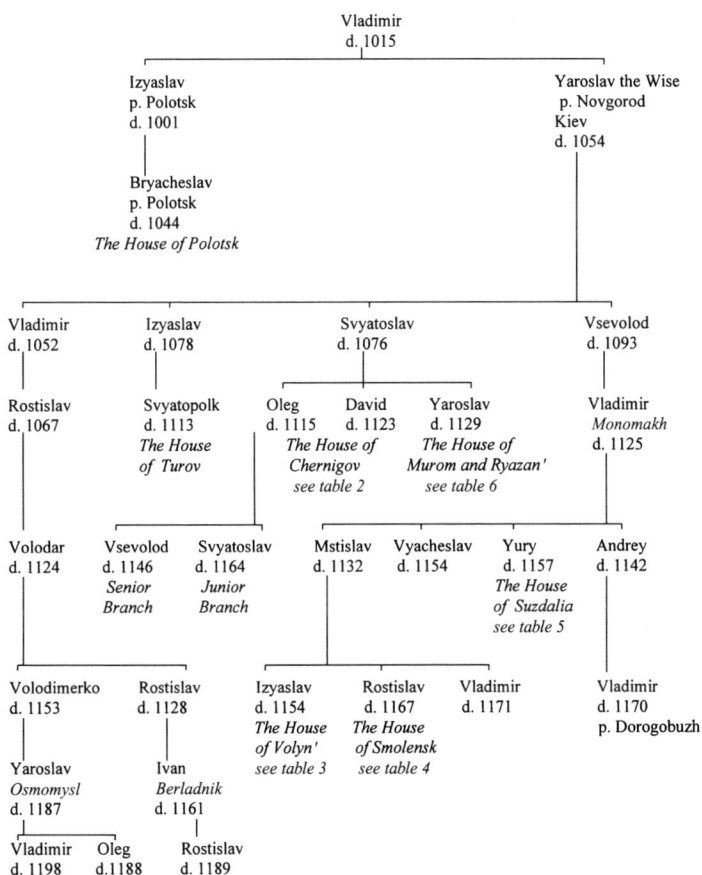

Vladimir
d. 1015

Izyaslav
p. Polotsk
d. 1001

Yaroslav the Wise
p. Novgorod
Kiev
d. 1054

Bryacheslav
p. Polotsk
d. 1044
The House of Polotsk

Vladimir
d. 1052

Izyaslav
d. 1078

Svyatoslav
d. 1076

Vsevolod
d. 1093

Rostislav
d. 1067

Svyatopolk
d. 1113
*The House
of Turov*

Oleg
d. 1115

David
d. 1123
*The House of
Chernigov
see table 2*

Yaroslav
d. 1129
*The House of
Murom and Ryazan'
see table 6*

Vladimir
Monomakh
d. 1125

Volodar
d. 1124

Vsevolod
d. 1146
*Senior
Branch*

Svyatoslav
d. 1164
*Junior
Branch*

Mstislav
d. 1132

Vyacheslav
d. 1154

Yury
d. 1157
*The House
of Suzdalia
see table 5*

Andrey
d. 1142

Volodimerko
d. 1153

Rostislav
d. 1128

Izyaslav
d. 1154
*The House
of Volyn'
see table 3*

Rostislav
d. 1167
*The House
of Smolensk
see table 4*

Vladimir
d. 1171

Vladimir
d. 1170
p. Dorogobuzh

Yaroslav
Osmomysl
d. 1187

Ivan
Berladnik
d. 1161

Vladimir
d. 1198

Oleg
d.1188

Rostislav
d. 1189

Abbreviations: d. = died; p. = prince of; ? = unconfirmed lineage.

393

Table 2 *The house of Chernigov*

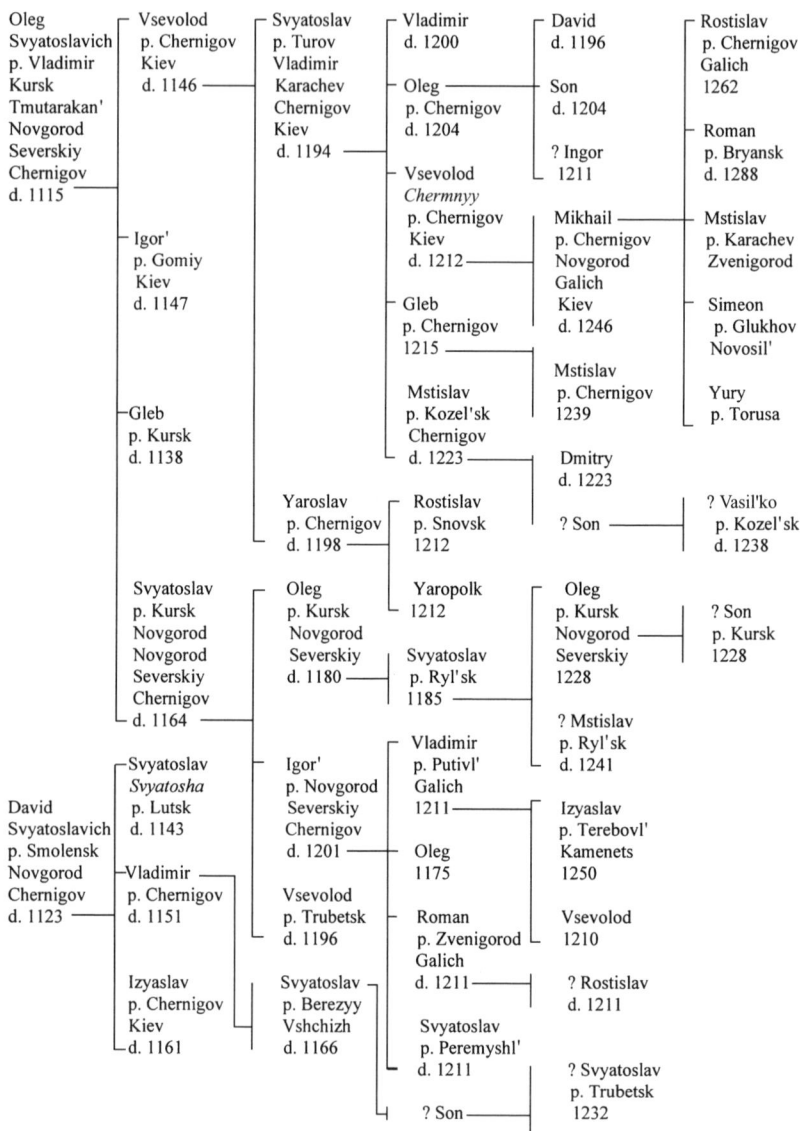

Oleg
Svyatoslavich
p. Vladimir
Kursk
Tmutarakan'
Novgorod
Severskiy
Chernigov
d. 1115

Vsevolod
p. Chernigov
Kiev
d. 1146 —

Svyatoslav
p. Turov
Vladimir
Karachev
Chernigov
Kiev
d. 1194 —

Vladimir
d. 1200

Oleg —
p. Chernigov
d. 1204

Vsevolod
Chermnyy
p. Chernigov
Kiev
d. 1212 —

David
d. 1196

Son
d. 1204

? Ingor
1211

Rostislav
p. Chernigov
Galich
1262

Roman
p. Bryansk
d. 1288

Igor'
p. Gomiy
Kiev
d. 1147

Gleb
p. Chernigov
1215 —

Mikhail —
p. Chernigov
Novgorod
Galich
Kiev
d. 1246

Mstislav
p. Karachev
Zvenigorod

Simeon
p. Glukhov
Novosil'

Gleb
p. Kursk
d. 1138

Mstislav
p. Kozel'sk
Chernigov
d. 1223 —

Mstislav
p. Chernigov
1239

Dmitry
d. 1223

Yury
p. Torusa

Yaroslav
p. Chernigov
d. 1198 —

Rostislav
p. Snovsk
1212

? Son —

? Vasil'ko
p. Kozel'sk
d. 1238

Svyatoslav
p. Kursk
Novgorod
Novgorod
Severskiy
Chernigov
d. 1164 —

Oleg
p. Kursk
Novgorod
Severskiy
d. 1180 —

Yaropolk
1212

Oleg
p. Kursk
Novgorod
Severskiy
1228 —

? Son
p. Kursk
1228

Svyatoslav
p. Ryl'sk
1185 —

David
Svyatoslavich
p. Smolensk
Novgorod
Chernigov
d. 1123 —

Svyatoslav
Svyatosha
p. Lutsk
d. 1143

Vladimir —
p. Chernigov
d. 1151

Igor'
p. Novgorod
Severskiy
Chernigov
d. 1201 —

Vladimir
p. Putivl'
Galich
1211 —

? Mstislav
p. Ryl'sk
d. 1241

Izyaslav
p. Terebovl'
Kamenets
1250

Oleg
1175 —

Vsevolod
p. Trubetsk
d. 1196

Roman
p. Zvenigorod
Galich
d. 1211 —

Vsevolod
1210

Izyaslav
p. Chernigov
Kiev
d. 1161

Svyatoslav
p. Berezyy
Vshchizh
d. 1166

Svyatoslav
p. Peremyshl'
d. 1211

? Rostislav
d. 1211

? Son —

? Svyatoslav
p. Trubetsk
1232

Table 3 *The house of Volyn'*

Mstislav
p. Kiev
d. 1132

Svyatoslav
p. Brest
d. 1183

Daniil
p. Vladimir
Galich
d. 1264 ——

Lev
p. Galich
1301

Roman
1260

Roman
p. Vladimir
Galich
d. 1205

Mstislav
1292

Vasil'ko
p. Vladimir
d. 1269 ——

Shvarn
d. 1269

Mstislav
p. Kiev
d. 1172

Vsevolod
p. Belz
d. 1195 ——

Aleksandr
p. Belz
Vladimir
1234 ——

Vsevolod
1264

Vsevolod
p. Belz
1244

Vladimir
p. Brest
d. 1173

Vsevolod
p. Cherven
1214

Izyaslav
p. Kiev
1154

Yaroslav
p. Lutsk
Kiev
d. 1180 ——

Ingvar'
p. Lutsk
Dorogobuzh
Kiev
1212 ——

Yaroslav
p. Lutsk
1231

Vladimir
1229

Izyaslav
d. 1196

Izyaslav
d. 1223

? Svyatoslav
p. Shumsk
d. 1223

Mstislav
Nemoy
p. Lutsk
Peresopnitsa
d. 1227

Yaropolk
p. Buzhsk
d. 1170

Vsevolod
p. Lutsk
1209

Table 4 *The house of Smolensk*

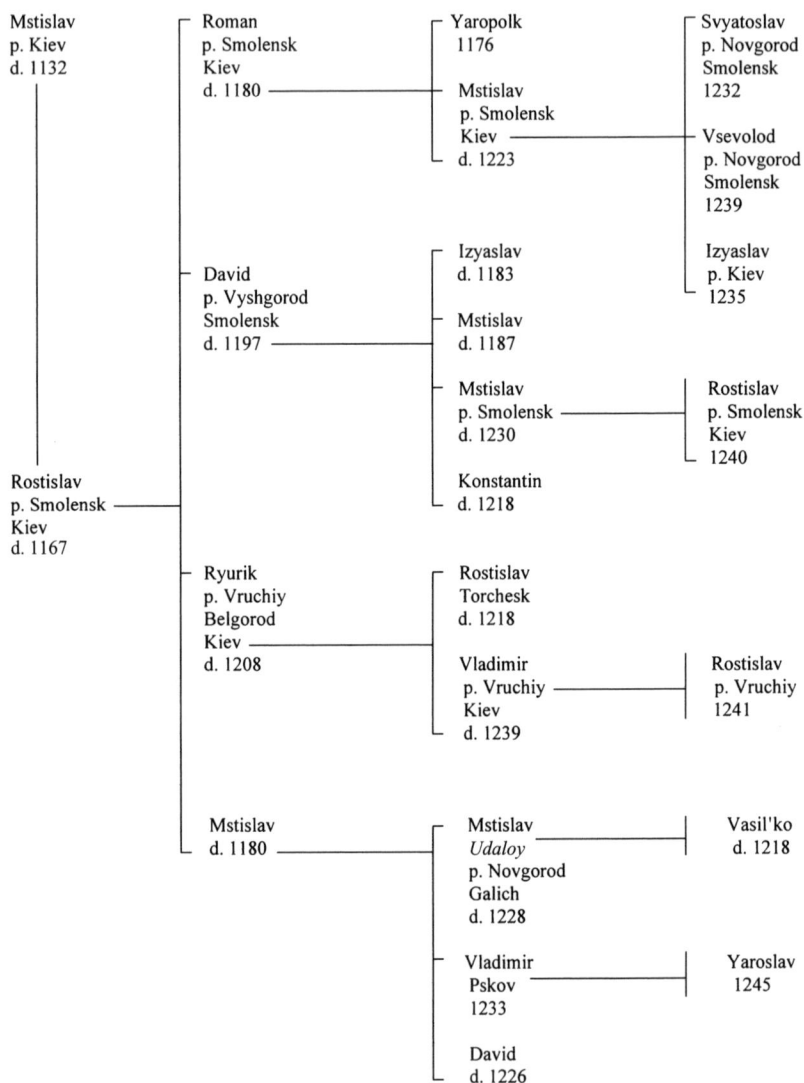

Mstislav
p. Kiev
d. 1132

Roman
p. Smolensk
Kiev
d. 1180 ──────────

Yaropolk
1176

Mstislav
p. Smolensk
Kiev ──────────
d. 1223

Svyatoslav
p. Novgorod
Smolensk
1232

Vsevolod
p. Novgorod
Smolensk
1239

David
p. Vyshgorod
Smolensk
d. 1197 ──────────

Izyaslav
d. 1183

Izyaslav
p. Kiev
1235

Mstislav
d. 1187

Mstislav
p. Smolensk ──────────
d. 1230

Rostislav
p. Smolensk
Kiev
1240

Konstantin
d. 1218

Rostislav
p. Smolensk ──────────
Kiev
d. 1167

Ryurik
p. Vruchiy
Belgorod
Kiev ──────────
d. 1208

Rostislav
Torchesk
d. 1218

Vladimir
p. Vruchiy ──────────
Kiev
d. 1239

Rostislav
p. Vruchiy
1241

Mstislav
d. 1180 ──────────

Mstislav
Udaloy ──────────
p. Novgorod
Galich
d. 1228

Vasil'ko
d. 1218

Vladimir
Pskov ──────────
1233

Yaroslav
1245

David
d. 1226

Table 5 *The house of Suzdalia*

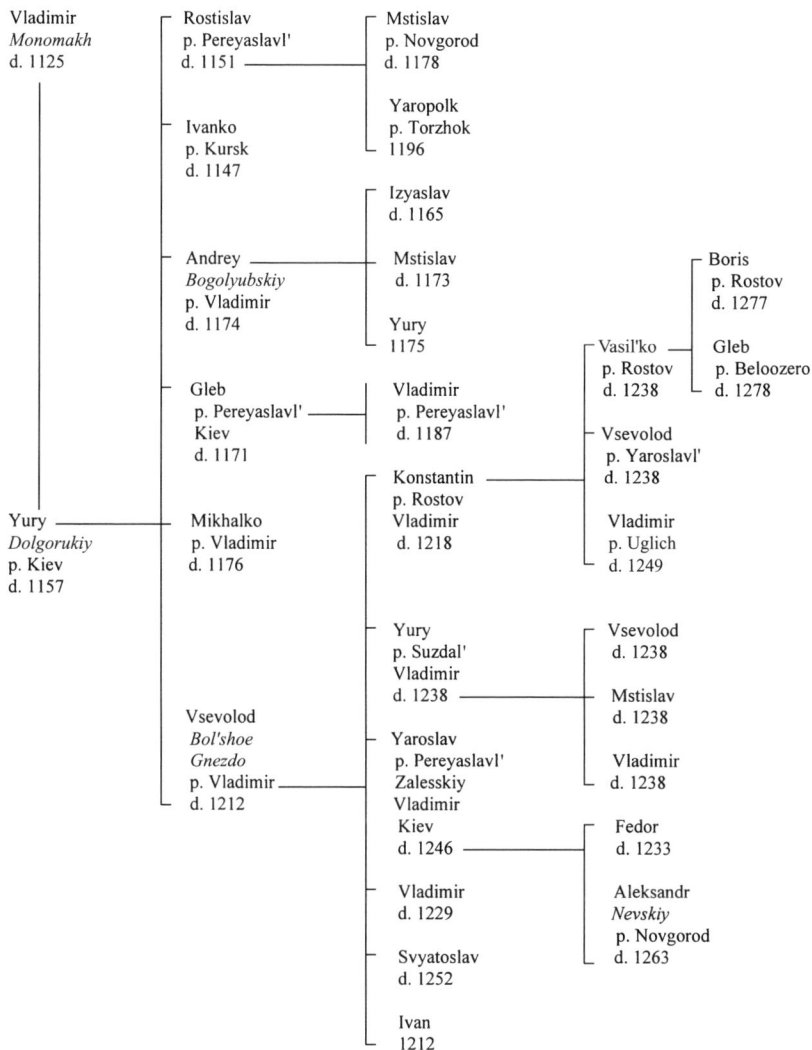

Vladimir
Monomakh
d. 1125

Rostislav
p. Pereyaslavl'
d. 1151 ——————

Mstislav
p. Novgorod
d. 1178

Yaropolk
p. Torzhok
1196

Ivanko
p. Kursk
d. 1147

Izyaslav
d. 1165

Andrey ——————
Bogolyubskiy
p. Vladimir
d. 1174

Mstislav
d. 1173

Yury
1175

Boris
p. Rostov
d. 1277

Vasil'ko ——
p. Rostov
d. 1238

Gleb
p. Beloozero
d. 1278

Gleb
p. Pereyaslavl'
Kiev
d. 1171

Vladimir
p. Pereyaslavl'
d. 1187

Vsevolod
p. Yaroslavl'
d. 1238

Konstantin ——————
p. Rostov
Vladimir
d. 1218

Vladimir
p. Uglich
d. 1249

Yury
Dolgorukiy
p. Kiev
d. 1157

Mikhalko
p. Vladimir
d. 1176

Yury
p. Suzdal'
Vladimir
d. 1238 ——————

Vsevolod
d. 1238

Vsevolod
*Bol'shoe
Gnezdo*
p. Vladimir
d. 1212

Mstislav
d. 1238

Yaroslav
p. Pereyaslavl'
Zalesskiy
Vladimir
Kiev
d. 1246 ——————

Vladimir
d. 1238

Fedor
d. 1233

Vladimir
d. 1229

Aleksandr
Nevskiy
p. Novgorod
d. 1263

Svyatoslav
d. 1252

Ivan
1212

Table 6　*The house of Murom and Ryazan'*

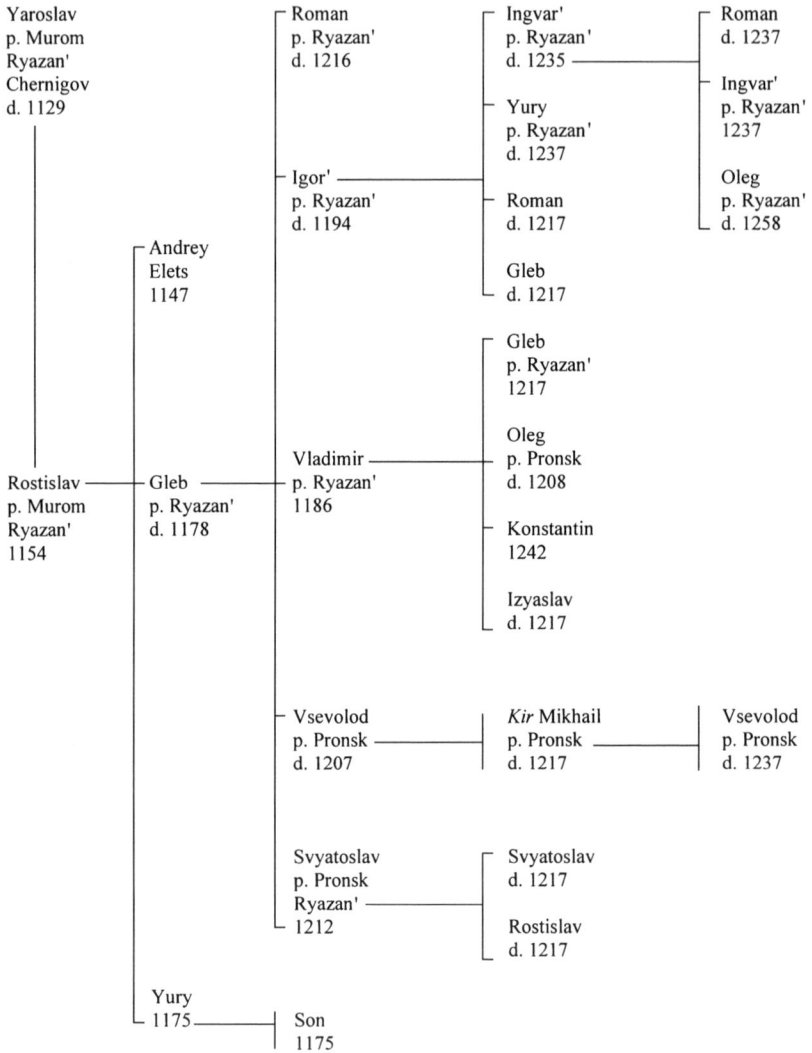

Yaroslav
p. Murom
Ryazan'
Chernigov
d. 1129

┌ Roman
│ p. Ryazan'
│ d. 1216

┌ Ingvar'
│ p. Ryazan'
│ d. 1235 ─────────

┌ Roman
│ d. 1237
│
├ Ingvar'
│ p. Ryazan'
│ 1237

┌ Yury
│ p. Ryazan'
│ d. 1237

├ Igor' ────────────
│ p. Ryazan'
│ d. 1194

├ Roman
│ d. 1217

Oleg
p. Ryazan'
└ d. 1258

┌ Andrey
│ Elets
│ 1147

└ Gleb
  d. 1217

┌ Gleb
│ p. Ryazan'
│ 1217

Rostislav ──────┬ Gleb ──────── ┐ Vladimir ───────
p. Murom　　　　│ p. Ryazan'　　p. Ryazan'
Ryazan'　　　　 │ d. 1178　　　　1186
1154

Oleg
p. Pronsk
d. 1208

├ Konstantin
│ 1242

Izyaslav
└ d. 1217

┌ Vsevolod
│ p. Pronsk ─────
│ d. 1207

Kir Mikhail
p. Pronsk ─────
d. 1217

Vsevolod
p. Pronsk
d. 1237

Svyatoslav
p. Pronsk
Ryazan' ────
└ 1212

┌ Svyatoslav
│ d. 1217

Rostislav
└ d. 1217

┌ Yury
└ 1175 ────────── ┤ Son
　　　　　　　　　　 1175

Select bibliography

SOURCES

Abramovich, D., *Kievo-pecherskiy Paterik*, K., 1930

Adrianova-Peretts, V. P. (ed.), *Voinskie povesti drevney Rusi*, M.-L., 1949

Adrianova-Peretts, V. P. (ed.), *Slovo o polku Igoreve*, M., 1950

Anninsky, S. A. (ed.), "Izvestiya vengerskikh missionerov XII–XIV vv. o tatarakh i vostochnoy Evrope," *Istoricheskiy arkhiv* 3 (M.-L., 1940), 71–112

"Arkhivnye materialy (opisi, gramoty, ukazy, i pr.) – prilozhenie k Opisaniyu Rizpolozhenskago monastyrya," *Trudy Vladimirskoy uchenoy arkhivnoy komissii*, bk. 2, Vladimir, 1900

Bielowski, A. (ed.), *Monumenta Poloniae Historica* (L'vov, 1872), vol. 2

Cross, S. H. and Sherbowitz-Wetzor, O. P. (trans.), *The Russian Primary Chronicle: Laurentian Text*, Cambridge, Mass., 1953

Dawson, C. (ed.), *The Mongol Mission*, New York, 1955

Długosz, J., *Longini canonici Cracoviensis, Historiae Polonicae* (Leipzig, 1711), bk. 6

"Ermolinskaya letopis'," PSRL 23 (Spb., 1910)

Fejer, G. (ed.), *Codex diplomaticus Hungariae ecclesiasticus ac civilis* (Budae, 1829), bk. 3, vol. 2 and bk. 4, vol. 1

Fennell, J. and Obolensky, D. (eds.), "The Lay of Igor's Campaign," *A Historical Russian Reader: A Selection of Texts from the XIth to the XVth Centuries* (Oxford, 1969), 63–72

Fennell, J. and Obolensky, D. (eds.), "Povest' o razorenii Ryazani Batyem," *A Historical Russian Reader: A Selection of Texts from the XIth to the XVth Centuries* (Oxford, 1969), pp. 76–85

Franklin, S. (trans. and intro.), *Sermons and Rhetoric of Kievan Rus'*, Harvard University Press, 1991

Georgievsky, V. T., "Zhitie pr. Evfrosinii Suzdal'skoy, s miniatyurami, po spisku XVII v.," *Trudy Vladimirskoy uchenoy arkhivnoy komissii* (Vladimir, 1899), bk. 1

"Gustinskaya letopis'," PSRL 2 (Spb., 1843)

Heppell, M. (trans.), *The "Paterik" of the Kievan Caves Monastery*, Cambridge, Mass., 1989

Hollingsworth, P. (trans. and intro.), *The Hagiography of Kievan Rus'*, Harvard University Press, 1992

"Ipat′evskaya letopis′," PSRL 2, second edition (Spb., 1908)

Katona, S. (ed.), *Historia pragmatica Hungariae* (Budae, 1782), vol. 1

Katona, S. (ed.), *Historia critica regum Hungariae stirpis Arpadianae ex fide domesticorum et externorum scriptorum* (Posonii et Cassoviae, 1783), vol. 5, and (Budae, 1782), vol. 6

Katona, S. (ed.), *Epitome chronologica rerum Hungaricarum Transsilvanicarum et Illyricarum* (Budae, 1796), pt. 1

"Kniga stepennaya tsarskogo rodosloviya," PSRL 21, chast′ pervaya (Spb., 1908)

Kukushkina, M. V. (ed.), *Radzivilovskaya letopis′* (Sankt-Peterburg, Moskva, 1994), vol. 1, Faksimil′noe vosproizvedenie rukopisi; vol. 2, Tekst, issledovanie, opisanie miniatyur

"Lavrent′evskaya letopis′," PSRL 1, second edition (L., 1926)

"Letopis′ Avraamki," PSRL 16 (Spb., 1889)

Loparev, Kh. (ed.), "Slovo pokhvalnoe na prenesenie moshchey Svv. Borisa i Gleba," *Pamyatniki drevney pis′mennosti 98* (Spb., 1894)

"L′vovskaya letopis′," PSRL 20 (Spb., 1910)

Makary, Mitropolit Vserossiyskiy, *Velikiya Minei Chetii*, September 14–24 (Spb., 1869)

Makhnovets′, L. Ie. (trans.), *Litopys rus′kyi (za Ipats′kym spyskom)*, S. A. Zakharova (ed.), K., 1989

"Mazurinskiy letopisets," PSRL 31 (M., 1968)

Moldovan, A. M., *"Slovo o zakone i blagodati" Ilariona*, K., 1984

"Moskovskiy letopisniy svod kontsa XV veka," PSRL 25 (M.-L., 1949)

Nasonov, A. N. (ed.), *Pskovskie letopisi*, 2 vols. (AN SSSR, 1941, 1955)

Nasonov, A. N. (ed.), *Novgorodskaya pervaya letopis′ starshego i mladshego izvodov*, M.-L., 1950

"Novgorodskaya chetvertaya letopis′," PSRL 4 (P., 1915)

"Novgorodskaya pyataya letopis′," PSRL 4 (ii) (P., 1917)

"Patriarshaya ili Nikonovskaya letopis′," PSRL 9 (Spb., 1862)

"Patriarshaya ili Nikonovskaya letopis′," PSRL 10 (Spb., 1885)

Perfecky, G. E. (trans.), *The Hypatian Code, Part Two: The Galician–Volynian Chronicle*, Munich, 1973

"Piskarevskiy letopisets," PSRL 34 (M., 1978)

Plano Carpini, J. de, *The Journey of Friar John of Pian de Carpini to the Court of Kuyuk Khan 1245–47 as narrated by himself*, W. W. Rockhill (ed. and trans.), London, 1900

Plano Carpini, J. de, *Istoriya Mongalov*, A. I. Malein (ed. and trans.), Spb., 1911

Priselkov, M. D. (ed.), *Troitskaya letopis′, rekonstruktsiya teksta*, M.-L., 1950

"Prolozhnoe skazanie ob osvyashcheniy tserkvi sv. Borisa i Gleba i perenesenii ikh grobov iz Vyshgoroda na Smyadinu, v 1190/1 godu," in N. K. Nikol′sky, "Materialy dlya istorii drevne-russkoy dukhovnoy pis′mennosti," I–IV, *Izvestiya*, otdeleniya russkago yazyka i slovesnosti Imperatorskoy Akademii Nauk. (Spb., 1903), tom 8, kn. 1, pp. 221–2

Radzivilovskaya ili Kenigsbergskaya letopis′, Komitet Imperatorskago Obshchestva Lyubiteley Drevney Pis′mennosti, 118 (Spb., 1902) [photoreproduction]

Rashid ad-Din, *The Successors of Genghis Khan*, J. A. Boyle (trans.), New York and
  London, 1971
"Rogozhskiy letopisets," PSRL 15 (P., 1922)
Rubruquis, William of, *The Journey of William of Rubruck to the Eastern Parts of
  the World 1253–55 as narrated by himself*, W. W. Rockhill (ed. and trans.),
  London, 1900
Rubruquis, William of, *Puteshestvie v vostochnyya strany*, A. I. Malein (ed. and
  trans.), Spb., 1911
"Simeonovskaya letopis'," PSRL 18 (Spb., 1913)
Sinyukov, V. I. *et al.* (eds.), *Skazanie o knyaze Mikhaile Chernigovskom i o ego
  boyarine Feodore*, M., 1988
"Sofiyskaya pervaya letopis' (vyp. pervyy)," PSRL 5, second edition (L., 1925)
"Sokrashchennyy letopisnyy svod 1493 g.," PSRL 27 (M.-L., 1962)
"Sokrashchennyy letopisnyy svod 1495 g.," PSRL 27 (M.-L., 1962)
Spuler, B., *History of the Mongols, Based on Eastern and Western Accounts of the
  Thirteenth and Fourteenth Centuries*, Helga and Stuart Drummond (trans.),
  London, 1972
"Suzdal'skaya letopis': Prodolzhenie po Akademicheskomu spisku," PSRL 1, sec-
  ond edition (L., 1928)
Tatishchev, V. N., *Istoriya Rossiyskaya*, 7 vols., M.-L., 1962–8
"Tipografskaya letopis'," PSRL 24 (P., 1921)
Tizengauzen, V. G., *Sbornik materialov, otnosyashchikhsya k istorii Zolotoy Ordy*
  (Spb., 1884), vol. 1
"Tverskaya letopis'," PSRL 15 (Spb., 1863)
"Vladimirskiy letopisets," PSRL 30 (M., 1965)
"Voskresenskaya letopis'," PSRL 7 (Spb., 1856)
Yakovleva, O. A. (ed.), "Piskarevskiy letopisets," *Materialy po istorii SSSR*
  (M., 1955), tom 2, pp. 5–210
Zaluski, J. A. (ed.), *Specimen Historiae Polonae Criticae*, Warsaw, 1735
Zotov, R. V., *O Chernigovskikh knyazyakh po Lyubetskomu sinodiku i o Chernigov-
  skom knyazhestve v Tatarskoe vremya*, Spb., 1892

SECONDARY WORKS

Afanas'ev, K. N., *Postroenie arkhitekturnoy formy drevnerusskimi zodchimi*, M., 1961
Afanas'ev, V., "Veroyatnyy put' knyazya Igorya Severskogo na polovtsev v 1185 g.,"
  Istoricheskiy Zhurnal, 6 (1939), 45–56
Alekseev, L. V., *Smolenskaya zemlya v IX–XIII vv. Ocherki istorii Smolenshchiny i
  Vostochnoy Belorusii*, M., 1980
Andersson, A., *Mediaeval Drinking Bowls of Silver Found in Sweden*, Stockholm,
  1983
Aseev, Yu. S., "Arkhitektura severn'oho pridniprov'ia ta Galits'ko-Volyns'kykh
  zemel' u XII–XIII stolittiakh," in vol. 1, *Mystetstvo naidavnishykh chasiv ta
  epokhy Kyivs'koi Rusi*, in series *Istoriia Ukrains'koho Mystetstva*, 6 vols. (Kyiv,
  1966)

Bagaley, D., *Istoriya Severskoy zemli do poloviny XIV stoletiya*, K., 1882
Barsov, N., *Materialy dlya istoriko-geograficheskago slovarya Rossii: I Geograficheskiy slovar' Russkoy zemli (IX–XIVst.)*, Vil'na, 1865
Barsukov, N. P., *Istochniki russkoy agiografii*, Spb., 1882
Baumgarten, N. de, *Généalogies et mariages occidentaux des Rurikides Russes du Xe au XIIIe siècle (Orientalia Christiana)* (Rome, 1927), vol. 9, nr. 35
Baumgarten, N. de, *Généalogies des branches régnantes des Rurikides du XIIIe au XVIe siècle (Orientalia Christiana)* (Rome, 1934), vol. 35, nr. 94
Beletsky, V. D. and Beletsky, S. V., "Pechat' knyazya Igorya," *Drevnosti Slavyan i Rusi*, B. A. Timoshchuk (ed.) (M., 1988), pp. 105–10
Belyaev, I., *Razskazy iz russkoy istorii*, second edition (M., 1865), bk. 1
Belyaev, L. A., "Iz istorii zodchestva drevnego Chernigova (tserkov arkhangela Mikhaila 1174 g.)," *Problemi istorii SSSR* 4 (M., 1974), 3–18
Berezhkov, M. N., *Blazhennyy Igor' Ol'govich, knyaz' Novgorodseverskiy i velikiy knyaz' Kievskiy*, Chernigov, 1893
Berezhkov, N. G., *Khronologiya russkogo letopisaniya*, M., 1963
Bohusevych, V. A., "Rozkopky v Putyvl's'komu kremli," *Arkheolohiia* 15 (K., 1963), 165–74
Bol'shakov, L. N. and Kovalenko, V. P., "Novyy pamyatnik Drevnerusskogo zodchestva v Chernigove," *Pamyatniki Kul'tury Novye Otkrytiya, Ezhegodnik 1988* (M., 1989), 541–3
Bol'shakov, L. N., Kovalenko, V. P., and Rappoport, P. A., "Novye dannye o pamyatnikakh drevnego zodchestva Chernigova i Novgoroda-Severskogo," *KSIA* 195 (M., 1989), 51–7
Braychevsky, M. Yu., "Chernigovskiy knyazheskiy dom i avtor 'Slova o polku Igoreve'," *Problemy arkheologii yuzhnoy Rusi*: Materialy istoriko-arkheologicheskogo seminara "Chernigov i ego okruga v IX–XIII vv.," Chernigov, 26–28 sentyabrya 1988 g., T. N. Telizhenko (ed.) (K., 1990), pp. 10–15
Bushkovitch, P., *Religion and Society in Russia: The Sixteenth and Seventeenth Centuries*, Oxford, 1992
The Cambridge History of Poland, Cambridge, 1950
Cherepanov, S. K., "K voprosu o yuzhnom istochnike Sofiyskoy I i Novgorodskoy IV letopisey," *TODRL* 30 (1976), 279–83
Cherepnin, L. V., "Letopisets Daniila Galitskogo," *Istoricheskie zapiski* 12 (1941), 228–53
Cherepnin, L. V., *Russkie feodal'nye arkhivy XIV–XV vv.* (M.-L., 1948) part 1
Cherepnin, L. V., "Mongolo-Tatary na Rusi (XIII v.)," *Tataro-Mongoly v Azii i Evrope*, S. L. Tikhvinsky (ed.) (M., 1970), pp. 179–203
Darkevich, V. P., "K istorii torgovykh svyazey Drevney Rusi," *KSIA* 138 (1974), 93–103
Darkevich, V. P. and Edomakha, I. I., "Pamyatnik zapadnoevropeyskoy torevtiki XII veka," *SA*, nr. 3 (M., 1964), 247–55
Dashkevich, Ya. P., "Kamenets – eshche raz," *Russia Mediaevalis* 5, 1 (München, 1984), 7–19

Dimnik, M., "Russian Princes and their Identities in the First Half of the Thirteenth Century," *Mediaeval Studies* 40 (1978), 157–89

Dimnik, M., "Kamenec," *Russia Mediaevalis* 4 (München, 1979), 25–34

Dimnik, M., "The Siege of Chernigov in 1235," *Mediaeval Studies* 41 (1979), 387–403

Dimnik, M., "The Struggle for Control over Kiev in 1235 and 1236," *Canadian Slavonic Papers* 21, nr. 1 (1979), 28–44

Dimnik, M., *Mikhail, Prince of Chernigov and Grand Prince of Kiev, 1224–1246*, Toronto, 1981

Dimnik, M., "The Place of Ryurik Rostislavich's Death: Kiev or Chernigov?," *Mediaeval Studies* 44 (1982), 371–93

Dimnik, M., "The 'Testament' of Iaroslav 'The Wise': A Re-Examination," *Canadian Slavonic Papers* 29, nr. 4 (1987), 369–86

Dimnik, M., "Oleg Svyatoslavich and his Patronage of the Cult of SS. Boris and Gleb," *Mediaeval Studies* 50 (1988), 349–70

Dimnik, M., *The Dynasty of Chernigov, 1054–1146*, Toronto, 1994

Dimnik, M., "Succession and Inheritance in Rus' before 1054," *Mediaeval Studies* 58 (1996), 87–117

Dimnik, M., "A Bride's Journey from Kiev to Vladimir (1211): Pitfalls in Using V. N. Tatishchev as a Source," *Roma, magistra mundi. Itineraria culturae medievalis.* Mélanges offerts au Père L. E. Boyle à l'occasion de son 75e anniversaire édités par J. Hamesse (Fédération Internationale des Instituts d'Etudes Médiévales. "Textes et études du moyen âge," X) (Louvain-la-Neuve, 1998), vol. 1, 137–53

Dimnik, M., "Igor's Defeat at the Kayala: The Chronicle Evidence," *Mediaeval Studies* 63 (2001), 245–82

Dmitriev, L. A., "Skazanie o ubienii v orde knyazya Mikhaila Chernigovskogo i ego boyarina Feodora," *SKKDR*, 412–16

Dovzhenok, V. I., "Drevnerusskie gorodishcha na srednem Dnepre," *SA*, nr. 4 (M., 1967), 260–73

Dworzaczek, W., *Genealogia: Tablice*, Warsaw, 1959

Ekzemplyarsky, A., "Chernigovskie knyaz'ya," *Russkiy biograficheskiy slovar'* (Spb., 1905; reprint, Kraus, 1962), vol. 22

Fedorov-Davidov, G. A., *Kochevniki Vostochnoy Evropy pod vlast'yu zolotoordynskikh khanov*, M., 1966

Fennell, J., "The Tale of Baty's Invasion of North-East Rus' and its Reflexion in the Chronicles of the Thirteenth–Fifteenth Centuries," *Russia Mediaevalis* 3 (München, 1977), 41–78

Fennell, J., "The Tale of the Death of Vasil'ko Konstantinovich: A Study of the Sources," *Osteuropa in Geschichte und Gegenwart. Festschrift für Gunther Stökl zum 60. Geburtstag* (Vienna, 1977), pp. 34–46

Fennell, J., "The Tatar Invasion of 1223: Source Problems," *FOG*, Band 27 (Berlin, 1980), 18–31

Fennell, J., "Russia on the Eve of the Tatar Invasion," *Oxford Slavonic Papers* 14 (1981), 1–13

Fennell, J., *The Crisis of Medieval Russia 1200–1304*, Longman, London, and New York, 1983

Fennell, J., "The Last Years of Riurik Rostislavich," *Essays in Honor of A. A. Zimin*, D. C. Waugh (ed.) (Columbus, Ohio, 1985), 159–66

Fennell, J., *A History of the Russian Church to 1448*, Longman, London, and New York, 1995

Fennell, J. and Stokes, A., *Early Russian Literature*, London, 1974

Filaret, Archbishop of Chernigov (Gumilevsky, D. G.), *Istoriko-statisticheskoe opisanie Chernigovskoy eparkhii*, 7 vols., Chernigov, 1861–74

Filaret, Archbishop of Chernigov, *Russkie svyatiye*, third edition (Spb., 1882), vol. 3

Fine, J. V. A., Jr., *The Late Medieval Balkans*, Ann Arbor, 1987

Flier, M. S., "Sunday in Medieval Russian Culture: *Nedelja* versus *Voskresenie*," in *Medieval Russian Culture* (California Slavic Studies 12), Birnbaum, H. and Flier, M. S. (eds.) (Berkeley, 1984), 105–49

Florovsky, A. V., *Chekhi i vostochnye slavyane* (Prague, 1935), vol. 1

Franklin, S., "Literacy and Documentation in Early Medieval Russia," *Speculum* 60, nr. 1 (Cambridge, Mass., 1985), 1–38

Franklin, S. and Shepard, J., *The Emergence of Rus 750–1200*, Longman, London, and New York, 1996

Froyanov, I. Ya., "Vechevye sobraniya 1146–1147 gg. v Kieve," *Vestnik* Leningradskogo Universiteta, 8, Seriya Istoriya, Yazyk, Literatura, vyp. 2 (1977), 28–36

Froyanov, I. Ya., "O sobytiyakh 1227–1230 gg. v Novgorode," *Novgorodskiy istoricheskiy sbornik* 2 (12) (L., 1984), 97–113

Froyanov, I. Ya., *Myatezhniy Novgorod. Ocherki istorii gosudarstvennosti, sotsial'noy i politicheskoy bor'by kontsa IX – nachala XIII stoletiya*, Spb., 1992

Fuhrmann, J. T., "Metropolitan Cyril II (1242–1281) and the Politics of Accommodation," JBfGOE, Neue Folge, Band 24 (Wiesbaden, 1976), 161–72

Georgievsky, V. T., "Suzdal'skiy Rizpolozhenskiy zhenskiy monastyr'," *Trudy Vladimirskoy uchenoy arkhivnoy komissii* (Vladimir, 1900), bk. 2

Getmanets, M. F., *Tayna reki Kayaly ("Slovo o polku Igoreve")*, Khar'kov, 1982

Golden, P. B., "Aspects of the Nomadic Factor in the Economic Development of Kievan Rus'," *Ukrainian Economic History: Interpretive Essays*, I. S. Koropeckyj (ed.) (Cambridge, Mass., 1991), 58–101

Golubinsky, E., *Istoriya kanonizatsii svyatykh v russkoy tserkvi*, second edition, M., 1903

Golubinsky, E., *Istoriya russkoy tserkvi*, revised and expanded second edition (M., 1901, 1904), vol. 1, pts. 1–2

Golubovsky, P. V., *Istoriya Severskoy zemli do poloviny XIV stoletiya*, K., 1881

Golubovsky, P. V., *Istoriya Smolenskoy zemli do nachala XV st.*, K., 1895

Golubovsky, P. V., "Opyt priurocheniya drevne-russkoy propovedi 'Slovo o knyaz'yakh' k opredelennoy khronologicheskoy date," *Drevnosti*: Trudy Arkheograficheskoy Kommissii Imperatorskago Moskovskago archeologicheskago obshchestva, M. V. Dovnar-Zapol'sky (ed.) (M., 1899), vol. 1, vyp. 3, cols. 491–510

Golubovsky, P. V., "Gde nakhodilis sushchestvovavshie v domongol'skiy period goroda: Vorgol, Glebl', Zartyy, Orgoshch, Snovsk, Unenezh, Khorobor?" Zh. M. N. P., chast' 347 (Spb., 1903), 111–35

Golubovsky, P. V., *Istoricheskaya karta Chernigovskoy gubernii do 1300 goda*, M., 1908

Gur'yanov, V. N. and Polyakov, G. P., "Novye issledovaniya drevnego Bryanska," *Rol' rannikh mis'kykh tsentriv v stanovlenni Kyivs'koi Rusi*, Materialy pol'ovoho istoryko-arkheolohichnoho seminaru. Serpen' 1993 r., s. Zelenyi Hai Sums'koho r-nu Sums'koi obl., O. P. Motsia (gen. ed.) (Sumy, 1993), 27–30

Halperin, C. J., *Russia and the Golden Horde*, Bloomington, 1985

Hóman, B., *Geschichte des Ungarischen Mittelalters* (Berlin, 1943), vol. 2

Hosch, E., "Russische Fürsten im Donauraum des 13. Jahrhunderts," *Münchner Zeitschrift für Balkankunde*, Band 2 (München, 1979), 97–107

Hrushevsky, M., *Ocherk istorii Kievskoy zemli ot smerti Yaroslava do kontsa XIV stoletiya*, K., 1891

Hrushevs'kyi, M., *Istoriia Ukrainy-Rusy*, 10 vols. (New York, 1954–8, being a reprint of the second enlarged edition of Lvov, 1905)

Hurwitz, E. S., *Prince Andrej Bogoljubskij: The Man and the Myth*, Firenze, 1980

Ilovaysky, D., *Istoriya Ryazanskogo knyazhestva*, M., 1858

Ivakin, G. Yu., *Kiev v XIII–XV vekakh*, K., 1982

Karamzin, N. M., *Istoriya gosudarstva Rossiiskago*, third edition (Spb., 1830–1), vol. 3

Karger, M. K., "Kiev i mongol'skoe zavoevanie," SA, nr. 11 (M.-L., 1949), 55–102

Kazan, M. D., "Yaroslavna", *Entsiklopediya "Slova o Polku Igoreve,"* (Sankt-Peterburg, 1995), vol. 5, pp. 295–7

Kazhdan, A., "Rus'–Byzantine Princely Marriages in the Eleventh and Twelfth Centuries," HUS, vols. 12/13, 1988/89 Proceedings of the International Congress Commemorating the Millennium of Christianity in Rus'–Ukraine (1990), 414–29

Kholostenko, N. V., "Arkhitekturno-arkheologicheskie issledovaniya Pyatnitskoy tserkvi v g. Chernigove (1953–1954 gg.)," SA, nr. 26 (M.-L., 1956), 271–92

Kloss, B. M., "Letopis' Novgorodskaya pervaya," SKKDR, 245–7

Korinnyy, N. N., *Pereyaslavskaya zemlya X-pervaya polovina XIII veka*, K., 1992

Kosztolnyik, Z. J., *Hungary in the Thirteenth Century*, East European Monographs 439 (Boulder, 1996)

Kotlyar, M. F., "Zahadka Svyatoslava Vsevolodovycha Kyivs'koho," UIZh 6 (1967), 104–9

Kotlyar, N. F., "O tak nazyvaemykh Chernigovskikh monetnykh grivnakh," *Moneta: Mezhdunarodnyy numizmaticheskiy al'manakh*, vyp. 4, 1995 (Vologda, 1996), 5–18

Kovalenko, V. P., "Osnovni etapy rozvitku litopisnikh mist Chernihovo-Sivers'koy zemli (VIII–XIII st.)," *Ukrains'kiy istorichniy zhurnal* 8 (1983), 120–5

Kovalenko, V. P., *Proiskhozhdenie letopisnykh gorodov Chernigovo-Severskoy zemli (IX–XIII vv.)*, Avtoreferat dissertatsii na soiskanie uchenoy stepeni kandidata istoricheskikh nauk, Kiev, 1983

Kovalenko, V. P., "Do typolohii litopysnykh mist Chernihovo-Sivers'koi zemli (VIII–XIII st.)," *Arkheolohiia* 61 (K., 1988), 1–10

Kovalenko, V. P., "Knyazheskie sela v okrestnostyakh Novgorod-Severskogo v XII v.," *Drevnerusskiy gorod Putivl'*, Tezisy dokladov i soobshcheniy oblastnoy nauchnoy konferentsii, posvyashchennoy 1000-letiyu g. Putivlya, A. V. Lugovskoy *et al.* (eds.) (Putivl', 1988), pp. 16–18

Kovalenko, V. P., "Osnovnye etapy razvitiya drevnego Chernigova," *Chernigov i ego okruga v IX–XIII vv.*, P. P. Tolochko (gen. ed.) (K., 1988), pp. 22–33

Kovalenko, V. P., "K istoricheskoy topografii chernigovskogo detintsa," *Problemy arkheologii Yuzhnoy Rusi*, T. N. Telizhenko (ed.) (K., 1990), pp. 15–23

Kovalenko, V. P., "Itogi i zadachi izucheniya drevnego Chernigova," *Istoricheskoe kraevedenie v SSSR: Voprosy teorii i praktiki*, V. A. Kovalenko (ed.) (K., 1991), pp. 201–10

Kovalenko, V. P., "Chernigovo-Severskaya zemlya v sisteme Drevnerusskikh knyazhestv XII–XIII vv.: istoriograficheskie traditsii i real'nost'," *Otechestvennaya i vseobshchaya istoriya: metodologiya, istochnikovedenie, istoriografiya* (Bryansk, 1993), pp. 83–5

Kovalenko, V. P., "Maisternia iuvelira XIII st. na dytyntsi Liubecha," *Starozhytnosti Rusi-Ukrainy*, L. L. Vashchenko (ed.) (K., 1994), pp. 132–40

Kovalenko, V. P., "K voprosu o vzaimootnosheniyakh feodal'nykh gorodov i okrugi v Chernigovo-Severskoy zemle," *Iz istorii Bryanskogo kraya* (Bryansk, 1995), pp. 63–9

Kovalenko, V. P., "Votchinnye mastera-yuveliry v gorodakh Chernigovo-Severskoy zemli," *Slavyanskaya arkheologiya, 1990, Rannesrednevekovyy gorod i ego okruga* (Materialy po arkheologii Rossii), vyp. 2 (M., 1995), pp. 67–85

Kovalenko, V. P., "Do vyvchennia chernihivs'kogo peredgoroddia," *Slov'ianorus'ki starozhytnosti pivnichnoho livoberezhzhia*, Materialy istorykoarkheolohichnoho seminaru, prysviachenoho 60-richchiu vid dnia narodzhennia O. V. Shekuna (19–20 sichnia 1995 r. m. Chernihiv), O. P. Motsia (gen. ed.) (Chernihiv, 1995), pp. 40–5

Kovalenko, V. P., "Chernihovo-sivers'ka zemlia v seredyni XIII st.," *Sviatyi kniaz'*, pp. 36–41

Kovalenko, V. P., "Chasha kniazia Ihoria," *Istoriia Rusi-Ukrainy* (Istorikoarkheolohichnyi zbirnyk), O. P. Motsia (gen. ed.) (K., 1998), pp. 142–51

Kovalenko, V. P. and Motsya, A. P., "Novgorod-Severskiy v X–XIII vv.," *Novgorodu-Severskomu – 1000 let* (Tezisy dokladov oblastnoy nauchno-prakticheskoy konferentsii [may 1989 g.]), A. B. Kovalenko *et al.* (eds.) (Chernigov and Novgorod-Severskiy, 1989), pp. 25–9

Kovalenko, V. P. and Rappoport, P. A., "Pamyatniki drevnerusskoy arkhitektury v Chernigovo-Severskoy zemle," *Zograf* 18 (Beograd, 1987), 5–11

Kovalenko, V. P. and Rappoport, P. A., "Etapy razvitiya drevnerusskoy arkhitektury Chernigovo-Severskoy zemli," *Russia Mediaevalis* 7, 1 (München, 1992), 39–59

Kovalenko, V. P. and Shekun, O. V., "Litopysna Sosnytsia," *Mynule Sosnytsi ta ii okolyts*, O. B. Kovalenko (gen. ed.) (Chernihiv, 1990), pp. 9–13

Kovalenko, V. P. and Shekun, O. V., "Do lokalizatsii litopysnoy Lutavy," *Slov'iany i Rus' u naukovii spadshchyni D. Ia. Samokvasova*. Materialy istoryko-arkheolohichnoho seminaru, prysviachenoho 150-richchiu vid dnia narodzhennia D. Ia. Samokvasova (14–16 veresnya 1993 r., m. Novgorod-Sivers'kyi), P. P. Tolochko (gen. ed.) (Chernihiv, 1993), pp. 101–2

Kovalenko, V. P. and Shinakov, E. O., "Litopysnyi Starodub (do pytannia pro lokalizatsiiu)," *Liubets'kyi z'izd kniaziv 1097 roku v istorychnii doli Kyivs'koi Rusi*, Materialy mizhnarodnoi konferentsii prysviachenoi 900-littiu z'izdu kniaziv Kyivs'koi Rusi u Liubechi, P. P. Tolochko (gen. ed.) (Chernihiv, 1997), pp. 89–101

Kovalenko, V. P. and Sytyy, Yu. N., "Letopisnaya Belavezha (K voprosu o lokalizatsii)," *Arkheologiya slavyanskogo Yugo-Vostoka*, A. G. D'yachenko (gen. ed.) (Voronezh, 1991), pp. 59–66

Kovalenko, V. P. and Sytyy, Yu. N., "Torgovo-ekonomicheskie vzaimosvyazi Chernigovo-Severskoy zemli s volzhskoy Bulgariey v IX–XIII vv.," *Put' iz Bulgara v Kiev*, A. Kh. Khalikov (gen. ed.) (Kazan', 1992), pp. 54–68

Kozakov, A. L., "De vidbuvalysia kniazivs'ki 'snemy' 1155 ta 1159 rr. (istoryko-arkheolohichnyi aspekt lokalizatsii litopysnoi Lutavy)," *Liubets'kyi z'izd kniaziv 1097 roku v istorychnii doli Kyivs'koi Rusi*, Materialy mizhnarodnoi konferentsii prysviachenoi 900-littiu z'izdu kniaziv Kyivs'koi Rusi u Liubechi, P. P. Tolochko (gen. ed.) (Chernihiv, 1997), pp. 101–8

Krasheninnikov, V. V., "Potomki Mikhaila Vsevolodovicha chernigovskogo i bryanskiy kray," *Sviatyi kniaz'*, pp. 33–6

Kuchkin, V. A., *Formirovanie gosudarstvennoy territorii Severo-Vostochnoy Rusi v XI–XIV vv.*, M., 1984

Kudryashov, K. V., *Pro Igorya Severskogo, pro zemlyu Russkuyu. Istoriko-geograficheskiy ocherk o pokhode Igorya Severskogo na polovtsev v 1185 godu*, M., 1959

Kuza, A. V., *Malye goroda Drevney Rusi*, M., 1989

Kuza, A. V., "Novgorod-Severskiy – stol'nyy gorod Igorya Svyatoslavicha," *Novgorodu-Severskomu – 1000 let* (Tezisy dokladov oblastnoy nauchno-prakticheskoy konferentsii [may 1989 g.]), A. B. Kovalenko *et al.* (eds.) (Chernigov and Novgorod-Severskiy, 1989), pp. 20–3

Kuza, A. V., Kovalenko, V. P., and Motsya, A. P., "Chernigov i Novgorod-Severskiy v epokhu 'Slova o polku Igoreve'," *Chernigov i ego okruga v IX–XIII vv.*, A. A. Zolotareva (ed.) (K., 1988), pp. 56–65

Kuza, A. V., Kovalenko, V. P., and Motsya, A. P., "Novgorod-Severskiy: Nekotorye itogi i perspetivy issledovaniy," *Na Yugo-Vostoke Drevney Rusi: Istoriko-arkheologicheskie issledovaniya*, A. D. Pryakhin *et al.* (eds.) (Voronezh, 1996), pp. 3–28

Kuz'min, A. G., "Ob istochnikovedcheskoy osnove 'Istorii Rossiyskoy' V. N. Tatishcheva," *Voprosy istorii*, pt. 9 (1963), 214–18

Kuz'min, A. G., *Ryazanskoe letopisanie*, M., 1965

Kuz'min, A. G., "Ipat'evskaya letopis' i 'Slovo o polku Igoreve' (Po povodu stat'i A. A. Zimina)," *Istoriya SSSR*, nr. 6 (M., 1968), 64–87

Lenhoff, G., "The Cult of Saint Nikita the Stylite in Pereyaslavl' and Among the Muscovite Elite," *Fonctions sociales et politiques du culte des saints dans les sociétés*

de rite grec et latin au Moyen Age et à l'époque moderne. Approche comparative,
   M. Derwich and M. Dmitriev (eds.) (Wroclaw, 1999), pp. 331–46
Leonid, Arkhimandrit (L. A. Kavelin), *Svyataya Rus' ili svedeniya o vsekh svyatykh
   i podvizhnikakh blagochestiya na Rusi (do XVIII veka)*. Obshche i mestno
   chtimykh, Spb., 1891
Likhachev, D. S., *Russkie letopisi i ikh kul'turno-istoricheskoe znachenie*, M.-L., 1947
Likhacheva, O. P., "Letopis' Ipatevskaya," *SKKDR*, 235–41
Limonov, Yu. A., *Letopisanie Vladimiro-Suzdal'skoy Rusi*, L., 1967
Limonov, Yu. A., "Pol'skiy khronist Yan Dlugosh o Rossii," *Feodal'naya Rossiya vo
   vsemirno-istoricheskom protsesse* (M., 1972), pp. 262–8
Lindeberg, O. A., "'Slovo o knyaz'yakh' (Problema sootnosheniya spiskov),"
   Literatura drevney Rusi: Istochnikovedenie (Sbornik nauchnykh trudov), D. S.
   Likhachev (ed.) (L., 1988), pp. 3–13
Lur'e, Ya. S., "Obshcherusskiy svod-protograf Sofiyskoy I i Novgorodskoy IV
   letopisey," TODRL 28 (1974), 114–39
Lur'e, Ya. S., *Obshcherusskie letopisi XIV–XV vv.*, L., 1976
Lur'e, Ya. S., "Letopis' Lavrent'evskaya," *SKKDR*, 241–5
Lyaskoronsky, V. G., *Istoriya Pereyaslavskoy zemli s drevneyshikh vremen do poloviny
   XIII stoletiya*, K., 1897
Lyaskoronsky, V. G., "K voprosu o Pereyaslavl'skikh Torkakh," Zh. M. N. P., chast'
   358 (Spb., 1905), 278–302
Lyaskoronsky, V. G., "Severskie knyaz'ya i polovtsy pered nashestviem na Rus'
   mongolov," in *Sbornik statey v chest' Dmitriya Aleksandrovicha Korsakova*:
   Istoriya Literatury – Arkheologiya – Yazykovedenie – Filosofiya – Pedagogika
   (Kazan', 1913), pp. 281–96
Macartney, C. A., *Hungary, A Short History*, Edinburgh, 1962
Makary, Mitropolit Moskovskiy, *Istoriya russkoy tserkvi v period mongol'skiy*
   (Spb., 1886; Slavica-Reprint nr. 16, The Hague, 1968), vol. 4, bk. 1
Makk, F., *The Árpáds and the Comneni*, Political Relations between Hungary and
   Byzantium in the 12th Century, Budapest, 1989
Makushnikov, O. A., "K voprosu o topografii letopisnogo Gomiya," *Tezisy
   Chernigovskoy oblastnoy nauchno-metodicheskoy konferentsii, posvyash-
   chenoy 20-letiyu Chernigovskogo arkhitekturno-istoricheskogo zapovednika*
   (sentyabr' 1987 g.) (Chernigov, 1987), pp. 46–8
Makushnikov, O. A., "Osnovnye etapy razvitiya letopisnogo Gomiya (do serediny
   XIII v.)," *Problemy arkheologii Yuzhnoy Rusi*, T. N. Telizhenko (ed.) (K., 1990),
   pp. 56–62
Makushnikov, O. A., "O meste letopisnogo Gomiya v sisteme gorodskikh tsentrov
   Chernigovo-Severshchiny," *Arkheolohichni starozhytnosti Podesennia*: Mater-
   ialy istoryko-arkheolohichnoho seminary, prysviachenoho 70-richchiu vid
   dnia narodzhennia H. O. Kuznetsova, O. P. Motsia (gen. ed.) (Chernihiv,
   1995), pp. 95–7
Markov, M. E., "O dostopamyatnostyakh Chernigova," *Chteniya* nr. 1 (M., 1847)
Matthews, W. K., "The Latinisation of Cyrillic Characters," *The Slavonic and East
   European Review* 30, nr. 75 (1952), 531–48

Mavrodin, V. V., "Levoberezhnaya Ukraina pod vlast'yu Tataro-mongolov," *Uchenye zapiski*, nr. 32, Seriya istoricheskikh nauk, vyp. 2 (L., 1939), 39–65

Mavrodin, V. V., "Nekotorye momenty razlozheniya rodovogo stroya na teritorii drevney Rusi," *Uchenye zapiski*, tom. 19, Leningradskiy gosudarstvennyy pedagogicheskiy Institut im A. I. Gertsena (L., 1939), 145–74

Medyntseva, A. A., "Chara Vladimira Davydovicha," *Problemy arkheologii Yuzhnoy Rusi*, T. N. Telizhenko (ed.) (K., 1990), pp. 128–35

Mezentsev, V. I., *Drevniy Chernigov: Genezis i istoricheskaya topografiya goroda*, Doctoral dissertation, The Institute of History of the Ukrainian Academy of Sciences, K., 1981

Mezentsev, V. I., "The Masonry Churches of Medieval Chernihiv," HUS 11, nr. 3/4 (1987), 365–83

Mezentsev, V. I., "The Territorial and Demographic Development of Medieval Kiev and Other Major Cities of Rus': A Comparative Analysis Based on Recent Archaeological Research," *The Russian Review* 48 (1989), 145–70

Miller, D. B., "The Kievan Principality in the Century before the Mongol Invasion: An Inquiry into Recent Research and Interpretation," HUS 10, nr. 3/4 (1986), 215–40

Miller, D. B., "Monumental Building and its Patrons as Indicators of Economic and Political Trends in Rus', 900–1262," *Jahrbücher für Geschichte Osteuropas* 38, H. 3 (1990), 321–55

Molchanov, A. A., "Ob atributsii lichno-rodovykh znakov knyazey Ryurikovichey X–XIII vv.," *Vspomogatel'nye istoricheskie distsipliny* 16 (1985), 66–83

Mongayt, A. L., *Ryazanskaya zemlya*, M., 1961

Morgunov, Yu. Yu., "Letopisnyy gorod V'yakhan'," SA, nr. 2 (M., 1982), 237–45

Morgunov, Yu. Yu., "Letopisnyy gorod Popash," SA, nr. 1 (M., 1985), 241–9

Motsya, A. P., "Obshchie zakonomernosti torgovo-ekonomicheskikh vzaimootnosheniy Kieva i Bulgara v IX–XIII vv.," *Put' iz Bulgara v Kiev*, A. Kh. Khalikov (gen. ed.) (Kazan', 1992), 6–12

Murav'eva, L. L. and Kuz'mina, L. F. (compilers), *Imennoy i geograficheskiy ukazateli k Ipat'evskoy letopisi*, M., 1975

Myshko, D. I., "Hustyns'kyi litopys iak istorychne dzherelo," UIZh 4 (1971), 69–73

Nasonov, A. N., *Mongoly i Rus'*, M.-L., 1940

Nasonov, A. N., *Istoriya russkogo letopisaniya XI-nachala XVIII veka*, M., 1951

Nasonov, A. N., *"Russkaya zemlya" i obrazovanie territorii drevnerusskogo gosudarstva*, M., 1951

Nasonov, A. N., "Vladimiro-Suzdal'skoe knyazhestvo," *Ocherki istorii SSSR: period feodalizma IX–XV vv.*, B. D. Grekov (ed.) (M., 1953), pt. 1, pp. 320–34

Nasonov, A. N., "Moskovskiy svod 1479 i ego yuzhnorusskiy istochnik," *Problemy istochnikovedeniya* 9 (M., 1961), 350–85

Nikol'skaya, T. N., "K istoricheskoy geografii zemli Vyatichey," SA, nr. 4 (M., 1972), 158–70

Nikol'skaya, T. N., "Liteynye formochki drevnerusskogo Serenska," *Kul'tura srednevekovoy Rusi* (L., 1974), 40–6

Nikol'skaya, T. N., "Voennoe delo v gorodakh zemli Vyatichey (Po materialam drevnerusskogo Serenska)," KSIA 139 (M., 1974), 34–42
Nikol'skaya, T. N., "Vorotynsk," *Drevnyaya Rus' i slavyane*, T. V. Nikolaeva (gen. ed.) (M., 1978), pp. 118–28
Nikol'skaya, T. N., *Zemlya Vyatichey. K istorii naseleniya basseyna verkhney i sredney Oki v IX–XIII vv.*, M., 1981
Nikol'skaya, T. N., *Gorodishche Slobodka XII–XIII vv.*, M., 1987
Noonan, T. S., "The Flourishing of Kiev's International and Domestic Trade, ca. 1100–ca. 1240," *Ukrainian Economic History: Interpretive Essays*, I. S. Koropeckyj (ed.) (Cambridge, Mass., 1991), pp. 102–46
Novosel'tsev, A. P. and Pashuto, V. T., "Vneshnyaya torgovlya Drevney Rusi (do serediny XIII v.)," *Istoriya SSSR* 1 (M., 1967), vol. 1, pp. 81–108
Obolensky, D., "Byzantium, Kiev and Moscow: A Study in Ecclesiastical Relations," *Byzantium and the Slavs* (New York, 1994), 109–65 (originally published in *Dumbarton Oaks Papers* XI [1957], 23–78)
Ol'shevskaya, L. A., "Paterik Kievo-Pecherskiy," *SKKDR*, 308–13
Ostrowski, D., *Muscovy and the Mongols: Cross-Cultural Influences on the Steppe Frontier, 1304–1589*, Cambridge, 1998
Pashuto, V. T., *Ocherki po istorii Galitsko-Volynskoy Rusi*, M., 1950
Pavlenko, S., *Kniaz' Mykhailo Chernihivs'kyi ta ioho vyklyk ordi*, Chernihiv, 1996
Pelenski, J., "The Contest for the 'Kievan Succession' (1155–1175): The Religious–Ecclesiastical Dimension," *The Contest for the Legacy of Kievan Rus'*, East European Monographs 377 (Boulder, 1998), pp. 21–43
Pelenski, J., "The Sack of Kiev in 1169: Its Significance for the Succession to Kievan Rus'," in *The Contest for the Legacy of Kievan Rus'*, East European Monographs 377 (Boulder, 1998), pp. 45–60
Pletneva, S. A., "O yugo-vostochnoy okraine russkikh zemel' v domongol'skoe vremya," KSIA 99 (1964), 24–33
Pletneva, S. A., "Polovetskaya zemlya," *Drevnerusskie knyazhestva X–XIII vv.*, L. G. Beskrovny (ed.) (M., 1975), pp. 260–300
Pletneva, S. A., "Donskie polovtsy," *"Slovo o polku Igoreve" i ego vremya*, B. A. Rybakov (ed.) (M., 1985), pp. 249–81
Pletneva, S. A., *Polovtsy*, M., 1990
Podobedova, O. I., *Miniatyury russkikh istoricheskikh rukopisey*, M., 1965
Pogodin, M., *Drevnyaya russkaya istoriya do mongol'skago iga* (M., 1872), vol. 1
Polyakov, G. P., "Knyaz' Roman Mikhaylovich bryanskiy," *Sviatyi kniaz'*, pp. 28–33
Polyakov, G. P., "Korachev i 'Lesnaya zemlya' v XII veke," *Tezisy istoriko-arkheologicheskogo seminara "Chernigov i ego okruga v IX–XIII vv."* (15–18 maya 1990 g.) (Chernigov, 1990), pp. 48–51
Priselkov, M. D., *Istoriya russkogo letopisaniya XI–XV vv.*, L., 1940
Pryimak, V. V., "K izucheniyu okrugi drevnerusskikh gorodov srednego Poseym'ya," *Gomel'shchina: arkheologiya, istoriya, pamyatniki*: Tezisy Vtoroy Gomel'skoy oblastnoy nauchnoy konferentsii po istoricheskomu kraevedeniyu, 1991 g., O. A. Makushnikov and A. I. Drobushevsky (eds.) (Gomel', 1991), pp. 60–3

Pryimak, V. V., "Deiaki pidsumky vyvchennia davn'orus'koho mista Vyr i Vyrivs'koi volosti," *Problemy rann'oslovians'koi i davn'orus'koi arkheolohii Poseim'ia*, O. P. Motsia *et al*. (eds.) (Bilopillia, 1994), pp. 38–42

Pyadyshev, G. E., "Pokhod Igorya v 1185 godu. Mesto bitvy," *Istoriya SSSR* 4 (M., 1980), 42–65

Rapov, O. M., *Knyazheskie vladeniya na Rusi v X-pervoy polovine XIII v.*, M., 1977

Rappoport, P. A., "Goroda Bolokhovskoy zemli," KSIIMK 57 (M., 1955), 52–9

Rappoport, P. A., "Trubchevsk," SA, nr. 4 (M., 1973), 205–17

Rappoport, P. A., *Russkaya arkhitektura X–XIII vv. Katalog pamyatnikov*, in the series *Arkheologiya SSSR Svod arkheologicheskikh istochnikov*, E1–47, B. A. Rybakov (ed.), L., 1982

Rappoport, P. A., "Arkhitektura," *Drevnyaya Rus'*, *Gorod, zamok, selo*, B. A. Kolchin (gen. ed.), in series *Arkheologiya SSSR*, B. A. Rybakov (gen. ed.) (M., 1985), pp. 154–67

Rappoport, P. A., "Stroitel'nye arteli Drevney Rusi i ikh zakazchiki," SA, nr. 4 (M., 1985), 80–9

Rappoport, P. A., *Zodchestvo Drevney Rusi*, L., 1986

Rappoport, P. A., "Stroitel'noe proizvodstvo drevney Rusi," *Russia Mediaevalis* 6, 1 (München, 1987), 90–134

Rappoport, P. A., *Drevnerusskaya Arkhitektura*, Sankt-Peterburg, 1993

Ravdina, T. V., "O vremeni vozniknoveniya Bryanska," KSIA 135 (1973), 66–71

Rozhkov, N., "Politicheskie partii v Velikom Novgorode XII–XVI vv.," *Istoricheskie i sotsiologicheskie ocherki, sbornik statey* (M., 1906), pt. 2, pp. 27–72

Rudenok, V. Ia., "Novovidkrytyi pidzemnyi khram v Antonievykh pecherakh v Chernihovi," *Chernihivs'ka starovyna*, Zbirnyk naukovykh prats', prysviachenyi 1300 – littiu Chernihova, P. P. Tolochko (gen. ed.) (Chernihiv, 1992), pp. 42–9

Rudenok, V. Ia., "D. Ia. Samokvasov ta arkheolohichne vyvchennia Borysohlibs'koho monastyria u Chernihovi," *Slov'iany i Rus' u naukovii spadshchyni D. Ia. Samokvasova*. Materialy istoryko-arkheolohichnoho seminaru, prysviachenoho 150-richchiu vid dnia narodzhennia D. Ia. Samokvasova (14–16 veresnya 1993 r., m. Novgorod-Sivers'kyi) (Chernihiv, 1993), pp. 95–6

Rudenok, V. Ya. and Makushnikov, O. A., "Pervye speleo-arkheologicheskie issledovaniya v Gomele," *Gomel'shchina: arkheologiya, istoriya, pamyatniki*: Tezisy Vtoroy Gomel'skoy oblastnoy nauchnoy konferentsii po istoricheskomu kraevedeniyu, 1991 g., O. A. Makushnikov and A. I. Drobushevsky (eds.) (Gomel', 1991), pp. 55–6

Runciman, S., *The Emperor Romanus Lecapenus and his Reign*, Cambridge, 1929; reprinted 1995

Rybakov, B. A., "Raskopki v Chernigove," KSIIMK 21 (1947), 40–2

Rybakov, B. A., "Drevnosti Chernigova," *Materialy i issledovaniya po arkheologii drevnerusskikh gorodov*, vol. 1, Voronin, N. N. (ed.), in *Materialy i issledovaniya po arkheologii SSSR* (M.-L., 1949), nr. 11, pp. 7–93

Rybakov, B. A., "Knyaz Svyatoslav Vsevolodovich (1125–1194)," *Materialy i issledovaniya po arkheologii drevnerusskikh gorodov*, vol. 1, Voronin, N. N. (ed.),

7777

777

in *Materialy i issledovaniya po arkheologii SSSR* (M.-L., 1949), nr. 11, pp. 93–9

Rybakov, B. A., "Raskopki v Zvenigorode (1943–1945 gg.)," *Materialy i issledovaniya po arkheologii SSSR*, nr. 12 (M.-L., 1949), 125–33

Rybakov, B. A., "Raskopki vo Vshchizhe v 1948–1949," KSIIMK 38 (1951), 34–41

Rybakov, B. A., "Vshchizh – udel'nyy gorod XII veka," KSIIMK 41 (1951), 56–8

Rybakov, B. A., "Stol'nyy gorod Chernigov i udel'nyy gorod Vshchizh," *Po sledam drevnikh kul'tur (Drevnyaya Rus')*, G. B. Fedorov et al. (eds.) (M., 1953), pp. 75–120

Rybakov, B. A., *Drevnyaya Rus': Skazaniya, Byliny, Letopisi*, M., 1963

Rybakov, B. A., "Russkie datirovannye nadpisi XI–XIV vekov," *Arkheologiya SSSR, Svod arkheologicheskikh istochnikov*, E 1–44, B. A. Rybakov (ed.) (M., 1964), 13–41

Rybakov, B. A., "Kievskaya letopisnaya povest' o pokhode Igorya v 1185 g.," TODRL 24 (L., 1969), 58–63

Rybakov, B. A., *"Slovo o polku Igoreve" i ego sovremenniki*, M., 1971

Rybakov, B. A., *Kievskaya Rus' i russkie knyazhestva XII–XIII vv.*, M., 1982

Sagaydak, M. A., *Velikiy gorod Yaroslava*, K., 1982

Salmina, M. A., "Slovo o knyaz'yakh," SKKDR, 429–31

Sazonova, L. I., "Letopisnyy rasskaz o pokhode Igorya Svyatoslavicha na polovtse v 1185 g. v obrabotke V. N. Tatishcheva," TODRL 25 (1970), 29–46

Senyk, S., *A History of the Church in Ukraine*, vol. 1, To the End of the Thirteenth Century (Rome, 1993)

Serebryansky, N., *Drevne-russkie knyazheskie zhitiya (Obzor redaktsiy i teksty)* M., 1915

Shakhmatov, A. A., "K voprosu o kriticheskom izdanii Istorii Rossiyskoy V. N. Tatishcheva," *Dela i Dni*, Kniga pervaya (Peterburg, 1920), 80–95

Shakhmatov, A. A., *Obozrenie russkikh letopisnykh svodov XIV–XVI vv.*, M.-L., 1938

Shchapov, Ya. N., *Gosudarstvo i tserkov' Drevney Rusi X–XIII vv.*, M., 1989

Shekun, A. V., "Drevniy sukhoputnyy put' mezhdu Chernigovom i Lyubechem," *Arkhitekturni ta Arkheolohichni Starozhytnosti Chernihivshchyny*, M. M. Holodna et al. (eds.) (Chernihiv, 1992), pp. 70–4

Shekun, A. V. and Veremeychik, E. M., "Selishcha IX–XIV vv. v mezhdurech'e nizoviy Desny i Dnepra," *Chernigov i ego okruga v IX–XIII vv.*, A. A. Zolotareva (ed.) (K., 1988), pp. 93–110

Shields Kollman, N., "Collateral Succession in Kievan Rus'," HUS 14, nr. 3/4 (1990), 377–87

Shinakov, E. A. and Minenko, V. V., "'Goroda' Chernigovo-smolenskogo pogranich'ya: faktory i etapy razvitiya," *Rol' rannikh mis'kykh tsentriv v stanovlenni Kyivs'koi Rusi*, Materialy pol'ovoho istoryko-arkheolohichnoho seminaru. Serpen' 1993 r., s. Zelenyi Hai Sums'koho r-nu Sums'koi obl., O. P. Motsia (gen. ed.) (Sumy, 1993), pp. 20–7

Shinakov, E. A. and Minenko, V. V., "Lokalizatsiya Orminy i Ropeska – letopisnykh tsentrov Chernigovskoy zemli," *Slov'iany i Rus' u naukovii spadshchyni D. Ia. Samokvasova*. Materialy istoryko-arkheolohichnoho seminaru, prysviachenoho 150-richchiu vid dnia narodzhennia D. Ia. Samokvasova (14–16 veresnya 1993 r., m. Novgorod-Sivers'kyi), P. P. Tolochko (gen. ed.) (Chernihiv, 1993), pp. 40–3

Shuliak, V. V., "P'iatnits'ka tserkva v Chernihovi," *Arkheolohiia* 16 (K., 1975), 118–21

Skripil', M., *Russkie povesti xv–xvi vekov*, M.-L., 1958

Solov'ev, S. M., *Istoriya Rossii s drevneyshikh vremen*, 29 vols. in 15 bks. (M., 1962–6)

Spuler, B., *Die Goldene Horde. Die Mongolen in Russland 1223–1502*, Wiesbaden, 1965

Stökl, G., "Kanzler und Metropolit," *Studien zur Geschichte Osteuropas*, III. Teil, Gedenkenband für Heinrich Felix Schmid in Wiener Archiv für Geschichte des Slawentums und Osteuropas V (Graz–Köln, 1966), 150–75

Sukhobokov, O. V., "K vozniknoveniyu i ranney istorii Putivlya," *Drevnerusskiy gorod*, Materialy Vsesoyuznoy arkheologicheskoy konferentsii, posvyashchennoy 1500-letiyu goroda Kieva (K., 1984), pp. 120–3

Sukhobokov, O. V., "Nekotorye itogi archeologicheskikh issledovaniy v Putivle," *Arkheologiya slavyanskogo Yugo-Vostoka*, A. G. D'yachenko (gen. ed.) (Voronezh, 1991), pp. 66–80

Sverdlov, M. B., "K voprosu o letopisnykh istochnikakh 'Povesti o bitve na Kalke'," *Vestnik Leningradskogo Universiteta*, nr. 2, Seria Istorii, Yazyka i Literatury, vyp. 1 (L., 1963), 139–44

Świętosławski, W., *Arms and Armour of the Nomads of the Great Steppe in the Times of the Mongol Expansion (12th–14th Centuries)*, M. Abramowicz (trans.), Łódź, 1999

Sytyy, Yu. N., "Chernigovsko Zadesen'e v sostave votchiny chernigovskikh knyazey," *Istoriko-arkheologicheskiy seminar "Chernigov i ego okruga v IX–XIII vv.,"* (26–28 sentyabrya 1988 g.), Tezisy dokladov (Chernigov, 1988), pp. 34–6

Sytyy, Yu. N., "K istorii izucheniya Chernigovskogo Zadesen'ya," *Problemy arkheologii Yuzhnoy Rusi*, P. P. Tolochko (gen. ed.) (K., 1990), pp. 62–6

Szymczakowa, A., "Księżniczki Ruskie w Polsce XIII wieku," *Acta Universitatis Łódzensis*, Zeszyty Naukowe Uniwersytetu Łódzkiego, Nauki Humanistyczno-społeczne, Folia Historica, Seria 1, zeszyt 29 (1978), 25–42

Tolochko, A. P., "'Porty blazhennykh pervykh knyazey': k voprosu o vizantiyskikh politicheskikh teoriyakh na Rusi," *Yuzhnaya Rus' i Vizantiya*, L. L. Vashchenko (ed.) (K., 1991), pp. 34–42

Tolochko, A. P., *Knyaz' v Drevney Rusi: Vlast, Sobstvennost', Ideologiya*, K., 1992

Tolochko, O., "Roman Mstyslavič's Constitutional Project of 1203: Authentic Document or Falsification?," *HUS* 18, nr. 3/4 (1994), 249–74

Tolochko, O. P., "Shche raz pro mistse smerti Riuryka Rostyslavycha," *Sviatyi kniaz'*, pp. 75–6

Tolochko, P. P., *Kiev i Kievskaya zemlya v epokhu feodal'noy razdroblennosti XII–XIII vekov*, K., 1980

Tolochko, P. P., *Drevnyaya Rus', Ocherki sotsial'no-politicheskoy istorii*, K., 1987

Tolochko, P. P. and Aseev, Yu. S., "Novyy pamyatnik arkhitektury drevnego Kieva," *Drevne-russkoe iskusstvo*, Khudozhestvennaya kul'tura domongol'skoy Rusi (M., 1972), pp. 80–7

Tvorogov, O. V., "Slovo o polku Igoreve," *SKKDR*, 435–7
Vernadsky, G., *Kievan Russia*, New Haven, 1948
Vernadsky, G., *The Mongols and Russia*, New Haven, 1953
Vlasto A. P., *The Entry of the Slavs into Christendom*, Cambridge, 1970
Voronin, N. N. and Rappoport, P. A., *Zodchestvo Smolenska XII–XIII vv.*, L., 1979
Vysotsky, S. A., *Drevne-russkie nadpisi Sofii Kievskoy XI–XIV vv.* (K., 1966), vyp. 1
Vysotsky, S. A., "Nadpis' s imenami geroev 'Slova o polku Igoreve' v Kievskoy Sofii," TODRL 31 (1976), 327–33
Vysotsky, S. A., *Kievskie graffiti XI–XVII vv.*, K., 1985
Włodarski, B., *Polska i Rus' 1194–1340*, Warszawa, 1966
Yanin, V. L., *Novgorodskie posadniki*, M., 1962
Yanin, V. L., *Aktovye pechati Drevney Rusi X–XV vv.*, vol. 1, Pechati X-nachala XIII v., M., 1970
Yanin, V. L. and Gaydukov, P. G., *Aktovye pechati Drevney Rusi X–XV vv.* (M., 1998), vol. 3, Pechati, zaregistrirovannye v 1970–1996 gg.
Zakharenko, A. G., "Chernigovskie knyaz'ya v Novgorode," *Uchenye zapiski*, Kafedra istorii SSSR, vol. 61 (L., 1947), 147–62
Zaytsev, A. K., "Do pytannia pro formuvannia terytorii davn'orus'kykh kniazivstv u XII st.," UIZh, nr. 5 (1974), 43–53
Zaytsev, A. K., "Chernigovskoe knyazhestvo," *Drevnerusskie knyazhestva X–XIII vv.*, L. G. Beskrovny (ed.) (M., 1975), pp. 57–117
Zaytsev, A. K., "Domagoshch i granitsy 'Vyatichey' XII v.," *Istoricheskaya geografiya Rossii XI-nachalo XX v.* (M., 1975), pp. 21–30
Zimin, A. A., "Novgorod i Volokolamsk v XI–X vekakh," *Novgorodskiy istoricheskiy sbornik* 10 (Novgorod, 1961)
Zimin, A. A., "Ipat'evskaya letopis' i 'Slovo o polku Igoreve'," *Istoriya SSSR*, nr. 6 (M., 1968), 43–64

Index

Mstislav Vladimirovich (prince of Dorogobuzh),
47, 113, 159, 245
son-in-law of Svyatoslav Vsevolodovich, 136
Mstislav Vsevolodovich (prince of Goroden),
159
Mstislav Yaroslavich (prince of Peresopnitsa),
159, 266, 272
Mstislavichi (descendants of Mstislav
Vladimirovich), 13, 113–22
rivals of Monomashichi, 29, 38, 41, 42
rivals of Yur'evichi, 117
Mtsensk, 34, 42, 43
Muravlya River, 52
Murom, 5, 12, 13, 29, 31, 34, 116, 285, 343
princes of, 70, 121, 223
troops from, 126, 131

Nastaska (concubine), 121, 186, 275
Navla River, 35
Nedna River, 43
Nepolod River, 43
Nerinsk, 42
Nestor (bishop of Suzdalia), 102
Nesvezh, 296–7
Nezda River, 271
Nezhin, 49
Nifont (bishop of Novgorod), 39, 78–9
nightingale, 180
Nikifor (metropolitan), 153, 184, 195, 204, 210,
214
Nikita (stylite), 181
Nikola (bishop of Rostov), 153
Nogay (Tatar khan), 382
Novgorod, 5, 25, 78–9, 95, 112, 115, 120, 131,
134, 136, 139, 152, 227, 228–9, 260, 285,
288, 300, 303, 310–15, 324, 332, 338, 344,
387
bishop (archbishop) of, 78, 104, 204, 313, 316
boyars of, 313, 319
bypassed by the Tatars, 345
commerce in, 5, 301, 339
commoners of, 313
famine in, 316, 319
lands of, 41, 69
legislation of Mikhail in, 312–13, 341
merchants of, 302, 313, 314
ruled by Svyatoslav Vsevolodovich, 144, 148–9
suburbs of, 310
trade in, 302, 339
troops of, 126, 148, 217, 278, 280
veche of, 302, 310–13, 325
Novgorodians, 46, 54, 60, 95, 115, 139, 144, 147,
204, 316
expel Roman Mstislavich, 120
expel Vladimir Svyatoslavich, 152

help Yaroslav Vsevolodovich occupy Kiev, 338
invite Svyatoslav Vsevolodovich, 144, 148
relations with Yaroslav Vsevolodovich, 228–9,
310–15
rivalry with Yury Vsevolodovich, 300–2
Novgorod Severskiy, 12, 24, 25, 27–8, 36, 38, 43,
54, 56, 61, 67–8, 78, 83, 105, 112, 117, 122,
176, 222, 237, 255, 263, 308, 379
besieged, 30, 32, 34–5, 71, 111, 132
capital of Oleg's patrimony, 233, 384, 386
captured by the Tatars, 350
Chernigov Gate of, 233
church in, 284
Kursk Gate of, 233
lands of, 31, 58
ruled by Igor' Svyatoslavich, 141, 232–3, 238
ruled by Mikhail Vsevolodovich, 293
ruled by Mstislav Svyatoslavich, 265, 278
ruled by Oleg Svyatoslavich, 315
suburbs of, 72
troops at the Kayala from, 166, 172
Water Gate of, 233
Novgorod Svyatopolch *see* Vitichev, 298
Novosil', 375, 378, 379, 380
Novyy Torg, 41, 139, 300, 311, 312, 319

oaths, 15–16, 18, 20, 22, 33–4, 39, 44, 53, 72, 117,
133, 212, 220, 226, 255, 318, 319, 326, 327,
331
infidelity to, 65, 106, 131, 218, 221, 226, 232
kissing the Holy Cross, 15–16, 17, 20, 33–4, 45,
53, 77, 101, 115, 135, 139, 143, 199, 215, 220,
226, 232, 236, 246, 247, 274
kissing the icon of the Mother of God, 15, 22
sacredness of, 56
Oka River, 31, 37, 42, 43, 77, 260, 261, 292
Oleg (prince of Ryl'sk and Vorgol), 382–3
sons of, 382
Oleg Igorevich, 133, 238
Oleg Ingvarevich (prince of Ryazan'), 368
Oleg Romanovich (of Bryansk), 376
Oleg Svyatoslavich (prince of Vruchiy), 8
Oleg Svyatoslavich (prince of Chernigov), 11–13,
33, 62
champions family's right, 26, 105
patrimony of, 58, 67–8, 212, 233, 292
patron of churches, 22, 46, 61, 62, 124, 141,
183, 281, 389
progenitor of Ol'govichi, 21, 228, 231, 392
retainer of, 34
right of succession denied, 19
son of, 269
stigma of, 218, 245
violated his oath, 23, 33, 218
wife of, 29, 208